THE ECONOMIES OF ASIA
1950–1998

THE ECONOMIES OF ASIA
1950–1998

Critical perspectives on the world economy

Edited and with a new introduction
by Robert Ash and Anne Booth

VOLUME II

South East Asia

London and New York

First published 2000
by Routledge
11 New Fetter Lane, London EC4P 4EE

Simultaneously published in the USA and Canada
by Routledge
29 West 35th Street, New York, NY 10001

Routledge is an imprint of the Taylor & Francis Group

Typeset in Times by RefineCatch Limited, Bungay, Suffolk
Printed and bound in Great Britain by Clays Ltd, St Ives plc

British Library Cataloguing in Publication Data
A catalogue record for this book is available from the British Library

Library of Congress Cataloguing in Publication Data
A catalogue record for this book has been requested

ISBN 0–415–14051–X (set)
ISBN 0–415–17948–3 (volume 2)

CONTENTS

VOLUME II SOUTH EAST ASIA

Introduction 1
Anne Booth

PART I: THE CHALLENGE OF MACROECONOMIC RESTRUCTURING

1 Economic reform, openness and Vietnam's entry into ASEAN 31
David Dollar

2 The Philippine economy: what's right, what's wrong 52
Emmanuel S. de Dios

3 Myanmar: will forever flow the Ayeyarwady 68
Khin Maung Kyi

4 Indonesia 91
Iwan J. Azis

5 The Thai economy: from boom to gloom? 121
Peter G. Warr

PART II: THE ROLE OF GOVERNMENT ENTERPRISES AND MONOPOLIES, AND PRIVATIZATION

6 Malaysia's privatisation experience 141
K.S. Jomo

7 Government corporations and government monopolies of agricultural products 160
Yoshihara Kunio

8 The Thai economy in the mid-1990s 184
Pasuk Phongpaichit

PART III: DEVELOPMENT OF THE FINANCIAL SECTOR

9 Industrialization, financial reform and monetary policy 201
Naris Chaiyasoot

10 Reforms of the financial sector in Indonesia, 1983–91 221
Anwar Nasution

11 Financial reform in Malaysia 250
Zainal Aznam Yusof, Awang Adek Hussin, Ismail Alowi, Lim Chee Sing and Sukhdave Singh

PART IV: FOREIGN INVESTMENT, TECHNOLOGY TRANSFER AND EXPORT PROCESSING ZONES

12 Foreign direct investment, institutional change and Vietnam's gradualist approach to reform 293
Carolyn L. Gates

13 Japanese industrial investments and technology transfer in Malaysia 312
Anuwar Ali

14 Indonesia's great leap forward? Technology development and policy issues 336
Hal Hill

15 Export processing zones: the economics of enclave manufacturing 370
Peter G. Warr

PART V: CHANGING LABOUR CONDITIONS

16 Approaching the turning point? Labour market change under Indonesia's new order 395
Chris Manning

17 Labour flexibility in the Malaysian manufacturing sector 427
Guy Standing

18 Thailand's industrialization: implications for health, education, and science and technology 461
Sirilaksana Khoman

PART VI: THE CHANGING NATURE OF SOUTH EAST ASIAN CAPITALISM

19 Changing patterns of Chinese big business in Southeast Asia 497
J. A. C. Mackie

20 The transformation of Malaysian business groups 534
Sieh Lee Mei Ling

21 The Chinese in business 563
Yoshihara Kunio

22 Family business reassessed: corporate structure and late-starting industrialization in Thailand 577
Akira Suehiro

PART VII: TRENDS IN POVERTY

23 Agricultural growth, landlessness, off-farm employment and rural poverty in the Philippines 611
Arsenio Balisacan

24 Rapid economic growth and poverty decline: a comparison of Indonesia and Thailand 1981–1990 640
Anne Booth

PART VIII: ASEAN ECONOMIC INTEGRATION

25 The deepening and widening of ASEAN 663
Chia Siow Yue

INTRODUCTION

Anne Booth

Attitudes to South East Asia in the economic development literature have varied enormously over the past four decades. In the 1960s the prevailing mood was one of pessimism. Indonesia was termed "the chronic dropout" from the economic development stakes,[1] while Malaysian prospects, after the formation of the federation, were viewed with concern because of the deep and apparently unbridgeable ethnic divide. Singapore, after it broke away from Malaysia in 1965, seemed to have little chance of rapid development as an independent economy and Thailand was considered still semi-feudal, with an entrenched elite which appeared to have little commitment to, and nothing to gain from, rapid economic modernisation. What had been French Indochina, by the 1960s had become an arena for a prolonged and devastating civil war between communist forces backed by what was then the Soviet bloc and non-communist forces backed by the USA. In 1960, Burma and the Philippines seemed to many observers to have the best prospects for rapid economic development.

By the early 1990s much had changed. The countries of former French Indo-China had been controlled by communist governments since 1975. But led by Vietnam, they were turning away from central planning, opening their economies to foreign trade and investment and developing market institutions. Indonesia, Malaysia, Singapore and Thailand were all included in the "East Asian Miracle" study, published by the World Bank in 1993. Together with Japan, Taiwan and South Korea, these countries had

> emerged with an apparent long-run model of development, seeming to have done almost everything right. Against them, one can contrast other countries and ask what went wrong (Bruno 1994: 10).

But by late 1997, it was obvious that much was going wrong in the very countries which the World Bank claimed were models for much of the rest of the developing world. In July 1997, the Thai government was forced to allow the baht to float; this measure led to a rapid devaluation against the dollar and other major currencies. In spite of predictions to the contrary, the contagion rapidly spread, and the currencies of Malaysia, the Philippines and Indonesia also underwent sharp devaluations. Stock market prices fell as both foreign and domestic investors sold equities and moved funds offshore. The currency devaluations in turn led to fears of widespread corporate bankruptcies, as many South East Asian firms which had borrowed off-shore in dollars, yen and other currencies to take advantage of lower interest rates found that they could no longer generate the funds necessary to service their hugely increased debt burdens.[2] The problem was most severe for firms producing non-traded goods, especially business and residential property. Domestic banks which had lent heavily to such firms were also threatened with bankruptcy. In addition, the currency devaluations posed problems for government budgets, especially in Indonesia where foreign debt service charges were a substantial component of government expenditure.

By early 1998 it was clear that the economic problems which had been exposed in the latter part of 1997 would have a substantial effect on real economic growth for at least the rest of the decade in most parts of the ASEAN region. The severity of the problems which emerged in the wake of the Thai devaluation shocked many commentators, both in the region and abroad, into a more searching evaluation of past economic performance. To what extent were these problems the result of past errors in government policies? Most governments in the region had in fact won widespread praise from international organisations such as the World Bank for their sound macroeconomic policies. Certainly they had avoided the large budget deficits which triggered balance of payments crises in other parts of the developing world in the 1980s. Was the crisis of 1997 then due to too rapid deregulation of key sectors of the economy, especially the financial sector? Or was it at bottom the result of years of political cronyism and nepotism which had led to the creation of huge financial conglomerates, controlled by people who obviously owed their success more to their political connections than to any genuine entrepreneurial abilities?

This introduction, and the papers which follow cannot offer definitive answers to these questions. Instead they offer a context in which to place the dramatic events of the latter part of 1997 and early 1998. They are intended to bring out the important differences in the economic development process both within South East Asia, and between South East Asia and other fast-growing Asian economies such as Taiwan and South Korea. Once these differences are understood, readers will be in a better position to speculate on the economic future of this important, but still widely misunderstood, part of the global economy.

GROWTH AND STRUCTURAL CHANGE: 1960–1990

The economies of South East Asia have been characterised by widely divergent growth paths over the three decades since 1960. Excluding the city state of Singapore, the fastest growth in real per capita GDP (in 1985 ICP dollars corrected for changes in the terms of trade) has been experienced by Indonesia, followed by Malaysia and Thailand (Table 1). Between 1960 and 1990, per capita GDP in these three countries more than trebled. In the Philippines by contrast, where per capita GDP was higher than in Indonesia and Thailand in 1960, and indeed higher than in South Korea, growth has been much slower, and for much of the 1980s negative. By 1990, the Philippines had a lower per capita GDP than either Thailand or Indonesia. Growth has also been slow in the three countries which comprise former French Indochina (Laos, Cambodia and Vietnam); in recent years the governments of both Laos and Vietnam have abandoned central planning and embarked on a series of economic reforms designed to create more open, market-driven economies. In Vietnam and Laos, these reforms have led to accelerated growth since the latter part of the 1980s. In Burma (Myanmar) by contrast, the government has been more reluctant to abandon the inward-looking growth strategies pursued since the 1960s, and economic growth is still erratic. In 1990, Burma had what was probably the lowest per capita GDP in the region, with the possible exception of Cambodia where continued political instability has prevented the kind of growth resurgence which has occurred in Vietnam and Laos.

The very different growth rates experienced by different parts of South East Asia since 1960 are in part the result of different colonial legacies, and in part the result of different policy regimes in the post-colonial era. By the mid-1990s they had led to striking differences in levels of per capita GDP across the ASEAN region. Singapore's per capita GDP was as high as that of Western

Table 1 Growth in per capita GDP, 1960–92

Country	*Per capita 1960*	*GDP 1992*[a]	*Average annual growth rate 1960–92 (%)*[b]
Japan	3,052	15,496	4.5
Singapore	1,649	13,095	6.9
Malaysia	1,497	5,614	4.4
Taiwan	1,258	8,211	6.3
Philippines	1,165	1,707	1.3
Thailand	969	3,931	4.1
South Korea	899	7,464	6.9
Indonesia	589	2,040	4.8
China	559	1,480	3.7
Burma	315	608	1.8
Laos	n.a.	1.377	n.a.

Note:
[a] Data for Laos and Korea refer to 1991; for Korea to 1990; and for Myanmar to 1989.
[b] Calculated by fitting a semi-log function to the data.

Source: Penn World Tables version 5.6 as published on the Internet.

Europe, while that of Burma, Laos and Vietnam was no higher than many countries in sub-Saharan Africa. Malaysian per capita GDP was about the same as in the Czech Republic, or Trinidad and Tobago.[3] While the growth performance of Indonesia, Malaysia and Thailand has been impressive in comparison with many other parts of the developing world, it has clearly been less rapid than that of South Korea and Taiwan (Table 1). Only Singapore has had a comparable record since the 1960s. It will be argued in this introduction that there are important differences between the "miracle economies" of North East Asia, and the economies of South East Asia, both in the initial conditions under which they began their accelerated growth, and in the economic strategies adopted since 1960. These differences in turn reflect the different experiences of South East Asia under European and American colonialism, compared with Japanese colonialism in Taiwan and Korea. They also reflect significant differences in development strategies in recent decades. But before developing these themes further, let us look more closely at the "North East Asian" model and its relevance to South East Asia.

THE SIMILARITIES BETWEEN NORTH EAST AND SOUTH EAST ASIA

Over the past decade, a considerable literature has developed which seeks to explain the remarkable surge in GDP growth in economies such as Japan after 1955, and South Korea and Taiwan after 1960. Although several contending viewpoints have emerged, there does appear to be broad consensus on the following points:[4]

(*a*) the governments of the successful export economies of North East Asia have pursued macroeconomic and exchange rate policies which have created a climate of incentives conducive to production for export;

(*b*) to the extent that specific sectors, or individual firms, have received assistance through subsidised credit, tariff protection, or other means, such assistance has been tied to strict performance criteria, especially for exports;

(*c*) governments have not allowed key areas of economic policymaking to be captured by special interest groups;

(*d*) governments have maintained relatively low ratios of expenditure to GDP, and have not provided a comprehensive social welfare system, relying instead on families to take care of the old, the young, the sick and the disabled;

(*e*) governments have invested heavily in infrastructure and in education, and created an incentive climate conducive to high investment by the private sector. The emphasis on scientific and technical education has in turn facilitated the development of a sophisticated domestic capacity for technological innovation;

(*f*) society is characterised by a high degree of equality between regions and social classes;
(*g*) ethnic minorities are small, and play no conspicuous role in business.

It would certainly be difficult to explain the rapid growth of countries such as Thailand, Malaysia or Indonesia since the 1960s in terms of these factors, although in a purely negative sense this list does help to explain the poor performance of the Philippines, or Burma (Myanmar). But there are similarities between the successful South East Asian economies and Japan, Taiwan and South Korea. In what follows, I discuss the major points of similarity, and then, in the next section, look at the main differences, including the different roles played by government, differences in the development of domestic entrepreneurship and human resources, and in income distribution.

(a) High levels of investment

The most obvious similarity between South Korea and Taiwan on the one hand and the high-performing economies of South East Asia on the other is the high proportion of GDP devoted to investment (Table 2). This variable is also correlated with economic growth in South East Asia; those economies which grew strongly through the 1980s had much higher ratios of investment to GDP in 1979–81 than those which grew slowly. But there was also a significant correlation between growth over the 1980s and investment ratios at the end of the decade, which suggests that rapid growth led to high rates of investment as well as vice versa. Collins and Bosworth (1996: Table 6) point

Table 2 Investment as a ratio of GDP (Annual average 1988–92)

Country	*Investment as a percentage of GDP*
Japan	37.7
South Korea	36.8
Singapore	33.4
Malaysia	31.2
Indonesia	27.5
Thailand	26.4
Taiwan	23.9
China	22.6
Philippines	16.1
Myanmar	7.3
Laos	2.2

Source: Penn World Tables version 5.6 as published on the Internet.

out that much of the growth in output per worker in South East Asia can be accounted for by growth in capital stock per worker, together with growth in education. Only in Singapore in the decade from 1984 to 1994 did total factor productivity growth account for more than 50 per cent of growth in output per worker.

As in the case of South Korea and Taiwan, the key question is: why were rates of growth of capital stock so rapid in economies such as Thailand, Malaysia, Singapore and Indonesia? A frequent response is that these economies have relied heavily on foreign direct investment (FDI), which accounted for a high proportion of total capital formation in these economies over the last two decades, and especially from 1986 onwards when the revaluation of the yen, the won and the Taiwanese dollar led to a marked acceleration in outward foreign investment flows from North East Asia into other parts of the region. But the available evidence indicates that only in Singapore did FDI account for more than ten percent of gross domestic capital formation in 1986–91. In fact FDI accounted for a higher percentage of total capital formation in several European economies over these years than in Malaysia, Indonesia, Thailand or the Philippines (Yoshida et al., 1994: Table 4.4).

The apparently small role played by FDI in gross domestic capital formation in most parts of South East Asia does not of course imply that FDI has not been an important vehicle for disseminating technologies and new management methods. Just how well FDI has played this role is a matter of some controversy in different parts of the region; the issues are debated for several countries in Chapters 13 to 15 in this volume. Some critics of FDI in Thailand, Malaysia and Indonesia have argued that foreign investment has "crowded out" domestic capital, but as Pasuk Phongpaichit argues in this volume, Chapter 8, if anything FDI has "crowded in" domestic investment in Thailand through the demonstration effect on local companies.

As in South Korea and Taiwan, foreign borrowing by both government and private enterprises has been an important source of investment funds in Thailand, Malaysia and Indonesia, and indeed it was the very rapid growth of foreign borrowing by domestic corporate entities in the early and mid-1990s which led to such serious problems as exchange rates depreciating after July 1997. But at least until the early 1990s, the available evidence indicates that in all three economies most investment funds have come from domestic savings. The Indonesian Planning Commission estimate that 92 per cent of investment funds over the Fifth Five Year Plan (1989–94) came from domestic sources, the majority of them private (Booth 1994: Table 4). There can be little doubt that many domestic firms in Indonesia plow back profits into enterprise expansion, and this accounted for a substantial part of total investment in the economy.

(b) Exports and growth

In both South Korea and Taiwan, many producers, especially in agriculture, were involved in production for export in the Japanese colonial era. In South East Asia, the promotion of exports was also an important goal of the colonial regimes. Although they were by no means "free trade" economies (most colonial governments in South East Asia discriminated in favour of imports and investment from the metropolitan power, as of course did Japan in Taiwan and Korea), production for export by both large-scale foreign estates and smallholders accelerated rapidly throughout the region in the late 19th and early 20th centuries. Several countries in South East Asia continued to expand their export economies in the 1950s; in 1958–62 exports per capita were higher everywhere in South East Asia than in South Korea, although they were only higher than Taiwan in Malaysia, Singapore and Brunei (Table 3).

But by the early 1960s the dichotomy between what Myint (1967) called the "inward-looking" and the "outward-looking" countries of South East Asia was already obvious. On the one hand, Malaysia, Singapore, Thailand and the Philippines continued to expand their exports in real per capita terms, while on the other, the export economies of Burma, Indonesia and the countries of former French Indochina (Vietnam, Laos and Cambodia) stagnated or

Table 3 Exports per capita (US$), 1909–13 to 1991–5

Country	*1909–13*	*1934–38*	*1958–62*	*1991–95*
Singapore	a	a	671	29,380
Brunei	b	b	133	8,463
Taiwan	6	6	26	4,279
Malaysia	88	88	121[a]	2,684
South Korea	0.5	7	1	2,048
Thailand	4	6	15	692
Indonesia	5	6	7	194
Philippines	5	8	19	187
Laos	c	c	3	50
Vietnam	3	4	5[c]	49
Cambodia	c	c	12	22
Myanmar	10	12	10	19

Note:
[a] In 1909–13 and 1934–38 Singapore is included with Peninsular Malaya under Malaysia. In 1958–62 Malaysia excludes Sabah and Sarawak.
[b] No data for Brunei prior to 1950.
[c] In 1909–13 and 1934–38 Cambodia and Laos are included with Vietnam. In 1958–62 Vietnam refers only to South Vietnam.

Sources: 1909–13 and 1934–38: Mitchell (1982) pp. 389–92, with additional data from Andrus (1948), Tables 3 and 27; Ingram (1971), Appendix C and D; *Changing Economy of Indonesia* Vol 12a; Leurence (1925) and Rahm (1952).
Exchange rates from van der Eng (1993), Appendix Table.
1958–62 and 1991–95: International Monetary Fund, *Direction of Trade Statistics Yearbook*, 1958–62, 1996, *International Financial Statistics,* various issues.

declined (Table 3). Since the early 1960s, Malaysia, Singapore and Thailand have all continued to expand and diversify their export economies. In Thailand, for example, per capita exports grew almost 50-fold in nominal US$ terms between 1958–62 and 1991–95, while over the same time the proportion of exports accounted for by manufactured goods rose from under 20 per cent to over 70 per cent. Similar diversification away from a narrow range of agricultural and mineral exports has occurred in Malaysia, Indonesia, the Philippines and Singapore.

There is very little relationship between an indicator of "openness" (exports and imports as a proportion of nominal GDP) in the early 1960s and subsequent economic growth in East and South East Asia. Excluding Singapore, the correlation is very weak.[5] Some countries which were very open in the early 1960s (such as Burma) subsequently grew very slowly while others such as Malaysia grew very rapidly. The difference between these two polar cases is explained by the policy regime. In Malaysia successive governments have maintained a market-determined exchange rate, and encouraged foreign investors to establish export-oriented manufacturing plants, often located in export-processing zones.[6] In Burma, the government pursued autarkic policies for over twenty years, and although there were some policy changes after 1987, the complex multiple exchange rate regime and a very corrupt administrative system together have deterred most foreign investors, as Khin Maung Kyi points out in this volume, Chapter 3.

Indeed the common lesson from Taiwan, South Korea and the fast growing economies of South East Asia would seem to be that it is the policy regime which is the main determinant of export growth, and that an export-friendly policy regime is essential in order to achieve the virtuous circle of rapid export growth leading to increased investment which in turn promotes further growth. What then determines the policy regime? Are there any similarities between the North East Asian developmental states, and the South East Asian regimes?

(c) An "insulated" economic bureaucracy?

The concept of the strong developmental state, derived from the experience of Japan, South Korea and Taiwan, emphasises the strong esprit de corps of officials in the elite government departments, and high degree of autonomy enjoyed by key decision-makers, especially in the bureaucracy, together with their "insulation" from sectional interest groups. Can we find any evidence of insulated bureaucracies in South East Asia? Certainly the Bank of Thailand has enjoyed a considerable, albeit fluctuating, degree of autonomy over several decades and was crucial in maintaining a stable monetary and fiscal policy regime through Thailand's years of accelerated growth, while in Thailand, Indonesia and Malaysia, technocrats in the Ministries of Finance have been able to insulate key areas of macroeconomic policy-making from overt political interference.[7] In Thailand and Indonesia, for example, the administration of duty drawback schemes, crucial to the rapid growth of a number of export-oriented industries, was placed in the Ministries of Finance to minimise corruption and malpractice.[8]

But at the same time some authors have claimed that policymakers in the fast growing economies of South East Asia have always been ready to listen to influential business lobby groups, who in their turn have been catalysts of policy reform, and active in promoting structural adjustment measures. In the case of Thailand, Laothamatas (1992), Doner and Laothamatas (1994) and Rock (1995) have argued that the successful implementation of a series of structural adjustment measures in the years from 1980 to 1985 was due in large measure to the government's successful attempts to build effective alliances between technocratic advisers (usually academic economists with strong neo-classical sympathies), key politicians, and business groups. While, as Pasuk points out in Chapter 8, it is difficult to fit Thailand with its notoriously weak planning apparatus, into the strong developmental state model, it is also wrong to assume that the government did nothing to facilitate rapid industrial expansion. Interventions in both capital and labour markets were crucial and often carried through at the instigation of, and with the full cooperation of, powerful industrial groups.

Macintyre (1994: 10) suggests that the states of South East Asia comprise an intermediate case between the strong developmental states of North East Asia (although Singapore would certainly be included in this group) and the notorious "klepto-patrimonial" regimes of Africa such as Nigeria or Zaire. Their governments are not hopelessly captured and corrupt, but on the other hand they are frequently beholden to sectional interest groups, and tainted by nepotism and cronyism. Nevertheless the Malaysian, Thai and Indonesian governments have been capable of coherent policy formulation and implementation in the face of external shocks, and have thus been able to maintain the momentum of growth over several decades. Even in the face of exchange rate instability, a tottering financial sector and contracting real GDP in 1998, the Thai and Malaysian governments have demonstrated a continued capacity for adopting tough policy measures.[9] In this they still resemble Taiwan and South Korea to a greater extent than regimes in other parts of the developing world.

THE DIFFERENCES BETWEEN NORTH EAST AND SOUTH EAST ASIA

(a) Land and natural resource abundance

An obvious contrast between the resource poor, densely settled countries of North East Asia and most parts of South East Asia is that the latter were able to initiate economic growth by exploiting their abundant reserves of land and natural resources. This in turn influenced the role of government in both the colonial and the post-colonial era; Amsden (1995: 794) argues that Malaysia, Indonesia and Thailand rich natural resources allowed a

> more modest initial role for the government than in Korea and Taiwan. The leading sectors of these South East Asian countries were agro-based and competitive in world markets without substantial productivity-augmenting support from government, and without significant reliance on imported inputs.

This argument has some merit, although colonial governments in many parts of the region were considerably more than mere "nightwatchmen" states. In the Netherlands East Indies (Indonesia) not only was per capita government expenditure quite high in comparison with other parts of Asia, but government intervened in, and regulated, key markets for goods and services (Booth 1998, pp. 154ff). Everywhere in South East Asia, governments both colonial and post-colonial taxed primary exporters quite hard, usually through export taxes, and used the revenues to develop infrastructure. In the mid-1960s, government expenditure as a proportion of GDP was higher in Malaysia than in Korea and only slightly lower than in Taiwan in spite of the higher burden of defense expenditure (Table 4). Since then, it would be rather difficult to call Malaysia an example of minimalist government, although the nature and purpose of government intervention in Malaysia, and indeed in Indonesia, has been rather different from in South Korea and Taiwan, a point which is addressed below.

A frequent argument made in the context of Malaysia and Indonesia in particular is that "the availability of natural resource rents – most notably from petroleum, natural (petroleum) gas, tin, and timber – has been very significant . . . allowing the government greater latitude and capacity than most other governments in the world" (Jomo and Gomez 1997: 367). There can be little doubt that successive governments in both countries have benefited from

Table 4 Government expenditure as a ratio of GDP

Country	*Year*	*Government expenditure as a percentage of GDP*	*Per capita GDP*[a] *($)*
Singapore	1960	7.0	1,649
Malaysia	1966	16.4	1,729
Taiwan	1966	19.8	1,750
South Korea	1970	12.5	1,694
Thailand	1973	12.9	1,716
Indonesia	1988	15.0	1,681
Philippines	1991	16.3	1,715

Note:
[a] Per capita GDP in 1985 international dollars adjusted for changes in the terms of trade.

Source: Penn World Tables version 5.6 as published on the Internet.

such "easy to tax" sectors, and that especially in periods of high world prices for key staples (rubber, tin, petroleum, gas, timber) huge increases in government revenues have occurred, with little or no government effort. Such "manna dropping from heaven" has caused considerable problems of macroeconomic stabilisation and raised production costs for other traded goods sectors, as analysed in the large "Dutch Disease" literature.[10] Similarly in periods of low prices both the government budget and the balance of payments have come under great pressure. There is a sense in which the economic history of both Indonesia and Malaysia over the past century is a history of government response to fluctuations in the prices of key export staples. The same could hardly be argued about South Korea and Taiwan.

(b) Educational attainment and social stratification in South East Asia

Virtually everywhere in South East Asia with the exception of the Philippines under American rule, the colonial regimes left behind an extremely meagre educational legacy. Not only was there inadequate provision of educational facilities, but such facilities as did exist were mainly (at the post-primary level almost exclusively) in large towns and cities, and places were usually allocated on the basis of race and income, rather than academic merit. The well-known study by Furnivall (1943: 111) showed that in the late 1930s the proportion of the population enrolled in recognized schools was around 11 per cent in Taiwan and the Philippines, 9.7 per cent in Thailand, six per cent in Malaya, four percent in Burma, 3.4 per cent in the Netherlands Indies and only 2.1 per cent in French Indochina. Furnivall (1943: 119) pointed out that the good performance of the Philippines and Thailand in comparison with the rest of the region was due to "specially favourable circumstances";

> in both countries the chief impulse to the progress of primary instruction has been the nationalist drive behind it. In the other countries foreign governments have inevitably been critical of nationalist enthusiasm, and nationalist leaders have had less zeal for primary instruction than for higher education, which, as they hope, will equip them for handling national affairs.

In British Malaya, the appointment of the noted scholar of Malay culture, Richard Winstedt, to the post of assistant Director of Education in the inter-war years appeared to usher in a period of educational progress for rural Malays. But as Rudner (1994: 288) has pointed out, access to English language education continued to be restricted to a tiny minority, almost entirely in urban areas. For the rural Malay, the number of years in elementary schooling was reduced and the curriculum was oriented to such manual skills as basket weaving and horticulture. "This benign, custodial outlook in education tended to reinforce the prevailing colonial assumption that the Malay peasantry should be retained, and improved, in their traditional kampung environment and saved from the disruptions of modernization".

In colonial South East Asia as in most other parts of the colonial world, education in the language of the colonial power was the key to non-agricultural employment, especially in highly remunerated professional, technical, administrative and clerical occupations. The skewed access to secular, non-vernacular education inevitably resulted in substantial disparities in income between and within ethnic groups, and between urban and rural areas. In rural areas the distribution of land became more skewed especially in regions where large estates were established. In the very densely settled regions of South East Asia (Java and Bali, the Red River delta in North Vietnam), a growing population could no longer be accommodated on the available land, and a landless rural proletariat emerged which depended mainly on wage income to survive. Given the large numbers competing for the available wage labour, wages and total incomes were extremely low.

In the more land adundant parts of the region, growing rural populations were accommodated through an expansion of the cultivation frontier. But often the land was of poor quality, and basic infrastructure such as irrigation and roads were not provided. In addition, in some frontier areas such as North East Thailand, new settlers were in effect squatters with no title to land. Thus they could not use their land as collateral to borrow, even where rural credit facilities were available.[11] Those farmers growing export crops such as rice in Thailand, and rubber in Malaysia and Indonesia, were taxed very heavily via graduated export taxes. The burden of taxation on rural incomes earnt from export crop cultivation was thus heavier than on incomes derived from other sources. Over time the effect of such discriminatory policies was to widen urban-rural and inter-regional disparities in incomes and living standards.

As a result of these trends, substantial differentials had emerged within indigenous populations in South East Asia by the 1960s, based on access to land and education. In addition, the last phase of the western colonial era saw the emergence of growing disparities between indigenous populations and immigrant Chinese, especially in Indonesia and Malaya. In most cases these disparities were not greatly reduced in the early post-independence years. Thus most countries in South East Asia entered a phase of accelerated growth in the 1960s with greater disparities in income than was the case in either Taiwan or South Korea.

It might have been expected that given the poor educational legacy from the colonial era, the newly independent states of South East Asia would have given high priority to educational expansion after 1950. To a considerable extent, this was the case, but given the low level from which educational expansion was starting in most parts of the region, great efforts and resources were required, and government revenues were not always sufficient. Thus private sector education played an important role in educational expansion, especially at the post-primary levels. In countries such as Indonesia, Malaysia and Thailand, universal primary education became a key government priority and was indeed achieved by the early 1980s. But progress in post-primary enrollments was much slower and more erratic.

In Thailand over the 1980s, post-primary enrollments stagnated; indeed at the senior high school level they contracted (see Chapter 19, this volume). In 1992, when per capita GDP in Thailand was roughly equal to what had been attained in South Korea in 1984, or in Taiwan in 1978, gross enrollment ratios at the secondary level were still only 37 per cent, compared with 94 per cent in Taiwan in 1978 (Table 5). In Indonesia growth in secondary enrollments through the 1980s was very rapid, although upper secondary enrollments contracted in the early 1990s. Even so, in 1992, gross enrollment ratios in Indonesia were higher than in Thailand, although still lower than in South Korea two decades earlier. Even in Malaysia, where government spending on education had risen to over five per cent of GDP in 1990, the gross secondary enrollment ratio was only 56 per cent, compared with 100 per cent in Taiwan in the mid-1980s.

It is clear from Table 5 that educational progress in the fast growing countries of South East Asia has been slower than in Taiwan and Korea.[12] Singapore, Malaysia, Thailand and Indonesia all had lower levels of educational attainment than Taiwan or South Korea in the 1960s; and in spite of considerable expansion in enrollments at the primary and secondary levels, the gap has not closed, especially in Thailand and Indonesia. Indeed in both countries there were signs of falling educational enrollments at the secondary level in the 1980s, and early 1990s. The effects of this are clear when we look at the educational attainment of the labour force in Indonesia and Thailand in comparison with South Korea when levels of per capita GDP in the three countries were roughly similar (Table 6). Already by 1974, only 13.6 per cent of the male Korean labour force, and 29.6 per cent of the female labour force had five years of schooling or less. In Thailand in 1981 the corresponding figure was 83.3 per cent for males and 89.5 per cent for females.

There has been considerable discussion of the impact of the very restricted access to post-primary education on income distribution in Thailand. As Sirilaksana Khoman (Chapter 18, this volume) points out, parents' education and household income are two very important determinants of access to post-primary education; in addition parents' expectations about the likelihood of a child getting a formal sector job influences the decision to send the child to secondary school. To the extent that expectations will be lower in rural areas, and in poorer households, the probability of children from these backgrounds getting to secondary school is very low. A recent study by a team of World Bank economists indicates that the education of the household head is an important determinant of changes in income inequality over time in Thailand (Ahuja, Bidani, Ferreira and Walton 1997: 44). In other words, because access to post-primary education is an important determinant of lifetime earnings,

Table 5 Government expenditures on education and gross enrollment ratios

Country	*Government educational expenditure as % of GDP*	*Gross enrollment ratios*	
		Primary	*Secondary*
Per capita GDP (Approx $5,600)			
Malaysia (1992)	5.5	93	60
South Korea (1988)	3.3	104	87
Taiwan (1985)	4.1	99	90
Singapore (1976)	2.7	110	54
Japan (1965)	4.3	100	82
Per capita GDP (Approx $3,930)			
Thailand (1992)	4.0	99	37
South Korea (1984)	5.8	99	91
Taiwan (1978)	3.3	101	76
Per capita GDP (Approx $2,040)			
Indonesia (1992)	2.2	114	43
Thailand (1978)	2.4	92	28
South Korea (1973)	3.6	104	51
Malaysia (1970)	4.4	87	34
Taiwan (1969)	3.3	98	n.a.
Per capita GDP (Approx $1,700)			
Philippines (1992)	2.3	112	77
Indonesia (1988)	0.9	118	47
South Korea (1970)	4.6	105	43
Taiwan (1966)	2.8	103	40
Per capita GDP (Approx $1,480)			
China (1992)	2.0	124	51
Indonesia (1981)	2.2	117	30
Philippines (1972)	2.0	115	51
Thailand (1969)	3.5[a]	81[a]	16[a]
South Korea (1969)	4.6[a]	105[a]	43[a]

Note:
[a] Data refer to 1970.

Sources: *Unesco Statistical Yearbooks*, various issues, with additional data on Taiwan from the *Taiwan Statistical Yearbook,* 1995, Tables 47, 53. Per capita GDP in 1985 international dollars adjusted for changes in the terms of trade, taken from Penn World Tables, version 5.6.

the relatively small proportion of the population gaining access to such education could be an important explanation for the increase in income inequalities which have occurred in Thailand between the 1970s and the 1990s.

It is ironic that in South East Asia only the Philippines emerged into the

Table 6 Distribution of the labour force by educational attainment

	South Korea (1974)	*Thailand (1981)*	*Indonesia (1994)*
Male			
No schooling	12.9	5.6	7.5
Primary	41.0	82.4	59.6
Secondary	38.5	8.3	29.7
College or more	7.6	3.8	3.2
TOTAL	100.0	100.0	100.0
Female			
No schooling	28.5	10.4	16.4
Primary	49.9	82.4	59.9
Secondary	20.0	4.2	21.1
College or more	1.6	2.9	2.6
TOTAL	100.0	100.0	100.0

Sources: *1974 Special Labour Force Survey Report,* Seoul: Bureau of Statistics, Economic Planning Board, Republic of Korea, December 1976, Tables 17 and 19.
Labor Force Situation in Indonesia, 1994, Jakarta: Central Bureau of Statistics, March 1995, Tables 04.7 and 04.8.
Report of the Labour Force Survey, July–September 1981, Bangkok: National Statistical Office, Table 4.

post-colonial era with a strong educational base; this asset was squandered under the Marcos regime when macroeconomic policy mistakes led to low levels of investment and capital flight. Rodrik (1995: 96) argues that the Philippines experience casts doubt on the theory that countries beginning their growth process with high levels of human capital relative to physical capital are likely to grow fast. While the experience of South Korea and Taiwan may support such a theory, that of the Philippines, Sri Lanka and several Latin American countries does not. On the other hand, the experience of Thailand demonstrates the cost of neglecting investment in education, especially at the post-primary level. As Warr points out in Chapter 5, the export slowdown in 1996, which was an important factor leading to the baht devaluation in July 1997, was in part the result of a failure to move into higher technology exports and labour costs rose. That failure was in turn due to the low levels of skill in the Thai labour force.

(c) Government economic intervention and regulation

In the fast-growing economies of North East Asia, (Japan, Taiwan, South Korea) there now appears to be a measure of consensus that governments have been important not just in removing policy-induced distortions, but also in coordinating and subsidising private investment (see e.g. Stiglitz 1996). In the South East Asian context, no such consensus yet exists. Instead, several contending schools of thought have emerged. First, there are those who argue that the success of Indonesia, Singapore, Malaysia, Thailand is a triumph of "orthodox policies" and that government interventions, although pervasive, have usually been deterimental to growth. This is especially true of interventions at the enterprise level. Subsidy allocations have seldom been tied to any credible performance criteria, but are usually made either on the basis of political cronyism, or to achieve non-economic goals such as the promotion of indigenous (i.e. non-Chinese) businesses. Export growth and diversification in South East Asia has not been due to government guidance but primarily to multinational companies relocating to the region to take advantage of lower operating costs, or to Chinese firms exploiting region-wide family networks. State-owned enterprises (SOEs) have benefited from capital injections either from the government budget or from subsidised bank loans, but for the most part SOEs perform poorly according to standard rate of return criteria (Hill 1996: 161–65).

This school does not downplay the importance of economic policymaking as a prerequisite for rapid economic growth. Rather it argues that Thailand, Singapore, Malaysia and Indonesia all grew fast because their economic managers have got the macroeconomic fundamentals right, or where these fundamentals were clearly wrong, governments were prepared to change tack. Especially during the 1980s, they devalued exchange rates, deregulated, privatised and restructured markets, thus creating a positive investment climate for both domestic and foreign investors. However other writers claim that several South East Asian governments went considerably further than simply creating a positive investment climate, and actively intervened in markets in order to achieve specific goals. Pasuk (Chapter 9, this volume) has described the "major interventionist role in remodelling key markets for capital and labour" played by the Thai government in the 1980s, while Rock (1995: 755) argues that "industrial policy in Thailand has been more coherent than neo-liberals admit".

A third school of thought, based largely on the Malaysian case, concedes many of the points made by writers in the first camp. It points to the very poor performance of many of the heavy industries set up by government under the umbrella of HICOM, the Heavy Industries Corporation of Malaysia, established in order to promote industrial "deepening" (Jomo et al., 1997: 101–3). But this literature is also critical of some of the neo-liberal solutions to the problem of government failure, especially the Malaysian government's ambitious privatization programme. According to Jomo (this volume, Chapter 7), this programme was itself "captured" by powerful political interests; the tendering process was far from transparent and indeed the entire process was designed to transfer vaulable assets to a small group of powerful businessmen connected to the ruling United Malay National Organisation. They suggest that Malaysia would have been better advised to embark on a policy of state enterprise management reform, rather than wholesale privatisation.

There can be little doubt the objectives of intervention in Malaysia were quite different from those in Korea or Taiwan. The primary goal for the two decades from 1970 to 1990 was to address ethnic imbalances in the economy, and all other goals including that of international competitiveness and industrial efficiency were subordinated to that (Jomo et al., 1997: 105; Lall 1995: 764–6). Obviously the Malaysian bureaucracy could not play the tough disciplining role of that in South Korea when its main goal was to promote the growth of industrial and commercial enterprises owned by the relatively backward Malay majority. Indeed Lall (1995: 765) thinks that criticism of Malaysian interventions is unwarranted at least in part because "the design of the interventions in Malaysia was not ideal and so does not constitute a proper test for the effectiveness of industrial policy".

An important point made by Lall (1995: 771), drawing on Wade (1994: 65–8) is that Malaysia (and by extension other countries in the South East Asian region)

> is reaping the benefits of industrial policy undertaken earlier by other countries in the region, in particular Japan, Taiwan, Singapore and Korea". A large part of the export growth is fuelled by the capabilities that selective interventions in these countries fostered, which then spilled over to neighbouring countries that offered cheaper labour and a conducive investment climate . . . The market forces that Malaysia's "market friendly" policies tapped were thus themselves the creatures of industrial intervention

There is some truth in this type of argument, although the dependence on FDI to fuel manufactured export growth has varied considerably by country, and anyway a considerable part did not originate from North East Asia. But whatever conclusion one reaches on this issue, the broader point remains, that government interventions in South East Asia have been different in scope and purpose from those in South Korea and Taiwan. This leads me to consider a further set of claims about the very different nature of capitalist economic development in South East Asia.

(d) Crony capitalism and ersatz capitalism

Although some authors such as Amsden (1995: 791) have argued that the growth experiences of Indonesia, Malaysia and Thailand form part of a single "late-industrialising paradigm", there is a considerable literature which argues that economic growth in South East Asia is not only different from earlier episodes in Europe, the USA and Japan but also "ersatz", or fake, and by implication, unsustainable. Yoshihara's well-known contribution points to three aspects of South East Asian industrial growth which, he claims differentiate it from earlier industrial success stories, and also cast doubt on its sustainability:

(*a*) it is very dependent on foreign capital and technology;
(*b*) it is driven by foreign companies and the overseas Chinese;
(*c*) where indigenous capitalists have emerged, they are often mere "rent seekers", exploiting political connections to build up large conglomerates.

Are these claims true and if so, do they matter? An obvious counter-argument to the first point is that all late industrialising countries have depended on imported technology, including of course Japan in the latter part of the 19th and early 20th centuries, and Taiwan and South Korea in more recent decades. Yoshihara (1988: 112) responds to this by arguing that, although it is true that Japan, Korea and Taiwan all imported machinery, their technological dependency was not as complete as in contemporary South East Asia where most industrialists are simply Japanese "compradores". Indeed he goes as far as to talk about "technologyless industrialisation" in the South East Asian context.

Yoshihara's arguments have undoubtedly struck a chord with a number of South East Asian scholars who are concerned about the extent of dependency on foreign technology, the continuing dominance of the Chinese minority in industry and commerce and the growth of large conglomerates, especially in Indonesia and Malaysia, owned by individuals whose success owes far more to their political connections than to any obvious entrepreneurial ability. In the Malaysian context Ali (Chapter 13, this volume) has made a case for "a more systematic and comprehensive approach to the issue of technology transfer acceleration", while in Indonesia the efforts of the Minister of Reasearch and Technology, Dr Habibie, to build up an aircraft industry have received much attention (McKendrick 1992).[13] But policy prescriptions designed to accelerate technology transfer are not always convincing, especially when they involve substantial government subsidies to promote "leapfrogging" into high technology industry. The work of Hobday (1994) on Singapore, the most successful South East Asian economy in terms of upgrading the technological sophistication of its export industries, suggests that: technology was accumulated in a gradual and painstaking manner, with "firms engaging in a hard slog of incremental learning in response to factor price increases and the improving infrastructure". Certainly the Singapore experience underlines the crucial importance of government investment in education and training, and as Hill (this volume, Chapter 14) makes clear, Indonesia and Thailand lag far behind Singapore in terms of technical and scientific skills. If these countries wish to improve the technological sopistication of their export sectors they will have to give much higher priority to technical and scientific education. An important lesson from Taiwan and South Korea is that attempts by government agencies to promote technology transfer cannot succeed in the absence of a well-educated labour force.[14]

(e) Ethnic and regional disparities in income and wealth

The last significant point of difference between the North East Asian and the South East Asian experiences of accelerated economic growth concerns the distributional outcomes. An important part of the colonial legacy in South East Asia were the substantial income disparities between urban and rural areas, between regions and between ethnic groups, which persisted in the immediate post-independence era. Most countries in the region embarked on a process of accelerated growth after 1960 with greater income differentials than in South Korea or Taiwan. Although international comparisons of inequality indicators are fraught with difficulties, the available data on the distribution of household income/expenditure show a less skewed distribution, with a lower proportion of total income accruing to the top decile in South Korea and Taiwan than in most parts of South East Asia (Table 7). In Malaysia and Thailand in 1989 and 1992 respectively, the ratio of the percentage share of the top decile to the bottom two deciles was very much higher than in Taiwan in 1972, or South Korea in 1976.

Greater inter-personal disparities are only one facet of the differences in the distribution of income between South Korea and Taiwan on the one hand and South East Asia on the other. We must also examine spatial inequalities and

Table 7 Distribution of income in East and South East Asia by decile group and country

Country	*Year*	*Per capita GDP ($)*[a]	*Percentage share of*		*Ratio of top 10% to bottom 20%*
			Top decile	*Bottom 20%*	
Singapore	1982–3	8,565	33.5	5.1	6.6
Japan	1969	6,995	27.2	7.9	3.4
South Korea	1976	2,584	27.5	5.7	4.8
Malaysia	1973	2,504	39.8	3.5	11.4
	1989	4,571	37.9	4.6	8.2
Thailand	1975–6	1,813	34.1	5.6	6.1
	1992	3,931	37.1	5.6	6.6
Taiwan	1964	1,574	26.7	7.7	3.5
	1972	2,698	22.7	8.9	2.6
Philippines	1970–1	1,433	38.5	5.2	7.4
	1988	1,699	32.1	6.5	4.9
Indonesia	1976	902	34.0	6.6	5.2
	1993	2,142	25.6	8.7	2.9

Note:
[a] Per capita GDP in 1985 international dollars adjusted for changes in the terms of trade.

Sources: GDP data: Penn World Tables version 5.6 as published on the Internet.
Income Distribution data: World Bank (1983: 200–1); World Bank (1997: 222–3); Taiwan: Ho (1978: 141).

inter-racial inequalities. In Indonesia, inter-provincial inequalities in GDP have been high since the late 1960s, largely because of the concentration of mining and manufacturing activities in a few locations. Although the decline in GDP in several oil-producing areas as a result of production cutbacks has led to some dimunition in regional inequalities, the disparities in per capita GDP by province remained quite high in the early 1990s (Akita and Lukman 1995, Table 2). Urban-rural differentials in per capita consumption expenditures have widened since 1980, and disparities in consumption expenditures within urban areas have also widened (Booth 1992: 329–34). In Thailand, where urban-rural and spatial income differentials have always been high, there is little evidence of any narrowing of the gap during the era of rapid growth after 1980 (Pranee 1995: Table 10.7; see also Chapter 24, this volume). In 1992, the share of total household income accruing to the poorest two deciles was 5.6 per cent, no higher than in the mid-1970s (Table 7). Similarly in Malaysia, rapid growth has been accompanied by only a modest narrowing of income disparities since the mid-1980s.

One possible reason for the more skewed distribution of income in many parts of South East Asia compared with Japan, South Korea and Taiwan at similar levels of real per capita GDP is that non-agricultural employment opportunities have been growing more slowly, and those that have been created are in poorly remunerated service sector occupations rather than in the more secure and highly paid manufacturing sector. Certainly in most parts of South East Asia except the Philippines, the proportion of the labour force in agriculture is higher than in Japan, Taiwan or South Korea at similar levels of income (Table 8). This in itself would not necessarily lead to a more skewed distribution of income; in land abundant economies such Malaysia and Thailand it could be argued that people can make a reasonable living in agriculture and do not need to migrate to other employment.[15] But the high urban-rural income disparities common in South East Asia suggest a rather different explanation. Many people stay in rather poorly remunerated agricultural jobs because they doubt that they can find non-agricultural employment, and those that do move into non-agricultural jobs tend to find them in low-paid services rather than in manufacturing. It is striking that a considerably higher proportion of non-agricultural employment in Indonesia, Thailand, Malaysia and the Philippines was in services compared with Taiwan, South Korea and Japan at similar levels of income (Table 8).[16]

The issue of the inter-ethnic distribution of income and wealth has attracted a considerable literature in South East Asia, although with the exception of Malaysia, no government releases any data on household income or expenditure broken down by ethnic group. Evidence of changes in the distribution of wealth between ethnic groups is even more difficult to obtain; the Malaysian government releases data on share ownership by ethnic group

Table 8 Composition of the employed labour force in East and South East Asia (per capita GDP of approximately $2,040, 1985 prices)

Country/Year	*% employed labour force in agriculture*	*% of non-agricultural employed labour force*
Philippines (1995)	43.6	71.9
Indonesia (1992)	53.7	68.2
Thailand (1978)	66.5	64.3
Malaysia (1970)	53.5	68.7
South Korea (1978)	50.0	60.6
Taiwan (1969)	39.0	56.7
Japan (1955)	42.9	59.8

Sources: Philippines: *Philippines Statistical Yearbook 1996*, Table 11.3 (Manila: National Statistical Coordination Board); Indonesia: *Labour Force Situation in Indonesia, 1992* (Jakarta: Central Bureau of Statistics); Thailand: *Report of the Labour Force Survey, July–September, 1978* (Bangkok: National Statistical Office); Malaysia: *Third Malaysia Plan 1976–80*, Table 8.1 (Kuala Lumpur: Government Printing Office); South Korea: *Korea Statistical Yearbook 1976*, p. 70 (Seoul: Bureau of Statistics); Taiwan: *Taiwan Statistical Data Book, 1972*, Table 2.9b (Taipei: Bureau of Statistics); Japan: *Japan Statistical Yearbook 1958*, pp. 44–45 (Tokyo: Bureau of Statistics).

although this is hardly a complete indicator of the distribution of wealth. Malaysia is the only country in the region to have pursued policies designed to alter the ethnic distribution of income and wealth. Sieh (this volume, Chapter 20) examines the impact of the New Economic Policy on the structure of business in Malaysia, and points out that the corporate vehicle has been extensively used by the government to "propel Malays into the business world". This in turn has had the effect of increasing income and wealth differentials within the Malay population. As both Sieh and Mackie (this volume, Chapter 19) argue, the pro-Malay policies have not prevented many ethnic Chinese businesses from flourishing in Malaysia, as they have in other parts of the region. Far from being out-competed by multi-nationals many Chinese family firms in Thailand, Malaysia and Indonesia have gone multinational themselves, increasing both their asset base, and their influence in the wider Asian arena.

What are the consequences of these disparities in income and wealth? Studies using cross-sectional data from a large number of developing countries have reached the conclusion that "inequality in income and land distribution is negatively associated with subsequent growth" (Alesina and Rodrik 1994: 485; see also Birdsall, Ross and Sabot 1995: 495). Clearly such a finding would have to be treated with great caution in the South East Asian context. Certainly Balisacan (Chapter 23, this volume) finds a strong correlation between poverty and skewed land distribution by region in the Philippines, and some writers argue that the skewed distribution of income and wealth has been one factor in retarding growth in that country.[17] But Thailand and Malaysia, starting from a fairly skewed distribution of income in the 1970s, have achieved rapid growth over the past two decades. In Thailand there is persuasive evidence that this growth has been accompanied by widening income disparities.[18]

Can the growth momentum be regained?

The ASEAN economies (still excluding Cambodia but including Burma (Myanmar), Laos and Vietnam) now face several years of slower growth, and mounting demands, from both internal and foreign sources, for wide-ranging economic reforms.[19] No longer can policy-makers assume that GDP will grow at seven, eight or nine per cent per annum almost regardless of the international economic climate. In countries such as Thailand, Indonesia and Malaysia, governments which were confidently expecting rapid economic growth to continue well into the next century must now embark on far-reaching policy reforms in order to win back the confidence of both domestic entrepreneurs and foreign investors. In the Philippines which had under the Ramos administration seen an acceleration in economic growth after a decade of stagnation, a new administration will have to sustain economic growth in a much more uncertain regional economic environment. For Vietnam and Laos, where the transition from centrally planned to market-oriented economies was well underway by the mid-1990s, the current upheavals in other parts of Asia will affect both trade and inward flows of foreign investment. The same is true of Burma where the military regime has yet to convince many foreign investors that it is truly committed to thorough-going economic reform and the disciplines of a market economy.

On the other hand, the upheavals of 1997/98 have at least had the advantage of concentrating the energies of governments throughout the region on the necessity of ongoing policy reform. To most external observers, the Asian crisis has been one of microeconomic errors, rather than of increasing government expenditures leading to large budget deficits and escalating inflation.[20] By the mid-1990s, financial deregulation had led to a proliferation of banks (especially in Indonesia), and bank lending grew rapidly. Growth in bank and non-bank lending to the private sector exceeded by a considerable margin the already rapid growth of GDP in economies such as Thailand, Malaysia and Indonesia. This credit boom was in part the result of rapid growth of private capital inflows. The combination of open capital accounts and substantial interest rate differentials encouraged many firms to borrow offshore, while high interest rates attracted foreign funds into the domestic banking system. Because exchange rates were not expected to depreciate rapidly, much of the borrowing by domestic corporates was unhedged. Some of these loans were used to finance the development of export-oriented and import-substituting industries, but much was used to finance expansion in speculative, non-traded goods sectors, especially property.

Many economists in South East Asia have been aware of the dangers of an open capital account in a world where short-term capital flows were growing rapidly. As Naris Chaiyasoot points out (Chapter 9, this volume) "the increase in the inflow of such a mobile source of funds can indeed prove to be a destabilising influence". He argued that the Thai monetary authorities would have to be prepared to permit greater fluctuations in the exchange rate, if monetary policy was to continue to be an effective tool of macroeconomic stabilisation in Thailand, as it had been in the past. Such fluctuations would not necessarily destabilise the traded goods sector if appropriate hedging mechanisms could be developed. If these warnings, delivered in the early 1990s, had been heeded by the Bank of Thailand, at least some of the problems which emerged in the latter part of 1997 could have been avoided.[21]

That the financial systems throughout the region will have to undergo substantial change and new regulatory regimes put in place is now widely accepted. As two economists from an influential international think-tank argued in early 1998:

> These financial-sector problems could not have progressed so far were it not for long-standing weaknesses in banking and financial-sector supervision. Loan classification and provisioning practices were too lax; there was too much "connected" and "policy-directed" lending; state-owned banks did not pay much attention to the creditworthiness of borrowers; bank capital was often inadequate relative to the riskiness of banks' operating environment; and there were strong expectations of government bailouts should banks get into difficulties. On top of this, the quality of public disclosure and transparency was poor (Goldstein and Weatherstone 1998: 2).

Given these problems, financial sector reform will be a lengthy process. Goldstein and Weatherstone argue that there must be a clear statement of commitment by the monetary authorities everywhere in South East Asia to upgrade financial supervision and regulation. But to many observers the problems described by these authors, although originating in the financial sector, go much deeper and their ultimate resolution will depend on reforms in the entire structure of government. Many bad debts incurred by banks in Thailand, Malaysia and Indonesia are the result of politically motivated lending, in turn often the result of crude nepotism and cronyism. While such practices are not unique to South East Asia, the evidence from other times and places indicates that their eradication will not be easy, and may indeed involve not just changes of political personalities but thorough-going constitutional change.

Slow or negative growth of GDP will inevitably lead to increased unemployment and in all probability an increase in the proportion of the population under the poverty line.[22] Coping with the social and political consequences of this will be extremely difficult, especially for those governments (in particular Indonesia) which are already seriously tainted with nepotism and cronyism in the eyes of many of their citizens. New elections in Indonesia should produce a government with greater popular legitimacy, but it may not be stable, and a prolonged period of political instability, either in Indonesia or elsewhere in the region cannot but have negative consequences for economic recovery. Over the past two decades many governments in South East Asia have demonstrated a capacity for implementing extensive policy reforms in order to accelerate economic growth. Broadly speaking these reforms conformed to the policy prescriptions of the "Washington consensus". Now that this consensus is itself coming under critical scrutiny,[23] the challenge for the ASEAN economies will be to formulate and implement a new set of reforms which will not only lead back to sustained economic growth, but will also ensure a more equitable distribution of the benefits of growth.

NOTES

1 The phrase was used by Higgins (1968: 678).
2 The total amount of private foreign debt in several countries in the region has turned out to be considerably higher than had been previously realised, either by governments or by international agencies, thus giving rise to concerns about the adequacy of international monitoring of such flows.
3 World Bank, *World Development Report, 1997*, pp. 214–15.
4 Volume 3 in this series will focus on South Korea, Taiwan, Hong Kong and Singapore.
5 See Booth (1997a), Figure 2.
6 Warr's paper (Chapter 15 in this volume) discusses the role of export processing zones in Malaysia in detail, and contrasts the Malaysian experience with that in the Philippines, Indonesia and South Korea.
7 Warr and Nidhiprabha (1996; 210ff) discuss the role of the Bank of Thailand; Pasuk (1992) examines the interaction between technocrats and business leaders in economic policy-making in Thailand in the early 1980s. Jomo et al (1997: 105ff) examine the role of the bureaucracy in Malaysia. Bresnan (1993: Chapter 3) and Cole and Slade (1996: 327ff) discuss the role of technocrats in economic policy-making in Soeharto's Indonesia.
8 Yoshihara (1994: Chapter 18) contrasts the performance of the bureaucracy in Thailand and the Philippines after 1960, and concludes that in Thailand government interventions were far more pro-market and supportive of rapid capital formation in the private sector than in the Philippines, especially in the martial law era.
9 Even Indonesia which in early 1998 reneged on implementation of the conditions for an IMF rescue package, by April 1998 was back in serious discussions with the IMF and appeared willing to accept the policy reforms required.
10 See Warr (1992) for a full discussion of this literature in the Indonesian case.
11 Tongroj (1990: Chapter 6) discuss the problems of land rights and land titles in Thailand.
12 For further discussion of the problems in Thailand see Chapter 18 by Sirilaksana Khoman in this volume and also Myers and Sussangkarn (1992). It is surprising that, in spite of the growing literature stressing the failures of the Thai educational system (much of it contributed by Thais), and increasing concern about

the state of education in Indonesia, many foreign observers continued to argue that all the high-performing Asian economies invested heavily in education. See e.g, Campos and Root (1996: 56).

13 There is some debate among economists on the extent of technological and other linkages between the export-oriented manufacturing sector dominated by large multi-nationals especially in the electronics sector, and domestic firms. Jomo et al (1997; 107ff) argue that the linkages are small but Rasiah (1995: 194) finds evidence that: foreign firms have "played important roles in the transformation of local firms", although the extent of the influence varied by type of firm.

14 Ranis (1995 : 529) points out that overall 60 per cent of Taiwan's industrial R and D is carried out by the private sector and the balance within various public sector institutions most of which are oriented to the needs of small and medium scale firms. In most parts of South East Asia, such firms are largely ignored by government and such agencies as do exist to assist them in upgrading technology are poorly equipped and understaffed.

15 It is well known that Taiwan was extremely successful in generating rural non-farm employment opportunities in the 1960s and 1970s. Ranis and Stewart (1993: Table 14) show that rural non-agricultural incomes grew well over three times as fast as agricultural incomes between 1962 and 1980. In the Philippines between 1965 and 1985 the growth was broadly similar. A comparison of agricultural household income data for Indonesia in 1984 and 1993 indicates that off-farm sources of agricultural household income grew no faster than on-farm sources. It appears that what Ranis and Stewart refer to as the linkage ratio was far more powerful in Taiwan than in either Indonesia or the Philippines. See Booth (1997b) for further discussion of this point.

16 Berry (1978: 210) argues that the high proportion of the non-agricultural labour force employed in services in several Latin American economies reflects the fact that efficient manufacturing technologies are inherently more capital-intensive than in the 19th century when Western Europe, North America and Japan were beginning to industrialise. This may well be true, but such an explanation hardly explains the higher proportion of the non-agricultural labour force employed in services in Malaysia in 1970 compared with Taiwan.

17 The skewed distribution of land combined with an American style system of government has led to the concentration of political decision-making in the hands of the landed elite and thus often a reluctance to adopt growth-promoting policies which could threaten their interests.

18 See Ahuja, Bidani, Ferreira and Walton (1997), Chapter 4.

19 The IMF is predicting a contraction in Thai GDP in 1998 of 3.1 per cent in Thailand and five per cent in Indonesia (Economist, April 18–24, 1998). Malaysian GDP may not contract but growth will be very low in 1998.

20 See e.g. Krugman (1998), and the interview with David Hale, *Fortune*, January 12, 1998, pp. 10–12.

21 Why was the advice not heeded? There can be no doubt that the political independence of the Bank of Thailand had become severely compromised by the mid-1990s. For an extended discussion of the decline of technocratic influence in Thailand in the 1990s, see Siamwalla (1997).

22 The Indonesian government predicted that unemployment will rise to 13 million by the end of 1998, from an estimated nine million at the beginning of 1998. Several very pessimistic estimates were also circulated about the proportion of the population under the poverty line in 1998/99. In fact by early 1999, it appeared that both the unemployment and poverty consequences of the crisis

may have been exaggerated. See Booth (1999) for a review of the available evidence.

23 See e.g. Stiglitz (1998).

BIBLIOGRAPHY

Ahuja, Vinod, Benu Bidani, Francisco Ferreira and Michael Walton (1997), *Everyone's Miracle? Revisiting Poverty and Inequality in East Asia*, Washington: World Bank.

Akita, Takahiro and Rizal Affandi Lukman (1995), "Inter-regional Inequalities in Indonesia: A Sectoral Decomposition Analysis for 1975–92" *Bulletin of Indonesian Economic Studies*, Vol. 31(2), August, pp. 61–82.

Alesina, A. and Dani Rodrik (1994), "Distributive Politics and Economic Growth, *Quarterly Journal of Economics*, Vol. 109, May, pp. 465–85.

Amsden, Alice (1995), "Like the Rest: South-East Asia's 'Late' Industrialization", *Journal of International Development*, Vol. 7(5), pp. 791–99.

Andrus, J. R. (1948), *Burmese Economic Life*, Stanford: Stanford University Press.

Birdsall, Nancy, David Ross and Richard Sabot (1995), "Inequality and Growth Reconsidered: Lessons from East Asia", *World Bank Economic Review*, Vol. 9(3), 477–508.

Berry, Albert (1978), "A Positive Interpretation of the Expansion of Urban Services in Latin America, with Some Columbian Evidence", *Journal of Development Studies*, Vol. 14(2), pp. 210–31.

Booth, Anne (1992), "Income Distribution and Poverty" in Anne Booth (Editor), *The Oil Boom and After: Indonesian Economic Policy and Performance in the Soeharto Era*, Kuala Lumpur: Oxford University Press.

Booth, Anne (1994), "Repelita VI and the Second Long-Term Development Plan", *Bulletin of Indonesian Economic Studies*, Vol. 30(3), December, pp. 3–40.

Booth, Anne (1997a), "Initial Conditions and Miraculous Growth: Why is South East Asia Different from Taiwan and South Korea?", Working Paper 72, Department of Economics, SOAS, University of London.

Booth, Anne (1997b), "Rural Development, Income Distribution and Poverty Decline in South East Asia", Paper prepared for the Conference of the Asia-Africa Collaborative Research Programme, Johannesburg, 3–6 November.

Booth, Anne (1998), *The Indonesian Economy in the Nineteenth and Twentieth Centuries*, Basingstoke: Macmillan Press.

Booth, Anne (1999), "The Impact of the Asian Crisis on Poverty: Some Preliminary Evidence from Indonesia and Thailand", paper present to the Development Studies Association Workshop on Poverty Strategies, University of Reading, April 1999.

Bresnan, John (1993), *Managing Indonesia: The Modern Political Economy*, New York: Columbia University Press.

Bruno, Michael (1994), "Development Issues in a Changing World: New Lessons, Old Debates, Open Questions", *Proceedings of the World Bank Annual Conference on Development Economics 1994*, pp. 9–19.

Campos, Jose E. and Hilton L. Root (1996), *The Key to the Asian Miracle: Making Shared Growth Credible*, Washington: Brookings Institution.

Cole, David C. and Betty F. Slade (1996), *Building a Modern Financial System: The Indonesian Experience*, Cambridge: Cambridge University Press.

Collins, Susan M. and Barry P. Bosworth (1996), "Economic Growth in East Asia: Accumulation versus assimilation", *Brookings Papers on Economic Activity*, No. 2, pp. 135–203.

Doner, Richard and Anek Laothamatas (1994), "Thailand: Economic and Political

Gradualism" in Stephan Haggard and Steven B. Webb (Editors), *Voting for Reform*, New York: Oxford University Press.

Eng, Pierre van der (1993), "The Silver Standard and Asia's Integration into the World Economy", *Working Papers in Economic History, Number 175*, Canberra: Australian National University.

Furnivall, J.S. (1943), *Educational Progress in Southeast Asia*, New York: Institute of Pacific Relations.

Hill, Hal (1996), "Indonesia's Industrial Policy and Performance: "Orthodoxy Vindicated", *Economic Development and Cultural Change*, Vol. 45(1), October, pp. 147–74.

Ho, Samuel P. S. (1978), *Economic Development of Taiwan 1860–1970*, New Haven: Yale University Press.

Hobday, Mike (1994), "Technological Learning in Singapore: A Test Case of Leapfrogging", *Journal of Development Studies*, Vol. 30(4), pp. 831–58).

Ingram, J. (1971), *Economic Change in Thailand, 1850–1970*, Kuala Lumpur: Oxford University Press.

Jomo, K. S. et al. (1997), *Southeast Asia's Misunderstood Miracle: Industrial Policy and Economic Development in Thailand, Malaysia and Indonesia*, Boulder: Westview Press.

Jomo, K. S. and E. T. Gomez (1997), "Rents and Development in Multiethnic Malaysia" in M. Aoki, H-K Kim and M. Okuno-Fujiwara (Editors), *The Role of Government in East Asian Economic Development*, Oxford: Clarendon Press.

Krugman, Paul (1998), "What Happened to Asia?", On-line at http://web.mit.edu/krugman/www/DISINTER.html.

Lall, Sanjay (1995), "Malaysia: Industrial Success and the Role of Government", *Journal of International Development*, Vol. 7(5), pp. 759–73.

Laothamatas, Anek (1992), "The Politics of Structural Adjustment in Thailand: A Political Explanation of Economic Success" in Andrew J. MacIntyre and K. Jayasuriya (Editors), *The Dynamics of Economic Policy Reform in South-east Asia and the South-west Pacific*, Singapore: Oxford University Press.

Leurence, F. (1925), "Etude Statistique sur le Developpement Economique de L'Indochine", *Bulletin Economique de L'Indochine*, pp. 127–61.

Macintyre, Andrew (1994), "Business, Government and Development: Northeast Asian and Southeast Asian Comparisons" in Andrew Macintyre (Editor), *Business and Government in Industrialising Asia*, Ithaca: Cornell University Press.

McKendrick (1992), "Obstacles to Catch-up: The Case of the Indonesian Aircraft Industry" *Bulletin of Indonesian Economic Studies*, Vol. 28(1), April, pp. 39–66.

Mitchell, B. R. (1982), *International Historical Statistics: Africa and Asia*, Basingstoke: Macmillan.

Myers, Charles N. and Chalongphob Sussangkarn (1992), *Educational Options for the Future of Thailand: A Synthesis*, Bangkok: Thai Development Research Institute.

Myint, Hla (1967), "The Inward and Outward-Looking Countries of South East Asia", *Malayan Economic Review*, Vol. XII(1), April, pp. 1–13.

Pasuk Phongpaichit (1992), "Technocrats, Businessmen and Generals: Democracy and Economic Policymaking in Thailand", in Andrew J. MacIntyre and K. Jayasuriya (Editors), *The Dynamics of Economic Policy Reform in South-east Asia and the South-west Pacific*, Singapore: Oxford University Press.

Pranee Tinakorn (1995), "Industrialization and Welfare: How Poverty and Income Distribution are Affected" in Medhi Krongkaew (Editor), *Thailand's Industrialization and its Consequences*, Basingstoke: Macmillan.

Rahm, Henry A. (1952), "L'Action de la France en Indochine", *Bulletin Economique de L'Indochine*, Vol. 55(1), pp. 10–109.

Ranis, Gustav (1995), "Another Look at the East Asian Miracle", *World Bank Economic Review*, Vol. 9(3), 509–34.

Ranis, Gustav and Frances Stewart (1993), "Rural Non-agricultural Activities in Development: Theory and Application", *Journal of Development Economics*, Vol. 40, pp. 75–101.

Rock, Michael (1995), "Thai Industrial Policy: How Irrelevant was it to Export Success?", *Journal of International Development*, Vol. 7(5), pp. 759–73.

Rodrik, Dani (1995), Getting Interventions Right: How South Korea and Taiwan Grew Rich", *Economic Policy*, No. 20, April, pp. 55–107.

Rudner, Martin (1994), "Colonial Education Policy and Manpower Underdevelopment in British Malaya" in *Malaysian Development: A Retrospective*, Ottawa: Carleton University Press.

Siamwalla, Ammar (1997), "Can a Developing Economy Manage its Macroeconomy?" in *Thailand's Boom and Bust*, Bangkok: Thai Development Research Institute.

Stiglitz, Joseph E. (1996), "Some Lessons from the East Asian Miracle", *World Bank Research Observer*, Vol. 11(2), August, pp. 151–78.

Stiglitz, Joseph E. (1998), "More Instruments and Broader Goals: Moving towards the Post-Washington Consensus", Helsinki: WIDER Annual Lecture, January 7.

Tongroj Onchan (1990), *A Land Policy Study*, Research Monograph No. 3, Bangkok: The Thai Development Research Institute Foundation.

Wade (1994) "Selective Industrial Policies in East Asia: Is the East Asian Miracle Right?" in Albert Fishlow et al., *Miracle or Design?: Lessons from the East Asian Experience*, Washington: Overseas Development Council.

Warr, Peter G. (1992), "Exchange Rate Policy, Petroleum Prices and the Balance of Payments" in Anne Booth (Editor), *The Oil Boom and After: Indonesian Economic Policy and Performance in the Soeharto Era*, Kuala Lumpur: Oxford University Press.

Warr, Peter G. and Bhanupong Nidhiprabha (1996), *Thailand's Macroeconomic Miracle: Stable Adjustment and Sustained Growth*, Washington: World Bank.

World Bank (1983), *World Development Report 1983*, New York: Oxford University Press for the World Bank.

World Bank (1997), *World Development Report 1997*, New York: Oxford University Press for the World Bank.

Yoshida, M., Ichiro Akimune, M. Nohara and K. Sato (1994), "Regional Economic Integration in East Asia: Special Features and Policy Implications" in Vincent Cable and David Henderson (Editors), *Trade Blocs? the Future of Regional Integration*, London: Royal Institute of International Affairs.

Yoshihara, Kunio (1988), *The Rise of Ersatz Capitalism in South-east Asia*, Singapore: Oxford University Press.

Yoshihara, Kunio (1994), *The Nation and Economic Growth: The Philippines and Thailand*, Kuala Lumpur: Oxford University Press.

Part I

THE CHALLENGE OF MACROECONOMIC RESTRUCTURING

1

ECONOMIC REFORM, OPENNESS AND VIETNAM'S ENTRY INTO ASEAN

David Dollar

1 INTRODUCTION

The transformation that Vietnam has undergone during the decade between 1985 and 1995 is truly remarkable. In the mid-1980s Vietnam was heavily dependent on Soviet aid and was isolated from most other countries, including the members of the Association of Southeast Asian Nations (ASEAN). Its economy was in disastrous condition and its people were desperately poor. The past decade saw the collapse of the Soviet Union, which was a big shock for its client states. Vietnam is virtually unique among the Soviet bloc countries in its swift adjustment to a new reality. For the ten years ending in 1995, Vietnam's average gross domestic product (GDP) growth rate was 6.4 per cent. This rate was the highest among the 40 poorest countries listed in the *World Development Report 1996*. As a result of this rapid growth, people's lives have improved; the decline in poverty incidence is estimated to be from about 75 per cent in 1985 to about 50 per cent today.[1] There are a number of factors that accounts for Vietnam's quick adjustment and robust growth; one of the most important is the economy's growing openness in general, and the country's expanding ties with neighbouring economies in particular. Vietnam's entry into ASEAN in 1995 was an important symbol of its integration into the regional economy.

While Vietnam's economic performance has been good, it remains a poor country facing significant challenges. Important reforms need to be consolidated. This article examines the main challenges that remain, and in particular looks at the effect of Vietnam's entry into ASEAN on the country's economic development and on its reform programme. The next section lays the foundation for this analysis by briefly reviewing the progress with economic reform to date. It stresses the key role of trade liberalization and growing openness in Vietnam's accomplishments so far. The third section of the article examines Vietnam's integration into ASEAN from a strictly *economic* point of view. What are Vietnam's comparative advantages and how

Source: ASEAN Economic Bulletin, Vol. 13(2), November 1996, pp. 169–84.

are its economic relations with neighbouring countries likely to develop? The fourth section then addresses the key economic management challenges with which Vietnam must deal. Will entry into ASEAN make this management easier or more difficult? How will ASEAN membership affect policy-making in Vietnam? The overall messages are summarized in a brief concluding section.

2 MACROECONOMIC POLICIES AND GROWING OPENNESS, 1988–94

Vietnam's policy-makers faced an extraordinarily difficult situation in the mid-1980s. The country at the time was receiving massive assistance from the Soviet Union, and yet macroeconomic outcomes were still very poor. The economy was growing slowly, agriculture was stagnating at a subsistence level, and the excesses of the public sector were reflected in hyperinflation that reached 600 per cent per annum in 1986. Furthermore, the Soviet Union was facing its own economic difficulties by this time and it was clear that Soviet aid would decline. The key measures of Vietnam's macroeconomic reform are well documented and I will not repeat them here.[2] Suffice it to say that the macroeconomic programme contained many orthodox features including credit restraint, increases in interest rates, fiscal contraction, and devaluation.

The response of Vietnam's economy to the adjustment programme was very quick and very positive. There are a number of ways to capture this adjustment, but Figure 1.1 summarizes some key elements related to the real economy. The Soviet assistance in the mid-1980s is reflected in the current account deficit (capital inflow) of around 10 per cent of GDP. It can be seen that this dropped off fairly quickly. Nevertheless, investment rose throughout the adjustment period, because the domestic savings rate climbed by a remarkable twenty percentage points of GDP. In the high-inflation period, Vietnam had negative savings. By 1995 savings had increased to a respectable 16 per cent of GDP.

The fact that Vietnam was able to halt high inflation without suffering a recession can be attributed in part to the dualistic nature of the economy at the beginning of 1989. Agricultural land had been distributed to peasant families through a series of reforms stretching back over the decade. Furthermore, Vietnam had a private sector that was large relative to other socialist economies. This sector had been operating largely underground up until 1988. Stabilization is normally a shock to the economy because interest rates are raised, various government subsidies are cut, and devaluation makes imported inputs more expensive. Vietnam's stabilization had the predictable effect on the state sector of the economy, which showed negative growth in 1989. What was different in Vietnam was that, alongside the state sector, there were large agricultural and private service and manufacturing sectors, in

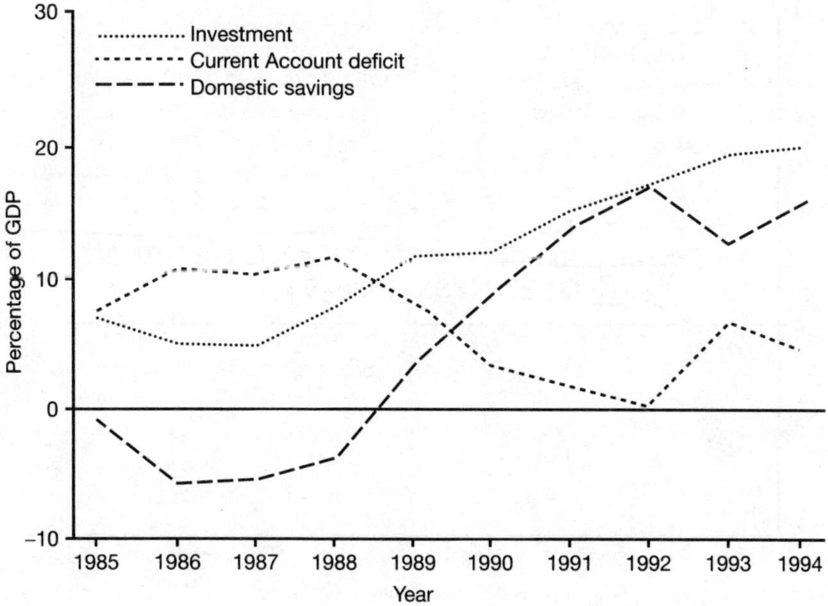

Figure 1.1 Savings and Investment, 1985–94

total producing about 60 per cent of GDP and employing 85 per cent of the labour force. These producers were not receiving credit from the formal sector or subsidies from the budget. Thus, for them, the year 1989 was one in which inflation was reduced and prices were liberalized, creating a good environment for expansion. That interest rates were much higher and subsidies lower did not matter to firms that were not getting any of the formal credit or budget subsidies to begin with.[3] These influences can be seen in the sectoral growth rates for this period. While agricultural value added increased about 8 per cent in 1989, industrial growth was negative (Figure 1.2). The industrial decline is even more striking when the growing crude oil production is removed from that sector. Non-oil industrial value added declined about 12 per cent in 1989.

That Vietnam was able to grow throughout its adjustment period can also be attributed to a large extent to the fact that the economy was being increasingly opened to the international market during this period. As part of its overall effort to stabilize the economy, the government unified its various controlled exchange rates in 1989 and devalued the unified rate to the level prevailing in the parallel market. This was tantamount to a 73 per cent *real* devaluation; combined with relaxed administrative procedures for imports and exports, this sharply increased the profitability of exporting. Since 1989 the exchange rate has largely been managed so as to maintain competitiveness. Thus, throughout the 1990–91 period, the exchange rate was allowed to

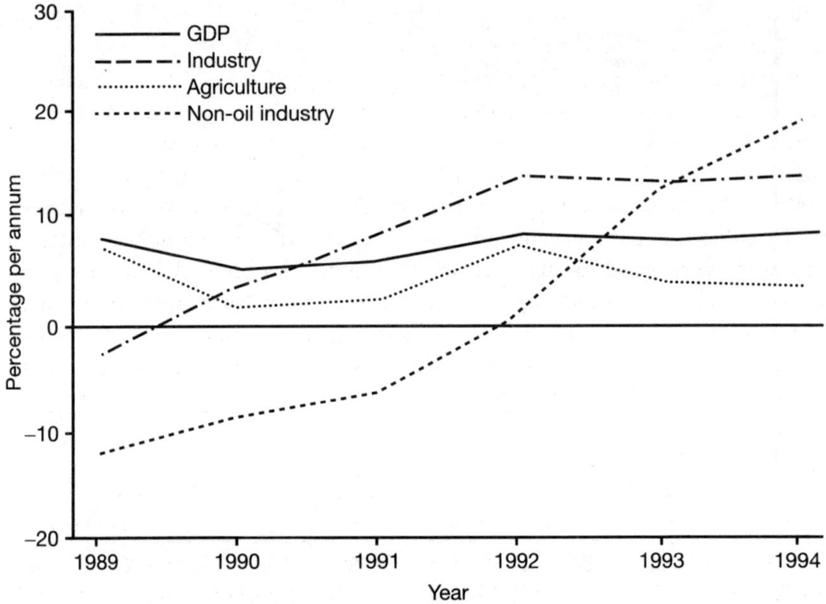

Figure 1.2 Growth Rates of GDP and Major Sectors, 1989–94

devalue continuously in line with the moderate inflation. This exchange rate policy produced strong incentives for export throughout most of the 1989–94 period. During these years real export growth averaged more than 25 per cent per annum, and exports have been a leading sector spurring the expansion of the economy.

While good macroeconomic policies have been key to Vietnam's success in recent years, structural reforms in the areas of foreign trade and investment were also required to complement those policies. In general Vietnam has taken a pragmatic and gradual approach to liberalizing foreign trade and investment. Policies have been revised on virtually a continual basis as experience has been gained. Vietnam began with a totally controlled system in which most of its trade was organized through bilateral protocols within the context of the Council for Mutual Economic Assistance (CMEA). Vietnam in fact had very few exports, and relied on aid, primarily from the Soviet Union, to finance its imports. It depended on the Soviet Union for most of its refined petroleum, steel, and fertilizer—all key inputs for the economy. Vietnam exported a small amount of primary products (dried fruit) or labour-intensive manufactures such as clothing to its CMEA partners. While the trade was limited, it did conform to Vietnam's comparative advantage: exporting products that used natural resources or abundant labour in exchange for more capital- and technology-intensive products.

As noted earlier, the threat of the end of Soviet assistance was a strong impetus to Vietnam's reform. It was clear in the later 1980s that Vietnam would in the future need to finance its imports in a different way, and that in particular it would need to increase its exports and also to find new sources of financing. The massive devaluation and generic structural reforms in 1989 created a good basis for exports, but other trade-specific reforms were needed as well. In the CMEA era Vietnam's external trade was monopolized by a small number of state trading companies. In 1989 the system was liberalized, first by allowing competition among state trading companies. Results in 1989 were very good, as hard currency exports doubled. All of this gain, however, can be attributed to two products: crude petroleum and rice. Vietnam was fortunate to have crude oil production coming on line just as the Soviet aid went into decline. (The offshore production was from a joint venture with the Soviet Union.) The gain in oil revenue was not a one-for-one substitute for the diminished aid, but it did to some extent cushion the shock of the impending CMEA collapse.

The increase in rice exports—from zero in 1988 to about US$300 million in 1989—was a dramatic success resulting from price reform, strengthened property rights, and the trade reforms that allowed more than 40 different trading companies to compete for this business. Vietnam's success as a rice exporter has been sustained in the years since 1989, and these exports have slowly increased. There is little potential for these exports to grow much further, however. Vietnam is a very densely populated country with 900 people per square kilometre of agricultural land, three times higher than China's density. Owing to its population density and modest natural resources, Vietnam's comparative advantage lies primarily in labour-intensive activities such as light manufacturing and services (tourism). The modest trade reforms introduced in 1989 were sufficient to support rice exports, but the resulting regime was not conducive to export of a more diversified set of products. The main problem with the trade regime was that only a small number of firms had certificates from the Ministry of Trade allowing direct access to the international market. For a country such as Vietnam, export of manufactured products requires import of machinery and materials. The control of these imports by a small number of state firms did not encourage development of a dynamic export sector. In addition to controlling the number of firms allowed to engage in foreign trade, the Ministry of Trade had two other control mechanisms: permits that served as unofficial quotas and import shipment licences that were mostly an accounting tool.[4]

One of the key structural reforms of the past few years has been the gradual dismantling of this complex system of control. First, all firms producing for export were given the right to import machinery and materials directly. Permits regulating the inflow of these products were then dropped, and shipment licences are being phased out. In practice this means that both state and private firms manufacturing for export can easily import needed inputs; furthermore, the sound exchange rate policy guarantees availability of foreign exchange at the market price. These policies have encouraged the expansion of manufactured exports. In the last couple of years, there have been a wide range of exports on the rise, including processed primary products (that is rubber, cashew nuts, and coffee), labour-intensive manufactures, and tourist services. Note in Figure 1.2 that the growth of non-oil industry has been extraordinarily rapid in the past two years, and this growth includes the processing and light-manufacturing export sectors.

This export surge was important both because it spurred production and because it financed growing imports for the economy. As anticipated, Soviet aid declined very rapidly after 1988, and this was not replaced by financing from other sources. Normally, the collapse of financing in this way would require a sharp cutback in imports. However, Vietnam's export growth was sufficient to ensure that imports could grow throughout this adjustment period.

Finally, it should be noted that there was a need for significant fiscal adjustment during this period. As in other countries with high inflation, the root problem was a large and inefficient public sector. The fiscal deficit was close to 10 per cent of GDP in the late 1980s (Figure 1.3), a level that could not be financed without resort to printing money. Part of the adjustment programme involved a very sharp reduction in government spending. With military demobilization, state enterprise layoffs, and civil service reductions, about 1.5 million people left the public sector between 1988 and 1992,

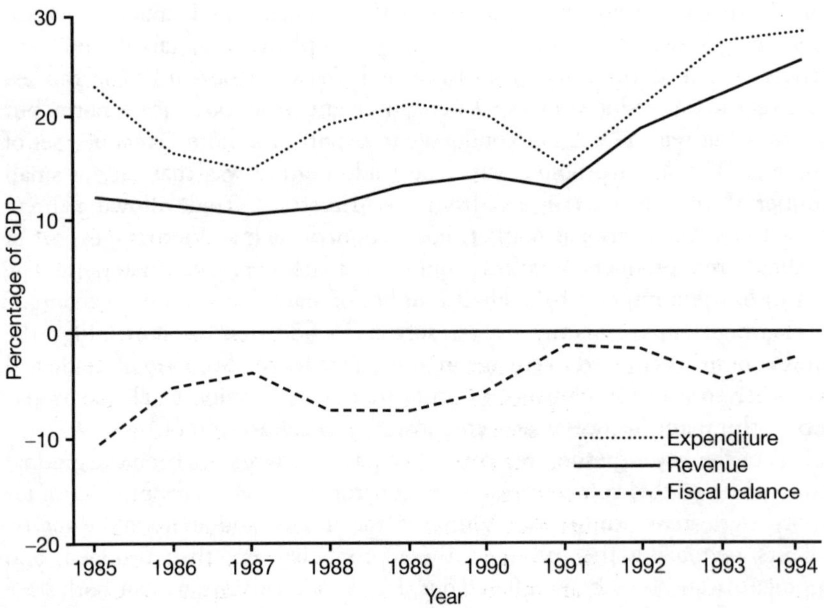

Figure 1.3 Government Revenue, Expenditure and Fiscal Balance, 1985–94

reducing its share of the labour force from 15 per cent to 10 per cent. This adjustment was accomplished without a recession because private producers, particularly in agriculture, light industries, and the service sector, responded quickly to strengthened property rights, price reforms, and new opportunities to export. The fact that the economy was growing made adjustment easier. The Ministry of Labor has found in its surveys that most workers laid off from the public sector were absorbed by the rapidly growing private sector within one year.[5] The robust growth, in conjunction with tax reform, has also led to increases in government revenue, with the result that public expenditure was actually larger as a share of GDP in 1994 than at the beginning of adjustment. The extraordinary devaluation of 1989, and good exchange rate management afterwards, resulted in strong effective demand for tradable goods, without which avoidance of a recession would probably have been impossible.

3 VIETNAM'S EXPANDING TRADE WITH ASEAN

Expanding international trade has been an important factor in Vietnam's development over the past decade. In this section I turn to the question of Vietnam's partners, in trade and investment. What is the potential for economic relations between Vietnam and its new ASEAN partners? And to what extent is that potential being realized? The logical starting point for this discussion is the different factor endowments of the ASEAN economies. Are Vietnam's endowments complementary or competitive with the other ASEAN members?

Important factor endowments are summarized in Table 1.1 (leaving out the small, oil-rich Brunei). Because Vietnam has grown well for a number of years now, there may be a tendency to lump it together with the other populous ASEAN members (Indonesia, the Philippines, and Thailand). This would be a mistake, as Vietnam's endowments are quite different. Vietnam is much poorer than the other ASEAN members. Some may be skeptical of the reported per capita GNP (US$170 in 1993, or about one-fifth the level in Indonesia or the Philippines). However, the World Bank's study of poverty in Vietnam estimated the poverty rate to be 51 per cent in 1993. Using a comparable methodology, poverty rates for other ASEAN members are Indonesia (15 per cent), the Philippines (21 per cent), and Thailand (16 per cent).[6] These data confirm that Vietnam is in fact a much poorer country, roughly two decades behind these other ASEAN members in terms of per capita income and poverty alleviation.

It is important to note that Vietnam's human development indicators are quite good, despite the country's poverty (Table 1.1). Illiteracy and child mortality, for example, are much lower than in Indonesia, and are comparable to levels typical of middle-income countries. Relatively speaking, Vietnam is well endowed with human capital. It may seem paradoxical that Vietnam is

Table 1.1 Vietnam in comparison to other ASEAN countries

	Vietnam	*Indonesia*	*Philippines*	*Thailand*	*Malaysia*	*Singapore*
GNP per capita (US$, 1993)	170	740	850	2,110	3,140	19,850
Population (millions, 1993)	71.3	187.2	64.8	58.1	19.0	2.8
People per sq. km. (1993)	215	98	216	113	58	2,800
GDP growth rate (%, 1980-93)	7.0[a]	5.8	1.4	8.2	6.2	6.9
Poverty incidence (%, recent year)	51	15	21	16	n.a.	n.a.
Adult illiteracy (1990)	12	23	10	7	22	<5
Under-5 mortality rate (1993)	48	111	59	45	17	7
Telephone mainlines (per 1,000 people, 1992)	2	8	10	31	112	415
Power (kWh per capita, 1992)	139	233	419	1,000	1,612	6,353

Note:
[a] 1985–95.

Source: *World Development Report 1995* (Washington, D.C.: World Bank, 1995).

rich in human capital but nevertheless very poor. The key to this apparent paradox is the word "relative". International trade depends on relative factor endowments, and Vietnam is relatively well endowed with human capital. The country has some natural resources as well, but these are modest relative to the population of nearly 75 million. Population density, for example, is far higher in Vietnam than in Indonesia or Thailand. The country has very little capital stock. There are no good data on the aggregate capital stock, but there are some suggestive indicators. In the infrastructure area, which is a key part of the capital stock, Vietnam has far fewer telephone lines per capita or power capacity per capita than other ASEAN countries.

The bottom line is that Vietnam has very good human resources, which currently earn very low wages because this important resource is not complemented by large capital stock, good infrastructure, or rich natural resources. This review suggests that there is a very sound basis for economic relations between Vietnam and its ASEAN partners. Vietnam's comparative advantage over the next few years should be in labour-intensive manufactures, labour-intensive services such as tourism, and certain natural resource products, such as rice and rubber. The country also needs to import capital-intensive and technology-intensive items, particularly machinery and intermediate products such as steel and fertilizer.

To what extent does Vietnam's current trade fit this pattern? Analysis of Vietnam's trade is hampered by the weak quality of the import and export data produced by the country. Most of Vietnam's trade now is with countries that report regularly to the UN trade data system. Thus, it is possible to reconstruct Vietnam's trade from its partners' data, as is done for exports in Table 1.2. There are obviously some potential pitfalls in this approach, but it nevertheless should indicate broad trends in Vietnam's trade. One serious problem is that Singapore did not report its Vietnam trade to the UN database before 1993. In 1988–89 Singapore had virtually no trade with Vietnam, and hence its non-reporting does not distort the comparison between that period and 1993. However, Singapore's trade gradually built up

Table 1.2 Vietnam's exports by commodity (US$ millions)

	1988	*1989*	*1990*	*1991*	*1992*	*1993*
Primary products of which:	466	763	1,145	1,304	1,581	1,966
Rice	0	316	272	225	300	340
Energy	64	199	403	519	771	983
Manufactured goods, of which:	101	137	175	267	598	1,085
Clothing	34	52	72	142	352	497
Footwear	6	13	9	7	32	155
Others	12	6	11	2	16	17
Total	579	906	1,332	1,571	2,195	3,068

Source: UN Trade Data Base.

during the early 1990s, so that its non-reporting before 1993 results in an artificial leap in the total from 1992 to 1993.

The table confirms that there has been an extraordinary increase in Vietnam's exports during this period of adjustment and reform, albeit beginning from a very low base.[7] Most of the increase between 1988 and 1990 came from rice and energy (oil and coal). Since 1990, there has been more diversified expansion. Between 1990 and 1993, rice and energy exports increased by US$650 million out of a total increase in exports of US$1.7 billion. The remaining US$1 billion increase was primarily manufactured products (US$800 million), with US$200 million from primary products other than rice and energy (that is coffee, rubber, and shrimp). Within manufactured exports, it is no surprise that the big increase was in clothing and footwear. Note also that the table includes *merchandise* trade. Data on tourist earnings are not very good, but their growth probably dwarfs the increase in agricultural exports since 1990.

Vietnam's imports can similarly be reconstructed from trade partners' data, and the result is reported in Table 1.3. Imports were sustained during the adjustment period because the growth of export earnings compensated for the loss of Soviet aid. Since 1991 there has been a very sharp increase in imports as private and official financial flows picked up. The pattern of imports is as

Table 1.3 Vietnam's imports by commodity (US$ millions)

Commodity	*1988*	*1989*	*1990*	*1991*	*1992*	*1993*
Food and tobacco, of which:	68	85	84	89	143	268
Tobacco and manufactures	1	2	1	4	41	88
Intermediate inputs, of which:	1,257	1,206	1,252	1,233	1,804	2,312
Textile materials	65	72	110	159	279	416
Petroleum and products	556	449	644	485	615	716
Organic chemicals	15	9	20	49	60	110
Medicinal, pharm. products	27	38	54	62	98	118
Fertilizers, manufacturers	365	418	223	210	190	130
Plastic materials etc.	11	9	18	65	108	118
Iron and steel	118	130	90	52	114	146
Capital goods, of which:	346	350	371	532	1,364	2,044
Power generating equipment	67	22	23	36	69	111
Industrial machines	118	85	98	141	348	473
Telecom, sound equipment	34	42	62	106	300	280
Electronic machinery n.e.s.	26	21	30	55	84	226
Road vehicles, of which:	57	86	89	79	312	615
Pass. motor vehicles, excl. buses	2	25	14	10	184	231
Road motor vehicles n.e.s.	4	11	13	5	32	42
Motor vehicle parts n.e.s.	5	1	2	14	6	14
Cycles, motorized or not	16	17	36	31	78	271
Others	20	16	78	9	25	20
Total	1,691	1,657	1,785	1,863	3,336	4,644

Source: UN Trade Data Base; Vietnam Ministry of Trade (for trade with Russia).

expected, with 1993 imports divided roughly in half between capital goods and intermediate products. One fact of note is that import of passenger cars and motorcycles amounted to about US$500 million in 1993, one-quarter of capital goods imports.

A key point about the import and export data concerns the direction of Vietnam's trade. The country has shifted very rapidly from trading primarily with CMEA countries to trading primarily with countries in its region and with western Europe. In 1993 two-thirds of Vietnam's exports went to OECD (Organization for Economic Cooperation and Development) countries, of which Japan was the largest customer. In the same year, two-thirds of Vietnam's imports came from the economies of ASEAN plus Korea, Taiwan, and Hong Kong. These data suggest that Vietnam's economy is very complementary with the more developed ASEAN states (that is Singapore and Malaysia). With Indonesia, the Philippines, and Thailand, on the other hand, there is likely to be a mixture of complementarity and competition. Indonesia recently exchanged fertilizer for rice with Vietnam, a good example of complementarity that reflects Indonesia's higher level of industrialization. At the same time, all of these economies are producing labour-intensive manufactures for the United States and other developed markets. With the end of the U.S. trade embargo, Vietnam will begin to compete for that business.

Vietnam's trade liberalization has been complemented by a similar liberalization of policies towards foreign investment. The move to attract foreign investment began during the very early years of reform, and a foreign investment law was passed in 1987. Vietnam's pragmatism is evidenced by the fact that it has been willing to amend this law and the implementing regulations several times already, in light of experience. The State Committee for Cooperation and Investment,[8] which licenses and regulates direct foreign investment (DFI), reports nearly US$12 billion of commitments and a much smaller, those still impressively large, US$3 billion of cumulative disbursements (inflow) as of end-1994.

Vietnam's foreign trade appears to be closely linked to this foreign investment. The largest foreign investors are by and large the same economies from which Vietnam imports. The four largest investing economies are in fact the four tigers: Taiwan, Hong Kong, Singapore, and South Korea (Table 1.4). Together they account for about half of all the investment (measured by value of commitments). The same four economies account for about one-half of Vietnam's imports, which were shown earlier to be concentrated in capital goods and intermediate products. Furthermore, a growing share of foreign investment is going to manufacturing, which has been the leading source of exports in recent years. In the early years of reform, foreign investment went primarily to the oil sector and to tourism. By the end of 1994, however, industry (excluding oil and gas) was the leading receiving sector (Table 1.5). Thus, it seems that the four Asian tigers are investing in manufacturing and tourism in Vietnam and contributing to the export boom.

Table 1.4 Foreign investment by source (commitments, end of 1994)

Countries	*Number of projects*	*Total investment of projects (US$ million)*
Taiwan	179	1,968
Hong Kong	171	1,796
Singapore	76	1,028
Republic of Korea	98	889
Japan	73	789
Australia	42	661
Malaysia	32	585
France	58	510
Switzerland	14	463
England	15	376
Total	1,201	11,992

Source: State Committee for Cooperation and Investment.

Table 1.5 Foreign investment by economic sectors (commitments, end of 1994)

	Number of projects	*Total capital (US$ million)*
Licensed projects	1,201	11,992
Projects in	1,012	11,043
Industry	548	4,334
Oil & gas	26	1,302
Agriculture & forestry	74	369
Aquaculture	21	62
Transport & telecom	128	951
Hotel & tourism	113	2,235
Services	134	1,254
Finance & banking	15	177
Housing development	14	70
Export processing zone	29	109
Industrial centre	2	167
Others	8	14

Source: State Committee for Cooperation and Investment.

There is an economic logic to these middle-income economies investing in Vietnam. As their wages have risen in response to their successful development, they have lost comparative advantage in the labour-intensive activities. Vietnam's excellent location, good human resources, and low wages have attracted producers from the newly-industrialized countries (NICs). It also likely that investors from the NICs are less daunted by the weak state of the legal and regulatory framework, compared to investors from OECD countries. In the case of Taiwan, Hong Kong, and Singapore, investors also have a link to the still substantial Chinese community in Ho Chi Minh City.

4 REGIONAL INTEGRATION AND VIETNAM'S REFORM PROGRAMME

Vietnam has already received substantial economic benefits from greater integration with ASEAN and with the larger East Asian economy, and would derive further benefits from closer integration; that was the main conclusion of the previous section. Beyond the narrowly economic benefits, however, are other intangible benefits from integration that may ultimately prove to be more important for Vietnam. The other ASEAN countries are excellent role models for Vietnam. It was noted above that Vietnam is roughly two decades behind countries such as Indonesia or Thailand. However, Vietnam will not automatically catch up. There are many examples of countries that have stagnated for long periods of time, including Vietnam between 1975 and 1985. Vietnam has grown well now for about a decade, but the country still faces important policy challenges. In my view, the three most crucial of these are macroeconomic management, trade liberalization, and state enterprise reform/privatization. The ASEAN countries all have good lessons to share in these areas; furthermore, close economic ties to ASEAN creates economic and political pressure to follow through with reform in these areas. This pressure is ultimately beneficial to Vietnam. One of the most important roles of international economic agreements is to bind governments to changes that are for the good, but that may be controversial for some domestic constituencies. Vietnam's membership in ASEAN increases the probability that it will continue to reform and to grow successfully. In this section, I take each of the key policy areas in turn—macroeconomic management, trade liberalization, and enterprise reform—and examine the impact of integration into ASEAN on Vietnam's policy-making.

Macroeconomic management is an area in which Vietnam has done well for several years. However, since the full success of stabilization around 1992, the country has not been tested with any major shocks. The country's track record is short and it would be a mistake to be sanguine about macro management. In joining ASEAN, Vietnam is linking itself to a group of countries that generally has excellent macroeconomic management. This link has its advantages as well as its pitfalls. The issue is analogous to the less developed countries of Europe attaching themselves to Germany and its strong currency. For Vietnam, a relatively stable currency link to the ASEAN economies is an excellent objective. This will encourage strong macroeconomic management. To some extent it ties the hands of policy-makers, which is good for long-run development, though this may be resented at times in the short run.

One important macro issue for Vietnam is that its recent inflation of 10–15 per cent has been too high. During this period the exchange rate against the dollar has been stable, not primarily because of intervention but because of strong capital inflows. By extension, Vietnam's exchange rate has been fairly stable against currencies, such as those of Indonesia and Thailand, that are also loosely pegged to the dollar. Given Vietnam's higher inflation, it has experienced real appreciation against these other ASEAN economies. In my view, this problem has not been severe so far. Vietnam's low initial level of development indicates that there is a lot of scope for productivity enhancement, and one would expect some tendency towards real appreciation without any dimunition of competitiveness. Nevertheless, Vietnam is flirting with the danger of 15 per cent inflation. In the next few years it needs to bring inflation down to high single digits or else accept continual slow depreciation of the nominal exchange rate. The stability of the dong-dollar relationship has taken on important symbolic value in the business community, however, so that the former course is strongly preferable. In the face of high capital inflows Vietnam's best course, as demonstrated by its ASEAN partners, is tight fiscal and monetary policies that keep inflation in check. It remains to be seen if Vietnam will strengthen its macro policies in this way. But the link with ASEAN increases the probability that it will by putting pressure on policy-makers to keep the exchange rate stable and inflation low, and by providing good practical examples of macro management in the face of high capital inflows.

The second important area in which Vietnam's policy needs to improve is trade liberalization. Objective studies of trade regimes generally find the ASEAN countries to be among the most open of developing countries. One can always point to specific examples of protection, but overall the ASEAN countries are relatively more open, and most observers find this to be an important factor in their rapid development.[9] While Vietnam has made good progress with initial steps to reduce direct controls of foreign trade, it still has a long way to go to harmonize its trade system with the ASEAN group. A further problem is the tariff code. Vietnam introduced import taxes as it began dismantling non-tariff barriers. The average level of tariffs (about 15 per cent) is modest. These tariffs, combined with the spectacular growth of import volumes, have provided the government with an important source of revenue and have been a factor assisting fiscal stabilization. The problem with the tariff code is that it has 28 different rates dispersed from zero to over 100 per cent. Furthermore, there is little logic to the code. In some cases finished products have much higher tariffs than intermediate products, producing large and inefficient effective protection. In other sectors, however, finished products have lower tariffs than intermediate products creating negative protection for assembly operations.[10] Streamlining this tariff code is an important reform that should be undertaken soon before vested interests develop that make dismantling of protection difficult.

Vietnam is very fortunate that its membership in ASEAN and its aspiration to membership in AFTA and the World Trade Organization will put pressure on it to move forward with dismantling of non-tariff barriers and with rationalization of the tariff code. This is an area in which there is quite a bit of confusion among Vietnamese policy-makers. There is still talk of targeting particular industries for development. This view is reflected in the political report for the mid-term party conference (1994):

> Capital allocated from the budget should be invested mostly in the construction of socio-economic infrastructure, a number of key industrial enterprises and a number of processing units for agriculture, forest and aquatic products and for export goods and services.

This kind of direct support of industry is not going to be acceptable to Vietnam's trading partners, nor will indirect support through tariff protection. Thus, there are likely to be some fairly clear clashes between the tendency in the party and the government to want to protect certain industries and Vietnam's commitment to ASEAN and eventually to the WTO to reduce protective barriers.

The evidence that trade liberalization is a better development strategy than infant-industry protection is clear. The ASEAN economies are among the best examples to demonstrate this. While these countries have experimented with industrial targeting, most observers agree that targeting did not produce good results in the ASEAN countries and was not an important part of their success.[11] Vietnam needs to learn and internalize this important lesson. That the results of trade liberalization in Vietnam so far have been excellent helps in this process. It is also very important that the government can point to international agreements that require it to continue down this road. An important question is how quickly Vietnam can meet its trade liberalization obligations. There is a tendency in international agreements to give low-income countries additional time to meet tariff reduction agreements. In many ways this special treatment is unfortunate. Vietnam will benefit strongly from trade liberalization, so that the sooner it is accomplished the better. Some policy-makers in Vietnam are concerned that, if they liberalize too soon, they will be overrun by competition from other ASEAN countries. But that is a matter for macroeconomic management, discussed above. With good macro management that preserves competitiveness, Vietnam will find itself competitive in a wide range of industries, and a net importer in other industries, as happens for all economies. Trade instruments are not a substitute for macroeconomic management. And with good macro policies, a liberalized trade regime will lead to the most efficient investment. The only real concern about timing should involve the revenue question. Vietnam has come to depend to some extent on import tariff revenue, not uncommon for low-income countries. It needs to co-ordinate tariff reductions with other tax reforms that ensure a steady revenue collection. In Vietnam's case this problem is not too great, however, because the reliance on tariff income is not excessive. In fact, the main problem with Vietnam's tariff code is the wide variability of rates. There are too many products with zero or very low rates. Vietnam could immediately make significant improvements in its tariff code by simplifying it to a small number of rates (that is 5, 10, 20, and 30 per cent). The other tariff changes could then be phased in on the agreed timetable.

I have saved for last the most difficult reform issue, state enterprise reform. In comparing Vietnam and the other ASEAN countries, I neglected to mention the most important difference of all: the ASEAN economies consist largely of private firms, whereas Vietnam has 7,000 state enterprises that dominate many fields. Vietnam is fortunate among transition economies in that it has a relatively large private sector, but its position is still small compared to ASEAN countries. There was a substantial down-sizing of the state enterprise sector during the years of fiscal adjustment, 1989–92. The number of firms has declined from 12,000 to 7,000, and about one-third of the 1988 work force has left the sector.[12] More recently, however, the state sector has seen a resurgence, largely owing to partnerships with foreign investors. In this context a significant fact is that 98 per cent of all joint ventures are with state enterprises rather than with the domestic private sector. The main attraction of the state sector, to foreign investors, is easy access to land and the value of a well-connected local partner in dealing with the bureaucracy.

Linking state enterprises with foreign investors has a positive impact on the firms, leading them to operate on a sound commercial basis. There is a danger, however, that powerful alliances among line ministries, large state enterprises, and foreign investors will create an environment that hampers the development of the domestic private sector. In the East Asian economies that have had sustained growth of exports and GDP over a long period, entry of new firms—most starting out as small and medium sized ones—has been a key element of success. Vietnam can get a certain amount of mileage out of linking its viable state firms with foreign partners. But fairly soon the large gains from this approach will have been achieved, and then the economy will need ongoing entry of small and medium domestic private firms—as well as entry of new foreign investors—to sustain industrial growth. Thus a central question over the next decade is whether a good framework for such an ongoing expansion of the private sector is being put in place.

There are several reasons to be concerned about the alliances between line ministries and foreign investors. First, several of these ministries have crucial roles to play in developing the basic economic infrastructure, including roads, ports, water supply, and power. However, commercial ventures in hotels or manufacturing are more attractive to these ministries in the current environment of weak accounting and accountability. Aid resources are available to finance the rehabilitation and expansion of infrastructure, but projects are proceeding slowly. The fact that ministries are distracted by commercial activities is one reason for weak implementation. A second and more serious issue is that there is obviously a conflict of interest between ministries and local authorities as regulators and as producers. As regulators, government bodies should favour ease of entry and should promote competition. As partners in producing joint ventures, however, these government agencies have an interest in restrictive arrangements.

In recent years progress with enterprise reform or privatization has been very slow. Once stabilization was achieved and foreign investment began to flow in to modernize state firms, the policy-makers lost any enthusiasm for enterprise reform. Obviously the economy has grown well in the past couple of years and it is hard to argue with success. But in the longer term there are reasons to be concerned. No government has been able to manage 7,000 firms efficiently, and there are already growing problems with corruption that reflect this difficulty of accountability. Looking to the future, entry of private firms is clearly hampered by the current system.

Integration into ASEAN will not have the same direct effect on the state enterprise problem as it is likely to have on the issues of macroeconomic management and trade liberalization. Nevertheless, the three issues are closely related. Vietnam has done very little directly to reform state enterprises. Yet, significant changes have already occurred because the macroeconomic and trade policies have spilled over into the enterprise arena. For example, stabilization required putting an end to budget subsidies for firms and to highly subsidized credit. These macro changes hardened the budget constraint for state firms and led to the down-sizing that has occurred. The trade liberalization that has occurred up until now has similarly created a lot of competition for state firms producing tradable goods, which has also spurred efficiency. State firms in some cases have survived by completely shifting their products in line with comparative advantage. The point is, the main enterprise reforms to date have been spurred by a commitment to macro stability and by initial trade reforms. To the extent that Vietnam's integration into ASEAN puts pressure on policy-makers to further improve macro management and further liberalize trade, it will indirectly encourage further measures of enterprise reform.

This analysis implies that there is some contradiction in the government's different policies, on the one hand trying to hang on to large numbers of commercial enterprises, and on the other hand trying to join the world market economy and to play by its macro and micro rules. It is likely that Vietnam and its partners will have to live with this contradiction for some time. It is also possible to imagine the three policies interacting in a way that moves the whole reform backward. For example, domestic pressure to increase direct and indirect subsidies to state enterprises could undermine macro stability through a rising fiscal deficit and/or excessive credit creation. Macro problems in turn could spillover into the external accounts, creating problems with the exchange rate and the balance of payments. Trade restrictions are not an efficient way to deal with such a problem, but many developing countries have gone down this wrong path when faced with incipient crises. Thus, one could imagine backsliding on enterprise reform, macro policies, and trade liberalization all reinforcing each other. The response of

ASEAN partners and the larger global community will be important if there are such incidents. International groupings must demonstrate some flexibility in the face of domestic political problems for one partner. However, it really is in Vietnam's long-term interest for its economic partners to expect continued movement towards internationally accepted policies. In particular, it will be important for ASEAN and others to have high expectations for Vietnam's progress with macro management and with trade liberalization. Further measures in these areas will increase the pressure for meaningful reform of state enterprises. In my view, this will require at least some gradual privatization of the large number of commercial firms now in state hands.

Integration with ASEAN can be a critical anchor for Vietnam's policies, encouraging it to stay the course in the key areas of macro management and trade liberalization. This path will expose further the contradictions of state ownership within a system that is integrating with dynamic market economies. The route to enterprise reform is not easy, economically or politically, and there is much that can wrong along the way. But if Vietnam is really committed to integration with the East Asian economy then, with fits and starts, these problems are likely to be solved.

CONCLUSIONS

Vietnam stands out among the economies in transition from planned to market systems. Like China it has grown well for the last decade. But China did not have to deal with the same kind of macroeconomic problems that Vietnam faced; not linked to the Soviet bloc in recent decades, China did not receive any economic shock when the Soviet Union collapsed. Among the economies closely tied to the Soviet Union, Vietnam is unique for its swift adjustment. While Vietnam's stabilization and macroeconomic management had many orthodox elements, its ability to grow throughout this adjustment must be attributed in large part to its increasingly outward orientation. Exports have grown from around US$500 million in 1988 to nearly US$5 billion in 1995. At the same time the inflow of private foreign investment increased from zero to around 7 per cent of GDP in 1995. Relative to its own GDP, Vietnam is one of the largest recipients of direct investment among developing countries, though the absolute inflow is still small relative to the amounts going to Indonesia, Thailand, or Malaysia. The general point is that Vietnam has made a lot of progress opening its economy over the past decade, and these reforms have had a dramatic payoff for its people.

Certainly part of Vietnam's success can be attributed to its fortuitous location among the most dynamic economies in the world. There is a good basis for Vietnam to trade with its neighbours. It is much poorer than the other ASEAN countries, yet has excellent human resources. This pattern reveals a relative wealth of human capital and a relative scarcity of finance, infrastructure, and natural resources. On this basis one would expect Vietnam to export labour-intensive products: clothing, footwear, rice, rubber, and tourist services are all good examples. In exchange Vietnam needs capital- and technology-intensive items, and capital itself (foreign investment). This predicted pattern of exchange is exactly what has emerged over the past decade. Most of Vietnam's foreign trade and investment is with nearby economies. About half of its imports and of its foreign investment come from Asian developing economies, including Hong Kong, Taiwan, Korea, and the ASEAN countries. As this trade expands, Vietnam's economy should be highly complementary to the more developed ASEAN economies (Malaysia, Singapore) and partly complementary and partly competitive with Indonesia, Thailand, and the Philippines.

Despite the progress to date, Vietnam faces important policy challenges. The immediate and visible ones are to consolidate macroeconomic management (notably bring inflation down to high single digits) and to further liberalize foreign trade and investment. Vietnam's membership in ASEAN will help in these tasks. The other countries provide good role models, and firming up the link to ASEAN will require progress in reforming macro and trade policies. Frankly, it will be good for Vietnam's development if its ASEAN partners expect a lot from it in terms of meeting tariff reduction schedules. There is no economic reason that Vietnam cannot meet these goals, and for all countries an international commitment helps overcome domestic political opposition from vested interests.

A key reform area in which there has not been much recent progress in Vietnam concerns state enterprises. After some tough initial measures driven by fiscal austerity, the enterprise reform programme slowed around 1993. Vietnam's membership in ASEAN may not have much direct effect in this area, but it should have indirect benefits. Good macroeconomic management and further liberalizing of trade are two key measures that will keep the pressure on the state enterprise sector. Ongoing reform in the macro and trade areas will require Vietnam to come to grips with the problems of managing 7,000 state firms. In my view, the solution to this problem in the long run at least must involve significant privatization. This reform will not be easy, but Vietnam is far more likely to undertake it as a member of an integrated ASEAN economy than in isolation. There are still many things that could go wrong with Vietnam's economic development, but its association with ASEAN countries greatly increases the probability of a positive outcome over the next ten years.

NOTES

The views expressed are those of the author and do not necessarily reflect the opinions of the World Bank or its member countries.

1 Dollar, Glewwe, and Litvack (forthcoming), chapter 1.
2 On Vietnam's economy and reform program in general, see Dapice, Haughton

and Perkins (forthcoming), Ljunggren (1993), Riedel (1992), and de Vylder and Fforde (1988); on the stabilization and structural adjustment more specifically, see Dollar (1993, 1994).

3 Ronnas (1992) used survey data to demonstrate the extent to which the private sector in services and manufacturing was cut off from formal credit channels in this period.

4 On the trade regime and its gradual reform, see World Bank (1994).

5 World Bank (1993*b*), chapter 3.

6 World Bank (1995).

7 Table 1.2 does not include Vietnam's exports to the Soviet Union during the 1988–91 period. Those exports were minor, probably amounting to several hundred million dollars equivalent at their peak. Excluding them from the table has the effect of modestly exaggerating the growth of Vietnam's exports. For the 1992–93 period, Vietnam's exports to Russia (now in hard currency) are included. At that time the exports amounted to US$100–200 million per year. The potential bias of excluding the Soviet trade is much more serious on the import side, where Vietnam received very significant flows from its major ally. In Table 1.3, I have included Vietnam's major imports from the Soviet Union during 1988–91: refined petroleum, steel, fertilizer, and other such inputs. As data on these were available in physical units, it was possible to value them at world market prices. Thus Table 1.3 should reflect quite accurately Vietnam's overall imports during the period in which its trade was shifting from CMEA partners to East Asian market economies.

8 The State Committee for cooperation and Investment and the State Planning Committee were recently merged into a new Ministry of Planning and Investment.

9 Dollar (1992) constructed an objective index of trade orientation and demonstrated that more outward developing economies grew more rapidly, after adjusting for differences in investment levels. In that study, the ASEAN economies were found to be among the most open in the developing world.

10 World Bank (1994).

11 The World Bank's (1993*a*) *East Asian Miracle* study canvasses the literature on this topic.

12 World Bank (1994).

REFERENCES

Dapice, David, Jonathan Haughton and Dwight Perkins, eds. *In Search of the Dragon's Tale: Economic Reform in Vietnam*. Cambridge, MA: Harvard Institute for International Development and Harvard University Press, forthcoming.

Dollar, David. "Macroeconomic Management and the Transition to the Market in Vietnam". *Journal of Comparative Economics* 18 (1994): 357–75.

——. "Outward-Oriented Developing Economies Really Do Grow More Rapidly: Evidence from 95 LDCs, 1976–1985". *Economic Development and Cultural Change* 40 (1992): 523–44.

——. "Vietnam: Successes and Failures of Macroeconomic Stabilization". In *The Challenge of Reform in Indochina*, edited by Borje Ljunggren. Cambridge, MA: IID and Harvard University Press, 1993.

Dollar, David, Paul Glewwe, and Jennie Litvack, eds. *Household Welfare and Vietnam's Transition to a Market Economy.* Forthcoming.

Ljunggren, Borje, ed. *The Challenge of Reform in Indochina.* Cambridge, MA: IID and Harvard University Press. 1993.

Riedel, James. "On the Trail of the Tigers". Working Paper, Johns Hopkins/SAIS, 1992.

Ronnås, Per. *Employment Generation Thmugh Private Entrepreneurship in Vietnam.* Geneva: ILO, 1992.

Vietnam, Communist Pasty of. "Political Report of the Central Committee to the Mid-term Party Conference". Hanoi, 1994.

de Vylder, Stefan and Adam Fforde. *Vietnam: An Economy in Transition.* Stockholm: Swedish International Development Authority (SIDA), 1988.

World Bank. *The East Asian Miracle: Economic Growth and Public Policy.* Washington, D.C.: 1993*a*.

——. *Vietnam: Transition to the Market.* Washington, D.C.: 1993*b*.

——. *Vietnam: Public Sector Management and Private Sector Incentives.* Washington, D.C.: 1994.

——. *Vietnam: Poverty Assessment and Strategy.* Washington, D.C.: 1995.

2

THE PHILIPPINE ECONOMY

What's Right, What's Wrong

Emmanuel S. de Dios

Most domestic and foreign enthusiasm over the Philippine economy's performance in 1994 was due to its resiliency and success in overcoming its most immediate problems. Confidence strengthened as the economy showed a strong recovery from the recession of 1991–92 (Figure 2.1) and left behind the crippling power outages that had held back industrial growth since 1992. The gross domestic product (GDP) for the first three quarters of the year rose 4.4 per cent, a modest performance for the region, but a vast improvement over the figure of less than 2 per cent over the same period in 1993. Large contributions made by remittances from overseas contract workers raised the growth of income significantly more than product growth. The gross national product (GNP) has grown faster than GDP since 1989, a phenomenon likely to be observed for some time to come.[1]

Led by manufacturing, industry recovered the most rapidly in 1994, growing at more than 5 per cent in the first three quarters, unhampered by power shortages for the first time since 1992 (Table 2.1). Services were pulled along, growing at 3.7 per cent over the same period. Agriculture, on the other hand, grew at an historically high rate of over 4.4 per cent, helped along by favourable weather and early harvests. All in all, it is estimated that GNP and GDP will increase by 5.5 per cent and 4.5 per cent, respectively, over the whole year, about a percentage point higher each than the target growth rates. Encouraged by this year's developments, the government decided to raise its GNP growth projections for 1995 to 6.5 per cent, with output expected to grow a percentage point lower than that.

Even as the most immediate problems have been resolved, however, serious attention has come to focus on whether and how the present recovery may be parlayed into sustained growth, a question that will be definitively settled only in the next few years. Changes in macroeconomic fundamentals, resource allocation, and resource use and mobilization, and social issues warrant a closer look at the Philippine economy, both because of favourable developments and the challenges that remain. Despite a generally optimistic outlook,

Source: *Southeast Asian Affairs 1995*, Singapore: Institute of Southeast Asian Studies, 1995, pp. 273–88.

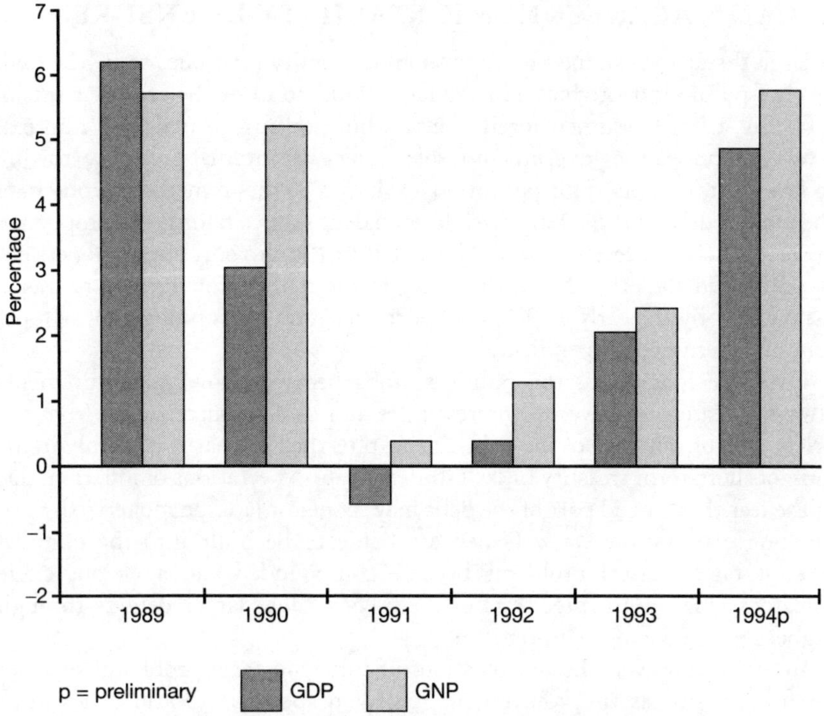

Figure 2.1 GDP and GNP Growth, 1989–94
Source: National Statistical Coordination Board.

Table 2.1 Growth rates of GDP by sector, 1989–94 (percentages)

	GDP	*Agriculture*	*Industry*	*Services*
1989	6.21	3.01	7.38	7.03
1990	3.04	0.48	2.56	4.86
1991	−0.58	1.37	−2.67	0.15
1992	0.34	0.39	−0.54	1.02
1993	1.97	2.01	1.78	2.10
1994*	4.42	4.13	5.53	3.67

Note:
* January to September.

Source: National Statistical Coordination Board.

questions on the ultimate success and follow-through of various policies and the sustainability of recent trends remain. It is important to identify in each area what is temporary and conjunctural, and what is lasting and structural.

CAN MACROECONOMIC STABILITY BE ENSURED?

A large threat to sustained macroeconomic stability continues to be the high level of public indebtedness. In the late 1980s, to meet the requirements of servicing a large assumed foreign debt while seeking to maintain minimal levels of services, the government resorted to heavy internal public borrowing to finance its deficits. This permitted a solution to the immediate problem of the foreign debt of the 1980s, with foreign debt service falling as a proportion of current account receipts from 34 per cent in 1986 to only about 16 per cent by 1994. On the other hand, the resort to internal borrowing had created a fiscal crisis[2] by the early 1990s, as debt service took up as much as 30–40 per cent of government expenditure.

Over the long haul, the public sector's heavy borrowing requirements always threaten to drive up interest rates and pull resources away from the private sector. The size of the public debt, plus the fact that it is mainly in the form of short-term treasury bills (T-bills), create expectations of inflation, due to the fear that a good part of the debt may sooner or later be monetized. Such inflation expectations, *à la* Fisher, are liable to be built into the nominal interest rates.[3] Fiscal problems become compounded and a vicious circle threatens when high interest rates themselves cause larger deficits through higher debt-servicing requirements.

In 1994, however, the repercussions of this long-term problem were successfully muted as the government reined in spending. National accounts figures show public construction from the first to the third quarter of 1994, for example, growing in real terms by only 5.5 per cent, compared with 20.4 per cent over a similar period in 1993. Similarly government consumption contributed negatively to the growth of aggregate demand, actually shrinking by 0.6 per cent over the three quarters of 1994. Although tax efforts have not shown dramatic changes after initial improvements arising from the tax reforms of 1986, non-tax revenues have risen owing to privatization of large public corporations (notably of the oil company Petron). As a result, for over three-fourths of the year the national government not only managed to show a primary surplus—as it has for the last few years—but a surplus even after debt service.[4]

The effects of the fiscal surplus were evident in the downward trend of T-bill rates and inflation, even if money aggregates near the end of the year ultimately deviated slightly from IMF targets. The rate on 91-day T-bills fell from almost 16 per cent in December 1993 to 8.9 per cent in September 1994. In September 1994, the consumer price index had risen on an annual basis by 9.6 per cent, slightly higher than the same period last year, but with a further downward trend evident near the year end (Figure 2.2). Though inflation was slightly higher, this was considered manageable since it was accompanied by a substantially higher growth in output, evidence of a good supply response.

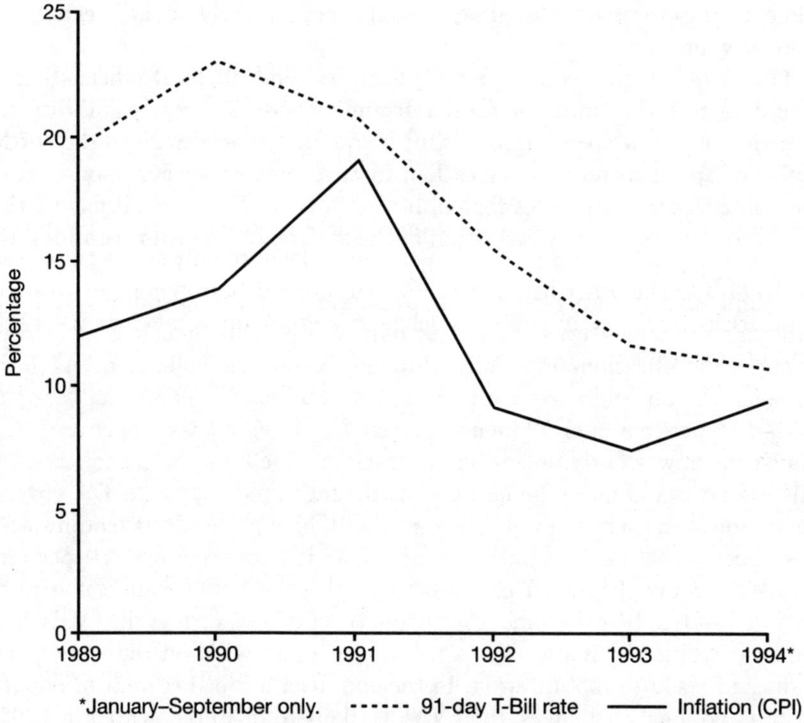

Figure 2.2 Inflation and Interest Rates

Taking a longer view, however, there is good reason to think that the factors ensuring this year's good fiscal performance may be transitory. Infrastructure spending cannot be held back indefinitely if the government wishes to support output growth and enable the Philippines to compete as an investment location. The country still lags behind most other countries of the region—and in per capita terms, sometimes even behind its own historical record—in many aspects of infrastructure, including roads, bridges, port facilities, and telecommunications. On a real per capita basis, essential social services such as education, health, housing, and sanitation are also in need of massive catch-up and upgrading.

Indeed, the underspending on infrastructure this year was more of a fluke or, as it has been more critically described, failure masquerading as success (Fabella 1994). Quite apart from any aim at macroeconomic stabilization, real problems of implementation have hampered the Ramos government's capital spending programme and prevented it from making a bigger push for infrastructure. These problems range from very real right-of-way problems aggravated by a tortuous judicial and legal system, lengthy project negotiations, bureaucratic jockeying and red tape, whether or not related to corruption, up to concept failures, fuzzy priorities, and poor co-ordination.

Some of these bottlenecks, unfortunately, are unlikely to be cleared permanently, or soon.

That 1995 is an election year for Congress and all local officials is also bound to test the limits of fiscal restraint. There is a real possibility the direction of public spending may shift markedly, especially given the bottlenecks in capital spending cited earlier, towards greater consumption instead, including various pay raises for public employees. These are all factors that will work against an easy repetition of the apparent success in trimming the budget in 1994.

Ultimately, the only way both to increase public spending on infrastructure and social services and still rein in the public deficit is to increase resource mobilization, especially through better tax collection. As it is, however, the tax effort has not increased substantially. Tax revenues are still around 16 per cent of GDP (non-tax revenues adding another 2 per cent). For some time now, a fairly broad consensus has emerged that better collection of existing taxes and not more new ones is the indicated approach. The government, however, spent most of its tax goodwill during the year defending what was effectively a new tax measure: an expanded coverage of a 10 per cent value-added tax (EVAT). Rightly or wrongly, the EVAT issue came to be regarded—both by government itself and by outsiders such as the IMF whose opinions seemed to matter—as a test of "political will" on the issue of tax effort and resource mobilization. In the end, over a broad current of popular protest and legal challenges, the EVAT is likely to be implemented in 1995.

What the issue of the expanded VAT highlighted, however, was the importance of credible enforcement as a prior condition to a successful tax reform. The most persuasive objections to the EVAT pertained not to the principle of value-added taxation *per se*, but to timing and preparation: poor information, unclear guidelines, and the experience of uneven tax implementation eroded credibility of the measure. It was evident, for example, that in many cases, the poor system of documentation could turn the 10 per cent VAT into an excise on gross, with a resulting impact on prices. The cogency of these arguments was indirectly recognized with the government's belated tacit admission that a good deal of refinement and revisions in the rules would have to occur in any case. Upon hindsight, it can be argued that the government could have lost a lot less goodwill and avoided a hardening of the ground for tax reform if it had proceeded more prudently and with greater preparation for the expanded VAT, while strengthening its credibility by coming down hard on tax evasion. As it stands, however, the support for any more new taxes has weakened considerably, and while the administration may have won a battle, it is unclear whether this has done anything to help win the larger war for tax reform.

Adding uncertainty to future fiscal outcomes has been the slow government action in plugging existing revenue loopholes, not to mention its occasionally puzzling proposals for tax-losing measures. While defending the expanded VAT, for example, the administration also implemented a net income taxation scheme that markedly reduced the tax base; countenanced the continuation of liberal tax incentives for certain preferred industries; permitted large purchases of duty-free goods by residents exempted not only from tariffs but also from the VAT; as well as facilitated duty-free imports of capital equipment ahead of scheduled tariff reductions.

Interpreted in the best light, these could merely reflect a lack of policy co-ordination, or perhaps simple uneven policy progress in various parts of the bureaucracy, which can be evened out or adjusted in due course. A less considerate view, however, is to interpret these as a continuing parcellization of the economy to favour certain interest groups, preventing the formulation and implementation of a coherent and unified policy in the process. What seems certain is that a good deal of effort and credibility-building must go into mustering the constituency needed to raise the tax effort further among a public that has become increasingly aware of the shortcomings and injustice of existing tax administration. It will remain an open question whether and how over the next few years the government can preserve a regime of acceptable inflation and low interest rates, while meeting the minimal infrastructure requirements of a growing economy and providing the social services needed by a population that has been deprived in both absolute and relative terms.

INVESTMENT AND SAVINGS

The problem of mobilizing sufficient resources to finance growth extends beyond the issue of the size of the public sector deficit. The country is even now investing the equivalent of only some 25 per cent of GDP, with the biggest reason being low savings mobilization; the ratio of savings to GDP currently hovers at 19 per cent. This already represents an improvement over the much lower rates of savings to GDP ratios of 15 per cent or so in the early 1980s. A substantial gap remains, none the less, between the country's current performance and the savings ratio of 35 per cent or better that is customary in neighbouring countries. Even the recent rise in the investment ratio has been fuelled largely by higher foreign rather than domestic savings (Table 2.2). Clearly, however, larger amounts of foreign investments will not

Table 2.2 Investment and savings as percentage of GDP

	1983	*1985*	*1989*	*1991*	*1992*	*1993*	*1994**
Gross investment	28.6	15.3	22.0	20.1	21.5	23.2	25.0
Gross domestic savings	20.3	15.0	18.6	17.8	19.6	17.1	19.4

Note:
* January to September

Source: Lim (1995).

be forthcoming to make up the difference between current investment ratios and levels required for high growth; domestic savings must obviously increase.

Part of the reason for the low share of domestic savings to output is a simple Keynesian one: the average propensity to save rises with income.[5] One may expect the country's performance to improve on this score, therefore, as and when the economy's growth rate improves; some of this is already apparent, but even a growth momentum is unlikely to suffice. Poor savings are also related to changing relative prices. The peso's overvaluation (a trend even exaggerated in 1994 and discussed further below), together with the on-going liberalization of trade, has meant a cheapening of tradables, especially competing imports, which has encouraged higher consumption out of income. Lim (1995) shows some evidence for this in both the increase in personal consumption spending and the increasing import content of consumption expenditures.[6]

A final aspect discouraging savings behaviour relates to the underdevelopment and segmentation of the financial markets, which has caused disintermediation and discouraged small savings. Ultimately, this must be traced to the unique system of financial-industrial conglomerates that dominate the industrial structure of the country.[7] On the positive side, the liberalization of the terms of entry and participation of foreign banks is expected to provide competition in the banking sector that may result in better returns to savings. The development of the stock markets and other financial instruments may also provide more attractive returns to a new (admittedly middle class) strata of savers.

MONETARY POLICY AND THE EXCHANGE RATE

In 1994, the Philippines, as were other countries of the region, was the destination for large portfolio capital inflows, which caused a substantial nominal appreciation of the peso throughout the year. Between 1992 and 1993, portfolio investments increased from US$566 million to US$2,257 million. A broader interpretation of these would include withdrawals from FCDUs, or foreign-currency deposit units (curiously treated in balance of payments accounting as "exports of non-factor services"). Under this broader measure of "portfolio" investments, the increase in inflows would be from almost US$2 billion to almost US$4 billion (Table 2.3). The dramatic increases in portfolio investments dwarfed the modest increases in direct foreign investments, which rose from US$500 million in 1993 to US$665 million by the first semester of 1994.[8]

Fluctuations in international returns must, of course, ultimately be adduced to explain these flows. Several factors peculiar to the Philippines, however, also enhanced the country's relative attractiveness. The backdrop was provided by the removal of foreign-exchange surrender requirements for exporters and more liberal treatment of capital flows beginning in 1992, as

Table 2.3 Portfolio capital flows, 1990–94*
(US$ millions)

	1990	*1991*	*1992*	*1993*	*1994**
Portfolio inflows	152	227	566	2,257	1,355
Withdrawals from FCDUs	642	866	1,263	1,680	1.432
Total inflows	795	1,093	1,929	3,937	2,787
Portfolio outflows	—	15	115	1,061	692
Net inflows	795	1,078	1,814	2,876	2,095

Note:
* First semester only.

Source: Bangko Sentral ng Pilipinas, *Selected Philippine Economic Indicators.*

part of the new administration's effort to send a signal about its liberalizing intentions. The loosening of the capital account coincided with the country's recovery of a measure of credit worthiness as the foreign debt problem wound down. Internally, a high interest-rate regime prevailed, caused by tight monetary policies, and this created a substantial wedge between foreign and domestic interest rates. A large share of T-bill issues came ultimately to be held by foreigners, so that the government was effectively borrowing from abroad.

Stock market activity was another major stimulus to speculative flows. In 1993 both Philippine stock exchanges[9] were rated the highest performers in the category of "new emerging markets". In 1994, despite narrower interest-rate differentials between foreign and local securities, portfolio investor interest was sustained as a result of a large number of initial public offerings (IPOs) by large but hitherto closely-held family corporations and public companies undergoing privatization.[10]

Large portfolio inflows, therefore, were the new element that combined with overseas workers' earnings and the lower debt service to cause a large nominal peso appreciation. The peso rose relative to the U.S. dollar from P27.7 as of the end of 1993 to P24.5 near the end of 1994, or a nominal appreciation of almost 12 per cent. International reserves rose substantially from US$5.8 billion as of December 1993 to US$7.57 billion by September 1994, boosting portfolio investor confidence even further. Nearing the end of the year, the peso was ranked high among the currencies in the region that had appreciated the most *vis-à-vis* the dollar. The real exchange rate, already previously misaligned, fell even further, causing an outcry among exporters and import-substituting industries alike.

The temporarily favourable fiscal situation in 1994 could have provided the newly-rehabilitated Bangko Sentral ng Pilipinas with the leeway in managing monetary policy that it had not possessed for some time. This additional latitude, however, was not fully utilized where and when it was especially needed in the matter of the handling the exchange rate. The authorities eschewed any direct response to stemming the portfolio inflows—such as a reimposition of administrative controls, or tax on capital inflows[11]—since it was feared this would be regarded as reneging on the previous capital-account liberalization.

The other major option—accommodating the new inflows by allowing money supply to expand, or perhaps even managing the exchange rate through appropriate purchases—was largely ignored. This approach would have dampened interest rates sooner and caused the peso to depreciate. Proposals from outside government, especially academe, had already been made as early as 1993 for the central bank to abandon monetary targets and attend to the exchange rate instead. The central bank boxed itself in, however, by its decision to adhere to an unreasonably restrictive IMF programme oriented primarily towards preventing inflation. It chose to pursue its customary rule of targeting money supply, largely losing control over the exchange rate as a result.

Earlier on, the authorities initially sought to stem the peso rise through occasional purchases of foreign-exchange to placate an increasingly restive export sector. These moves lacked credibility, and therefore failed to change the direction of exchange rate movements since it was clear to all market participants that the domestic liquidity thus created would just as soon be drained to maintain monetary targets.

Short of measures to directly discourage portfolio inflows, the central bank took steps to reduce the supply of foreign exchange, as well as to compensate for the damage and pain among exporters, who have since become a vocal and potent lobby group. Among others, the authorities refrained from drawing down some foreign loans and spoke of prepaying foreign liabilities, tightened rules on banks' overbought foreign exchange positions, imposed a (largely superfluous) "volatility band" on dollar trading among banks in anticipation of further appreciation, and opened a foreign-exchange credit facility for exporters. An announcement was also made to (very) gradually phase out the forward cover on foreign exchange bought by the country's large oil companies beginning next year and ending in 1996. In the main, however, the central bank took the position of "riding out" the capital surge.

It became increasingly clear—even to those in government—that compensatory measures alone could not turn the trick. With existing money ceilings, on the other hand, the central bank could never purchase enough foreign exchange to influence exchange rate movements. A consensus in government grew, therefore, to push for greater monetary flexibility, preferably within the IMF programme, but without it if necessary. As the year drew to a close, the government seemed to have reached some agreement with the IMF to loosen monetary targets for 1995. Whether and to what extent the concessions would be large enough to resolve the exchange rate problem could not be immediately ascertained. In the light of more impending initial public offerings in the stock market for 1995, more portfolio inflows can be expected.

There seems to be no question that the nominal exchange rate must ultimately be adjusted in order to regain competitiveness. The only question is when and how this is to be accomplished. In a "hard landing" scenario, as in the recent case of Mexico, adjustments come when the bubble bursts, and speculators realize they have simply been feeding on their own expectations.[12] A "softer" landing, on the other hand, could probably be managed if the authorities themselves initiated prompt credible exchange rate adjustments while reserves and credibility remain high. What is crucial ultimately is whether the direction of real-resource allocation contributes to sustaining growth and competitiveness in a timely fashion.

LIBERALIZATION AND REAL RESOURCE ALLOCATION

In fact, the pace of economic liberalization was sustained and strengthened throughout 1994 and, together with the resumption of growth, was the main source of returning confidence both for domestic and foreign investment. The stimulus given by liberalization to investment has been most tangible in the form of deregulation, easier entry into various industries, and privatization, especially telecommunications, energy, and infrastructure provision.

In telecommunications, new entrants have been allowed to provide cellular, gateway, and even backbone telephone services in parts of the country; as a result, dramatic changes as well as large new investments have become most visible both by new entrants and by incumbents who have been compelled by competition to accelerate expansion. In electronic media, competition among the majors has also led to expansion of capacity and the use of newer and more powerful technology (for example satellite broadcasts, cable TV). In the case of the energy sector, both foreign and domestic private investors played a significant role in the construction of new capacity, contributing to the resolution of the energy crisis. Private investments have also been sought for large infrastructure projects under the build-operate-transfer scheme. Land development has been another large attraction for new investments, stimulated partly by significant government privatization efforts. In terms of contributions to aggregate output, the activity in these sectors, which may be classified as a part of non-tradables production, is reflected in Table 2.4. With a share of around 20 per cent of GDP, the contribution of these sectors amounted to 30 per cent of total output growth.[13] Notably, many of the most actively traded shares in the stock exchange are those of firms in these same sectors.

The positive experience with freer entry rules in many of these sectors has led to a greater acceptance of freer entry and liberal rules and the replication of this experience in other areas. Among the most important are the banking industry, where the entry and operation of foreign banks is to be allowed; the petroleum industry; and possibly ultimately retail trade, shipping, and cement.

Table 2.4 Contribution to growth of selected non-tradable sectors, first to third quarter 1994, at constant prices (percentages)

Sector	*Share*	*Growth*	*Contribution to total output growth*
Construction	5.59	9.40	0.52
Electricity, gas, water	2.92	14.3	0.42
Transport and communications	5.79	4.27	0.25
Dwellings and real estate	5.56	2.82	0.23
Total	19.86		1.42

Source: National Statistical Coordination Board.

It should be noted that a large number of these sectors are strictly non-tradables and feed at best into tradables production. To some extent, their good performance now is merely a reflection of how far the country has fallen behind, and represents a catching up. This is most true, for example, in transport and communications infrastructure and energy capacity. It is also a favourable feature of this past growth that it has been led mainly by the private sector, and that the government role has not been overbearing. However, the developments also point to the subsequent need to vindicate a good deal of these non-tradables investments through increased production of tradables (exportables and importables).

The continuing threats to macroeconomic stability in the next few years could make this change-over less smooth and certain. The lack of predictability in the nominal exchange rate, and expectations of inflation have pushed the real exchange rate—the price of tradables relative to non-tradables—towards substantial misalignment. The nominal peso appreciation throughout 1994 accentuated an already long-standing problem of real appreciation, further pushing down the prices of both exportables and importables relative to non-tradables. The resulting loss in competitiveness since 1986 has been estimated by some writers (Fabella 1994) to amount to as much as 25 per cent compared to 1986 (Figure 2.3).

The incipient symptoms of Dutch disease should not be underestimated. A failure to correct the strong peso in the next few years could undermine efforts to promote tradables, particularly exports. It would certainly increase the dangers of a Mexican type "hard landing". The elements of this are well-known: a huge current account deficit fed by equally huge portfolio inflows, a resulting currency appreciation, and finally a sudden withdrawal of confidence as "fundamentals" become questioned. The likelihood of such a scenario for the Philippines becomes larger if portfolio investors—whose fancies are now attuned to the non-tradables sector—were suddenly to realize after a time that the current account had continued to deteriorate, since the appreciation their own actions had caused had ironically ruined the chances

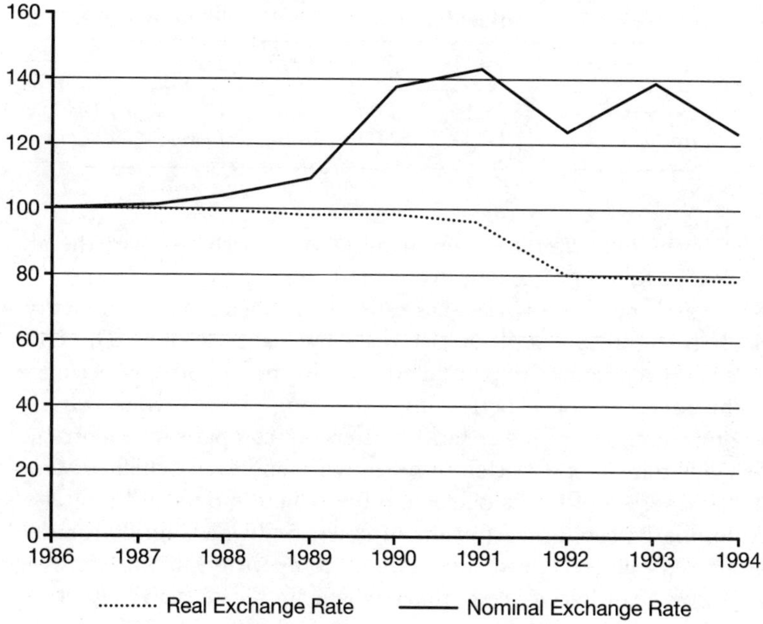

Figure 2.3 Indexes of Nominal and Real Exchange Rates (Peso-dollar rates; 1986 = 100)

for exports and efficient import substitution, or if for some reason the overall growth rate should start to sputter.

In the meantime, during the first three quarters of 1994, merchandise exports proved resilient and continued to grow in real terms at 15 per cent, fuelled mostly by electronics. In dollar values, exports rose from US$11.37 billion in 1993 to US$13.8 billion in 1994, while imports rose from US$17.59 to US$20.8 billion over the same period (Table 2.5). The continuing growth of exports, the peso appreciation notwithstanding, has caused some complacency about future export growth. It is fairly clear, however, that the improvements in the export picture have been possible mainly because of conjunctural factors, such as the resolution of the power crisis and the recovery of demand in electronics; these factors cannot be expected to persist indefinitely, and therefore the growth rate of exports may suffer. For the moment, because exports have sunk costs and goods are priced to market, producers will have chosen largely to absorb losses rather than curtail production immediately. Unless the overvaluation is corrected soon, however, the lagged adverse effects of the real appreciation on export quantities may begin to be felt in a few years.

By contrast, the adverse effects of real appreciation have been more visible in the import-competing sector, where some of the impact has been felt in the

Table 2.5 Exports and imports, 1990–94 (US$ millions)

	1990	*1991*	*1992*	*1993*	*1994*
Exports	8.19	8.84	9.82	11.38	13.15
Imports	12.21	12.05	14.52	17.60	20.80

form of lower than average or even negative growth. Among the affected industries have been textiles, wood and cork products, leather, rubber products, and metal industries. Losses in the rubber products industry were particularly significant and characterized by plant closures. The effects of currency appreciation were particularly felt in the import-competing sector, since this sector is also experiencing a lowering of protection owing to the ongoing programme to lower tariff barriers. In comparison, exportables did not benefit from the protection to begin with, and even benefited somewhat from the lowering of tariffs on some intermediate inputs and capital equipment. Similarly, though part of importables, traditional agriculture has also been affected relatively less, since import competition in this sector is still governed by quantitative restrictions, which are not sensitive either to tariff changes or exchange rate changes.

In current peso prices, the current account deficit rose further to 9.4 per cent of GDP for the first three quarters of 1994, compared to 8.8 per cent over the same period in 1993. A strong export recovery has fortunately prevented it from getting out of hand, but its size has begun to cause concern, and points to the need for prompt adjustment. The continuing increase in the size of the current account deficit implicitly sums up the twin problems confronted by the economy: (1) the need to increase tradables production, and (2) the need to raise domestic savings. The state of the current account represents the surest sign of the danger to sustainable growth.

For policy, what the entire 1994 episode reveals is the need for closer synchronization between macroeconomic adjustments and real structural reforms. This was seen most clearly in the failure of trade reforms and exchange rate policy to reinforce each other mutually. The reduction of tariff and other trade barriers should normally be accompanied by a currency depreciation as part of the change in the mechanism for balancing the current account. Tariff reductions, in turn, ought to stimulate import demand and reinforce the depreciation. This otherwise automatic mechanism failed to work, however, owing to the disturbance caused by capital inflows, which the monetary authorities' policies failed to counter. Just as macroeconomic policy is too inflexible to support trade reforms, some trade policies are also too inflexible to reinforce macroeconomic adjustments. In particular, the impact of a depreciation on price might be mitigated if imports—especially of food—are more freely allowed. Just this type of manoeuvre will be ruled out, however, if the agricultural sector continues to be uncompetitive and income support to the peasantry continues to be understood largely in terms of prohibitions against cheaper imports.

The need for greater flexibility and sophistication in managing macroeconomic variables with an eye to their real effects is likely to increase, since the country has inexorably committed itself to further reductions of trade barriers under different multilateral trade liberalization efforts. After months of public debate and deliberations, the Philippine Senate ratified the GATT in early December of 1994. The ratification of the Uruguay Round instruments, notwithstanding remaining uncertainties in provisions on aspects of property rights and national treatment, can be viewed as proof of a further commitment to a liberalization approach. On a regional basis, the Philippines has reaffirmed its commitment to the 2003 trade liberalization timetable of the ASEAN Free Trade Area (AFTA), as well as supported the Asia-Pacific Economic Co-operation (APEC) group's call for regional free trade by 2010. In the country itself, thinking within the executive is progressing steadily towards the goal of bringing down all most-favoured-nation (MFN) tariffs to a uniform tariff of 5–10 per cent by 2003. All these developments point to a decreasing scope for reliance on traditional tools of trade policy for achieving external balance and directing resource allocation, therefore placing a special onus on macroeconomic policy to maintain an even keel,

SOCIAL AND POLITICAL ASPECTS

It is fair to ask whether the character of the growth achieved so far has allowed its benefits to be shared broadly. Little in the current growth differs from the previous pattern, in which modest increases in output were associated with increasing inequality and also failed to stem increases in the absolute number of poor families.[14] The massive tilt of prices towards non-tradables has penalized employment in both import-competing and exportables industries, for which reason the employment impact has been modest. Even for non-tradables, however, the expanding sectors—real estate, transport, communications, construction—are those that have more limited potential for massive and sustained employment. As a result, notwithstanding income growth, the government failed to attain its own employment targets. In the October labour force survey, underemployment stood at 20.9 per cent of the labour force, while unemployment at 9.4 per cent had hardly changed from the same period a year ago. An outstanding challenge, therefore, is to ensure that subsequent growth generates enough employment and livelihood to alleviate poverty more rapidly and on a broader scale.

To its credit, the government seems to realize in principle the need to spread out development geographically, for which reason it has designated "growth corridors" in various regions of the country to serve as focal points of industrial development, with the implied priority in infrastructure. Complicating the situation is the fiscal bind, already discussed, which prevents the provision of initial infrastructure sufficient to make growth corridors viable and link underdeveloped areas with growth centres, as well as restrict the amount and range of basic social services needed to prepare the poor for participation in a regime of competitive markets. The hope is that the slack in government finance should be taken up by private capital, going by the example of how the private sector contributed to solving the energy shortage. Clearly, however, not all projects are equally attractive to the private sector or suited to private sector schemes, and therefore they may augment but cannot substitute for a critical minimum of public effort and resources in these areas.

At the moment, the government's only explicitly redistributive programme is agrarian reform. Land redistribution has become a sacred cow—and indeed most quantitative targets have been attained—but its efficacy in resolving the worst features and causes of the contemporary rural poverty (for example rural unemployment, low incomes and productivity, lack of access to markets, low technological diffusion, environmental degradation) remains ambiguous, at best. At worst, the long-drawn out implementation of agrarian reform and uncertainty over its future have discouraged new investments in agriculture (by incumbent owners and prospective beneficiaries alike) and adversely affected productivity.

From a narrow viewpoint, a prompt and direct address of poverty and inequality is probably not absolutely necessary to sustain the current growth momentum. It will, however, ultimately affect the social and political acceptance of the government's programme. The disorganization among leftist groups and the existence of avenues for legal and electoral participation preclude for the moment any significant armed threat. Still one cannot underestimate the prospect and consequences of local pockets of disturbance or less political expressions of resentment (for example crime and lawlessness) among social groups that are left behind in a sudden rush to prosperity by the haves and the would-haves. Considerations such as these may perhaps be less important in other contexts. Where the basis of governance is based on broader coalitional (not to mention democratic) consensus, however, they could well prove vital.

NOTES

1 While large overseas remittances were certainly present much earlier, GDP had always been less than GNP since the positive inflows from workers were exceeded by larger outflows for foreign-debt service. The situation changed from 1989 onwards, however, with substantial reductions of debt-service requirements.

2 For a more detailed discussion, see E. de Dios et al., *Poverty, Growth and the Fiscal Crisis* (Makati: Philippine Institute for Development Studies and International Development Research Centre, 1993).

3 This point was made some years ago by P. Krugman, et al., *Transforming the Philippine Economy* (Pasig: National Economic and Development Authority and United Nations Development Programme, 1991).

4 This does not include the servicing of liabilities assumed by the national

government on behalf of the old central bank, which are held in a separate account.

5 Suppose $S = -S_o + S^1Y$ is the savings function, where S^1 is the marginal propensity to save out of income, and $S^o, S^1 > 0$. The average savings ratio is $s = -S^o/Y + S^1$. There $(ds/dY) = (S^o/Y^2)$, and $Y(ds/dY) = S^o/Y > 0$. The latter states that s rises (at a decreasing rate) with an increase in the growth rate of income.

6 J. Lim, "Structural Shifts in Key Macro Parameters: Implications on the Sustainability of Growth", in *Towards Sustained Growth*, edited by R. Fabella and H. Sakai (Tokyo: Institute of Developing Economics, 1995).

7 See E. Tan "Interlocking Directorates, Commercial Banks, Other Financial Institutions, and Nonfinancial Corporations", *Philippine Review of Economics and Business* 30, no. 1 (1993): 1–50; and E. de Dios, "Resource Mobilisation and Industrial Organisation", in *Resource Mobilisation and Resource Use in the Philippines*, edited by R. Fabella and H. Sakai (Tokyo: Institute of Developing Economies, 1994).

8 These figures exclude debt conversions; their inclusion would leave the picture unchanged, however.

9 The Manila Stock Exchange and the Makati Stock Exchange existed as separate entities with different listings and prices until they were unified functionally in 1994.

10 This healthy trend towards public listing is a significant development that bodes far-reaching change in the country's financial and industrial structure. On possible reasons for this trends, see E. de Dios, "Resource Mobilisation and Industrial Organisation", in Fabella and Sakai, eds. (1994), op. cit.

11 Malaysian authorities, in particular, did not hesitate to take this route in dealing with their own problems with portfolio inflows.

12 On this, see P. Krugman, "The J-Curve, the Fire Sale, and the Hard Landing", *AEA Papers and Proceedings* 79, no. 2 (May 1989): 31–35.

13 That is, 1.42 divided into a GDP growth rate of 4.5.

14 The latest official data on poverty and income distribution are from 1991, and showed a headcount incidence of some 40 per cent, barely changed from 41 per cent in 1988. Approximations made by Balisacan (1995) strongly suggest that both inequality and the number of poor families continued to increase in 1993 as well, with the incidence of poverty even increasing slightly relative to 1991. A. Balisacan, "Agriculture in Transition: Arresting Poverty in the Rural Sector", in Fabella and Sakai, eds. (1995), op. cit.

3

MYANMAR

Will Forever Flow the Ayeyarwady?

Khin Maung Kyi

INTRODUCTION

When Myanmar (then known as Burma) attained its independence in 1948, international agencies identified it as one of the most promising regional candidates for economic take-off. Its modern technical and university education system, high rate of literacy, well-trained civil service and a cadre of educated middle class, basic infrastructure, and a well-run legal system were considered as good ingredients for Myanmar's expected take-off. In the 1950s, Myanmar's gross domestic product (GDP) was growing consistently at an annual average rate of over 4 per cent, in contrast with the chequered performance of its neighbours. In the early 1960s, the country was poised for labour-intensive industrialization with a number of textile and consumer product firms manufacturing export-quality goods. Then came the *putsch* and the socialist revolution, followed by stagnation and decline. Twenty-six years passed before Myanmar finally erupted and the change to market economy was forcibly brought in. Myanmar is now in the throes of the struggle for modernization and change. With the military still holding on to the reins of power on the one hand and the contending democratic opposition and the ethnic groups with diverse claims and interests on the other, Myanmar has not come out of its pains of growing up, to meet the challenges of the outside world.

This paper will review significant developments and changes in 1993 and re-examine the complex of situations influencing its sluggish economic performance and the equally slow pace of political transformation. Myanmar's problems and prospects for long-term development and modernization are also analysed.

Source: Southeast Asian Affairs 1994, Singapore: Institute of Southeast Asian Studies, 1994, pp. 209–30.

THE ECONOMY IN GRIDLOCK

Performance of the economy in the year 1992/93

While most of the wearisome indicators such as budget deficit, money supply, inflation, adverse balance of trade remain on the rising trend, improvement in the rate of GDP growth provides a ray of hope for a possible arrest of the downward slide of the economy.

The provisional growth rate of GDP in 1992/93 over the previous year 1991/92 was 10.9 per cent, a marked improvement over the average negative growth rate of 1.5 per cent over the previous four years. As shown in Table 3.1, this growth rate of 10.9 per cent principally came from 15 per cent growth in agriculture, 13.7 per cent growth in industry, and 10 per cent growth in trade, all forming a large percentage of the total makeup of GDP. The expansion of the acreage of paddy, especially summer paddy, accounts for the growth in agriculture. The revenues of state economic organizations rose by 30 per cent, probably through the realignment of prices and also through some increment in output. The increase in trade by 10.3 per cent is probably the ultimate result of improvement in agricultural production, which generates all other activities in chain. The sustainability of this rate of growth is very doubtful since the growth rate is calculated on a very low base year and other fundamentals have not changed. Furthermore, these are provisional figures for 1992/93 and the practice of scaling down provisional figures in the final estimates has been very common in the past. In addition, unless there is sustained growth in the coming few years it cannot be presumed that it is a break from the stagnant past.

Potential foreign investors exploring possibilities have increased and deals have been struck on hotel, oil, and gas projects. But long-term industrial investments are not forthcoming yet. The total amount of foreign investment

Table 3.1 Myanmar: growth rates of the economy and its sectors (in percentages)

Sector	*1980 –82**	*1982 –84**	*1984 –86**	*1986 –88**	*1988 –89*	*1989 –90*	*1990 –91*	*1991 –92*	*1992 –93*
GDP	7.2	5.0	4.4	–2.6	–11.4	3.7	2.8	–1.0	10.0
Goods	8.8	5.4	4.1	–2.9	–13.3	6.5	2.6	–1.9	13.2
Agriculture	10.7	5.9	2.8	–3.0	–13.2	5.2	2.0	–3.9	15.2
Forestry	3.8	1.0	5.5	–4.3	–1.6	28.4	8.3	–2.6	5.9
Manufacturing	7.5	4.3	5.2	–5.0	–15.9	11.3	0.1	–4.1	13.7
Construction	11.6	5.6	5.4	–5.1	–23.4	32.7	35.8	17.1	3.8
Services	7.1	5.2	5.2	3.1	–3.3	–7.5	4.2	4.4	3.7
Trade	3.4	3.8	4.2	–6.5	–12.0	5.3	2.4	–2.6	10.3

Note:
* Average rate for two years.

Source: *Reports to the Pyi Thu Hluttaw* and *Review of the Financial Economic and Social Indicators.*

promised or initialled in 1992/93, according to provisional figures, amounted to US$900 million, compared with the US$4,076 million received by the compatriot socialist market economy of Vietnam in 1993. In Myanmar, the largest foreign investor happened to be its immediate neighbour, Thailand, with 19.3 per cent of total foreign direct investment in Myanmar.

It should be noted that the US$900 million only represents the total amount signed in the contracts or the memorandums of agreement and does not indicate the actual amount of inflow to date or the level of activities being carried out. The largest foreign investments fall in the areas of extraction of natural resources, such as gas exploration, timber extraction, selling of fishing rights, and also of development of the tourist industry such as the construction of hotels.

The construction boom in urban areas is quite noticeable. Some of the upcountry cities on the border trade route show marked signs of prosperity. Mandalay's city business centre is largely taken over by the Overseas Chinese and Chinese immigrants. Monywa, linked to the Indian border trade, is thriving on trade with India. Varieties of cheap consumer goods are swamping the market, while teak, timber, and agricultural produce are being moved across the border to China.

The productivity of various sectors of the economy remains stagnant. The state industrial sector is facing the possibility of a slow and lingering death with the shortage of raw materials, spare parts, managerial know-how, and fresh capital. Small industries are springing up but are very localized, facing stiff competition from cheap consumer goods from China.

The basic fundamentals have not changed. As illustrated in Table 3.2, the best achievements in 1993 do not reach the level of 1985/86, the best year before the social upheaval in 1988. The reported increase in rice production

Table 3.2 Myanmar: important indicators, 1985/86 and 1992/93 (at constant prices)

Indicator	*1985/86*	*1992/93*
In million kyat		
GDP	55,989.3	55,170.1
Agricultural output	22,243.5	21,541.6
Social and administrative services	5,561.4	4,973.1
Consumption	49,531.9	44,264.7
Investment	8,649.5	9,549.5
In kyat		
GDP per capita	1,509.0	1,303.0
Consumption per capita	1,298.0	1,046.0
Investment per capita	233.0	226.0
Net output per worker	3,710.0	3,350.0

Source: *Review of the Financial Economic and Social Indicators.*

still needs to be carefully looked into, as export figures for rice for the year did not improve and yet the price of rice has gone up to 80 kyat per *pyi*, much higher than the level in 1991. A recent market report indicates that Chinese rice is being imported and sold in Mandalay and other parts of the upcountry. More surprisingly, it is also reported that rice imported from Bangladesh is sold in border towns in Arakan state.

The prices of basic consumer goods are still rising. In spite of the 25 per cent increase in salaries in the early part of 1992, the urban wage or salary earners are being increasingly squeezed. The unintended consequences of the rapid rate of inflation is that moonlighting by government employees has become very common. Worse still, for government officials who provide service or grant permits to the public, asking for or taking payments for services rendered in their normal course of duty is done with nonchalance and impunity.

It is likely that the seeming prosperity of certain commercial sections of the community is taking place at the expense of the lower stratum. As the total productivity of the economy does not improve, trade takes the form of over-exporting some of the food items such as fish, prawn, beans, and pulses, which the average or low-income earners consume as a mainstay in their diet. In its stead, non-essential consumer items such as electronic and luxury goods, which the wealthier section of the population can afford, are imported. This deliberate policy of deficit spending and the resultant price increases falls heavily on lower-income groups, whose daily essentials have been rising steeply in price in the last five years. Unless productivity can be increased, this disparity between the commercialized group and the great majority of both urban and rural lower-income groups will widen.

Comparative performance in the last five years

The switch to market economy, practically, began in 1989, an aftermath of social unrest in 1988, and this new experience will have passed the first five years by the end of 1993. It is appropriate at this juncture to review the performance of these five years and draw the likely trends to the future.

During the five-year period, the military leadership, the State Law and Order Restoration Council (SLORC), have tried hard to improve the economic lot of the people. Though these efforts were at times characterized by political expediency, short-term perspective, and half-way measures, the departure from the socialist economic past is unmistakable and the commitment to market economy is irrevocable. The following are the main thrusts of economic activities the new Myanmar Government has pursued during the past five years:

1 Opening up of the economy to the international market, through legalization of private enterprise, encouragement of foreign investments, and introduction of foreign investment law.

2 The construction of infrastructure projects especially roads, bridges, and schools. Also, the reconstruction and renovation of historical monuments.
3 Very recently, a drive for agricultural productivity through the encouragement of second or summer cropping.

However, the actual performance in respect of the total economy is, to say the least, discouraging though a slight ray of hope appeared in the year 1992/93. The following are the results of the five years under the new economic management.

The aggregate performance of the economy and its various sectors hardly moved. The average GDP growth rate for the five years including the best year of 1992/93 during this period remains at a sluggish 1 per cent per year. Sector-wise, the average growth rates of the agriculture, forestry, and manufacturing sectors stand at 1.06 per cent, 7.68 per cent, and 1.02 per cent, respectively, indicating that forestry was the only industry with a higher growth rate, possibly because of the larger number of concessions granted and the higher level of exploitation.

Construction showed a growth rate of 12.2 per cent for the period. This is due partly to the government's emphasis on the construction of roads, bridges, schools, and some other infrastructure projects but principally to the growth of private-sector construction activities quite visible in urban areas such as Yangon, Mandalay, and some large trading towns.

The services sector and the trade sector show abysmal growth rates of 0.3 per cent and 0.7 per cent, respectively. These observations are made on the basis of Table 3.1, which also shows the growth rates of early years of this decade in two-year averages. Unmistakably, growth in all sectors has been declining, with 1992/93 being the only exception. When compared with the average yearly growth rates for the previous decade (Table 3.3), the last decade, 1981–90, showed a real decline in performance.

Table 3.4 shows the financial indicators of Myanmar from the years 1986/87 to 1992/93. It clearly illustrates the effects of the fiscal and monetary practices of the government. The budget deficits have been rapidly climbing since 1987/88 though the percentage increases have declined in the last two years, 1991/92 and 1992/93. Currency in circulation, on the other hand, has

Table 3.3 Myanmar: average growth rates (base year = 1985)

Sector	*1971–80*	*1981–90*	1988–93
GDP	4.7	−0.1	1.00
Agriculture	4.5	−0.3	1.06
Industry	5.8	−0.2	1.02
Services	4.6	0.2	0.30

Source: Calculation based on *Reports to the Pyi Thu Hluttaw* and *Review of the Financial Economic and Social Indicators*

Table 3.4 Myanmar: annual rate of change in percentage of financial and performance indices, 1987/88 to 1992/93

Year	*Total budget deficit*	*Money supply*	*Consumer price index*	*Exports*
1987/88	54.5	–44.9	–13.2	–33.1
1988/89	82.5	49.9	16.8	30.5
1989/90	23.3	55.6	27.2	29.7
1990/91	24.2	45.9	17.6	4.0
1991/92	15.0	34.9	32.3	–1.0
1992/93	2.7	40.7	21.9	13.0

increased very steeply, at the annual average rate of 45.4 per cent almost consistently in the last five years, from 1988/89 to 1992/93.

In absolute terms the total amount of budget deficit over the last five years, from 1988/89 to 1992/93, was 53.6 billion kyat, principally covered by the increase in the currency in circulation, that is, 40.7 billion kyat. The shortfall was probably financed by bank loans or other financial instruments. Since under the new financial management system, state-owned enterprises could borrow money from banks independent of budgetary allocations, the inflationary pressure is greater than increases in money supply suggest.

The consumer price index (CPI) in Yangon, a measure of inflationary pressure, is rising at an average rate of 21.4 per cent per year. This should be considered a conservative figure, not reflective of actual happenings at the average consumer's level. It should be noted that the CPI may include the subsidized prices of rice distributed to government servants. The price of rice, an important indicator of basic prices in Myanmar, has increased by 6.8 times between 1987 and 1992. In fact, during October 1993 the price of rice went up to 80 kyat per *pyi*, 17.5 times of the price in 1987. On the whole, prices of other commodities such as beans and pulses, and groundnut oil, the other staple items of the Myanmar diet, had increased approximately 2.6 to 3.2 times between 1987 and 1992. (See also Table 3.5.)

This huge increase in the price of rice almost created a problem of crisis proportions. Rice is a staple food for the great majority of the people. It also forms a basic raw material for food-producing industries such as animal feed and fish-breeding industries. Recent press reports indicate that the government has been paying serious attention to this problem.

Another important set of indicators is the balance of trade and the quantum of exports during this period. The balance of trade shows increasing deficits throughout the five-year period, with an average deficit of 22.4 billion kyat in the last three years, from 1990/91 to 1992/93. In spite of various efforts to promote exports through the encouragement of private enterprise, exports remained stagnant at about the 2.9 billion kyat level from 1989/90 to 1991/92. Except for forest products, hardwood, beans and pulses,

Table 3.5 Yangon: prices of selected consumer goods (In kyat per viss)

Commodity	*1985*	*1987*	*1989*	*1990*	*1991*	*1992*
Rice *ngasein* *	4.5	4.55	19.42	11.16	15.91	31.13
Rice *emahta* *	4.87	5.38	21.00	13.98	17.90	32.99
Gram (split)	12.30	11.21	28.77	36.49	38.60	35.89
Pegyi	7.80	11.50	22.20	26.56	34.79	35.38
Sadawpe	14.82	20.50	34.03	38.32	55.51	58.88
Groundnut oil	42.86	65.00	59.89	75.88	146.56	172.00
Sesame oil	41.69	62.00	56.90	67.74	137.62	159.12

Note:
* Rice is measured in *pyi* (small basket).

Source: *Reports to the Pyi Thu Hluttaw* and *Reviews of the Financial, Economic and Social Indicators*.

the quantum of exports in other items did not change appreciably. The rice export is limited to a fraction of what had been achieved in the past. Rice export in 1992/93 amounted to 207.7 thousand metric tons, not reaching even the level of export in 1987/88, that is, 303.3 thousand metric tons.

Table 3.6 illustrates the state of agricultural production during the five-year period under the present government. The table compares sown acreage

Table 3.6 Myanmar: Comparative sown acreage and yield of main agricultural crops, 1986/87 to 1992/93

		Sown acreage (thousand acres)		*Yield* * *(per acre)*	
Crop	*Basket size*	*1986/87*	*1992/93*	*1986/87*	*1992/93*
Paddy	46 lb.	11,968	12,603	58.72	57.10
Wheat	72 lb.	293	341	21.44	12.95
Maize	55 lb.	442	369	29.10	24.35
Sorgham	62 lb.	545	496	16.43	11.36
Matpe	72 lb.	237	518	13.98	11.17
Pedesein	72 lb.	143	443	7.48	8.12
Butter bean	69 lb.	159	92	18.60	14.18
Soya bean	71 lb.	78	93	11.03	10.29
Gram	69 lb.	498	451	11.32	9.94
Pesingon	72 lb.	64	71	10.09	7.76
Groundnut	25 lb.	1,394	1,251	37.15	32.33
Sesamum	54 lb.	2,848	3,422	4.12	4.07
Sunflower	32 lb.	615	477	30.28	20.35
Cotton	viss	471	426	123.49	111.94
Jute	viss	126	137	278.64	202.35

Note:
* Cotton and jute yields are measured in viss per acre. The rest are in basket per acre. Equivalent pounds per basket are shown for each crop.

Source: *Reports to the Pyi Thu Hluttaw* and *Reviews of the Financial, Economic and Social Indicators*.

and yields of all the important crops between the years 1986/87 and 1992/93. It should be noted that although 1992/93 was the best year in agricultural performance during this period, yields for all crops except one single crop, *Pedesein* (a variety of beans), have declined compared with the year 1986. All other years between the two landmark years, not shown here, have consistently declined throughout this period.

Between the two periods, the sown acreage in paddy and other crops has increased by 5.3 per cent and 11.8 per cent, respectively. Since the sown acreage approximately indicates the response or interest shown by the farmers to economic stimuli for a particular crop, the higher rate of increase in sown acreage in crops other than rice suggests more responsiveness to non-rice farm products. Another interesting observation is that the proportions of sown acreage among various crops other than rice have changed, which again should be taken as a response to the expectations of market price. The sown acreage in *Matpe*, *Pedesein*, and *Pesingon* have substantially increased. *Matpe* and *Pedesein* are major export items among beans and pulses, and *Pesingon* too is an export item probably sold overland to India. On the other hand, one redeeming factor is the rise by 6.1 per cent in the paddy output in 1992/93 over the level of 1986/87. This again was mainly due to the increase in acreage since the yield in 1992/93 is still lower than that in 1986/87. Changes in the output of other crops are likewise due to the shift in acreage rather than change in productivity.

On the whole, in spite of some improvement in the year 1992/93, agricultural production is considered as declining or to say the least, as stagnant. This condition could be partially explained by the fact that the quantum of important inputs such as fertilizers and other agricultural inputs made available to farmers has also declined. The total amount of fertilizer utilized for all crops in 1986/87 was 381,000 tons while in 1992/93 this amount declined to 116,000 tons. The decline in supply of inputs has been consistent throughout this period. Other inputs such as agricultural loans, have increased in kyat amounts but the rate of inflation would have nullified the effects of these increases.

Though these factors contributed to the decline or the stagnant conditions of agriculture, the more fundamental problem is that Myanmar's agriculture, within the existing technology and available land, seems to have reached the production plateau. Modern biotechnology has not become part of agricultural research. Seed development and plant breeding is far behind countries such as Thailand. How much of high-yielding seeds distributed are pure enough to be effective is not known. The irrigation ratio, that is the ratio of net sown area to irrigated area, has remained at 12.5 per cent for the last twenty years. Support facilities such as efficient marketing, ready supply of inputs, market information, access to loans and credit are still limited though the market economy has begun to make some inroads.

All these indicators suggest that production and exports have not responded to market forces as effectively as expected. No substantial change in production, productivity, or surplus for export have taken place in agriculture. The external trade that takes place is confined only to limited amounts of available surplus. It is common knowledge these days that some foreign businessmen go to Myanmar with high hopes of procuring abundant agricultural produce, only to learn to their disappointment that the local businessmen cannot supply the quantity required or conform to the quality standards specified. Moreover, the available surplus cannot be procured, graded, or shipped in time. Quality control is lacking or non-existent. Transport and storage facilities are inadequate. The lack of infrastructure and support is another stumbling block responsible for the slow growth of the export sector.

Problems and prospects for future development

Five years is a reasonable length of time to put in place the basic social framework for facilitating the functioning of a market economy. This has not been achieved in Myanmar over the last five years. Investment laws, rather hurriedly passed in the early stage, were followed by the formation of a few private banks and state-sponsored joint-venture corporations but long-term foreign direct investment in manufacturing or agribusiness areas has not come in. Institutional development measures such as the establishment of a civil service with a fair degree of efficiency and responsiveness, the legal administration system to dispense impartial justice, and development and training of manpower for the next phase of growth were neglected or sidelined. Some roads were built and school buildings constructed, but they were relatively inconsequential in the context of a major need for overhauling and drastic upgrading of the existing system.

Out of the total construction budget of the central government for the last four years, 62.7 per cent was spent on constructing buildings including schools, offices, industrial buildings, dwellings, and so forth. New road construction and renovation and improvement took up 21 per cent and 7.9 per cent, respectively. However, the average physical miles of new roads constructed per year in the last five years amounted to only 103 miles while the average miles of new roads constructed per year since 1961/62 was 603 miles.

With regard to measures to stabilize the functioning of the economy such as the introduction of prudent fiscal and monetary management, performance is woefully short of what is required. On the whole the development of infrastructure and reconstruction of institutions are yet to begin earnestly.

However, Myanmar investment laws and other government rules provide a reasonably attractive package for foreign investors. It is not the lack of incentives but the absence of a basic price mechanism and a social framework that most likely dissuades foreign investors from coming in.

Myanmar's entry to the market was very cautious and hesitant, almost to the point of ineffectuality. Holding on to the highly unrealistic exchange rate of 6 kyat to one U.S. dollar undermines other efforts the government is pursuing to introduce market economy. Importers would have to buy back whatever is available in the market to export so that they can get hard currency. The foreign exchange certificate recently introduced to facilitate the currency market is a poor substitute as it is costly, cumbersome, and still serves only those who bring in dollars for spending in Myanmar. There is no market for those who wish to buy dollars with kyat for transfers abroad. The repatriation of capital, interest, and dividends are possible only with the permission of the authorities. Under the present exchange rate, any deal that does not earn direct dollar revenue will be very unprofitable in terms of foreign currency. The capital brought in is undervalued at the official exchange rate while profits made will not be allowed to be repatriated at the same official exchange rate. Under this restriction, a potential investor will be discouraged from going into a venture involving a large amount of fixed capital. If a sizeable portion of the product is sold locally it would be more difficult to get the profits out of the country. Only short-term extraction of natural resources such as timber extractions, sea or coastal fishing, or procurement of local produce for export will be favoured.

Apart from exchange control, other controls on the market are still operative. The farmers, particularly rice farmers, have to surrender part of their produce at the very low fixed price. In fact farmers are still subsidizing the urbanized or government employees. Any significant rise in prices in the open market will invite intervention or chastizing from high military officials. The local commanders still have the liberty to control the movement of goods in and out of the regions. The control of foreign trade or border trade has been quite extensive. With frequent changes in rules and restrictions and numerous rules to follow, opportunities for corruption are many, resulting in high transaction cost for business.

Another feature that would impede further development of the economy is the government's emphasis on short-term results or expediency in almost all its endeavours. Most important measures taken by the government seem to be quick fixes to relieve some pressing problems at hand. The foreign investment law was introduced rather hurriedly with an overriding desire to help improve the precarious imbalance of foreign exchange. The long-term importance of technological transfer was not recognized and the relevant conditions to that effect were not laid down in the law. In addition, how foreign investments would fit into the long-term industrial development was unclear as there was no clear vision for future development.

The whole pattern of government expenditure suggests that these expenditures are made to address some immediate need to avoid political discontent rather than to increase the productive level of the nation. Increasing wages and benefits, without an increase in productivity, just to pacify the disquiet of a certain section of the people or to reward some group to secure their loyalty only leads to sharing the existing stock of goods at the expense of the majority. The construction of roads and bridges has long-term benefits but it can be counter-productive if used as a pork barrel for a certain constituency. Border trade was introduced to alleviate the extreme circumstances created by economic isolation from other countries. The terms of trade are unfavourable to Myanmar both ways because it lacks a bargaining position. There is nothing wrong with the logic of cross-border trade as long as the trade takes place in a competitive setting, with such prerequisites as decontrol of foreign exchange, foreign trade banking, and proper trading facilities including quality control.

Timber concessions and the selling of fishing rights are glaring examples of short-term thinking without regard to long-term consequences. How much over-exploitation the concession owners have done cannot be estimated yet. According to Myanmar's trade statistics in 1991/92, approximately 481.3 thousand metric tons of timber was exported. But the real amount may be considerably higher. It should also be noted that Thai deep-sea fishing has always been so efficient and ruthless that by the late 1970s fishing resources were nearly exhausted in the Gulf of Thailand itself. The environmental damage and resource depletion that may have been done by Myanmar's concessions is not known yet.

A major weakness is that the government does not seem to have a conception as to how the economy will merge with markets of the region and the world. Although it is supposed to be only a caretaker or a transitional government, the fact remains that it has stayed in power for five years and intends to have a major role in the future. Hence there is no good reason for the lack of longer-term economic thinking. On the other hand, it is possible that, weary of the socialist planning of the past, the military leadership takes it that the market economy is a form of a *laissez-fair*, a hands-off or a free-for-all policy. But this would be erroneous. All East Asian economies that have developed through the market system have had the calculated and enlightened hand of the government. The economies are developed through the build-up of selective industries that are able to compete in the international market.

The policy of allowing remote regions of the country to be linked with neighbouring economies could have both positive and negative consequences. Unless these regional developments are tied up with the core development of Myanmar's economy, and these regions themselves establish their own competitive advantage consonant with their own potentials and in conjunction with the pattern of development of the whole of Myanmar, these regions will unwittingly become the hinterland of other countries instead of developing as full partners in regional growth.

Another major problem that will slow down the long-term growth of the economy is the depletion of trained and educated manpower and the deterioration of the educational system. The Myanmar leaders still seem to place much store on the supposedly rich natural resources of the country. However, with the population having increased to 50 million in the 1990s from 16 million in 1940s, the man-resource ratio has declined. Even with some introduction of modern technology and some improvement in productivity since the 1940s, the level of rice production now barely meets the needs of the population. Moreover it should be realized that countries gain competitive advantage not through the richness of natural resources, but through the development of technology and the skills of their work-force. All countries that have developed rapidly in the last two decades followed the route of technological development and the upliftment of skills. The need for skilled manpower will become more pressing as future industries become more and more technology-based and skill-intensive. The idea of inviting labour-intensive industries to be relocated in labour-abundant countries is a tempting option for countries in the early stage of development. This option is a fleeting one since these industries are moving to more labour-abundant countries as the original host countries reach a certain level of development and labour become more expensive. The training of skilled technicians and engineers takes a long time to bring about results, and so far the government has paid scant attention to this need.

The last, though not the least, will be the political stability of the country. Ultimately private investors and donors from international agencies will come forward only if a conducive and stable political climate prevails. The seeming quietness or the acquiescence under extreme social and physical control should not be equated with stability under normal circumstances.

WILL FOREVER FLOW THE AYEYARWADY?

In Myanmar, in over forty years of post-war political history, momentous events seem to have been precipitated by political rather than economic imperatives: the split of the pre-independent national coalition in 1947, the outbreak of multiple insurgencies after independence, the breakup of the ruling national front in 1958 and the subsequent *coup d'état* leading to the establishment of the one-party socialist state. When foreign capitalist influences waned after independence, Myanmar did not have any deep-seated economic conflicts. The land nationalization act of 1950 clearly removed any possible remaining contentious social divisions between land-owners and peasants. The failure of the communist rebellion also suggests the absence of an underlying deep economic cleavage in the society. The splits, take-overs, and breakups that characterized the political process were more the outcome of factionalism, personality clashes, and the inherent inability of the Myanmar to work on a give-and-take, conciliatory, or consensual basis among themselves. At this juncture, in the most critical stage of Myanmar's move towards a modern state, finding an amenable political solution acceptable to all major actors has become the central theme again.

Recent political events

If events during 1993 can be taken at face value, the ruling authorities can congratulate themselves for their tenacity to hold on and for the turn of events in their favour.

First, the national convention convened for drawing up the constitution, which began early in 1993, has only a minority of elected representatives while groups more amenable to the wishes of the ruling group constitute the rest. Moreover, the military authorities have stipulated a set of six-point guidelines, which among others clearly state the dominant role of the military in the new state system

In the initial stage, even among these selected groups of delegates a consensus on what topics or headings should be included in the deliberations could not be reached. Since the basic principles of the proposed constitution were not first agreed upon, some topics concerning issues and matters perceived as threatening to their own special interests were disputed by the respective groups of delegates.

What emerged from the sessions of the convention by late 1993 was that the new state structure will embody the following principal characteristics:

1 A republic with an executive president, elected by an electoral college, as the head of state. The presidential candidate must be capable of handling high-level military affairs.
2 The state system will be a Union constituting seven regions and seven states with equal status. Separate executive, judicial, and legislative powers to be shared among the "Union, regions, states, and self-administered areas".
3 A bicameral Union Parliament and separate parliaments for each region and state.
4 Complete autonomy for the military.
5 Nomination by the Commander-in-Chief of military officers to the Union Parliament and all other elected assemblies down to the district level. Also assignment of military officers to executive positions in the administrative hierarchy down to the district level.
6 The statutory right for the Supreme Commander to assume state power in a national emergency defined as and when disturbances and violence are used to usurp state power or when there is danger of disintegration of the Union and national solidarity as well as the loss of national sovereignty.

The last three points and the executive presidency were not endorsed by the National League for Democracy (NLD) and the Shan National League for Democracy (SNLD), which together won over 80 per cent of the seats in the

1990 election. They voiced the view that though the important contribution of the military to the stability of the forthcoming state system must be duly acknowledged, in a genuine democracy the elected Parliament should be the supreme state authority. All other groups representing workers, peasants, intelligentsia, civil servants, and selected nationalities, chosen by the ruling authorities went along with SLORC guidelines and came up with principles similar to those described above. In a subsequent plenary session, a synthesis in the form of the aforementioned principles emerged which will be further elaborated and finalized.

Secondly, a formula for dealing with the ethnic insurrections that have been going on in the name of self-determination for over four decades in Myanmar's peripheral regions has been worked out by the SLORC. It was first used with ex-communist Wa and Kokang ethnic groups and entailed a cease-fire, conversion of the rebel military wing into a local militia, and co-option of rebel leaders as local indigenous leaders. In fact a temporary *de facto* autonomy is granted to these groups whose members are allowed to reside and do business anywhere in Myanmar.

Apart from Kokang, Wa, and several minor armed ethnic groups, the government has recently reached a cease-fire agreement with the Kachin Independent Organization (MO) and is likely to conclude a pact along similar lines. This may well have been prompted by China's desire to promote communications and trade links with Myanmar via the Kachin state. As China accelerates its development, Myanmar has increasingly become an important gateway to the sea for southwestern Chinese provinces. Border trade with China is growing very rapidly and as such all these interests have reinforced China's desire to foster an orderly and peaceful atmosphere in the Myanmar-China border area.

The anti-SLORC alliance of armed ethnic groups and other dissidents known as the Democratic Alliance of Burma (DAB) has been much weakened by the KIO's direct deal with the government outside the collective framework previously agreed upon among its members. Earlier, the DAB had laid down the following pre-conditions for any dialogue with the government:

1 The Alliance will only enter into any discussion with the government as a group.
2 All political prisoners must be released before any discussion with the government.
3 Any negotiation or talks will take place in a neutral place outside Myanmar.

It therefore seems that the Karen National Union is now left holding the defunct DAB. Under pressure from both sides of the Myanmar-Thai border where they had been ensconced for decades the Karens finally seem to have relented. They have expressed willingness to enter into negotiations with the Myanmar Government for political autonomy as part of a collective settlement.

This leaves the non-ethnic democratic opposition groups, the National Coalition Government of the Union of Burma (NCGUB) and students at the border with an uncertain future. The NCGUB, though favourably looked upon by Western and West European governments, did not make much headway in their cause and are likely to be marginalized once armed ethnic conflict with the SLORC ceases.

Thirdly, on the international front, the SLORC has probably scored a favourable stand-off. Some improvements during the year, such as the release of political prisoners and the holding of the constitutional convention elicited some positive expectations even on the part of the Western governments generally antagonistic to the military regime. The waning of the American resolve to push human rights issues and the general disengagement of the United States from the predominant role in international peace-keeping operations also further lessens the possibility of strong sanctions from the Western community.

Emerging patterns

Strategies are not always explicitly and deliberately devised. Many often emanate from an incremental learning process. Probably in the beginning, when the military leaders took power they just wanted to stave off social chaos as well as the sweeping tide of a people's power revolution. Fear of an imminent disintegration of the armed forces was probably the prime motive behind their action. They were also compelled to promise the holding of multi-party elections as the overwhelming desire of the people could not be ignored. However, as their grip on the situation became stronger, the resolve to ensure the military's continuing role in defining the parameters of power in the future state also strengthened. After successful travails against dissidents and detractors, the original position of safeguarding corporate and individual interests has evolved into one of extending the military's direct participation into the future national political process and governance.

It is now fairly clear that the military have set out to determine the future power configuration by seeking a format that would legitimize their participation while accommodating to some extent the popular demand for democracy. This can be inferred from the ways in which the national convention has been carried out and the manner in which the ethnic issue was tackled.

Major elements of the emerging strategy can be identified thus:

1 The military will be a dominant and self-perpetuating institution not accountable to the elected or civilian authority.
2 Representative democracy will largely operate in the limited spheres

of interest articulation and legislative affirmation of executive decision-making.

3 The economy will be left mainly to the private sector but the military may be involved as a corporate entity as well as individually. Ex-members of and those connected to the military establishment are expected to play an active and significant role in private business. Business practices of the Thai and Indonesian military establishment will probably serve as relevant examples. Such opportunities are expected to contribute towards cohesion and corporate loyalty.

The strategy seems to assume that the border areas, which enjoy a semi-autonomous status, will prosper economically and become integrated within the Myanmar state gradually; while opposition in the Myanmar heartland will wither away as the economy progresses. Groups that still remain intransigent will be "handled" militarily or through persuasion.

The military leadership is probably also making the assumption that with the opening of the economy to international investors and businesses, Myanmar as a whole will prosper, as for other open economies in the region. With more, though limited, participation of elected representatives in public affairs, the economically satisfied and better-off population will eventually not want to pursue the democratic ideal for its own sake. As such, the democratic opposition movement as well as its renowned leader will be marginalized.

Whether such an optimistic scenario materializes will depend upon the following conditions: First, the rate of economic growth will have to be consistently high for a fairly long period, say at least ten years. Second, the fruits of economic progress must be more equitably shared among different strata of the population. Third, economic and political developments in neighbouring countries as well as developments in the international economy should not impinge too adversely on Myanmar.

Problems and limits of the emerging strategy

As regards conditions for the rapid growth of the economy, the importance of appropriate physical infrastructure cannot be overstated. The existing stock of physical infrastructure is so limited and dilapidated that large-scale international official development assistance (ODA) will be needed. Likewise, technological development and training will require an equally large dose of investment. Retraining adult workers technically and training and educating the youth need time to take effect. Without these improvements, large inflow of private entrepreneurial resources may not materialize.

What Myanmar needs by way of business capital is a large amount of private investment for value-added and growth industries which will tie up capital for a longer period. Such large-scale long-term investment, in turn, will need a stable and open political atmosphere and Myanmar's access to markets in the industrialized world. All these cannot materialize without the goodwill generated by satisfying some of the minimal demands for human rights and representative government. Without substantial improvement in these fields, the flow of assistance and consequently the flow of capital will only be a trickle and Myanmar will not be able to attain a high rate of growth.

The next problem identified is concerned with how the military as an all-encompassing and self-perpetuating institution could overcome systemic failures inherent in the new arrangement and roles assumed under the new supra-organizational doctrine. Myanmar's military grew out of the patriotic struggle against imperialism, both West and East. Its image of self-sacrificing young nationalists in rag-tag uniforms undergoing military training to fight for freedom has lingered on. The term, *Tatmadaw*, Royal Army, was bestowed with fondness and admiration. On the other hand, the image of the wheeling-and-dealing businessman and official jostling for a larger and larger share of the economic pie does not square well with the traditional ideal of the self-less soldier-patriot. This business role is also in conflict with the military's primary role, namely, professionalism. The greatest danger is that the business or self-seeking role could sow dissensions within the rank and file of the military establishment itself. If accumulating personal wealth is seen as the goal, even if it is a hidden one, of those in leadership position, the conflict of interests among themselves could lead to rift and instability. This discord could grow as the democratic opposition weakens or the threat of the contending forces subsides. On the other hand, the military's role as a group with vested economic interests is double-edged in its effects. Its very success in garnering a share in the economic pie will further isolate the military from the general population or become a source of envy for other social groups. Also, the opportunities for corruption will increase under the new arrangement in which the military maintains control over all spheres of state power. The separation of powers is formalized but the military will participate or influence all three branches of government. The decisive power resting with the military may provide stability and continuity but its side-effects could be disastrous.

Another important question is how would Myanmar's military fare in its new dominant but mixed role as a collective decision-maker in the new political set-up. Myanmar's military has had no experience of running the country under relatively pluralistic or permissive circumstances. It has been used to operating as a stern disciplinarian or a top-down decision-maker. Going by the experience of successful East Asian countries, power-sharing among different élites, relatively free flow of information, rational economic decision-making, an efficient bureaucracy, and an impartial and effective legal system are deemed to be basic ingredients of all-round development. It has been repeatedly observed that the wide degree of freedom granted to civil servants and technocrats or insulating them from political pressures in making rational economic choices and effectively implementing them contributed in no small measure to the success of progressive economic policies.

However, in Myanmar since 1962 the role of top civil servants whose experience could be very useful even under the new circumstances, had been down-graded and many of them replaced by loyal cadres who subscribed to the new socialist order. The continuity of the judicial tradition has also been disrupted because only elected representatives could serve as judges under the socialist regime. All this is in sharp contrast with the situation in Indonesia where the military rulers co-opted intellectuals, economists, and other professionals into the ruling group from the outset. In fact, the so-called Berkeley Mafia, a group of able economists, reputedly engineered the Indonesian modernization-cum-development process. It is difficult to envisage the Myanmar military to radically change its mindset, given its history of "absolutism" or the tradition of "we alone can do" doctrine.

How efficiently can the system be run under the new political set-up of market economy? In successful East Asian states the government usually restricts itself to providing basic services and maintaining law and order and stability. The direction of the economy is guided according to long-term objectives but the operation of the economy is left to the private sector with a minimum of interference from the government. The government in this setting provides effective and efficient service to all including the business community. The reorganization of the bloated bureaucracy, keeping costs down, and operating according to accepted principles of law are considered as requisites for a viable market economy. In fact, the success of one of the best-performing market economy, Singapore, may be attributed in no small measure to these qualities of good government However, the system likely to emerge in Myanmar will probably be plagued by a number of both external and systematic weaknesses that are counter-productive to the emergence of efficient government organizations.

The first will be the problem of legitimacy on the part of the power-holders, which will make it difficult for them to take unpopular but necessary action, such as the retrenchment of surplus workers. Legitimacy here means not the legal authority which is most likely to be affirmed in a referendum but moral and emotional acceptance and voluntary compliance on the part of the population regarding the mandate to rule. Lack of wholesale popular support and acceptance will make it difficult for the government to act "lean and mean". We have noted that so far the government has not dealt with the problem of redundancy in the government or the corporatization or privatization of state economic enterprises, which will involve shedding surplus labour. Successful developmental experiences of the newly industrialized East Asian countries show that governments often have to take necessary but unpopular measures for long-term national interest. In such circumstances political legitimacy or strong public support of the government is crucial. To catch up with other economies, Myanmar will have to demand public sacrifice or undertake measures adversely effecting the interests of powerful constituencies. Only a popular government with a strong and genuine mandate or a leader with overwhelming support from the masses will be able to accomplish long-term national objectives.

A second potential weakness is that in the new system itself, which seems to emphasize social and political control rather than openness and responsiveness. Military participation in the administration will not be conducive to the development of an independent and efficient civil service, given the habit of the Myanmar military to want to do things its own way. As it is, since the abolition of the old administrative system in the 1960s the administration has functioned only at the beck and call of the powerholders and their agents. Administrative impartiality, the strict rule of law, or the reliability and predictability of administrative actions have lost their relevance. This overwhelming control will not further the re-emergence of an efficient, impartial, and consistent administrative system that is surely needed for an open market economy. Moreover inefficiency due to rent-seeking, high transaction costs, and favouritism could be another systematic weakness that will adversely effect the functioning of the market economy.

In the present state of the economy within the context of the changing world order, an emulation of the Indonesian model dating back to the 1960s is hardly innovative. First, the Cold War confrontation between the superpowers no longer exists so that it is inappropriate to expect ready support from the great powers for the planned Myanmar system. Everywhere, the military's role is changing and even in developing countries it is moving into a more strategic function rather than continuing as a social controller. Secondly, conditions leading to the introduction of the new system in the two countries are very different. The Indonesian military took power to remedy the social chaos and economic ruin caused by years of mis-rule, whereas in Myanmar's case the military took over to re-establish its authority after a brief period of social upheaval against the long-standing military-socialist regime. Thus a cleavage between the military and the people has occurred unintentionally or unwittingly. Thirdly, in Indonesia the political process for consultation and consensus as well as the mechanism to imbibe them had existed in the form of a national culture. As such, the military conveniently fitted into the setting as a stabilizing force. Unlike in Myanmar, there have been continuity and concord within the state-society nexus. In Myanmar, the polity's demand is for a new political system which every citizen expects to be responsive and representative. Thirdly, the Myanmar people had gone through a long process of different political experiences, and at this juncture they aspire for a new social order which is responsive and representative. It should be noted that the Myanmar polity had experienced five pre-war national elections choosing their representatives to assume ever-increasing political powers from 1920 to 1940. Furthermore, after independence there had been five general elections (excluding those under the one-party socialist system), which allowed the choice of representatives in a relatively free and fair atmosphere. The Myanmar people have been exposed to the rule of law, the Western legal system, and democratic values for a long period of time. As such, they are more than ready for representative government at this stage though they will surely recognize that the military could be a pillar for the stability of the democratic state.

With the interplay of such factors in the new set-up fast economic growth is doubtful. The government's lack of bargaining power and the cash-strapped situation could even lead to economic decisions that may have far-reaching consequences in the long run. The promotion and development of Myanmar's indigenous entrepreneurs and the development of high-value-added industry or labour-intensive and skill-intensive industries will be delayed or neglected. The slow rate of growth coupled with inequitable distribution favouring privileged groups may create a social divide never experienced before in the past. As such, the emerging pattern could resemble the Latin American or Philippine road to stagnation and social inequity than the East Asian model of prosperity for all.

The most serious matter will be the eventual outcome of the informal granting of semi-autonomous status to the armed ethnic groups in their own territories. In the earlier years, when the neighbouring countries themselves were still economically under-developed, it was the Myamar heartland, that is, the Ayeyarwady valley, not the periphery, that served as the economic dynamo of the country. In fact, the Ayeyarwady valley was the centre of economic activities. One reason past insurrections in the peripheral states did not succeed was their economic insignificance and geographical isolation. The situation today is different: with the neighbouring countries developing very fast and with the development of regional groupings or growth areas, the peripheries of Myanmar can now thrive economically and politically, confederated to a larger market.

Thus, the present policy of postponing the solution of the Union problem is tantamount to playing with a time bomb. We have to assume that the minority groups too know that the present arrangement is transitional and that they would be eventually "handled" by the central government. In the mean time because of border trade, the complementary nature of regional economies, and if the progress of development in Myanmar proper faltered, these regions may grow faster than the Myanmar heartland and become rapidly tied up with the economies of neighbouring countries. The stronger the economic ties between these states and neighbouring countries, the more intractable the problem of ethnic autonomy will be. Will Myanmar's centre be able to "handle" the periphery when it becomes integrated with powerful neighbours?

CONCLUSION

What attitude the Myanmar military takes towards the problem of development will ultimately influence what strategies they follow. There is the danger that immediate or short-term considerations will take precedence over long-term needs. From the military's point of view, the threat of Myanmar's democratic opposition to the predominant position of the incumbents looms very large. However, in the long run the interests of democratic groups and those of the military will converge or overlap to a great extent. In the short run, the whole political situation appears to be a zero-sum game, whereby one side gains at the equivalent expense of the other. Nevertheless, in the long view, national development is a non-zero-sum situation which benefits all: the economic pie becoming much larger and all having their fair shares.

In fact, impending social and economic changes and attendant threats and opportunities should form the basis of an evolving Myanmar strategy for the future, subsuming short-term sectional interests. In the next twenty to twenty-five years, the following changes can be expected.

First, the Southeast Asian nations will continue to grow at a sufficiently rapid pace along with all other East Asian economies to join the ranks of the NICs. Consequently, region-wide development will take place. Geographical proximity will have an important bearing on development.

Second, while Japan will rejuvenate and maintain its advanced industrial economy, China will emerge as a very powerful industrial power. Both Japan and China will have direct interest in Southeast Asia for its natural resources, as a market for their products, and also as staging areas for some of their transferred industries.

Third, problems relating to the sharing of common natural resources and globalization such as sharing water and fishing rights, exploration of ocean floors, migratory pressures, market access, and transportation are likely to become bones of contention. In this context, Myanmar occupies a very delicate position sandwiched between two giant neighbours, India and China. Myanmar's strategic geography in relation to China also will become more important as China develops. The land-locked southwestern parts of China could have a shorter route to the sea through Myanmar than through Chinese seaports. This also will be thousands of miles shorter than the usual sea route through the Straits of Malacca and the South China Sea. Unwittingly, Myanmar will become a very important variable in the development calculus of southwest China. In addition, with the most favourable land-man ratio within the region, Myanmar could also be a tempting target for spillover migration from its more populous neighbours.

Within this overall context, Myanmar has to carve out its distinctive economic role and national existence for the future. It will have to hitch on to the rising tide of growth in the region and make the best out of its comparative advantage based on its natural resources, human resources, and capabilities, and its own unique geographic position. Apart from opportunities, serious threats to the very existence of the Myanmar state must also be recognized. Disintegration of the Union through *de facto* integration of peripheral regions with economically dominant neighbours is very real. Through no fault of its own, Myanmar's independent existence can be swept away in an intra- or inter-regional conflict. The remark by an astute observer of the Myanmar scene forty years ago that it should not be surprising if Myanmar accidentally or inadvertently becomes part of China in the next hundred years is still pertinent. Myanmar has to steer its way very nimbly through these uncertain waters and forge its own destiny amidst rapid external changes.

In this new mission, national consensus, reconciliation, and an early agreement among all contending forces for the future course of action is a must for both national survival and renewal. All parties must be convinced that their interests can be served by working together, not against each other. Just as there is a need for a national leader who can marshal overwhelming support to carry out national reforms in a non-contentious way, there will be an even greater role for the military in moulding Myanmar's long-term strategy for national development. Myanmar needs a modernized military professionally capable of defending its vital interests in the twenty-first century. It must also be impressed upon all parties that no Myanmar with a balanced frame of mind needs ever question the importance of the military as a stabilizing factor in Myanmar politics. What the ordinary citizen wants is the rule of law and a genuinely representative government with ultimate authority descending from the people. Minorities, on the other hand, are also tired of armed conflict, uncertain status, and impoverished conditions. They are asking for a dignified and definite place in the new Myanmar community of equal and enlightened members. This is the most opportune moment for national reconciliation and reconstruction.

However, this may yet be a barren hope especially when one contending party is on the seemingly unstoppable ascendency to power. Myanmar's traditions of *Apyok taik yei* (fight to the finish) could be too strong to be reversed by reason and foresight. We have to bear in mind that things are not what they seem to be in Myanmar. The most elaborate social edifice ever introduced in Myanmar under the socialist regime fell through when the people's long-term interests were not served. Myanmar is prone to alternating between cycles of docile acquiescence and social eruptions. Myanmar's polity is unlike that of the Thais or the Indonesians in the 1960s. The same formula may not work. It should be realized that when the peripheral regions are gone and forests are denuded ruthlessly, the Ayeyarwady may literally dry up, with what remain of Myanmar degenerating to a sub-Sahara stasis. It has been the overwhelming desire of Myanmar citizens for decency, dignity, and self-expression in the matter of national policy. We hope that the scenario painted earlier about Myanmar's road to disaster is never actualized.

There is an urgent need for a national leader who is able to comprehend all these implications and has taken Myanmar's interest to heart: one who commands overwhelming respect and admiration of the whole military as well as the society at large. Only such a leader can bring all parties together to establish a common national destiny and an inspiring mission acceptable to all. Will Myanmar ever reclaim its rightful place in the community of nations, burying all narrow sectional interests? More emphatically, will the Ayeyarwady flow forever?

4

INDONESIA

Iwan J. Azis

INDONESIA SINCE THE 1960s: CRISES AND REFORMS

Discussion of economic reforms in Indonesia cannot be detached from the nature of the events and crises that prompted them. Unfortunately, no easy generalizations can be made as to whether any given shock, be it external or internal, constitutes a crisis. Furthermore, reforms have to be viewed from a historical perspective as well as in the context of the country's geography and resources.

The three episodes of economic crisis and response in Indonesia identified in this paper reflect this context. However, most of the discussion focuses on the period of the 1980s; the two earlier episodes of crisis and response will be discussed only briefly.

The political and economic crisis of the 1960s

The political collapse that accompanied the state of total economic chaos in Indonesia in the 1960s was unquestionably a major crisis. The events of those years resulted in a huge loss of life, placing them in the category of political, economic, and social crises of the first order. Runaway inflation, peaking at 595 percent in 1965, and the apparent decline of per capita income during the early 1960s, could easily have given way to political upheaval and the resurgence of the Indonesian Communist Party, which was believed at that time to be the strongest Communist party outside the Communist bloc. Microeconomic distortions were myriad, and the corrupt administrative structure created serious economic disarray. The extent of macroeconomic imbalance was also extreme, making it impossible for even the most productive economic sector, the export sector, to grow.

The political and ideological climate during those days favored socialism, albeit of a non-Marxist variety, and a large number of the government's policies were still influenced by the idea of struggle against imperialistic and capitalistic forces and the quest for an egalitarian state. As one senior

Source: *The Political Economy of Policy Reform*, John Williamson (Editor), Washington: Institute for International Economics, 1994, pp. 385–416.

economist put it, ". . . the ideological climate in Indonesia [at that time] was probably the same as what prevailed in bygone days in India."

With the collapse of the old regime in the mid-1960s, new opportunities opened up, and the whole economic policy framework was changed. Having identified monetization of the budget deficit as the major source of the country's extremely high inflation, the new government, with its "stabilization and rehabilitation" program announced in 1966, replaced the policy of easy money with a policy of fiscal balance. This bold change was initiated by a group of economists most of whom graduated from the Faculty of Economics of the University of Indonesia and later became known as the "economic technocrats."[1]

Given the state of chaos that prevailed during the last few years of the old regime, the reforms introduced immediately after the new government took power naturally enjoyed considerable public support. In this respect, the Indonesian case confirms the "crisis" and "honeymoon" hypotheses in John Williamson's introductory paper to this volume. Serious resentments were practically never expressed, and the outcomes of the reforms were quite dramatic: the inflation rate dropped to less than 115 percent in 1967 and plunged further to double-digit rates in 1969 (17 percent) and 1973 (19 percent). The neoclassical influence on the reform program was reflected more in its rehabilitation aspects, where efforts were clearly made to allow at least some play to market forces. Output in both the agricultural and the manufacturing sector increased, and GDP growth revived, reaching 9.2 percent in 1970 and 14 percent in 1973.[2]

The balance of payments shock of the 1970s: the Pertamina crisis

Another, later shock, also often labeled a "crisis," stemmed from the overexpansion of nonoil investments by the state oil company Pertamina, following the first oil boom in the mid-1970s. Headed by General Ibnu Sutowo, a close confidant of President Suharto, the company borrowed heavily in the international credit markets, including many short-term loans. When the debt-service burden reached an intolerable level, forcing Pertamina to default, the crisis began to be felt nationwide. As expected, Bank Indonesia, the central bank, had to take over the company's debt; this resulted in a drawdown of foreign reserves, which by September 1975 amounted to only $0.5 billion.

Interestingly enough, the erroneous decision to borrow short-term in the international credit markets was said to be the result of the technocrats' persistence in persuading the president not to allow the company to borrow in the medium-term credit market because of its shaky financial position. The episode was thus the first sign of the president's support for the economic technocrats.

The Pertamina crisis itself was managed by a special team of economic technocrats, and the handling was considered a success. The aftermath of the crisis caused official borrowing to proceed very cautiously with regard to exposure in the short-term credit market.

This crisis was obviously different, both in nature and in scope, from that of the 1960s. Whereas in the earlier episode it was the severity of the crisis itself that, in keeping with the "crisis hypothesis," created the political backing for change, in the Pertamina crisis it was the president's personal support for the views of the economic technocrats that made the difference. This, coupled with the disciplined nature of the reform itself, apparently played a major role in the success of the maneuver. That success reinforced the president's trust in the team of technocrats, strengthening their hand even further.

Certainly, compared with the episode of the 1960s, the Pertamina crisis did not produce a major reform. Indeed, the only reform resulting from the crisis was greater control over Pertamina finances or, more generally, greater discipline of foreign borrowing. No changes in the management superstructure of the other state enterprises were made.

The crisis of the 1980s

The crisis of the 1980s was largely propelled by the worldwide economic recession of 1982–83 and by the plunge in oil prices in 1983–86, from almost $30 to less than $10 per barrel. Given that 60 to 70 percent of government and export revenues were generated from the oil sector, the price collapse dramatically affected the Indonesian economy almost across the board.

The government made an immediate and fairly forceful response to this external shock. A series of measures within a wide-ranging stabilization and structural adjustment (SSA) program was introduced, with spectacular results. The stabilization part of the program was reflected in a balanced budget policy, maintained mostly through such austerity measures as budget cuts and the postponement of major industrial projects. On the revenue side, the government moved quickly to mobilize nonoil revenues through a major tax reform.

A new income tax law, enacted in 1984, extended tax coverage and improved collection rates, The new system was designed to avoid excessive income tax rates while enlarging the tax base, The value-added tax (VAT) of 10 percent was introduced in 1985 in the manufacturing and construction sectors and on fuel oils; an additional tax of 10 to 20 percent applied to luxury goods sold in domestic markets, The new value-added tax basically replaced the old sales tax, in the expectation that it would avoid taxation of full value at each stage of the production chain. Excessive use of tax incentives to achieve particular objectives (e.g., tax holidays) was also discontinued.

The tax reforms dramatically reversed the shares of oil and nonoil receipts in the budget. In the first two years of the tax reform, the main increase in nonoil revenues was due to the VAT. In the following years, income and land tax revenues also increased, resulting in a dramatic jump in total nonoil revenues of around 30 percent from the 1987–88 period to the 1989–90 period. As can be seen in Table 4.1, the annual rate of growth of nonoil revenues increased sharply, from 16.5 percent during the prereform period to more than 20 percent during the reform period. The VAT and the income tax remain today the two major sources of government revenues aside from the oil tax.

The tax reform was also meant to enhance the efficiency of the tax system. The government's efforts resulted in an increase in the number of registered taxpayers (doubling for VAT and more than doubling for the income tax), and an increase in the number of tax returns submitted.

Along with these steps, civil service employee salaries were frozen for at least three consecutive years. Obviously this move was politically very difficult, but it was implemented without serious resistance from any pressure groups.

Reforms within the context of the stabilization program were also made in monetary policy. During the oil boom, monetary policy had been based primarily on two mechanisms: credit ceilings and interest rate controls for state banks, which were major players in the financial market at that time. The government also had determined that subsidized interest rates were necessary for some high-priority sectors. While the policy was effective in limiting credit expansion in certain sectors, in general the banking system suffered from considerable excess liquidity due to the augmented net foreign assets prompted by the two oil booms, and by uncontrolled liquidity credits (*kredit likuiditas*) to many high-priority sectors. The dominant state banks remained plagued by inefficiency and were unable to accumulate deposits from the private sector because of the controlled interest rate.[3] The excess of funds being created in the banking system had an adverse effect on the country's balance of payments position.

The plunge in oil prices led to a shortfall in government revenues and balance of payments deficits. This, in turn, constrained the interest spreads of Indonesian banks and forced the government to promulgate monetary and financial reforms in June 1983. These reforms were aimed at dismantling the old system of monetary control, replacing it with a more indirect approach based on reserve management through open market operations. In 1984, a new monetray instrument, the Sertifikat Bank Indonesia (SBI), was introduced, followed by the issuance of promissory notes, known as Surat Berharga Pasar Uang (SBPU), in early 1985. The SBI is a debt certificate that may be used by the central bank to reclaim its share of net foreign assets and to create government debt instruments, to secure greater control over reserves.

Although the new financial mechanism was able to cover only the equivalent of 20 percent of reserves, it did prove effective when the government needed to act quickly in response to a serious financial crisis. The "Sumarlin

Table 4.1 Indonesia: selected economic indicators during periods of external shock and policy reform, 1980–90[a] (percentages except where noted)

	Prereform period, 1980–83	*External shocks and early reform period, 1983–86*	*Active reform period, 1986–90*
Economic growth			
Gross domestic product	3.2	5.1	6.4
Oil	–4.3	3.3	2.5
Nonoil	5.2	5.6	7.4
Gross domestic income	4.1	3.7	6.1
Growth by sector			
Agriculture	2.6	3.7	3.4
Mining	–4.4	0.4	1.8
Manufacturing	3.6	14.0	11.0
Construction	6.1	0.1	10.0
Electricity	18.9	11.0	14.0
Services	8.2	5.8	7.4
Consumption expenditures	7.2	2.7	5.3
Private	7.5	2.4	5.3
Government	5.5	4.6	5.2
Gross capital formation	6.6	3.2	11.6
Private	16.1	4.1	15.2
Government	–2.9	1.9	5.0
Exports of goods and services[b]	–8.8	4.2	7.8
Imports of goods and services[b]	9.7	0.5	4.3
Merchandise exports[c]	–1.2	–11.2	14.8
Oil	0.9	–19.9	7.8
Nonoil	–6.8	9.2	22.1
Merchandise imports[c]	14.7	–13.1	17.4
Oil	33.3	–35.6	15.0
Nonoil	10.3	–7.6	17.7
Money supply (current prices)			
M2	23.9	23.5	32.3
M1	14.9	15.4	19.6
Claims by monetary authorities (current prices)	26.9	20.7	13.8
Government budget (current prices)	13,8	9.9	18.9
Nonoil revenues	16.5	25.8	21.5
Oil revenues	10.0	–2.5	13.1
Loans	26.4	14.6	23.9
Development expenditures	10.7	7.0	15.2
Oil price (dollars)	0.0	–22.7	13.0
Devaluation (rupiah per dollar)	13.2	12.1	9.5
Inflation	11.2	4.9	8.3
Share of population living below poverty line[d]			
Urban	12.1	7.3	7.3
Rural	39.4	26.8	20.8
Total	33.0	21.7	16.7
Gini coefficient[d]	0.331	0.321	0.319

Note:
[a] Figures are annual rates of growth except where noted.
[b] In local currency terms at constant 1983 prices.
[c] In dollar terms.
[d] For 1984, 1987, and 1990.

Sources: CBS, Indonesian Central Bank, and World Bank.

shock" of 1986 was a good example. Fueled by rumors of impending devaluation, signs of capital flight became visible during that period. The economic technocrats, led by Minister Sumarlin, took action by calling in SBPUs before maturity and persuading state banks to buy SBIs. Naturally, this move triggered a surge in the interest rate (upon the announcement, interbank rates soared to 40 percent), but at the same time it indicated that the government had policy measures other than devalution at its disposal to discourage capital flight.

Meanwhile the government took a strong stance on maintaining the stability of exchange rates and domestic prices. This prudent and persistent policy has paid off. Inflation remains very much under control in single digits (Table 4.1), resulting in a stable real exchange rate and greater competitiveness. Remarkably enough, control of inflation was achieved without giving up much in terms of ecnomic growth: GDP rose on average by 5.1 and 6.4 percent per year during 1983–86 and 1986–90, respectively.

The structural adjustment aspects of the SSA program were designed to move the country toward a more outwards-oriented development strategy. Using various deregulation measures, the government aimed at an improvement of national efficiency through greater reliance on market forces. The spirit of the derugulation policy was to promote the fostering of internal dynamics in the domestic economy by removing structural rigidities.

One may wonder why, in a country as large as Indonesia, the technocrats emphasized the export-oriented strategy more than the reforms targeted at the domestic market. The usual argument stresses the non-productive quality of the domestic market and lower domestic purchasing power compared with the international market. Another, no-less-common argument holds that competitive pressures from abroad are necessary to raise the efficiency of various sectors in the economy. Too many obstacles, including those of a political nature, persist when the ballgame is contained within the country (e.g., under a strategy based on import substitution).[4] But perhaps the strongest justification relates to the fact that the increasing debt payments left the government no option but to earn more foreign exchange.[5] Given the fall in oil prices in 1986 and the uncertainty of future prices, nonoil exports were the logical alternative.

Two major devaluations were implemented, in March 1983 (28 percent) and September 1986 (31 percent).[6] The resulting increase in nonoil exports has been dramatic. In only six years, nonoil exports almost tripled, from $5 billion in 1983 to $14.4 billion in 1990, and their share of total exports rose from 25 percent to 56 percent. This implies annual growth rates of nonoil exports of 9.2 and 22.1 percent during 1983–86 and 1986–90, respectively (Table 4.1). It is believed that, at least for the 1987–88 period, the impact of the devaluations was greater than that of the trade deregulation promulgated in May 1986 (see Azis 1992b, 15).

Although the system of monopoly importing rights remained in place after the 1986 reforms, a series of measures to liberalize trade were adopted. A number of tariff categories were cut, and rates were reduced across the board. Import restrictions were lifted on a wide range of products, and the import licensing system was revamped. Further relaxations of investment restrictions and other efforts to create a more favorable investment climate were made systematically.

The overall results of these efforts have been very encouraging. Along with the boost from other demand components, the liberalization measures accelerated economic growth, which reached more than 7 percent in 1989 and 1990. In fact, as already described, during the whole of the post-reform period the country has enjoyed an average growth rate of more than 6 percent (Table 4.1).

Trends in other selected variables are also depicted in Table 4.1. Table 4.2 lists the various reforms implemented in the 1980s and the purpose of each. In general, the SSA program, designed to respond to the external shocks of the 1980s, has been a success for Indonesia, at least as viewed from its repercussions upon macroeconomic trends.[7]

THE PRECONDITIONS AND REASONS FOR EFFECTIVE REFORM

Many of the measures taken in response to the crisis of the 1980s were bold and drastic, and, as one would expect, the social impacts were enormous. Indeed, in the early period of reforms, open unemployment increased considerably, particularly in the urban areas, although this was due in part to rural-urban migration. The freeze on government employees' salaries and the austere budget constraints caused a drop in domestic purchasing power, one result of which has been a decline in manufacturing profits. The real earnings of urban workers have fallen, especially in the construction and services sectors, and including in the informal sector.

Although all these repercussions took place only during the early reform period, one may wonder how a series of pro-market reforms was able to survive in the mid-1980s and to the present day without serious challenge. To many observers, the success of the Indonesian economic reforms of the 1980s is even more puzzling, given that a number of economic nationalists, in the army and in civilian groups (including the business sector), hold influential positions both in and out of government, and would theoretically oppose a more liberal and open economic policy. Furthermore, Indonesia has a long history of separatism and regional rebellions. Although the history in each region is different, in general there is always a sense of alienation among regions outside Java, not only because the economy's center of gravity is in Java, but also because the administration frequently has been dominated by the Javanese. Therefore, it is legitimate to ask how economic reforms affect interregional imbalances in a large, ethnically diverse, archipelagic country such as Indonesia.

Table 4.2 Indonesia: summary of economic reforms, 1983–90

Reform	*Contents*	*Repercussions*
Fiscal		
1983–84	Postponement of large-scale and capital-intensive projects	Reduced pressures on government budget
	Reduction of subsidies on fuel and rice	
April 1984	Introduction of value-added tax	Increased coverage, collection rates, and government revenues
	Rationalization of income tax	
	Additional 10 to 20 percent tax on luxury goods	Reduced tax bargaining
	Removal of withholding tax	
	Improvement of tax administration and apparatus	
1986	Introduction of new property tax at a single rate of 0.5 percent	Slight increase in property tax revenues
	Introduction of new law on stamp duties	Reduced number of transactions involving stamp duties
	Subsidy on fertilizers and pesticides reduced	Further reduction of pressures on government budget
	Efficiency of government agencies in implementing development projects increased	Increased efficiency
	Suspension of carrying unspent development funds over to next year (SLAP)	
1987	Further reductions in capital expenditures	Strong relief in budget constraints
	Restraints of subsidies and administrative cost	
Financial		
March 1983	Devaluation of rupiah by 28 percent	Improved export competitiveness
June 1983	Credit ceilings removed	Rise in deposit rate
	Interest rate controls removed	Liquidity credits still increased
	Subsidized liquidity credit reduced	Fall in cost of intermediation
	SBI and SBPU introduced (see text)	
1983–84	Jakarta Stock Exchange activated	Trade in stocks occurs below par value

Reform	*Contents*	*Repercussions*
	Opening of bond market	
1985	Capital Market Executive Board (BAPEPAM) initiates further reform and reduces requirement for new issues (to Rp 200 million)	Some commercial banks receive underwriting privileges for stock and bond issues
September 1986	Devaluation of rupiah by 31 percent	Increased export competitiveness
October 1986	Ceiling on swaps removed	Increased swap trading
December 1987	Capital market deregulation	Increase in capital market activity
	Stock purchase allowed to foreigners	
	Establishment of a secondary over-the-counter market	
October 1988	Lending limit regulation	Many banks and joint ventures emerged
	Reserve requirement lowered	Intense competition between banks
	Licenses for new banks and joint ventures	Interest rates soar
	More competition allowed between commercial and state banks	Signs of fall in interest rate spread
	Easier branching for existing domestic and foreign banks allowed	
November 1988	Reform of the currency market	More market-based swap rate
December 1988	Deregulation of insurance industry	Significant increase in market activity
	Further capital market deregulation	Increased market index
	Rationalization of financial services sector (including foreign)	Many companies going public
Trade		
March 1985	Reduction in number of tariffs levels	Increased efficiency and import flows
	Reduction of tariff ceiling	
April 1985	Swiss survey firm assigned to manage customs	Early positive psychological effects

Table 4.2 (Cont.)

Reform	*Contents*	*Repercussions*
	Port charges reduced	Reduced inefficiencies in shipping, port handling, and customs procedures
	Shipping industry opened to international competition	Increased export competitiveness
	Port administration simplified	
May 1986	Introduction of duty drawback system to 'producer-exporters'	Clear signs of export increase along with augmented foreign investments
October 1986	Import licensing reduced	Further increase in export-oriented investments
	Tariffication	Increase in necessary (nonconsumption) imports
	Further tariff reduction	
January 1987	Further reduction in import licensing	Same as in October 1986
July 1987	Still further reduction in import licensing with no tariff increase	Same as in October 1986
	System of textile quota allocation improved	
November 1988	Inter-island shipping deregulated	Increased competition
	Removal of monopolies in imports of steel and plastic	Increased confidence in government efforts to deregulate the economy
May 1990	Deregulation in pharmaceuticals and animal husbandry	Increased competition
	Adjustment in tariffs	Improved investment climate
	Reduction in number of surcharges	
	Further removal of nontariff barriers	
Investment		
1985	Simplification of application procedures for foreign investment	Reduction in waiting period and number of documents
May 1986	Allowance of 95 percent foreigh ownership in export-oriented investments	Increased exports and further increased investment
	Local distribution opened to export-oriented firms	Japanese department store 'SOGO' opened

Reform	*Contents*	*Repercussions*
	Export credit scheme opened for participation by joint ventures	Increased confidence in the economy
	Retail trade opened to foreign firms	
1986	One-year tax exemption on imported equipment	Enthusiastic response from foreign investors
	Visa requirements from 29 countries lifted	
	Investment from Eastern European countries no longer needs intelligence approval	
September 1986	Maxi devaluation (More than 30 percent)	Increased export competitiveness
July 1987	Deregulation of investment and capacity licensing	Improved investment climate
	Stock exchange opened to foreign investors	
November 1988	Further deregulation in shipping industry	Increased competition
	Joint ventures allowed to distribute their own products domestically	
May 1989	Replacement of priority list with negative list	Improved investment climate further
June 1989	Attempts to improve efficiency of state enterprises	Some state enterprises showed improved efficiency
	Encourage privatization	Increased signs of more 'going public'
1989	Foreign portfolio investors allowed to purchase 49 percent of nonbank companies listed on stock exchanges	Improved foreign confidence in the economy
November 1989	Steps to improve performance of state enterprises	186 out of 210 state enterprises affected
	Specifice steps to improve efficiency in 75 enterprises	Sales of equity in 52 state enterprises
		Mergers of joint ventures in 59 state enterprises
1990	Up to 30 percent of shares of three large state cement enterprises offered to public	Increased expectations of further privatization

Then there is the question of the type of reform being undertaken. Any crisis demands a response, but there is no general precept that the response will be of a pro-market type. In fact, unlike the economic reforms of the 1980s, the response to the two preceding crises, especially that of the 1970s, did not relect a strong move toward reliance on market forces. The reaction to an economic crisis can go either in a pro- or an anti-market direction.

The key role of the technocrats and the president's support

Political institutions in Indonesia are such that they can be used by an *effective* government to steer policy direction (including economic reform) in either of these two ways. There is no strong system of checks and balances between executive, legislative, and judical powers. Serious ideological controversies are absent as well, and civil society is not organized to the same extent as, for example, in Latin America. On the other hand, there is a strong consensus on the need to put a priority on economic development.

Because of its longevity (from 1966 until the present), the government of President Suharto is unquestionably very effective. The policy direction proposed in the 1980s was to reform the economy using pro-market mechanisms. This recommendation came from a group of people that have also been effective in the political arena, namely, the economic technocrats. The analytical capabilities of this group are superb, and more importantly they possess a talent for selecting policy changes that recognize the political and other noneconomic constraints. The technocrats' approach is pragmatic, professionally based, and little influenced by party politics and ideology.

The shared views and persistent courage of the economic technocrats under the leadership of Widjojo Nitisastro, former economic and planning minister and now a senior govemment adviser, have been the economic team's primary source of strength and the reason why its reforms have gone practically unchallenged. The concrete outcomes of their strategy—a rising standard of living together with sustained rapid growth and low inflation, an evident reduction in poverty, and the enhancement of infrastructure throughout the country—have further strengthened the standing of the economic technocrats in the political arena.

However, to contend that the work of the technocrats is the only factor in Indonesia's success story would be an exaggeration. Without other supporting factors the story would undeniably have been different. The economic team has received the full support of the president since the very early days of the new government. In a heterogeneous and at the same time paternalistic society such as in Indonesia, this factor is of utmost importance. When very difficult economic decisions have to be made, it is only the president's blessing that allows them to be successfully implemented.

Many of the policy measures taken in the 1980s were certainly not easy to implement. Nevertheless, after conducting careful analyses, some with a fair degree of sophistication, the technocrats made their case to the president using straightfonvard economic arguments. These were often accepted by the president, and the proposals were subsequently put forth with no serious challenge in the Parliament. The full support of the president, as in the Pertamina crisis, has been the prime reason for the effective implementation of the reforms.

The drastic "Sumarlin shock" in 1986 and the fiscal austerity program implemented in anticipation of falling oil prices during the mid-1980s are examples of unpopular decisions that originated with the economic technocrats. It was difficult to bypass several vested interests, but the initiatives were believed necessary to stabilize the financial sector of the country. Here too the blessing of the president strengthened the implementation of some difficult decisions.

Another example was the courageous decision of the technocrats to devalue the currency in 1983 and 1986.[8] This decision originally encountered great resentment among some interest groups, but the devaluations were implemented anyway, and with only very minor disturbances. The economic consequences were positive: export growth accelerated while inflation was kept at the single-digit level. Robust export performance has also helped improve the living standard of many Indonesian farmers through greater competitiveness of their export crops. Hence, poverty was reduced and the anticipated worsening of the income distribution due to the reform was averted. The floating exchange rate regime has also been well-managed. From the time the first reform was introduced (in the banking and monetary sector in June 1983), the inflation rate has been kept below the two-digit level, except in 1984.

Then there was the Pertamina case. As previously discussed, a team of some influential economic technocrats, again with the president's support, undertook a bold financial rescue of Pertamina in 1975, when the company was on the brink of bankruptcy. It should be noted that the company was headed by General Sutowo, who is a close confidant of the president.

Thus, it is clear that the economic technocrats have enjoyed the president's full confidence, without which many tough economic decisions could not have been implemented. The backing of the president was also of crucial importance in implementing the SSA prograrn during the 1980s.[9]

The basis of the president's confidence can be traced to a specific event: a 1966 seminar, called the Seminar Angkatan Darat, at which the economists who later would serve as technocrats were active participants. They managed to impress the president with their bold proposals, even though these made less of a bow to political susceptibilities than those broached by other groups, at least in the first stage. Although one could argue whether such an approach was indeed less political, the "straight economics" character of the technocrats' proposals is viewed even today as one of the group's hallmarks.[10]

Another illustration is worth mentioning. In the deliberations over the

1993–94 budget, there were extensive discussions about the possibility of eliminating subsidies for fuel. It was realized that such a move would likely induce an increase in domestic fuel prices and thus contribute to inflation. And, as expected, various interest groups have strongly opposed the proposal. However, by making their case in terms of "straight economic" arguments that are appealing to the public, the technocrats succeeded in making the 1993–94 budget the first to eliminate fuel subsidies entirely. Thus, another battle for the liberalization of the economy has been won.

The increase in the price level, it appears, however, was taken into account before the decision to remove the fuel subsidies was made. Indeed, the following argument was offered. The inflation rate for 1992 was at an all-time low (less than 5 percent). Further inflationary pressures from the fuel price hike in 1993 would, therefore, still enable the government to expect a one-digit inflation rate, a range considered harmless for pursuing prudent macroeconomic policy. However, judging from the sharp increase in the inflation rate for January 1993 (almost 3 percent, suggesting a yearly average well into double digits), special efforts to maintain low inflation are certainly needed. Thus, while there is no doubt that the technocrats are masters of the art of winning political arguments (in this case to remove subsidies), they often face a situation where, by winning one battle, they end up facing another problem.

Interestingly, the same budget also raised civil servants' salaries, providing another potential source of inflationary pressure. To offset these pressures, or at least those transmitted via expectations, the salary increase was disguised by calling it "changes in the salary structure." As deceiving a tactic as this may appear to be, and however limited the impact would be, past experience suggests that such a maneuver can be effective.[11] The removal of subsidies in fact is often found to be the best solution in a straightforward, unconstrained optimization exercise. Hence, a complex calculation and the corresponding economic analysis (not merely based on psychological and other noneconomic factors) was surely conducted prior to the decision. With foreign debt payments ballooning to almost half of all routine expenditures, and with stagnant inflows of foreign loans, it is only appropriate to slash all government-funded subsidies.

From this review of the various policies taken in response to the economic crisis in Indonesia, John Williamson's hypothesis that "the existence of a team of economists with a common, coherent view of what is needed to be done and commanding the instruments of concentrated executive authority" seems unquestionably to apply in the Indonesian case. The pragmatic approach of Indonesia's team of economic technocrats has certainly won the support of the public and the president.

In fact, the same pragmatism can be detected in the early history of the Suharto regime. The regime has been faithful to the 1945 Constitution decree, which declared that the national economy should be organized in a cooperative way, in contrast to unbridled laissez-faire competition. And in fact the new regime has always deliberately avoided speaking in terms of "embracing capitalism and abandoning socialism."

The Indonesian reforms in light of the Williamson hypotheses

Several hypotheses have been proposed as to the preconditions for successful reform and to explain how a country can mobilize and maintain the necessary political support for reform. Naturally, none of these hypotheses can be either unambiguously confirmed or rejected in the case of Indonesia.

Although some may argue that the policy package introduced by the team of economists installed in the late 1960s already constituted "economic reforms," this is true only if "reform" is defined in a very broad and somewhat ambiguous way, as denoting any change in government policy designed to alter economic activity. The term could cover, for example, changes in administrative procedures and in institutional structure, in addition to standard economic policy changes. Such a definition fails to specify whether the reform is more focused on stabilization or structural adjustment, or both. Under such a broad definition, one can maintain without any hesitation that there was indeed a major reform in the late 1960s. It could be argued further that the reform was deliberately designed in response to a perceived crisis (economic as well as political), and hence is an illustration of the "crisis hypothesis" at work. In fact, the crisis of the 1960s was the most traumatic of the three examined here; it even threatened the existence of the nation.

The economic technocrats during that period were kept busy, and were even obsessed, by the goal of slowing the country's runaway inflation, which plagued the economy and depressed the living conditions of most of the population. They confronted the task by balancing the budget (inclusive of receipts of foreign aid) in order to prevent the budget from being a major source of money creation. However, given the absence of an appropriate institutional setting and effectively functioning administrative procedures, and given the enormous amount of capital required, the task was unquestionably very difficult.[12] Yet the record of the technocrats in controlling inflation was impressive. In a relatively short period of time, inflation dropped to low double digits.

The "crisis" that prevailed in the 1980s was different, and certainly much less severe. It was propelled by external shocks, inflation did not reach triple digits, infrastructure conditions were already better than in the 1960s, and a stable institutional structure and administrative procedures were in place, as were many other necessary conditions for sustained development. The severity of the worldwide economic recession in the early 1980s, followed by the plunge in oil prices over the 1983–86 period, certainly did not match the crisis of the 1960s. In this respect, acceptance of the "crisis hypothesis" for the 1980s events is still justified, but much less than for the phenomena of the 1960s.

What is interesting to observe is that, while the crisis in the 1980s was by no means of traumatic proportions, the nature and scope of the response were far more extensive, spawning a series of trade and industrial policy reforms. One speculation is that there was a pent-up pressure for comprehensive reform in the 1980s, and the economic technocrats had clearly undergone a learning process over the course of time.

It is less clear that the "honeymoon hypothesis" applies to the Indonesian reforms of the 1980s. There has been no "new team of economic policy-makers" in Indonesia since the late 1960s. True, there was a period when a group of special advisers to the president, the "Aspri" (from *asisten pribadi*, which translated literally means "private assistants"), held a crucial role in shaping various strategies. These individuals were not always in agreement with the views of the economic technocrats, but the strategies they advised mostly, although not exclusively, pertained to the political arena. In economic matters the strategies they advocated were too general to reverse, or even affect, those championed by the economic technocrats. The Aspri are also known to be more inclined toward "operations"—that is, toward individual, ad hoc measures than toward articulating an alternative economic system.

There was, of course, something of a honeymoon between the technocrats and the political forces supporting the New Order, which included students, the media, and the armed forces (and in particular the army), especially during the early stage. Yet, with the exception of the armed forces,[13] the relationship fluctuates. For example, the honeymoon between the technocrats and the 1966 students' movement petered out after the Malari affair in 1974. Some members of the media are also increasingly critical of the government's policy direction, although in general the relationship between the technocrats and the media has been mutually supportive.[14] The increasingly significant role of engineers in the cabinet (discussed in the next section) has led to a rather different view about development policy in general, and this has recently been reflected in media coverage.

The absence of opposition, however, should not be exaggerated. It is certainly not true that the SSA program went totally unchallenged by those inclined toward a populist macroeconomic policy. The usual allegation is that the SSA program favors growth at the expense of equity—a classic trade-off argument. However, this claim is unsupported by the data. Several studies found, at least during the early years of the SSA program, no sign of a worsening income distribution (Thorbecke et al. 1992a). A simple Gini coefficient actually shows a slight improvement in income distribution (Table 4.1), from 0.321 in 1987 to 0.319 in 1990.[15]

The poverty figures also have been encouraging. The proportion of the population living below the poverty line declined from 33.0 percent in 1984 to 21.7 percent in 1987, and to 16.7 percent in 1990 (Table 4.1; the figures are based on a head count index using World Bank estimates).[16] This achievement is primarily due to the persistent allocation of public expenditures to infrastructure and to other social overhead capital that surely benefit the middle- and lower-income groups, including the rural population.[17] A government program known as Inpres played perhaps the most important role in this regard. Despite the existence of ad hoc criteria for the allocation of some Inpres categories among the country's 27 provinces, implying the need for further improvement, this government program has become the major impetus for averting a worsening of income distribution and poverty conditions during and after the economic reform. In a study utilizing the 1985 input-output table, I have found that Indonesia's outward-oriented strategy, compared with the alternative strategy of import substitution, is far more favorable to employment creation (Azis 1989b).

It has also been shown that the SSA program is capable of generating a wider dispersal of investments throughout the country. Thus, the fear of alienation among the regions outside Java has gradually abated. However, judging from the trend during the early years of the reform, the SSA program also appears to reinforce the concentration of export activities on the crowded island of Java, mainly because of the island's relatively superior infrastructure (Azis 1992b). It is expected that these conflicting outcomes will disappear as various deregulations begin to take effect in many regions outside Java. Moreover, the maintenance of a competitive exchange rate will strengthen further the position of the export-oriented farm sector in the outer islands.

Hence, while the point should not be exaggerated, opposition to the policy course is indeed fragmented and, in general, weak. Some of those who were regular critics in the past have even jumped on the bandwagon, militating for further deregulation and pleading for the removal of monopoly powers and other protectionist policies that remain. Cynical observers may charge that these people have merely been co-opted. Other opponents, some of whom attempted to amalgamate economic reform with greater political democracy, likewise receive no popular support, mainly because it is still fresh in everybody's mind that the economic strategy during the period of liberal pluralistic democracy (in the 1950s) was ineffective. The exuberance of the democratic politics of those years led to undisciplined and disorderly conditions that were inimical to development.

At present, the political parties other than the government party, Golkar, do not have an alternative strategy that can capture widespread popular support.[18] It is no overstatement to assert that the views of the various parties are converging—or at least are no longer diametrically opposed. In this respect, a sort of consensus has emerged.

Some have also maintained that an important part of the success of the Indonesian economic reforms relates to the fact that the reforms were undertaken before the actual crisis arrived (see, for example, Bourguignon and Morrisson 1992). If this is true, it is not too difficult to understand why the reforms were also easier to implement, since room to maneuver is more ample when reforms are taken prior to the crisis. However, I am not convinced that this was indeed the case. It is true, for example, that a range of policy reforms were implemented before oil prices hit their lowest level in August 1986. However, the decline in oil prices had begun in 1983, immediately following the worldwide recession. Indonesia's policymakers undoubtedly did anticipate still lower oil prices, but to assert that policy reforms were taken long before, or even independently of, the crisis is certainly an exaggeration. The hypothesis that the technocrats actually introduced a "pseudo-crisis" is perhaps easier to believe than the hypothesis of precrisis reform. Nonetheless, the unprecedentedly high quality of economic reforms in Indonesia cannot be discounted, whether the reforms were undertaken before or during the crisis.

Finally, the severity of the crisis certainly suggests some reasons why the reforms were effective and largely unchallenged. Whereas the financial rescue of Pertamina, in particular, was made possible through the president's support of the economic technocrats, the handling of the crises in the 1960s and 1980s unquestionably had something to do with the nature and extent of the deteriorating economic conditions during those times.

Market reform and the role of foreign capital and advisers

Although it is true that the economic technocrats were by no means free-market ideologues, the policy direction that emerged in response to the crisis of the 1980s was clearly pro-market. Some government interventions were condoned, as long as they were market compatible.[19] Hence, the technocrats' position on the role of the state is more or less clear. Maintaining such a position should, at least in principle, imply a certain degree of compatibility with the emerging ideas of market reform. It would also be difficult to envision the alluring performance of the economy without contemplating the role of external funding. Some of these issues are discussed below.

Ideas about pro-market reforms in Indonesia in fact began to spread long before such reforms were actually put in place. One former economic minister recalls that, in the late 1970s, the idea of market reform was already being discussed quite extensively, albeit privately, among economic policymakers. In their judgment, however, the timing was not propitious. It should be recalled that, in the 1970s, Indonesia experienced two episodes of oil boom (1974 and 1979), so that a sense of urgency for reform was not really present. The technocrats fully realized that the choice would not be well received politically, and that support from the president also would be difficult to obtain.

The importance of foreign investment

The first and, perhaps, foremost idea is concerned with what, precisely, should be the role of external funding in the process of development. In this regard, the economic technocrats have fully recognized, from the beginning, the link between foreign aid and private foreign investment. The 1966–67 law on foreign investment strongly reflected that recognition. With the objective of attracting foreign capital inflows, a series of incentives (and disincentives) were introduced. In 1969, the system of foreign exchange controls was abolished, making the rupiah completely convertible at market rates. The idea was to attract capital repatriation by making capital transfers easier and lawful—tax authorities asked no questions about the origin of repatriated funds. In addition, a set of fiscal incentives and duty exemptions was introduced. To break the fear of nationalization, the provision of legal protection was made.

But perhaps the most interesting case was the implementation of an open capital account system as early as in 1969. Recognizing the need for foreign investment in oil and other sectors based on the country's abundant resources, Indonesia liberalized its capital account long before the SSA program was begun in the 1980s, and at a time when the current account remained full of protection and distortions. In this sense, Indonesia did not follow the usually prescribed sequence for liberalization. One consequence is that the government is constantly under pressure to maintain a competitive real exchange rate. This partly explains the persistently jittery policy toward inflationary pressure on the part of Indonesian policymakers.

At any rate, all the efforts paid off. Foreign direct investment inflows as recorded in the capital account turned positive after at least three years in a row of persistent outflows (1966–68). Other factors also attracted foreign investors, including the country's wealth of natural resources and, later, the low cost of labor. Following the first oil boom in 1974 (which of course was an oil crisis for neighboring oil-consuming countries), a strong import substitution strategy was implemented. All of a sudden, the domestic market became potentially attractive. To make sure this factor worked in the face of low purchasing power, the government mostly granted investors' requests for protection from competing imports. A similar practice was later extended to domestic investors, and thus began the heyday of infant-industry protection; so, too, began the process of industrialization.

There is no doubt that foreign investment helped propel the country's economic growth, which in turn allowed foreign financing to become available on easier terms. Indonesia's lack of ideological aversion toward foreign investment facilitated its continued inflow, which continues to the present. The requirement that the government control the country's natural resources and those economic activities considered important for the livelihood of society at large (as stated in the constitution) did not reduce the interest of foreign investors in many resource-based sectors, particularly petroleum, timber, and mining. The attraction of Indonesia'a large domestic market was recognized later, mostly by the Japanese. Then, through massive subsidized investment credits made possible by the oil bonanza in the mid-1970s (mostly via the state-owned development bank Bapindo), the domestic industrial class, consisting of both Chinese and indigenous peoples, came to the fore. This marked the start of the real process of industrialization.

The solid economic performance following implementation of the SSA program in the 1980s was also made possible by strong inflows of foreign capital, particularly those related to the relocation of many industrial investments from Japan (and later from the newly industrializing countries as well), that swept the ASEAN countries as a consequence of the appreciation of the yen in 1985 and after. Economic growth was very strong, the rate of increase of nonoil exports was at an all-time high, and the growth of manufacturing production accelerated. Some observers, rightly or wrongly, even referred to the late 1980s as an economic boom period. Another noted economist labeled the phenomenon "Japanese-led growth."

Obviously, however, the flood of investments would not have occurred had Indonesia not followed the policy course described earlier. The push factor from abroad directed investment flows to the ASEAN area, but these countries able to provide incentives and welcoming macroeconomic environment (pull factor) were those to whom the investment gravitated. Thus, the economic reform of the 1980s helped to attract these capital inflows, which in turn stimulated strong economic growth.

The role of foreign borrowing and foreign assistance

Another important external source of Indonesia's economic growth has been foreign loans. Both the old and the new regime recognized the importance of this source of financing for the country's economic development. But there were major differences in the sources and uses of this financing under the two regimes. More than 60 percent of the debt incurred under the old regime was owed to the Communist bloc. A considerable share of those funds was used for the purchase of military hardware. When Indonesia eventually defaulted, the new regime requested a special meeting to discuss a rescheduling scheme. Two important and historic meetings finally took place in Tokyo and Paris in the autumn of 1966. In terms of the substance of the relief program that was agreed upon by all parties involved, the meetings, especially the one in Paris, were considered an unprecedented success. They allowed the new economic team to start working on a new economic plan without being overly constrained by the debt problem.

The new regime also took a different approach to borrowing. The terms of the new loans, which came from the Western countries, were always set as soft as possible, and a special group known as the IGGI (Inter-Governmental Group on Indonesia) was formed. This group has become an important avenue for discussing the problems, challenges, and amounts of foreign aid required by the Indonesian government in order to undertake continuous development efforts. After the first IGGI meeting, the Indonesian government received $167 million in foreign loans. The amount has been consistently increased every year since then, and by the early 1990s annual lending (the bulk of it concessionary) through the IGGI was in the neighborhood of $4 billion.

Thus, like foreign direct investment, foreign loans have played an important role in the development of Indonesia. But the role of the latter dates back not only through the 25 years in which the present government has been in power, but to the old regime as well. It is difficult to imagine the stabilization and rehabilitation program of the 1960s succeeding without the massive foreign capital inflows the Indonesian government received during that time. In fact, some believe that foreign financial support played a central role in establishing the program's political acceptance.

However, many observers have mistakenly overstated the role of foreign loans. A counterexample may clarify this point. By the end of the old regime, Indonesia's debt-GDP ratio had reached more than 30 percent. Although this figure was lower than the 1990 ratio of approximately 70 percent, it nevertheless reflects the presence of massive flows of foreign assistance under Sukarno's government. Yet at that time the economy was in virtually total disarray. There was no prudent management of publicly guaranteed external debt, and consequently default was inevitable. Cases where massive flows of foreign assistance produced less-than-desirable outcomes can be easily found in other countries as well.

Hence, while foreign loans are an important support for the development process, by themselves they do not ensure healthy economic performance. How foreign loans are utilized is absolutely critical. The historical evidence of the public sector's development expenditures in Indonesia indicates a persistent intention to improve infrastructure conditions so as to achieve more rapid and sustained growth and, at the same time, maintain and protect important social programs (see Azis 1989a). Most foreign assistance is channeled to these programs.

Recently some of the government's technocrats have expressed concerns about the size of the country's foreign debt. It is absolutely necessary for the government to make productive use of budget expenditures, be it sectorally or regionally, if Indonesia is to avoid becoming a "debt-ridden" country. Efforts have been made to create a mechanism to secure the productive use of private foreign loans, while preserving the principle of accepting only concessional (soft) loans.

Another important pillar in the management of debt under the present government is the consistent policy of avoiding any move that might lead to a debt rescheduling. This strong stance is driven by the full recognition that the principle effectively puts a limit on budget expenditures (and keeps spending decisions relatively free of unbridled political lobbying). Furthermore, the country's invariably prompt payment has caused its creditworthiness to stay mostly in the upper tier.

Foreign advisers and donor agencies

Since the first oil boom in 1974, the number of foreign economic advisers in Indonesia has increased considerably. Indeed, their presence is obvious in various government offices. Some are under long-term contract, while others are engaged in short-term endeavors. The sources of funding for retaining these advisers vary: while some are funded by domestic sources, either budgetary or extrabudgetary, a number of others are funded by particular donor agencies or by foreign governments.

Unfortunately, not all of these advisers are of high quality, and some of their work and recommendations are quite trivial and show an inadequate understanding of local issues. Even when their suggestions appear to be the result of rigorous analysis, their conclusions seem to have been reached beforehand. Given the amount of resources involved, if funded by loans or other domestic sources, such cases are easily perceived as a financial waste to the country. It is to these kinds of foreign advice (and advisers) that increasingly negative critiques, including from members of the Parliament, have recently been directed. In the early stage of reforms, foreign advisers may have offered more concrete contributions to the design of policy reforms. But as part of their "learning process," economic policymakers should have developed a better grasp of the problems they face and of appropriate alternative solutions.

To be fair, there are a number of cases where foreign advisers have produced some truly innovative work. Many believe, for example, that the help of foreign advisers in designing the tax reforms of the mid-1980s was of great importance. Yet it is still often found that, even in cases where potentially valuable work is done, there is no effective dissemination of knowledge to the local staff, either because the latter are already burdened by a heavy workload, or simply because no mechanism has been created for transferring the knowledge. Of course, a few exceptions to this tendency do exist.

It is generally believed, rightly or wrongly, that the hiring of foreign advisers has few advantages. Foreign advisers often refrain from disclosing important data and information to the public that is considered confidential.[20] This is more difficult to guarantee when domestic rather than foreign consultants are involved. To many local experts and even academic researchers, this type of government (officials') attitude may cause a great deal of annoyance. As ironic as it may sound, of all possible explanations, this has been perhaps the most often cited. Moreover, foreign advisers are considered capable of making objective and more comprehensive analyses, since they are not tied to any local value system, nor are their schedules cluttered by other engagements (most, although not all, foreigners who are hired are supposed to allocate a considerable amount of their time to the assigned task). Whether they are indeed more capable than local experts remains, of course, a subjective matter. But the more recent complaints seem to be concerned more with the mismatch between the quality of work or advice that foreign advisers provide and the fees they earn (especially when those fees are taken from the public sector's budget), which are far higher than what local consultants could make.

Finally, foreign observers often criticize the independence of Indonesian policy reforms from the influence of donor agencies such as the IMF and the World Bank. Interestingly, domestic critics often make the opposite indictment: that the country's economic policymakers simply follow meekly whatever these international agencies prescribe. The truth, most likely, lies somewhere in between the extreme positions.

The independence of policy reforms in Indonesia is not entirely clear. Certainly, a "learning process" has taken place during the course of Indonesia's development over the last 25 years. Along the way, various sound ideas concerning market reform undoubtedly have had a considerable effect, which policymakers have eventually grasped and digested. Thus, the idea of market reform might have been in place even before donor agencies came up with their prescriptions. On the other hand, should a different kind of idea emerge in Indonesian policy circles, one that is diametrically opposed to those held by the IMF and the World Bank, it is difficult to imagine that as good a relationship and as strong support from these international agencies to Indonesia and its SSA program as we are witnessing today would be possible. One thing, though, is absolutely true. Unlike those of some other countries, the Indonesian SSA program in the 1980s never came under strong pressure from the famous IMF conditionality: there was never any quid pro quo situation in which additional funding was made contingent on further reforms.

THE COEXISTENCE OF LIBERALIZING AND PROTECTIONIST POLICIES

Despite the successes of Indonesian macroeconomic reform, it would be absolutely incorrect to assert that the economy today is free of protectionist policies. Besides the presence of strong protectionist lobbies (as in other countries), another important factor in the persistent mix of liberalizing and protectionist policies in Indonesia is the effective presence of two groups of presidential economic advisers: the economic technocrats and the "engineers." Many observers see the emergence of these two camps of contending advisers as a recent phenomenon, particularly since the appointment of B. J. Habibie as minister of science and technology. But the division of views between the two groups toward national industrialization and a broader range of development issues actually began much earlier.

Whereas in the past the engineers' group lacked a single influential leader and a common strategy was not easy to identify, in general the economic technocrats were much more focused on strategy and policy design, largely through the leadership of Widjojo Nitisastro. This group of very able and mostly low-profile technocrats has basically been given the responsibility for the country's major economic portfolio since the launching of the first Five-Year Development Plan (Repelita) in 1969. Today, even without a direct ministerial or executive position, Widjojo is still believed to be the key designer of economic policy and is even considered by many to be a major player of the country's portfolio of economic policies.

Talk about the roles of the economic technocrats and the engineers reemerged more intensively in the mid-1980s. In fact, more or less the same economic technocrats have been present since 1969, through several cabinets. Although different names may appear on the list of ministers, the consistency of their views is notable. Hence, at least in absolute terms, there seems no reason to believe that the technocrats' role is declining. If this is so, the recent talk must have been prompted by something that provides a strong boost for, and recognition of, the engineers' group.

At the outset, it does seem that the persistence and determination of Science and Technology Minister Habibie, backed by his internationally acknowledged capability, has made the role of the engineers in the Indonesian political arena far more significant. Some also point to his appealing personal style; perhaps more important, however, these attributes are also bolstered and sustained by his apparently strong support from the president.[21]

While it may not always be true that the engineers favor a more protectionist approach than the technocrats, many believe this is not an exaggeration. Foreign scholars (e.g., Woo et al. 1992) also make this comparison. In fact, the positions traditionally held by engineers, or at least those that are largely controlled by them (e.g., the Ministry of Industry, the Investment Coordinating Board, and, in the past, the Ministry of Trade), are connected with aspects of policymaking where certain reasons for protection, such as for infant-industry purposes, seem natural. In many cases, this is true either because they share the interests of the lobby groups they represent, or because they simply see the importance of fostering high-technology industries that require support and protection from the government.

This tug-of-war between protectionist and liberalizing policies, with outcomes oscillating between the two poles, is found in other countries as well (for example, in Korea). Sometimes the economists' idea of market reform triumphs; at other times the engineers' and economic nationalists' view prevails. Which view prevails at any given time is most often determined by the state of the economy. During a booming economy protectionist notions receive widespread support, while in difficult times more prudent policies and pro-market reforms tend to gain stronger backing.

The identification of so-called strategic industries, all of which are under the control, directly or indirectly, of Minister Habibie, is also seen as deviating from pro-market reform.[22] Yet the president has given his full support to this undertaking. This, however, does not mean that the SSA program cannot be implemented. Certainly there is still ample room for further structural adjustment. As some senior politicians like to put it, "the coexistence of liberalizing and protectionist policy simply indicates the multitudinous objectives of development strategy."

The difficulties in completely eliminating monopoly powers and various forms of nontariff barriers are facts of life that cloud efforts to reform the economy fully. Notwithstanding these difficulties, Indonesia has now gone through a period where major reforms have been implemented with success. This certainly has required superb abilities on the part of economic policymakers in identifying areas where changes could be made and acknowledging those things that cannot or should not be changed. Cynics may call this approach opportunistic, but Indonesians consider it pragmatic.

Besides being the result of the presence of engineers in the cabinet, many of the remaining protectionist policies today can best be understood in historical perspective. The strong flavor of government intervention that often leads to protection (and, in the past, has led to nationalization as well) has its roots in Indonesian political and economic nationalism, which emerged after independence. The Dutch legacy of a plantation economy, with its exploitation of resources and profit repatriation, was considered antithetical to prosperity. The natural response was, as might be expected, a drive toward industrialization.

To secure and maintain the new industrial investments, it was implicitly asserted, some forms of protection were needed. High trade (tariff and nontariff) barriers and restrictions on entry for foreign ownership were imposed. On the financial side, the required capital was largely provided by the government. Strong support for such an approach also came from a great number of intellectuals, who at that time were certainly not champions of the laissez-faire paradigm.

The emotional need to counter the colonial legacy was further combined with resentment against those Indonesians of Chinese origin who, as in many other Asian countries, often managed to hold economic power out of proportion with their numbers. Moreover, from the perspective of regional development (especially of the outer islands), the absence of infrastructure and the resulting low level of economic activity further justified government intervention.

Although the installation of able economists in the economic policymaking arena during the late 1960s led to many changes in the direction and nature of the country's development strategy,[23] some elements of protectionist policies prevailed throughout the 1970s and 1980s and even to the present day. Following a series of policy changes within the context of the SSA program, Indonesia has entered a different policy environment, although many undesirable outcomes are still easily observed. These outcomes are often associated with protectionist measures that are either no longer the direct results of, or have little to do with, deliberate new policies. Rather, many of them are tailwinded by historical circumstances or are the legacy of past policies. As a result, the 1980s saw the implementation of appropriate macroeconomic policies, but trade and industrial policies remained unliberalized.[24]

This situation was observed particularly in the early years after the decline in oil prices. For this reason, many analysts believe that the major thrust of reforms in Indonesia during the early period has been macroeconomic, oriented toward stabilization, and backed by the open capital account system in place since the late 1960s. The structural adjustment phase, that of trade and industrial policy reform, came only after changes in industrial policy in an export-oriented direction had taken place. But even with an export-oriented strategy, economic nationalism and the urge to foster strategic industries remain great.

In summary, the SSA program has indeed worked quite effectively in Indonesia, because the various measures taken were either bold, bringing radical transformation, or simply timely and appropriately chosen. But to conclude that there are no protectionist policies in Indonesia would certainly be incorrect.

CONCLUSIONS

In various respects, the three episodes of crisis and response in Indonesia since the 1960s differ from one another. The preconditions and reasoning for the effective handling of the crises, however, bear some degree of similarity. Each episode was marked by the presence of an able and coherent team of economic technocrats, under the leadership of Widjojo Nitisastro, supported by the stable and effective government of President Suharto.

This paper has emphasized the events of the 1980s. Overall, the responses to the crisis of those years were bold and drastic, resulting in dramatic improvements in macroeconomic conditions and robust economic growth. The Indonesian case is rather unique, however, since the achievement of macroeconomic equilibrium produced neither worsening poverty nor a deteriorating income distribution, at least in the years immediately following the reforms. This outcome was largely due to a strategy of budget allocation in which infrastructure and social overhead capital, particularly in the rural sector, were consistently given top priority. In part, the strategy has been preserved because the memory of the events of 1965–66 causes the government to continue to focus on the needs of the rural sector.

The neutral role of the military has helped to sustain the economic growth of the country in the last 25 years. This factor is often underestimated by many observers. Foreign assistance has also played an important role in the reform, but it would certainly be misleading to assert that external resources guarantee the success of the reforms. As noted above, unlike reform programs in some other countries, the Indonesian SSA program in the 1980s has never been associated with IMF conditionality.

Emerging ideas of pro-market reform have also contributed a great deal to the shaping of policy directions. In this respect, Indonesia's economic technocrats have undergone a "learning process." Over the course of time, various ideas about market reform have gained widespread acceptance, which policymakers eventually grasped and digested.

The absence of a strongly organized civil society and the dominance of a single party have made it relatively easy to reach a national consensus on giving economic development a high priority. The Indonesian system lacks strong checks and balances between executive, legislative, and judicial powers. Serious ideological controversy is also absent. The country's political institutions are such that they can be used by an effective government to steer policy (including economic reform) either toward or away from a pro-market direction. Given its longevity, the New Order government is unquestionably very effective, and the policy direction proposed in the 1980s was to reform the economy in a pro-market direction.

However, the present-day Indonesian economy is by no means free of protectionist policies. Besides the presence of strong business lobbies and the persistence of economic nationalism, the presence of two groups of presidential economic advisers with differing views helps explain the coexistence of liberalizing and protectionist policies. The result has usually been a seesawing between liberalization and protection: the hands of the technocrats were strengthened when serious problems were perceived, or when there was a scarcity of capital, whereas when the economy was booming or capital was in adequate supply, the engineers and the protectionists have often gained the upper hand.

It is worth mentioning in closing that the 1993 election has clearly led to the strengthening of the position of the engineers' group in the cabinet. Although a few of Widjojo's group remain in the cabinet, and Widjojo himself is still present in an advisory position, many perceive that the new cabinet reflects the coming of a new era. Consistent with the thesis that the engineers and nationalists gain strength in relatively prosperous times, this most recent cabinet restructuring occurs at a time when annual economic growth is in the neighborhood of 6 percent, nonoil exports are growing at better than a 20 percent annual rate, and the current account deficit is well under control. Whether this relatively healthy state of affairs can be preserved under the new cabinet remains to be seen.

ACKNOWLEDGMENT

Iwan J. Azis is a Visiting Professor at Cornell University and the Director at the IUC (Inter University Center) for Economics at the University of Indonesia. The author is indebted to Emil Salim and M. Sadli for insights into the role of technocrats. Special thanks to Sid Saltzman, Gustav Ranis, and Max Corden for suggested revisions, and to Erik Thorbecke and Wing

Thye Woo for extremely helpful suggestios. Comments by an anonymous referee are also acknowledged.

NOTES

1 This group, under the leadership of Widjojo Nitisastro, was later labeled the "Berkeley mafia" by some observers because some of its members had been educated at that university.

2 Different figures for GDP growth may be found in other publications. These numbers are based on my own calculations using a somewhat different method; they are measured at 1983 prices.

3 Many of the state banks were dependent on captive markets, notably the state-owned enterprises.

4 Japan, for example, has a long history of using outside pressures to enhance the efficiency of the domestic economy.

5 By 1990, the total external debt of Indonesia reached $67.9 billion, $9.4 billion of which was "private nonguaranteed" debt (World Bank 1992). Debt-service flows in that year were already quite alarming: $4.1 billion for repayment of principal and $2.5 billion in interest payments for long-term public and publicly guaranteed external capital. For the private nonguaranteed debt the corresponding figures are $1 billion and $0.5 billion. These obligations, coupled with increasing deficits on current account and the expectation of increased scarcity of external funding, gave the export-oriented strategy much stronger leverage.

6 After 1978 the exchange rate was no longer fixed at 415 rupiahs to the dollar. The introduction of a "managed floating" system in that year inevitably required a maior adjustment of the prevailing overvalued rate; hence, the devaluation in 1978 took place at the same time as the emergence of a more market-determined exchange rate system. Interestingly enough, the decision was unrelated to, and to some extent was not in accordance with, the advice of the IMF. In fact, since the 1960s, Indonesia has never had the need to submit to IMF conditionality.

7 Some observers view the Indonesian case as unique, in that liberalization did not follow the standard path of current account followed by capital account liberalization. In fact, since the end of the 1960s, Indonesia has had a free foreign exchange system, making it easy for badly needed foreign capital (investments in oil and other natural resources, as well as foreign aid and loans) to flow into the country.

8 Prior to each devaluation, the government would announce its forecast of the balance of payments position, and especially of the expected size of the current account deficit. Their predictions of large deficits on these occasions might permit one to argue that the technocrats were attempting to engineer a "pseudo-crisis."

9 At least three technocrats have directly confirmed this in separate private conversations with the author.

10 Emil Salim, Minister of Environment and Population and an economics professor at the University of Indonesia, is one of the most dynamic of the government's technocrats and is very popular among students, even those who are strongly critical of the government. Salim once told me that, in almost all cabinet discussions involving economic decisions, the technocrats have always tried to maintain the "straight economics" (his own term) approach.

11 One cannot neglect the important role of the mass media and other forms of public relations in forming a favorable public opinion. As is easily observed, over

time, more open and critical views toward monopolies and other types of distortions are increasingly expressed by growing numbers of media commentators. Intellectuals and scholars often voice similar concerns through various forums (seminars, conferences, workshops, interviews, etc). To a certain extent, this criticism can help alleviate the burden on the technocrats in their struggle to eradicate distortions and protection in some sectors of the economy.

12 One of the technocrats who twice held ministerial positions (labor and mining), M. Sadli, who also designed the investment laws that prompted the inflow of foreign capital in the early 1970s, once indicated that the enormous problems faced by the former Soviet Union and other former socialist countries in transition today are quite similar to the Indonesian case in the late 1960s. Nothing could be done properly without immense flows of foreign capital. The main difference is perhaps that Indonesia, under the old regime, was not a completely centrally planned command economy. Private enterprises and other institutions characterizing a mixed economic system were already present in Indonesia, even during the early postwar period.

13 The armed forces have always been given the responsibility of securing and protecting development policies and the outcomes of the New Order's initiatives.

14 There is perhaps only one exception, namely, the *Merdeka* daily newspaper. This is not hard to understand, since the paper is considered a remnant of the old Indonesian Nationalist Party (PNI), which has a strongly nationalist ideology.

15 However, this index ought to be read with caution, since the data source used (the SUSENAS socioeconomic survey) is plagued by a severe underestimation of incomes among the high-income group. See Azis (1992a).

16 However, using different assumptions. one can come up with a slightly higher number for poverty incidence for 1990 (see Azis 1992a).

17 An alternative political calculation that has worked to the benefit of reform in Indonesia is the fact that, in the wake of the traumatic events in the 1960s, the government has been continually careful to pay attention to the needs of the rural population.

18 During the 1992 election, the Indonesian Democratic Party (PDI) offered a series of economic proposals that many believe were the result of serious and sincere effort. However, for whatever reason—perhaps the proposals' heavily microeconomic rather than macroeconomic agenda—the PDI's plan was never considered as an alternative to the SSA program.

19 The continued operation of Bulog, the government body that controls the price of rice and other basic commodities, as well as the presence of state-owned enterprises (*badan usaha milik negara*) in various sectors reflects policymakers' recognition of the need for state intervention in some areas.

20 However, in one case a foreign adviser got into trouble because he made some statements in a public forum related to the work assigned to him.

21 Recently, Minister Habibie was also assigned, with the blessing of the president, to head a very influential organization called ICMI (Ikatan Cendekiawan Muslim Indonesia), whose members are largely Moslem intellectuals. A member of the economic technocrats' team, Emil Salim, was designated vice head of the organization.

22 The list of these industries has lengthened markedly over time and now covers no fewer than 10 industrial sectors: aircraft, steel, machinery (two separate industries), explosives, shipbuilding, telecommunications, arms, electronics, and the railway industry.

23 The most dramatic change was the promulgation of new investment laws clearly designed to allow (and attract) inflows of foreign capital.

24 By comparison, the situation in Korea during the 1980s seems quite congruous with this phenomenon, whereas in the case of India the export orientation did not prevail.

REFERENCES

Azis, I. J. 1989a. "Economic Development and Recent Adjustment in Resource Rich Countries: The Case of Indonesia." In T. Fukuchi and M. Kagami, eds., *Perspectires on the Pacific Basin Economy: A Comparison of Asia and Latin America*. Tokyo: Institute of Developing Economies.

Azis, I. J. 1989b. "Export Performance and the Employment Effect." Paper presented at a conference on "The Future of the Asia-Pacific Economies," sponsored by the Asia-Pacific Development Center and the Thailand Development Research Institute, Bangkok (8–10 November).

Azis, I. J. 1992a. "Regional and Social Impacts of Structural Adjustment in Indonesia: A Preliminary Analysis." *CRP Working Papers* Ithaca, NY: Cornell University.

Azis. I. J. 1992b. "Review of Regional Development: Equity and Foreign Exchange Accumulation." In T. K. John, G. Knaap, and I. J. Azis, eds., *Spatial Development in Indonesia: Review and Prospects.* London: Avebury.

Bourguignon, F. and Morrisson, C. 1992. *Adjustment and Equity in Developing Countries: A New Approach.* Paris: OECD Development Centre.

Nelson, J. M., ed. 1990. *Economic Crisis and Policy Choice: The Politics of Adjustment in the Third World.* Princeton, NJ: Princeton University Press.

Sadli, M. 1992. "Resources and Management, The Indonesian Case." Paper presented at a conference on "The Asia Pacific Region: Efficiency in Transition," organized by the Asian Association of Management Conference, New Delhi (1–4 November).

Thorbecke, E., et al. 1992a. *Adjustment, Growth and Income Distribution in Indonesia.* Paris: OECD Development Centre.

Thorbecke, E., et al. 1992b. "The Indonesian Adjustment Experience in an International Perspective." Washington: Institute for Policy Reform (mimeographed; reprinted in *Indonesian Economic Journal* 1 [April]).

Woo, W. T., et al. 1993. *Macroeconomic Policies: Crisis and Long Run Growth: The Case of Indonesia, 1965–1990.* Washington: World Bank (forthcoming).

World Bank. 1992. *World Development Report 1992.* Washington: World Bank.

5

THE THAI ECONOMY

From Boom to Gloom?

Peter G. Warr

Following elections in November 1996 a new coalition government took office in Thailand, led by incoming Prime Minister and New Aspiration Party leader General Chawalit Yongchaiyut. The new administration began its work in an atmosphere of great concern about the state of the Thai economy. Throughout 1996 Thai economic commentary was dominated by signs that the export-led boom that began in the late 1980s may be coming to an end. Most important of these signs were an apparently dramatic slow-down in the annual rate of growth of total exports and revelations that some investment and securities institutions may be unable to meet interest obligations. Confidence in Thailand's capacity to sustain high levels of economic performance was seriously damaged. The economic situation had clearly contributed to the downfall of the previous government of Banharn Silpa-Archa and posed immediate dangers for the new government. Identifying the causes of these and other economic problems is the central theme of this article.

ECONOMIC BOOM, 1988–95

The background to the economic gloom of 1996 was the unprecedented boom which began in 1988. Over the eight years ending in 1995 the Thai economy was the fastest growing in the world (Table 5.1). The average rate of real GDP growth was unprecedented, at 10.4%, and inflation was low, averaging 5.3%. Two factors produced the dramatic growth: growth of exports, especially exports of labour-intensive manufactured goods; and very high inflows of foreign capital, including direct foreign investment. The two went together, in that much of the foreign investment was in the labour-intensive manufacturing sector. Export growth over this period averaged an extraordinary 28% per annum and as a share of GDP exports surged from 23% in 1988 to 34% in 1995. Economic inequality increased during this period but this should not be taken to mean that the benefits of growth

Source: *Southeast Affairs 1997*, Singapore: Institute of Southeast Asian Studies, 1997, pp. 317–33.

Table 5.1 Thailand: main economic indicators

	1985	*1990*	*1991*	*1992*	*1993*	*1994*	*1995*	*1996*
GDP (US$bn)[a]	38.9	85.6	98.7	111.3	125.0	143.0	167.1	185.0
Population (millions)[a]	51.6	56.1	56.9	57.8	58.6	59.4	60.2	61.1
Growth (% p.a.)	1.9	1.6	1.5	1.5	1.4	1.4	1.5	1.4
GNP per capita (US$)[a]	742	1,508	1,709	1,889	2,087	2,356	2,714	3,028
Share in GDP (%)[b]								
Agriculture	15.8	12.7	12.7	12.0	10.0	10.4	10.3	10.0
Industry	31.8	37.0	38.8	38.5	39.2	39.4	40.3	40.4
(Manufacturing)	21.9	27.2	28.4	28.0	28.5	28.6	30.2	30.0
Services	52.3	50.2	48.5	49.5	50.5	50.2	49.4	49.6

Sources:
[a] International Monetary Fund, International Financial Statistics (IFS) series.
[b] World Bank, World Development Tables.

were confined to the rich. The boom coincided with dramatically reduced incidence of absolute poverty, which fell from 22% in 1988 to under 10 in 1994, using the most common definition of poverty incidence.[1]

ECONOMIC GLOOM, 1996

In 1996 GDP growth in real terms fell to "only" 6.8%, the first year since 1993 of annual growth below 8%. Inflation was moderate at just under 6%. The government's budget ended the calendar year in deficit and the new government promised to cut public spending, in particular that involving military purchases. The current account deficit was a focus of public concern, at 8.3% of GDP, compared with 8.1% in 1995. Export growth slowed from 20% or more in the immediately preceding years to less than 2% in 1996. During 1996 the baht remained under speculative pressure and rumours of impending devaluation were common. The Thai property and stock markets also ended 1996 in a slump which damaged confidence in the country's immediate economic prospects.

The export slow-down and the problems of the financial sector have different origins but they are linked in the present economic crisis through speculation on the exchange rate. The export slow-down was primarily the result of a slow-down in international demand for Thailand's exports, a real appreciation of the baht caused by the fact that it has remained pegged to the U.S. dollar while the Japanese yen has depreciated, and—most importantly—increases in real wages within Thailand. The last of these causes means that Thailand is facing a structurai adjustment problem requiring that resources be reallocated away from labour-intensive export industries and towards more skill-intensive exporters.

The financial crisis was a consequence of the boom combined with inadequate public sector supervision. Several large investment institutions have become over-extended by excessive and unhedged borrowing abroad and domestically, leaving these firms highly vulnerable to exchange rate and interest rate risk. They were also suffering the effects of bad loans within Thailand. During late 1996 speculation about devaluation resulted from the county's poor trade performance and this speculation induced a capital outflow, raising domestic interest rates. Bankruptcies in the property and financial sector seemed inevitable unless the government agreed to large "bail-outs".

The export slow-down

Table 5.2 shows the levels of Thailand's exports by destination for the years 1994 to 1996. The slow-down was widespread among Thailand's export destinations but was greatest in exports to Japan, NAFTA and the Chinese economies. By looking at the composition of exports by commodity (Table

Table 5.2 Thailand's export trade flows

Destination share (%)	*1994*	*1995*	*1996*
ASEAN	18.2	19.9	19.3
Chinese economies	9.5	10.5	8.7
Japan	17.1	16.8	16.7
European Union	14.9	14.5	15.8
NAFTA	22.6	19.1	18.5
Rest of World	17.7	19.2	21.0

Note: Chinese economies mean China (PRC), Hong Kong and Taiwan.

Source: *Bangkok Post Year-End Economic Review*, December 1996.

5.3) it can be seen that the slow-down was concentrated in manufactured exports from labour-intensive industries.[2] The reasons for the export slow-down are discussed in depth below.

The budget deficit

Thailand's financial year runs from 1 October to 30 September. In the current 1996/97 financial year, the first quarter ending 31 December 1996 revealed a government cash deficit of 54 billion baht (US$ 2.1 billion). This compares with a surplus of 16.2 billion baht a year earlier. The first quarter fiscal result produced concern that the current full financial year may produce a budget deficit for Thailand for the first time in nine years. Thailand's revenue base is highly responsive to the overall growth rate and even small slow-downs in growth produce significant reductions in revenue.[3]

In the past, the policy response in similar budgetary circumstances has been a contraction of public investment spending. Responses of this kind have already been announced for 1997 and 1998. Thailand's financial planners are known for their conservatism and the policy issue is not whether expenditure cuts will occur but where the cuts will be concentrated. In Thailand's current economic circumstances it is clearly important that cuts in expenditure not exacerbate the export slow-down already experienced in 1996. Because Thailand's infrastructure is already heavily congested, reductions in infrastructure spending would threaten just that.

The government has announced that the 50 billion baht expenditure cuts planned for each of 1997 and 1998 were to be concentrated on military expenditure. There was also to be a 40 billion baht cut in the budget of the state enterprises. But the bulk of government savings will come from a slow-down in military expenditures. It remains to be seen whether the military will accept that outcome. The paradox may be that as Prime Minister a former general is capable of implementing military spending cuts that would not be accepted from politicians with purely civilian backgrounds.

Table 5.3 Commodity structure of Thailand's export slow-down

	1994	*1995*	*1996*
Total exports (million baht)	1,137,602	1,406,310	1,401,392
Growth rate (%)	20.9	23.6	−0.35
Growth rate by major commodity:			
1 Computers and parts	44.9	38.7	31.3
2 Garments	12.4	1.3	−21.9
3 Rubber	43.3	46.5	1.4
4 Integrated circuits	27.5	28.4	3.4
5 Gems & jewellery	8.3	11.5	8.4
6 Rice	18.9	24.1	8.4
7 Sugar	41.2	67.2	11.7
8 Frozen shrimps	29.9	2.3	−17.8
9 Television & parts	26.2	12.7	14.1
10 Shoes & parts	40.5	37.0	−40.9
11 Canned seafood	24.7	4.1	−0.3
12 Airconditioner, & parts	62.1	49.6	33.6
13 Plastic products	−29.1	102.2	51.4
14 Tapioca products	−13.6	−2.8	16.7
15 Textiles	4.5	22.1	−4.4

Note: Growth rates by major commodity for 1996 based on nine months data, January to September.

Source: *Bangkok Post Year-End Economic Review*, December 1996.

The current account deficit

The Thai baht is loosely pegged to the U.S. dollar. As in all (approximately) fixed exchange rate countries, Thailand's economic commentary focuses perhaps excessively on the current account balance. The 1996 slump in export growth obviously contributed to the current account deficit experienced in 1996 but the deficit was almost as high in 1995 and then recorded export growth was at 20%. The export slow-down is not the sole cause of the current account deficit. The continued high rate of capital inflow into Thailand is a more significant explanation for the high current account deficits of recent years and the economic debate in Thailand has largely missed the relevance of this point.

As Thailand continues to industrialize, its high rate of capital inflow generates a corresponding current account deficit. The high level of foreign investment into Thailand contributes to the current account deficit because of the imported inputs of capital equipment and intermediate goods required during the production process. More significantly, as foreign investment enters the country and foreign exchange is converted to baht at the (approximately) fixed exchange rate, the domestic money supply is increased as these baht are spent within Thailand. The demand for all goods increases, including both imports and goods which might otherwise have been exported. The current account deficit thereby increases but this is not a "problem", to the extent that autonomous capital inflow is the originator of this process. The problem potentially arises when a capital inflow, in the form of borrowing from abroad, is not autonomous but is undertaken in order to finance a payments problem due, say, to loss of international competitiveness of the country's exports.

How can we tell which of these factors is the more important cause of Thailand's current account deficit? An indicator of the health or otherwise of the country's trade position is the state of its foreign reserves. When autonomous capital inflow is the cause of the current account deficit the level of reserves increases. When a loss of competitiveness is the cause, and capital inflows are accommodating, the level of reserves declines. Table 5.4 indicates that Thailand's foreign exchange reserves continued to increase in 1996, measured both in millions of US$ and in months of imports, in spite of the supposed current account crisis. The level of Thailand's international reserves is more than adequate by international standards and by Thailand's own very conservative historical standards.[4] It is appropriate that these issues should continue to be monitored closely, but the evidence does not indicate that a significant payments problem currently exists. What exists is a crisis of confidence.

Exchange rate management

Thailand has a long and proud history of stable monetary policy, a stable exchange rate and low inflation. The independence of the central bank, the Bank of Thailand (BOT), has been seen as an important contributor to that record. During the government of Prime Minister Banharn Silpa-Archa the autonomy of the BOT was threatened by what was seen in the press as political interference from the government. Negative public reaction to this perceived interference contributed to the Banharn government's growing unpopularity. But a more serious threat to the Bank's independence in setting monetary policy derived indirectly from the economic reforms of the early 1990s.

For several decades, Thailand has maintained a virtually fixed exchange rate relative to the U.S. dollar.[5] If international movements of capital were entirely free, then the fixed exchange rate would mean that the BOT did not have effective control of Thailand's domestic money supply. The reason is that if the Bank tried to reduce the money supply by raising domestic interest rates, speculative capital would flood in from abroad to take advantage of the high interest rates. This inflow would raise the domestic money supply as the funds were converted to baht at the fixed exchange rate, thus defeating the monetary objective. Likewise, if the Bank wished to raise the domestic money supply by lowering interest rates this objective would be defeated by a capital outflow.

Table 5.4 Thailand: external indicators, 1985–96

	1985	*1990*	*1991*	*1992*	*1993*	*1994*	*1995*	*1996*
Merchandise exports, fob. (US$bn)[a]	7.1	22.8	28.2	32.1	36.4	44.5	55.4	56.2
% change	−3.8	15	23.8	13.7	13.4	21.3	24.5	1.0
% GDP	18.1	26.6	28.8	29.1	29.4	31	34	29.5
Merchandise imports, fob. (US$bn)[a]	8.4	29.6	34.2	36.3	40.4	47.9	63.0	68.1
% change	−9.1	29.9	15.8	6	11.8	18.5	31.6	8.1
Merchandise trade balance (US$bn)[a]	−1.3	−6.8	−6	−4.2	−4.3	−3.7	−8	−11.9
Net invisibles (US$bn)[a]	−0.2	−0.5	−1.6	−2.6	−2.5	−4.3	−5.6	−4.1
Current account (US$bn)[a]	−1.5	−7.3	−7.6	−6.3	−6.3	−8	−13.6	16.0
% GDP	−4	−8.5	−7.7	−5.8	−5.6	−6	−7.2	−8.6
Foreign exchange reserves (US$bn)[b]	2.2	13.3	17.5	20.4	24.5	29.3	36	39.5
Months imports	3.1	5.4	6.1	6.7	7.2	6.8	6.3	6.9
Exchange rate (baht/ US$bn)[b]	27.16	25.59	25.52	25.4	25.32	25.15	24.92	25.5
Real exchange rate (1990 = 100)[c]	94	100	100	102	103	104	105	100
External long-term debt (US$bn)[d]	13.2	19.9	23.5	24.9	26.1	31.8	33.5	35.5
% GDP	34	23.2	23.0	22.5	21.1	10.8	20.4	18.7
External long-term debt-service ratio[d] (% exports)	25.2	13.9	10.7	12.1	16.5	17.9	11.7	14

Sources:

[a] IMF, Balance of Payments data series.

[b] IMF, International Financial Statistics data series.

[c] Real exchange rates are calculated with Thailand's export shares as weights, using price indices and exchange rates data from source[b].

[d] World Bank, World Development Tables and Asian Development Bank, *Asian Development Outlook, 1996 and 1997* for 1995 and 1996 debt service data.

Historically, what prevented the above mechanism from destroying the BOT's monetary independence was that the Bank imposed several forms of controls on capital movements into and out of Thailand. These measures preserved for the Bank a considerable degree of monetary autonomy.[6] But in the early 1990s most of these capital market controls were dismantled in a liberalization programme intended partly to facilitate Thailand's challenge to Singapore and Hong Kong as a regional financial centre. The Bangkok International Banking Facility (BIBF) was established in 1993 to promote this objective. The unintended effect was that it left the BOT with very little control of the domestic money supply so long as the fixed exchange rate policy remained in place.

One policy recommendation was to move to a truly floating exchange rate. Another was to reinstate some controls on international capital movements. The latter proposals seem to have won, at least temporarily. In June the Bank set a 7% cash reserve requirement on short-term lending through the BIBF. In October the fear of capital flight induced the Bank to withdraw policy changes which would have liberalized the raising of loans offshore. The Bank also reduced the maximum ratio of non-baht borrowing to total liabilities. Further measures designed to limit speculative capital movements remain possible.

During 1996 there were suggestions that the Bank of Thailand may move to a flexible exchange rate system. It was announced that the band within which the baht is pegged had been widened, and this was interpreted by some as an indication that a switch to a flexible exchange rate policy was imminent. Such a prospect was apparently under discussion, but for the time being it seems the debate was resolved by reinstating some controls on capital movements removed during the capital market liberalizations of the early 1990s.

During 1996 rumours of an impending devaluation of the baht were frequent and these rumours had powerful financial effects. The expectation of a devaluation induces an outflow of speculative capital and deters the holding of money. It is well known that such expectations can actually force a devaluation that might not otherwise have been required. The speculative capital outflow may explain in part the property market and stock market slump experienced in 1996. The export slow-down presumably contributed to the lack of confidence in Thai financial markets as well, but the expectation of a devaluation was probably its most powerful financial effect.

EXPLAINING THE EXPORT SLOW-DOWN

The apparent export slow-down has attracted many attempted explanations from observers of the Thai economy. They are reviewed here, arranged in what would seem to be increasing order of importance—that is, with the least important explanations first, followed by the more important.

Politics

The government of Prime Minister Banharn Silpa-Archa had taken office after the election of July 1995 but was disrupted by repeated scandals and by allegations of corruption and other misdemeanours. The public perception was also one of incompetence in economic management and other areas. In November 1996 the government was forced by the threat of a parliamentary censure motion to call a general election. Economic management was a major issue in the campaign and the Banharn government was blamed for a range of economic problems including the export slow-down, the deterioration in the current account and slumps in both the property market and the stock exchange.

Corruption and incompetence of the levels attributed to the Banharn administration are nothing new for Thailand. In the past, corruption at the top of government did not lead to serious economic failure because policy continued to be controlled primarily by technocrats, rather than the politicians. Consequences of the kind experienced in 1996 did not occur. For this reason it seems unlikely that the Banharn government was truly responsible for more than a little of the export slow-down. The government's apparent incompetence seems to have been more a source of public embarrassment than of extensive policy failure.

There were worrying instances in which the Banharn government had attempted to interfere with the bureaucracy's economic management, including an apparent challenge to the independence of the central bank, the Bank of Thailand, but it would seem that, to some extent, the Banharn government was merely "unlucky" to have been in office when more powerful economic forces induced the economic problems of 1996. The prospects for economic management are better under the new government, but the reported deficiencies of the Banharn government were insufficient to explain the 1996 export slow-down.

Monetary policy

The Bank of Thailand responded to above normal inflation in 1995 by tightening monetary policy. Inflation eased, but the apparent effect on real output was greater than expected. By early 1996 an export slow-down was already evident and slower growth for 1996 was being forecast. The Bank of Thailand eased its monetary policy and interest rates declined. Monetary tightness in late 1995 and early 1996 may have contributed to the export slow-down but was presumably responsible for only a small part of the large decline in export growth that was reported. There is no obvious reason why exporters should be more negatively affected by a tight monetary policy than producers for the domestic market, and also no reason why labour-intensive exporters should be affected the most.

As discussed above, liberalization of the movement of capital into and out of Thailand has reduced the Bank of Thailand's capacity to control the domestic money supply but exchange rate expectations have powerful effects on financial markets. Expectations of exchange rate adjustments have major effects on capital movements, and rumours of impending devaluation of the baht have circulated in Bangkok financial circles since at least May 1996. By inducing capital outflow these expectations have a contractionary effect on the domestic money supply. These financial movements could not reasonably be cited as a cause of the export slow-down but they do provide a credible explanation for the property and stock market slumps of 1996.

Trade liberalization

During the late 1980s and early 1990s, Thailand liberalized its import protection regime significantly. The expected effect of this liberalization is a gain in overall economic efficiency, reflected partly in a surge of exports. The efficiency gains raise overall productivity and the *level* of exports permanently, but they will not necessarily raise growth *rates* permanently. That is, the gains are expected to be primarily static rather than dynamic. The surge in export growth rates experienced in the late 1980s and early 1990s thus reflected, in part, the efficiency gains from the earlier liberalizations. By the mid-1990s the efficiency gains from these liberalizations had been fully realized. The level of exports had been permanently raised by these liberalizations, but the growth *rate* of exports had been raised only temporarily. The growth rate of exports would have been expected to slow down on this account some time around the mid-1990s. This effect may therefore explain some but not all of the slow-down that actually occurred at that time.

Congested infrastructure

The unprecedented rate of Thailand's industrial expansion since the late 1980s, concentrated on export oriented production, has placed enormous strain on the country's already congested infrastructure facilities. Despite very high levels of public investment in infrastructure facilities during the period of the Seventh Five-Year Plan (1992 to 1996), it has not been possible to keep up with the demand. Average levels of infrastructure investment over this period exceeded baht 250 billion per year (US$10 billion). Of this, transportation accounted for 40%, energy 35%, telecommunications 18% and other utilities 7%. Roads, ports and telecommunications are increasingly overcommitted. The congestion of infrastructure has clearly contributed to the export slow-down but could not in itself explain the apparent severity and suddenness of the 1996 export problems.

Falsified export data

A new value-added tax (VAT) system was introduced in the early 1990s at the rate of 7%. Under this scheme exporters may receive rebates of value-added taxes at the rate of 7% of the value of goods exported. The rebates are paid on production of documentary evidence that the exports actually occurred. By 1995 a market had developed in falsified export documents, so that VAT rebates were being claimed for exports which did not actually take place. Empty containers were reportedly being shipped abroad as part of this form of tax fraud. It has been estimated that of the 1,406 billion baht of exports officially declared for 1995 at least 100 billion baht were fictitious.[7]

If this estimate was correct and the official export data for both 1994 and 1996 were both correct, the true growth rate for 1995 would have been lower than the reported rates. Similarly, the true export growth rate for 1996 would then have been higher than the reported rate because the true 1995 base on which it is calculated would have been below the reported level. If the 100 billion baht estimate for export overstatement in 1995 was correct, export growth for the years ending 1995 and 1996 would be 14.8 and 7.2%, respectively, rather than the 23.6 and 1.6% actually reported. If the true overstatement of 1995 exports was 150 billion baht the true growth rates for 1995 and 1996 would have been 10.4 and 11.4%, respectively.

The overstatement of exports for the purpose of claiming VAT rebates presumably began a year or two earlier than 1995, when it was officially uncovered. This means that the true growth rates for 1994 and 1995 were also presumably lower than the reported rates and the 1996 export slow-down was correspondingly smaller than the official data indicate. In short, the overstatement of exports probably disguised a moderate slow-down in exports which actually began a year or two earlier. A slow-down really does seem to have occurred, though not as sudden or as large as the 1996 slow-down indicated by the official export data.

Real appreciation

Over the year 1995 to 1996 the Thai baht/US$ exchange rate depreciated somewhat, from an average of to 24.9 to 25.5—a depreciation of 2.4%. Much more significant, however, was that the Japanese yen depreciated relative to the dollar, from an average of 93.5 to 107.5 yen/US$—a depreciation of 15%. This means that the baht appreciated relative to the Japanese yen by more than 12%.

When these calculations are conducted in real terms, to take account of differences in rates of inflation, the story is even more dramatic. The 2.4% nominal depreciation of the baht relative to the U.S. dollar was offset by the difference in rates of inflation between the two countries, as measured by CPI movements—5.8% for Thailand and 2.8% for the United States. Thailand's real exchange rate relative to the U.S. dollar barely changed; there was in fact a small real appreciation of 0.6%. But Japan's rate of inflation was only 0.2%, so the yen depreciated in real terms relative to the U.S. dollar by a striking 17.6%. The baht appreciated in real terms relative to the yen by more than 18%! In 1996 Thailand's overall real exchange rate with respect to all trading partners appreciated by about 5% compared with 1995.[8]

Along with the goods of other countries which peg their exchange rates more or less to the U.S. dollar, Thai goods became less competitive in Japanese markets as a result of this large real appreciation. For the same reason, Thai goods also became slightly less competitive in U.S. export markets relative to U.S. goods and markedly less competitive in U.S. markets relative to Japanese goods. The large real appreciation of the baht relative to the yen explains part of Thailand's export slow-down in 1996, but it does not explain why labour-intensive industries suffered the most.

Demand slow-down in importing countries

In 1996 export growth declined relative to the previous year in almost all Asian countries. Thailand was not alone, although Thailand's reported export slow-down was one of the largest (Table 5.5). As the table also shows, the principal reason was a slow-down of demand from major importing countries. Japan is a major market for all of the East Asian exporting countries and slow growth of the Japanese economy over several years has produced a slow-down in Japanese import growth.

To the extent that international demand side factors were responsible, the

Table 5.5 Asian economies export and import slow-down (percentage change)

	Exports		*Imports*	
Country/Territory	*1995*	*1996*	*1995*	*1996*
China	21.0	−11.8	15.3	−2.2
Hong Kong	13.3	0.0	4.0	1.0
Taiwan	20	3.9	21.3	−2.2
Indonesia	18.5	7.5	26.8	10.3
Japan	4.5	−8.2	17.5	3.4
Korea	25.5	4.3	28.2	7.3
Malaysia	20.4	8.7	25.3	−0.4
Philippines	20.6	24.8	18.9	38.7
Singapore	19.3	11.5	16.6	11.7
Thailand	19.4	1.5	22.8	12.8

Note: Indonesian export data relate to non-oil exports only.

Source: Except for Taiwan, growth rates computed from International Monetary Fund, Direction of Trade data series in US$, current prices. Taiwan data from Ministry of Finance, Republic of China, Taipei.

1996 slowdown in the growth of exports from Thailand and similar exporting countries does not indicate a decline in their export competitiveness. There is little these countries can do about a decline in international demand. To some extent, they must wait for demand to recover and maintain their efficiency in the meantime. Desperate schemes intended to "promote" exports have the potential to introduce inefficiencies that will only impede their capacity to respond efficiently to increased international demand when recovery occurs.

The slow growth in international demand for electronic products is well known and was also significant for Thailand, but it should be recalled (from Table 5.3) that electronic products were not the slowest growing of Thailand's exports. Exports of labour-intensive products such as garments, textiles and footwear actually fell the most. Once again, slow growth of international demand does not account for that difference. Internal factors, operating within the Thai economy, must be responsible (see below).

Real wages

Recently available data on real wages provide the single most significant explanation for Thailand's export slow-down and its concentration in labour-intensive industries. Research at the Thailand Development Research Institute has recently produced a reliable series of real wage data for Thailand. These data are reproduced in Figure 5.1 for the years 1982 to 1994. The data describe an index of nominal wages for the manufacturing sector deflated by the consumer price index and are indexed in the chart below so that the level for 1982 is 100. Over the 13 years from 1982 to 1994, real wages increased by 70%, but this increase was heavily concentrated in the years since 1990. Over the years 1982 to 1990 the increase was from an index of 100 to 117, an average compound rate of increase of 2%. But over the following four years to 1994 the real wage increased to an index of 170, an average annual rate of increase in real wages of almost 10%!

Why the sudden increase in real wages? During the early stages of Thai economic growth the rising industrial and services sector demand for labour could be satisfied from a very large pool of rural labour with relatively low productivity. The potential supply of unskilled rural labour was so large that as workers moved from agriculture to more productive jobs in the manufacturing and services sectors, it was possible for these sectors to expand their levels of employment without significantly bidding up real wages. But as this process continued that pool of "cheap" rural labour was largely used up, so that by the early 1990s labour shortages were becoming evident. Agricultural industries were themselves experiencing serious problems of seasonal labour shortages. Further increases in the demand for labour outside agriculture then led to rising wages.

Thailand's export industries are especially vulnerable to increases in real

Figure 5.1 Thailand: Index of Real Wages, 1982–94.
Source: Thailand Development Research Institute, Bangkok.

Table for Figure 5.1

Thailand: Real wages, 1982–94 (1982 = 100)

Year	*Index*
1982	100.0
1983	98.5
1984	110.8
1985	112.3
1986	113.8
1987	114.5
1988	106.2
1989	104.6
1990	116.9
1991	123.1
1992	144.6
1993	163.1
1994	170.1

Source: Thailand Development Research Institute, Bangkok.

wages for two basic reasons. First, many of Thailand's most successful export industries are highly labour intensive, implying that a given increase in real wages has large effects on their costs. Second, these export industries face highly competitive international markets for their products, where they must act as price-takers. This means that cost increases cannot be passed on in the form of increases in product prices. Producers for the domestic market may have greater scope for doing so.

The implication of rising real wages is a loss of competitiveness in the labour intensive export oriented industries that have been the basis of much of Thailand's growth over the past decade. This information helps explain the export slow-down of the mid 1990s. With the end of the era of "cheap labour", Thailand's labour-intensive exports face the prospect of declining competitiveness. The importance of this point is confirmed by the fact that the export slow-down was concentrated in labour-intensive industries such as garments, footwear and textiles.[9]

For the export-oriented labour-intensive industries, large real wage increases raise serious problems. Unlike most of the potential causes of the export slow-down reviewed above, the increase in real wages is presumably (and hopefully) permanent. This means that the export competitiveness of these labour-intensive industries has declined permanently, given their present technology. They must adjust or face steadily declining market share. To adjust, these industries must find less labour-intensive and more capital- and skill-intensive ways of producing their goods. Thailand as a whole must move out of these industries as wages continue to rise and move into more skill-intensive industries. Here, the performance of Thailand's education sector in supplying the skilled labour force required becomes crucial.

Past indications raise serious concern about the capacity of the Thai education sector to deliver the skilled work-force that will be required. Thailand's primary school participation rates are high but retention rates at the secondary level are low by Southeast Asian standards. The reasons for this include the concentration of upper secondary schools in urban areas and the resulting high cost for rural people to participate, since students must stay away from home to attend school. In addition the secondary curriculum has been described as unsuitable for vocational type students.[10] These features of the education system combined with Thailand's high rate of industrialization have produced severe shortages of skilled labour. The long-term prospects for the Thai economy depend on its capacity to upgrade its manufacturing base. But the country's capacity to move from forms of manufacturing dependent on abundant unskilled labour and towards more skill-intensive forms of production will depend crucially upon the capacity of the education system to produce the skilled work-force required.

The increase in real wages may be bad news for some manufacturers, but it is obviously good news for Thailand's poor, who derive most of their incomes from their own labour. Observers of Thailand's economic development have for some years expressed concern at the rising inequality evident from consumer expenditure surveys. The income share of the richest quintile group (richest one fifth of the population) increased continuously at least from 1975/76, the earliest year for which reliable data are available, until 1992.

The income share of each of the other four quintile groups continuously declined. Nevertheless, the same household survey data sources also reveal that the proportion of the population whose incomes fell below a designated poverty line—held constant in purchasing power terms—declined significantly over the same period. The poor became better off in absolute terms over this period, which is why absolute poverty incidence declined, but the rich became better off at an even faster rate, which is why relative inequality simultaneously rose (Table 5.6).

There is roughly a two-year lag between conduct of the household surveys and publication of the survey results. The data for 1994 recently became available and Table 5.6 includes these results. Poverty incidence continued to decline, but the increase in relative inequality evident until 1992 was reversed over the interval to 1994. The experience of Thailand illustrates an empirical phenomenon first noticed in 1955 by Simon Kuznets: economic growth often produces rising inequality in the early stages of development followed by reduced inequality as the process matures.

In the Thai case, the fundamental reason for the transition from rising to declining inequality as growth proceeds is clear. It is the increases in real wages that began in the early 1990s. As the process of industrialization continues, "surplus" rural labour is eventually absorbed and real wages then begin to rise. As real wages rise, the real incomes of all labour-income earners rise accordingly and inequality declines, but this may occur only after a prolonged period when, as in the case of Thailand, real wages remain relatively constant for many years and inequality increases.

Table 5.6 Thailand: income distribution and poverty, 1981–94

	1981	*1986*	*1988*	*1990*	*1992*	*1994*
Income share by Quintil groups (%)						
Quintile (poorest)	5.41	4.55	4.60	4.20	3.94	3.99
Quintile 2	9.10	7.87	8.13	7.38	7.02	7.29
Quintile 2	13.38	12.09	12.46	11.50	11.06	11.60
Quintile 2	20.64	19.86	20.66	19.26	18.95	19.60
Quintile 5 (richest)	51.47	55.63	54.16	57.67	59.04	57.52
Ratio of income share of Quintile 1 to Quintile 5	9.5	12.2	11.8	13.7	15.0	14.4
Gini coefficient	0.453	0.500	0.485	0.522	0.536	0.525
Poverty incident (head count ratio %)	23.0	29.5	22.2	16.6	13.1	9.6

Source: *Bangkok Post Year-End Economic Review*, December 1996, p. 22.

PROSPECTS FOR 1997 AND BEYOND

The new government is expected to boost investors' optimism in the future of the Thai economy by restoring confidence in the government's capacity for competent economic management. Public investment is expected to decline in real terms in an effort to restore a more sustainable level of the budgetary deficit.

The International Monetary Fund predicts that global economic growth will recover from 3.8% in 1996 to 4.2% in 1997. The growth of world trade is expected to increase slightly, from 6.8% in 1996 to just over 7%. The United States and Japanese economies are expected to slow down slightly, however. Because of these two countries' importance as sources of demand for Thailand's exports, the prospects for demand for Thailand's exports are probably only slightly, if at all, more favourable in 1997 than the experience of 1996.

Some further real appreciation of the baht relative to the yen may occur in 1997. Slow recovery of Thailand's exports in 1997 relative to 1996 is probably the best that can reasonably be expected. Gradual recovery may be expected in subsequent years provided Thai producers can adjust their product mix appropriately in response to rising real wages. The very high rates of export growth experienced in the late 1980s and early 1990s will probably not be repeated.

The Thai economy may be expected to continue to grow at 6% per annum or better in real terms – high by international standards but below the unprecedented rates of over 10% achieved during the boom of 1988 to 1995. This growth slow-down need not be a source of gloom. The boom period growth rates were recognized to be environmentally unsustainable; in so far as they were based on unlimited supplies of cheap labour, they were economically unsustainable as well. In adjusting to lower growth rates Thailand may find ways to manage the social and policy conflicts produced by economic growth better than was possible during the hectic days of the boom.

NOTES

1 This is the headcount measure of poverty incidence, discussed later in this article.
2 The fifteen commodities represented in Table 5.3 comprised between 52 and 54% of total exports in each of the three years shown.
3 See Peter G. Warr and Bhanupong Nidhiprabha, *Thailand's Macroeconomic Miracle: Stabte Adjustment and Sustained Growth* (Washington, D.C.: World Bank and Kuala Lumpur: Oxford University Press, 1996).
4 Measured in months of imports, Thailand's reserves were the highest in Southeast Asia, with the possible exception of Brunei, for which data were not available. At the end of 1996 Thailand's reserves were US$42.7 billion, equivalent to 7.3 months of imports. Note that Table 5.4 describes annual average levels of reserves, rather than year-end levels. Corresponding end-of-year data for other Southeast Asian countries (with months of import coverage in parentheses) were:

Malaysia US$21.4 billion (3.3 months), Indonesia US$17.2 billion (4.6 months), Singapore US$78.2 billion (7.1 months), and the Philippines US$ 7.8 billion (2.8 months). [*Source*: HG Asia, *Economic Snapshot*, February 1997.]

5 The main exceptions were devaluations in mid-1981 (roughly 10%) and late 1984 (roughly 15%). For further detail, see Peter G. Warr and Bhanupong Nidhiprabha, *Thailand's Macroeconomic Miracle: Stable Adjustment and Sustained Growth* (Washington, D.C.: World Bank, and Kuala Lumpur: Oxford University Press, 1996).

6 For further detail, see Peter G. Warr and Bhanupong Nidhiprabha, *Thailand's Macroeconomic Miracle: Stable Adjustment and Sustained Growth* (Washington, D.C.: World Bank, and Kuala Lumpur: Oxford University Press, 1996).

7 *Bangkok Post Year-End Economic Review*, December 1996, p. 26.

8 Since we are interested in the implications for Thailand's export industries, this calculation uses Thailand's export shares to weight the bilateral real exchange rates with respect to individual trading partners.

9 The frozen shrimp industry is a special case, where U.S. import restrictions were important, effectively banning non-farm shrimp imports from Thailand. Fortunately, these bans are due to be lifted in 1997.

10 For further detail, see Sirilaksana Khoman, "Education Policy" in *The Thai Economy in Transition*, ed. Peter G. Warr (Cambridge: Cambridge University Press, 1993), pp.325–54.

Part II

THE ROLE OF GOVERNMENT ENTERPRISES AND MONOPOLIES, AND PRIVATIZATION

6

MALAYSIA'S PRIVATISATION EXPERIENCE

K. S. Jomo

6.1 INTRODUCTION

In the 1980s, privatisation was strongly recommended in most developing countries where key sectors had been dominated by public enterprises. In the early and mid-1980s, external price shocks led to a marked deterioration in macroeconomic performance, precipitating fiscal and debt crises. In this context, loss-making public enterprises have been seen or portrayed as a particularly conspicuous drain on government resources. Privatisation has often been touted as the best answer to the many problems of these varied public enterprises.

The following discussion deals primarily with the implications of the privatisation of such utilities and public services, rather than statist capitalist activities without any public welfare pretensions whatsoever, which, in any case, have not been the main target of privatisation in Malaysia.

By the early 1980s, the generally lacklustre performance of the Malaysian public sector, including many public enterprises, required a policy response. The real question, however, has been whether such inefficiencies are necessarily characteristic of the public sector, and hence cannot be overcome except through privatisation. If the current record of the Malaysian public enterprises is primarily due to the nature, interests and abilities of those in charge, rather than to the fact of public ownership, then privatisation in itself cannot and will not overcome the root problem. Also, while privatisation may increase enterprise efficiency in order to increase profits for the private owners concerned, such changes may not necessarily benefit the public or consumers on balance.

Since a significant portion of such activities are monopolies, privatisation will hand over such monopoly powers to private interests who are likely to use them to maximise profits. The privatisation of public services tends to burden the people, especially if charges are raised for the privatised services. Obviously, private interests are only interested in profitable or potentially

Source: *Privatization Policy and Performance: International Perspectives*, Paul Cook and Colin Kirkpatrick (Editors), New York: Prentice Hall, 1995, pp. 225–43.

profitable activities and enterprises. This may mean that the government will be left with unprofitable and less profitable activities. And this will worsen overall public sector performance. Public sector inefficiencies and other problems need to be overcome, but privatisation in Malaysia has primarily enriched the few with strong political connections to secure many of these profitable opportunities, while the public interest increasingly becomes vulnerable to private capitalists' powers and interests.

While most affected public sector employees have felt threatened by privatisation, many other Malaysians, fed up with the waste, inefficiency and corruption usually associated with the public sector, have been indifferent to, if not supportive, of this policy. Many Malaysians also associate the growth of the public sector with increased state intervention and the ascendance of Malay hegemony under the New Economic Policy (NEP), and see privatisation as a desirable policy change that would reverse these trends, which have apparently discouraged private investment, and thus slowed down growth. Some others identify state intervention with socialism and support privatisation as a measure to restore capitalist hegemony. While statist capitalism is not socialism, undermining the public sector, especially public services, through privatisation has important welfare implications for the people, especially public sector employees, consumers and the poor.

6.2 PRIVATISATION IN MALAYSIA

The Malaysian government was among the first to climb on the privatisation bandwagon, enthusiastically endorsed and promoted by the Bretton Woods institutions, particularly the World Bank. Two years after becoming Prime Minister in 1981, Dr Mahathir Mohamad announced the Malaysian government's own commitment to privatisation in 1983. Unlike the 'Look East' policy and the 'Malaysia Incorporated' concept – also associated with Mahathir's administration – which seemed to fade in significance by the mid-1980s, privatisation achieved new vigour, especially after the appointment of Daim Zainuddin as finance minister in mid-1984 and the deepening economic crisis of 1985–86. To be sure, Mahathir's own commitment to private – rather than public – enterprise began much earlier, reflected in his *The Malay Dilemma* (1970) and especially his *Menghadapi Cabaran* (1976; published in English translation as *The Challenge* in the mid-1980s). This unwavering commitment is all the more remarkable because of his two predecessors' commitment to public enterprise as the main vehicle for furthering national, especially ethnic Malay communal business interests.

From 1971, the Malay elite-dominated Malaysian government's New Economic Policy was committed to reducing poverty and inter-ethnic economic disparity, ostensibly to achieve national unity, understood primarily in terms of reduced inter-ethnic resentment. New statutory bodies, government corporations, government-owned or controlled publicly listed companies as well as government-owned or controlled private companies, all became means to achieve government objectives, including the NEP's corporate wealth redistribution target of increasing indigenous (Bumiputera) share ownership to 30 per cent by 1990 from 2.4 per cent in 1970. The NEP's Outline Perspective Plan for 1971–90 also envisaged the creation of a Bumiputera commercial and industrial community (BCIC), while the Fourth Malaysia Plan for 1981–85 expected Bumiputera 'trust agencies' to account for 83 per cent of Bumiputera share capital in 1990 (i.e. only 17 per cent – or 5.2 per cent of total share capital – was to be held by Bumiputera individuals). By 1990, however, Bumiputera share capital had risen to 20.3 per cent of total share capital, with trust agencies accounting for 6.3 per cent and individuals for 14.0 per cent (i.e. 31 per cent and 69 per cent of the Bumiputera share respectively). However, it should also be pointed out that various criticisms have been made about official share distribution data. Besides the valuation problem raised by using nominal or par values – which, it is claimed, especially underestimates the market value of Bumiputera corporate wealth – and underestimation owing to the use of nominee companies, the Malaysian government has not explained how share capital owned directly by the government and other bodies – such as Bank Negara Malaysia (the central bank) or the Employees Provident Fund – is categorised.

In 1985, two years after the privatisation policy was announced, and possibly in response to public criticism, the Privatisation Section of the powerful Economic Planning Unit (EPU) of the Prime Minister's Department issued its *Guidelines on Privatisation* (Malaysia, 1985) which outlined policy aims, modes of privatisation and the means for implementation. Since then, various laws have been reformed to facilitate the incorporation of government departments and agencies as public limited companies and to facilitate privatisation more generally. The government also commissioned the drafting of a privatisation masterplan, the main elements of which were announced in various fora in 1989 (e.g. Sheriff, 1991). The EPU (Malaysia, 1991a) finally published the *Privatisation Masterplan* (*PMP*) document in February 1991, after the October 1990 general election and before announcing its post-NEP (or post-1990) policy in the form of three key documents:

1 Mahathir's (1991) inaugural paper to the National Business Council entitled *The Way Forward*, now more popularly referred to as the 'Vision 2020' speech, declaring the intention for Malaysia to achieve 'developed country' status by the year 2020 (i.e. after three decades).
2 The *Second Outline Perspective Plan* (*OPP2*) (Malaysia, 1991b) for 1991–2000 for the National Development Policy (NDP) replacing the NEP.
3 The *Sixth Malaysia Plan, 1991–1995* (Malaysia, 1991c).

Hence, the *PMP* is regarded as one of four major programmatic documents issued in 1991 outlining Malaysian economic development policy in the foreseeable future. Claiming success for its privatisation programme thus far, the *PMP* announced the government's intention to 'expand and accelerate further the pace of privatisation process' (sic).

Malaysia's privatisation experience is now critically reviewed here, after which the main features of the *Privatisation Masterplan* are summarised.

6.2.1 Privatisation experience

Privatisation – or denationalisation – refers to changing the status of a business, service or industry from state, government or public to private ownership or control. The term sometimes also refers to the use of private contractors to provide services previously rendered by the public sector.

In Malaysia and elsewhere, privatisation has been identified with a broad range of processes including those involving ownership transfer of enterprises from the public to the private sector. Privatisation can be strictly defined to include only cases of the sale of 100 per cent or at least a majority share of a public enterprise, or its assets, to private shareholders. However, in Malaysia, it is often understood to include cases where less than half of the assets or shares of public enterprises are sold to private shareholders, and even cases where public enterprises are allowed to undertake activities previously monopolised by the state.

In Malaysia, when a public enterprise, legally formed as a government department or statutory authority, is privatised, this necessarily first entails corporatisation, or the formation of a limited company incorporated under the Companies Act. On the other hand, the privatisation of a public enterprise which has been constituted as a limited company would merely entail a transfer in share ownership from the public to the private sector without any change in the legal form of the enterprise.

In contrast to privatisation, which essentially only involves property rights, the broader concept of marketisation is widely believed to entail not only denationalisation, but also market liberalisation, involving greater competition. Privatisation is then expected to be accompanied by the relaxation or abolition of monopolistic practices, including statutory monopoly powers, such as those usually conferred on and enjoyed by public utilities. Privatised entities are thus expected to find themselves in competitive markets or environments.

Competition generally encourages more efficient behaviour among private entities or companies, in order to achieve both productive and allocative efficiencies. Enhanced efficiency is therefore conceived of as the result of the interaction between private ownership and the competitive environment. Hence a privatisation exercise which merely involves selling a portion of the shares of a public enterprise to the public, but is not accompanied by greater exposure to market forces, may not bring about desired efficiency increases. Conversely, efficiency gains may be achieved through other changes – for example, management reforms – without any change in ownership. Even improvements in capital resource allocation may be achieved by eliminating a soft budget constraint and strengthening management accountability – for example, through greater organisational transparency.

In the case of Malaysia, therefore, desired increases in efficiency may not be achieved through privatisation, since there has been little evidence of increased competition associated with privatisation. Some of the selected enterprises already privatised or expected to be privatised are natural monopolies, such as airlines, toll roads, public utilities and telecommunications. Thus, if privatisation merely involves transforming a public monopoly into a private monopoly, consumer welfare may well be adversely affected. Improved enterprise efficiency may not enhance consumer welfare, but may simply increase the monopoly profits accruing to the privatised enterprise.

Full or complete privatisation means a complete transfer of ownership and control of a government enterprise or asset to the private sector. In Malaysia, such privatisations are not the norm, the most prominent cases involving the North-South Highway, Kumpulan Fima and Peremba.

In the case of Malaysian Airlines (MAS) and the Malaysian International Shipping Corporation (MISC), privatisation has actually only involved partial divestment, with majority ownership and hence ultimate control still in the hands of the government, which remains the majority shareholder. Even if the government share should decline to less than half, in preparing some enterprises for privatisation the government has created a 'golden share', allowing it to retain control even with considerably diminished minority ownership.

In Malaysia, privatisation has officially referred to:

1 Sale or divestment of state concerns. The public service concerned usually has to first be incorporated legally as a public limited company to facilitate such a sale: for example, the establishment of Syarikat Telekom Malaysia Berhad on 1 January 1987 to take over the activities of the Telecoms Department (Jabatan Telekom) or the incorporation of Tenaga Nasional Berhad, taking over the National Electricity Board (Lembaga Letrik Negara).
2 Public issue or sale of a minority or even a majority of shares in a state-owned public company: for example, Malaysian Airlines System (MAS) in 1985 and the Malaysian International Shipping Corporation (MISC) in 1987.
3 Placement of shares with institutional investors: for example, the sale of about 5 per cent of MAS stock to the Brunei government in 1986.
4 Sale or lease of physical assets: for example, the lease of the Lady Templer Hospital to Rampai Muda in 1984.
5 Joint public/private sector ventures: for example, the establishment of Perbadanan Otomobil Nasional (Proton) in 1983, with 70 per cent held by HICOM, the Heavy Industries Corporation of Malaysia, and 15 per cent

each by two Mitsubishi companies, the Mitsubishi Corporation and the Mitsubishi Motor Corporation.

6 Schemes to draw private financing into construction projects: for example, North Port Kelang toll road bypass, the Jalan Kuching toll flyover and the North-South Highway, as well as the low-cost housing scheme 'privatised' since the mid-1980s.
7 'Contracting out' public services previously provided within the public sector: for example, the contracting out of various local government authorities' activities, such as parking services and garbage disposal, Telecoms $2.5 billion telecommunications development projects (Kennedy, 1991), Port Kelang's container terminal services.
8 Allowing private competition where the public sector previously enjoyed a monopoly: for example, the launching of a third television channel (TV3) in 1984 owned by Sistem Televisyen Malaysia Berhad, now controlled by the New Straits Press Berhad, and controlled in turn by the UMNO-owned Fleet Group, and now by the UMNO-controlled Renong Bhd.

The Malaysian government has summed up its argument for privatisation as follows in its *Guidelines on Privatisation*:

> Privatisation has a number of objectives. First, it is aimed at relieving the financial and administrative burden of the government in undertaking and maintaining a vast and constantly expanding network of services and investments in infrastructure. Second, privatisation is expected to promote competition, improve efficiency and increase the productivity of the services. Third, privatisation, by stimulating private entrepreneurship and investment, is expected to accelerate the rate of growth of the economy. Fourth, privatisation is expected to assist in reducing the presence and size of the public sector, with its monopolistic tendencies and bureaucratic support, in the economy. Fifth, privatisation is also expected to contribute towards meeting the objectives of the New Economic Policy (NEP), especially as Bumiputera entrepreneurship and presence have improved greatly since the early days of the NEP and they are therefore capable of taking up their share of the privatised services. (Malaysia, 1985)

These arguments in favour of privatisation have been refuted on the following grounds:

1 The public sector can be more efficiently run, as has been demonstrated by some other public sectors: for example, in Singapore (Rodan 1989), Taiwan (Wade 1990) and South Korea (Amsden, 1989). Also, privatisation is not going to provide a miracle cure for all the problems (especially the inefficiencies) associated with the public sector, nor can private enterprise guarantee that the public interest is most effectively served by private interests taking over public sector activities. Also, by diverting private

sector capital from productive new investments to buying over public sector assets, economic growth would be retarded rather than encouraged.

2 Greater public accountability and a more transparent public sector would ensure greater efficiency in achieving the public and national interest while limiting public sector waste and borrowing.
3 The government would only be able to privatise profitable or potentially profitable enterprises and activities because the private sector would only be interested in these enterprises.
4 Privatisation may postpone a fiscal crisis by temporarily reducing fiscal deficits, but it would not necessarily resolve it because the public sector would lose income from the more profitable public sector activities, and would be stuck with financing the unprofitable ones, which would undermine the potential for cross-subsidisation within the public sector.
5 Privatisation tends to adversely affect the interests of the public sector employees and the public, especially poorer consumers, which the public sector is more sensitive to.
6 Privatisation would give priority to profit maximisation at the expense of social welfare and the public interest, except on the rare occasions when the former and the latter coincide; hence, for example, only profitable new services would be introduced, rather than services needed by the people, especially the poor and politically uninfluential.
7 Privatisation exercises in Malaysia may not even pretend to achieve their other alleged advantages and benefits by invoking NEP restructuring considerations, supposedly to increase Bumiputera wealth ownership and business opportunities. With increased Bumiputera competition, where prior collusion cannot be arranged, it seems that political influence and connections have become increasingly decisive.

In many cases of privatisation in Malaysia, it is popularly believed that there are strong influences from private interests who try to determine what is to be privatised, in what manner and to whom. For example, Sapura Holdings commissioned a consultancy report by Arthur D. Little of Boston entitled 'The advantages and feasibility of privatising Jabatan Telekom Malaysia' in 1983 for the attention of the Malaysian government; with the benefit of hindsight, it is generally acknowledged that Sapura is undoubtedly the main beneficiary of the privatisation of telecommunications in Malaysia (Kennedy 1991).

Often, privatisation in Malaysia does not even involve the formalities of an open tender system, as sanctioned by the official 'first come, first served' policy by which the government justifies awarding privatisation opportunities to those who have supposedly first proposed the privatisation of a government property or activity. Instead, many beneficiaries are believed to have been chosen on the basis of political and personal connections.

For example, in 1986, it was announced that M$ 1.4 billion worth of water supply projects involving 174 schemes had been awarded to Antah Biwater without open tender. Though hailed as the nation's first privatised water supply project, the government will remain responsible for the operation and maintenance of the schemes. Antah Biwater – which is 51 per cent owned by the Negeri Sembilan royal family's Antah Holdings Bhd and 49 per cent owned by the British water supply and treatment group, Biwater Ltd – had in fact secured a turnkey contract with a British government financing arrangement thrown in as an aid package. It is anticipated that all the design and engineering work will be handled by Biwater – since Antah has no relevant engineering track record – at the expense of Malaysian engineers and consultants who have long handled such projects.

In December 1986, the Malaysian parliament passed amendments to the Official Secrets Act (OSA) which extended the definition of official secrets to include, among other things, government tender documents (even after completion of the tender exercise) and any other documents or material which ministers and public officials may arbitrarily deem secret or confidential. The classification of a document or other material as an official secret cannot be challenged in any court of law, while the amendments impose a mandatory minimum one year jail sentence for any OSA offence. Such legislation, accompanying the privatisation drive, further limits the already limited scope for meaningful governmental transparency and public accountability.

Privatisation is also supposed to free market forces and encourage competition in the economy generally, especially in the sectors concerned. But this is negated by the fact that potential beneficiaries have a common interest in getting the public sector to privatise services, which can be far more important. Not surprisingly, with the limited experience of privatisation thus far, there is already widespread concern about and some evidence of:

- the existence of formal and informal collusion (e.g. cartel-like agreements);
- possible patterns in bidding for contracts, suggesting collusion among bidders; and
- some companies enjoying special influence and privileged information, thus being able consistently to bid successfully for profitable opportunities from privatisation.

Some other adverse consequences of privatisation to be considered include the following:

1 Increased 'costs' to the public of reduced, inferior or costlier services: for example, the unit charge for local telephone calls was increased by 30 per cent just before STMB was incorporated.
2 The implications of two sets of services: for example, one for those who can afford privatised services and the other for those who cannot, and hence have to continue to rely on public services (e.g. medical services and education).

3 The effects of minimal investments by private contractors concerned with short-term profits.
4 Increased costs of living and poorer services and utilities – especially in remote and rural areas – due to 'economic costing' of services (e.g. telephone, water supply and electricity).
5 Reduced jobs, overtime work and real wages for employees of privatised concerns.
6 The deflationary consequences of fewer jobs or lower wages, or both.

6.2.2 Privatisation masterplan (*PMP*)

As of the end of 1990, according to the *PMP*, 37 privatisations had taken place since the announcement of the policy, of which 27 involved private interests taking over existing government entities, while the other 10 involved the construction of new infrastructure. The government had also approved another 18 privatisations, of which 7 are new infrastructure projects. This did not include government divestments since 1981 to transfer government equity to Bumiputeras, involving some 30 companies transferred to Permodalan Nasional Berhad and another 120 or so to private Bumiputera interests – which remain to be systematically documented. Also, minor privatisations – such as contracting out of services (e.g. security, cleaning and laundry) – are not included. Of the 27 privatisations, 17 involved ownership divestment by sale of equity or assets to the public, or by way of private placement and management buy-out; 2 involved leasing arrangements, 5 involved management contracts and 2 more a combination of sale and lease; also the Lembaga Letrik Negara (LLN, or National Electricity Board) was corporatised as Tenaga Nasional Berhad (National Power Ltd.) as a step towards privatisation. Of the 10 new infrastructure projects, 8 involved 'build-operate-transfer' (BOT) (to government after some time), while the other 2 involved 'build-operate' (BO) (for perpetuity).

The *PMP* considers four main modes of implementing privatisation, namely: sale of assets or equity; lease of assets; management contract; and 'build-operate- transfer' (BOT) or 'build-operate' (BO) new infrastructure.

However, the document also cites other examples of privatisation which have nothing to do with any of these: for example, the so-called privatisation of TV3 through issue of a licence for a private television broadcasting company, and contracting-out services. The *PMP* also mentions broad alternative methods, considerations and criteria for the valuation of assets for sale or lease – net tangible assets (NTA), price-earning (PE) ratios, discounted cash flows (DCF) – emphasising that only the latter two take account of potential earnings, which the *PMP* favours. Yet, there is no evidence that any of these methods have been strictly adhered to in determining the actual price (or lease rate) of privatised government assets. On the contrary, very substantial discounts (in the case of sales) and premiums (in the case of privatised infrastructure projects) seem to have been the norm, with the proportion apparently not unrelated to the political influence of the beneficiary. It is believed that the predominance of the (politically most influential) Malays among public sector employees, the presence of relatively large unions in the big public utilities earmarked for privatisation, the virtual halt to public sector employee recruitment as a result of the post-election austerity drive since June 1982, and the virtual public sector wage freeze since 1980 (despite considerable inflation, especially in the early 1980s), encouraged the government to ensure employment security for five years and better service terms and conditions as inducements to workers not to resist privatisation. Hence, though workers can choose not to join the privatised entity, very few do so; the vast majority have yet another option – of continuing with the government's scheme of service or accepting the new company's scheme – which most tend to select.

The government has had to legislate many changes to existing laws to facilitate privatisation. The primary concern, however, has been with overcoming legal obstacles to privatisation. Little attention has been given to ensuring greater competition or public or consumer accountability, which are matters of considerable concern since many of the privatised entities remain virtual monopolies. Since the *PMP* acknowledges that there is not much scope for increasing competition with natural monopolies, it promises an appropriate regulatory framework to protect consumer interests, particularly in terms of price, quality and availability of services, as well as 'commercial freedom' for private monopolies. Implicit in this formulation is the acknowledgement that such regulation does not yet exist, and, if introduced, is unlikely to threaten enterprise autonomy. While privatisation undoubtedly exerts heavy demands on private sector financial resources to mobilise both debt and equity capital, it is not self-evident that deepening and broadening the Malaysian capital market are desirable in themselves. On the contrary, it has been suggested that with privatisation, capital resources – which might otherwise have been invested into expanding productive capacity – have instead been diverted into acquiring or transferring existing public sector assets. The *PMP* reiterates the government's intention to advance Bumiputera corporate participation through ethnically preferential privatisation. This is expected to include collaboration between Bumiputera institutional investors and others as well as management buy-outs (MBOs) and employee share ownership plans (ESOPs). The *PMP* also promises an institutional mechanism to ensure sustained Bumiputera participation after privatisation. Anticipating public objections, the *PMP* advocates minority (no more than 25 per cent) foreign investments in privatised entities where:

- foreign expertise is needed and local expertise is not available;
- foreign participation is crucial for export market access and promotion;

- international linkages and exposure are required by the business;
- the supply of local capital is not sufficient to buy up the shares offered.

An interesting innovation proposed by the *PMP* is the establishment of a special fund to finance related expenses such as feasibility studies, preparing candidates for privatisation and disbursing compensation related to privatisation. To motivate staff, the *PMP* recommends employee share ownership as well as other incentives. However, it acknowledges that such schemes have not benefited poorer employees very much, while loyalty and commitment to the company have been undermined by the subsequent sale of shares. To overcome these problems, the *PMP* recommends Employee Share Ownership Plans (ESOPs) for future privatisations, involving the establishment of a trust to hold shares for employees who will only be able to sell them when they retire or resign. The *PMP* also recommends management as well as management-cum-employee buy-outs, i.e. MBOs and MEBOs. The *PMP* also proposes a Privatisation Action Plan (PAP) consisting of a two-year 'rolling plan' reviewed at the end of each year, identifying the targets for privatisation and for preparation for eventual privatisation in the following years. According to the *PMP*, 424 government-owned entities (GOEs) were studied by private consultants to determine the desirability and suitability of their privatisation. The consultants identified 246 as privatisable, with 69 to be privatised within two years, 107 in two to five years and the balance after five years; but the government has deemed some of this number not suitable for privatisation on various grounds.

The government also claims to be considering others not covered by the study for possible privatisation. Such government-initiated privatisations are supposed to be subject to competitive bidding. According to the *PMP*, however, the government is still prepared to consider private sector-initiated privatisation if it is convinced that no other private sector party can privatise a particular project, as in the following circumstances:

1 The proposer offers a unique cost-effective solution to an economic problem or potential savings to the government.
2 The proposer has unique possession of certain technical know-how or patent rights essential to the proposal.
3 The privatisation would not be viable on its own as its viability is dependent on another component possessed by the proposer.

Although still open to abuse, if strictly interpreted, these criteria represent a significant departure from the earlier 'first come, first served' policy, which has still not been unequivocally rejected.

The *PMP* claims to be influenced by both feasibility and desirability criteria in determining priorities for privatisation. Feasibility is, in turn, said to be determined by both ease of privatisation and attractiveness to the private sector, whereas desirability seems to be defined by the government's perception of private sector superiority. Using a 2×2 matrix, the *PMP* distinguishes the following four categories of candidates:

1 *Immediate privatisation* candidates will be the main focus in the early years of the PAP as they rank highly on the feasibility and desirability criteria.
2 *Priority restructuring* candidates are deemed to require preparation (e.g. restructuring) for privatisation despite the government's desire to privatise them.
3 *Back burner* candidates are deemed feasible for privatisation, though the benefits of privatisation are considered to be less than self-evident.
4 The *consider future* candidates rank poorly on both feasibility and desirability criteria.

The PAP also distinguishes six different categories of candidates for privatisation requiring different treatment, as follows:

1 *Flagships* – comprising GOEs of national importance, in terms of size and complexity, thus meriting special treatment (such as JTM and LLN) – are to be privatised over several years, usually at the rate of one per annum.
2 *Easily privatisable government majority-owned companies*, especially in manufacturing and agricultural production, are most likely to be given priority for privatisation.
3 *Restructuring candidates* mainly refers to unprofitable companies needing financial and operational restructuring; however, the government prefers to minimise pre-privatisation restructuring, which usually involves financial aspects.
4 *Services* previously protected from commercial competition are to be deregulated and privatised in the consumer interest.
5 *Listed and minority share holdings* are to be given low priority since the private sector is already quite involved.
6 *New projects* – usually involving infrastructural development – are to be privatised on a BOT basis.

To facilitate implementation, the PAP distinguishes those ready for privatisation from those requiring preparation (e.g. most flagships). The stages required for their preparation may include:

1 commercialisation (e.g. raising user charges, commercial accounting and commercial performance criteria); and
2 legal corporatisation;

and other changes at this stage before actual divestment may also include:

3 replacing bureaucratic administration with profit-oriented management;
4 replacing centralised production-oriented decision making with market-driven consumer preferences; and

5 introducing clear financial and operational performance criteria and commercial accounting.

While the *PMP* admits that 'it is still too early to make an assessment of the effectiveness of the privatisation programme', it nonetheless claims several significant achievements, as follows:

1 *Efficient gains* The *PMP* cites four examples:
   (*a*) reduction of average vessel turnaround time at the Kelang port container terminal from 11.7 hours to 8.9 hours two years after privatisation;
   (*b*) improvements in television broadcasting with greater competition after the licensing of a private third television channel, TV3;
   (*c*) improved telecommunication services since the corporatisation of STM in 1987;
   (*d*) completion of the Labuan water supply project ahead of schedule.
2 *Stimulus to growth* The *PMP* claims privatisation has stimulated economic growth by providing greater opportunities to (and thus motivating) the private sector, generating multiplier effects (e.g. TV3's stimulus to the domestic film making and advertising industries), compensating for the decline in public expenditure and encouraging private entrepreneurship.
3 *Reducing governmental responsibilities* The *PMP* claims a significant reduction in the government's administrative and financial burden due to privatisation, citing the reduction of the public sector workforce by 54,000, of whom 29,000 were Telecoms employees. One-off proceeds from the sale of government properties came to M$1.18 billion, while recurrent revenues are expected from taxation and leases (e.g. Kelang Container Terminal); meanwhile, the government's tax burden has been reduced as privatised companies take over loan refinancing. The *PMP* also claims that privatising new infrastructure projects has saved the government M$8.2 billion, while other capital spending (development expenditure) commitments have been significantly reduced.
4 *Redistribution* Since most privatisations have involved at least 30 per cent Bumiputera participation, the policy is said to have furthered the NEP's inter-ethnic wealth redistribution objectives. The *PMP* also claims that privatisation has enabled the government to spend more on poverty alleviation although there is no real evidence of this.

6.3 CONCLUDING REMARKS

Despite the *PMP*'s claim that privatisation is 'premised on the superiority of market over administrative directives in governing economic activity to achieve efficiency' and that the 'Government's intervention in the economy will be minimal', actual deregulation efforts are well behind those of privatisation. While there has been a great deal of rhetoric about deregulation accompanying privatisation, such efforts have been quite limited and mainly oriented to inducing foreign investments. And in many instances, especially with public utilities, the government has retained effective control despite changes in ownership. Privatisation in itself only involves the transfer of property rights, and in many instances in Malaysia (e.g. the privatisation of large public utilities and management buy-outs), management personnel have not even been significantly changed.

Improvements in management generally reflect management initiatives encouraged by increased enterprise and administrative autonomy as well as new incentive systems – that is, changes which do not require privatisation as a prerequisite, but can alternatively be achieved by greater decentralisation, devolution or administrative authority. These changes have long been advocated by trade unions (e.g. see Mustapha Johan and Shamsulbahriah, 1987) and others in the public sector, which became increasingly centralised in the early 1980s with the Cabinet Committee Report on new salary structures for the public sector, chaired by then Deputy Prime Minister Mahathir, and the later centralisation of authority over the public sector, in the Prime Minister's Department under Mahathir, especially through the strengthening of the Public Services Department (JPA). Also, the so-called Non-Financial Public Enterprises (NFPEs), or Off-Budget Agencies (OBAs), were less subject to the Treasury's budgetary discipline, especially after then Finance Minister Tengku Razaleigh Hamzah challenged Mahathir's preferred candidate (Musa Hitam) for the ruling party's deputy leadership, and traditionally, the deputy prime ministership as well.

If one accepts the view that it is competition and enterprise reorganisation – rather than mere changes in ownership status – which are likely to induce greater enterprise efficiency, then it becomes difficult to conclude that economic efficiency has been improved because of privatisation in Malaysia. Some of the – often exaggerated – efficiency gains have been brought about by greater employee and managerial motivation with new incentive systems and greater scope for managerial initiatives with administrative autonomy and can hardly be attributed to privatisation *per se*. The advocates of privatisation in Malaysia have not been honest in presenting a full and balanced record of what has happened with privatisation. Instead, anecdotal claims have been selectively advanced to imply that the Malaysian experience has been an unqualified success, as in the *PMP*. The existence of mistakes or negative consequences and implications is not acknowledged, in order to avoid their recurrence. While the policy makers or those in charge presumably know better, the *PMP*'s failure publicly to consider the failings bears ominous implications about how the policy has been formulated, adopted and implemented.

While the *PMP* undoubtedly represents an advance, at least on paper, over some of the most blatant abuses of early Malaysian privatisation policy, especially the 'first come, first served' policy, it offers little ground for comfort about the future of privatisation in Malaysia, especially in light of what has taken place and seems likely to occur in the foreseeable future. While privatisation undoubtedly reduces the role of the public sector in the economy, it is not clear whether this is an end in itself or merely the means to an end. If the former, then the policy is essentially intended to aggrandise its politically influential beneficiaries, or is clearly ideological in inspiration, or is meant to please the ideologically motivated governments and powerful international economic institutions (such as the World Bank and the Asian Development Bank) the Malaysian government seeks to find favour with. There is evidence that all three factors may be operative in the Malaysian case.

Advocates of privatisation in Malaysia, including the *PMP*, also claim that it will reduce the government's financial and administrative burden. While there undoubtedly are one-off revenues for the government from the sale of public assets, it is not self-evident that the retention of such assets would not have been in the government's and the public's medium- and long-term interest for a variety of reasons mentioned above. Perhaps most importantly, the considerable evidence of heavy discounting in asset prices for sale or lease suggests otherwise. Also, the sale of the government's most valuable assets, while it is obliged to retain those less profitable activities and assets of little interest to the profit-seeking private sector, contributes to the self-fulfilling prophecy of the unprofitability of public sector economic activities. The diminution of the public sector also reduces the scope for government intervention, for example, for equity reasons or in support of industrial policy.

The *PMP*'s claim that privatisation contributes to growth is vague and even spurious. After the announcement of the policy in 1983, Malaysia went through a deep recession in 1985–86, before experiencing rapid manufacturing-led growth since the late 1980s. Although the mid-1980s recession was exacerbated by the deflationary consequences of public spending cuts, which can be analytically distinguished from privatisation *per se*, there is also no clear evidence that privatisation in particular has significantly contributed to recent economic growth. No claim has yet been made that privatisation is a necessary and indispensable ingredient for the broader economic liberalisation measures of the mid-1980s that probably induced the foreign investment increase associated with the recent boom. On the contrary, it may be argued that private acquisition of public assets has probably diverted potential investment funds, while it is now generally agreed that the stock market – undoubtedly expanded by privatisation – has not been important for corporate financing of the dynamic foreign-dominated manufacturing sector.

Privatisation in Malaysia might be said to have been most successful in contributing to the government's NEP objective, particularly Bumiputera wealth acquisition, though it should be emphasised that wealth concentration levels are very high and strongly related to political influence and access. One might even argue that the prioritisation of this objective has probably seriously undermined achievement of the other stated aims of its privatisation policy. However, it is unclear how the creation and distribution of substantial economic rents through ethnically-biased privatisation have been in the national interest, whether this is understood in developmentalist or equity terms. There is now official acknowledgement that most of these rents have not been efficiently deployed through productive investments to significantly accelerate industrialisation or to consolidate genuine Bumiputera entrepreneurship. Instead, much has been wasted on rent-seeking costs associated with political involvement in business, while the very source of such rents and the limited abilities of those who control them have contributed to their deployment in real property, construction, finance and other investments with a short-term time horizon, thus adversely affecting investment priorities and activities generally in an economy officially committed to sustained manufacturing-led growth. The foregoing analysis also implies that privatisation is unlikely to enhance the NEP's other equity objectives (e.g. inter-ethnic parity in occupational and employment distribution, poverty reduction), and may instead undermine public welfare as a result of the strengthening of private monopolistic interests.

In the increasingly authoritarian and centralised Malaysian polity, with public accountability and governmental transparency considerably diminished deliberately by those in power, the strengthening of private business interests, especially of those who are politically well connected, is very likely to transform, and even increase, rather than eliminate the opportunities for rent appropriation. Ironically, the remaining democratic features of the system in such a context may well serve to sustain rent-seeking behaviour and costs.

This is not intended to legitimise further authoritarianism to reduce such waste. Rather, it serves to emphasise that enhanced public accountability, governmental transparency and other democratic safeguards are crucial for reducing rents – which can still be productively deployed – and, more importantly, rent-seeking behaviour in the context of privatisation.

Instead of transferring or selling off activities and enterprises which have not been well run by the public sector, the government seems to be doing exactly the opposite. The better-run public sector activities and enterprises are being privatised, leaving the public sector with the poorly run loss-making remainder. The result will only further strain government revenues and appears to confirm the charges of public sector ineptitude, while enriching those well placed to gain from the privatisation exercises. This process has included and is expected to continue to involve the transfer of public monopolies into private hands, without adequate safeguards to protect and ensure the public interest after privatisation. Current policy also seems to fail to recognise that it is rarely privatisation *per se* that enhances efficiency, but rather competition. Also, the problems of poor management and inefficiency in the rest of the public sector have not been addressed by such a privatisation policy.

Instead, Malaysia's mixed economy can be reformed by other more equitable and desirable means. Public sector activities and enterprises directly competing with the private sector may be privatised, especially if they are poorly managed or draining public resources. To ensure that Bumiputera interests are not undermined in the process, privatisation could well involve management or leveraged buy-outs and other similar devices without incurring further loss of revenue, but without the huge 'subsidies' characterising earlier privatisations. In some cases, where little interest is shown, the enterprises involved may well have to be shut down as they were probably set up for dubious reasons in the first place.

However, where public sector enterprises and activities have been well run and properly managed, the government should not privatise for its own sake – that is, for ideological reasons – as this is not necessarily in the public interest. For the public monopolies and social services, particularly, privatisation should be avoided, though management reforms and greater competition are probably desirable, if not urgent. If such activities have been less than well run, organisational reforms should be instituted to enhance performance. In this regard, the public sector as a whole must be reorganised to allow for greater flexibility and variation than is permitted by current rules and regulations, as well as to reward initiative, productivity and performance.

Hence, this objection to privatisation does not recommend complacency or inaction with regards to problems of the public sector. Reforms are certainly urgently needed, and there is no single or simple solution to the varied problems of the public sector, as implied by some advocates of privatisation. The experience of some other countries, for example, neighbouring Singapore, has clearly demonstrated that the public sector can be run well and flexibly. Reforms towards this end are urgently required.

The current obsession with privatisation also has the unintended consequence of postponing or otherwise putting aside the urgent need for public sector reform. The privatisation of some public sector activities and enterprises will do little to improve the situation in the unaffected remainder of the public sector. Moreover it conveys the wrong impression that these problems can only be overcome by privatisation. The current eagerness to privatise also ignores the problems of market failure, better recognised in earlier times.

Malaysia's experience thus far suggests that the government-revenue-generating, government-deficit-reducing, private-sector-control-increasing, and capital-market-deepening official objectives of Malaysian privatisation have largely been subordinated to the ostensibly Malay-wealth-enhancing objective through rent redeployment, particularly to the politically well connected. The privatisation policy's multifarious objectives undoubtedly require various trade-offs, but the apparently consistent bias suggests serious abuse for the purposes of political patronage and personal aggrandisement at the expense of the other objectives of privatisation, ostensibly in the national interest.

There should instead be a comprehensive critical review of the public sector, including the statutory bodies and other public enterprises, with a view to reform in order to enhance efficiency and cost-effectiveness, as well as dynamic, equitable, balanced and sustainable national economic development. Such a critical review should consider the variety of modes of privatisation, marketisation and other reform measures as options in dealing with the public sector as it has evolved in Malaysia. In such an approach, privatisation becomes one among several options available to the government for dealing with the undoubted malaise of the Malaysian public sector. This flexible approach seems superior to the current, narrow and dogmatic approach which apparently views privatisation as the only – and presumably best – solution to a complex variety of problems faced by the Malaysian public sector.

This existing approach also tends to neglect the persistent problems faced by the rest of the public sector not targeted for privatisation, which may in fact require more urgent attention. Ironically, their problems are probably the most serious – and hence in greater need of remedy – which may explain the lack of private sector interest in privatising them. Furthermore, if successful on its own terms, the existing approach is likely to saddle the public sector with the most uneconomic, unprofitable and unattractive activities, thus only confirming prejudices and charges of public sector incompetence and inefficiency, besides worsening the public sector deficit with the loss of possibilities for cross-subsidisation.

Unfortunately, however, there does not seem to have been any significant progress in checking the various problems which have emerged from the privatisation process thus far, or in avoiding them with future privatisations. The entire privatisation process itself seems to be beyond accountability, and the lack of transparency hampers the few who might feel inclined towards, or rather would dare risk, speaking out against the present situation. The significant increases in consumer prices for privatised or soon to be privatised utilities, services and infrastructure have been reluctantly accepted by consumers without much public dissent, except in the case of the Cheras tolls just before the 1990 general election. The staggered nature of such price increases as well as of the privatisations themselves render mass protest against privatisation most unlikely.

However, when the cumulative effects of these privatisations are finally realised at the public level, it is quite possible that the political consequences may undermine the mandate to rule of those responsible.

REFERENCES

Amsden, A. (1989), *Asia's Next Giant: South Korea and late industrialization*, New York: Oxford University Press.

Jomo K.S. (1990), *Growth and Structural Change in the Malaysian Economy*, London: Macmillan.

Kennedy, L. (1991), 'Liberalization, privatization and the politics of patronage in Malaysian telecommunications', paper presented at the 41st Annual Conference of the International Communications Association, Chicago, Ill., 24 May.

Mahathir, M. (1970), *The Malay Dilemma*, Singapore: Donald Moore.

——, (1976), *Menghadapi Cabaran*, Kuala Lumpur: Penerbit Utusan Melayu.

——, (1991), *The Way Forward*, Kuala Lumpur: ISIS.

Malaysia (1985), *Guidelines on Privatisation*, Kuala Lumpur: Economic Planning Unit.

Malaysia (1991a), *Privatisation Masterplan*, Kuala Lumpur: Economic Planning Unit.

Malaysia (1991b), *The Second Outline Perspective Plan, 1991–2000*, Kuala Lumpur: Economic Planning Unit.

Malaysia (1991c), *Sixth Malaysia Plan, 1991–1995*, Kuala Lumpur: Economic Planning Unit.

Mustapha Johan, A. and K. A. Shamsulbahriah (eds) (1987), *Penswastaan: Kebajikan pekerja atau untung kapitalis*, Kuala Lumpur: MBPbK.

Rodan, G. (1989), *The Political Economy of Singapore's Industrialization*, London: Macmillan.

Sheriff, M. K. (1991), 'Privatization: performance, problems and prospects', in L. K. Hock and S. Nagaraj (eds), *The Malaysian Economy Beyond 1990*, Kuala Lumpur: Malaysian Economic Association.

Wade, R. (1990), *Governing The Market: Economic theory and the role of government in East Asian industrialization*, Princeton, NJ: Princeton University Press.

7

GOVERNMENT CORPORATIONS AND GOVERNMENT MONOPOLIES OF AGRICULTURAL PRODUCTS

Yoshihara Kunio

THAILAND IN THE MID-1950s

In the mid-1950s, Thailand had numerous government corporations in various sectors. The World Bank mission which visited the country at that time reported the situation as follows:

> [T]he Government is . . . involved directly or indirectly in a large number of commercial and other industrial enterprises. In manufacturing it monopolizes tobacco, potable and industrial spirits and playing cards; it dominates timber, sugar, paper, gunny bags and minerals other than tin; it has large interests in cement, glass, pharmaceuticals, batteries, tin, tanneries and textiles, sometimes in direct competition with established producers; and finally, it operates a number of small plants making such diverse products as shoe polish, alum, rubber footwear, metal cabinets, paper clips, ceramics, and many others. In all, it controls some 60 establishments (including 15 distilleries), of which perhaps 40 can be classed as large in the sense of employing more than 50 workers.[1]

During the period of absolute monarchy, the Thai government was hardly involved in business ventures. The only exceptions were the two companies the king participated in: Siam Commercial Bank and Siam Cement. Under the guidance of conservative British Financial Advisers, the Thai government largely restricted its role to providing general government services (maintenance of peace and order, defence, education, etc.); building infrastructure (primarily railways); and collecting taxes to pay for these. Since it was afraid of getting into financial trouble—which could be an excuse for foreign intervention—the government did little in the way of developmental functions. The economy was left primarily to Chinese merchants and Thai peasants.

The situation changed with the Revolution of 1932. The Revolutionary

Source: *The Nation and Economic Growth: The Philippines and Thailand*, Singapore: Oxford University Press, 1994, pp. 81–104.

Party, whose leadership consisted of Western-educated civil and military bureaucrats, stripped the king of absolute power, but retained him as a constitutional monarch. To justify such a drastic action (drastic at that time in the Thai context), they had to explain the benefits that would be brought about under their new government. They promised, among other things, to bring the economy under Thai control. In their view, the Chinese—at least those not integrated into Thai society (the first-generation Chinese and those of the second generation who resisted integration)—were not Thai, and the economy was underdeveloped because foreigners were controlling it. They reasoned that if the economy was brought under Thai control, it would improve. They therefore encouraged Thais to go into trade and industry, but because the Thai entrepreneurial class was virtually non-existent, this strategy did not work well. As an alternative, they soon created a large number of government corporations.

By the mid-1950s, this economic experiment was developing problems. Most government and government-backed corporations were losing money, and thus draining the Treasury. Unlike some other South-East Asian countries, the government did not have the natural resources to indefinitely finance these money-losing ventures. The most notorious case was that of National Economic Development Corp. (NEDCOL), a private company set up in 1954 by a number of prominent people connected with the War Veterans Organization. Its authorized capital was B50 million, but only B3 million was paid up by private shareholders. Most of its capital came from loans, especially foreign loans, guaranteed by the government. By the end of 1957, when the first loan repayment was due, NEDCOL had become bankrupt with a total debt of about B700 million (of which $30 million was foreign loans).[2]

POLICY REVERSAL UNDER SARIT

The conservative economic bureaucrats centred around the Bank of Thailand who wanted the government to leave entrepreneurial activities to private initiative engineered a World Bank mission. After studying the situation in the country, the mission recommended that the governtnent rely on private enterprise for economic development (industrial development in particular). This recommendation was adopted by the newly established Sarit Thanarat government, which in the late 1950s began disengaging itself from the financial, commercial, and industrial sectors of the economy. Thereafter, the government restricted direct involvement largely to the public utilities sector (railways, air transportation, telecommunication, electric power generation and distribution, etc.).

Events did not proceed exactly as the conservative economic bureaucrats wanted. In the late 1980s, there were two government corporations losing money heavily: the State Railway of Thailand and the Bangkok Mass Transit

Authority. These two bodies provide transportation for the masses, thus raising fares to cover expenses was politically difficult. Their losses were at least partly the result of the populist demand initiated by student and union leaders and supported by publicity-seeking politicians, often the case in a developing country.

Fortunately for Thailand, the situation did not get out of control. Most other state enterprises were earning profits, and as a whole, they were not a direct drain on the Treasury. In contrast, a number of government corporations in the Philippines were a big drain on the Treasury. The government had to heavily subsidize, for example, the National Power Corp., National Electrification Administration, Metropolitan Waterworks and Sewerage, and National Food Authority.

In Thailand, although Sarit decided in the late 1950s when he became Prime Minister that the government should withdraw from the economy, some government corporations remained in manufacturing and finance. One such example is the Petroleum Authority of Thailand, which is engaged in oil and gas exploration, refining, petrochemical manufacturing, and distribution. But in manufacturing, Thai government involvement was less than that of its counterpart in the Philippines. At the beginning of martial law, the Philippine National Oil Company was set up to play a role similar to that of the Petroleum Authority of Thailand. However, compared with the former, the latter is better run; normally, the Petroleum Authority of Thailand sets up joint ventures with private companies, and there is greater economic rationality in these operations.[3] Also unlike in the Philippines where the government-owned National Steel Corp. has a monopoly over major steel products, all steel companies in Thailand are privately owned. However, there are still several small government corporations undertaking industrial production in Thailand, but their negative effects on the economy are not large. The biggest of them is Thailand Tobacco Monopoly. The Philippine government, through the National Development Company, is a co-investor in fertilizer production (Philippine Phosphate Fertilizer Corp.) and copper smelting (Philippine Associated Smelting and Refining Corp.).

THE FINANCIAL SECTOR: CONTRASTS

In Thailand

The biggest difference between the Thai and the Philippine attitude with regard to government intervention can be seen in the financial sector. In the late 1980s, four Thai institutions were considered government specialized banks: the Government Savings Bank, Government Housing Bank, Bank of Agriculture and Agricultural Cooperatives (BAAC), and Industrial Finance Corp. of Thailand (IFCT). They were small banks, accounting for about 11 per cent of the total assets of financial institutions. Of these four, the

Government Savings Bank is the largest, having half of their total assets. Its deposits were invested largely in government bonds and promissory notes. The Government Housing Bank channelled its funds into government housing schemes for low-income people and government employees, while the BAAC lent money to the agricultural sector. The IFCT was the smallest of the four, and could not be really considered a government bank as in the late 1980s about 85 per cent of its equity was owned by the private sector. It was being run essentially as a private bank engaged in long-term lending. For these reasons, there was little room for cronies or government-connected entrepreneurs to obtain large loans from these banks. The only exception may be the BAAC which lent money to large agri-businesses, but no major problems have surfaced even here.

Khrung Thai Bank, the government-owned commercial bank which was created in 1966 by merging two badly run commercial banks (Provincial Bank and Agricultural Bank), remains a government bank, although it is not clear why the government keeps it so. As it did with the First Bangkok City Bank in the mid-1980s, the Bank of Thailand could have restructured its ownership by inviting new private investors, but it gave control of the bank to the Ministry of Finance. In the late 1980s, Khrung Thai Bank took over the trouble-ridden Sayam Bank and became the second largest commercial bank (surpassing Thai Farmers Bank), accounting for about 15 per cent of the total assets of commercial banks and about 10 per cent of the total assets of all financial institutions. Thus, if Khrung Thai Bank was added to the four specialized government banks, the share of government financial institutions was about 21 per cent.

Khrung Thai Bank had some similarities to government banks in the Philippines. In the mid-1980s, it had a large portfolio of non-performing assets. Large borrowers which could not pay back their loans at that time were Cha-am Pineapple Cannery Co., the Metro Group (a diversified commodities-trading conglomerate), and Siam Vidhya (a real estate company). Their indebtedness was reportedly as much as B10 billion ($340 million at the then exchange rates). These companies were headed by politically connected entrepreneurs. Cha-am Pineapple Cannery's chairman, Colonel Phol Rerngprasertvit, was a Member of Parliament at that time and a leader of the small opposition party, United Democratic Party. The bank was being run bureaucratically, and could not have been as large as it was without large deposits from government corporations (which accounted for about half its deposits). The loss it suffered from bad loans to the three companies was contained as they made up less than 10 per cent of its assets. It even had enough discipline left to file criminal charges against Tamchai Kambhato, who had approved loans beyond the limits of his authority during his five-year term which ended in January 1986.[4] In July 1992, after he was sentenced to 20 years in prison, he immediately petitioned the Court of Appeals, and of this writing, the case is still pending.

In the Philippines

Philippine government financial institutions played a much more important role in the sector. In the early 1980s, a Filipino economist described their position in the financial sector as follows:

> Another important feature of the [financial] system is the presence of a large public sector—the Philippine National Bank (PNB), a commercial bank, the Development Bank of the Philippines (DBP), an investment bank, and the semi-public rural and development banks. The last two are saving banks with a development-oriented lending objective. The PNB has been the largest commercial bank whose assets comprise from 20 to 30 percent of the total commercial banking sector. The DBP assets have been about 15 percent of total banking assets. Counting [semi-public] rural and development banks, the share in assets of the public and semi-public banks amount to more than half of the total.[5]

In the last five years of President Ferdinand Marcos's rule, the operations of both the PNB and the DBP expanded rapidly. Between 1980 and 1985, PNB's assets doubled from ₱38 billion to ₱76 billion, while DBP's assets increased more, from ₱27 billion to ₱72 billion. Then, after Marcos fled the country, under the new Corazon Aquino administration, these government banks went through massive rehabilitation. The new management team which took over the DBP reported the situation as follows:

> During the first semester of 1986, we found that the DBP was in a dismal state, financially and otherwise, resulting from mistakes of the past. Foremost among its problems was the massive amount of Non-Performing Assets still carried in its books which accounted for more than 90 per cent of its portfolio. Another was the large and unwieldy organizational structure which at the very least needed to be trimmed down and streamlined.[6]

The state of affairs in the PNB was not much better than in the DBP. The government took over the non-performing assets of both banks to put them on a financially sound basis. Non-performing assets of ₱110 billion in book value were transferred to the government, which also took over ₱117 billion worth of their liabilities.[7] As a result, both became smaller banks. PNB's assets were halved in 1986, and its share of total assets in the banking sector declined from 26 to 12 per cent between 1985 and 1987, though it still maintained the leading position in the commercial banking sector. DBP's assets were drastically reduced, from ₱72 billion to about ₱10 billion between 1985 and 1986. In size, the DBP became comparable to the larger private commercial banks. Privatization of the PNB began in 1987, and in 1991, 30 per cent of its equity was held by the private sector.

Both the PNB and the DBP had faced some problems before martial law, but they were not serious ones. After martial law was declared, they began losing economic rationality almost completely. Marcos needed to dispense favours to a large number of his supporters throughout the country, not just his cronies; he used the two institutions to meet their financial needs. Some of them, of course, gave him a certain percentage of the loans they received from the banks or a share in their projects. Money came easy for them. A large number of new projects were 'cooked up' just to obtain money from the two banks; often, it did not matter whether or not the projects were economically viable. By launching projects, they made money, and if the projects floundered later on, they could be given to the banks. For example, in the mid-1970s, although the sugar market did not look good, a number of sugar mills were built by Marcos's supporters with money from the two banks (primarily the PNB). These projects, of course, turned out to be non-viable.

If the banks had been using the private sector's money, they would have been more careful. But a large part of their funds came from the government, the Central Bank, or foreign financial institutions (with the government's guarantee). If the money from these sources was not enough, the banks guaranteed foreign loans to the private sector. Since the PNB was a commercial bank, its lending operations were not as liberal as those of the DBP, but as a government bank too, it was also expected to play the part of an investment banker, like the DBP. Already in the pre-war period, the PNB was performing such a role in the sugar sector (by financing construction of sugar mills), but its developmental function broadened during the Marcos period. Besides diversifying its lending activities (so that Marcos's associates such as Ricardo Silverio, the assembler of Toyota cars, could borrow from it), it also bought equity through its subsidiary, the National Investment Development Corp. The DBP was in worse shape than the PNB because it gave large 'behest loans'—given at the behest of Marcos—to his cronies and continued to do so even after they began experiencing difficulties in the early 1980s. Its funds came almost exclusively from the government, the Central Bank, and foreign borrowing.[8] Even if it had gone bankrupt, the public would not have been seriously affected as they were not its major depositors. It was easier for economic rationality to break down in such a bank.

Not all the non-performing assets taken over by the government were useless. The Assets Privatization Trust (APT), which took over these assets, sold a large number of them and remitted about ₱18 billion to the Treasury. The APT had also taken over some assets from the Philippine Export and Foreign Loan Guarantee Corp. (a government corporation set up by Marcos, essentially for guaranteeing foreign borrowings) and the National Development Co., thus not all assets sold came from the DBP and the PNB, but their assets constituted the bulk of APT's assets. The APT recovered about 15 per cent of the non-performing assets of the two government financial institutions, with some assets yet to be privatized. These are the more difficult assets to dispose of, but the APT may be able to sell some of them eventually and remit more to the Treasury. But the fact remains that a large sum, probably about ₱95 billion, was lost by the PNB and the DBP.[9]

Undoubtedly, Marcos was the most culpable in causing such huge losses. But those bank executives who often executed the so-called 'behest loans' were accessories to his criminal acts, and the new Aquino government should have filed charges against them. But it was more concerned with the 'big fish', and had enough problems dealing with them. The wheel of justice turns slowly in the Philippines, and no 'big fish' have been convicted yet. Compared with them, the bank executives were 'small fish', and the government has not filed any charges against them. None took proprietary interests in the PNB or the DBP nor did they protect their integrity. Everything is blamed on Marcos, but he needed collaborators to wreak such serious damage on the country. After he was overthrown, the collaborators, big or small, should have been tried in court, as a warning to others. PNB's ₱2–billion loan to the Construction & Development Corp. of the Philippines—owned by Marcos's crony Rodolfo Cuenca and in which Marcos had a stake—was a clear violation of the rules by PNB executives since it exceeded a single borrower's limit, which was 15 per cent of its net worth.[10]

The Thai government filed criminal charges against the head of Khrung Thai Bank for the losses incurred by the bank in the first half of the 1980s. In the late 1910s, during the colonial period in the Philippines, the American administration convicted and jailed Venacio Concepcion, the first Filipino head of the PNB, for the large losses of the bank ($30 million, a very large sum at that time); he had granted fat loans to many of his friends with little collateral in return. Much of the discipline of the Philippine bureaucracy in the early post-war years was created during the American period, but this started crumbling as a new generation of Filipino politicians took over the country. The degeneration reached an acme during Marcos's martial law period. The PNB and DBP debacle in the mid-1980s was a part of this decline of discipline in the government bureaucracy.

ELECTRIC POWER GENERATION: EGAT AND THE NPC

In the Philippines, the problems of government corporations were not confined to the financial sector. The differences in approach between Philippine and Thai government corporations were most clearly demonstrated in electric power generation and air transportation. The government corporation Electricity Generating Authority of Thailand (EGAT) has a monopoly on electric power generation. There have been no serious complaints about EGAT; rather it is known for its record of efficiency and profitability. In the Philippines, however, the National Power Corp. (NPC), which has a monopoly on power generation, has often been criticized, its reputation reaching a nadir in 1992. A power shortage began developing towards the end of 1989, and worsened in mid-1992 when the country began experiencing daily brownouts lasting four or more hours. It is estimated that in the two and a half years since 1990 the damage to the national economy caused by brownouts has amounted to over ₱100 billion. In November 1992, President Fidel Ramos said, '[E]lectric brownouts . . . have cut down the productivity of manufacturing enterprises by nearly a third.'[11] In the first 9 months of 1992, exports declined by 2.45 per cent and gross domestic product by 0.41 per cent (however, the gross national product increased by 0.91 per cent largely due to the remittances of Filipino contract workers overseas).

The power shortage became critical only recently, therefore it is not a major factor for the poor performance of the Philippine economy in the 40-year period ending in 1991. However, the NPC's problems are indicative of the problems of other government corporations. But a couple of them are unique to the NPC.

One is the question of environmental protection. Given a liberal intellectual atmosphere and broad exposure to English writings which have increasingly become environmentally conscious in recent years, it is not surprising that the country has produced strong environmentalist groups. Since thermal power plants tend to cause air and water pollution, hydroelectric plants environmental disruption, and nuclear power plants safety problems, it has become difficult in the past several years for a power project to get clearance from the Department of Environment and Natural Resources, which is under the strong influence of environmentalist groups. New power projects were opposed for one environmental reason or another, and no new major power plants have been built since the end of the Marcos administration. The 630 megawatt nuclear power plant in Bataan, which was to increase the country's total generation capacity by over 10 per cent, was almost completed in 1986 when new President Corazon Aquino stopped it partly because of environmental and safety concerns. Anti-nuclear groups have been adamantly opposed to its reopening. If the government tried to push through a power plant project over the objection of environmentalists, the latter got in touch with their counterparts in developed countries which were financing it (the Philippines was too short of foreign exchanges to carry it out alone) to put pressure on their governments.

The second problem, while not entirely unique to the NPC, cannot be too generalized either. Prior to the 1970s, the NPC was in charge of hydroelectric power generation, primarily for the provinces. But after martial law was declared, it took over the thermal power plants of the Manila Electric Co. (Meralco), and electric power generation became its monopoly. If Meralco had kept their thermal plants and kept expanding as it did in the 1960s, the situation might have been better today, but the political power balance in the early 1970s did not allow it. Meralco was controlled by Eugenio Lopez, Marcos's political enemy at that time. The Lopezes (Eugenio and his brother Fernando, Vice-President under Marcos) belonged to the old oligarchs whom

Marcos wanted to purge from his New Society; hence, Meralco had to be taken away from them. Power generation and distribution were separated; Meralco retained the latter function and the company was given to Imelda Marcos's family while the NPC took over the former.[12]

Not so unique to the NPC is the charge that the Bataan nuclear power plant was a project tainted with corruption. Its major contractor was Westinghouse Electric Corp. When the Philippine government was leaning towards another contractor (General Electric), Westinghouse approached Marcos through its Filipino agent Herminio Disini, a crony whose wife is a cousin of Imelda as well as her personal physician. Westinghouse paid Disini $17 million as a sales fee, and part of it (probably, a large part of it) went to Marcos as a bribe. Marcos seems to have taken a certain percentage from all major government-related projects, including this nuclear power plant. This factor plus the tendency of bribers to overcharge their clients inflated the costs of government projects. For the nuclear plant, it is said that the government paid twice as much as other governments did for a similar plant.[13] Soon after Aquino became President, she stopped the project, and sued Westinghouse for bribery. In this project, which did not produce any power, the NPC incurred a foreign debt of $2 billion to be paid over the 10-year period ending in 1995.[14] Under martial law, like many other government corporations, the NPC did not have clear control over its operations.

A more common problem the NPC faced as a government corporation was the lack of revenues for the maintenance and expansion of its plants. It could set rates on its own (they were not set by the Energy Regulatory Board which regulated energy prices), but any attempt to increase rates was opposed by politicians who were backed by populist groups such as trade unions. Their thinking was that electric power (or any public utility service) should be made available cheaply with government subsidies. But with the budget in deficit, that was not possible. During the Marcos period, his solution was to borrow from abroad, but this could not go on indefinitely. When foreign creditors found out that the country was heavily indebted and that there was a risk of default, foreign loans were no longer easily available, and government projects, such as power plants, had difficulties in raising finance. The only way to keep expanding the power supply to meet increasing demand is to make consumers (household, industrial, and commercial users) pay for the costs. If this principle is not clearly established, privatization of power plants, which is gaining popularity now, will be futile.[15]

Aquino appointed Ernesto Aboitiz as head of the NPC in 1987. Many people say that he was an incompetent administrator. He was not, however, inexperienced in running a power company. Before coming to the NPC, he had managed one such company in Davao City in southern Mindanao. It is said that during Aquino's presidential campaign in 1986, Aboitiz was her active supporter and that his NPC appointment was her reward for his support (in the election, Davao City voted overwhelmingly for Aquino). But his critics contended that operating a large organization like the NPC required more capability than running a small power company and they charged that he did not know what to do with it. They say that if he had wanted to expand the power supply, the government was willing to finance it, but he did not do anything to prevent the shortage which was forecasted. Some even charge that he deliberately caused the power shortage because it was good for his family's business which included selling generators. But probably from his point of view, the NPC was too politicized and undisciplined (with so many employees and so many entitlements) an organization for an outsider like him to put right in a short time. In the past, the head of the NPC had changed frequently, being a political appointee.

The NPC's malaise was a result of its failure to develop a strong bureaucracy, a common fate of government corporations and administrative agencies in the Philippines, with the NPC being one of the worst. One journalist, fed up with the frequent brownouts in 1992, wrote that 'besides being callous and shameless, it [NPC] is also grossly negligent, extravagant and incompetent'.[16]

CONTRASTING PHILIPPINE AIRLINES AND THAI INTERNATIONAL

Philippine Airlines (PAL) was another badly run government corporation. Many people used to say jokingly that PAL stood for 'Planes Always Late'. International travellers tended not to take PAL if there was an alternative airline flying the same route. During the Marcos period, PAL passengers were left stranded abroad, sometimes for days, while their aircraft were diverted to fly Imelda and her entourage. Sometimes an extra jumbo jet was sent along for the luggage. During the Aquino administration, PAL's performance improved, but in the year ending March 1991, only about two-thirds of its international flights could leave within 15 minutes of schedule.[17] The Aquino administration took over its losses amounting to $520 million to make it saleable to private investors.

In contrast, Thai Airways International, owned by the Thai government, is a model airline of a developing country. It was one of the 24 top airlines which received super excellent classification in 1991 from the International Travel Research Institute.[18] It has earned profits during most of its 32-year history; 1990/1 was its twenty-seventh consecutive year of profit, contrasting sharply with PAL's dismal financial record in the past 20 years. Thai International expanded its fleet by buying new aircraft according to plan, and by the end of 1991, had reduced the average age of its aircraft to 5.6 years (one of the youngest fleets in the industry). It has become a full partner in AMADEUS, the computerized global travel distribution system which feeds information on the airline's schedule, tariff, and reservations to 30,000 travel trade terminals, world-wide. In 1992, having met the listing requirements of the Securities Exchange of Thailand (SET) (which include profit records in the recent past), its shares were listed on the SET.

One of PAL's problems was that it had to serve many domestic destinations because the Philippines is an island nation. Thailand built a good road system so that land transportation was a good substitute for air conveyance within the radius of a few hundred kilometres from Bangkok. For outlying areas also, there was no strong need to create many destinations, since it was enough to link Bangkok to a small number of regional cities, to which nearby small towns were connected by good roads. In 1991, PAL was serving about 43 domestic destinations, twice Thai International's domestic destinations. The domestic tariffs were controlled by the Civil Aeronautic Board (CAB), which tended to set tariffs so low that PAL could not make profits on most routes even with full capacity. The problem was similar to the one the NPC faced with its regulatory agency.

PAL's problem, however, was more deep-seated than that. PAL has a history that is 20 years longer than Thai International, but it is more unstable as an organization because ownership changed a few times and new management did a poor job of running the company. Originally, it was privately organized and managed by Andres Soriano, head of Soriano y Cia, under a contract. (Soriano's style was for Soriano y Cia to become a minority shareholder of a company and obtain the contract for its management. In this way, Soriano successfully built a few major companies, such as San Miguel Corp.) In the 1950s, the Philippine government became PAL's majority stockholder. At first, because of Soriano's good relations with the country's presidents, the airline's operation continued smoothly but in early 1961, he resigned from his position as president. The immediate reason was two airplane accidents at the end of 1960, but he also seemed to have become fed up with increasing attacks by nationalists on him. Though he was born in the Philippines and had served as a captain in its Army and as Secretary of Finance in President Manuel Quezon's government-in-exile in Washington, he became an American citizen soon after the Pacific War. Together with his American friends, he managed PAL, an arrangement which was, however, disagreeable to Filipino nationalists.[19]

After Soriano resigned, the government took over the management of PAL, and soon after Diosdado Macapagal became President, he gave control of it to Benigno Toda, one of the major financiers of his presidential campaign. Toda eventually bought the government's equity and became PAL's controlling shareholder. PAL was once again a privately owned and managed company, but this did not do much good for PAL. Toda was not interested in building up the airline as a business organization. Instead, he was milking it for his family businesses. For example, his flagship company, Rubicon, had a management contract with PAL, receiving 5 per cent of its profits before taxes.[20] In 1970, he had a conflict with the pilots, who eventually staged a mass resignation, thus making it necessary to reduce domestic and international flights.

Imelda Marcos often utilized PAL's planes when she went abroad. It is said that soon after Marcos asked Toda to send him a bill for her use of the aircraft—Toda sent a bill but not for the full amount (reported to have been around $6 million)—an angry Imelda made sure that he lost the company. But a more plausible reason was probably that the company was not under good management and had to be restructured to meet the increasing demand for international travel in the mid-1970s. In 1977, the government took over the company and made Roman Cruz, head of the Government Service Insurance System as well as one of Imelda's lackeys, its executive officer.

During Cruz's term, PAL incurred large losses which are often attributed to his incompetency.[21] When he took over the company, PAL needed a large infusion of capital for building up its fleet, for this he borrowed from abroad.[22] In 1979, the second oil crisis sent the Philippine economy (affected further by political instability) into a tailspin. Domestic operations were affected by this economic downturn, as well as by the inability to obtain fare increases from the regulatory agency (CAB) despite the increase in aviation fuel prices. The peso devaluation at this time was another source of difficulty since PAL had borrowed heavily in foreign currencies and planned to use its peso revenues for partial debt servicing. Imelda's indiscriminate use of PAL's aircraft continued to be a problem.[23]

A large part of the losses was probably due to circumstances beyond Cruz's control. His culpability was a little different from that of the executives of the PNB and the DBP, who often knowingly created non-performing assets. Cruz nevertheless seems to have been a corrupt official. In June 1985, the *San Jose Mercury News* (which exposed Marcos's wealth in the United States) reported that he is one of several government officials who had 'huge' hidden wealth there. (Another is Geronimo Velasco, Minister of Energy, who had supervised the NPC.)

Ironically, the better-run Thai International was always headed by the Air Force Chief. Many government corporations were headed by former military officers, but Thai International was one of the few headed by an active-duty military officer. Many retired officers went to Thai International from the Air Force (in the early 1990s, at least half of its top 24 managers were said to have come from the armed forces, mostly from the Air Force). One might suppose therefore that it was one of the badly run, military-controlled companies observed in developing countries. But the Thai military were careful about management. In its first decade, the flights were only within Asia. Furthermore, it invited the Scandinavian Air System (SAS) to be a shareholder, and was run under SAS tutelage. In the early 1970s, after gaining experience in regional flights, it started intercontinental flights. A few years later, it bought out the SAS holding, but maintained a co-operation agreement with it, under which some SAS personnel continued to work for Thai International.

The advantage of Thai International was in its organizational stability. But as a military-controlled company, it had problems of its own. Factionalism within the Air Force was sometimes reflected in the power struggle among the top management. The professional managers who rose from the ranks were not happy with military officers occupying high positions as a sinecure. Furthermore, corruption was a recurrent problem. For example, the management under Air Force Chief Kaset Rojananil (who had been serving as chairman since 1989) was accused in early 1992 of malpractices ranging from costly land acquisition to questionable selection of aircraft engines. But the Thai Air Force gave stability and protection to Thai International, and by relying a great deal on professional expertise, it has built a fairly well-run airline.

THE RATIONALE FOR GOVERNMENT MONOPOLIES

During the martial law period in the Philippines, President Ferdinand Marcos created several monopolies, of which the two most disreputable were the National Sugar Trading Corp. (Nasutra) and United Coconut Oil Mills (Unicom). Since their products were mostly exported, the rationale behind these monopolies was the strengthening of the country's bargaining position in the world market, thus bringing greater benefits to domestic producers. Sugar-cane producers and millers and coconut farmers were supposed to benefit from these monopolies, but the results were otherwise.

Marcos was not a poorly educated military dictator in a developing country, but he may not have had a good understanding of how the economy works. In particular, he may not have understood that it is competition which drives the economy. Competition does not have to be atomistic. Even in an oligopolistic industry, if competition prevails between large firms, the results can be beneficial to the economy. Since these large firms emerge through competition over time, they usually have an internal mechanism to keep themselves efficient. But an artificially created monopoly is prone to fail due to mismanagement, or if it continues to exist, it becomes a burden on the economy. Nasutra and Unicom were such examples.

If Marcos understood the merit of competition, he probably did not see much importance in the role of middlemen. There is no doubt that Unicom in particular greatly simplified the trading channels for coconut. Since the industry was dominated by the Chinese, although he was probably not anti-Chinese, it was politically easier to get rid of the middlemen. Undoubtedly, there is little merit in a fragmented distribution channel. If it can be simplified by the emergence of large traders, distribution may become more efficient, but competition between them must remain. Otherwise, a large trader becomes a monopolist (or monopsonist), and then even if distribution becomes better organized, producers get lower prices and/or consumers have to pay higher prices.

Unicom could not determine the price of its product (coconut oil) in the international market because of the availability of substitutes (such as palm oil and soybean oil), although that was its original purpose. As the dominant buyer in most areas in the Philippines, it became a monopsonist and depressed its purchasing prices. After Unicom was formed, the spread between domestic and export prices of copra became larger. In 1979, when Unicom started operation, the spread was about 10 per cent, but in the next year it rose to 26 per cent, and remained at this level in the following two years.[24] Since the spread was about 10 per cent originally, the spread beyond that could be considered as the loss to coconut farmers due to the formation of Unicom.[25]

NASUTRA

There was a political purpose to the creation of Nasutra as well. Martial law was declared in order to create a New Society, which meant that the Old Society, which had opposed Marcos, had to be destroyed. Sugar was the financial basis of many politicians in the Old Society because as a major export commodity, wealth was created in the industry and used to fund political activities. More specifically, because the allocation of American quotas, which gave preferential treatment to Philippine sugar until 1974, was often a political decision and because the Philippine National Bank (PNB), a government financial institution, was heavily involved in the financing of the industry, sugar became a politicized industry, prompting sugar barons to get into politics. Many of the politicians who represented the sugar industry were Marcos's political enemies: the Lopez brothers (Eugenio and Fernando) were prime examples.

The sugar monopoly was probably a means to bring the industry under government control. The best way of doing this was to give a trading monopoly to its major financier, the PNB. This is what the government did initially. For sugar trading, the PNB set up a subsidiary called Philippine Exchange Co. (Philex). Philex mismanaged trading and incurred large losses, and was thus dissolved. Sugar trading was then put under the newly created Philippine Sugar Commission (Philsucom), of which Nasutra was a trading arm. Marcos put Roberto Benedicto, one of his closest cronies, in charge of Philsucom. Benedicto, who had headed the PNB from 1966 to 1970, also kept a careful watch on the PNB, because its loans were an important means by which Philsucom kept the industry under control. Benedicto also went into banking on his own. He bought a controlling interest in the Republic Bank and renamed it Republic Planters Bank (RPB). Given low-interest loans from the Central Bank and designated as the depository of the sugar industry by a presidential decree, the RPB quickly became one of the largest commercial banks (the fifth largest in 1980 in terms of assets).

The shortage of sugar in the domestic market gave the government an excuse to take over sugar trading in 1974–the same year that saw the end of the American quota system which paid higher prices to Philippine sugar than did the international market (about 38 per cent higher in the 1960s).[26] Fortunately, it was the year when the international sugar market was recording the highest prices in its history (about 65 cents per kilogram). Sugar producers had been required to meet the domestic demand at the prices set by the government, but with the surge of prices in the international market, they did not want to sell their sugar in the country. As a result, the domestic market suffered a shortage, prompting the government to step in.[27]

Philex had made money at first. Since sugar prices were going up in the international market, the sugar it bought in the country could be sold abroad at higher prices. At that time, the question was to whom the profits belonged. Many sugar producers thought that Philex was their trading agency, and thus, profits should be handed over to them. But this was probably not what Marcos had intended. In the following years, however, Philex incurred huge losses, and there was no more money to distribute. Sugar prices came down to 45 cents per kilogram in 1975, 25 cents in 1976, and 18 cents in 1977. Philex probably did not understand the volatility of the international market at that time. Since sugar prices fell in the mid-1970s, it ended up with sugar for which it had paid higher prices, and it kept the sugar, hoping that prices would go up. But prices did not rebound, and when it began unloading the large stock it had accumulated (probably over 1 million tons), it had to take substantial losses (moreover, some stock had deteriorated due to poor storage facilities).[28]

Nasutra, which took over sugar distribution from Philex in 1977, strengthened its role by setting up offices in London and New York (the two world centres of sugar trading), getting directly into the transport, bulk storage, and handling of sugar, and even expanding into sugar milling and refining.[29] Complaints about Nasutra were not about its losses, as in the case of Philex, though sugar prices were volatile around 1980. Probably, having learnt some lessons from the earlier Philex debacle, Nasutra was more cautious about speculation. Instead, the complaints were that it underpaid sugar producers. It was said that 'while . . . Nasutra sold at $63.70 per picul in the 1979–80 period, it bought at $18.16; when it sold at $40.05, it paid $14.20'.[30] There may have been some such profitable operations for Nasutra, but the average spread between its purchase and sales prices was probably much smaller. Undoubtedly, however, Nasutra was a milking operation for Marcos and his cronies (especially, Benedicto). One study estimates that during 1972–82, the net income loss for sugar producers was about 30 per cent.[31]

UNICOM

The coconut industry was organized differently from the sugar industry. Unlike Nasutra, Unicom was heavily involved in production (coconut oil); in the case of sugar, processing was done primarily by private sugar mills.

Furthermore, Unicom did not have complete control over distribution as Nasutra did with sugar. Unicom did not have much control over the direct export of desiccated coconut or copra. It was the dominant manufacturer of coconut oil, controlling 80–90 per cent of the country's milling capacity, making it a dominant player in the coconut industry, which, like the sugar industry, was very much export-oriented. In the 1970s, coconut oil was the dominant coconut export; in 1980, it comprised 85 per cent of total coconut exports.[32] In the earlier decades, coconut oil was less important, but as the Board of Investments (BOI) gave incentives to coconut oil mills to add more value to their exports, a number of new mills were created in the 1970s, and coconut oil became the dominant coconut export.

The ease with which Unicom could establish such a dominant position in a short time was due to the rapid expansion of milling capacity which took place under BOI incentives. Furthermore, in 1979, a number of newly established mills were facing difficulties because coconut oil prices did not increase much despite a large increase in copra prices. They were glad to be bought out. In addition, the presidential letter of instruction which led to the formation of Unicom stipulated that it control at least 55 per cent of the country's oil milling capacity. This made large foreign-affiliated oil producers (such as Legaspi Oil and Granexport) vulnerable to take-over. The provision of the letter of instruction that 'the government shall give its total support for [Unicom] which includes financial and other assistance' also made it difficult for private mills to operate independently of Unicom. For example, the domestic price of coconut oil was set by the government, and if subsidies were required, they were restricted to firms which co-operated with Unicom. Three private mills (Interco Group, Southern Island Oil Mills, and Lu Do & Lu Ym) became participating mills under the co-ordination scheme of Unicom.

Criticisms of government intervention in the coconut industry during the martial law period were not confined to Unicom. Another major issue was the levy on copra and its use. This started, however, before martial law, with the so-called Cocofund levy. In 1971, a law was passed to collect a fixed levy (55 centavo per 100 kilograms of copra) for a period of 10 years starting in 1972. The levy was to be used to set up the Coconut Investment Co. to be owned by the coconut farmers of the Philippine Coconut Producers Federation, Inc. (Cocofed), which would invest the levy in the processing and trading of copra. It was reasoned that coconut farmers would gain under this scheme since they would share in the profits of the processing and trading operations (which othewise would go to middlemen).

The Cocofund levy was modest, but in August 1973 during martial law, a much larger tax (the Coconut Consumers Stabilization Fund (CCSF) levy) at the rate of ₱60 per kilogram was imposed on copra. Initially, it was intended as a temporary levy to stabilize the domestic prices of coconut-based products through subsidies when the world price of copra rose abruptly during 1973–4. Even after copra prices had stabilized, the levy remained, and became a sort of a development tax on the industry (administered by the government agency Philippine Coconut Authority, PCA). Part of the CCSF levy (₱20 per 100 kilograms of copra) was earmarked for the industry's development programmes, including the nation-wide coconut hybrid replanting programme and the acquisition of a bank for coconut farmers.

In 1975, the PCA was authorized to buy a small bank, the First United Bank, by using the CCSF levy. The PCA paid about ₱29 million for 72 per cent of its equity, and renamed it United Coconut Producers Bank (UCPB). Eduardo 'Danding' Cojuangco, another of Marcos's close cronies, negotiated the acquisition and was made president of the bank. Later, in order to meet the Central Bank's ₱100 million minimum paid-up capital requirement for a universal bank (a commercial bank allowed to undertake diversified functions, such as selling securities and undertaking equity investment in industrial firms), the PCA poured an additional ₱80 million of the CCSF levy into the bank. With this increase in capital and as the depository of all coconut levies, the UCPB quickly became one of the largest commercial banks (the seventh largest in terms of assets in 1980). With the existence of the UCPB and a large CCSF levy, what was envisioned when the Cocofund levy was imposed became a reality. In 1978, the Coconut Industry Investment Fund (CIIF) was created with part of the CCSF levy, and it was put under the control of the UCPB. The next year, the UCPB and the CIIF bought almost two-thirds of the country's total milling capacity, and put the acquired mills under the newly created organization, Unicom.[33]

In principle, there is nothing particularly wrong with a development programme funded by a tax on the industry. However, for most coconut farmers, benefits from the CCSF levy were few compared to the amount they paid. From 1972 to 1982 when the levy was lifted, coconut farmers paid about ₱9.7 billion. The levy fluctuated during the period; starting at 4 per cent of export prices in 1973, it went up to 21 per cent in 1974, stayed roughly at this level until 1980, though it fell to 13 per cent in 1979, and rose to 31 per cent in 1981.[34] At first, coconut farmers did not understand what was going on; they did not pay the levy directly but received the balance due to them from traders. It was traders and processors who paid the levy, and knowing in advance how much they had to pay, they deducted it from their offer prices to coconut farmers. Thus, it was coconut farmers who bore the burden of the levy. However, they gradually caught up with what was going on, and began complaining bitterly. The levy was finally lifted in 1982.

The levies and monopolies were supposed to benefit Filipino producers (sugar producers and coconut farmers), and they might have done so if they had been well managed. Instead, they were used to benefit a small group of privileged people. In the case of sugar, the key beneficiary was Roberto Benedicto, and in the case of coconuts, they were Eduardo Cojuangco and Juan Ponce Enrile, a lawyer by profession and a Minister of Defense, who also served as chairman of the PCA. How the levies were used and the monopolies were run are not well documented, though there is a general consensus of opinion that Benedicto, Cojuangco, Enrile, and their 'sub-cronies' (the landlords who dominated Cocofed and some large sugar planters and millers who collaborated with Benedicto) benefited enormously. They received high salaries, lucrative commissions, preferential treatment from the monopolies, and used the monopolies to generate profits for their own businesses. The Marcoses also had a share: Imelda used the levies for her extravagant projects (such as the Miss Universe Pageant), while Marcos received $8.3 million in contributions from the coconut levies for his 1986 presidential campaign.[35]

THE DECLINE OF THE SUGAR AND COCONUT INDUSTRIES

The sugar and coconut industries became depressed in the 1980s, but the levies and monopolies were not the major cause, though they were undoubtedly a contributing factor. The two industries, which had developed as export industries, faced weakening prices during the decade. This was not obvious of the sugar industry until the early 1980s, though there were signs of weakening prices in the mid-1970s. The international sugar price, which, in 1980, rebounded almost to the level of 1974 (65 cents per kilogram, the highest price in its history), started to plummet in the following years, hitting the bottom in 1985 (about 9 cents per kilogram). In the second half of the 1980s, the price recovered somewhat, rising to about 28 cents per kilogram in 1990, but by then, the Philippine sugar industry had become a much smaller one (as evidenced by the dramatic decline in exports to about 10 per cent of the mid-1970s level). Copra prices took a sharp decline during the same period. The decline in purchasing power was worse. In 1982, when 1 ton of copra sold for $314, the sum purchased less than half of what it did in the first half of the 1950s.[36] The 1990 price of $230 per ton was even below the 1982 price.

The basic problem for sugar and coconut oil (the dominant coconut product exported) was that their demand in the international market declined and/or their supply increased. The demand for coconut oil declined because of the increasing availability of soybean oil and palm oil as its substitutes in the United States (the major market of Philippine coconut oil). Furthermore, the campaign against coconut and palm oil launched by the American Soybean Association was fairly successful in planting an image in the minds of American consumers that coconut and palm oils are bad for the health. Affected by this, rightly or wrongly, consumers in other developed countries generally began to form a similarly negative view of coconut and palm oils.

Increasing concern about the unhealthy effects of sugar consumption also had a dampening effect on demand; between 1973 and 1984, per capita consumption of sugar declined in developed countries.[37] But a decline in the demand of sugar from the food industry (soft drink makers in particular) was more sharply felt by the sugar industry. In the 1960s, there was a technological breakthrough in the production of corn-based sweeteners (the most popular was High-Fructose Corn Syrup, known as HFCS), and over time, they became a serious competitor of sugar. On the supply side, an increase in sugar beet production in Europe reduced its dependence on cane sugar from the tropical region. Beet sugar is not competitive with cane sugar, but under the protection and subsidies given for the self-sufficiency programme in food production, beet production in Europe increased rapidly, even to the extent of exporting the excess.

The Philippine sugar industry was known to be a high-cost industry. The cost of sugar production in the Philippines was already high in the pre-war period. In the mid-1930s, it was about twice as high as in the other two major centres of production, Cuba and Java.[38] Despite this, the Philippine sugar industry prospered because of the free trade arrangement with the United States. In the post-war period, the cost situation did not improve much in the Philippines as it continued to enjoy privileged access to the US market under a quota system. In the meantime, new low-cost sugar producers were emerging. In the late 1970s, the heavily mechanized Australian sugar industry could produce sugar at less than half the cost in Negros, the major sugar-producing area in the Philippines.[39]

THE RISE OF THAILAND AS A SUGAR EXPORTER

The rapid rise of Thailand as a major sugar exporter is another indicator of the strength of Thai agriculture. In the post-war period, protected by an import ban, the sugar industry expanded rapidly, and by 1960, the country had become self-sufficient in sugar. Exports began slowly in the 1960s, increasing dramatically in the following decade. Sugar exports rose from 150,000 to 1.16 million tons between 1971 and 1981.[40] In the 1980s, Philippine sugar exports declined (from 1.5 million tons in 1980 to about 0.15 million tons in 1990), while Thai sugar exports increased and reached the level of 3.0 million tons in 1991, making Thailand the third largest exporter in the world.

This increase in Thai sugar exports was not, however, solely the result of a production increase guided by market forces. Faced with the sharp decline in prices in the mid-1980s, the Thai sugar industry pressured the government to give it assistance in the form of reduced business taxes, low-interest loans, and subsidies. The subsidies came from consumers, who paid the higher domestic prices set by the government. The Thai sugar industry is unique in that it was the only agricultural sector sustained by government assistance. All others were either taxed or left to market forces. According to one estimate made in the late 1980s, the Thai sugar industry would have shrunk to one-quarter of its size at that time if government assistance was withdrawn.[41]

DISTRIBUTION OF GRAINS BY THE GOVERNMENT: CONTRASTS

The Thai government started taxing rice soon after the Pacific War. In the early 1950s when there were multiple exchange rates, the government paid rice exporters B35 per pound sterling and sold the pound sterling at B55–60 to importers. The difference was revenue to the government. When a direct tax on rice exports was added, the combined tax burden on rice was about 58 per cent of the domestic wholesale price or 33 per cent of the free on board price. In 1955, the exchange rates were unified, and the implicit export tax was replaced by a rice tax (called rice premium in Thailand), which imposed a similar level of burden on rice in the following years.[42]

This burden, similar to that borne by Filipino sugar and copra farmers, did not retard the rice industry in Thailand. On the contrary, both production and exports rose in the following decades. Over time, however, rice exports became less important as new exports emerged. Rice production became particularly difficult in the late 1980s because the cost of production increased as a result of sustained economic growth in the country, while rice prices tended to stagnate as the United States and Vietnam entered the export market. Since the rice tax was lifted in 1986, it did not have anything to do with the difficulties of the rice industry in the early 1990s. There was, however, one fundamental difference about this tax from the Philippine situation. The rice tax collected over the three decades was government revenue, and therefore used to finance government expenditure.

Immediately after the Pacific War, the Thai government agreed to deliver 1.5 million tons of rice to the Allies, free of charge, as a sort of war indemnity, and could have used this as an excuse to set up a monopoly over rice exports. However, it did not do so, though its rice policy was not *laissez faire* as in the pre-war period. The government ensured that rice was available in the domestic market at reasonable prices and let only surplus rice be exported. Since domestic prices were set below export prices, the government took a large part of the difference from rice exporters through the rice tax, not through a monopoly as the Philippine government did in the 1970s. The Thai method of ensuring the availability of rice in the domestic market was somewhat cumbersome, but worked better than the monopoly system of the Philippines. In Thailand, rice exporters had to obtain licences to sell rice abroad. The government allocated the difference between production and domestic consumption of rice to exporters on the basis of their past export performance.[43]

The Philippine government's intervention in agriculture had a clear anti-middlemen bias. In Thailand, rice trading was under the jurisdiction of the Ministry of Commerce, which did not get involved in distribution directly. In the Philippines, however, a government agency undertook commercial operations. This started with a government corporation, the National Rice and Corn Corp. (NRCC), set up in 1936. It had a monopoly on rice and corn imports which it distributed through government-sponsored agencies such as agricultural co-operatives. (This monopoly was politically important for the party in power because it could be used to lower food prices in the years of national elections and as a source of patronage for party supporters in the provinces.) The NRCC's role was taken over by the Rice and Corn Administration (RCA) in the early 1960s. In the same decade, the RCA went into rice milling and warehousing because it was felt that distribution could not be left to unscrupulous merchants. In addition, the RCA ensured the implementation of the Rice and Corn Trade Nationalization Law (passed in 1960) which Filipinized the rice and corn industry in 1964 (akin to what the Retail Trade Nationalization Law did for retail trade). In 1972, at the start of martial law, the RCA became the National Grains Authority (NGA) to strengthen the government's power to 'stabilize the supply and prices of grains and benefit farmers and consumers'. In 1981, it was renamed the National Food Authority (NFA) and put under Imelda Marcos, Minister of Human Settlements. Under the new head, the NFA became more broadly involved in distribution (for example, by setting up direct distribution outlets called Kadiwa stores), diversifying its functions to all basic foods.

In the distribution of domestic grains, however, the NFA relied a great deal on private distributors. For example, in the case of the most important commodity, rice, although the NGA or the NFA increased the number of its warehouses, the private sector bought more rice from farmers (90 per cent sold in the country in the early 1990s). But in the areas where warehouses were not adequate (in the second half of the 1970s, rice production rapidly increased, and a few hundred thousand tons were exported), the government agency became the major procurer of rice. For the country as a whole, despite the government's efforts (to increase warehousing facilities in particular), post-harvest losses were becoming a serious problem. The private sector was not responding to meet this problem, despite there being a large number of merchants involved in the distribution, because profit incentives tended to be weak; the government set support prices for farmers and price ceilings for consumers. It was within this range that private distributors and processors could operate—they could operate only by the grace of the government. The NFA, for example, was given the power to register, license, and supervise merchants (including processors) in the distribution of rice.

This situation may seem good to those who view middlemen as hoarders, black marketeers, manipulators of prices, or exploiters of the masses, but it was very damaging to the rice industry and the rural economy as a whole. Because of corruption, inertia, lack of incentives, and bureaucratic red tape, a government agency was a poor substitute for merchants, despite the rhetoric to the contrary. Being government-directed, if not -dominated, the rural distribution channel in the Philippines became inefficient.

ECONOMIC CONSEQUENCES

In Thailand, agriculture was the leading sector of the economy in the 1950s and 1960s, and provided the basis for industry-led growth in the following decades. This was made possible partly by owner (mainly) cultivation and infrastructural development, but an important contribution arose from the way distribution was structured. Rice was exported largely through Chinese networks, but new agricultural exports (for example, maize and tapioca) were initially handled by foreign trading companies with the assistance of Chinese domestic distributors. It was through this Chinese network that foreign price signals were transmitted to the rural sector, finances were arranged, and processing was undertaken. For example, to increase maize production to satisfy the large market in Japan in the 1960s, Thai peasants needed small tractors (two-wheel and light four-wheel) which could till land when the soil was still too hard (before the beginning of the rains) for draught animals to plough. These were imported by Japanese trading companies from Japan, and distributed by Chinese middlemen with their finances. The Chinese distribution network also made possible further mechanization (for example, in the introduction of threshing machines), rural motorization, increased storage facilities, and better processing technologies, which conjoined to reduce post-harvest losses and improve product quality.

In the Philippines, the distribution network connecting the rural sector and the international market was weak. A reason for this weakness was government restriction of the entry and operations of foreign trading companies. Another reason was the weakening of domestic distribution by government discrimination and intervention. In this, the first blow came with the Retail Trade Nationalization Law. The Chinese who survived it by becoming naturalized then faced government intervention. In the 1970s, their predicament was compounded when rice, sugar, and coconut oil exports became government monopolies. Some distributors and processors were bought out by the government; others who remained as private entities became sub-agents, distributing and processing under the guidance of their supervising agencies. Evolving into a bureaucratic system, in efficiency and dynamism, the rural distribution channel in the Philippines was a far cry from its Thai counterpart. This factor is a major reason why Philippine agriculture never became the leading sector of the economy in post-war years.

NOTES

1 *A Public Development Program for Thailand*, Baltimore: Johns Hopkins Press, 1959, p. 91.

2 Frank H. Golay et al., *Underdevelopment and Economic Nationalism in Southeast Asia*, Ithaca: Cornell University Press, 1969, p. 308.

3 A typical ownership structure is 49 per cent for the Petroleum Authority

of Thailand, 2 per cent for a quasi-government organization (such as Crown Property Bureau), and 49 per cent for private investors.

4 *Asian Wall Street Journal*, 4 and 5 December 1987.

5 Edita Tan, *The Structure and Growth of the Philippine Financial Market and the Behavior of Its Major Components*, Working Paper No. 81–94, Makati: Philippine Institute for Development Studies, June 1981, p. 2.

6 Development Bank of the Philippines, 1986–7 Report, p. 22.

7 According to the annual reports of the PNB and the DBP for the 1986 financial year, the government took over ₱47 billion worth of non-performing assets and ₱55 billion worth of liabilities from the PNB, and ₱61 billion worth of non-performing assets and ₱62 billion worth of liabilities from the DBP.

8 Mario Lamberte, *The Development Bank of the Philippines (DBP) and the Financial Crisis: A Descriptive Analysis*, Staff Paper Series No. 84–07, Makati: Philippine Institute for Development Studies, November 1984, p. 10.

9 '5-Year Performance Report', Asset Privatization Trust, Makati [1992].

10 This was one of Jaime Ongpin's 'eleven major infuriating problems' when he was attacking Marcos in the mid-1980s. Ongpin became Secretary of Finance after Aquino became President (Nick Joaquin, *Jaime Ongpin: The Enigma*, Makati: Jaime V. Ongpin Institute of Business and Government, 1990, p. 211). Belatedly, in mid-1992, the Philippine government filed graft charges against Panfilo Domingo, then president of the PNB, and Marcos's former crony, Rodolfo Cuenca, for having defrauded the government of some $29 million (roughly ₱727 million) in behest loans.

11 Edward R. Kiunisala, 'Hang Napocor'. *Philippines Free Press*, Part II, 14 November 1992. National Power Corp. is often abbreviated as Napocor in the Philippines.

12 For Meralco's history, see *66 Years of Service*, Manila: Manila Electric Co., 1969 and *A Brief History*, Manila: Manila Electric Co., 1976.

13 Ricardo Manapat, *Some Are Smarter Than Others: The History of Marcos' Crony Capitalism*, New York: Aletheia Publications, 1991, p. 325.

14 *A Short Story of the National Power Corporation, 1936–1986*, Quezon City: National Power Corp., 1986, p. 59. This debt incurred in connection with the nuclear power plant was later taken over by the government.

15 Another way to ensure enough revenues is to bribe the regulators. It is said that this can be more easily done if the NPC is privatized.

16 Edward R. Kiunisala, 'Hang Napocor', *Philippines Free Press*, Part I, 31 October 1992: 4.

17 *Asian Wall Street Journal*, 30 January 1992.

18 'Thai Airways International: 32nd Anniversary', *Sawasdee* [Thai International's flight magazine], May 1992. After the political unrest of May 1992, Thai International faced some difficulties in going ahead with its plan to list its stocks on the SET because of chairman Kaset's close link to the disgraced army strongman, Suchinda Kraprayoon, who pro-democracy groups hold responsible for the shooting of demonstrators by the military that month. By scaring away foreign tourists, the unrest caused a decline in the airline's passenger load to about 50 per cent (from a little over 60 per cent before the unrest).

19 This and the next paragraph are partly based on 'A History of Philippine Airlines' [1989].

20 Bernard Wideman, 'Philippine Airlines: A Presidential Landing', *Insight*, July 1978: 52.

21 Manapat, *Some Are Smarter Than Others*, pp. 368–71.

22 Soon after the government take-over, PAL's capital was increased 10 times, from ₱25 million to ₱250 million.
23 'Philippine Airlines: 50 Years . . . and Counting' [1991].
24 *Philippine Daily Inquirer*, 28 April 1992.
25 According to one estimate, Unicom paid between 9 and 15 per cent below the price it would have paid under competitive conditions (Robert Dohner and Ponciano Intal, 'The Marcos Legacy: Economic Policy and Foreign Debt in the Philippines', in Jeffrey Sachs and Susan Collins (ed.), *Developing Country Debt and Economic Performance*, Chicago: University of Chicago Press, 1989, Vol. 3, p. 468).
26 A University of the Philippines study estimated that in the period 1960–71, if the International Sugar Agreement price was taken as the relevant border price for the Philippines, there was a net income transfer to Philippine sugar farmers averaging 38 per cent of the value of the output (Dohner and Intal, 'The Marcos Legacy', p. 462).
27 Ricardo Manapat, *Some Are Smarter Than Others: The History of Marcos' Crony Capitalism*, New York: Aletheia Publications, 1991, p. 103.
28 Dohner and Intal, 'The Marcos Legacy', pp. 462–3.
29 Ibid., p. 464.
30 Manapat, *Some Are Smarter Than Others*, p. 107.
31 From a University of the Philippines study quoted in Dohner and Intal, 'The Marcos Legacy', p. 463.
32 Ramon Clarete and James Roumasset, *An Analysis of the Economic Policies Affecting the Philippine Coconut Industry*, Working Paper No. 83–08, Makati: Philippine Institute for Development Studies, 1983, p. 6.
33 This and preceding paragraphs are based on 'IBON Primer on the Philippine Coconut Industry', Manila, IBON Databank Phils., Inc. [1979]; Clarete and Roumasset, *Economic Policies Affecting the Philippine Coconut Industry*, pp. 1–21; and 'How the Coco Levy Worked', *Philippine Daily Inquirer*, 26, 27, and 28 April 1992.
34 Clarete and Roumasset, *Economic Policies Affecting the Philippine Coconut Industry*, p. 15.
35 Manapat, *Some Are Smarter Than Others*, p. 184. The Philippines' former ambassador to the United States, Emmanuel Pelaez, is quoted to have said that the coconut levy resulted in 'the biggest robbery in Philippine history' (Teodoro Benigno's column, *Philippine Star*, 26 August 1992).
36 *1950–1983 Commodity Trade and Price Trends*, Baltimore: Johns Hopkins University Press, n.d. [1985], the statistical table on copra prices.
37 Joop Theunissen, 'Linkage and Alternatives: The Philippine Sugar Industry in the 1990s', Discussion paper, Tilburg University, July 1989, p. 9.
38 *Report of the Joint Preparatory Committee on Philippine Affairs*, Washington, DC: US Government Printing Office, 20 May 1938, p. 1072.
39 Alfred W. McCoy, 'The Restoration of Planter Power in La Carlota City', in Benedict J. Kerkvliet and Resil B. Mojares (eds.), *From Marcos to Aquino: Local Perspectives on Political Transition in the Philippines*, Quezon City: Ateneo de Manila University Press, 1991, p. 116.
40 Theunissen, 'Linkage and Alternatives', p. 18.
41 Ammar Siamwalla and Suthad Setboonsarng, *Trade, Exchange Rate, and Agricultural Pricing Policies in Thailand*, World Bank Comparative Studies, Washington, DC: World Bank, 1989, p. iii.
42 Ibid., pp. 29–31; James Ingram, *Economic Change in Thailand, 1850–1970*, Stanford: Stanford University Press, 1971, p. 246.
43 Ammar and Suthad, *Trade, Exchange Rate, and Agricultural Pricing Policies in Thailand*, p. 31.

8

THE THAI ECONOMY IN THE MID-1990s

Pasuk Phongpaichit

INTRODUCTION

According to the World Bank, Thailand was the world's fastest-growing economy in the decade 1985–94. Real gross domestic product (GDP) per capita increased at an average rate of 8.2 per cent a year.

From 1987 to 1990, the GDP recorded real annual growth rates of 9.5, 13.2, 12.2 and 11.6 per cent. Since then, the pace has levelled out to the 8–9 per cent range, but the momentum of growth remains strong.

This spurt has transformed the Thai economy. In the early 1980s, Thailand could still justifiably be viewed as an agrarian economy, with crops playing the major role in exports. By the mid-1990s, Thailand belongs to the club of NIEs (newly industrializing economies), with computer and electronic parts topping the list of export products.

This article looks at three aspects of this phase of growth and its consequences for the Thai economy in the mid-1990s. Rapid growth has wrought large changes in the structure and dynamics of the Thai economy. The first section traces the major patterns.

Secondly, Thailand now figures in the debates over Asian industrialization, and the special features of the "Thailand case" bring new elements to the debate. In brief, the World Bank has argued that "second-tier NIEs" such as Thailand have grown by following the Bank's structural adjustment policies; by courting direct foreign investment; by creating a favourable environment for exporters without intervening directly in the capital market; and by refraining from positive industrial policy-making. Several other economists, particularly those associated with UNCTAD (United Nations Commission on Trade and Development), have countered that governments in these countries have in fact played an important and effective role through interventionist industrial policies and active restructuring of the markets for capital and labour. The second section looks at the recent changes in these two markets in Thailand.

Source: *Southeast Asian Affairs 1996*, Singapore: Institute of Southeast Asian Studies, 1996, pp. 369–81.

Thirdly, the speed and special character of Thailand's growth have given rise to doubts about the country's capacity to sustain the current momentum. Industrialization has already placed great strain on infrastructure, on the supply of skilled labour, on the environment, on social equity, and on the government's ability to maintain macro-economic stability. The last section looks at the major current problems as perceived by the policy-makers.

TRANSFORMATION

The main driver of growth and change since 1986 has been the export of manufactures, which has grown at an average rate of 30 per cent a year. Between 1980 and 1994, the share of manufactures in total exports increased from 36 to 81 per cent, the share of manufacturing in GDP value-added increased from 22 to 29 per cent in 1994, and the share of agriculture in GDP dropped from 21 to 11 per cent. As in South Korea and Taiwan, Thailand's manufacturing exports began with labour intensive products. The textile industry, established since the 1960s, was the major contributor to manufactured exports in 1980. After 1986, textile and garment exports spurted ahead and were the largest of all export categories at the end of the decade. Other export categories grew in the same period through a mix of labour-intensity and local availability of raw materials – jewellery, wood products, canned fruits, and seafood. Several others were simply labour-intensive industries using a mix of local and imported raw materials such as toys, games, leather products, shoes, and confectionery. In a very short space of time, Thailand had developed export-oriented labour-intensive manufacturing covering a broad product range, and involving a very large number of different companies.

From 1991 onwards, many of these industries faced difficulties as wage rates shifted upwards, and neighbouring countries such as Vietnam and China emerged as competitive sites. The large garment industry was especially hard hit. Yet by 1995, the garment industry had restructured to undertake higher-value and higher-margin production, and exports again increased.

Even so, from the late 1980s, growth in these classic labour-intensive industries was outstripped by growth in medium- and high-tech products,

Table 8.1 Exports (in billion baht)

	1981	*1985*	*1989*	*1994*
Agriculture	73.0	73.4	104.5	129.5
Labour-intensive	22.6	41.5	118.7	297.4
Medium hi-tech	7.9	13.7	61.7	384.4
Other manufactures	24.2	40.4	85.2	36.9
Others	25.3	24.4	33.5	85.1

Source: Bank of Thailand.

such as computer components, electronics, automobile parts and electrical goods. By 1994 this subcategory accounted for one-third of all exports.

Initially, Thailand's contribution to the production of such medium-tech products was largely assembly work. The design, complex manufacturing processes and international marketing were located elsewhere. Because of this, some economists expressed reservations about Thailand's technological capability, compared to South Korea or Taiwan at similar stages of development. Yet the shift to medium-tech itself worked as a stage in industrial upgrading. The production and management in these medium-tech industries required more skilled manpower and more sophisticated support industries than classic labour-intensive segments, such as garments or shoes. In the 1990s the level and scope of skill-training increased, both through educational institutions and on-the-job schemes. The industrial structure also deepened. Many of the new investments in mid-decade went into component factories, process shops, and other support industries required by this medium-tech segment. Engineering sub-sectors were among the fastest-gowing.

In both the labour-intensive and medium-tech phases, foreign direct investment played a major role. Textile businesses from Japan and garment export houses from Hong Kong and Taiwan had begun relocating operations to Thailand since the 1970s. They invested much more aggressively in Thailand after 1985 to escape rising costs at home and to benefit from GSP (Generalized System of Preferences) privileges. Many other labour-intensive firms relocated from Japan and the "Four Tigers" (Taiwan, Korea, Hong Kong and Singapore) in the late 1980s. The average annual inflow of net foreign direct investment rose from 6.6 billion baht in 1980–87 to 47.1 billion baht in 1988–93.

Foreign investment also drove the upgrade to medium-tech. After the labour-intensive firms had demonstrated the suitability of Thailand as a manufacturing base, more sophisticated manufacturing soon followed. Minebea, for instance, first moved its ball-bearing works to Thailand, and only in the late 1980s was it followed by the manufacture of its computer component. Seagate shifted part of its disk-drive assembly from Singapore in 1989, and several other drive plants followed in the next three years.

The prominent role of foreign investment sparked several debates. Some criticized the slow pace of technology transfer by foreign firms. Some feared that footloose foreign industries would merely use Thailand's cheap resources and then move on to cheaper countries when the cost structure changed. Some pointed to the heavy impact on the balance-of-payments from import of both capital goods and inputs. Some feared that foreign investment would "crowd out" domestic capital.

The last concern appears to have been unfounded. If anything, foreign investment has "crowded in" domestic investment through a demonstration effect. Many export companies were joint ventures, often growing out of alliances formed earlier to import or produce for Thailand's home market. In many other cases, local firms were able to copy or emulate foreign exporters. And in a few cases, domestic firms bought out companies initially set up by foreign investment.

In addition, the growth of manufactured exports led to a secondary boom in the domestic market in which local capital played the major role. Thai firms have taken the leading role in real estate development, wholesale and retail trade, services, media, telecommunications, infrastructure development, and many types of consumer goods manufacture.

After 1988, gross domestic investment made a step upwards from about 25 per cent to about 40 per cent of GDP. The contribution from foreign direct investment increased from about 2–3 per cent of GDP to a peak of 9 per cent in the early 1990s and then tailed off. The greater part of this upward shift came from increased domestic investment.

By the early 1990s, this upward trend in domestic investment had already begun to break beyond the boundaries of the home market. In 1988 Thai equity abroad totalled only US$24.1 million. By 1993 the figure had risen almost twelvefold to US$281 million.

Three major factors seem to have been important in drawing Thai firms rapidly into overseas ventures. First, firms which grew rapidly during Thailand's domestic market boom quickly exhausted local opportunities and looked for ways to deploy their expertise abroad, especially in the neighbouring Asian countries. Firms in telecommunications, the media, and real estate development sought new ventures in Indochina and elsewhere in ASEAN. Secondly, some service companies developed expertise which made them competitive in international markets. Thai hotel chains bought or launched ventures in Asia, Europe and the United States. Thirdly, the opening of China provided a magnet for several Thai-Chinese entrepreneurs. The Charoen Phokphan (CP) group of companies, originally an agri-business enterprise which had diversified into several growth areas including telecommunications and petrochemicals, became one of the largest single foreign investors in China, spanning across a wide spectrum of industries, including bicycles, industrial forests, real estate, petrochemicals, retailing, entertainment, electronics, telecommunications and agri-business. In addition, CP began to function as an unofficial trade mission to China, acting as godfather (and sometimes also as venture partner) for other Thai firms seeking to penetrate the China market.

RESTRUCTURING

The phenomenon of Asia's newly industrializing economies is now (rightly) a major topic of debate in economics. The battle-lines in the debate over the original four "Tigers" had only just been drawn when the arrival of the second-tier NIEs (Thailand, Malaysia, Indonesia) made the debate more complex. The appearance of Thailand as the most successful of the second-tier NIEs proved especially disruptive. Prior to 1987, very few had expected Thailand to perform so well and to take such a lead. Besides, certain features of Thailand's growth appeared to run athwart the main lines of the debate.

By the late 1980s, the World Bank had developed the argument that the success of the "Tigers" was due to well-functioning markets policed by powerful governments. In the early 1990s, a counter school argued that the "Tiger" governments were certainly powerful, but that they used that power to distort markets and favour individual firms in order to force the pace of growth.

The emergence of the second-tier NIEs offered the World Bank a second chance to argue that these states were less interventionist than the "Tigers". Their governments had achieved growth by concentrating on macro-economic discipline and infrastructure development, while allowing foreign investment to work its market magic. Superficially, Thailand appeared a good recruit for this argument: its governments had a long record of disciplined macro-economic policy-making, and the inflow of foreign investment played a prominent role in the post-1987 boom.

The counter school argued that the "Tigers" forced the pace of growth in three ways. First, the governments had a vision of economic growth, which was distilled from the experience of other countries and actuated through disciplined growth plans. Secondly, the governments played a major role in investment in lead sectors. Thirdly, the governments enforced their plans by controlling or governing the capital market, and through a mass of other subsidies, incentives and regulations collectively termed "industrial policy".

It is difficult to fit Thailand into this model. The planning process has been notoriously weak and arguably has become weaker as the economy accelerated towards industrialization. The government has been an active investor in utilities, and this is not unusual. Outside infrastructure, it has invested in petroleum and petrochemicals and even then in a minor role. The government has never tried to nationalize the banks or seriously direct their activities. It did introduce many techniques of industrial policy copied from the "Tigers", but only after 1991 when the boom was well under way, and without the focus attributed to the "Tigers".

However; one should not conclude that Thailand's push towards industrialization has been free of government intervention. In fact, since the mid-1980s the government has played a major interventionist role in remodelling the key markets for capital and labour in order to facilitate industrial expansion.

Restructuring capital markets

From the 1950s on, a handful of domestic commercial banks dominated the capital market. With no new banking licences issued and with foreign banks effectively excluded, twenty-nine commercial banks enjoyed a highly protected market.[1] Their assets accumulated at the rate of 20 per cent a year over twenty years. In 1990, sixteen of these banks accounted for 95 per cent of total assets. In the absence of a developed capital market, banks dominated commercial lending. The families which owned the major banks, and other entrepreneurial families which worked closely with them, came to dominate business growth. By 1980, some thirty conglomerates, together owning over a thousand companies, sprawled across the dynamic sectors of the urban economy.

In the post-1987 boom, two major sources of capital growth came from firms' retained earnings and bank lending. Between 1985 and 1994 the total volume of corporate savings increased seven times, from less than 50 billion baht a year to nearly 600 billion baht, and the assets of the domestic banks multiplied more than six times from 714 million to 4,605 million baht.

Since the 1970s, the government has tried to diminish the monopoly power of the major banks. One strategy was to license finance companies under rules which enabled them to compete favourably with the banks. This strategy faltered in the early 1980s when many finance companies failed as a result of weak management and recession. But from mid-decade, the finance sector boomed. Between 1985 and 1994, total assets increased from 133 million to 1,211 million baht. In 1991–92, the government adjusted the regulations to expand the areas of business open to finance companies. In 1993–94, it began encouraging finance companies to open offices in the provincial areas to expand access. Many new exporters who were not connected to the leading conglomerates and banking groups were able to expand with funds raised from the finance sector.

From 1987 onwards, the Finance Ministry and the central bank introduced other measures to expand the capital market and to reduce further the monopoly power of the commercial banks. In 1987, they kick-started the Thai stock market, which had been in existence since 1975 but had been inactive since a crash in 1979. In 1991–92, they improved the regulation of the stock market to make it more attractive to foreign funds. In 1993, they began licensing mutual funds, and took some experimental steps in developing a bond market. Between 1988 and 1995 the number of firms listed on the stock market rose from 141 to nearly 400, and market capitalization expanded from 234 to 3,297 billion baht. The market quickly assumed a role in the mobilization of domestic savings. In 1986 the share of total savings mobilized by the stock market was 8.6 per cent. By 1991 this had risen to 28.8 per cent.

The rapid growth of the market, and especially the inflow of foreign funds from 1991 onwards, provided another avenue of access to capital. Several new firms in areas such as property and telecommunications which had expanded during the secondary domestic market boom made deft use of the stock market to achieve very rapid growth. Through their new relations with overseas merchant banks and broking firms, some firms went on to raise funds on the stock and bond markets of London, New York, Tokyo and elsewhere.

In 1992–93 the government widened the capital market further by legalizing offshore banking and issuing licences to fifteen Thai and thirty-two foreign banks. Through this window, Thai firms gained another access to outside funds. In 1989 the commercial banks' net borrowing abroad was only 15 billion baht. In 1994, with the advent of offshore banking, it jumped to 545 billion baht.

In 1994, the authorities started to break down the commercial banks' protected market. They announced plans to issue full licences to five foreign banks, and began urging finance companies to upgrade to full banking status. At the start of 1995, the Finance Minister said that a major ministry objective was to liberalize the financial sector even further in order to destroy old monopolies.

The liberalization of the financial system amounted to breaking down the local commercial banks' monopoly. The authorities view liberalization and expansion of the financial sector as the best way to increase the availability and reduce the cost of capital for export expansion and infrastructure projects.

Restructuring labour markets

The shift to industrialization accelerated the demand for urban labour. Throughout the 1980s, the urban population grew by about 4 million people. From 1984 to 1993, the numbers working in industry doubled from 2 to 4 million. Before 1980, three out of every five net new entrants to the work-force had gone into agriculture. From the early 1980s onwards, however, all the net addition to the work-force accrued in industry.

Thailand had a large pool of rural labour which had long acted as the source of additional urban labour supply. But in the boom this supply ran into two problems. First, supply tagged behind demand. By the end of the 1980s, firms were already complaining about difficulties in securing adequate supplies of unskilled labour; and there was growing upward pressure on wage rates. Secondly, the levels of skill and education were inadequate for market requirements. Many export firms had relatively sophisticated technology, and required both skilled workers and well-educated managers and technicians. With the rapid shift up to medium-tech industries, these requirements became more pressing. Thailand's educational system had not been geared to expect such a demand. Only a small proportion (10.3 per cent in 1993) of the labour force had the secondary education which provided the basis for industrial skills. The number of graduates in key areas such as engineering was small compared to the demand. By 1990, the wages for skilled and educated personnel were increasing at 15–20 per cent a year.

The government responded to these problems with a series of measures to restructure the labour markets. To increase the basic labour supply and minimize wage pressure, the government first attempted to increase the flow out of the villages. It placed restrictions on the further expansion of agriculture, and withdrew land from some communities settled in areas officially designated as "forest". However, these schemes ran into political opposition and had to be scaled back.

Instead, the government began to develop a two-tier labour market. In the upper tier, labour was increasingly subject to government regulation and protection. The government imposed a minimum wage which was adjusted upwards annually, ahead of inflation. Safety laws and labour regulations were enforced by a factory inspectorate. A series of tripartite (employer-labour-government) bodies were created to manage different forms of labour problems and disputes. A new Social Security Act passed in 1989 created a basic system of labour welfare. In this upper tier, the government took a larger role in regulating wages and conditions with the aim of maintaining the flow of new recruits, and pre-empting labour discontent. In parallel, the government tacitly allowed the development of a second tier where wages were lower, conditions worse, and regulation absent.

The second tier was large as many major industries avoided the minimum wage and other labour laws by using subcontract or casual labour. Most of the 800,000 workers in the garment industry were employed on a subcontract basis. Surveys of major factories in Bangkok found that about a quarter of the work-forces was treated as casual or temporary employees. In the early 1990s, about half of the urban work-force was paid less than the minimum wage, and the proportion was increasing. Most small and medium-scale factories escaped the attention of the factory inspectorate.

This second tier drew in recruits from the villages, many of whom worked in the urban sector on a temporary basis. Increasingly, it also drew recruits from two other sources: child labour and illegal immigrants from neighbouring countries. The sensitivity over child labour means that statistics are highly unreliable, but some estimates put the figure at around half a million. Data on illegal migrants are marginally better. By 1994, it was generally agreed by both official and unofficial sources that there were around a million illegal immigrants in the labour force. The largest component had come from Myanmar, with others from China and Indochina. Many worked in the border areas and in specific industries such as fishing. But some filtered into the main urban centres and into industrial recruitment. While there were occasional attempts to deport groups of such workers, for the most part the authorities tacitly allowed the immigration to continue. In the fishing industry, entrepreneurs managed to negotiate a scheme to legitimize the employment of such migrants. By 1995, employers groups began to press the government to create a structure for legitimizing labour in-migration on a wider basis.

To forestall the possibility that a tight labour market would lead to labour agitation, the government restricted labour organization. Since labour repression had formed a fundamental part of government industrial policy for several decades, this was merely a matter of fine-tuning.

Labour organizations were strongest in the public sector. In the upsurge of the late 1980s, these organizations pressed for wage rises, opposed plans to privatize certain state enterprises, and assumed a leadership role for labour as a whole. In reaction, the military government in 1991 excluded state enterprise workers from the labour relations law, which meant that their associations were restricted to welfare issues, had no role in wage or dispute negotiation, were debarred from striking, and were removed from the umbrella labour federations. When the military government was succeeded by a democratically elected Cabinet in 1992, the state-enterprise workers agitated for a reversal of this measure, but without success.

To combat the short-fall in skills and education, the government undertook a variety of measures. From 1991 it increased the provision of extension courses for skill-training, and launched a crash programme to extend secondary schooling. Within four years, the proportion staying on from primary to secondary schooling rose from 50 to 65 per cent. The government planned to boost the figure to 95 per cent by the turn of the century. In 1995 the government launched a cheap loans scheme designed to encourage private investors to build more schools faster than the government could. It planned to follow this up with a student loan scheme to encourage more students to stay at school longer. The government also tried to interest firms in contributing to a major expansion in its skill-training schemes. The big firms, however, refused as most had already set up their own in-house schemes. They suggested instead that the government should subsidize these.

To expand higher education, the government channelled more money into the education budget, but also recognized that it would achieve results faster by opening up higher education to private investment. By 1994, there were twenty-six private universities and technical colleges with a total of over 125,000 students. Several other private universities were in various stages of construction. The number entering universities (excluding open universities) each year grew from 22,000 to 33,000 between 1991 and 1995.

As with the unskilled labour supply, the government also recognized that the only short-term solution was importation. The rules for the employment of expatriate workers were relaxed. Between 1991 and 1994, the number of new work permits issued to foreigners doubled. By 1994 the total number of foreigners with work permits had reached 160,000. Possibly as many again were reckoned to be working illegally on tourist visas. Thailand pulled in scientists, engineers and skilled workers especially from China, the Philippines, and Eastern Europe.

STRESS

The speed and unexpectedness of Thailand's recent growth has exerted strains on markets, institutions and policy-making capabilities. This final section reviews the problems and issues in five key areas of concern to the public and policy-makers: macro-economic stability, infrastructure, environment, labour, and income distribution.

Macro-economic stability

Throughout 1995, estimates of the current-account deficit and the inflation rate edged upwards. At the end of the year, the deficit stood at 7.1 per cent of GDP, and inflation at an annual rate of 5.6 per cent. While these figures are far from crisis levels, the persistent upward trend has led to concern about the authorities' ability to maintain Thailand's record of macro-economic stability.

This concern arises because the nature of macro-economic management has totally changed as a result of the structural changes in the economy and society. For many decades, the macromanagers have concentrated on maintaining a stable baht in order to facilitate trade. Traditionally, they achieved stability by keeping the budget deficit within close limits through fiscal discipline, minimizing foreign debt, and reacting to any sign of over-heating with strong deflationary measures. The changes of the last decade have rendered these strategies inadequate. First, following financial liberalization, the authorities have less control over the levels of foreign indebtedness. In particular, they face eccentric movements of short-term international funds. Secondly, the potential political costs of deflationary correction have risen. In the past, such corrections weighed heaviest on the large agrarian sector. Now they would impact on the growing urban business sector, particularly the large number of small businesses, and the growing urban labour force.

In moving towards financial liberalization, some neighbouring countries have adopted more flexible exchange-rate policies to enable capital flows to be regulated through market mechanisms. The Bank of Thailand resists this approach. It believes that the economy will stabilize in the medium term through export growth, and that a stable baht is indispensable for achieving that growth. Hence, the Bank has pegged the baht to a basket of currencies in which the U.S. dollar dominates.

The Bank of Thailand argues that the increases in inflation rate and the current account deficit in 1995 were due to short-term effects – the international uptrend in rice prices, the impact of the country's severe flooding, and the import of capital equipment for infrastructure and industrial investment. The Bank argues that the situation will improve in 1996. But in the meantime, the Bank's usual monetary tools for deflationary correction have not been effective. High interest rates set to reduce demand have resulted in the inflow of short-term funds which have negated the policy's intended effect As a result, the Bank has retracted partially from its policy of financial liberalization. It has imposed reserve requirements and other controls to reduce speculative short-term financial flows through the offshore banking facility. It has also begun experimenting with restrictions on credit cards and other forms of consumer credit to inhibit domestic demand.

For the medium term, besides relying on the growth of exports, the authorities are looking for ways to increase savings in order to close the savings-investment gap. While gross domestic savings have increased from 20 to 35 per cent of GDP since 1986, gross domestic investment has climbed even higher to 40 per cent. The authorities are looking for ways to restrict spending, as in the examples above, and also to increase the range and accessibility of savings instruments.

Infrastructure

The rapid acceleration of the economy has placed great strains on the infrastructure. Port, land transport and telephone facilities were already inadequate at the onset of the boom, and have fallen further behind.[2] Air and telecommunications facilities will be critical for growth prospects in the future.

The government has faced several different kinds of problems over infrastructure. First, it has run into difficulties over funding. Since 1988, the government has run a fiscal surplus which both contributes to the domestic savings rate and serves as a counter to inflationary pressures in the economy. To preserve this surplus, the government is reluctant to embark on large spending ventures. Secondly, partly to overcome the shortage of funds and partly to achieve speed, the government in the late 1980s determined to privatize infrastructure provision as far as possible. This policy has had mixed results, with varying profitability by different ventures. By and large, telephone and telecommunications projects have delivered good margins, and hence have been completed relatively fast. By contrast, land transport ventures are scarcely profitable. The second-stage expressway project ended in acrimony when the contractor tried to blackmail the government to increase the margin. The airport tollway project is bankrupt and up for sale. Two of the three mass transit proposals are moribund because banks will not finance them. Thirdly, the government faces difficulty in managing infrastructure investments, largely because the large potential for corruption revenue has resulted in heavy political in-fighting.

Environment

The poor state of the infrastructure has contributed to the deterioration of the environment In addition, many of the factories migrating to Thailand are attracted by the laxity of environmental regulation in comparison with the country of origin. Finally, there is little effective attempt to enforce zoning or other simple forms of environmental control.

As a result, the state of the environment has deteriorated rapidly in parallel with accelerating economic growth. Bangkok's canals are reported to be among the most polluted stretches of water in the world. The city's traffic is notorious. The urban air carries high levels of fungi and toxic elements which result in respiratory diseases and allergies. Toxic wastes and toxic emissions from factories have created problems in many provincial areas.

In 1992, Thailand introduced an Environment Law which enshrines the principle of "polluter pays". To date, however, the law is ineffective. In part, this is a direct result of inadequacies in the judicial process. In part, it reflects the government's reluctance to deter the continued inflow of investment.

Labour supply

In the short-term, the government has overcome stickiness in the labour markets by opening up the borders to labour inflow on an official and unofficial basis. In the medium term, the government has to decide whether it will sustain this policy and learn to manage its social consequences, or attempt to overcome labour market problems internally.

Income distribution

Thailand's average real income per capita has just about doubled in the boom decade of 1985–95 to reach US$2,315 in 1994. In purchasing power parity (PPP) terms, which take into account price levels to give more realistic cross-country comparisons, the 1994 per capita income was US$6,390—about half the level of Taiwan and two-thirds of South Korea.

As far as social indicators are concerned, most showed an improvement. The infant mortality rate dropped from 22.5 per 1000 in 1971 to 8.3 in 1992. During the 1980s the percentage of homes with electricity increased from 43 to 82 per cent, the proportion of pre-school children suffering from malnutrition declined from 51 to 19 per cent in 1990, and average life expectancy increased from 60 to 65 years.

However, the number living below the poverty line fell by only 1–2 per cent in the 1980s. In 1990, almost 12 million people remained below the poverty line. Most of the gains in growth accrued to a narrow minority, and overall income distribution became sharply worse. Between 1982 and 1992 the average income of the top 10 per cent of the nation's households almost tripled. By contrast, the income of the bottom 30 per cent barely changed. The gap between the top and bottom 10 per cent widened from seventeen times to thirty-eight times. The majority of the poor are in the rural areas.

The government has put all its attention to the promotion of urban growth. It is reluctant to divert resources to the rural sector, which consequently falls steadily further behind. In both Taiwan and Korea, the governments have used positive policies to close the gap between rural and urban incomes in order to pre-empt political reactions. But in both these countries, the rural population is relatively small. In Thailand, some 30 million people, or 60 per cent of the total, still live in the rural areas. Any policies to upgrade rural incomes through productivity investments and subsidies will be comparatively more expensive for the economy than in Korea or Taiwan.

The growth decade has witnessed a steady rise in rural complaints and protests. These protests have mainly focused on specific urban threats to rural life—forest destruction, dam building for hydro-electricity, land diversion for plantations and resorts, and pollution of air and rivers by factories. Non-governmental organizations (NGOs) have helped to organize some of these protests, and to give a theoretical framework to the movement. In late 1995, farmers' organizations travelled to Bangkok to protest against the movement towards regional economic integration on the grounds that such globalizing trends increase the likelihood that rural populations will be increasingly marginalized.

CONCLUSION

Thailand's rapid growth over the past decade was not unique. Most countries in the region performed well and the East Asian countries as a group (including China, Korea, Taiwan and ASEAN) had an average rate of growth of 7.8 per cent per annum in the 1980s. Even India performed well in the decade 1985–94, with an average rate of growth of 5.3 per cent in the 1980s compared to 3.6 per cent in the 1965–80 period. In this respect, Asia parted company with trends in the rest of the developing world. Sub-Saharan Africa grew at only 2.1 per cent, Latin America and the Caribbean at 1.6 per cent (World Bank 1992, cited in Singh 1995, p. 33).

The explanation for this growth must clearly be at the regional level, and would need to take into account the industrial dispersion from Japan and the "Tigers"; the increasing flows of trade, capital, technology and labour around the region; and the impetus from the opening up of China.

Thailand's experience of this phase of growth differed from the pattern of the original four "Asian Tigers" in several ways. First, foreign investment played a stimulating role from the very beginning. Secondly, domestic enterprise responded powerfully without the prodding by a strong "development state". Thirdly, the transition from classic labour-intensive exports to medium-tech manufactures took place within a handful of years. Fourthly, Thailand overcame shortages of labour, skill and technology by importation. Fifthly, the government provided little planning lead and took no significant role in allocating capital resources. Yet it was far from the passive market-friendly force imagined in World Bank theorizing. The government took a major part in restructuring the key markets of capital and labour over a very short period.

In the mid-1990s, the Thai economy faces many stresses created by the rapid and comparatively unexpected nature of the previous decade's growth. For the medium term, most observers expect the economy to maintain its momentum, though perhaps at a gradually diminishing pace. The problems of macro-economic management and infrastructure provision currently attract considerable attention, but ultimately are soluble within the current political and policy-making structure. The problems relating to the environment, distribution and labour supply are more fundamental and ultimately more critical. How Thailand confronts these problems over the next few years will determine the prospects for long-term growth and social harmony.

NOTES

1. The fourteen foreign banks accounted for less than 5 per cent of total bank assets. They are disadvantaged compared to the local banks because they are allowed a limited number of branches, are not allowed to be listed on the stock exchange, and their dividends are subjected to withholding taxes.
2. "The Bangkok mass transit ("sky train") will be completed by 1993", in Pasuk Phongpaichit, "Thailand: Miss Universe 1988", *Southeast Asian Affairs 1989* (Singapore: Institute of Southeast Asian Studies, 1989). This was a little optimistic. Construction only started in 1995.

Part III

DEVELOPMENT OF THE FINANCIAL SECTOR

9

INDUSTRIALIZATION, FINANCIAL REFORM AND MONETARY POLICY

Naris Chaiyasoot

9.1 INTRODUCTION

This chapter aims to provide an overview of Thailand's financial sector and an analysis of the many reforms and deregulation efforts that have been undertaken. Thailand's financial reforms have been prompted primarily by the desire to mobilize domestic savings and compete for increasingly scarce foreign capital inflows. These funds are needed to finance sustained industrialization efforts and infrastructure building, which are seen as prerequisites for Thailand's ability to maintain high economic growth in the future.

Section 9.2 provides a summary of Thailand's economic development from the 1950s to the present with a special emphasis on its financial development. Section 9.3 takes a more detailed look at Thailand's financial sector and monetary policy. Finally, Section 9.4 looks at the trouble-free implementation of Thailand's financial-reform package in the context of the rich literature that exists with regard to the financial-reform experiences of other countries.

9.2 THAILAND'S ECONOMIC DEVELOPMENT IN PERSPECTIVE

9.2.1 Postwar economic development

Thailand's postwar development can be roughly divided into three phases. The first phase (1950–70) can be characterized as one based on rapid infrastructure building and subsequent industrialization through an import-substitution strategy. The building of infrastructure – particularly transportation networks, electricity supply and irrigation – was assisted partly by foreign aid and loans and was motivated, apart from economic-development objectives, by national-security considerations. Agriculture in particular

Source: Thailand's Industrialization and its Consequences, Medhi Krongkaew (Editor), London: Macmillan, 1995, pp. 160–82.

benefited from this infrastructure, especially with regard to the production of rice and several other crops that were major foreign-exchange earners.

Import-substitution industrialization succeeded in maintaining industrial growth at double-digit levels during its initial phase. However by the late 1960s it had become clear to Thai policy makers that avenues for continued industrialization through import substitution would be severely constrained by the small domestic market. As a result, policy makers began to turn to an export-oriented approach as an alternative means of sustaining industrialization efforts.

Throughout the period fiscal and monetary policy remained conservative. Government deficits during the period averaged below 2 per cent of GDP while monetary growth ranged from 10–15 per cent per annum. As a result, annual inflation averaged only about 5 per cent during these two decades. The period also saw the Thai baht pegged to the US dollar from 1963 onwards, and the exchange rate between the baht and the US dollar remained unchanged until the 1980s.

The second phase of Thailand's economic development (1970–85) not only saw a shift towards a more outward-oriented development strategy but also the need for economic adjustments in the face of severe external shocks in the form of two energy crises. The period 1973–85 saw Thailand's terms of trade deteriorate by about 36 per cent. Yet the export-oriented strategy and other favourable external factors resulted in the ratio of exports to GDP rising from a low of 10 per cent in 1970 to a high of 20 per cent in 1982. Nevertheless average GDP growth for 1973–85 fell to about 5 per cent per annum, well below those attained during the previous period. The average inflation rate increased sharply, with peaks of 25 per cent and 20 per cent, respectively, in 1973 and 1980. A substantial and persistent current-account deficit emerged, averaging about 6 per cent of GDP. This in turn led to a significant increase in Thailand's external debt and debt service.

Thailand's policy reactions to the first and second oil shocks were very different. After the first oil shock there was an attempt to cushion the impact of energy-price increases and restore past growth rates. Energy subsidies were introduced, which kept the domestic cost of energy well below world prices. At the same time public expenditure increased sharply and a substantial fiscal deficit emerged, which was increasingly financed by external borrowing. The second oil shock saw Thailand's trade balance deteriorate sharply as the baht continued to appreciate. Thailand was in a much weaker position then and was less able to cushion the impact of this external shock. While the level of foreign debt and debt services remained manageable, the rapid rate of debt accumulation was an increasing concern. At the same time the domestic economy was becoming increasingly strained by the distortions created by unrealistic energy pricing, price controls and tariff increases.

In 1980 the government decided to undertake a comprehensive economic-adjustment programme. Loans from the IMF and the World Bank assisted the government in its efforts to reduce the twin fiscal and current-account deficits, to eliminate price distortions, to undertake interest-rate-ceiling adjustments and to dismantle tariff barriers. The baht was devalued by almost 15 per cent in November 1984. It was also delinked from the US dollar. The system of fixed exchange rate, which was the hallmark of Thailand's foreign-exchange policy, was replaced by a system of managed float based on a basket of key foreign currencies. Although the authorities refused to disclose the weights of the foreign currencies used to determine the value of the baht, it was obvious that the US dollar dominated the basket.

Policy-reform successes began with the easing of ceilings on interest rates and inflation, thereby helping to restore positive real interest rates after 1982. Domestic energy prices were raised to world-market levels, eliminating distortions and disincentives to energy conservation. The range of tariff rates was narrowed and quantitative restrictions on some imports were lifted. Tariff rates were not significantly reduced, however, as improvements in the government's fiscal position proved more elusive. It was found that the problem was a chronic tendency to overestimate revenue and a lack of responsiveness of the tax system, due mainly to numerous tax exemptions. To deal with the problem the government adopted a conservative revenue estimate mechanism, which now consistently underestimates revenue, on average, by about 2 per cent of GDP. Expenditure was also significantly reduced by adopting policies that allowed only moderate increases in the salaries of government employees, by reducing capital expenditure to about 1 per cent of GDP, and by increasing the prices of public enterprises' services and reducing their capital investments.

9.2.2 The boom years, 1986–90

Economic reforms undertaken during the first half of the 1980s helped place Thailand in a strong position to take full advantage of the US-led world economic recovery, which began in earnest in the latter part of the decade. Inflation was brought down to about 4 per cent in 1986. Government fiscal deficit, which reached a peak of 5 per cent of GDP in 1984–5, turned into surplus in 1986–7, peaking at 5 per cent of GDP in 1990.

Thailand's economic performance from 1987–90 was impressive even when judged in terms of its past commendable standards. Real GDP growth was 9.5 per cent, 13.2 per cent, 12.2 per cent and 11.6 per cent, respectively, in the four years from 1987 to 1990. This growth resulted primarily from a boom in manufactured exports, which averaged about 30 per cent annually, and the massive inflow of private foreign investment particularly into the export-oriented manufacturing sector. By late 1989, however, it had become clear that bottlenecks were fast emerging and the economy was in danger of overheating. Lack of adequate transportation, port capacity, and electricity and water supply were becoming more and more apparent. Shortages of skilled personnel, especially engineers, was another emerging problem. More importantly, the capital inflows and balance-of-payments surpluses resulting from direct foreign investment was accelerating monetary growth, a trend that the Bank of Thailand increasingly found difficult to sterilize in view of the growing openness of the capital account. Accelerating import growth in order to implement investment projects was a major factor contributing to large current-account deficits, which were estimated at a worrying 8.5 per cent of GDP in 1991. The effectiveness of monetary policy will be discussed in more detail below. At this point it is sufficient to add that the massive inflow of foreign funds and intensified economic activity pushed up the rate of inflation up to beyond 6 per cent in 1990. The economic expansion also led to a frenzy of speculation in tbe real-estate and stock markets causing the value of these assets to more than double from 1986–90.

In response the Bank of Thailand asked commercial banks to put voluntary lending limits on 'non-productive' activities (such as golf-course investments). It also reintroduced the 10 per cent withholding tax on interest payments on foreign loans. The ceiling on deposit interest rates was abolished, while at the same time the ceiling on lending rates was increased from 15 per cent to 16.5 per cent. Finally, Bank of Thailand bonds worth 13.5 billion baht were sold in open market operations.

These measures, combined with effects of the Persian Gulf crisis, slowed down the Thai economy in 1990. The military coup in February 1991 further eroded economic confidence and depressed the economy to a growth rate of about 8 per cent in 1991. Expectations of economic recovery in 1992 were somewhat dashed by the violent clash between civilians and the military in May, in which scores of people were killed. However the economy recovered remarkably quickly from the May incident, and attained a rate of growth of 8 per cent in 1992. With the return to democracy following the general election in September 1992, coupled with continued world economic recovery, it was believed that Thailand's economic expansion to the end of the Seventh Plan in 1996 should satisfy the planned annual growth rate of 8.2 per cent.

9.2.3 Current policy issues

There is a realization among Thailand's policy makers and top technocrats that Thailand's future prosperity lies in its ability to cope successfully with an increasingly competitive world economy. The means by which Thailand's economic prowess could be enhanced is through continued commitment to liberalization and deregulation, in effect exposing the Thai economy to greater internal and global competition.

There is also a need to address the problem of insufficient infrastructure. This needs to be financed in part by increased domestic (private) savings, although the government's fiscal position remains strong. The major policy goal is, of course, to maintain the pace of economic expansion primarily through continued rapid industrialization. Moreover, Thailand's future industries need to be more capital and technology intensive, in line with the growing scarcity of labour in Thailand and the loss of comparative advantage in labour-intensive industries to places such as China, Indonesia and the South Asian countries.

Financing industrialization and infrastructure building would require the Thai government to try as far as possible, to increase the availability and reduce the cost of capital. Liberalization and promotion of the financial sector is considered the best way of doing this. A more open and efficient financial sector would, it is believed, contribute significantly to the mobilization of domestic savings and attract increasingly scarce foreign capital. Apart from developing the financial sector to support these key objectives, it was also advocated by Thai policy makers that the financial sector should be developed for its own sake because Thailand can fill a niche as a subregional financial centre, particularly as a provider of financial services for the reconstruction of Indochina. The government has been particularly keen to establish off-shore banking units (OBUs). The government has shown a readiness to give 15–20 licences for the establishment of OBUs, and responses from both Thai and foreign banks have been enthusiastic. In broad terms, regulations laid down by the government are aimed particularly at the promotion of 'out-out' transactions, especially the channelling of funds from various sources to Indochina. Some incentives exist for 'out-in' transactions – that is inflows of funds from foreign sources into Thailand – but these incentives have been tempered by a concern that domestic banks should not face competition that is too intense, a concern that is in keeping with past protective policies of the government.

Other development objectives include the need to improve human resources, to close the urban–rural income gap and to deal with the growing problem of environmental degradation. While these are important national issues, they are not a primary concern of this chapter. Instead, we will concentrate on the development and reform of Thailand's financial sector, particularly its role in supporting a continued rapid pace of industrialization. Monetary policy and policy mechanisms will also be discussed in this regard, particularly the way in which financial reform and deregulation as well as Thailand's increasing openness will make the conducting of monetary policy more challenging and complex.

9.3 THAILAND'S FINANCIAL SECTOR AND MONETARY POLICY

During the 1980s the size of Thailand's financial sector nearly doubled as a percentage of GDP. In particular, the ratio of financial assets to GDP increased from 69.2 per cent to 121.2 per cent. At the same time the ratio of M2 to GDP increased from 34.2 per cent to 67.4 per cent (Robinson, Byeon and Teja, 1991; Tseng and Corker, 1991).

While the financial system has broadened considerably the capital market has remained quite small with the exception of the fast-expanding stock market. This can be seen in the growing role of the stock market in savings mobilization at the expense of the financial institutions. For instance, the share of total savings mobilized by financial institutions and the stock market were 70.7 and 8.6 per cent, respectively, in 1986. These shares changed markedly in 1991 as financial institutions managed to account for only 50.7 per cent of total savings whereas the share of the stock market rose to 28.8 per cent (Patira, 1992).

Nevertheless the variety of financial instruments available to both users and providers of funds is limited at present. To remedy the situation, the Thai authorities have laid out a wide-ranging programme of financial reforms aimed at boosting domestic savings, enhancing the competitiveness of the Thai financial sector and establishing Thailand as a subregional financial centre, primarily to serve the needs of reconstruction in Indochina.

9.3.1 Financial institutions

The Bank of Thailand – the country's central bank – forms the core of the Thai financial system. As of early 1992 there were 29 commercial banks and three specialized banks owned by the government: the Government Savings Bank, set up to mobilize household savings through an extensive branch network; the Bank for Agriculture and Agricultural Cooperatives, which makes mostly concessional loans to the agricultural sector; and the Government Housing Bank, which finances home purchases by those with moderate incomes. These specialized government banks accounted for nearly 9 per cent of financial assets in 1990.

The 29 commercial banks, which accounted for 71 per cent of total financial assets in 1990, dominate the Thai financial sector. Most domestic banks were originally established by business groups and trading houses to help finance their operations, and they maintain close links today. The banking sector is highly concentrated, with the five largest domestic banks accounting for some two thirds of total bank assets. The sector is also mainly closed to foreign competition as the 16 local commercial banks, with their extensive branch networks (2112 domestic and 22 foreign branches), account for 95 per cent of bank assets. The 14 foreign banks, which account for 5 per cent of bank assets, are disadvantaged with respect to domestic banks in three respects: (1) they are unable to offer retail banking services since they are allowed only one branch in Thailand; (2) they are not juristic entities, so they cannot be quoted on the stock exchange and are thus not allowed certain tax breaks; and (3) they pay a withholding tax on dividends transferred overseas.

The 94 finance and securities companies are the second largest group of financial institutions, accounting for about 15 per cent of total financial assets. They are relatively new institutions, having emerged in the early

1960s as affiliates of commercial banks. They were set up primarily to undertake higher margin but higher risk consumer finance as well as to provide services that the parent bank could not undertake directly. Their activities subsequently expanded into certain types of corporate finance. The finance and securities companies expanded rapidly during the 1970s but were stalled in the early 1980s following financial crises in 1979 and, particularly, in 1983. The 1983 financial crisis, triggered initially by large losses in a finance company and its affiliates, subsequently affected one third of all financial companies accounting for one fourth of financial assets. Important factors leading to this financial crisis included the slowdown in growth and tight monetary policy, the weak management practices of the finance companies (particularly with regard to extending credit and guarantees to projects in which the institution's directors and shareholders had vested interests), and the weak supervisory and regulatory framework of the central authorities.

One of the authorities' responses was the setting up of the Financial Institutions Development Fund to rehabilitate ailing financial institutions. Among the various schemes to revive the ailing institutions, the 'lifeboat scheme' was the principal means by which liquidity was provided in exchange for control by the Ministry of Finance who will try to strengthen the institution's management, credit-collection procedures and financial plan with an aim to return those institutions to health.

Supervision and regulation were strengthened also. The Bank of Thailand revoked the licences of some 24 financial institutions and intervened in 30 more from 1983–6. The Bank of Thailand's legal, regulatory and supervisory powers were strengthened. It was empowered to enforce compliance by direct intervention, and when necessary it can order an increase in bank capital and remove bank directors and officers.

Finally, other specialized financial institutions that make up the Thai financial sector include the Industrial Finance Corporation of Thailand (IFCT, a privately owned development bank financed primarily through foreign borrowing with government guarantees); over 2000 savings and agricultural cooperatives; 18 credit foncier companies (financing and leasing of immovable assets); life insurance companies and numerous pawnshops. These are estimated to account for a little more than 5 per cent of total financial assets.

9.3.2 Monetary policy

Thailand's monetary authorities have declared that monetary policy serves several policy objectives, namely growth, stability and economic development (Bank of Thailand, 1990). A primary objective is, however, to maintain domestic price stability. This was accomplished in all but two short periods in which domestic inflation rate rose to double-digit levels: 25 per cent in 1974 and 20 per cent in 1982. Thai monetary authorities have consistently kept monetary-base growth in line with real economic growth. For example, monetary-base growth from 1960–71, 1972–9, and 1980–90 were 11 per cent, 14.5 per cent, and 19 per cent, respectively. Compared with real economic growth during the same period, the excess of monetary growth over real economic growth averaged 6.3 per cent, 7.2 per cent and 11 per cent, respectively. As a result, the inflation rate in Thailand over the past 30 years has been very similar to that which prevailed in industrialized countries, particularly the United States (Virabongsa and Pakorn, 1988).

The comparability of Thailand's inflation rate with the United States did not occur by chance. Thailand pegged the baht to the US dollar for over 20 years – from 1963 to 1984. The pegging of the baht to a basket of currencies since then has turned out, in practice, to be an implicit continuation of past policy to keep the baht closely aligned with the US dollar. Arising from this is the fact that Thailand's monetary policy has been used to defend the exchange rate, in particular to redress external-balance problems when they arise. For example the authorities kept the rate of growth of M1 at 4.0 per cent and 2.4 per cent below nominal GDP growth from 1972–9 and 1980–6, respectively, as a means of both curbing inflation and restraining widening external deficits. In short, monetary policy in Thailand has traditionally been assigned the task of maintaining both domestic price stability and external balance under a regime of fixed exchange rates and subsequently a 'dirty float', which kept the baht in close parity with the US dollar.

The main monetary policy instruments in Thailand are open-market operations in the repurchase markets and, to a lesser extent, lending by the Bank of Thailand. Changes to interest-rate ceilings were also resorted to, especially in the 1980s, but ceilings on both deposit and lending rates have been completely abolished as of June 1992. The Bank of Thailand also intervenes in the foreign-exchange market. Changes to reserve ratio requirements have rarely been used as an instrument of monetary policy. As such, the basic reserve requirement of 7 per cent of deposit liabilities (2 per cent deposit with the Bank of Thailand, 2.5 vault cash and the rest in government securities) has remained unchanged for the past 20 years.

The primary instrument of monetary policy is open-market operations in the repurchase market. As the sole seller in the market, the Bank of Thailand can readily inject or absorb liquidity as the situation warrants. Securities traded in this market are government bonds. However, following a substantial improvement in Thailand's external position and growing liquidity in the banking system in 1986, the Bank of Thailand actively drained liquidity through consistent government-bond purchases. The need to continue draining liquidity and the growing importance of open-market operations led to the introduction and sale of the Bank of Thailand's own bonds from 1987.

The other monetary instrument, central-bank lending, is carried out via a general loan window and a refinancing facility. These instruments have not really played a significant role as tools for economic stabilization. The former facility essentially provides short-term liquidity for financial institutions but requires government securities as collateral. Banks must also show that they have no alternative sources of funds. Lending under this window amounted to only 2.4 billion baht or 0.15 per cent of total bank deposits, underscoring the 'last-resort' nature of this window. Changes in loan-window interest rates have been more frequent, especially in recent times. These changes have been used to signal shifts in the Bank of Thailand's monetary policy.

Interest-rate ceilings cannot initially be considered instruments of monetary policy since they were set by legislation to 'prevent excessive competition' and ensure 'stability' of the financial system. Lending rates were set at 15 per cent, which kept domestic interest rates significantly positive during periods of low inflation prior to the 1970s. Moreover, foreign interest rates were stable at 5–6 per cent, thereby keeping a margin that was sufficient to uphold the level of capital inflow necessary to maintain the external balance. However, periods of high interest rates and inflation during the 1970s led to periods of significantly negative real interest rates, threatening to dry up capital inflows and bringing about severe credit tightening in Thailand. Credit rationing was particularly severe in 1979, causing a great deal of commercial hardship, and was a prelude to the subsequent crises in the financial sector that were mentioned above.

As a result the authorities amended the law to enable the Bank of Thailand to announce changes in interest-rate ceilings in 1980. The Bank of Thailand increased bank deposit and lending rates by 3 per cent that year followed by another upward adjustment in bank and financial-company lending rates to reach 19 per cent and 21 per cent, respectively, in 1984. Variations in interest-rate ceilings were used as instruments to affect money and credit until ceilings on all interest rates for bank deposits were abolished in March 1990. This was followed by a removal of ceilings on lending rates for commercial banks and other financial institutions in June 1992. In short, the Thai authorities have been very mindful of ensuring that domestic interest rates closely track foreign interest rates. In particular, domestic interest rates have been significantly positive in most years. The systematic liberalization of interest rates, beginning in 1989, signalled a comprehensive approach to reform that was consistent with Thailand's level of economic maturity and rapid industrialization.

The Bank of Thailand's refinancing facility is designed to allocate more financial resources to priority sectors at preferential interest rates by providing credits to commercial banks against their promissory notes. Commercial banks lend to these priority sectors at rates not exceeding 10 per cent while refinancing interest rates are 3–5 per cent depending on the sector in question. Some 90 per cent of the loans go to exports, with the rest allocated to manufacturing and agricultural activities, and rural development. The amount of refinancing outstanding was 22 billion baht in 1990.

9.3.3 Financial reforms

Apart from the abolition of interest-rate ceilings discussed above, Thailand also undertook financial liberalization in the following areas.

Relaxation of foreign exchange control

On 22 May 1990 Thailand officially accepted Article VIII of the International Monetary Fund Agreement, which obliges it to allow unrestricted international payments with respect to current-account transactions. This was, in effect, the first stage of foreign-exchange control liberalization aimed at boosting confidence among investors and entrepreneurs as well as improving Thailand's credit worthiness in international markets. Measures to relax foreign-exchange controls include allowing commercial banks to grant all foreign-exchange transactions relating to international trade and to approve repayments of foreign loans and remittances of securities sales for up to US$500 000; increasing the maximum limits on foreign-exchange transactions relating to services accounts; and increasing the limit on travel allowances, education and other remittances.

On 1 April 1991 the Bank of Thailand announced the second stage of foreign exchange control liberalization which included, among other things, allowing repatriation of investment funds, dividends and profits as well as loan repayments and interest payment without requiring prior authorisation; allowing unrestricted direct foreign investment by residents to their affiliated companies abroad to an amount not exceeding US$5 million, although the purchase of immovable assets and securities abroad still require Bank of Thailand approval; and allowing Thai individuals and juristic persons in Thailand to maintain foreign-currency accounts under certain conditions.

Liberalization of commercial banks and other financial institutions

The Thai authorities embarked on a strategy to promote and widen the scope of activities of commercial banks and other financial institutions not only as a means of improving the mobilization of domestic savings and foreign-capital inflows, but also to strengthen the competitiveness of Thai commercial banks and other financial institutions. In this regard the authorities anticipate that successful completion of the Uruguay Round of GATT negotiations will inevitably require Thailand to open up its financial sector to foreign competition in the near future. Thus, ongoing liberalization is partly in anticipation of, and in preparation for increased competition in the Thai financial market. In particular, from 3 November 1987 commercial banks were permitted to undertake the following activities: preparation of feasibility studies for investment projects; loan syndication; provision of consulting services on acquisitions, mergers or consolidation; and management of trust funds.

The implementation of the Securities and Exchange Act (SEA), passed on 16 May 1992, is expected greatly to expand the scope of activities of commercial banks. Banks can now manage as well as act as a trustee of a mutual fund. Several major banks have already obtained licences and are setting up mutual funds. SEA also allows banks to act as selling agents of government and state enterprise agencies (bonds, debentures and notes). The scope of commercial bank services were further broadened, allowing them to act as sales agents for debt instruments of government and state enterprises, to provide information services for clients, and to act as financial advisers. Finally, banks can now issue negotiable certificates of deposits.

The maximum limit of net open foreign asset position with respect to the capital funds of commercial banks was increased from 20 per cent to 25 per cent on 9 April 1990. On 13 November the same year, the ratio of securities holdings to total deposits required for new branch opening was reduced from 16 per cent to 9.5 per cent. Since 5 June 1991 bond issues by state enterprises, which were not guaranteed by the Ministry of Finance, can be counted as required reserves for branch opening. Moreover, the ratio of securities holdings was further reduced to 8 per cent and 7 per cent, respectively, on 13 September 1991 and 14 February 1992.

On 23 June 1991 the type of reserves required to maintain a 7 per cent reserve ratio was relaxed to include liquid assets such as Bank of Thailand bonds, debentures, bonds or other debt instruments issued by state organizations and state enterprises. Foreign currencies held by commercial banks are also counted as cash on hand.

In line with government policy to promote Thailand as a regional financial centre, the government plans to issue as many as 20 licences to foreign banks to set up offshore banking institutions under the Bangkok International Banking Facility, or BIBF. This plan was initiated in 1990 by the Bank of Thailand, which, in view of the successful financial liberalization carried out so far, felt that Thailand was ready and the timing and opportunity were right. Banks under the BIBF will be authorized to undertake the following activities:

- In the form of foreign currencies: take in deposits and loans from abroad and extend loans to both overseas (out-out) and local (out-in) markets.
- In baht: take in deposit and loans from banks (both Thai and foreign) abroad and make loans to banks abroad (out-out in baht). Note that BIBF will not be allowed to lend in baht to local markets.
- Engage in cross-currency foreign-exchange trading.
- Provide aval and guarantee facilities for foreign-currency loans extended to overseas borrowers.
- Handle trade finance for overseas customers.
- Engage in loan syndication by acquiring foreign-currency loans extended to overseas borrowers.

Many key foreign banks have expressed keen interest in BIBF and viewed it as a first step towards being granted a full commercial bank operating licence in Thailand. Major Thai banks have shown some concern that offshore banking institutions will intensify competition in acquiring foreign loans for the domestic market (out-in), an area they have dominated in the past. The package of incentives subsequently granted by the government in this regard, such as retention of the 10 per cent withholding tax for such BIBF loans, will however temper the competitiveness of BIBF vis-à-vis local banks. It is also an indication that the Thai central-bank authorities are well aware of the competition and are determined to ensure that this competition against local banks will not be excessive.

Concerning the effects of BIBF on local banking, it is probable that BIBF will slow down corporate lending by local banks. Large corporations will seek to obtain more funds through BIBF. Local banks will therefore have to place greater emphasis on retail banking and fee-based income, where there will be greater competition with finance companies (Thanisr, 1992a). Another implication is that the expected inflows of out-in transactions by BIBF will certainly increase the domestic money supply. Again, the withholding tax will help slow down such inflows. The BIBF will also enable Thai businesses to acquire foreign loans at lower cost. Moreover, the greater integration of the Thai financial market with the global market will help narrow the spread between domestic and foreign interest rates, thereby benefiting investors and savers. In addition the BIBF is expected to promote a significant increase in out-out transactions, in particular loans from overseas into Indochinese countries. It is here that BIBF and Thai banks are expected to complement rather than compete with each other. The opening of Thai bank branches in Indochina will create an important financial network that will help facilitate BIBF activities in Indochina (Thanisr, 1992a).

With respect to finance companies, the Bank of Thailand has advocated that they be allowed to expand into areas previously reserved for commercial banks. Established and reputable financial companies will, for example, be allowed to deal in foreign exchange business. As a result, top-tier finance companies will be almost indistinguishable from banks.

Concerning the capital market, the principal aim of the Securities and Exchange Act of 1992 was to create and develop the primary-securities market. Previously a company wanting to mobilize funds directly from the public had to meet very stringent conditions to become a public company. Subsequently companies that were listed and authorized by the Stock Exchange of Thailand (SET) were allowed to issue new shares for public subscription and to float debentures. But this did not meet the primary objective of developing the primary market, for it was tantamount to making use of the secondary market to determine the role of the primary market. The new SEA allows both public and ordinary limited companies to issue debt instruments for fund-mobilization purposes (Patira, 1992). The success in this regard could provide yet another important source of direct finance for Thailand's industries in line with the government's industrial-promotion policy. It would, at the same time, further erode the corporate-finance activities of local commercial banks, which may have to adjust by providing consultancy and fee-based services to companies wishing to obtain finance from the primary market.

As regards the equity market, the passage of the Securities Exchange Act has streamlined the supervision of the SET by a separate and independent institution modelled along the lines of the US Securities and Exchange Commission. The SEC also promises to expedite the time needed to evaluate and authorize company listing in the SET. Delays and strict evaluation procedures have led some firms to gain 'back door' entry by taking over firms that are already listed in the stock market. Other firms have explored the over-the-counter (OTC) market as an alternative means of raising capital, and this is attracting some interest at present.

All in all, however, it must still be concluded that the Thai financial market is not yet well developed. The main financial instruments available to individuals are still essentially limited to bank deposits, promissory notes issued by finance and securities companies, and shares. The primary sources of finance are loans from banks or finance companies, share issues and, for larger companies, foreign borrowing. While other financial instruments exist – such as commercial paper, transferable certificates of deposit, short-term notes and debentures – they have in practice played a limited role. Nevertheless recent reforms, as noted above, suggest that the Thai financial sector could continue to be a dynamic and fast-growing sector of the economy.

9.4 INDUSTRIALIZATION, FINANCIAL REFORM AND MONETARY POLICY

9.4.1 Assessment and evaluation of Thailand's financial reforms

Widespread acceptance of the effectiveness of market forces as the most effective means of promoting economic development has led many countries to comprehensively liberalize and deregulate their economies. Many such liberalization efforts have succeeded in spurring growth, yet a significant number have produced adverse repercussions that are serious enough to undermine the policy reforms. A brief survey of the literature below revealed that the financial reforms in Thailand have been undertaken in the correct sequence, as prescribed by empirical evidence.

Because of the importance of the sequencing of reforms, a body of literature on this subject has been developed. For example Edwards (1987) argued that the domestic economy should be reformed before the external sector is liberalized. In particular, on the domestic side fiscal deficit must be controlled before inflation is dealt with. Once this has been done domestic financial reforms can be undertaken, leading to the raising of domestic interest rates. Within the external sector, the current and capital accounts should not be liberalized at the same time. Liberalizing the capital account first would most likely lead to rapid inflows of capital, generating real appreciation of the domestic currency, making it more difficult for the tradeable goods sector to adjust to world competition. Instead the current account should be liberalized first, and only after the new productive structure has been established should the capital account be slowly set free.

The *1991 World Development Report* concluded that macroeconomic stability formed the basis upon which successful reforms, particularly those concerning the financial sector, could be carried out. Empirical evidence also revealed that the goods sector should be reformed first because the financial sector adjusts itself more quickly than the product sector. This is particularly so with respect to the liberalization of the trade and capital accounts.

According to McKinnon (1988), who carried out several studies on the interest-rate policies of some Asian and Latin American countries, financial liberalization and significantly positive real interest rates are, on average, associated with higher economic growth. He also found that full liberalization of the banks during high and variable inflation is not warranted because unduly high real interest rates are likely to prevail in such circumstances. There are limits to which interests rates can be raised without incurring the danger of adverse risk selection among borrowers. High real interest rates not only allow the riskiest borrowing to remain, but actually encourages the practice. And this could create a moral-hazard problem for the banks themselves, especially when bank supervision is weak and ineffective.

Villanueva and Mirakhor (1990) further expanded on McKinnon's work and concluded that macroeconomic stabilization and stringent bank supervision must occur before complete interest-rate liberalization can take place. Where the economy is unstable and bank supervision is weak, interest-rate liberalization should be gradual and accompanied by both strong macroeconomic policy to stabilize the economy and strict supervision of the banking system. Where supervision is already effective but macroeconomic instability exists, the economy should be stabilized before introducing gradual interest-rate liberalization. Where macroeconomic stability has been attained but supervision is inadequate, supervision should be boosted while interest rates are regulated. Macro stability and effective supervision help the reforming country avoid the adverse consequences of financial liberalization, namely sharp increases in interest rates, bankruptcies of financial institutions and loss of monetary control.

Thailand's situation exhibits many of the characteristics necessary for successful financial reforms. First, domestic stability has always been maintained as inflation has been kept low. Second, real domestic interest rates have been kept at levels that are consistently higher than world rates. Third, Thailand successfully dealt with its fiscal problems and strengthened supervision of the financial sector prior to embarking on comprehensive financial liberalization in the latter part of the 1980s. Fourth, the tradeable-goods sector has been relatively free of distortions. Protection of the domestic market has been confined to moderate tariff rates and quantitative restrictions existed only in exceptional cases. It is therefore not surprising that liberalization of Thailand's financial sector and capital account were carried out smoothly without any subsequent instabilities or adverse impacts (Bank of Thailand, 1992). The prospects are also good that implementation of further liberalization policies such as the BIBF, undertaken with the Thai financial authorities' usual care and caution, will bring about no serious repercussions.

9.4.2 Implications for monetary policy and economic stability

As mentioned earlier, the task that Thai policy planners have set for themselves is the maintenance of economic growth rates comparable to past performance while at the same time addressing the problem of growing inequality and environmental degradation. Concentrating on economic growth, the Seventh Plan has set a target growth rate of 8.2 per cent per year between 1992 and 1996. In this regard, industry and exports are expected to be the primary means by which this growth rate is to be achieved, that is, these two sectors are expected to expand at an annual rate of 9.5 per cent and 14.7 per cent, respectively. Meanwhile, inflation is to be kept to below 5.6 per cent per annum while the current-account deficit as a percentage of GDP is predicted to fall from a high of 8.5 per cent in 1991 to an average of 5.2 per cent during the Seventh Plan period.

The Seventh Plan also set ambitious goals, particularly in relation to growth in the industrial sector and exports. Financial reform and liberalization, it is hoped, will help significantly to mobilize domestic savings, which have been estimated to fall short of investment demands over the next five years. Further maturity and expansion of the stock-exchange market, growth of mutual funds and insurance companies, and expanded activities of commercial banks, particularly the setting up of offshore banking units, are all expected to play an important role in mobilizing domestic savings.

In addition, reforms in the financial and real sectors are expected to attract additional capital inflows, preferably of the direct-investment variety. Yet, with the economic slowdown of Japan and other countries that are major investors in Thailand, and the additional time needed fully to restore foreign-investor confidence in the Thai economy, it is increasingly clear that direct-investment inflows cannot be relied upon to play a dominant role in boosting domestic investment. Indeed, the inflow of direct investment fell 20 per cent, from a peak of 58 700 million baht in 1990 to 46 700 million baht in 1991. Direct foreign investment fell further at the rate of 33 per cent in the first quarter of 1992. The continued postponement of economic recovery among the major industrialized countries is bound to have adverse effects on direct foreign investment.

Instead, investment financing will be more dependent on portfolio investment and short- and long-term capital inflows. Indeed Thailand's liberalization of the foreign-exchange market and capital account will undoubtedly encourage greater flows of such capital. Yet the greater openness and capital mobility has important implications. Domestic interest rates will be increasingly determined exogenously, corresponding more or less to world interest rates. While the authorities may wish to keep the Thai baht fixed to the US dollar in keeping with the past practice, they will find the supply of money increasingly difficult to control. For example, attempts to tighten the domestic money supply, leading to increases in domestic interest rates, will only induce greater capital inflows, which will eventually restore the differential between domestic and foreign interest rates. In the extreme case, monetary policy will not be able to influence domestic money supply and price levels if interest rates are exogenously determined and the exchange rate is fixed (Mundell, 1962).

Even prior to liberalization of the financial and external sectors, evidence of the openness of the Thai capital account was recognized. Robinson, Byeon and Teja (1991), utilizing quarterly interest-rate data from 1978–90, concluded that the Thai capital account was quite open. With subsequent liberalization, they expressed the view that maintainmg a relatively fixed exchange rate is increasingly likely to constrain the conducting of monetary policy in Thailand.

Evidence of greater capital mobility has already emerged. The inflow of portfolio and short- and long-term capital increased by more than 130 per cent from 107 185 million baht in 1989 to 247 011 million baht in 1991. The inflows were induced by the wide disparity between domestic and world interest rates, the stability of the baht and, more importantly, liberalization of Thailand's foreign-exchange sector. It is noteworthy that increased volumes were very evident for short- and long-term private capital inflows. As recently as 1987, for example, it was central-government borrowing and direct investment that dominated Thailand's capital account. In 1991 short- and long-term private borrowing accounted for over 80 per cent of capital inflow into Thailand. From only 4.1 billion baht in 1987, short-term private borrowing accelerated to 157.66 billion baht in 1991, notwithstanding the fact that 1991 saw considerable turmoil in the form of a coup d'etat in Thailand and fighting in the Gulf. Continuing financial liberalization particularly the advent of the BIBF, will most certainly further boost such short-term inflows. As it now stands, private short-term inflow accounts for more than half of total capital inflow into Thailand.

The increase in the inflow of such a mobile source of funds can indeed prove to be a destabilizing influence. In fact the inflow helped increased the rate of growth of M1 in 1991 from 1.1 per cent in the third quarter to 13.8

per cent in the fourth quarter. Shielding the domestic economy from external instability and restoring the effectiveness of monetary policy can be attained only by greater willingness on the part of the Thai authorities to accept increased fluctuations in the exchange rate. For example, attempts to curb the domestic money supply will put pressure on interest rates. This will lead to capital inflows, which will in turn cause the domestic currency to appreciate. This appreciation will reduce the competitiveness of the tradeable-goods sector, thereby further reinforcing the deflationary impact of restrictive monetary policy.

Such fluctuations in the exchange rate may not be readily acceptable to Thai authorities and traders since over the decades they have grown accustomed to the exchange rate being more or less fixed. The argument that greater exchange-rate fluctuations create uncertainties need not apply in the case of Thailand, however. While greater fluctuations in exchange rates are likely to occur, the Thai financial system should be mature and dynamic enough to develop the means by which traders can hedge risks in foreign-exchange fluctuations. However, excessive fluctuations in the exchange rates that cannot be hedged must indeed be undesirable as they could have an adverse destabilizing impact on Thailand's industrial and tradeable-goods sectors.

The other implication has to do with the impact of financial reforms on the demand for money. A stable and predictable relationship between monetary aggregates on the one hand, and income and wealth, prices and interest rates on the other is a crucial element in the formulation and effectiveness of monetary policy. Financial liberalization creates potential for change and, more importantly, instability in money demand. In the case of Thailand, it can be surmised that freeing interest rates so as better to reflect economic returns could prompt portfolio shifts. The shift could be accounted for by money-demand functions that contain appropriate interest terms. Yet the estimated coefficient based on past events when interest rates were not really allowed to vary may not have reflected the true relationship between money demand and interest rates. As interest rates become more flexible, previously dormant influences of interest rate on money demand could become transparent.

Measures to improve the functioning and depth of financial markets could result in both portfolio shifts and affect the sensitivity of money demand to changes in income and interest rates. For example, Thailand's intention to increase competition between various financial institutions (for example banks and finance companies) could lower transaction costs in financial markets, thereby allowing money demand to respond more rapidly than before to interest changes. Moreover, better regulation of and information about financial institutions (such as the setting up of a credit-rating agency) may alter the relative risk of different financial assets, leading to both discrete portfolio adjustments and a change in the interest elasticity of money demand.

The introduction of new, attractive assets could lead to a gradual portfolio shift away from monetary assets, independently of income and interest-rate changes. The gradual, perhaps disjointed shift away from money assets will make more difficult the task of arriving at a stable estimate of the demand for money. At the same time, to the extent that the policy of financial-market development encourages reintermediation – that is, attracting domestic savings away from informal 'curb' money markets – the direction of the effects on broad monetary aggregates may be to increase the demand for all financial assets, including money.

In short, as summed up by Tseng and Corker (1991), financial liberalization could lead to one-off or more gradual shifts in the level of money holdings, as well as to changes in the measured income and interest elasticity of money demand. The practical difficulty, as mentioned above, lies with gradual changes in income and interest-rate elasticity of demand, which would take longer to detect. This would render money demand relationships unstable over a longer period.

Tseng and Corker (1991) looked at nine Asian countries, including Thailand, and attempted to estimate their money demand in light of the financial reforms being carried out in those countries in the 1980s. They found that the estimated long-run elasticities of narrow money demand varied substantially among countries: the elasticities exceeded unity for four countries and were less than unity for five, of which Thailand was one. This suggested monetization in the former cases and attempts to economize on cash balances in the latter cases. Interest rates had significant negative coefficients in the M1 equations for all countries.

On the other hand, the long run elasticities of broad money demand (M2) exceeded unity in all countries except Korea. This reaffirms the decline in the velocity of broad money that was found in Asia in the 1970s. The large income elasticities do not necessarily reflect monetization; instead the growth in money demand may have resulted from the rapid growth in wealth.

For several countries, including Thailand, broad money demand was found to be negatively related to an opportunity-cost variable defined as the return on alternative assets minus the average interest rate paid on broad money balances. This suggests that broad money demand is affected by relative asset returns as opposed to the general level of interest rates.

Significant for Thailand was the fact that stable long-term relationships could not be found for either narrow or broad money demand. Narrow money does not appear to have a stable long-term relationship with income and interest or inflation rates. Income and interest-rate elasticities of demand for narrow and broad money were, however, all statistically significant and large. Income elasticities for narrow and broad money were 0.85 and 1.72, respectively. Interest-rate elasticities were strongly negative at – 1.53 for narrow money and – 2.46 for broad money, reinforcing the belief that financial liberalization will increase the sensitivity of money demand to interest rates.

9.5 CONCLUSIONS

Financial reforms in Thailand are being carried out both to mobilize savings to finance industrialization efforts and to enhance the ability of domestic financial institutions to cope with global competition. These goals are indeed laudable and can contribute significantly to the sustained growth of the Thai economy envisaged by Thai economic policy makers. Moreover, Thailand appears to have placed itself in a position to maximize the chance of successful financial reform and liberalization. Its reform package is comprehensive, if perhaps a little too cautious with respect to opening up domestic banks to greater foreign competition. More importantly, Thailand possesses the ingredients that have made financial reforms successful, namely a stable macroeconomic environment and competent financial-institution supervision. Moreover, liberalization of the real sector is well under way and Thailand's traded-goods sector is in a strong competitive position.

Financial reforms and liberalization have important implications. As the prospect of increased direct foreign investment is diminishing because of the slow pace of world recovery (especially in Japan), and because of the increased competition for such investment in Europe, the former states of the Soviet Union and even the North American Free Trade Area (NAFTA), capital mobility will be increasingly relied upon to finance domestic investment. The greater openness has increased this capital mobility. Greater capital mobility also means that interest rates will be increasingly determined exogenously. However capital mobility when the exchange rate is more or less fixed, as is the case in Thailand at present, would make sterilization of capital flows difficult. The implication is that the ability of the Bank of Thailand to control the money supply will be reduced. Since fiscal policy tends to be a cumbersome tool for macroeconomic stabilization, especially in developing countries such as Thailand, it is likely that the Thai authorities will choose to restore the efficacy of monetary policy as a primary means of macroeconomic stabilization.

Increasing the effectiveness of monetary policy will, however, require greater fluctuations in the exchange rates. This may not be in keeping with the past policy of the Bank of Thailand in trying to maintain a stable exchange rate in order to facilitate trade and other external transactions, but it looks as though greater variations in the exchange rate will be difficult to avoid in the future. This need not have a destabilizing impact on the tradeable-goods sector, so long as hedging mechanisms are developed to eliminate risks arising from fluctuations in exchange rates. It is in this regard that the development of exchange-rate hedges will play a central role in Thailand's financial-reform efforts. At the same time the central authorities will have to take care to coordinate monetary policy with foreign-exchange rate policy.

Financial reforms will also significantly affect the relationship between money demand, income and interest rates. The increasing variety of monetary instruments will make monetary policy more difficult to conduct. Moreover, the impact of financial reforms on money demand can be both immediate and gradual, making the relationship difficult to quantify. Available evidence has shown that, in the case of Thailand, money-demand relationships could be unstable over a longer period of time. The inability to establish a stable demand for money function could in turn jeopardize the ability of the central bank to conduct effective monetary policy. In other words, with liberalization and openness comes the inevitable prospect of increased uncertainty and instability.

ACKNOWLEDGMENT

I would like to express my appreciation to Assistant Professor Bhanupongse Nidhiprabha of the Faculty of Economics, Thammasat University and Dr Thanisr Chaturongkul of the Bangkok Bank. Both were kind enough to read this chapter and provided valuable comments and suggestions. Any errors and omissions are, of course, mine alone.

10

REFORMS OF THE FINANCIAL SECTOR IN INDONESIA, 1983–91

Anwar Nasution

INTRODUCTION

After a long period of financial repression and import-substitution industrialisation, Indonesia embarked on a broad economic restructuring programme in the early 1980s. This broadbased economic reform has been successful in promoting rapid expansion of private sector investment and consumption expenditures as well as non oil exports. These sectors have been the driving forces behind the brisk economic activity since 1987 (Table 10.1). Private investment has increased substantially with the bulk of the investment outside the oil-related manufacturing industries and directed towards export activities, particularly labour-intensive and resource-based industries where Indonesia has a comparative advantage. Some of these projects represent a relocation of "foot-loose" industries to Indonesia because of industrial restructuring in East Asia. In terms of exports, the reform has contributed to greater diversification. For example, in contrast to the situation in the 1970s and early 1980s, over 60 per cent of export revenues are now generated from non oil exports.

The economic reforms were initiated in the financial sector, and although reforms in the real sector followed, the pace of the reform has been much faster in the financial sector. The objectives of the financial policy reforms are to promote domestic savings, improve the efficiency of resource allocation, and provide a framework that allows for the implementation of effective market-based monetary control.

Beginning the economic structuring programme with reforms in the financial sector before reforms in the real sectors of the economy is contrary to the conventional wisdom. Economic theory recommends that deregulation should begin in the real sectors of the economy.[1] This article argues that the reverse sequence – i.e., financial reform followed by reforms in the real sectors – combined with the slow pace of economic deregulatiun and the inconsistency of government policies have served to weaken the structure of financial institutions in Indonesia. The problem was exacerbated by the absence of

Source: *The Indonesian Quarterly*, XXI/3, 1993, pp. 284–310.

Table 10.1 Macro-economic indicators, 1983–1991 (percentage)

	1975–1983 (Av.)	*1983–1987 (Av.)*	*1988*	*1989*	*1990*	*1991*[a]
1. Aggregate growth rates						
Gross domestic product	6.5	5.0	5.7	7.4	7.3	6.6
Non-oil GDP	7.0	5.7	7.4	8.2	7.8	6.5
Agriculture	3.5	3.3	4.7	4.3	2.5	0.9
Manufacturing	10.6	12.0	12.8	11.6	13.0	10.2
Mining	6.8	3.4	4.8	11.0	14.6	8.9
Construction	10.8	1.1	9.5	11.8	13.6	11.5
Other services	8.6	6.0	6.9	8.5	7.8	6.6
Gross national income	8.5	3.4	6.2	7.7	6.5	5.6
Consumption	8.9	4.0	4.3	5.9	7.5	5.2
Fixed investment	10.7	−3.7	10.3	13.0	19.7	10.7
Public	12.6	−9.8	11.4	6.8	11.9	11.2
Private	9.1	0.9	9.7	16.8	24.4	10.4
2. Structure of the Economy						
Oil GDP		21.8	19.3	18.6	18.3	18.3
Non-oil GDP		78.2	80.7	81.4	81.7	81.7
Agriculture		21.9	21.2	20.5	19.6	18.4
Manufacturing		11.4	13.6	14.1	14.9	19.9
Mining		1.2	1.2	1.3	1.4	n.a.
Construction		5.3	5.3	5.5	5.8	6.0
Other services		38.5	39.4	40.0	40.1	40.1
3. Macroeconomic balance						
Deficit current account/GNP		2.5	2.3	2.0	3.8	4.3
Non-interest current acc./GNP		2.0	2.1	2.2	0.3	0.1
Overal public sector balance/GDP		−2.7	−3.1	−1.3	0.2	−0.7
Medium- and long-term debt service/ exports		34.8	34.4	31.6	27.8	30.1
Medium- and long-term debt/GNP		65.5	60.3	54.6	58.6	61.1
National saving/GDP		20.1	19.9	21.7	22.1	22.2
Public		7.4	5.4	6.5	9.3	8.9
Private		12.8	14.5	15.2	12.7	13.3
Domestic investment/GDP		24.4	22.2	23.5	25.2	26.2
Public		9.5	8.4	8.6	9.2	9.6
Private		14.8	13.8	14.9	16.0	16.6
4. Money and prices						
Inflation rate		8.5	5.5	6.0	9.5	9.5
Interest rate			18.5	18.6	18.5	22.8
Narrow money growth (M^1)		13.8	13.5	39.8	18.4	8.4
Broad money growth (M^2)		23.3	23.9	39.8	44.2	15.5
Reserve money growth		12.1	−5.4	23.3	19.0	2.9
M^1/ GDP		10.3	10.1	12.0	12.0	11.2
M^2/GDP		23.6	29.6	35.0	42.5	42.5

Note:

[a] Weighted average interest rates on 12-month time deposits.

Sources: Central Bureau of Statistics, *National Income of Indonesia 1985–1990;* Bank Indonesia, *Indonesian Financial Statistics*, various issues.

relatively efficient money and capital markets which in turn prolonged the transition period and raised the costs of adjustment from financial repression to the market-based system. The "overshooting" of interest rates since the early 1990s wiped out marginal projects and created severe problems even for the most efficient and feasible business activities. Asymmetric information due to a relatively weak social infrastructure further retarded development of financial markets.

Nevertheless, with the recent financial reforms, many of these problems have been mitigated. Business opportunities are now wide open both in the "hardware" and "software" aspects of the financial system, Through joint venture operations, foreign banks can penetrate the fast-growing Indonesian financial market. Today, foreign lending institutions also have better access to providing loans and investment financing to Indonesian financial institutions and firms. Through capital markets, foreign investors can now buy securities issued by Indonesian financial institutions and firms at modest prices. In addition, the financial system also needs professiortal advisors, equipment and training to adjust to the new environment.

DEVELOPMENT FINANCING AND FINANCIAL REPRESSION PRIOR TO THE 1980s

In terms of total assets and number of offices, the core of the Indonesian financial sector is the banking system. Monetary assets (as defined by M^1 and M^2)[2] are the most important domestic assets in the portfolio of savers. The rapid rates of growth of money as financial assets (M^2) and the rising M^1/DGP and M^2/GDP ratios (Table 10.1) indicate that financial deepening has occurred. Because of the leading role of the banking sector in the financial system, bank credit is the main source of external financing both for long-term investment as well as for short-term working capital. Other sources of financing include loans from family members, tax evasion, economic rents, and other forms of self-financing. Only a handful of large and reputable domestic companies have access to international financial markets.

The banking system mainly consists of the central bank (Bank Indonesia or BI), and the commercial and development banks of which seven are state-owned banks (Table 10.2). Together, this group of institutions held over 90 per cent of the gross assets of the financial system in 1991. Non-Bank Financial Institutions (NBFIs), which are largely jointly owned by domestic and foreign banks, account for only about 2 per cent of gross assets. Other financial institutions such as savings banks, leasing companies, securities companies, insurance companies, and retirement funds are a fast-growing segment of the financial system, but these firms as a group are relatively small.

For more than two decades prior to 1983, Indonesia had a repressed financial system. Monetary policy was primarily based on direct controls in the

Table 10.2 Structure and growth of the financial sector, 1982–1991

	Number				*Assets (Rp billions)*				*Asset growth (percentage)*		
	1982	*1988*	*1990*	*1991*[a]	*1982*	*1988*	*1990*	*1991*[a]	*1982–88*	*1989–91*	*1990–91*
Bank Indonesia	1	1	1	1	13,707	42,445	49,045	55,220	18.8	8.0	11.9
Deposit money banks	118	111	166	185	17,105	65,693	135,992	152,377	22.4	28.0	11.4
State commercial banks	5	5	5	5	12,257	39,862	64,760	68,135	19.7	17.9	5.1
Private forex banks	10	12	23	23	1,168	10,189	37,311	44,873	36.1	49.4	18.5
Foreign banks	11	11	26	29	1,172	3,215	9,777	11,604	16.8	42.8	17.1
Other commercial banks	60	51	80	96	720	4,972	10,823	10,109	32.2	23.7	−6.8
Development banks	29	29	29	29	1,336	5,046	10,247	14,038	22.1	34.1	31.5
Savings banks	3	3	3	3	452	2,409	3,074	3,618	27.9	13.6	16.3
NBFIs	13	13	13	13	805	3,063	4,730	4,793	22.3	14.9	1.3
Insurance companies	83	106	117	n.a.	528	1,883	2,566	n.a.	21.2	n.a.	n.a.
Leasing companies	17	83	83	n.a.	114	1,735	2,711	n.a.	45.4	n.a.	n.a.
Other credit institutions	5,808	5,783	5,984	6,243	86	637	656	n.a.	33.4	n.a.	n.a.
All institutions	6,040	6,097	6,364	6,442	32,345	115,456	195,900	212,390	21.2	21.3	10.9

Note: n.a. = not available.
[a] Up to November 1991

Sources: Bank Indonesia, *Indonesian Financial Statistics*, various issues: *Annual Report*, various issues.

form of detailed asset ceilings. As a result of the asset ceilings policy, the role of the required reserve ratio as an instrument of monetary policy was eliminated and the only purpose for a high reserve ratio was as a covert taxation on financial assets. In addition, selective credit policies artificially depressed interest rates on both deposits and loans. At the same time, the authorities imposed ceilings on offshore borrowings of the private sector. The global credit ceiling and selective credit policy were first introduced in 1967, when Indonesia was under the IMF Standby Arrangements. A more complex system was introduced on April 1, 1974, at the beginning of the "oil boom" era.

The repressed financial system was partly a result of the way in which Indonesia financed its economic development. Since the first Repelita (i.e., the Five-year Development Plan), financing of economic development has strongly depended on revenues from the petroleum sector and foreign aid and concessionary loans from the Inter-Governmental Group to Indonesia (IGGI).[3] These two major external sources of financing helped to finance Indonesia's twin deficits in both the public budget and the balance of payments.

The significance of the oil revenues was particularly important during the oil boom period of 1973–1982; over this period, nearly two-thirds of the government's revenues and four-fifths of the country's export proceeds were generated from the oil sector. Oil revenues were also significant during the short spell in 1990-1991 following Iraq's invasion of Kuwait in August 1990.

Foreign aid and loans have also been significant sources of funds. Classified as "development revenues" in the public budget, aid and loans were earmarked for financing the country's "development expenditure", and, in fact, enabled the government to follow a balance-budget policy since 1968.

Both the oil revenues and inflows of official development assistance have been the main sources for the country's foreign exchange reserve. Borrowing from the private sector has had a secondary role in financing the investment-savings gap in Indonesia (Table 10.3), The present regime, known as the "New Order" government, has neither issued bonds in the domestic market nor borrowed from the central bank, although in the 1970s, Indonesia floated bonds in international financial markets on a trial basis.

Development and expansion of the financial system has been strongly influenced by the availability of foreign aid and loans as well as fluctuations in the oil price. Because monetisation of the balanced-budget policy limits the flexibility of monetary policy, the revenues received from the oil sector and foreign aid and loans are part of the government's fiscal policy. In the absence of a well-developed money market, sterilisation of these injections through open market operations is ruled out, although the monetary effects were partly sterilised by increasing the import content of the budget expenditures and accumulation of secondary reserves, mainly at the state-owned banks.

Table 10.3 Savings-investment balance, 1986–1991 (Rp billions)

	1986	*1987*	*1988*	*1989*	*1990*
Gross national savings	20,296	27,212	33,732	42,704	52,829
Private national savings	16,782	22,375	27,420	35,034	42,024
Government savings	3,514	4,837	6,312	7,670	10,805
Gross domestic investment	24,782	30,980	36,802	45,649	60,206
Private national savings	15,387	21,411	26,463	35,104	50,376
Government savings	9,395	9,569	10,339	10,545	9,830
Financing of the:					
Total S–I gap	–4,056	–3,768	–3,070	–2,945	–7,377
Private S–I gap	1,395	964	957	–70	–8,352
Government S–I gap	–5,881	–4,732	–4,027	–2,875	975
Government S–I gap	–5,086	–4,732	–4,027	–2,875	975
External financing	3,790	3,256	4,215	3,679	2,404
Change in reserves [a]	2,091	1,476	–188	–804	–3,397
Private S–I gap	1,395	964	957	–70	–8,352
External financing	2,566	2,956	–1,694	–325	267
Change in reserves [a]	–3,961	–3,920	737	395	8,085
Total S–I gap	–4,486	–3,768	–3,070	–2,945	–7,377
External financing	6,356	6,212	2,521	3,354	2,671
Change in reserves [a]	1,870	2,444	–549	409	–4,706
Current account (foreign savings)	4,486	3,768	3,070	2,945	7,377
National savings ratio (percentage)	23.2	28.1	29.1	32.8	34.7

Note:
[a] A negative value represents an increase in reserves.

Sources: Central Bureau of Statistics, *National Income of Indonesia*, various issues.

In 1967, the government issued a regulation requiring the public sector (including state enterprises) to hold deposits only with state-owned banks. Because of the dominant role of the public sector in the economy, this implied a large captive market for these banks. At the same time, this regulation provided exclusive access of the group of state-owned banks to foreign aid and loans as well as to government oil revenues.

Since nearly all of BI's priority credits were handled by the state-owned banks, discretionary credit policy became part of the government's policy to subsidise its own banks. The ceilings on foreign borrowings were allocated according to the size of assets and past performance of individual financial institutions. Through its control over refinancing and the sharing of credit risks, the central bank administratively directed cheap money to favored economic sectors.

While there was no deposit insurance in Indonesia, three instruments effectively implied protection for state-owned banks. *First*, savings and time deposits with state banks were explicitly guaranteed by the government. *Second*, for demand deposits, the general notion was that the government would stand by its banks and would not allow them to go bankrupt at the expense of depositors. *Third*, on the loan side, most of the loans for priority sectors were eligible for insurance coverage at subsidised premia through a government-funded insurance agency.

While this credit system served to preserve the leading position of the state-owned bank group, on the negative side, the long period of financial repression hindered the development of the money and capital markets as a means to mobilise domestic savings and improve the use of scarce resources. The credit subsidies, accompanied by high levels of protection, created distortions in assets, labour, and commodity markets and allowed inefficient firms to remain in business. The discretionary policies also made the authorities (both the Ministry of Finance and the central bank) unfamiliar with market-based control of monetary aggregates. The policies are also responsible for the state-owned banks becoming arm's-length extensions of the government bureaucracy which allocated credit on the basis of non-economic consideration.

DEREGULATION OF THE BANKING INDUSTRY, 1983–1991

Indonesia has been following a gradual approach in reforming its economy, including the financial sector and the banking system. The first stage of the reforms was introduced on June 1, 1983, and involved the removal of direct controls of interest rates on most credits and deposits, elimination of most credit programmes, and curtailment of the central bank's funding of state-owned banks. In the second stage, the central bank's facilities were further restructured and money markets began to be developed. Major reforms, known as "Pakto" (*Paket Oktober* – October Package), were introduced in October 1988 and have since been followed by other measures. These measures include an improvement in prudential regulations and the supervisory framework, a further reduction in the scope of credit programmes, further relaxation in the controls on interest rates and the foreign exchange system, a loosening of barriers in the banking industry, and reorganisation of state-owned banks to make them more independent (see Box 10.1 for a chronology of the reforms in the financial sector). These measures have helped to increase competition and improve the structure of the financial industry.

Policies to restructure the financial industry

Pakto encourages competition in the banking system by relaxing the barriers to entry into the industry. This includes a further opening of the domestic market to foreign banks by relaxation of the reciprocity clause which acts as a non tariff barrier that restricts foreign entry into the domestic banking industry. The mechanism by which foreign banks can currently penetrate the domestic market, according to Pakto, is through the establishment of joint ventures with local lending institutions.

Pakto also partly removes traditional functional specialisation between financial institutions. This increases competition between commercial banks, development (merchant) banks, and NBFIs, both in terms of assets and liabilities. For example, prior to Pakto, only *Bank Tabungan Negara* (BTN) was allowed to provide housing loans; following Pakto, state-owned commercial banks are allowed to provide mortgage-type lending facilities and other non-traditional financial services. In addition, ever since their inception in the early 1970s, NBFIs have become direct suppliers of short-term credit in economic sectors that are not covered by the selective credit programme and in activities that the banks could not service under the previous credit regulations. The capital market is still in an early stage of development and too small to support the activities of the existing twelve NBFIs (three development type and nine investment finance companies).

However, the new rules and regulations prohibit banks and NBFIs from engaging in securities underwriting, brokerage and trading, and giving loans for stock trading. Starting from December 4, 1991, such activities were to be transferred to their holding companies. NBFIs were given one year to make the adjustment either to continue in the merchant banking business or to shift to commercial banking activities. All of the NBFIs have opted to change their status to full-fledged commercial banks.

Policies to strengthen the preventive measures

Pakto improves the prudential or preventive measures which are aimed at controlling the level of risk assumed by lending institutions, which in turn

Box 10.1 The chronology of financial sector reforms, 1983–1991

June 1983	Elimination of credit ceilings and ending of control on interest rates for time deposits and credits; reduction in the types of priority/programme credits which are eligible for Bank Indonesia liquidity credits.
February 1984	Reintroduction of Bank Indonesia certificates (SBI) to support open market operations and introduction of rediscount windows.
January 1985	Introduction of money market instruments (SBPU) consisting of promissory notes of bank customers, of banks, NBFIs and trade bills. Rediscount facilities to banks were also set up by Bank Indonesia to the day-to-day reserve management as well as maturity management.
May 1987	With the objective of improving fund management, Bank Indonesia raised the interest of SBPUs, SBIs, discount facilities, and the swap premium.
July 1987	Introduction of auction system for the trade of SBIs and SBPUs.
October 1988	Introduction of measures to foster competition, i.e.: (1) lessening the restrictions on entry and branching for foreign/domestic banks; (2) allowing NBFIs to issue Certificate of Deposits (CDs); (3) permitting banks and NBFIs to raise capital in the stock market; (4) easing entry to leasing, insurance, venture capital, consumer finance and securities activities; (5) reducing reserve requirements from 15 to 2 per cent; and (6) improvements to other aspects of protective and preventive measures.
March 1989	Introduction of decrees clarifying matters with regard to NBFI's, legal lending limits, joint venture capital ownership and bank mergers, the definition of bank capital, reserve requirements, bank investment in stocks, and bank exposure to foreign exchange fluctuations.
January 1990	Reduction in the scope of credit programmes which are eligible for Bank Indonesia, i.e. liquidity credit. Introduction of legal lending limits requirements. A regulation was stipulated to require all domestic banks to lend 20 per cent of their porfolio to small firms and cooperatives, and foreign and joint venture banks to extend at least 50 per cent of their credit for export-oriented activities.
February 1991	Various measures were stipulated to improve banking management and supervision by, amongst other things, requiring banks to step up capital base according to BIS regulations.
November 1991	Reimposition of ceilings on offshore borrowing for the public sector (including state banks), improvements in swap mechanism, and elimination of swap premia.

affects the probability of their failure. The measures include an extension of Bank Indonesia's responsibility for setting a unified reserve requirement ratio and for supervising both banks and NBFIs to place the two types of financial institutions on an equal footing. The reserve ratio was reduced from 15 per cent to 2 per cent in October 1988 to reduce the cost of funds.

Bank Indonesia has adopted prudential regulations and a supervisory framework as outlined by the Committee on Banking Regulation and Supervisory Practices, under the auspices of the Bank for International Settlements (BIS) in 1974. In line with the BIS recommendations, the new measures aim to strengthen the capital bases of banks.[4] The capital adequacy ratio (CAR) of a bank, which links the capital base of the lending institution with its risk-weighted assets,[5] has been raised. In addition, the minimum initial paid-in capital for a new bank is now set at Rp10 billion or roughly US$500,000 (assuming an exchange rate of Rp2,000 per US dollar). The initial capital for a secondary bank (BPR) is Rp50 million. These regulations on minimum initial capital requirements and CAR are designed to ensure that banks have an adequate capital base for operations and for the protection of depositors. Additional investment is also needed by the banks in the following areas: improvement in their software to modernise their systems; improvement in services, human resources, and management capabilities; introduction of new financial products and other forms of innovation to reduce marginal cost and spread; and expansion of branch networks in order to survive in a more competitive market.

However, upon implementation of the new regulations, it was found that the reserves and retained earnings of state-owned banks were inadequate to meet the required CAR, and as a result, they could not go public and sell shares in the capital market. To beef up their capital bases, the government obtained a US$600 million financial sector loan from the World Bank. The remaining capital requirements were generated from assets revaluation, conversion of some of their debts to equity, and the government taking over part of their non-performing loans. Compulsory areas of specialisation and the credit policy of the past have hindered state-owned banks in seeking portfolio diversification. This obstable and other aspects of past credit policy have burdened state-owned banks with mounting problem loans, as well as illiquid financial instrument which carry artificially low interest rates and have a high risk of capital loss.

The new credit system and access to discount windows

Although Pakto reduced existing distortions in the credit markets, it also added new ones; hence, credit policy in Indonesia remains segmented and pro-cyclical. In January 1990, Bank Indonesia narrowed the scope of the credit programme to four areas, mainly for rice production, marketing, maintenance of a buffer stock, and investment financing in the eastern part of

Indonesia. At the end of 1990, this concessionary credit was also made available for *Badan Penyangga dan Pemasaran Cengkeh* (BPPC – Clove Buffer Stock and Marketing Agency) to finance its buffer stock of cloves, the main ingredient of clove cigarettes. The recipient of this credit is a consortium of private traders who have powerful backing and have been granted the exclusive right to operate a buffer stock for that agricultural commodity. Interest rates charged in these special credit programmes, however, are now much closer to market rates and their insurance is voluntary with market-based premia.

Three new credit regulations related to the system of credit allocation were introduced in 1989–1990. The first rule is implied in the legal lending limits regulations (LLR) which were made effective in October 1990. This rule restricts the aggregate amount of loans and advances to insiders, whether it be a single borrower (person or firm) or a group of borrowers. The rule is not applicable to all forms of the credit programme. The objectives of the maximum LLR are to increase access to bank credits by inhibiting concentration of financial power, protect the interests of ignorant depositors, and prevent misuse of funds by insiders. The second rule requires new joint venture banks and branches of foreign banks outside Jakarta to allocate at least 50 per cent of their loan portfolios to export-related activities. The third rule mandates domestic private and state banks to allocate a minimum 20 per cent of their loan portfolios to small-scale enterprises and cooperatives. These credit rules force lending institutions to operate with a portfolio that they would not otherwise voluntarily accept.

The reduction in the scope of the credit programme automatically reduced Bank Indonesia's credit liquidity to refinance them. To assist financial institutions to cope with more competitive markets, Bank Indonesia, as the bankers' bank, established two rediscount facilities in February 1984. In contrast to the programme-oriented liquidity credit, these facilities are for general purposes. The Rediscount Facility I is designed to facilitate day-to-day reserve management by financial institutions. The Rediscount Facility II is intended for promoting long-term lending by offering temporary relief to banks that face risks associated with maturity mismatches between assets and liabilities. The maximum duration of Rediscount Facility I is three working days and that of Facility II is ninety days.

Access to public sector deposits and foreign exposures

The October 1988 deregulation removed the state-owned banks' exclusive access to public sector deposits by allowing state-owned enterprises to hold up to a maximum 50 per cent of their deposits at non state financial institutions. Implementation of this, however, has been very slow, partly to prevent liquidity problems at state-owned banks and because of the fear that rapid transfers of the massive funds from one institution to another may lead to financial instability.

Along with the unification of the exchange rate in April 1970, Indonesia liberalised its foreign exchange system. As a result, there is no surrender requirements for export proceeds and taxes or subsidies on the purchase or sale of foreign exchange. Foreign nationals and Indonesian citizens are free to open accounts in either rupiah or foreign currencies with all banks which are authorised to deal in foreign exchange transactions. These institutions are free to extend credits in foreign currencies with a 15 per cent withholding tax on interest rates. Pakto rationalises the requirements for obtaining a license for dealing in foreign currencies transactions. One drawback of this more liberalised system and increasing monetary substitution, however, is that control of monetary aggregates is more difficult.

Prior to 1989, the only obstacle to capital inflows had been a complex system of ceilings on foreign borrowings. For a short period of time, beginning from March 25, 1989, the authorities replaced this system with a restriction to a daily net open position (NOP) amounting to 25 per cent of the capital of borrower. This combined with a subsidy on the foreign exchange premium induced a massive inflow of short-term capital in 1989–1991. Given the shallowness of the money market, Bank Indonesia could not sterilise these flows with open market operations. Thus, the central bank was faced with the difficult choice of either permitting the rupiah to appreciate or purchasing foreign exchange from the public. The first alternative would enlarge the external current account and complicate the structural adjustment process. The second option would rapidly expand the money supply and inflame the inflation rate. In April 1990, to cool the overheated economy, the authorities tightened monetary policy, eliminated the subsidy on the foreign exchange swap premium, and introduced an austere fiscal policy.

However, these policies were inadequate and on October 12, 1991, the authorities reinstituted a complicated set of ceilings on foreign borrowings for various categories of borrowers (state and private banks and state and private companies). Offshore borrowings of state-owned banks and enterprises were now required to obtain approvals from a newly established Coordinating Team for Management of Offshore Loans (TKPPKTLN), an interdepartmental body that is chaired by the Coordinating Minister for Economy, Finance, Industry and Development Supervision (*Menko Ekuin*). While ceilings on offshore borrowings of purely private sector enterprises are not binding, the enterprises are required to report their borrowings to the authorities.

Other discretionary measures to control the money supply were used by the Minister of Finance in June 1987 and February 1991. In both cases, the Minister issued orders to large state-owned enterprises to convert their deposits at state-owned banks into Bank Indonesia's certificates. These measures, known as "Sumarlin shocks" (named after the Minister of Finance, Professor J. B. Sumarlin), were effective in squeezing liquidity. At the same time, however, the measures eroded deposits of the state-owned banks and sharply raised their costs of funds.

THE MONETARY AUTHORITIES

The Ministry of Finance (MOF), the most powerful institution in the government, issues licenses to operate in the financial industry. It is not only in charge of the financial management of the central government, but its power extends to the economy as a whole by its "guidance" of state-owned enterprises and financial institutions. Some of the MOF's power is shared with the Planning Agency (*Bappenas*). The MOF is also involved in the consolidation of failing state-owned and private domestic firms through mergers or takeovers undertaken under the ministry's suggestion. Before the financial reforms, the MOF also oversaw price stabilisation in the stock market. The MOF consists of six powerful Directorate Generals and Authorities, namely, Custom and Excises, Taxation, Budgeting and Treasury, State-Owned Enterprises, Financial Institutions, and BAPEPAM (*Badan Pelaksana Pasar Modal* or Capital Market Executive Agency) which is equivalent to the Securities and Exchange Commission in the United States.

Implementation and administration of the government's "guidance" on monetary and credit policies are in the hands of Bank Indonesia which also controls, monitors and supervises the soundness of the banking and payment systems. In addition, Bank Indonesia owns a commercial bank in the Netherlands, three development finance companies, a credit insurance company for small business loans, and a housing finance company. The Governor and Managing Directors of the central bank are appointed by the President and their terms in office are similar to the terms of cabinet members. The Governor of Bank Indonesia attends regular meetings of the cabinet ministers, while the Government Commissioner supervises the operation of Bank Indonesia as an enterprise. The budget of Bank Indonesia is subject to approval from the government, indicating that Bank Indonesia is not an independent institution. The headquarters of both the MOF and Bank Indonesia occupy huge office complexes (see Box 10.2).

STRUCTURE OF THE BANKING INDUSTRY

As of March 1992, the banking system consisted of 164 commercial banks, twenty-nine development banks, three savings banks, and 664 secondary banks, including rural banks. In addition, there were thirty-one representative offices of foreign banks in Jakarta. Commercial banks provide long-term investment credit which are refinanced by the central bank and with special permission are allowed to deal in foreign exchange transactions. In theory, development (merchant) banks mobilise long-term savings from the public and provide long-term investment loans; in reality, however, they operate as

Box 10.2 Government agencies: points of contact

The following are the addresses of the agencies which are in charge of financial institutions:

The Ministry of Finance Headquarters
2–4 Jalan Lapangan Banteng Timur, Jakarta
Telephones: 373–309; 380–8388; 365–364; 371–248/256

The Ministry of Finance
The Directorate General of Financial Institutions
Jalan Dr. Wahidin Raya, Jakarta
Telephones: 360–296; 366–549; 381–0162/0164/0164

Bank Indonesia,
2 Jalan M. H. Thamrin, Jakarta
Telephones: 373–408; 374–108; 380–6798/6988

Badan Pelaksana Pasar Modal (Bapepam)
14 Jalan Merdeka Selatan
Jakarta
Telephones: 365–509; 363–030; 386–0442

commercial banks. Savings banks are now allowed to take demand deposits, but their loans are primarily for mortgage financing. Secondary or rural banks are not allowed to accept demand deposits.

Ownership

In terms of ownership, the commercial banking system consists of five state-owned banks,[6] 130 private national banks, ten foreign banks, and nineteen joint-venture banks. Four of the state-owned commercial banks (BBD, BDN, Exim and BRI) were originally Dutch institutions that were nationalised in 1958–1960, when Inddnesia was at war with the Dutch over the territory which is now the Province of Irian Jaya. The fifth commercial bank, *Bank Negara Indonesia* (Bank BNI), was established in 1946 to serve as the newly proclaimed Republic's central bank during the war of independence in 1945–1949. After Indonesia nationalised the Javasche Bank, which was the central bank, and renamed it in 1953 to the present Bank Indonesia, Bank BNI reverted to the status of a commercial bank.

Following the model system in socialist countries, under the era of a "guided economy", all state-owned financial institutions (except BDN),[7] including the central bank and state pawnshops, were integrated into one single institution, *Bank Negara Indonesia* (BNI). While the banking acts of 1968 disintegrated the single BNI and defined the major areas of concentration for each bank, in practice, this was not strictly implemented, subsequently, the Banking Act of 1992 changed the status of state-owned banks into limited liability companies and allowed them to go public.

Private banks first emerged in Indonesia in the 1950s, but monetary purges, inflation, and social instability up to the mid-1960s eroded their capital bases and led to bankruptcies. To improve their conditions, the authorities encouraged the ailling private banks to consolidate and merge (by offering various tax and credit facilities) and seek technical assistance from state and foreign banks. In fact, merger and consolidation were at that time part of the requirements to open a new branch, acquire foreign exchange bank status, or form a joint venture with foreign banks. In 1971 entry to the banking industry was completely closed. Today, through its networks of ownership and business, nearly all of the private domestic banks are closely connected to large business conglomerates.

The ten foreign banks presently operating in Indonesia established their operations in Jakarta in the late 1960s and early 1970s. By nationality, four of the ten foreign banks are American institutions (see Box 10.3). The other six banks come from five countries, namely, the Algemene Bank Nederland-Amro (Holland); Bangkok Bank Limited (Thailand); the Bank of Tokyo (Japan); the Standard Chartered Bank (England); Deutsche Bank (Germany); and the Hong Kong and Shanghai Banking Corporation (England/Hong Kong).

Sixty-seven of the private domestic banks and the nineteen joint venture banks were established following the banking sector reforms in October 1988. By nationality, the foreign partners of the nineteen joint venture banks are as follows: ten Japan; three France; two each for Singapore and Holland; and one each for Korea and Australia. Foreign and joint venture banks are

Box 10.3 American Banks in Indonesia

These American Banks include the American Express Bank; Citibank, NA; Bank of America; and the Chase Manhattan Bank. With their superiority in technology and information and global networks, the group of American banks in Indonesia controls the market for credit cards, travelers cheques, technical assistance, and new financial products (such as certificates of deposit, consumer credit, residential and commercial mortgages, electronic banking services, margin loans, NOW/ATS transaction accounts, data processing, and syndicated loans), and is superior in terms of operation and management systems as well as personnel training to local banks. American banks were the first to introduce derivative instruments * by using existing facilities in the money and foreign exchange markets. For example, in February 1993, Citibank of Singapore, offered flexible 6-month fixed-rate loans denominated in rupiah at an interest rate of 16 per cent per annum. This rate was 6 percentage points lower than that offered by state-owned and local private banks. Morgan Trust is the main lender to Bank Indonesia and Lasard Fre'res et Cie, Shearson Lehman Hutton, Inc. and Warburg & Co., Ltd. are the financial advisors to the government of Indonesia.

Note:
* Some contracts give the contract holder the obligation of choice to buy or sell a financial asset. The price of the contract derives its value from price of the underlying financial asset. Consequently these contracts are called "derivative instruments" (Fabozzi and Modigliani 1992).

said to specialise in providing services to multinational firms from their home countries. Some of these banks, particularly the American institutions, have successfully expanded their bases to include local customers. Of the private domestic banks, only twenty-three are licensed to deal in foreign exchange transactions. These specially licensed private domestic banks together with the state-owned commercial banks and foreign and joint venture banks are collectively known as "foreign exchange banks."

Bapindo is the only state-owned development (merchant) bank and *Bank Tabungan Negara* is the sole savings bank owned by the national government. Each of the twenty-seven provinces has a regional development bank (RDB), most of which were established in the 1960s. As their name suggests, RDBs were intended to specialise in the provision of long-term investment loans, and accordingly were expected to mobilise long-term savings from the public. In reality, however, *Bapindo* and RDBs operate as commercial banks and fiscal agents, collecting and disbursing funds for provincial and local governments. One development bank owned by the provincial government of Central Java has recently been licensed to deal in foreign exchange.

Branch networks

Indonesia has a branch banking system. Because of past discrimination, state-owned banks have far wider branch systems than do other banks. At the other end of the spectrum, prior to the 1988 reforms, foreign banks were not allowed to operate outside Jakarta and the number of their branches was limited to two. After the reform, foreign banks have been allowed to open branch offices in five major cities outside Jakarta including Medan, Bandung, Semarang, Surabaya, and Ujung Pandang. In addition to these cities, joint venture banks are allowed to operate in Denpasar, Bali, the main center of tourist industry in Indonesia. The regional development banks are restricted to operating within their respective provinces. Secondary banks operate within a subdistrict.

The geographic dispersion of bank offices in Indonesia is strongly oriented towards the major cities. To some extent, the authorities have tried to redress this imbalance by encouraging national private banks to establish branches in small towns and the rural sector. The rapid expansion of branch offices of state-owned banks in the 1970s was also related to this policy. The result of this policy, however, has been mixed since there has been no similar response from the real sector outside agriculture. To channel agricultural credits, *Bank Rakyat Indonesia* (BRI) has a wide network of rural credit banks.

Market share

The impacts of the increased competition in the financial industry have been directly felt by the state-owned bank group (Table 10.4). On the liability

Table 10.4 Market shares of banking institutions by ownership

	Assets		*Loans*		*Saving and time deposits*		*Demand deposits*		*Total deposits*	
	1988	*1991*	*1988*	*1991*	*1988*	*1991*	*1988*	*1991*	*1988*	*1991*
State banks	39,862	70,158	21,149	48,790	12,294	22,403	4,366	6,399	16,660	28,802
Private forex banks	10,189	45,654	7,629	36,844	4,463	19,639	1,403	5,777	5,866	25,416
Private non-forex banks	4,972	12,868	4,334	11,189	2,619	6,735	960	2,001	3,579	8,736
Foreign and joint venture banks	3,215	12,070	2,109	9,181	763	1,538	342	645	1,105	2,183
Development banks	5,046	14,505	3,678	11,534	800	2,317	961	1.930	1,761	4,247
Total	63,284	155,255	38,899	117,538	20,939	52,632	8,032	16.752	28,971	69,384
(as a percentage of the total)										
State banks	63.0	45.2	54.4	41.5	58.7	42.6	54.4	38.2	57.5	41.5
Private forex banks	16.1	29.4	19.6	31.3	21.3	37.3	17.5	34.5	20.2	36.6
Private non-forex banks	7.9	8.3	11.1	9.5	12.5	12.8	12.0	11.9	12.4	12.6
Foreign and joint venture banks	5.1	7.8	5.4	7.8	3.6	2.9	4.3	3.9	3.8	3.1
Development banks	8.0	9.3	9.5	9.8	3.8	4.4	12.0	11.5	6.1	6.1

Sources: Bank Indonesia, *Indonesian Financial Statistics*, various issues.

side, these banks are directly competing with NBFIs and private banks for lucrative pension funds and deposits of the public sector. At the same time, the group of state-owned banks loses revenue from holding secondary foreign exchange reserves. On the asset side, higher interest rates on bank credits turn more private companies to the newly liberalised stock of exchanges for long-term investment funds and to foreign banks, This has led to an erosion in the pool of creditworthy corporate clients which, in turn, creates pressure on all banks to replenish their portfolios with lower quality loans and to reduce lending rates in order to win new customers.

In 1991, more than 2 per cent of the assets of foreign exchange banks and over 49 per cent of the assets of this group (including joint venture banks) were controlled by branches of the four American banks. Citibank is the leader among foreign banks in Indonesia and is followed by Chase Manhattan.

MONEY, CAPITAL, AND FOREIGN EXCHANGE MARKETS

In general, the dominance of credit or debt finance involves dangers both at the micro- and macroeconomic levels. Japan's success in developing a credit-based and highly leveraged financial system is the only exception from this general rule. A high debt-to-equity ratio and a highly leveraged financial system leaves enterprises and banks that have to operate in a volatile market with a high degree of exposure to down-side risks. At the macro level, economy-wide shocks simultaneously affect the performance of a substantial number of enterprises and banks. Offshore borrowings through banking channels pose greater monetary effects than through capital and money markets.

From a microeconomic point of view, the financial sector policy reform in Indonesia has two objectives: (1) to pave the way for the corporate sector to switch from a reliance on bank loans to issuing securities directly in the financial markets; and (2) to move from a controlled financial system towards a market-based one. Attainment of these objectives require the creation of well-functioning money and capital markets with low transaction costs.

The money market

Bank Indonesia started to develop the short-term money market by reactivating the use of central bank certificates, *Sertifikat Bank Indonesia* (SBI), as a money market instrument in 1984. This was followed by the introduction of private sector commercial papers, *Surat Berharga Pasar Uang* (SBPU), and large-denomination negotiable Certificates of Deposit (CD) in 1985. The SBPU consists of the following: promissory notes issued by banks or NBFIs in connection with interbank borrowing and bills of exchange issued by third parties and endorsed eligible financial institutions. All CDs are issued by domestic banks and are denominated in rupiah. Other instruments being used are Repurchase Agreements (RA)[8] and Banker Acceptances (BA) (see Box 10.4).

Initially SBIs were auctioned on the basis of pre-announced rates. Daily auction of SBI is now supplemented with a weekly auction. The cut-off rate in the auctions is set by Bank Indonesia, based on bids and offers received. Following Pakto, fifteen banks and NBFIs were authorised to act as market-makers though the number was raised to twenty in February 1993.[9] Despite these efforts, the secondary market for SBIs and SBPUs is not yet well-functioning. Over 83 per cent of the outstanding money market instruments traded in May 1992 (Rp17,2 trillions) were SBIs and the remaining 17 per cent were SBPUs. The dominant role of SBIs indicates the high price paid by Bank Indonesia to promote money market development. The amount of the subsidy paid by the central bank to operate the SBI market may in fact have been higher than its revenue from making transactions in the foreign exchange market.

Prior to the establishment of the SBI and SBPU markets, banks were heavily dependent on the segmented interbank money market to smooth out their liquidity problems. During that pre-reform period, the fund providers

Box 10.4 Money market instruments in Indonesia

Instrument	*Return on comparable Maturities*	*Credit risk*	*Maturity*
Certificate of Bank Indonesia (SBI)	Lower rates in market	Central bank (Bank Indonesia) certificates	Seven days, fourteen days, one month, three months, six months, and twelve months
Certificate of deposit (CD)	Comparable with time deposit rates	Issuing commercial bank and non bank financial institutions (NBFIs)	One month up to twelve months
Commercial paper	Comparable with time deposit rates	Issuing commercial bank and NBFIs	Varies
Repurchase agreement (RP)	Comparable with time deposit rates or lending rates	Issuing commercial bank and NBFIs	Varies
Banker's acceptances (BA)	Comparable with time deposit rates or lending rates	Issuing commercial bank and NBFIs, company	Varies
Promissory notes	Comparable with time deposit rates or lending rates	Issuing commercial bank and NBFIs	Varies

were mainly the overliquid state-owned institutions (state-owned banks and RDBs) and the buyers were mainly private and foreign banks as well as NBFIs. Partly to popularise the SBI and SBPU markets, effective from October 1, 1984, Bank Indonesia set a limit on each bank's borrowing to 7.5 per cent of the bank's third-party liabilities. This upper limit was raised to 15 per cent on August 7, 1985. The value of the interbank call money market in May 1992 amounted to 19.5 per cent of the outstanding SBIs and SBPUs traded in the money market.

The authorities use market – and non market – based policies to encourage money market development. Early in 1984, Bank Indonesia reduced the rate it was then paying on excess reserves in rupiah and stopped paying any interest on excess exchange reserves deposited with the central bank. At the same time, Bank Indonesia announced that it would cease paying any interest on the rupiah excess reserves after three months. To help sterilise the liquidity impact of the reduction in the required reserve ratio, Pakto required banks to temporarily use their excess liquidity to purchase SBIs with three- and six-month maturities. As has been pointed out earlier, the Sumarlin shocks required the switching of deposits of non bank state enterprises, mainly at state banks, into SBIs.

The capital market

To diversify sources of financing and channels of capital inflows, the authorities deregulated the stock of exchanges in 1988 and 1989. However, securities traded in the capital market have not been used by Bank Indonesia as instruments for open market operation. The present Jakarta Stock of Exchange (JSE) was established on August 10, 1977,[10] and was followed by the establishment of the Surabaya Stock of Exchange (SSE) in 1989.

Three government organisations that were established in 1976 share the responsibility of guiding and regulating the present stock of exchange. The Capital Market Policy Council (BAPEPAM) assists the Minister of Finance in drawing up policies and regulations for the operation of the stock of exchange. BAPEPAM sets operating procedures for the stock of exchange and supervises the implementation of these procedures. It also evaluates applicants for listing to make sure that they meet the listing requirements and monitors the progress of the listed companies. The third institution, the National Investment Trust Company (PT Danareksa), has the role of "democratising the ownership of Indonesian corporations in order to promote equal distribution of income." It has the right to buy at least 50 per cent of every new issue in the first instance, but it has no obligation to purchase any percentage of an issue. Once PT Danareksa has taken up a percentage of an issue, it places the shares in its investment portfolio and may then issue bearer certificates, relating to the specific companies backed by certain percentage shares in its portfolio, in small denominations which it sells to the general public.

From the demand side, there were at least three reasons why the securities traded in JSE were unattractive prior to the reforms in December 1987. *First*, the government (through PT Danareksa) stabilised the security prices making the yields on these securities close to the interest rates on time deposits at state-owned banks. *Second*, prior to the reform, the dividend was subject to a 15 per cent withholding tax while interest income from bank time deposits were tax-free. *Third*, the absence of a secondary market made the securities illiquid assets. The lax accounting and legal systems also reduced investors' confidence in the capital market.

The first stage of reforms in the capital market was introduced in December 1987. In this reform package, initial listing requirements were relaxed, procedures for new issues were streamlined, an over-the-counter (OTC) market was established, and foreign investors were now allowed to own up to 49 per cent of all outstanding shares issued by an Indonesia firm (except banks) and up to 49 per cent of all listed shares.[11] In addition, Pakto eliminated the differential tax treatment by levying the same 15 per cent tax on interest income earned from bank deposits which had been applied for income from securities. In the second stage of reforms, in December 1989, the government privatised the securities exchange and separated them from BAPEPAM, and opened up the securities business to foreign firms.

From the supply side, there were only twenty-four firms listed on the JSE before 1988. Of these twenty-four firms, seventeen were joint ventures firms which went public in order to meet the divestment programme and to take advantage of the generous special tax relief offered for public listing companies. At that time, there was no incentitive for domestic companies to raise capital through the selling of securities in the capital market because of the availability of cheap investment credit with low risks from state-owned banks. By October 1992, however, there were 151 companies listed and thirty-two firms issued bonds in the JSE and SSE, while four companies were listed and six firms floated bonds in the parallel market. The total value of shares and bonds traded in these two markets amounted to over Rp41 trillion. Currently, the types of bonds listed in the markets are straight and convertible bonds which are mainly issued by state-owned banks and non-bank companies. Twenty-three of the thirty-eight bonds carry fixed coupons (interest rates), ranging from 15.5 per cent to 19.5 per cent per annum. The remaining fifteen bonds carry float rates which are tied to the average interest rate on one-year time deposits at state-owned banks.

There are some 200 securities firms operating in the capital markets. Of these, thirty-four are affiliated with banks, eleven are affilliated with NBFIs, and the rest independent firms which are exclusively engaged in the securities business alone. A mix of the market efficiency problems and high interest rates have eroded the index of stock prices by 54 per cent between August 1990 and May 1992. Correction of these problems require improvements in disclosure rules, restrictions on insider trading, and other elements of the regulatory framework to improve the efficiency of the capital markets.

The very high real interest on loans and the reduction in the levels of protection that followed the reform have worried investors about the efficiency and competitiveness of the issuing banks and non-bank firms. Most of the securities in the JSE are absorbed by institutional investors, particularly state-owned insurance companies and pension funds, such as PT Taspen, a state-owned company which manages pension funds of civil servants.

The foreign exchange market

Aside from controlling its domestic credit to the public sector, financial institutions and non-financial entities, Bank Indonesia affects monetary aggregates – i.e., the money supply, interest rates, and the external value of the rupiah – through its control of private capital flows, particularly that of financial institutions, and through its operations in the foreign exchange market. As noted earlier, deregulation and sound foreign exchange rate management have promoted rapid growth of both non-oil exports and inflows of private foreign investment. These and the massive short-run capital inflows in 1989–1990 have added to the supply of foreign exchange.

Currently, there is no forward market for the rupiah. Concurrently with the rupiah devaluation in November 1978, Indonesia replaced the US dollar as the external anchor with a basket of major currencies (the composition of which has not been disclosed) and moved to a managed floating exchange rate system. More recently, however, this story has changed. The authorities have been repeatedly reported that the aim is to have a 5 per cent annual rupiah nominal depreciation against the US dollar, and no reference has been made to the "basket." In a managed floating exchange rate system, Bank Indonesia sets the external value of the rupiah at the beginning of each business day at the weighted average of transactions in the inter-bank market on the preceding business day. Interbank and customer rates are allowed to float freely within specific margins. The width of the margins puts an upper limit on the amount by which the central rate can be adjusted each day. The developments of nominal and real effective exchange rates are depicted in Figure 10.1.

Until December 1991, a special effective exchange rate was made available to domestic borrowers by providing explicit subsidies on the exchange rate. This was extended through the exchange rate swap facility at Bank Indonesia. Under this facility, which was introduced in January 1979, Bank Indonesia provided forward cover to foreign exchange borrowing contracts or swaps to banks and NBFIs as well as to customers with a foreign-currency liability. Although the facility was originally intended as an inducement for inward foreign investment, in reality, it was used by financial institutions either to fund themselves or to speculate against the rupiah.[12] From a macroeconomic

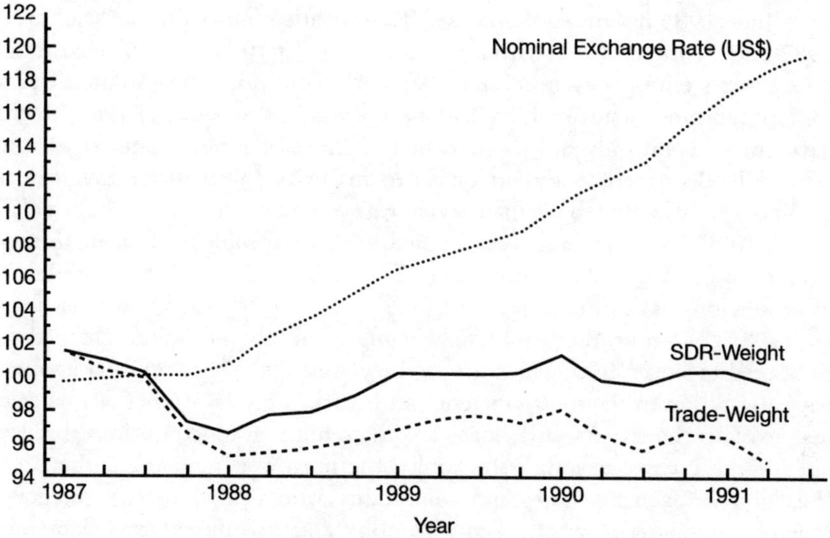

Figure 10.1 Index of Nominal & Real Effective Exchange Rates, 1987–1991 (1987 = 100)

view, the monetary substitution induced by such a subsidised exchange rate swap premium made control of monetary aggregates even more difficult.

REMAINING ISSUES

Adjustment to a new environment is not a simple task and cannot be done overnight. Adjustment may involve high costs and may give rise to acute short-run problems. For example, as a result of the changes in the capital adequacy ratio, the composition of a bank's portfolio may need to be altered. Banks with substantial off-balance-sheet assets which are now used to assess the minimum capital requirements will be required to raise new capital. Alternatively, the banks may try to lower their capital cost by either shrinking the size of their portfolio or by placing greater emphasis on those assets with a low risk weight.

On the other hand, banks with relatively low shareholder equity will now need to raise additional equity. The costs associated with doing so, however, may be rather high as the composite price index of securities traded in the JSE has eroded by nearly 50 per cent since 1989. The new CAR and LLR rules and regulations as well as the existence of ownership interlocking with non-bank companies also make it more difficult for mergers and acquisitions to take place within the industry.

The portfolio adjustment problem is particularly difficult for the "old" commercial banks, especially the state-owned banks, that were established prior to the economic deregulation. The increase in interest rates on deposits since June 1983 has raised their costs. The so-called Sumarlin shocks of mid-1987 and February 1991 withdrew more than Rp10 trillion of deposits of state-owned enterprises from state banks. In addition, the profitability of "old programme loans" which had been extended prior to January 1990 have eroded. Not only did these loans bear rates of interest rates that were artificially depressed, but their terms to maturity (particularly investment credits) were usually longer than of deposits.

The "old" banks are also preoccupied with the problem of an increasing amount of bad loans. The elimination of credit subsidies and the lower levels of protection that followed the deregulation have threatened marginal firms with a serious bankruptcy problem. The high real rates of interest charged on bank credits since 1990, which are in the vicinity of 20 per cent per annum, have affected even the most efficient and feasible projects. Other factors that may explain the rise in "bad" loans are changing market conditions that are outside the control of either the banks, the borrowers, and the authorities. Volatility in exchange rates and commodity prices fall into this category. Most of Indonesia's imports and its public and private external debts are denominated in yen, which has appreciated in the past few years. At the same time, nearly all of Indonesia's exports are quoted in US dollars, which as been depreciating. The rise in the number of problem loans is also due to the rapid expansion of commercial real estate and consumer loans that were financed by massive external borrowings during the "euphoric" years of 1989–1991.

Part of the costs of bad loans are measurable in financial terms. Financial costs include the erosion of the allowance for loan and lease losses, the costs of loans that are placed on a non-accrual status, costs attached to foreclosed assets, legal expenses, and the opportunity costs of the bad loans. Unquantifiable costs include the erosion in the bank's image because of the lack of confidence among both depositors and investors, the loss of marketing impetus as the banks focus all of their attention towards "cleaning up" the problem loans, and the loss in quality personnel.[13]

To assist the old banks and borrowers during the transition period as they adjust their portfolios to the new rules and regulations, McKinnon (1991) suggests the adoption of several measures. *First*, commercial banks should be tightly monitored and regulated; this may include temporary credit rationing. *Second*, both the old commercial banks and their clientele should be recapitalised. For the former, McKinnon suggests either using "old low-yield loans" for credit against the reserve requirements or simply having the state assume the problem loans. *Third*, the banking industry should be closed to new entrants, both domestic and foreign, since new entrants are not burdened with low-yield loans and can easily outcompete the old banks.

In addition, to increase their competitiveness, banks will need to reduce costs through modernisation and innovation of systems of operation as well as management. Compliance to the new rules and regulations, the cleaning up of existing bad loans, and prevention of new problems are all elements of the strategy to reduce costs. Banks will need to establish a new loan policy as a guide to the extension and control of credit in the new environment. Loan monitoring procedures, including loan review procedures and procedures that determine potential problems early on so that preventive action can be taken, must be spelled out in detail. Improvements in credit agreements, documentation, inspection, and appraisal of collateral are other components of this programme. Retraining of bank officers and improvements in credit monitoring are also integral parts of a long-term plan to minimise loan quality problems. To make the state-owned enterprises (including state banks) more accountable, more independent, and eligible to enter money and capital markets, they will need to be restructured, privatised, or liquidated. Only corporations with good reputations and credit ratings should be allowed to switch from a reliance on bank loans to securities issued directly in financial markets.

As the economy becomes more integrated into the world economy, the financial institutions will also need to master knowledge about international financial (currencies, bonds, and stocks), commodity, and labour markets. Aside from knowing the markets and products, the banks will also have to be familiar with global banks and security houses who are the main players, global investors as clients, global rules and regulations, and global systems. These interlockings not only create more opportunities but also increase the negative impacts of volatilities in international markets on the domestic economy. In the case of availability of such markets will enable banks and borrowers to purchase shares in other banks' loans to commercial borrowers and to transform credit into equity. This, in turn, implies reforms in other sectors of the economy and improvements in social infrastructure. The essence of the market system is individual property rights. To develop a market-based system, therefore, Indonesia will also need to improve its accounting and legal systems, particularly commercial laws, and other aspects of the social system.

The volume and variety of money market instruments, for example, can be increased by encouraging more of the eligible state-owned enterprises (including state banks), quasi-government institutions (such as the Logistic Agency, BULOG), and private firms to raise funds from the money and capital markets. An independent commercial credit-rating institution can be established to rate the quality of these debt instruments or securities. Ineligible State-Owned Enterprises (SOEs) and BULOG could start floating bonds with full government guarantees. This serves other purposes as well. *First*, it would impose financial discipline to these institutions and increase the transparency of their operations. *Second*, it would reduce the pressures on public expenditures and make these enterprises contribute to the public treasury. *Third*, it would encourage the SOEs and BULOG to restructure, privatise, or liquidate.

The need for improvements in the social structure is indicated by the recent failures and indicents of fraud that have occurred among banks (such as

PT *Bank Umum Majapahit*, PT *Bank Duta*, PT *Bank Putera Sampoerna*, and PT *Bank Summa*) and non-bank companies (such as PT *Bentoel*, PT *Mantrust*, and PT *Astra*). These examples show the weakness of the accounting and legal systems, as well as the low quality of the central bank's ability to administer and enforce the new rules and regulations which it has created. Asymmetric information arising from these weaknesses retards the development of financial markets. This also reinforces the tendency of the banks to keep their loans short-term in nature and closely monitored to ensure that borrowers are not diverting the loans from productive investment projects.

BUSINESS OPPORTUNITIES

Business opportunities in Indonesia seem promising, following the recent deregulation in both the financial and real sectors of the economy. As has been indicated previously, from a microeconomic point of view, deregulation in Indonesia has had three connotations: (1) lower barriers to market entry in both the financial and real sectors of the economy; (2) relaxation of constraints on the activities of the business sector, including reorganisation of state-owned enterprises and state-owned banks; and (3) privatisation in the sense of a transfer of enterprises from public ownership to the private sector.

Judging by the large number of new domestic and foreign banks, the financial sector reforms in 1988–1991 have been successful in improving competition in the industry. The reforms have broken the monopoly power of the state-owned bank group. At the same time, the negative impacts of interlocking ownerships between banks and non-bank firms of the private sector on resource allocation have been minimised.

To conclude, with the implementation of the new banking law and the enactment of new rules and regulations, financial institutions – ranging from the central bank to rural banks and the money and capital markets – will need to adjust. A credit-rating institution needs to be established to further develop money market instruments. New reporting systems and controls need to be developed to monitor the implementation of the new rules and regulations. Problem loans need to be addressed. Management and operations have to be modernised. All of these require imports of machinery, systems, computer programmes, financial instruments, and training programmes as well as the services of bankers, economists, financiers, management and technical consultants, industrial specialists, lawyers, and accountants.

NOTES

1 In the external sector, deregulation should begin in the trade account and then followed by deregulation in the capital account. The two arguments for this sequence are: (1) the speed of adjustment is slower in the trade/real sectors and so reforms should begin in these sectors; and (2) reforms in the financial sector (and

capital account) may lead to volatility in exchange rates and interest rates which will increase internal distortions in the real sector (trade account). See, for example, Edwards (1986) and McKinnon (1991).

2 M^1 refers to the amount of currency outside banks and private sector demand deposits. M^2 is equal to M^2 plus time and savings deposits.

3 The IGGI, a consortium of Indonesia's Western creditors, was established in 1967 and chaired by the Minister of Development Cooperation of the Netherlands. Subsequently the Netherlands was accused of using its aid as a "tool of political intimidation." As a result, Indonesia unilaterally dissolved the IGGI in March 1962 and, at the same time, requested the World Bank to establish and chair the Consultative Group on Indonesia (CGI). The function of the CGI is exactly the same as that of IGGI and, except for the Netherlands and Canada, all former members of IGGI are in the CGI.

4 Capital is defined as the sum of the paid-in capital, general and specific reserves and retained earnings, plus subeordinated and two-step loans. Subordinated and two-step loans are basically government-guaranteed foreign borrowings mainly channeled through state-owned banks.

5 Bank of Indonesia has set a schedule for banks to raise the capital adequacy ratio to 5 per cent of their risk-weighted assets by March 1992, 7 percent by March 1993, and 8 per cent by the end of 1993.

6 The five state-owned banks are: *Bank Bumi Daya* (BBD), *Bank Dagang Negara* (BDN), *Bank Exim, Bank Rakyat Indonesia* (BRI), and *Bank* (BNI) 1946.

7 Thanks to the political skill of its director, BDN escaped integration and continued operating with some independence, i.e., as a "little central bank" with its own foreign exchange.

8 A repurchase agreement is the sale of a security with a commitment by the seller to buy the security back from the purchaser at a specified price and at a designated future date. A repurchase agreement is actually a collateralised loan, where the collateral is a security.

9 Previously, Ficorinvest, and NBFI owned by the central bank, was the sole institution authorised for this purpose.

10 Prior to the present form, the JSE was reopened on June 4, 1952, after being closed since the beginning of World War II. However due to economic and social instability, its activities were again officially suspended in 1968.

11 The upper limit of foreign capital participation in the listed share of a domestic bank has not been set by the government as of yet.

12 The latter is due to the time lag in either an upward adjustment of the swap premium or a nominal depreciation of the rupiah, or a combination of both.

13 In the long-run, a slow expansion of new loans may create more problems for the banks than the bad loans themselves.

REFERENCES

Benston, George J., Robert Eisenbeis, Paul M. Horvits,. Edward J. Kane, and George C. Kaufman. 1986. *Perspectives on Safe and Sound Banking: Past, Present, Future.* Cambridge: MIT Press.

Binhadi and Paul Meek. 1992. Implementing Monetary Policy. In *The Oil Boom and After: Indonesian Economic Policy and Performance in the Soeharto Era*, ed., Anne Booth. Singapore: Oxford University Press.

Chant, John, and Mari Pangestu. 1992. An Assessment of Financial Reform in

Indonesia: 1983–1990. In *Financial Reform: Theory and Experience*, ed., Gerard Caprio Jr., Izak Aithyas, James Hanson and Associates. Washington D.C.: Johns Hopkins Press, forthcoming.

Cole, David C., and Betty F. Slade. 1992. Financial Development in Indonesia. In *The Oil Boom and After*, ed. Anne Booth.

Cukierman, Alex, Steven B. Webb, and Leila M. Webster. 1992. Measuring the Independence of Central Banks and Its Effect on Policy Outcomes. *The World Bank Economic Review* 6(3): 353–98.

Edwards, Sebastian. 1986. The Order of Liberalisation of the Current Account and Capital Accounts of the Balance of Payments. In *Economic Liberalization in Developing Countries*, ed. Armeane Choski and Demetris Papageorgiu. New York: Basic Blackwell.

Edwards, Sebastian, and M. S. Khan. 1985. Interest Rate Determination in Developing Countries. *IMF Staff Papers* 32 (September): 377–403.

Fabozzi, Frank J., and Franco Modigliani. 1992. *Capital Markets: Institutions and Instruments.* Englewood Cliffs, N.J.: Prentice Hall.

Hanna, Donald P. 1992. *Indonesian Experience with Financial Sector Reform.* A paper prepared for the ECLAC/UNU-WIDER/UNCTAD Seminar on "Savings and Financial Policy in Developing Countries," Santiago, Chile, October 5–6.

Harris, John, Fabio Schiantarelli, and Miranda Siregar. 1992. *Financial and Investment Behavior of the Indonesian Manufacturing Sector and the Effect of Liberalization: Evidence from Panel Data, 1981–1988.* A paper prepared for the Conference on "The Impact of Financial Reform," sponsored by the World Bank, Washington D.C., April 2–3.

Komatsu, Massaki. 1992. "Monetary Policies and Money Markets in Indonesia," *Working Paper* 11 (July). Tokyo: Department of Research Cooperation, Economic Research Institute, Economic Planning Agency.

McKinnon, Ronald. 1991. *The Order of Economic Liberalization: Financial Control in the Transition to a Market Economy*. Baltimore: Johns Hopkins University Press.

Nasution, Anwar. 1983. *Financial Institutions and Policies in Indonesia*. Singapore: ISEAS.

——. 1990. Recent Deregulation of the Banking Sector in Indonesia. In *Privatization, and Deregulation in ASEAN and the EC: Making Markets More Effective*, ed. Jacques Pelkmans and Nobert Wagner. Singapore: ISEAS and European Institute of Public Administration.

——. 1991a. The Adjustment Programme in the Indonesian Economy Since the 1980s. In *Indonssian Assessment 1991*, ed. Hal Hill. Canberra: Department of Political and Social Change, Research School of Pacific Studies, Australian National University.

——. 1991b. Survey of Recent Developments. *Bulletin of Indonesian Economic Studies* 26(2): 3–43.

——. 1992. The Years of Living Dangerously: The Impacts of Financial Sector Policy Reforms and Increasing Private Sector External Indebtedness in Indonesia, 1983–1992. *Indonesian Quarterly* XX, no. 4 (Fourth Quarter, 1992): 405–37.

Portes, R., and A. K. Swoboda, eds. 1987. *Threat to International Financial Stability.* Cambridge: Cambridge University Press.

Price Waterhouse. 1991. *Bank Capital Adequacy and Capital Convergence.* London: Price Waterhouse World Regulatory Advisory Practice.

Ravallion, Martin, and Monica Huppi. 1991. Measuring Changes in Poverty: A Methodological Case Study of Indonesia During an Adjustment Period. *World Bank Economic Review* 5(1): 57–82.

Stiglitz, Joseph, and Andrew Weiss. Credit Rationing in Markets with Imperfect Information. *American Economic Review* 71 (June): 393–410.

Warr, Peter G. 1992. Exchange Rate Policy, Petroleum Prices, and the Balance of Payments. In *The Oil Boom and After*, ed. Anne Booth.

Woo, W. T., B. Glassburner, and A. Nasution. 1991. *Macroeconomic Policies, Crises and Long-run Growth: The Case of Indonesia, 1965–1990*. Washington, D.C.: World Bank.

11

FINANCIAL REFORM IN MALAYSIA

Zainal Aznam Yusof, Awang Adek Hussin, Ismail Alowi, Lim Chee Sing and Sukhdave Singh

Liberalization of Malaysia's financial markets, tackled in earnest in the early 1980s, has been gradual and cautious. It has been a process of structural deregulation and prudential reregulation, with the authorities willing to change course when borrower net worth (and the banks) have come under pressure. The result appears to be a financial system that is more stable and competitive, with a wider public choice of financial instruments, as well as institutions, and more effective conduct of monetary policy by the Central Bank.

Malaysia began the reform process with a relatively deep financial sector, compared with the simple structure of the mid-1950s. It also had a relatively open economy, with little financial repression and negative real interest rates only at the time of the first oil shock in 1973. Yet there were many structural weaknesses in the economy and the financial system, which came to the fore only during the recession of the early 1980s. Malaysia's experience suggests that in financially repressed countries contemplating liberalization, governments should first administratively raise interest rates, sort out the health of banks, and at the same time build a strong central bank on both the regulatory and monetary side.

Malaysia's Central Bank was a key player in its financial reform. By keeping inflation down, the Bank helped the spread of long-term financial markets and facilitated the growth of money markets. The introduction of repos and swaps has broadened the range of monetary instruments, while the reforms in government securities' markets have made it easier for the Central Bank to conduct open-market operations, although these are still small. Moreover, new laws and regulations governing the conduct and accountability of banks and other financial institutions have allowed the Central Bank to act quickly to deal with delinquent firms and so give credibility and sustainability to Malaysia's financial reforms. The impact of these reforms on the Malaysian economy and their contribution to growth and development is the focus of this study.

Source: *Financial Reform: Theory and Experience*, Gerard Caprio, Izak Aithyes and James Hanson, Cambridge University Press, 1994, pp. 276–320.

Malaysia's macroeconomic background is covered in Section 11.1, followed by an overview of the financial system. Section 11.3 deals with the nature of liberalization and Section 11.4 with the effects of reform on the economy and financial system. The new regulatory and supervisory framework of reform is analyzed in Section 11.5 and, finally, the lessons of Malaysia's experience are drawn in Section 11.6.

11.1 THE MALAYSIAN ECONOMY: 1970–90

Malaysia generally has enjoyed rapid economic growth with rising per capita income and price stability. Real GDP growth accelerated from an average of 5.2% a year in 1961–70 to about 8% in the 1970s. However, it slowed down considerably in the early 1980s before bouncing back to 7% in 1986–90. The economic growth of the 1960s and 1970s was accompanied by rising per capita income and living standards, greater urbanization and access to health and education, and an improvement in the distribution of income. At the end of 1990, nominal GNP stood at U.S.$41 billion and per capita income at U.S.$2,300. In 1970–90 the government pursued a policy of diversification in agriculture and industry, and the role of public sector in the economy was reduced. Table 11.1 reviews GDP, prices, the balance of payments, and the government deficit.

The soaring seventies

Malaysia's growth performance in the 1970s was led by a rapid expansion of palm oil output, in the face of a modest expansion of rubber, a prior leading sector. Hence, the share of palm oil in agriculture value added increased from 9.6% in 1970 to 25% in 1980, while in rubber it decreased from 34.3% to 24.9%. With generous tax and other incentives, export-oriented and labor-intensive industries, such as electronics, textile, and wood products, also flourished. In 1970–80, the manufacturing sector grew by 12.5%, accounting for 20.5% of GDP in 1980. The expansion of crude oil production (by 31.6%) compensated for the decline in tin output. Much of the increase in Malaysian exports in the 1970s (7.6%) came from palm oil, crude oil, and manufactures.[1]

Redressing social and income distribution imbalances (in line with the New Economic Policy development plan for 1971–90) led to an expansion of the government's role in the economy in the 1970s. Total public investment increased from 5.7% of GNP in 1970 to 8.8% in 1980, while public consumption doubled to 20.2% of GNP. At the same time, private investment and consumption increased by 12% and 7.7%, respectively.

The external accounts were relatively favorable: in 1970–80, imports increased by 9.8%, mainly due to rising capital goods imports, in line with growth in private investment. However, imports of consumption and

Table 11.1 Malaysia: key macroeconomic indicators (% change unless otherwise indicated)

	1971–79 Avg.	*1980*	*1985*	*1989*	*1990*
1. Real GDP	8.4	7.4	–1.1	8.8	10.0
Agriculture	5.2	1.3	2.0	5.8	1.7
Mining	5.6	–2.2	–1.9	8.6	4.1
Manufacturing	12.0	9.2	–3.8	12.0	17.8
Construction	9.2	17.3	–8.4	11.6	16.0
Services	8.7	10.7	1.7	8.6	10.6
2. Real aggregate domestic demand					
Private consumption	7.7	12.7	0.3	14.3	12.5
Private investment	17.3	17.9	–8.6	31.0	30.3
Private consumption	7.2	25.1	–0.9	7.6	5.0
Private investment	11.7	38.1	–10.4	33.5	14.0
3. Domestic prices	5.9	6.7	0.4	2.8	3.1
4. Balance of payments					
Merchandise exports ($b)	11.7	28.0	37.6	66.8	78.3
Merchandise imports ($b)	9.3	22.8	28.7	56.2	73.1
Merchandise account ($b)	2.4	5.2	8.9	10.6	5.2
Current account ($b)	0.2	–0.1	–1.5	–0.6	–4.5
5. Federal government					
Overall deficit ($b)	2,013	7,104	5,707	5,260	5,516
(Without transfer to dev. fund)	–1,635	–3,704	–4,407	–3,410	–3,437
% of GNP	8.0	13.8	6.6	5.5	5.0
	–7.0	–7.2	–6.1	–3.5	–3.1

intermediate goods fell because of the import substitution policies of the government in the 1960s and early 1970s. In the 1970s Malaysia's overall balance of payments was consistently in surplus. Although the service account was persistently in deficit (due to investment income payments and freight and insurance outflows), the merchandise account surplus was in general somewhat larger. So, too, was the capital account, and substantially so, thanks to sustained inflows of corporate investment, as well as government borrowing abroad. As a result, external reserves of the Central Bank increased to $10.3 billion at the end of 1980, sufficient to finance about 5.5 months of retained imports.

Malaysia's gross national saving increased from 18% of GNP in 1970 to a peak of 34.8% by 1979, due to both a rapid increase in domestic income during the Third Malaysia Plan and attractive real interest rates on deposits, which were gradually deregulated during the decade (see below). Over the same period, investment increased from 17.8% to 30% of GNP. The savings–investment gap was always positive except for a few years in the early 1970s when a small gap of $3 million emerged.

Inflation, as measured by the consumer price index, was higher in the 1970s (5.8%, compared with less than 1% in the 1960s). It rose from 3.2% in 1972 to a peak of 17.5 in 1974, thanks mainly to the (first) oil shock of 1973. However, the CPI's increase moderated to only 4% per annum in 1976–9, due partly to government anti-inflation measures.

Adjustment in the 1980s

Malaysia's economic growth of the 1970s was halted in the early 1980s by a prolonged global recession, despite countercyclical policies adopted by the Government. The balance of payments and government budgetary positions also deteriorated. By 1982, the public sector deficit stood at 19% of GNP; the balance-of-payments current-account deficit was 14% of GNP, with an increase in external borrowing and foreign debt. After 1982, Malaysia's economic performance slackened further, revealing structural weaknesses embedded in the economy.

In mid-1982, the government embarked on a massive fiscal retrenchment exercise as part of a multiyear structural adjustment program. The government also took effective control over its activities and those of the non-financial public enterprises (NFPEs) to bring about an efficient management of the economy, while, at the same time, reducing the size and role of the public sector in the economy. The deficit was financed mainly by non-inflationary domestic sources, while external borrowing was curtailed to reduce the debt/service ratio.

By the end of 1985, the budget and balance-of-payments deficit were reduced, respectively, to 6% and 2.1% of GNP. External debt increased by 14.2% in 1985, inflation was below 1%, and the Central Bank's international reserve amounted to $12.5 billion, enough to finance five months of retained imports. As noted below, the credibility gains from persevering with such a tough adjustment program appear to have been considerable.

Just as the economy was emerging from this adjustment process, it was hit again by the collapse of commodity prices at the end of 1985. International terms of trade fell by 4.5% in 1985 and by 14.9% in 1986. Thus, nominal national income declined by −5.8% in 1985–6, with lower aggregate domestic demand resulting in a 10.7% fall in real private sector expenditure.

In the mid-1980s, the government began promoting the private sector as the engine of economic growth. A new privatization policy, pursued partly to reduce the size of the public sector in the economy, saw nine projects privatized by 1986. The government also relaxed regulations on foreign equity participation in Malaysia, and parts of the Industrial Coordination Act 1975 were liberalized. Up to 100% foreign equity ownership of export-oriented companies was allowed; visa and work permit requirements for foreign employees of companies with foreign paid-up capital of U.S.$2 million or more were eased; approval of new investment projects made easier; foreign investment guidelines were loosened; and the Central Bank's scheme to promote exports and domestic linkages was revamped.

By the end of 1986, real GDP was rising by 1.2%. Notwithstanding this upward economic trend, unemployment increased from 8.5% in 1986 to 9.1% in 1987, leading to the adoption of measures to stimulate further growth and reduce unemployment. These included low-cost housing schemes, speedier approval of licenses for small business, easier transfer of land to the private sector for cultivation of commercial crops, new public infrastructure projects, and a crash program to retrain the unemployed. To reduce unemployment of university graduates, temporary employment schemes were adopted by some government agencies, private companies were encouraged to offer training and jobs, and the Ministry of Education's teacher-training scheme was intensified. The government also continued to keep a tight rein on public sector wage increases.

To encourage the private sector further, the 1988 budget saw (1) the reduction of corporation tax from 40% to 35% and the scaled abolition of the 5% development tax, beginning with 1% reduction in 1990; (2) the scrapping of the 3% excess profit tax on companies; (3) the extension of the reinvestment allowance period for another two years and increasing its rate from 25% to 40%; (4) the introduction of a $500 million soft loan scheme under the Enterprise Rehabilitation Fund to help Bumiputera industries (Bumiputera is the official term for Malays and other indigenous groups); (5) amendments to the Industrial Relation Act 1967, the Trade Union Act 1959, and the Employment Act 1955 to ensure greater flexibility in wage determination; (6) the launch of the ASEAN–Japan Development Fund (ASEAN is the Association of South East Asian Nations) to provide financing for small and medium industries (SMIs) for investment in manufacturing, agriculture, and tourism; and (7) the loan limit under a special loan scheme for small traders and hawkers increased from $2,000 to $3,000 ($5,000 in special cases), while the capital eligibility criterion was raised from $5,000 to $10,000.

To strengthen its budgetary position, particularly to overcome the deficit in the current account, the federal government (1) lowered wage levels for new recruits in the public sector; (2) introduced tighter controls of expenditures of statutory bodies; (3) privatized or closed unprofitable government enterprises; and (4) began prepaying and refinancing the government's more expensive external market loans. With better domestic macroeconomic policies and stronger world economic recovery since 1987, the Malaysian economy picked up again. Real GDP growth accelerated to over 9% a year on average over the last three years of the 1980s, while inflation averaged less than 2% per year.

11.2 THE FINANCIAL SYSTEM

The Malaysian financial system can be divided into the banking system and the system of nonbank financial intermediaries. The Central Bank and the commercial banks constitute the monetary institutions, but the banking system also includes finance companies and merchant banks, which are regulated by the Central Bank, as well as the discount houses, money and foreign exchange brokers, and the Credit Guarantee Corporation, which provides guarantee cover for commercial banks on loans to small businesses.

Nonbank financial intermediaries, which are supervised by various government departments and agencies, can be divided into five groups – the development finance institutions, the savings institutions, provident and pension funds, insurance companies, and others, which include the building societies and unit trusts. The *capital market* comprises a primary securities market, in which issues of government and corporate securities are offered for sale, and a secondary market, in which such securities are traded. Funds raised by the private sector in the capital market were dwarfed by those raised by the federal government. However, in the secondary market (mainly the Kuala Lumpur Stock Exchange but also the Bumiputera Stock Exchange Division of the Komplek Kewangan Malaysia Berhad), the volume of business in corporate securities outweighed that in government securities, which are held mainly by the institutions (particularly provident and pension funds) and held mainly to maturity.

Total resources of the financial system, expressed in current prices, grew phenomenally to M$309.1 billion in 1990, compared with M$11.6 billion in 1970 and representing an average annual growth rate of 17.8% (see Table 11.2). Unlike Korea, which also saw rapid financial deepening over the same period, the banking system led the way in Malaysia, accounting for almost 75% of the 1990 total (and the Central Bank for 12.1%), significantly higher than the 64.1% in 1970. However, the share of the nonbank financial intermediaries declined from 35.9% to 25.5% over the same period. The *commercial banks*, which accounted for 44.2% of total assets in 1990 (38.4% in 1977), have seen strong deposit growth and branch-network expansion since 1970. By 1990 there were 38 commercial banks, of which 22 were domestic incorporated banks, and representative offices of foreign banks increased from 12 to 29. Bank branches doubled to 1,000, an average population-to-banking office ratio of 18,277.

Finance companies compete with commercial banks for savings and fixed deposits but, specializing in hire-purchase and housing loan finance, they complement the credit operations of banks. Between 1978 and 1990, finance companies increased their numbers from 33 to 45, and their branch network

Table 11.2 Assets of the financial system

By institutions	*Outstanding ($ million)*				*% Share*			
	1970	*1977*	*1985*	*1990*	*1970*	*1977*	*1985*	*1990*
Banking system	7,455	26,098	118,509	230,243	64.1	69.6	71.4	74.5
Monetary institutions	6,882	21,919	91,343	174,127	59.2	58.5	55.0	56.3
Central bank	2,227	7,701	16,525	37,545	19.2	20.5	9.9	12.1
Currency board	195	55	—	—	1.7	0.1	0.0	
Commercial banks	4,460	14,163	74,234	129,197	38.4	37.8	44.7	41.8
Islamic banks	—	—	584	7,385	0.0	0.0	0.4	2.4
Non-monetary institutions	573	4,179	27,166	56,116	4.9	11.1	16.4	18.2
Finance companies	531	2,610	17,833	39,457	4.6	7.0	10.7	12.8
Merchant banks	—	914	6,296	11,063	0.0	2.4	3.8	3.6
Discount houses	42	649	2,830	4,871	0.4	1.7	1.7	1.6
Credit guarantee corp.	—	6	207	726	0.0	...	0.1	0.2
Non-bank financial intermediaries	4,167	11,394	47,583	78,813	35.9	30.4	28.6	25.5
Provident, pension and insurance funds	3,156	8,161	32,658	56,449	27.2	21.8	19.7	18.3
Employees provident fund	2,265	5,843	24,708	46,766	19.5	15.6	14.9	15.1
Other statutory & private provident & pension funds	452	897	2,919	4,999	3.9	2.4	1.8	1.6
Life insurance funds	324	960	3,646	2,342	2.8	2.6	2.2	0.8
General insurance funds	115	461	1,385	2,342	1.0	1.2	0.8	0.8
Development finance institutions 1/	133	892	4,044	6,016	1.1	2.4	2.4	1.9
Savings institutions 2/	645	1,759	8,096	10,001	5.5	4.7	4.9	3.2
Other financial intermediaries 3/	233	582	2,785	6,347	2.0	1.6	1.7	2.1
Total	11,622	37,492	166,092	309,056	100.0	100.0	100.0	100.0

Note:
1/ Include Malaysian Industrial Development Finance Berhad (MIDF), Agricultural Bank of Malaysia, Borneo Development Corporation, Sabah Development Bank Berhad, Saban Credit Corporation, Development Bank of Malaysia, and Industrial Bank Berhad.
2/ Include National Savings Bank, Bank Kerjasama Rakyat and the co-operative societies.
3/ Include unit trusts, building societies, Pilgrims Management Fund Board, Credit Guarantee Corporation and Cagamas Berhad.

from 195 to 542. Their share of total assets also increased sharply – from 4.6% in 1970 to 12.8% in 1990. The first of Malaysia's 12 *merchant banks* was established only in 1970, and by 1990 their branches numbered 17. Accounting for about 3.6% of total assets in 1990 (2.4% in 1977), the merchant banks were mainly involved in wholesale banking, money market operations, and corporate finance. Malaysian *discount houses* are financial intermediaries that mobilize short-term funds from other financial institutions and companies that have excess liquid funds and want to temporarily "park" them as earning assets. They were required by the Central Bank to invest only in government securities. Since they enjoyed rediscounting and lender-of-last-resort facilities at the Central Bank, they were essential in making a secondary market for government securities and providing liquidity for the financial system. The Employees Provident Fund (EPF), the largest of the *provident and pension funds*, is the largest mobilizer of private savings in the country. Accounting for 15.6% of the total assets of the financial system, it has been an important source of government financing.

Priority-sector lending and the financial system

The Central Bank did not issue guidelines on lending until the mid-1970s, when it began promoting a more development-oriented approach for banking in Malaysia. The 1975 guidelines required commercial banks and finance companies to extend a minimum of 50% of new net credit during that year to priority sectors. Almost immediately this fraction was lowered to 20%, and subsequently this was amended to a certain percent of the *outstanding* loans in a reference period. Limits were also placed on interest charged to some priority borrowers. Since the introduction of guidelines, the priority sectors have included (1) the Bumiputera community; (2) small-scale enterprises, including the Special Loans Scheme; (3) agricultural food production; (4) individual housing loans, including low-cost houses (of $25,000 and less); (5) manufacturing; and (6) the broad sector covering agriculture, fishing, and forestry; building, construction, and property development and manufacturing (Table 11.3).

Commercial banks and finance companies that did not meet the priority lending targets were required to place with the Central Bank deposits equal to their respective shortfalls for one year at a rate of interest to be determined by the Bank. Such funds were then on-lent to banks and finance companies that exceeded their targets. Sometimes the Central Bank would also on-lend to specialized agencies that lend to the private sector. But overall, the requirements were generally not binding on the financial system, especially regarding loans to Bumiputeras, since the actual amount of loans to this community tends to be higher than prescribed in the guidelines.

Since 1979 the Central Bank has issued annual priority-lending guidelines each March, suitably modified and adjusted in line with developments in the

Table 11.3 Priority-sector guidelines and achievements of commercial banks (% and M$ million)

	Bumiputera community		*Manufacturing sector*		*Agricultural food production*		*Small-scale enterprises*		*Individual housing loans*		*Low cost housing*	
	Target %	*Achievement %*	*Target **	*Achievement %*	*Target **	*Achievement %*	*Target **	*Achievement*	*Target **	*Achievement**	*Target units*	*Achievement units*
1975	50.0	56.8					10.0	12.1				
1976	20.0		25.0		10.0				10.0			
1977												
1978	20.0	21.7	20.0	19.0	10.0	8.3			10.0	13.3		
1979	17.0				6.0		20.0					
1980	17.0	29.8	$2,573m	$3,951m	6.0	9.5	20.0	28.9	$1,417m	$2,233m		
1981	17.0	25.0	$4,018m	$5,166m	8.0	11.1	12.0	13.7	10.0	13.4		
1982	18.0	27.5	$5,166m	$5,386m	10.0	12.4	12.0	12.6	10.0	13.7	20,000	19,503
1983	18.0	29.7	31.12.82		6.0	6.7	5.0	3.8	31.12.82		20,000	21,708
1984	20.0	31.7			6.0	6.2	5.0	3.2			20,000	25,738
1985	20.0	32.7			6.0	6.7	5.0	3.5			20,000	26,334
1986	20.0	31.9			6.0	5.4	$150m	$235m	80,000	32,658	48,000	12,458
1987	20.0	32.3			6.0	5.4	$150m	$217m	80,000	68,342	48,000	29,772
1988	20.0	31.8			6.0	5.2	$300m	$831m	75,000	43,156	45,000	17,903
1989	20.0	37.0					$600m	$1,012m	75,000	95,069	45,000	39,525
1990	20.0	39.6					$200m	$132m				
1991	20.0						$150m					

Note:
* Initially in percent, then switches to $: "31.12.83" means that loans were to be maintained at the level of that date.

economy. Of key importance is that the guidelines were kept broad-based, with considerable discretion left to individual institutions in assessing and monitoring the credits. Most important, the system did not seriously distort interest rates since the fixed rate reflected the actual cost of funds to the banking institutions. In April 1987 interest rates on priority lending were pegged to the Base Lending Rate (BLR) but subject to a maximum level.

With banking deregulation, the Central Bank has reduced the number of priority sectors, as well as the proportion of loans covered by the guidelines. The latest (1991) set only two targets for banks – to the Bumiputera community and loans provided under the Principal Guarantee Scheme (PGS) of the Credit Guarantee Corporation for small businesses – and only one target for finance companies – just to the Bumiputera community. Data indicate that commercial bank lending to the Bumiputera community accounted for 39.6% of all loans outstanding at the end of the base year (1988), well in excess of the minimum requirement of 20%. Finance companies had the same 20% but, in fact, their total lending to the Bumiputera accounted for 57.2% of all loans.

Priority lending and the government

To meet various social and economic objectives, the federal government has given loans to government agencies, as well as corporations partly owned by government. This practice has helped to avoid excessive implicit taxation of the financial system to carry out government priorities. Made from the federal budget, these loans carry interest rates that depend on the purpose for which the loans are given. In early years, loans for projects to relieve poverty were interest-free, while those for restructuring, infrastructure, strategic, and other related projects carried an interest rate of 2–5%. Commercial projects carried interest rates that reflected the full cost of government funds. The current practice is to charge one-half the cost of funds for loans to poverty-eradication programs run by financially strong government agencies, and as grants for other agencies. Loans for restructuring and other such projects have an interest rate between one-half and the full cost of funds. No government loans are given for commercial projects.

Many corporations have received such loans, as well as statutory bodies and cooperatives involved in extending credit to the private sector (Table 11.4). Bank Industri and Bank Pembangunan are development banks set up by the government to provide long-term financing for investment projects that have long gestation periods. Hicom, MSE, and Perwaja were set up to push the development of heavy industry in Malaysia. PNB and MARA respectively encourage equity ownership and the development of professional skills among the indigenous Bumiputera. The Agricultural Bank lends for agricultural projects, while FELDA, FELCRA, and RISDA are statutory bodies set up to develop land schemes and resettle the landless poor. ASEAN

Table 11.4 Government loans to corporations and selected other agencies (M$ million)

	(M$ million)			
Corporations	*1975*	*1980*	*1985*	*1989*
1. MIDF	130.2	99.8	—	—
2. Food industries of Malaysia Bhd.	2.9	27.8	—	—
3. Chenderoh Electricity (M) Sdn. Bhd.	—	34.6	—	—
4. Syarikat Perumahan Pegawai Kerajaan	27.4	34.9	17.6	—
5. MISC	147.2	433.9	371.2	—
6. Permodalan National Berhad (PNB)	73.0	374.1	592.0	72.7
7. Bank Pembangunan Malaysia Bhd.	15.0	98.1	372.0	494.7
8. Malaysia Shipyard Engineering (MSE)	97.0	127.3	123.9	117.3
9. Malaysia Building Society Bhd. (MBSB)	0.5	0.5	85.5	112.6
10. Malaysian Rubber Development Corp. Bhd.	34.8	56.1	42.5	33.3
11. Syarikat Jengka Sdn. Bhd.	25.2	25.2	33.4	29.4
12. Pineapple Cannery of Malaysia Sdn. Bhd.	6.0	4.5	4.5	4.5
13. Malaysia Batek and Handicrafts Bhd.	1.4	1.5	1.5	1.5
14. Syarikat Malaysia Explosives Sdn. Bhd.	—	14.0	13.3	12.0
15. Bank Industri Malaysia Bhd.	—	102.4	129.7	147.9
16. Syarikat Permodalan Kemajuan Perusahan	—	—	23.5	26.0
17. Syarikat Takaful Malaysia Bhd.	—	—	1.0	1.0
18. Yayasan Pelaburan Bumiputra	—	—	600.0	525.0
19. ASEAN Bintulu Fertilizer Sdn. Bhd.	—	—	471.8	89.9
20. Komplek Kewangan Malaysia Bhd.	—	—	27.0	22.4
21. Kumpulan Fima Bhd.	—	—	164.5	128.0
22. Perwaja	—	—	—	105.2
23. PETRONAS	—	—	—	385.8
24. PLUS	—	—	—	362.6
25. Sabah Forest industries	—	—	—	266.7
26. Heavy Industry Corporation of Malaysia (HICOM)	—	—	—	626.7
Statutory bodies				
(only those that extend credit to the private sector)				
1. Bank Pertanian Malaysia	20.0	125.8	262.5	410.1
2. Federal Land, Consolidation, and Rehabilitation Authority	51.4	165.3	403.3	634.3
3. Federal Land Development Authority	921.4	2,012.4	3,349.1	3,906.4
4. MARA	151.1	326.0	325.1	219.8
5. RISDA	—	—	86.3	167.8
Co-operatives				
1. Bank Kerjasama Rakyat Malaysia	—	155.0	164.3	130.8
Total	1,704.5	4,219.2	7,665.5	9,034.4
(Relative size compared to total outstanding loans of the banking system to the private sector)	22.0%	16.0%	11.6%	9.8%

Bintulu Fertilizer is a joint venture with other members of ASEAN, formed partly to promote regional economic cooperation. Although these loans increased from $1.7 billion in 1975 to $9 billion in 1989, they declined from 22% to 9.8% of all outstanding loans of the banking system. Still, they can be viewed as an important "safety valve," reducing what otherwise could have been intense pressure for greater reliance on directing credit through the banks. Moreover, even with the low nominal interest rates charged, in real terms borrowers of direct credit lines paid mildly negative to slightly positive interest rates, compared with substantially negative real rates seen on some directed credit lines in developing countries.

Financing government

Malaysian government securities (MGS), the major instrument of financing for the government, constituted the largest share (89%) of domestic debt outstanding at the end of 1990. The financial sector accounted for 86.7%, 91.8%, and 90.1% of all MGS at the end of 1975, 1978, and 1990, respectively (Table 11.5), mainly because of statutory requirements imposed on institutions to hold MGS for prudential and liquidity reasons. For example, the Employees Provident Fund (EPF), the biggest provider of government finance, invested the bulk of its resources in MGS – 53.4%, 53.4%, and 58.2% of all MGS outstanding at the end of 1975, 1978, and 1990, respectively.

To meet liquidity requirements of the Central Bank, commercial banks, finance companies, and merchant banks also hold some in MGS. At end-1990, the banking system held 16.2% of all MGS outstanding, compared with 18.2% in 1978.

11.3 THE NATURE OF LIBERALIZATION

Interest-rate reforms

In 1971 fixed deposits placed with commercial banks for more than four years were allowed to carry market-determined interest rates. From January 1972, interest rate ceilings were lifted for commercial bank deposits with maturity exceeding one year. From August 1, 1973, interest rates for deposits placed with finance companies were freed and from August 20, discount rates on Treasury bills were determined by open tender in the money market.

The major phase of reform came in October 1978. The Central Bank freed interest rates of the commercial banks, allowing them to determine rates to depositors and borrowers. Subsequently, rates tended to behave in an asymmetrical manner. When the cost of funds rose, the banks immediately passed it to their customers in higher lending rates. But when the cost of funds declined, lending rates moved downward only with a prolonged lag.[2] And,

Table 11.5 Finance sector's holdings of Malaysia government securities (outstanding) (M$ million)

	1975	*1978*	*1980*	*1981*	*1982*	*1983*	*1984*	*1985*	*1986*	*1987*	*1988*	*1989*	*1990*
Banking system	1,225.7	1,991.5	2,812.7	4,149.3	4,256.8	4,499.3	5,063.6	4,902.9	4,966.0	7,801.5	7,863.4	10,004.3	10,039.5
Commercial banks	1,131.6	1,806.5	2,445.9	3,818.1	3,942.8	4,027.5	4,554.3	4,248.7	4,093.2	6,661.6	6,055.5	7,819.7	7,845.7
Finance companies	67.8	78.4	205.3	151.4	124.9	165.4	173.1	193.9	482.6	640.5	1,260.0	1,419.2	1,360.6
Merchant banks	26.3	106.6	161.5	179.8	189.1	306.4	336.2	460.3	390.2	499.4	547.9	765.4	833.2
Other financial institutions	5,148.3	8,958.5	13.005.4	13,840.3	17,513.3	21,347.2	25,882.1	28,170.3	31,514.9	35,095.0	41,173.8	43,182.3	45,889.0
Central bank	251.2	346.2	1,627.4	560.7	1,802.6	3,254.7	4,768.2	2,340.4	2,052.9	1,631.3	1,781.8	1,262.9	2,198.9
EPF	3,925.7	6,369.4	8,581.6	10,314.9	12,468.8	14,415.6	17,199.7	20,605.9	24,009.4	28,254.0	32,504.9	34,107.9	36,130.4
Insurance companies	209.3	357.1	501.2	607.8	680.0	650.5	689.0	813.3	777.1	1,001.4	1,158.2	1,353.7	1,437.1
National Savings Bank	578.5	807.9	924.1	857.0	879.9	926.1	919.2	921.3	907.8	1,125.3	1,338.1	1,520.1	1,595.4
SOCSO	22.1	145.5	259.5	354.5	466.5	582.5	711.5	824.0	911.8	1,050.3	1,081.3	1,180.4	1,353.5
Discount houses	151.0	748.2	889.7	976.3	1,148.4	1,208.8	1,361.6	2,134.7	1,996.3	1,461.9	953.0	1,670.4	1,190.9
Caganas Berhad										52.6	116.4	128.5	80.0
Others	10.5	184.2	221.9	169.1	67.1	309.0	232.9	530.7	859.6	518.2	2,240.1	1,958.4	1,902.8
Total	6,374.0	10,950.0	15,818.1	17,989.6	21,770.1	25,846.5	30,945.7	33,073.2	36,480.9	42,896.5	49,037.2	53,186.6	55,928.5
Total MGS outstanding	7,354.5	11,931.9	16,795.5	20,586.4	26,170.4	30,037.3	33,090.2	36,681.1	41,300.8	48,794.0	55,830.2	58,213.4	62,106.1

when the banks did lower lending rates, they were not evenly applied to all borrowers. As a result, the Central Bank introduced the base lending rate (BLR) on November 1, 1983. Every bank's or finance company's lending rates (except those charged to the priority sectors) were anchored to its declared BLR, which was based on the cost of funds, after providing for the cost of statutory reserves, liquid assets requirements and overheads. As the actual cost of credit to borrowers was determined by the BLR and an interest margin based on the borrower's credit standing, this was intended to remove much of a bank's discretion on which of its borrowers benefited or was penalized whenever interest rates changed.

Free market determination of interest rates was further interrupted during the tight liquidity period from October 1985 to January 1987, when controls on deposit interest rates were reinstituted. In the tight liquidity environment of 1985, interest rates rose sharply as the financial institutions bid for funds. The Central Bank got the commercial banks and finance companies to peg interest rates for deposits of up to 12-month maturities to the deposit rate of the two leading domestic banks with effect from October 21, 1985. The maximum differential vis-à-vis the lead banks was 0.5 percentage point for the commercial banks and 1.5 percentage points for the finance companies. This pegged interest rate arrangement was dismantled in February 1987.

However, the sluggish response of lending rates to the decline in deposit rates led to the Central Bank imposing new guidelines on September 1, 1987. These required the BLR of commercial banks to be no more than 0.5 percentage points above the BLR of the two lead banks. The margin by which lending rates can exceed the BLR was limited to not more than four percentage points, depending on the credit standing of borrowers. Penalties on delinquent loans were not to exceed 1% per annum. The finance companies were subject to similar guidelines. On February 1, 1991, the BLR was finally freed from the administrative control of the Central Bank. Except for some priority-sector lending, all interest rates are now determined by market forces.

Exchange-control liberalization and exchange-rate reform

On May 8, 1973, exchange-control regulations ceased to discriminate between countries in and outside of the Sterling Area and allowed for a freer flow of funds in and out of Malaysia. On January 1, 1987, new measures reduced the formalities with which businessmen have to comply when exporting their goods and provided investors with greater access to credit to expand productive capacity. In addition, the public was permitted to deal freely in gold. Existing exchange controls are meant mainly to ensure that export receipts are received promptly in Malaysia, to assist the Central Bank in monitoring the settlement of international payments and receipts and to encourage the use of financial resources for productive purposes.

In June 1972 Malaysia broke its historical link with sterling and adopted the U.S. dollar as the intervention currency. A year later, the ringgit was allowed to float upward. This implied that the Central Bank was no longer obliged to buy U.S. dollars with ringgit at the floor rate of M$2.4805 for U.S.$1. Moreover, the Association of Banks ceased to issue best-agreed merchant rates, and each bank was free to determine its own exchange rate for any foreign currency (including the Singapore dollar) for any amount. In September 1975 the value of the ringgit was determined by a basket of representative major currencies, weighted by the main currencies of settlement, as well as the trade shares of the major trading partners of Malaysia. This arrangement is still the basis for Malaysia's exchange-rate policy.

Prior to the mid-1980s, it was considered desirable to keep the ringgit relatively stable against the Singapore dollar. However, intervention through the U.S. dollar kept the ringgit relatively strong vis-à-vis the U.S. dollar. The unsustainability of an appreciating exchange rate in a weak economy, combined with speculative attacks on the ringgit, led to a shift in policy in late 1984: The ringgit was allowed to move freely against the U.S. and Singapore dollars. This led to a sharp depreciation of the ringgit exchange rate, which contributed to the gains in the level of international competitiveness since 1985.

From February 1987 the commercial banks, finance companies, and merchant banks were allowed to observe the *minimum liquidity requirement* (MLR) on a two-week average basis, with a maximum daily variation of 2 percentage points above or below the requirement. Previously the requirement had to be met daily. From January 1989 a similar ruling applied to the *statutory reserve ratio* (SRR), with a maximum daily variation of 0.5 percentage point and a common ratio for all banking institutions. The primary liquidity ratios of the finance companies and commercial banks were abolished in January 1989 and June 1990, respectively. Beginning July 1, 1990, the commercial banks, finance companies, and merchant banks were allowed to observe the SRR and MLR based on their average eligible liabilities (EL) over a fortnight, instead of a single day.

Different priorities

From April 1, 1987, the ceiling rates for priority-sector lending were pegged at 1.75 percentage points above the average BLR of the two lead banks or 9% a year, whichever is lower. In March 1989 these ceiling rates were removed from all priority-sector loans, save for those to individuals for owner-occupied houses (costing $100,000 or less) and for those to small-scale enterprises (SSEs) under the Principal Guarantee Scheme of the Credit Guarantee Corporation, although compulsory lending to the former borrower ceased in March 1990. Quantitative lending guidelines apply now only to the Bumiputera community and SSEs.

Developments in the capital market

A priority of the Bank in the 1980s was to develop the capital market in Malaysia, particularly a secondary market in government securities. One problem was that the yields on Malaysian government securities (MGS) were well below other financial assets. Moreover, the bulk of MGS were held by "captive" institutions, so limiting the amount available for trading on the secondary market and also reducing the Central Bank's ability to conduct open market operations and so, control money supply and credit.

Measures were taken to increase the role of the market in providing liquidity for MGS, reduce the scope of captive markets and move toward a market-based pricing of primary issues of MGS. These included adjustments of statutory and liquidity requirements, allowing well-capitalized finance companies to participate in the interbank money market and establishing the Interbank Funds Transfer System, the Scriptless Securities Trading System, the Kuala Lumpur Automated Clearing House, and the Day-One Settlement System. MGS with market-based coupons were first issued in 1987. In January 1989 there were other major reforms:

1 *Appointment of principal dealers.* Twenty-three financial institutions (9 commercial banks, 7 merchant banks, and all 7 discount houses) were appointed to underwrite new issues of MGS and to make a secondary market in them.
2 *Issue of MGS by auction.* MGS with maturities of up to 10 years are now auctioned through the principal dealers. Longer dated securities are still sold by subscription, although only to the Employees Provident Fund and the National Savings Bank.
3 *The Central Bank's open market operations* are now conducted through the principal dealers only. The Bank's role in the money market has now changed to one of maintaining liquidity in the system. Institutions with excess liquidity (or short of funds) have to square their positions in the market and not with the Central Bank. Only principal dealers have access to the Bank's discount window.
4 *Freeing of discount house operations.* Because discount houses had become securities dealers, restrictions on their investments were removed in June 1990. They are now free to decide their portfolio structure, subject only to the adequacy of capital on a risk-weighted basis. They can, also, invest in securities with maturities of up to 10 years, previously limited to 5 years or less.

The Central Bank also took steps to develop a market for corporate bonds, when it issued guidelines on the issue of private debt securities. A private credit-rating agency was also set up in November 1990.

Sequencing of reforms

Countries wishing to reform their financial systems must decide upon the timing of measures to ensure a smooth transition with minimal instability and disruptions to the economy. Should financial sector reforms be undertaken prior to real sector reforms or vice versa? Or should reforms in both be undertaken simultaneously? And should liberalization of the capital account precede or follow liberalization in the current account? Or both at the same time?

Although interest rates were liberalized in Malaysia in 1978, it is not clear if there was a deliberate policy then of reforming the financial sector. Liberalization became widely accepted only in the early 1980s, following government policy to restructure the economy through a multiyear structural adjustment program. It was targeted at the real sector to overcome prolonged and deep recession, arising from a sharp deterioration in the country's international terms of trade and to address the large twin-deficits problem and widespread inefficiencies in the economy. Liberalization of the real sector began with drastic cutbacks in public sector expenditure; privatizations; reduction in public sector employment; and promoting private sector investment by relaxing investment guidelines.

Reform of the financial system was not pursued concurrently in the early stages of real sector liberalization. Indeed, there was greater control and supervision of the financial system because of difficulties arising from mismanagement, overexposure to some sectors, and bad debts during the recession. The government, worried about bank failures and the erosion of public confidence, brought in the system of "lead banks." This was deemed necessary because interest rates were escalating to excessively high levels due to fierce competition for funds by the deposit-taking cooperatives (DTCs), speculation on the ringgit and the decline in the external sources of liquidity due to the. collapse of commodity prices and deteriorating balance of payments.

So *real-sector reform preceded financial reform in Malaysia*. It was only in 1987, with economic recovery, that the government could take further guarded steps toward financial liberalization. Deposit rates were again allowed to be freely determined, but the base lending rate continued to be pegged to the two lead banks. It was only in February 1991, when the economy had recovered, that lending rates were determined freely by individual financial institutions. Lending guidelines on directed credit have also been relaxed progressively and, for all financial institutions, the uniform reserve requirements have been introduced and the scope of their activities and instruments dealt in have been broadened.

In Malaysia, *liberalization of the current account of the balance of payments came before the liberalization of the capital account*. Tariff rates were relatively high in the 1960s, a time of import-substitution strategy, but were reduced progressively in the past 20 years across the board, save for some products associated with the development of heavy industries.

Reform of the capital account has been more modest. This appears to reflect concerns that the opening up of the capital account should be carried out prudently to avoid massive capital outflows that could accompany a sudden dose of capital account liberalization. Even so, exchange control regulations have been increasingly dismantled. The few remaining controls are on the repatriation of export proceeds, foreign borrowing of above M$1 million by residents, and domestic borrowing of more than M$10 million by non-resident controlled companies. Although export proceeds must be repatriated within six months, controls on borrowing have been flexibly enforced where they are for productive purposes.

Financial deepening

Although the financial system in Malaysia has been transformed from the simple structure of mid-1950s, many changes have nothing to do with the liberalization of interest rates in 1978, but rather to the growing needs of the economy. Between 1978 and 1990 there was a big increase in the number of commercial banks and finance companies, both domestically and foreign owned. Of all insurance companies, 80% were domestically owned in 1990, compared with 50% in 1978. The number of companies listed on the Kuala Lumpur Stock Exchange (KLSE) increased from 254 in 1978 to 307 in 1989 but fell to 285 in 1990 following the split between the Malaysian and Singapore stock exchanges. The market capitalization of the KLSE increased from $18.3 billion to $131.7 billion and the funds raised by Malaysian companies increased from $53 million to $8.5 billion.

The deepening of the financial system has been a contributor to (and a consequence of) the increasing monetization of the economy. The ratio of M3 to gross national product (M3/GNP) rose from 0.46 in 1973 to 0.56 in 1978, and it peaked at 1.07 in 1986. By 1990 it had drifted down to 1.05, as the growth in savings was affected by the recession in 1985–6 and low interest rates which led to investment in nondeposit assets. Financial deepening in Malaysia can also be seen in the relationship between total assets of the financial system and GNP (FA/GNP). This ratio increased from 1.23 in 1975 to 2.91 in 1990 (Table 11.6), among the highest in the developing world. The dominance of banking in the Malaysian financial system is seen in the ratio of the banking system's assets to GNP – 1.69 in 1990, which represented about 58% of all assets of the financial system. Commercial banks alone accounted for 40% of the financial system's assets at the end of 1990. Part of this expansion likely reflects the rapid expansion of branching, leading to a sharp fall in the number of people per branch and a commensurately greater ability to deliver financial services.

Table 11.6 Malaysia: selected measures of monetization and financial deepening, 1975–90

	1975	*1980*	*1989*	*1990*
M1/GNP	0.20	0.19	0.19	0.22
M2/GNP	0.46	0.54	0.70	0.76
M3/GNP	0.5	0.6	0.9	1.1
M3/M1	2.60	3.35	4.83	4.76
Currency/M1	0.51	0.49	0.46	0.41
M3 per capita	924	2,375	4,184	6,496
Per capita deposits	811	2,236	4,656	6,797
Persons per banking office ('000)	30	25	20	18
Total financial assets/GNP	1.23	1.44	2.35	2.91
Assets/GNP				
Central bank	0.22	0.25	0.23	0.37
Commercial banks	0.50	0.63	1.03	1.17
Finance companies	0.08	0.11	0.25	0.36
Merchant banks	0.02	0.04	0.09	0.10
Discount houses	0.02	0.03	0.04	0.04
Bank Islam	—	—	0.01	0.01
Total banking system c/	0.62	0.80	1.41	1.69
	1971–75	*1976–80*	*1981–85*	*1986–90*
Net issues ratio a/	−1.7	1.5	0.9	1.7
Financial system, of which:				
– Central bank	−0.3	0.3	0.0	0.2
– Commercial banks	−0.5	0.7	0.6	0.7
Income elasticity of net issues b/	−1.6	1.2	0.7	0.6
Financial system, of which:				
– Central bank	−1.8	1.1	0.3	0.5
– Commercial banks	−1.0	1.3	1.1	0.6
– Total banking system c/	−1.3	1.3	1.0	0.7

Note:
a/ Ratio of change in assets to change in GNP.
b/ Ratio of rate of growth of assets to rate of growth of GNP.
c/ Banking system refer to CBs, FCs, MBs, DHs and BI.

11.4 REFORM, THE ECONOMY, AND THE FINANCIAL SYSTEM

Macroeconomic impact

Heavily and uneconomic regulation of financial systems, usually encompassing substantial intervention in the credit granting and pricing process, can adversely affect savings and, consequently, economic growth and development. Hence, financial liberalization can enhance economic growth and development. A major role of any financial system is to *mobilize savings* for investment. In Malaysia, financial savings increased by an average of 14% in the 1960s, 18% in the first half of the 1970s, and 23% in the second half of that decade. However, growth fell to 17% in the first half of the 1980s and 13% in the second half, but still exceeded GDP expansion and left the savings ratio at a peak. The proportion of financial savings to gross national saving (GNS) also increased rapidly – from 35% in the first half of the 1960s to 60% in the 1970s and 66–67% in the 1980s. Although income growth has played a big part in the rapid increase in savings, equally important has been the development of an efficient domestic financial system, both by maintaining attractive yields for savers and by fostering an increased variety of financial services.

Financial liberalization should *promote investment* growth through the availability of a larger pool of funds and investment efficiency should be enhanced as funds are allocated according to returns determined by the market. Gross investment grew on average by 21% in 1961–5 and by 31% in 1971–5, before falling to around 17% in the second half of the 1970s and, in line with the economic slowdown, to 11% in the 1980s. The ratio of bank credit to gross domestic product in Malaysia has been increasing over the past 30 years, reflecting the importance of bank credit for financing economic activities and coinciding with the rapid liberalization of the banking system, the development of a secondary market for government securities, and of private debt securities in Malaysia. The ratio of total credit outstanding to GDP and of the flow of credit to investment have also increased over the same period. Other sources, such as direct issues of shares, are still insignificant as a means of financing in Malaysia.

Interest rates

Patterns of behavior

The historical pattern of interest rates in Malaysia can be divided into prereform (up to 1978) and postreform (Figure 11.1). The three-month fixed-deposit rate (FD) of the commercial banks is taken to be representative of deposit rates and the seven-day interbank money-market rate (IB) is a proxy for money-market rates Except for the spike in interbank rates during the tight liquidity and high inflation period of 1973–4, interest rates before reform appear to be more stable. The average level of the FD and IB rates increased respectively following 3 reforms, from 5.45% to 6.8% and from 6.3% to 6.67% a year. More important, the variation in the interest rates increased significantly following reform. The statistical variance of the FD and IB rates prereform, was 0.3% and 3.3%, respectively, increasing to 5.7% and 5.5%, respectively, postreform.

Prior to 1979, FD rates diverged significantly from the interbank rates,

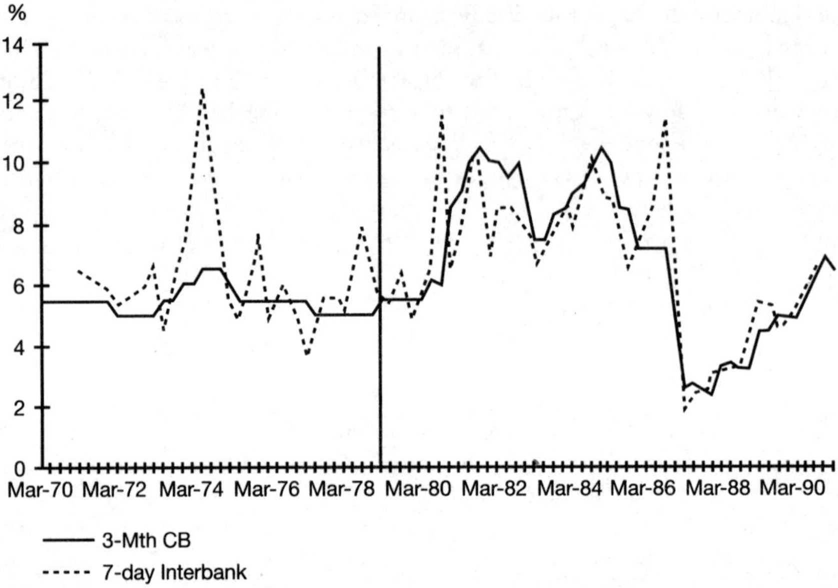

Figure 11.1 Variation in nominal interest rates

mainly due to the fact that while the interbank rates were market determined, deposit rates were controlled by the Central Bank. After liberalization, with the financial institutions free to set deposit rates, these tended to follow the interbank rates more closely. The differential between the variance of the *average* FD and IB rates narrowed markedly, from 3% to 0.2% between the two periods; with the *average* levels of the two rates differing by only 0.1% after reform, compared to 0.8% before reform.

There was a sharp decline in the level and volatility of interest rates in 1987, due mainly to a sudden inflow of liquidity from strong export receipts and hesitant loan demand. Day-to-day fluctuations were dampened by the Central Bank, but high volatility in part reflected the daily reserve holding period. The new minimum liquidity requirement (on a two-week average basis, from February 1987) reduced the volatility caused by banks seeking funds to fulfill daily requirements. Similarly, from January 1989 banks were allowed to observe an average statutory reserve ratio over a two-week period. The Day One Settlement System, introduced in 1986, helped interest rate stability by ensuring that, at the end of the check-clearing day, banks with a net surplus automatically lent those funds to those facing a deficit. This prevented scramble for funds by banks that were short, which would have pushed up interest rates.

Real interest rates

The sharp increase in inflation in 1973–4 led to negative real interest rates (Figure 11.2) as in many developing and industrialized countries. Immediately following reform, nominal interest rates remained higher than inflation, ensuring depositors a positive real rate of return and even when regulated, interest rates mostly offered positive returns to depositors. After liberalization, particularly in 1985–6, interest rates were high relative to Malaysian historical experience, but this was a natural market response to the tight liquidity conditions then prevailing.

The spreads between banks' and finance companies' average cost of funds and their lending rates (at times used as a measure of the institutions' efficiency) have widened during most of the 1980s.[3] One reason is the improved quality of services provided by the banks, for example, in electronic banking. However, spreads generally widen during (and after) periods of economic slowdown, for example, in 1981–2 and 1985–7 in the case of commercial banks. Banks become more risk averse in bad times and charge higher interest rates on loans. They also try to recover the costs of bad loans by passing these on to nondelinquent depositors and new borrowers. Conversely, interest margins have been narrowing over the late 1980s and early 1990s, as the improved economic environment led to a decline in bad debts.

Term structure

Following reform in the government securities market in 1987 and the introduction of the principal dealer auctioning system, there have been changes in the term structure of MGS yields. The yield curve has flattened and the difference in the yield between the shorter and longer maturities has narrowed. Only securities with maturities of less than 10 years are sold and so ensure market-determined yields. Those with longer maturities are sold by subscription to the National Savings; Bank and the Employees Provident Fund, both being required by law to hold a fixed amount of securities. Thus, the government has no incentive to offer higher interest rates. The result is a flat yield structure that does not seem to reflect the "normal" liquidity and risk preference of investors.

A similar pattern is seen in the term structure of deposit interest rates. The kink between one-month and three-month rates prior to liberalization became smoother as the differential between the two rates narrowed. However, adjustments in domestic interest rates remained modest immediately after liberalization. But when the resource gap emerged in the early 1980s, the commercial banks not only; adjusted deposit rates upward but also offered relatively higher deposit rates for shorter-term maturities. As a result, the yield curve became flatter in the early 1980s.

Between October 1985 and January 1987, when rates on deposits of up to

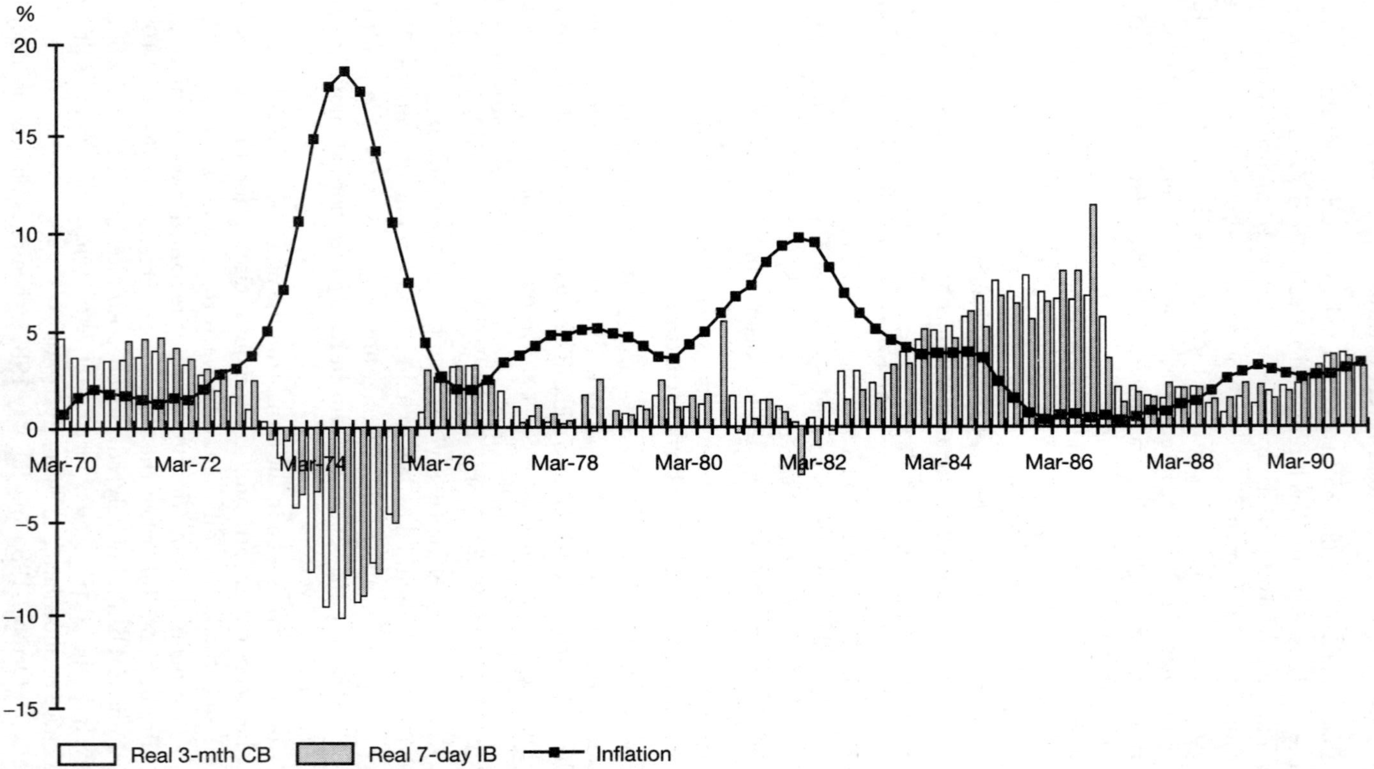

Figure 11.2 Real interest rates

12 months' maturity were pegged to the rates of the two lead banks, the differential in interest rates between the one and 12-month rates was only 0.25 percentage point. However, there was a wide differential (3–4 percentage points) between deposit rates of 12- and 15-month maturities as commercial banks competed at the longer end by offering higher rates. (Rates on 15-month maturity and above were, not subject to regulation.) The yield curve was therefore unusual, with a steep slope occurring at later maturities. With the unpegging of deposit rates on February 1, 1987, the yield curve showed a gradual upward slope. Then, uncertainty about future interest rates led to a further flattening of the yield curve, as the banks offered relatively, attractive interest rates on the shorter maturity deposits in order to avoid taking in too much of the longer-term deposits.

Banks and finance company rates

Finance companies have always offered higher interest rates on deposits than commercial banks, and their lending rates have also been higher. Following liberalization, a narrowing of the interest differential between the two may have been expected, as the banks set interest rates at competitive levels. In fact, it did not happen because the scope for competition for loans is limited. Finance companies are involved mainly in hire-purchase finance, which allows them to charge higher interest rates, and so offer higher deposit rates for funds. The commercial banks, with interest-free demand deposits and corporate clients' deposits, have been under little pressure to compete.

Risky and riskless rates

The trend in the differential between the 12-month Treasury bills rate and the average lending rate of the commercial banks in 1975–90 has been on an upward trend at least until 1986 (Figure 11.3). Following reform, the differential widened mainly as a result of high lending rates. Since 1986 lending rates have declined due to recession (1985–6) and excess liquidity. More important, the decision by the Central Bank in 1987 to issue government securities with market-related coupon rates helped to push up the rates on TBs. Thus, the differential between the two rates has declined sharply since 1987.

The earlier liberalization of interest rates (in 1978) did not by itself promote competition among banks. It was only after the 1985–6 recession, when lending opportunities were scarce, that banks started to compete by offering prime customers loans with fine interest margins. Moreover, improvements in the health of banks' balance sheets in the late 1980s constituted another reason for increased competitive behavior. So, the benefits of financial reform may not manifest themselves immediately and, if there are macroeconomic shocks to the system, this may further delay adjustment.

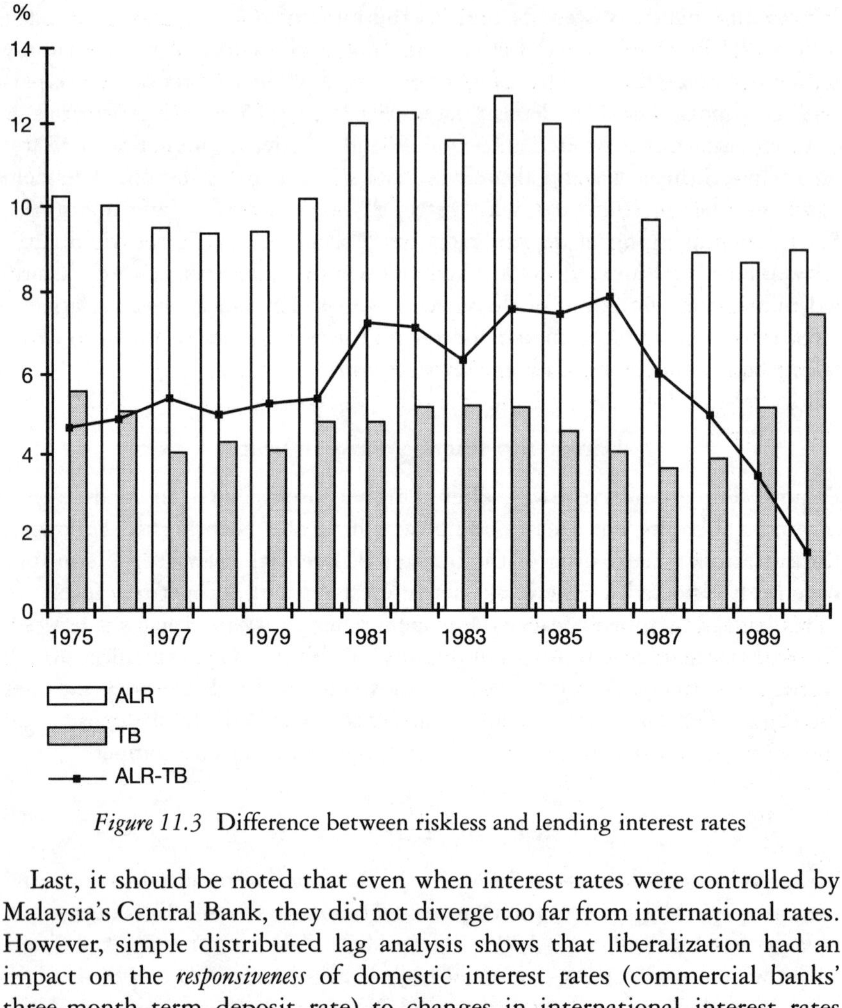

Figure 11.3 Difference between riskless and lending interest rates

Last, it should be noted that even when interest rates were controlled by Malaysia's Central Bank, they did not diverge too far from international rates. However, simple distributed lag analysis shows that liberalization had an impact on the *responsiveness* of domestic interest rates (commercial banks' three-month term deposit rate) to changes in international interest rates (Eurodollar 3-month rate). It seems that changes in international interest rates have more immediate effect on domestic interest rates following reform.

Banking system

Concentration

Before liberalization of interest rates, concentration in the commercial banking industry was high, with the 10 largest banks accounting for more than 80% of the industry's total deposits and loans and almost 30% of all assets. Following liberalization, concentration has been gradually reduced. Although no new banks have been allowed to enter the Malaysian financial system since the early 1980s, and foreign hanks cannot expand their branch network, the share of deposits of the 10 largest banks had declined continuously from about 84% of the total in 1975 to 72% in 1986, before rebounding back to 77% in 1990. A similar trend can be seen for the top five and the top three banks (Table 11.7). The 10 largest banks' share of total assets also declined from 80% in 1975 to 72% in 1984–6, rose to 74% in 1989 and fell again to 72% in 1990.

The degree of concentration in commercial banking has remained high. At the end of June 1991, the industry continued to be dominated by two banks, accounting for 35.2% of all banking assets, their 343 offices representing more than one third of all bank branches. In addition, there are 10 medium-sized banks and 26 smaller ones, 16 of which are foreign bank branches or subsidiaries. Most foreign banks are small in terms of assets and operate only one office.

Composition of liabilities

Since liberalization, interest rates have become more volatile, competition among banks has increased, and customers have become more sophisticated. This has led to new delivery systems and product innovation – for example, banker's acceptances (BAs), repurchase agreements (Repos), and negotiable certificates of deposit (NCDs). Other new financial products include mortgage-backed bonds, private debt securities, gilt-edged securities (based on MGS), and property trust funds. Increasing competition also led to greater computerization, and the widespread use of automated teller machines (ATMs) and other electronic funds transfer services as well as credit cards galore.

New instruments, such as Repos, NCDs, and BAs, have more flexible maturity periods and negotiable rates of return, thereby allowing banks greater flexibility in managing assets and liabilities. And although traditional deposits (current, savings, and fixed) remained a principal source of funds, they had declined by 1990 to an average of 48% of total liabilities of all banks, compared to 75% in 1975–8.

There have also been big shifts between savings and fixed deposits and from currency and demand deposits to fixed and savings deposits. Demand deposits, for example, declined continuously after the 1978 liberalization of interest rates to account for less than 12% of all sources of funds at the end of 1990. The share of savings deposits also declined continuously until 1985, when automated teller machines, introduced in 1983, had become accepted by depositors. The share of fixed deposits, on the other hand, rose from an average of 41% (1975–8) to 43.4% at the end of 1984, before declining continuously to 26.2% it the end of 1990. New financial instruments (e.g., Repos, NCDs, and BAs) accounted for 17.2% (or $22.2 billion) of the total resources mobilized by banks at the end of 1990. Repos and NCDs in

Table 11.7 Commercial banks' industry structure

	1975	*1978*	*1979*	*1980*	*1981*	*1982*	*1983*	*1984*	*1985*	*1986*	*1987*	*1988*	*1989*	*1990*
Share in total deposits of:														
Top 3 banks	44.30	43.90	44.76	44.48	43.90	43.90	42.10	39.27	39.08	38.45	34.35	40.18	40.08	41.82
Top 5 banks	63.00	61.90	61.82	60.17	57.80	57.50	54.90	53.57	52.89	53.15	49.31	54.99	54.52	57.45
Top 10 banks	83.70	81.70	78.77	77.19	78.00	77.50	76.20	75.67	72.64	72.43	65.95	75.64	71.66	77.12
Smaller banks	16.30	18.30	21.23	22.81	22.00	22.50	23.80	24.33	27.36	27.57	34.05	24.36	28.34	22.88
Ratio of profit to total assets	1.33	1.48	1.37	0.92	1.42	1.48	1.38	0.65	0.47	–0.06	–1.20	–1.02	–0.17	0.21
Share of bad debts provision to total assets	0.36	0.52	0.61	0.45	0.76	0.76	0.77	1.09	1.44	2.14	3.98	4.00	4.02	3.55
Capital and reserves to total liabilities	3.12	3.21	2.84	3.00	3.92	4.08	4.98	5.38	5.58	5.59	6.31	6.14	5.47	5.35
Liquidity ratio of commercial banks	36.20	36.00	25.80	23.40	27.00	26.40	23.20	24.20	22.50	20.40	24.10	23.10	19.90	18.60
Share of long-term loans in total loans and advances	23.55	30.38	31.02	31.30	34.09	37.14	38.54	39.77	40.21	41.52	44.04	44.00	44.57	41.86
Share of long-term deposits in total fixed deposits	7.17	22.23	27.31	28.84	16.75	16.50	23.24	25.60	30.11	55.12	51.89	53.61	48.96	46.49
Percent share of total assets of commercial banks held by														
10 largest banks	79.82	76.80	75.05	74.64	75.14	74.93	73.13	72.14	71.45	72.32	73.58	74.00	73.11	71.57
5 largest banks	58.50	57.16	57.04	57.12	56.59	55.94	55.48	52.21	50.17	52.15	54.23	54.33	54.05	52.14
3 largest banks	41.72	40.70	41.12	41.98	43.09	42.78	43.75	39.53	38.22	39.26	40.73	42.08	42.26	41.16

particular grew rapidly – by average annual growth rates of 36.2% and 20.7% respectively in 1981–90.

As interest rates began moving up after 1980, depositors' preference also shifted toward shorter maturities. The share of total long-term deposits to total fixed deposits of commercial banks fell from 28.8% in 1980 to 16.5% in 1982; subsequently, it rose to 55.1% (at the end of 1986) due partly to adjustments in the term structure of interest rates and partly to the tax exemption of interest earned on fixed deposits of more than 12-month maturities. However, when the exemption was removed in 1988, the share of long-term deposits fell again – to 46.5% at the end of 1990. Notwithstanding this high ratio, the decline of fixed deposits relative to total liabilities suggests that the deregulation of interest rates, in general, has led to a shortening of the maturity structure of the commercial banks' deposit liabilities and has increased the variability of their cost of funds.

Composition of assets

Most resources of commercial banks have been used to finance loans and advances to sectors of the economy. The share of loans and advances to total assets rose from an average of 59% in 1975–7 to 60–66% in 1978–90. In terms of the direction of credit, the change over time in the share of credit to sectors of the economy to total loans and advances have generally followed changes in the share of each sector in total GDP and the changes in the capital productivity of sectors. However, following the liberalization of interest rates, which coincided with a property boom, the share of credit to the property sector (real estate development, construction and housing) rose from 21% at the end of 1978 to a peak of 36.6% at the end of 1987. This sharp increase in property loans was in contrast to the low increase in the relative importance of the building and construction sector in total GDP and reflected the improved profitability of the sector, through capital appreciation. The liberalization of interest rates allowed banks to charge higher interest rates for property loans, yet the real interest rates were low relative to gains from capital appreciation and perhaps included some speculative element as well (Figure 11.4). This has made property projects profitable, at least ex ante, and hence bankable.

By loan type, there was a progressive decline in the use of overdrafts for short-term financing – from 37.2% of total loans and advances at the end of 1978 to 29.7% by the end of 1990 – mainly reflecting rising interest rates after deregulation and growing sophistication of the Malaysian corporate sector, both in liability and cash management. A 1% commitment fee on unused overdrafts facilities from February 1982 also contributed to the decline. So, too, did the Central Bank's urging of commercial banks to place more emphasis on term lending because of the large overhang of unutilized overdraft facilities and its impact on liquidity management.

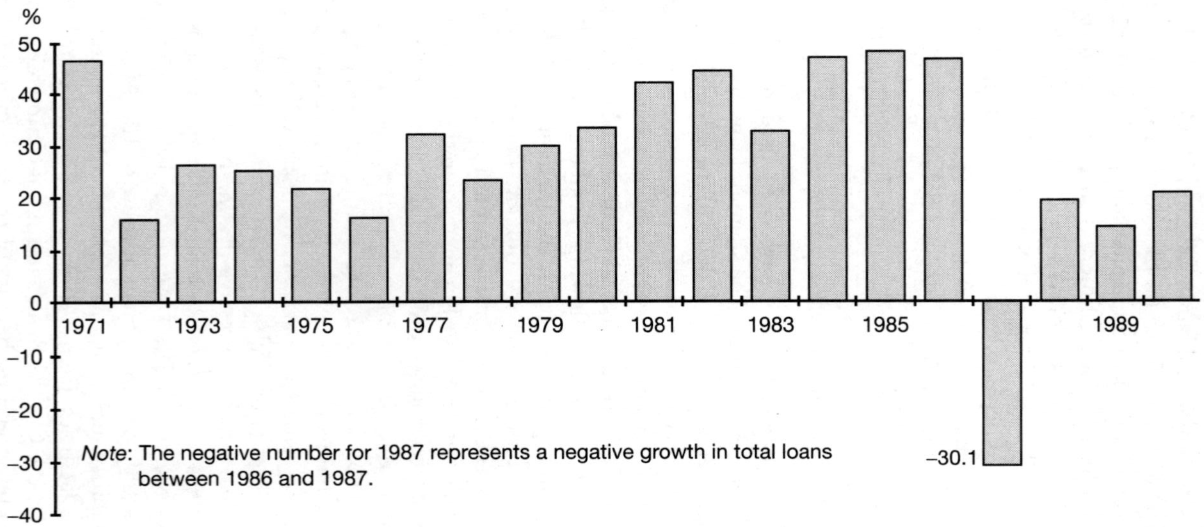

Figure 11.4 Malysian commercial banks: The share of lending to the property sector in total new loans

Asset quality

The share of bad-debt provisions of banks to total assets is shown in Table 11.8. The sudden jump in the mid-1980s was due partly to the introduction of Central Bank guidelines provisioning against previously unprovisioned loans, but it mainly reflects the severe recession of 1985–6 and the souring of property loans. Despite warnings from the Central Bank, banks continued to lend to the broad property sector, which in 1986 accounted for 55% of the total flow of new loans, compared with 32% in 1980. When the property market collapsed in the mid-1980s, many banks and finance companies were left with a large percentage of their property loans that were nonperforming.

As is often the case, the decline in the quality of bank loans resulted from insufficient diversification, in this case overconcentration of loans to one sector or a small group of large customers. The ratio of total provision for bad and doubtful debts (plus interest in suspense) to total loans and advances rose from an average ratio of 2.8% in 1980–4 to 6% at the end of 1985 (Table 11.8). This worsened to a peak of 15.5% at the end of 1988, before falling to 13.7% at the end of 1990.

Despite the problems of the 1980s, the banking system ended the decade with a substantial improvement in profitability and financial strength. The speedy pick-up in the property market, the bullish stock market in 1989, the expansion of manufacturing, which contributed to recovery, as well as the resolution of many nonperforming loans, helped boost the industry's earnings.

Table 11.8 Nonperforming loans of the commercial banks (%)

	Interest in suspense/total loans & advances %	*Provisions for bad debts/ total loans & advances* %	*Nonperforming loans/total loans & advances* %
1980	0.5	1.7	—
1981	0.6	1.7	—
1982	1.4	1.6	—
1983	1.1	1.7	—
1984	1.2	2.5	—
1985	2.2	3.8	10.3
1986	4.4	6.2	20.8
1987	6.0	7.3	26.8
1988	7.9	7.7	32.6
1989	7.9	7.3	24.5
1990	7.5	6.2	20.8

Finance companies

Mobilizing resources

Total resources of the finance companies had expanded rapidly, to M$39.5 billion by the end of 1990, 101 times those at the end of 1969. Growth averaged 24.6% annually, compared with 17.9% per annum for commercial banks over the same period. Much of the growth of finance companies since 1969 stemmed from increased deposits, particularly fixed deposits, which at the end of 1990 accounted for over 90% of all deposits placed with them; the balance was savings deposits. Fixed deposits grew at an average of 25% annually, against 16% for banks over the same period. The rapid growth of finance company deposits reflected not only high income growth but especially the higher interest rates that finance companies could offer, especially prior to October 1978, when banks were facing a ceiling on interest paid on deposits.

With increasing competition for funds after the liberalization of interest rates, finance companies' growth slowed somewhat in 1979–90, with total financial resources increasing by 23.1% a year, against 26.7% annually in 1970–8. Total resources of $39.5 billion mobilized by the finance companies were less than one quarter of resources mobilized by the banking system at the end of 1990. Similarly, growth in finance companies' deposits (excluding NCDs and Repos) eased to 21.2% per annum in 1979–90 (29.6% per annum in 1970–8), while loan operations grew at an average 24.4% a year between 1979 and 1990 (27.7% in 1970–8). Fixed deposits accounted for 93.1% of new deposits mobilized by the finance companies in 1979–90 and their market share had risen to 29.8% of total deposits of $95.3 billion mobilized by the banking system at the end of 1990 (15.4% in 1978).

After reform in 1978, there was a change in the structure of the finance companies' deposits. With depositors' shifting toward shorter maturities in the latter half of 1980s, the share of deposits of more than one-year maturity to total deposits fell from a peak of 66% in 1986 to 40.9% in 1990. Since March 1990, selected finance companies have been allowed to issue NCDs; by the end of 1990, these NCDs accounted for $1.6 billion (or 4.2%) of all resources mobilized by finance companies.

Although finance companies' total resources grew at a faster rate than the banks' in both the pre- and post-1978 periods, the differential between their rate of growth and banks' narrowed from 8 percentage points in 1970–8 to 5.8 percentage points in 1979–90.

Interest margins and profitability

Despite stiff competition after the 1978 reforms, the gross interest margins of the commercial banks and the finance companies widened in 1980–90 (Table

Table 11.9 Gross interest margins (% per annum)

	Finance companies			*Commercial banks*		
	Average lending rate	*Average cost of deposits*	*Interest margin*	*Average lending rate*	*Average cost of deposits*	*Interest margin*
1980	12.32	9.10	3.22	10.22	6.20	4.02
1981	15.58	11.23	4.35	12.07	7.77	4.30
1982	15.88	10.64	5.24	12.34	7.17	5.17
1983	15.87	9.40	6.47	11.64	6.61	5.03
1984	15.22	10.64	4.58	12.80	7.98	4.82
1985	14.66	9.72	4.94	12.10	6.81	5.29
1986	13.96	9.13	4.83	12.02	6.45	5.57
1987	12.62	5.75	6.87	9.73	3.63	6.10
1988	12.47	4.69	7.78	8.95	3.27	5.68
1989	11.95	5.47	6.48	8.70	3.79	4.91
1990	11.87	6.92	4.95	8.99	4.50	4.49

11.9). For example, despite the lower interest rates in 1982 and 1983, lending rates remained "sticky" downward and the gross interest margin of finance companies widened dramatically from 3.2 percentage points in 1980 to 6.5 percentage points in 1983.

With the new system of interest rates for the finance companies in October 1984, lending rates moved in line with changes in the cost of funds but at a slower rate. For example, although the cost of deposits of the finance companies had declined from 10.6% in 1984 to 4.7% per annum in 1988, the average lending rate was slower in responding – falling only by 2.8 percentage points to 12.5% a year. This reflected mainly high-cost property and commercial loans booked in earlier years, a significant proportion of which was nonperforming. The result was a widening of the interest rate margins from 4.6 percentage points in 1984 to 7.8 percentage points in 1988, a peak for the 1980s. However, the interest margins had narrowed to under 5 percentage points by 1990, reflecting greater competition among banking institutions.

Higher interest margins in 1986-8 did not always mean higher profits for finance companies (Table 11.10). For example, although finance companies had an interest margin of 7.8 percentage points in 1988, they had, on average, overheads (including staff cost) of 2.4% a year and bad-debt provisions and interest-in-suspense of 7.5%, leaving a net loan margin loss of 2.1 percentage points and a negative return on assets. Although finance companies generally remained profitable after 1978, their return on assets has not exceeded that of commercial banks since 1985.

Table 11.10 Pretax profit/loss

	Finance companies	*Commercial banks*	*Finance companies*	*Commercial banks*
	M$ million		*as percent of assets*	
1980	133	461	2.4	1.4
1981	119	539	1.6	1.3
1982	171	583	1.9	1.2
1983	229	(232)	2.0	(0.4)
1984	227	642	1.5	1.0
1985	112	(261)	0.6	(0.4)
1986	(75)	(332)	(0.4)	(0.4)
1987	(245)	310	(1.2)	0.4
1988	(160)	661	(0.6)	0.7
1989	241	895*	0.8	1.0*
1990	428	1278*	1.1	1.2*

Note:
* Excluding one commercial bank.

Deposit-taking cooperatives

Like commercial banks and finance companies, the cooperative movement has come a long way since it was introduced in 1922. Growth has been remarkable, especially among Deposit-Taking Cooperatives (DTCs). The number of DTCs has increased from three at the end of 1975 to 39 at the end of 1985 and total membership expanded from 54,988 to 1.03 million. Despite the formation of new DTCs during 1986, the collapse of another 24 in that year severely affected the industry's performance; their numbers fell to 17 and membership to 554,678 by the end of 1990. Total assets, which had touched M$2.2 billion at the end of 1986 had fallen to M$1.1 billion at end-1990.

Total resources mobilized by the DTCs rose from $247 million at the end of 1975 to $1.1 billion at the end of 1980 and increased at an average annual rate of 28.3% in 1981–5, reflecting the relatively high deposit rates offered, the government's 1983 decision to allow a large DTC (Cooperative Central Bank) to accept deposits from statutory authorities and insurance companies, and the nationwide mushrooming of branch offices. Moreover, DTCs were less regulated (by the Cooperatives Development Department) than was the banking system, and so confronted fewer impediments to their expansion.

Nonfinancial corporate sector

Evaluating the relationship between investment decisions of the NFCC (which refers mainly to companies engaged in manufacturing) and their financing is difficult due to data constraints and for comparative reasons. In Malaysia there have been several studies relating to the link but three which complement each other are those of the Central Information Collection Unit

(CICU) of PNB database, Bank Negara Malaysia's private investment surveys and the IMF study on interest rates in Malaysia. Generally these show that company size is an important determinant to accessibility to credit, that companies resorted mainly to internally generated funds to finance investments, and that the level of interest rates influenced investment decisions.

A study by the CICU showed that larger companies had easier access to external sources of financing than small and medium-sized companies, as expected. Bigger companies have better track records and reputation, and financial institutions impose on them less stringent requirements. The data used for the analysis was for 1983–90 and the companies in the database were listed companies. In terms of the average cost of credit (the ratio F/BT), the larger companies benefitted more than the small and medium-sized (Table 11.11). This could be due to the higher levels of investment (*I/K*) and lower rate of return on assets (*S/K* and *P/TA*) by the small and medium-sized companies. This "discrimination" was more pronounced during the recessionary years of 1985–6, when the average cost of credit for the large companies was 10.8%, compared with 21.6% for the small and medium-sized enterprises (SMEs). In terms of the level of indebtedness of the companies (the ratio of total debt to total fixed assets, or *BT/K*), the small and medium-sized companies were more highly indebted compared with the large. During the 1983–6 period, this ratio ranged between 177% to 204% for SMEs, compared with 34% to 41% for the large companies. Even during the 1987–90 postrecessionary period, the levels of indebtedness of SMEs were far in excess of the large companies, despite the former's lower levels of investment. Loans from domestic financial institutions dominated the total debt outstanding of the SMEs during the 1980s, while large firms had access to loans from government and especially foreign institutions.

Large firms also appear to have been more profitable, as measured by rates of return (*P/K* or *P/TA*). Indeed, SMEs had negative rates of return during the recessionary period and the smaller firms did not share in the profit turnaround during the recovery period. In this environment it is not surprising that SMEs only had access to bank debt and not to any significant direct financing.

Overall, a Bank Negara survey for 1986–90 revealed that internally generated funds accounted for between 45–64% of total financing. In 1988 the Figure reached 84%, in part thanks to a lower level of capital expenditure. Bank loans were viewed negatively by companies, no doubt because of high interest rates. For the manufacturing sector, even despite a sharp increase in its growth in the mid-1970s, there was a reduction in the share of credit it received from banks, as this was the period when property and construction lending was becoming popular. Central Bank guidelines issued in 1978 attempted to correct this imbalance, even as interest rates were being initially freed. However, the rising net worth of the manufacturing sector led it to rely increasingly on internally generated funds, and their debt ratios subsequently declined.

Table 11.11 Summary: statistics of real and financial performance

By size	*Period*	*I/K*	*S/K*	*P/K*	*P/TA*	*BT/K*	*BL/BT*	*F/BT*	*Yi/Y*	*Ii/I*	*dBTi/dBT*
Small & medium	83–84	0.259	0.318	0.044	0.004	1.767	0.996	0.142	0.02	0.021	0.055
	85–86	0.18	0.033	(0.382)	(0.03)	2.043	0.963	0.216	0.022	0.017	0.015
	87–90	0.049	(0.552)	(1.089)	(0.148)	4.118	0.991	0.153	0.005	0.001	0.005
Large	83–84	0.123	0.186	0.109	0.044	0.338	0.964	0.112	0.98	0.979	0.945
	85–86	0.084	0.11	0.05	0.021	0.411	0.973	0.108	1.978	0.983	0.985
	87–90	0.145	0.14	0.085	0.038	0.436	0.662	0.088	0.995	0.999	0.995

Notes:

I = Purchase of fixed assets (gross investment)
K = Total fixed assets
S = Operating profit
P = Profit after tax and interest payments, net of depreciation
TA = Total assets
F = Interest payments
BT = total debt
BL = Loans from financial institutions
Yi/Y = Share of sales of group i to total sales
Ii/I = Share of investment of group i to total investment
dBTi/dBT = Share of new debt of group i total investment

Size: Small & medium = shareholders' funds < M$2.5 million.
Large = Shareholders' funds ≥ M$2.5 million.

11.5 THE REGULATORY AND SUPERVISORY FRAMEWORK OF REFORM

While encouraging financial institutions to diversify and innovate, the Central Bank has, at the same time, beefed up the regulatory mechanism. Although liberalization has been considered a desirable goal, it has been tempered by the stronger concern for a stable financial system. For this reason, the approach to liberalization in the Malaysian financial system has been one of cautious and gradual structural deregulation and prudential reregulation.

Bank Negara Malaysia was established under the Central Bank of Malaysia Ordinance 1958 as the Central Bank of the nation. Among its main objectives is the promotion of monetary stability and a sound financial structure. Its powers were extended and strengthened by the *Banking and Financial Institutions Act 1989* (BAFIA), now the major legislation governing the financial system. For the Bank, the Act provides the framework to supervise three broad groups of financial institutions:

1 *Licensed institutions*. The major deposit-taking institutions – commercial banks, merchant banks, discount houses, finance companies, discount houses, and money brokers.
2 *Scheduled institutions*. Major nonbank sources of credit and finance, which include issuers of charge cards and credit cards and travelers' checks, operators of cash-dispensing machines, development finance institutions, building societies and housing credit institutions, factoring companies, and leasing companies. Also included are *representative offices* of foreign banks or institutions, which conduct business of finance companies or scheduled institutions.
3 *Nonscheduled institutions*. Statutory bodies (financial institutions set up by statute and supervised in most cases by authorities other than the Ministry of Finance) and any person or corporation, which are neither liable to be licensed under the BAFIA nor subject to the provision governing scheduled businesses and representative offices but are engaged in the provision of finance.

Apart from the Central Bank, which regulates the formal banking system, there are many other bodies that regulate various bits of the securities and equity market. Under the Securities Industry Act 1983 and the Companies Act 1965, the Kuala Lumpur Stock Exchange (KLSE) is responsible for ensuring that companies listed on the KLSE are of sound financial standing. The Capital Issues Committee (CIC) supervises the issue of shares and other corporate securities, including disclosure requirements of all pertinent financial information. The Registrar of Companies (ROC) administers the SIA 1983, ensures that stockbrokers comply with their statutory obligations and, under the Companies Act 1965, has both administrative and regulatory powers governing companies and their officers. The Foreign Investment Committee (FIC) implements government's guidelines (e.g., of the New Economic Policy) on acquisition or takeovers and is responsible for major issues of foreign investment. Finally, the Panel on Take-overs and Mergers (TOP) scrutinizes all takeovers and mergers, and the interests of minority shareholders are protected.

The Central Bank monitors the financial institutions (FCs), requiring them to submit regular financial returns so as to ensure that they are operating within prudential limits and observing legal requirements. The Bank also issues guidelines to regulate FCs. It can, too, conduct more thorough examinations of financial institutions, including (1) appraisal of asset quality; (2) verification of the types and size of various liabilities; (3) appraisal of management; (4) asset or liabilities management; (5) compliance with legal and regulatory requirements and broad national policies; and (6) evaluation of records, systems, and internal control. The major operations reviewed are credit operations including trade financing and loan portfolio; deposit operations; remittance operations; investments, money and foreign exchange market operations; and off-balance-sheet businesses.

Troubled financial institutions

Most institutions that have run into trouble did so following the 1985–6 recession. In the banking system, there was a big overhang of nonperforming property loans and imprudent share-based lending, which resulted in substantial provisions for interest-in-suspense and bad debts. On top of that, there were some cases of weak and fraudulent management. Some of these institutions suffered such large losses that their capital was eroded to the edge of bankruptcy.

Because of legal constraints, the Central Bank's initial approach to troubled institutions was limited to directing a change in management, entrusting them with stemming losses while detailed rescue plans were formulated. Later, legislation was introduced to allow the Central Bank, with the approval of the minister of finance, to grant secured loans to, or purchase any shares of, a licensed bank or finance company. Such measures were essentially short-term; to eliminate any conflict of interest between its role as a supervisor of the banking system and as a shareholder of banks, there was a phased withdrawal by the Central Bank from its equity holdings as the delinquent institutions were rehabilitated and put on a sound financial standing.

There was a moral hazard in allowing errant shareholders, responsible for the predicament of the ailing institutions, to benefit from the retention of their equity stake after rescue by the Bank. So, under new legislation, the Bank could apply to the High Court to reduce the institution's capital to the extent that it was lost or was unrepresented by available assets. In effect, shareholders had to bear responsibility for imprudent banking and mismanagement.

11.6 LESSONS FROM MALAYSIAN FINANCIAL REFORM

Although the reasons for liberalization were mixed, the financial reforms introduced in the 1970s (including allowing commercial banks to determine interest rates for depositors and borrowers) were a deliberate move to promote a more free and competitive financial system. Encouraging the growth of a more market-oriented financial system can also be seen with the introduction of two new money-market instruments – banker's acceptances (BAs) and negotiable certificates of deposits. Other financial reforms were also undertaken to increase the responsiveness of bank loan and deposit rates to market forces. In 1983 (November), all banks' and finance companies' lending rates (except the priority sectors) were anchored to their base lending rate, because lending rates tended to behave in an asymmetrical fashion and due to a concern about borrower net worth in the face of severe macro shocks. Indirect controls over interest rates in 1985–7 (when interest rates for deposits up to 12-month maturities were pegged to the deposit rate of the two lending banks) were removed when the economy recovered and when liquidity – and borrower net worth – increased in the system. There was further deregulation in early 1991 (February), when the base lending rate was freed from the Central Bank control and commercial banks and finance companies were allowed to set base lending rates on the basis of costs of funds. This was done to encourage market-oriented yield curves that will benefit the capital market, especially the development of secondary markets for public and private securities.

Liberalization cannot be seen as a uniformly linear process (i.e., once set in motion, its course cannot be redirected or qualified). This study has revealed that liberalization can have a stop-and-go approach. Interest rate reforms, for example, were initially implemented in 1971, when fixed deposits with commercial banks for maturities exceeding four years carried market-determined interest rates and (from January 1972) rate ceilings were lifted for all commercial bank deposits with maturity exceeding one year. In August 1972 the interest rates for deposits placed with finance companies were freed and, in the same month, the discount rates on Treasury bills were determined by open tender. In the early and mid-1980s, however, indirect controls on interest rates were reintroduced because it was believed that high interest rates were inconsistent with recession. Thus macroeconomic considerations, unsurprisingly, can exercise a decisive influence on the course and pace of reform.

The sequencing and speed of Malaysian liberalization supports the view that the complete opening of the capital account should follow the opening of the trade account, that a gradualist approach is more appropriate, and that the timing should take into account the state of the economy.[4] The Malaysian economy can be characterized as one that has enjoyed long periods of economic stability and strong supervision of banking. Between 1970 and 1990 the economy went through only two economic downturns, in 1975 and 1985. With the exception of 1973–4 and 1980–1, price stability was maintained; in the 1970s, prices increased at 5.9% a year, and by 3.3% per annum in the 1980s. This allowed financial liberalization in "phases." Villanueva and Mirakhor's (1990) conclusion that the stability enjoyed by the Malaysian economy has enabled the government to liberalize interest rates fully in less than three years without the adverse consequence of an immediate increase in interest rates, however, needs to be qualified. Liberalization of interest rates began as early as 1971 and further measures were taken in 1973, 1975, with important changes made in 1978, 1981, and, more recently, in 1991. It would, therefore, be difficult to sustain the conclusion that the Malaysian experience is one of a strategy of complete interest rate liberalization implemented in a very short period similar to that of Chile, Argentina, Uruguay, and the Philippines.

Another lesson of the Malaysian experience is that economic policy changes cannot succeed if conditions are not right to allow reforms to take root. Without the shock of the recession in the early 1980s and without government commitment to introduce policy changes in response to the recession, reforms would not have seen the light of day. What appeared to be a retreat from reform during the early 1980s was only a strategic one, and institutional development, led by an independent and capable Central Bank, continued. And political stability was an invaluable ingredient: despite internal disputes in the National Front, the ruling coalition party and, especially, within United Malays National Organization (UMNO), there was political stability and continuity in Malaysia, and a clear sense of direction – and marked consistency – in the policy package, which has helped a great deal in providing credibility to economic and financial reforms. The banking system responded to clear, credible, and consistent policy signals, helping to make the reforms sustainable in the long run.

ACKNOWLEDGMENT

The authors wish to acknowledge the comments of their colleagues at Bank Negara Malaysia and of Jerry Caprio. However, the views expressed here are those of the authors and may not represent the views of Bank Negara.

NOTES

1 In the 1970s, the share of palm oil in total exports increased from 9.8% to 25.3% and of manufactured goods from 11.1% to 20.6%, while minerals' share, largely crude oil rose from 22.8% in 1970 to 34.5% in 1980.

2 During 1981, when the average cost of deposits (ACD) of the banks *increased* by 1.57 percentage points, the average lending rate (ALR) immediately rose by 1.85 percentage points. However, in 1982, when the ACD *fell* by 0.6 percentage points, the ALR *increased* another 0.27 percentage point.

3 As John Chant recognized, wide spreads also can reflect portfolio problems, the type of clientele of the banks, etc.

4 Villanueva and Mirakhor (1990) have provided a typology of the initial macroeconomic environment: taking into account whether the macroeconomic environment is stable (SM) or unstable (UM) and has adequate bank supervision (AS) or inadequate bank supervision (IS). They also classify economies into four types: (a) UM/IS strategy, where macroeconomic instability interacts with weak bank supervision; (b) UM/AS, where the potential interaction between economic instability and moral hazard is largely offset by bank supervision; (c) SM/IS strategy, where the economy is stable but moral hazard in banks presents a potential problem because of inadequate supervision; and (d) SM/AS strategy, where the economy is stable and the banking system is adequately supervised. They typify Malaysia as following the SM/AS sequencing strategy.

Part IV

FOREIGN INVESTMENT, TECHNOLOGY TRANSFER AND EXPORT PROCESSING ZONES

12

FOREIGN DIRECT INVESTMENT, INSTITUTIONAL CHANGE AND VIETNAM'S GRADUALIST APPROACH TO REFORM

Carolyn L. Gates

12.1 INTRODUCTION

Vietnam in 1994 consolidated gains from its programme of stabilization and structural adjustment over the past six years, while building on its gradualist approach to reform. Foreign Direct Investment (FDI)—which grew by 40 per cent in 1993[1]—has been a unifying thread in Vietnam's gradualist reform process, and it is now facilitating bolder institutional change within the political economy. Over the past year, the government has reaffirmed its priority of attracting higher rates of contracted and realized FDI, but more importantly, it has stepped up efforts to demonstrate credible commitment to formal institutional reform. In the longer term, policies focusing on capital inflows and institutional change have been sequenced and paced to promote Vietnamese political objectives of stability, and economic goals of growth and structural change. Although the emphasis on these elements has been intensified recently, the actual policies are a result of long-term strategic objectives and an evolving reform process officially initiated in late 1986. Throughout this article, we are basing our reasoning on empirical evidence; the subjective motivations and objectives of Vietnam's leadership are positioned within this context.

While this article concentrates its arguments within the framework of *doi moi*, Vietnam's "renovation" or reform process that was initiated by the Sixth Congress of the Communist Party in December 1986, reform of Vietnam's economy can be traced back to the mid and late 1970s after the reunification of North and South Vietnam. This caveat, however, does not affect the validity of the discussion presented here. Beyond the obvious observation that economies in the real world are constantly changing and reforming, a more relevant point is that the nature of Vietnamese reform in these two periods

Source: *Southeast Asian Affairs 1995*, Singapore: Institute of Southeast Asian Studies, 1995, pp. 382–400.

was distinct, featuring different objectives, forces and mechanisms driving the process, even though post-1986 reform was influenced by experience gained in the earlier period. Essentially, reform before 1986 was propelled from the grass-roots level (for example local managers of state-owned enterprises, cooperatives and bureaucrats), and was tolerated by the central authorities to ease the pressures of the shortage economy, widening macroeconomic imbalances and rampant microeconomic inefficiencies. In the end, toleration of this *tâtonnement*-like process was based on an objective of making socialist transformation possible. In contrast to the post-1986 period, the leadership took the decision to endorse and lead reform after it recognized that the internal logic of Vietnam's socio-economic system was fundamentally flawed and could not be made to work by tinkering.[2] By trial and error, it initiated a stronger form of reform and allowed greater freedom to interest groups favouring marketization, ultimately bringing about an irreversible (even if non-linear) transformation to a market-oriented economy. Our argument is *not* that all elements of the old centrally-managed system have been eliminated, nor that all contradictions within the internal system were removed after the December 1986 decision. Instead, we maintain that qualitative and quantitative differences exist between the two periods, thereby justifying the convenient separation of Vietnam's reform process into the pre- and post-1986 periods to clarify the following analysis.

Vietnam's opening to the outside world over the past six or seven years has dramatically shifted the economic environment in which the country operates, and now occupies a central position in its gradualist reform process.[3] Comprising a number of bold and far-reaching reforms including a redirection and liberalization of trade and finance, the most prominent aspect of "opening up" can be subsumed under the category of FDI. Regardless of whether Vietnam's leadership was primarily acting on a "demonstration effect"—predominantly Chinese—or on its own analysis that only foreign capital could provide the massive resources needed for Vietnam's "catch up" process, it established a highly liberal and relatively comprehensive foreign investment law (FIL) in December 1987, one year after formally embarking on *doi moi*. Although the FIL has been amended several times since 1987—and new policies, institutions, and structures have been added to its framework—its basic underpinnings encouraging foreign firms to invest throughout Vietnam's economy remain unchanged. Furthermore, since the abrupt policy shift on foreign economic relations in 1987–88, Vietnam's leadership has been highly responsive to advice about improving its foreign investment regime. Such openness is quite remarkable for a country that was isolated from the international market economy only a few years previously.

Vietnam's early initiation of reforms permitting foreign direct investment—whereby partial liberalization of its capital account (that is inward capital flows) preceded stabilization, domestic price liberalization, trade reform, and institutional reform—is interesting in itself. A growing consensus among both orthodox and political economy-oriented economists maintains that sequencing and speed of reform in economies in transition to market-oriented systems are key determinants of successful transformation.[4] Within sequencing, they view institutional change as an ideal first phase of reform and external financial liberalization as among the last areas of adjustment. As for the speed of reform, there is greater controversy. "Shock therapy" or the "big bang" (Table 12.1) finds more support within the orthodox economics community than does "gradualism"; but a growing number of economists—especially analysts of the Chinese transition—are concluding that the gradual approach has facilitated high growth rates and reduced adjustment costs compared to the "big bang". On both counts, Vietnam has opposed orthodoxy by, for example, instituting a gradual pace of reform and liberalizing inward capital flows before establishing a domestic market-oriented institutional framework of property rights, contract and company law, and legislation regulating (or deregulating) factors markets. (Table 12.2) However; in one principal area of reform, stabilization, Vietnam has taken a more orthodox path. Strong stabilization measures aimed at reducing inflation in 1989 followed "shock therapy" prescriptions. They succeeded far beyond expectations: inflation fell from almost 500 per cent in late 1986 to 18 per cent in mid-1989;[5] and by 1993, it had been stabilized at 5–6 per cent per annum. Within this structure of reform, Vietnam has made great progress in establishing institutions and policies that reorient its external economic environment; stabilize the economy; and support a market-based system of relative prices that had been strengthened as the weight of the private sector and competition in the consumers' goods markets had grown.

In this article, we will examine the interrelated issues of Vietnam's early and strong emphasis on foreign direct investment after the initiation of market-oriented reform in 1987, the evolution of FDI, and the choice of

Table 12.1 Typical "Big Bang" sequencing of reforms for economies in transition to market systems

Stages	*Reform*
1	Institutional reform
2	Fiscal/monetary stabilization
3	Privatization
4	Trade reform
4	Domestic price liberalization
5	Domestic financial system
3/4/5	Capital flow liberalization

Source: Rudiger Dornbush, "Strategies and Priority for Reform", in *The Transition to a Market Economy*, edited by P. Marer and S. Zecchini, pp. 169–83 (Paris: OECD, 1991).

Table 12.2 Vietnam's gradualist sequencing of reforms

Stages	*Reform*
1	(Partial) capital flow liberalization
2/4	Domestic financial system
2/3	Fiscal/monetary stabilization
4	Price liberalization *
2/4	Trade reform
5/6	Institutional reform **
5/6	Privatization

Notes:

* Ill-planned and less comprehensive price reforms occurred in 1981 and 1985 before the formal initiation of *doi moi*.

** Includes reform of the legal system, property rights, company law, contract law.

Source: Carolyn Gates and David Truong, *Reform of a Centrally-Managed Developing Economy: The Vietnamese Perspective* (Copenhagen: *NIAS Report* 9, 1992).

a slow-track approach to domestic-oriented institutional change. In the following section, we discuss Vietnam's shift in emphasis from internal and Council for Mutual Economic Assistance (CMEA) investment financing to external equity finance (that is FDI), which was codified at a relatively early stage of reform. Section 12.3 goes on to analyse why foreign investors have positively responded to the new policies. Section 12.4 looks at evolving economic trends of FDI. In addition, sections 12.3 and 12.4 shed light on the long-term sustainability of Vietnam's utilization of foreign direct investment not only as a cornerstone of reform but also of development, which will ultimately determine the success or failure of Vietnam's transformation process. Section 12.5 examines the issue of institutional change and Vietnam's reform process. It discusses the reasons for the deferment of Vietnam's most difficult institutional challenges—establishing property rights and a legal framework appropriate to a market-oriented economy—to the current period. In the last section, we close with concluding remarks.

12.2 VIETNAM'S SHIFT TO FOREIGN DIRECT INVESTMENT

A shift in Vietnam's attitude towards (non-CMEA) inward foreign investment began to develop several years before the end of CMEA assistance, which along with domestic savings mobilized mainly from agriculture, had financed its socialist investment programme. With the numerous demands facing Vietnam's reformers in 1987, why did they decide to emphasize foreign investment at this early stage of official reform?[6]

A combination of factors prompted the decision-makers to initiate major changes in Vietnam's external economic and financial relations and mechanisms in the 1987–88 period. First, they were influenced by China's successful opening to foreign investment, which contributed to its achievement of an average annual rate of growth of GNP of about 9 per cent in the 1980s. Vietnamese policy makers and technocrats, who monitor China's reform policies for their successes, failures and applicability to Vietnam, assessed China's liberalizing foreign economic policies potentially suitable for Vietnam.[7] Thus, China's qualified success with special economic zones, foreign joint ventures, direct relations of Chinese enterprises with foreign firms, and other forms of foreign direct investment have provided a positive demonstration effect about the role of EDI for Vietnam's leadership. A second factor was the growing recognition that Vietnam's economic needs were simply too great to rely on its traditional sources of investment. This point will be elaborated below. Third, several important factors caused Vietnam's decision makers to begin to accept the necessity of diversifying economic relations and modalities: the warning signs of change in the Soviet Union and Eastern Europe; displeasure about the large-scale, inefficient and other problematical aspects of Soviet investment projects in Vietnam; and the growing realization that the economic gap between Vietnam and its neighbours was widening rather than closing. Perhaps the last factor; the expanding development gap between regional economies and Vietnam, most impressed the leadership about the urgency of Vietnam's situation. In particular, it was concerned about Vietnam's small manufacturing sector—the focal point of its rapid industrialization socialist development strategy—which was growing and changing too slowly to catch up with the Asian newly industrialized economies (NIEs) or many ASEAN economies in the foreseeable future. Finally, Vietnam's Communist Party was unwilling to consider power-sharing, that is moving towards a multi-party system, a position that was reaffirmed with the ongoing changes in the Soviet Union and Eastern Europe in the second half of the 1980s and early 1990s. During that time, Vietnamese students and workers were returning to Vietnam with personal stories about the changes there; and a number of Vietnamese policy makers had first-hand experiences with the new socio-economic environment in the socialist bloc, which they considered disastrous. The speed and direction of change in those countries shocked many Vietnamese leaders, and they vowed to avoid reform that would threaten the monopoly of power of the Communist Party. While decision makers recognized that they must slowly open up the internal system, they firmly believed that a multi-party system would only lead to chaos, and ultimately, that political pluralism would destroy Vietnam's renovation project.[8] They concluded that making progress on the economic front, which foreign investment could potentially accelerate, would reduce immediate pressures to liberalize its domestic political system.

With the collapse of the CMEA, Vietnam's altered viewpoint favouring foreign direct investment was strengthened, while its financial situation changed dramatically. Since that time, Vietnam has had to begin repaying its external debt, which is large compared to its gross domestic product (GDP), amounting to some 10 billion Transferable Roubles (TR)[9] and US$4 billion. Merely servicing the debt will require an estimated US$200–300 million per year. Moreover; Vietnam's fiscal deficit is again rising—projected at 6–7 per cent of GDP in 1994—after the government succeeded in reducing it from 8 per cent of GDP in 1988–90 to 2.5 per cent in 1991 and 3.8 per cent in 1992. Although the government must reduce future deficits—given the alternative of renewed inflation with money financing or higher interest rates and increased financial repression with debt financing[10]—Vietnam's policy makers are now seeking to increase FDI and foreign loans and grants as a means to counter the negative effects of higher budgetary deficits, particularly "crowding out" investment in priority areas.

Given these financial constraints and Vietnam's very large requirements to transform economically, its decision makers view FDI as a tool to reorient and bolster its industrialization drive, a stimulus to its "late" industries,[11] and a means to increase the pace of economic growth and structural change.

Considering these conditions, strong arguments supporting the use of foreign direct investment emerge. Vietnam's objectives can be summarized as follows:

1 In light of domestic financial constraints, it is seeking to use FDI to fill the savings-investment gap of an economy aiming at high growth and technical change;
2 It seeks to capture (assumed) positive externalities of foreign direct investment and outward-orientation (technology and knowledge transfer, demonstration effects, and external institutional influences).

For a low-income country striving to achieve high growth, Vietnam has a low domestic savings rate, about 14 per cent of GDP in 1993. Much higher levels of investment will be required to maintain Vietnam's 1992 growth rate of 8.3 per cent.[12] A high growth strategy assumes high investment. Vietnam's large investment needs also reflect its record of high inflation and inefficient investment and development strategies (both of which dampened and wasted investment) and the destruction and neglect of basic infrastructure.

To realize a "warranted" annual growth rate of 8–8.5 per cent, thereby doubling Vietnam's GDP in 12 years, and assuming an annual population growth of 2 per cent and an Incremental Capital Output Ratio (ICOR) of 2.5–3,[13] gross investment must grow from 16–17 per cent of GDP in 1993 to 27–28 per cent of GDP in 1998. Although Vietnam must increase domestic savings in this period, an annual savings-investment gap of 3–5 per cent of GDP is still likely. This gap will have to be filled by foreign savings (which includes FDI, official development assistance [ODA], commercial loans and current account deficits). While policy makers hope to obtain international loans to cover budget deficits in the short term, they view FDI as a means in the long-run to provide capital to expand export and capital-intensive industries, and high value-added services, thereby increasing economic growth. They have, therefore, created an investment strategy based on attracting a total of US$20–25 billion in FDI for the decade of the 1990s (Table 12.3), which will be matched by local capital to achieve an annual growth rate of 7.5 per cent or higher; and private foreign and domestic investment is to be supported by the government's requests for ODA of a projected US$7 billion by the year 2000.

A second objective of Vietnam's policies on inward foreign investment is predicated on the assumption that FDI (and foreign trade) are directly linked to the fundamental processes of economic growth and structural change, and can generate positive external economies.[14] Thus, many Vietnamese policy makers and advisers—who perceive foreign investment and trade as more than mere conduits of international flows of goods, services and capital—believe that they will increase output, productivity, technical change and accumulation; and encourage a shift from a dominating agricultural sector to that of industry.[15] The opening of Vietnam's economy in 1988—ending years of isolationism and reliance on the inefficient CMEA division of labour—meant that it is encountering new external institutional, technological, and "knowledge" forces. Through appropriate policy formulation and implementation, Vietnam's decision makers hope to harness these forces to move forward the country's development and adjustment processes.

12.3 ENABLING FACTORS: WHY DO FOREIGN FIRMS INVEST IN VIETNAM?

It is easy to understand why Vietnam's leadership would wish to pursue this path. What were the factors that made it possible? Why would foreign firms want to invest in Vietnam? Rather than applying a theory of foreign direct investment to the case of Vietnam, it is more useful to identify its

Table 12.3 Foreign direct investment in Vietnam, 1988–94 (Annual inflows in US$ millions)

Year	*1988*	*1989*	*1990*	*1991*	*1992*	*Total (1988–March 1994)*
Committed	362.8	537.7	600	1,220.6	1,905	8,500
Realized	232.2	356	443.6	1,132.4	1,891.8	n.a.
No. of projects	37	69	108	150	192	895

Note:
n.a. = not available.

Source: From databank of the State Committee for Cooperation and Investment (1994).

Table 12.4 FDI structure in Vietnam, 1988–1994
(percentage share of registered capital)

Sector	*1988–90*	*Dec. 1991*	*Dec. 1992*	*Mar. 1994*
Oil & gas	31.9	21.3	26.2	15.0
Manufacturing	13.2	13.9	40.0	41.9
Agriculture, forestry & fisheries	21.9	28.2	6.2	6.9
Hotels	23.7	25.6	16.5	18.9
Services	*	*	4.1	5.5
Telecommunications & transport	9.0	10.6	4.0	7.4
Construction		0.2		
Financial services			2.6	1.8
Other	0.3	0.2	0.4	2.6
Total	100.0	100.0	100.0	100.0

Note:
* Data for services aggregated with hotels, 1988–91.

Sources: General Statistical Office; Central Institute of Economic Management; State Committee for Cooperation and Investment.

major foreign investors and their strategies. From this approach, we can draw conclusions about determinants of source (investing) firms in Vietnam. As Table 12.4 shows, by March 1994, over 80 per cent of cumulative foreign investment in Vietnam had flowed into manufacturing (41.9 per cent), oil and gas (15 per cent) and hotels and services (24.4 per cent). Between January 1988 and March 1994, Western European, Soviet (Russian), Japanese and Asian transnational corporations (TNCs) had committed almost US$2.9 billion in the latter two sectors to explore and exploit Vietnam's petroleum resources, and to develop its tourism industry. The strategies of such investments need only a brief explanation. First, foreign petroleum companies began to flock to Vietnam in the earliest stages of FDI to develop its relatively unexploited oil and gas sectors that have proven reserves and high potential. At the same time, these companies could reduce political and economic risks in Vietnam because of their power in international markets. Second, large international hotel chains and smaller foreign tourism firms chose to invest in Vietnam's primitive tourism infrastructure primarily because they expected very high rates of return with little foreign exchange risk.

More significant, theoretically and empirically, are the motivations of foreign firms to invest in Vietnamese manufacturing.

The largest share of foreign capital flowing into manufacturing originates from the Asian NIEs and Japan. The investment strategies of the NIEs firms are based on the changing economic conditions in Asia, Vietnam's comparative advantage, and the international division of labour that has prevailed since World War II. Specifically, they are utilizing Vietnam's low-wage advantage by transferring labour-intensive industries from high-cost East Asian economies to a country where not only are wages low, but workers are disciplined, somewhat skilled, and potentially highly productive. Moreover, the Asian NIEs perceive Vietnam as an attractive alternative production site to produce goods for international and regional markets and to counter current or potential problems with currency appreciation and protectionism. The push factors are significant as Taiwan, South Korea, Hong Kong and Singapore become high-cost producers of standardized, mature manufactures in an international economy, in which they no longer enjoy easy access to large and rich markets. Pull factors also make Vietnamese manufacturing attractive to Asian producers. They include Vietnam's improved macro-economic and investment environment brought about by stabilization and structural adjustment programmes; small capital requirements to set up manufacturing projects; access to rich natural resources and to growing markets; and a strategic geographical position that can facilitate penetration of neighbouring Indochinese and southern Chinese markets.

The Asian NIEs are concentrating their investments in production of standardized, rudimentary goods: foodstuffs, garments, textiles, footwear; simple electronics and wood products. East Asian investment (NIEs and Japan) is also flowing into heavy industry (for example cement, steel and metallurgy); paper and pulp production; assembly of motor vehicles; components and spare parts production; and more complex electronic products. Typically, these firms enter joint venture agreements with Vietnamese partners, although increasingly, the Taiwanese are opting to establish wholly-owned subsidiaries in Vietnam. In the future, it is likely that many will locate projects in export-processing zones (EPZs)—two of which currently involve Taiwanese principals and a third with large Hong Kong capital.

Japanese firms (and bureaucrats) are laying the groundwork to expand investment significantly in Vietnam. Beyond similar factors that drive Asian NIEs investors in Vietnam (that is low-wage labour), several aspects of Japan's shift to offshore Asian production suggest its future investment strategies and operational principles in Vietnam. Important motivating features and determinants of this process are characterized by the following:'[16]

1 Japanese enterprises look for host countries where they can expand local and third country sales;
2 Japanese foreign investors are influenced by geographical location of projects, preferring proximity to Japan;
3 Japanese firms are concentrating their foreign investments in small and medium enterprises.[17]

Currently, Japanese firms are directing their non-petroleum production investment in Vietnamese small and medium enterprises (SMEs) that assemble electronic goods, automobiles, and motorcycles from Japanese inputs and technology. Most of these products are sold on the local market or in neighbouring areas (in Indochina and Southern China). Although committing only relatively small investments in Vietnam, Japanese firms are utilizing Vietnam as a low-wage producer of goods to sell in Vietnam's growing market, and its potential to expand production for neighbouring country sales.

Given the strong appreciation of the yen and fundamental "industrial imperatives" facing Japanese firms, it is likely that they will have to transfer more than low added-value industries to cheaper production areas like Vietnam. One strategy is laid out by a Mitsubishi-commissioned study of Vietnam's future automobile market, detailing the logic and mechanics of integrating Vietnam into Mitsubishi's regional and local production and distribution networks.[18] Unlike NIEs' export-oriented production in Vietnam, however; a large share of Japanese output in Vietnam remains to be marketed in the country. Indeed, many Japanese TNCs currently prohibit export of Vietnamese-produced goods to third countries—with the exception of its Indochinese and Chinese neighbours. From time to time, this emphasis on local sales has run into difficulties. For example, the author visited a small Japanese-Vietnamese joint venture in electronics assembly where production had stopped and a large volume of goods were warehoused. They could not be sold due to inadequate domestic demand and Japanese prohibition on export. According to local industry experts, this case is not atypical.

Japanese firms are currently utilizing Vietnam primarily as a seller's platform due to large infrastructural and institutional constraints in Vietnam. Hence, they are cautious about large-scale investment in export-oriented production because they estimate that five years of infrastructural development in Vietnam are needed before the country is ready to develop key export sectors like electronics and motor vehicles. This time period, they claim, may be shortened with increased bilateral ODA and multilateral loans for infrastructural development. Acting on this perspective, Japan officially pledged US$500 million in ODA credit to Vietnam for fiscal 1994, making Vietnam the sixth largest recipient of Japanese ODA. Moreover; in the first half of 1994, Japan announced that it would supply soft loans amounting to US$478 million for infiastructure projects, and a Japanese consortium disclosed that it would build a deep-water port in the southern region of Vietnam at an estimated cost of US$900 million. Both suggest that Japanese firms will be active in developing physical infrastructure in Vietnam. Under these conditions, Japanese firms will move steadily over the next five years from a position of using Vietnam as a seller's platform to a production platform for Vietnamese and third country markets; and at the same time, they will continue to purchase a very large share of Vietnam's oil output. These factors indicate that Japanese firms will increasingly integrate Vietnam into their regional supply, production and marketing networks.[19]

12.4 EVOLVING TRENDS OF FDI IN VIETNAM

Shifting structure, composition and distribution of FDI

The structure, composition and distribution of foreign investment in Vietnam have been shifting since 1988, due to three main factors: a decline of FDI in agriculture; an increase of foreign investment in manufacturing, which is currently supplanting oil and gas as the favoured sector of FDI; and the growing importance of Asian firms as sources of foreign capital.

The share of agriculture, forestry and fisheries in total FDI in Vietnam has declined dramatically from 21.9 per cent in 1988–90 to 6.9 per cent by March 1994. With the changing division of labour within Asia, intense international competition in agriculture and low world prices for commodities, the decline of foreign investment in Vietnam's primary sector may be the beginning of a secular (long-run) trend. As in China, only a small share of FDI is currently flowing into Vietnam's agriculture, forestry and fisheries, notwithstanding its sectoral share of GDP (34.5 per cent in 1992) and labour force (72 per cent in 1992). Beyond negative international conditions, the small appeal of Vietnam's agriculture to foreign investors reflects a host of internal problems within that sector: very low productivity; low purchasing power of the rural population; limited foreign markets for rice, the principal crop produced in Vietnam; and poor physical infrastructure. Clearly, foreign firms are not returning to the traditional pattern of investment in plantation and primary production in Vietnam. In brief, foreign investors find other sectors of Vietnam's economy more profitable—or potentially profitable—and more suitable to their strategies than agriculture.

Two other factors briefly mentioned above are closely interrelated and explain important shifts in the structure, composition and distribution of FDI in Vietnam. They are: (1) at least in the short-run, manufacturing is supplanting oil and gas as the sector receiving the pre-eminent share of foreign investment; and (2) Asian firms are replacing Western European TNCs as the fastest growing sources of foreign investment in Vietnam.

The first wave of foreign investment after the passage of Vietnam's FIL in late 1987 centred on the oil and gas sector; a recipient of 34 per cent of cumulative FDI in January 1988–May 1990.[20] Foreign firms also began to invest in Vietnam's long-neglected hotel, tourism and service sectors (almost 24 per cent of cumulative EDI, 1988–90).[21] During this period, Western European transnational investors began to explore for potentially large offshore oil and gas reserves.

European (including Russian) domination of Vietnam's oil and gas industry has been declining as Asian oil companies invest in Vietnam's energy potential. Japanese and other Asian investment in the petroleum industry had surged since the end of the Gulf War; showing their interest in expanding oil and gas supplies in East Asia. Currently, Vietnam's state oil company and consortia of 15 European-Japanese-Asian transnationals are driving the development of Vietnam's offshore oil and gas industry, which is centred in the southern coastal city of Vung Tau. Given the projected long-run growth of demand for natural gas in Japan, Taiwan and South Korea, it is probable that Vietnam will receive substantial regional investment in liquified natural gas (LNG) in addition to offshore oil. However; it remains to be seen whether a trend of higher investment in manufacturing, compared to energy development, is emerging in Vietnam. Currently, foreign investors are making commitments to finance very large projects in energy development of oil and gas, and related infrastructure. If these projects materialize as planned—and assuming the continuation of a heightened role for Asian investors in Vietnam and of growing demand for energy within Asia throughout the 1990s—oil and gas may re-emerge as the favoured sector of foreign investors in Vietnam.

In late 1990 and 1991, Asian NIEs began to invest in Vietnam's manufacturing branches, targeting the production of textiles, garments, footwear and home appliances; assembly of electronic goods; and processing of foodstuffs. Foreign investment in the manufacturing branches increased sharply in 1992 with a second wave of Asian investment. The Asian NIEs invested

Table 12.5 Selected Asian investors in Vietnam, 1993

Country	*No. of projects committed*	*Value committed (US$)*	*Sectoral concentration*	*Geographical concentration*
Taiwan	90 (127)	1.4 billion (1.6 billion)	Labour-intensive consumer goods & electronics; heavy industry; EPZs; tourism	Labour-intensive: Ho Chi Minh City and Hanoi; heavy industry: the north
Hong Kong	148 (144)	1.16 billion (1.2 billion)	Labour-intensive consumer goods & electronics: tourism	Ho Chi Minh City Hanoi Haiphong
Japan	45 (56)	474 million (542 million)	Oil, gas, mineral resources; motor vehicle assembly	Ho Chi Minh City Hanoi
South Korea	38 (62)	379 million (699 million)	Heavy indusry (steel, cement, metallurgy); electronics; construction	Hanoi, Haiphong and northern region

Note: Numbers in parentheses indicate updated data as of July 1994.

Source: David Truong and Carolyn Gates, field survey of foreign direct investment, Vietnam, October–November 1993.

heavily in electronics, chemicals, construction materials, motor vehicle assembly, and development of EPZs. Japanese capital flowed into electronics and motor vehicle assembly. (Table 12.5) In 1993, the second wave of Asian investment continued in the following sectors:

1 heavy industry (Korea);
2 motor vehicle assembly (Korea, Taiwan, Japan);
3 infrastructure and oil and gas (Japan, Korea, Taiwan, Indonesia); and
4 shipping and related services (Singapore, Hong Kong, Japan).

Asian capital following trade flows

A second important trend of foreign investment in Vietnam is Asian capital following Asia-Vietnam trade flows. (Table 12.6) This parallels a general growth in Vietnam's foreign (non-CMEA) trade turnover since 1987, which was followed by a very significant increase in foreign investment in that country. Moreover; Vietnam's expansion of trade with Asia contributed greatly to its successful trade reorientation from the CMEA countries to market economies; and from a trade deficit nation to an economy with a more or less balanced trade account (in 1992, it recorded its first current account surplus). These factors have made Vietnam's macroeconomic environment more attractive to foreign, particularly Asian, investors.

The share of total Vietnamese exports from, and imports to, the Asia-Pacific region steadily increased in the 1990–92 period (Table 12.7).

The rise of the relative position of Asian trade to Vietnam has been matched by its absolute importance. The value of Vietnam's trade with Japan and Singapore surpassed the billion-dollar threshold in 1992, rising in 1993 to US$1.3 billion and US$1.7 billion, respectively. Its trade with Taiwan grew fivefold in the 1988–92 period to US$402 million (1992); that with

Table 12.6 Asian NIEs foreign investment in Vietnam (up to July 1994)

Country	*Number of projects*	*Committed capital (millions US$)*
Taiwan	127	1,629
Hong Kong	144	1,246
South Korea	62	699
Singapore	60	567
Total/NIEs	393	4,141
Total/FDI *	859	8,980

Note:
* Up to August 1994.

Sources: *Vietnam Investment Review*, 4–10 July 1994; Reuters.

Table 12.7 Share of Vietnamese trade with Asia-Pacific (percentages)

	Vietnamese exports to Asia-Pacific	*Vietnamese imports from Asia-Pacific*
1990	43.6	37
1991	77	61
1992	79.4	77.5
1993	82	78

South Korea grew to US$470 million (1992). Furthermore, *official* trade turnover between Vietnam and China grew to US$427 million in 1993; the real figure is closer to US$1 billion.

From the preceding data, it is evident that the three focal points of Vietnam's foreign trade relations are the NIEs, Japan and China. Of these dominant trading partners, Taiwan and Hong Kong are also the two most important foreign investors in Vietnam. Furthermore, Japan, South Korea and Singapore are among the top ten investors. Thus, it is not surprising that about three-quarters of EDI had originated from Asia-Pacific corporate investors since 1992, mostly from the NIEs and Japan, up from a little over 50 per cent in 1991.

Although the data and research on trade and foreign direct investment in Vietnam are too weak and fragmentary to establish a direct correlation and directional relationship between trade and FDI, we argue that the expansion of Asian trade with Vietnam is pulling regional capital, and international investment via Asian subsidiaries or intermediaries, into Vietnam. By the logic of Asian investment strategies, Vietnam's location and human and physical resources augur well for it to become a magnet for even larger Asian capital. Hence, this process, which is driven as much, or more, by push factors as Vietnam's pull factors, suggests that Vietnam is well-placed to continue to attract foreign investment capital, thereby sustaining or surpassing its high levels of commitment in the 1991–93 period, while the high-growth foreign investment scenario is made even more realistic as large infrastructural projects come on stream.

12.5 INSTITUTIONAL CHANGE

Regardless of the economic system, a favourable investment and economic environment cannot be established without appropriate formal and informal institutions. Economies making the transition to market-oriented systems by definition will not be endowed with appropriate institutional and legal frameworks. Since no market or only small parallel markets existed previously, there are no (well-defined) property rights and laws essential to the smooth functioning of a market system (for example contract, company and bankruptcy laws). Moreover; informal conventions and behavioural norms are ill-suited to the demands of everyday life in a market economy. Given these conditions, many social scientists stress the urgent requirement to implement institutional reforms early in the transformation process. However; while in the early period of 1987–91 the Vietnamese leadership established numerous policy and institutional reforms on foreign direct investment, trade, finance, macro-level mechanisms, firm-level management rights and incentives, *inter alia*, it postponed creating the institutional nucleus of a market system.

The establishment of market-oriented institutions like property rights and bankruptcy mechanisms ("rules of the game" needed in Vietnam to complete its market incentive structure and to promote adaptive efficiency) was delayed to later stages of reform because of the leadership's political objectives and the realities of reform. Regarding the last point, we argue that policy reform is not linear, and at any time, it can be changed or reversed by strong opposition.[22] A focus on policy reform that could be made acceptable—or less objectionable—to the power bloc and influential parts of Vietnamese society was preferred to contentious issues of domestic institutional change. Decision makers, thus, deferred the most difficult and controversial aspects like property rights precisely because they were difficult and controversial. Consequently, the issues of ownership and control, ownership/usufruct rights of property (with the exception of the 1993 land law authorizing landholding rights of farmers), privatization or equitization, and other components of property rights have only begun to be addressed. Another factor in this sequencing of reforms emerged as a result of inexperience and "bounded rationality" – the inability of leaders to interpret and act "rationally" on limited and often misleading information and knowledge. In terms of knowledge, it was easier to address a matter like foreign direct investment than very complex issues of domestic institutional change.

In light of these conditions, it was highly rational for the Vietnamese leadership to establish FDI as an early and central reform because it was relatively easy in the context of Vietnam's political economy; it was likely to succeed in tangible ways; and it did not require large bureaucratic haggling to implement it. For the exact opposite reasons, domestic market-oriented institutional change was postponed to a time when reformers believed they would have greater political and bureaucratic influence to succeed (that is after their opponents and society at large recognized the benefits of earlier economic reforms). Moreover; Vietnam's policy makers and legislators have quickly learnt that "getting the prices right" and establishing functioning markets for goods and services will not automatically engender effective institutions to promote growth and structural change. As the leadership became more knowledgeable about, and experienced with, the market mechanism, and as the notion of the rule of law began to supplant the rule of arbitrary bodies, formal institutional change is progressing in Vietnam. Thus, only in the last year or two, laws were passed and policies implemented to permit private use and transfer rights of land; codified bankruptcy of enterprises; facilitated greater flexibility and mobility of labour; and began to establish building blocks essential for the development of capital markets. Nevertheless, a major lacuna in Vietnam's institutional environment required for a market system still remains. Specifically, defining property rights in a more transparent and effective manner; equitizing non-strategic state-owned enterprises on a more credible scale, and completing the legal system to permit market functions are essential tasks that remain to be tackled.

12.6 CONCLUSION

We argued that Vietnam has created its own gradualist path of transformation to a market-oriented economy, emphasizing foreign investment at an early stage of reform, and postponing difficult institutional changes like the creation of clearly-defined property rights and equitization of state-owned enterprises. Fundamentally, Vietnam's decision makers are sequencing and timing reforms in this manner to fulfil political objectives of maintaining control over the reform process and retaining the party's monopoly of power. In terms of its internal logic and objectives, Vietnam's leadership has been relatively successful in carrying out this reform programme. Vietnam has attracted growing amounts of foreign investment—perhaps close to its absorptive capacity. Policy makers were successful in stabilizing the economy, particularly in the area of inflation. And not only did the country avoid a protracted "transformational recession" typical of post-socialist European economies, it enjoyed good growth rates, and unemployment has not yet soared. On the other hand, Vietnam made little progress on demanding challenges that threaten its economic health: it was unable to complete its formal institutional setting by defining property rights and filling in the gaps of its legal system; nor has it made headway in developing its factors markets and overhauling its physical infrastructure.

A cornerstone of this strategy was the employment of foreign investment to achieve tangible economic results as rapidly as possible. A successful economy will support stable political change, thereby buttressing the position and objectives of Vietnam's Communist Party. And Vietnam was able to use this strategy—perhaps by luck, perhaps by foresight—by a fortuitous conjuncture of factors. Notably, Vietnam's financial liberalization was well-timed to interact synergistically with the changing international and Asian regional division of labour and the normal ramifications of reintegrating into the international market economy. Thus, the interaction of internal and external factors permitted Vietnam to employ FDI as a means to fill the savings-investment gap of its low-savings economy with high-growth ambitions. Second, Vietnam's policy makers hoped that the economy would benefit from external effects (assumed positive externalities) of foreign direct investment like technology transfer.

The nature of foreign investment in Vietnam has changed in the five years of its existence, reflecting both internal and external factors. The shift in the preponderance of FDI in resource-intensive industries (petroleum and agriculture) to labour-intensive ones (manufacturing) is due primarily to a conjuncture of forces occurring in East Asia and Vietnam. With rising labour costs in their home countries, East Asian economies have been transferring labour-intensive industries, while labour-rich Vietnam has been improving its macroeconomic and investment environments. As the success of Vietnam's reform programme gained international attention, and as Asian firms became familiar with Vietnam through trade, East Asian investors committed greater amounts of capital to Vietnam, mainly to utilize its comparative labour advantage. Thus, by late 1992, a second important shift in foreign investment in Vietnam had occurred: Asian FDI exceeded European investment and Asia became the most important source of foreign capital for Vietnam. Simultaneously, manufacturing surpassed petroleum, agriculture and services to become the sector receiving the largest share of FDI.

Our analysis showed why Vietnam's leadership was able to employ its policies on FDI successfully. Foreign investors are finding at least three economic attractions in Vietnam: low-wage labour for manufacturing industries; natural resources that are in high demand; and high profits for moderate risks in its service industries. All else being equal, the likely demand for these suggests that Vietnam will attract greater amounts of foreign capital for the rest of the decade. It is unlikely to suffer from a shortage of international capital as many developing countries (DCs) have been experiencing in the 1990s. In contrast to much of the developing world, the dynamic Asia-Pacific region has had few difficulties in attracting foreign capital, amounting to 50–60 per cent of world-wide investment in DCs in the 1990s; and Vietnam is likely to benefit from the fact that it is an important host country to firms from leading capital exporters—Japan, Taiwan, Hong Kong, South Korea and Singapore. These facts suggest that international capital is readily available to economies like Vietnam that provide favourable growth and profit opportunities.

In the meantime, if Vietnam can maintain macroeconomic stability, establish greatly needed institutional changes appropriate for a market-oriented and high-growth economy, and reduce rent-seeking, unproductive, and illegal activities—three very big ifs—it will also create an environment that encourages investment efficiency and effectiveness and, therefore, sustainable growth and development.

Of these three requirements, institutional change directed towards the internal political economy will be the most difficult to accomplish. We argued that to keep its reform and development programme on track, Vietnam must define property rights in a more transparent and effective manner; and amend/complete the legal system to permit a smoother functioning of the market. Change directed at fitting Vietnam's institutions to a market economy is essential to build an economy capable of accomplishing the leadership's stated objectives. Moreover; appropriate institutional change and economic growth are often mutually reinforcing: effective rules of the game promote growth and efficiency, which can facilitate new institutional reforms. Less urgent but still highly important in this context is the necessity to begin a serious equitization (privatization) programme of non-strategic state-owned enterprises, especially if Vietnamese policy makers are to deal effectively with a recently growing budget deficit and to give appropriate signals to both foreign and domestic investors.

Finally, Vietnam is likely to continue an economic path that emphasizes foreign investment. In the future, however; Vietnamese technocrats will probably attempt to direct FDI more at achieving various growth and developmental targets and effects. Regardless of fine-tuning, the basic thrust of Vietnam's FDI policy will not change significantly for the remaining years of this decade. Moreover, due to the many reasons we have already discussed, Vietnam is likely to attract large amounts of foreign capital inflows, at least in the medium-run. What remains to be answered is the big question about the long-run impact of FDI on Vietnam's growth and development, something that policy makers and economists will be examining for many years to come.

NOTES

1 Growth calculated on basis of investments of 1 January 1993–31 December 1993.

2 See Adam Fforde and Stefan de Vylder, *Vietnam: An Economy in Transition* (Stockholm: Swedish International Development Authority, 1988).

3 For more on Vietnam's reform process, see David Truong and Carolyn L. Gates, "Effects of Government Policies on the Incentive to Invest, Enterprise Behaviour and Employment: the Case Study of Vietnam", *World Employment Programme Working Paper* (Geneva: International Labour Office, 1992); Gates and Truong, "Transition of a Developing Socialist Economy to a Developing Mixed Economy: The Case of Vietnam", in *Restructuring Third World and Communist Economies: The Neoliberal Eruption*, edited by Alex E. Fernandez Jilberto and André Mommen, Special issue of the *International Journal of Political Economy* (Spring 1993).

4 See Norbert Funke, "Timing and Sequencing of Reforms: Competing Views and the Role of Credibility", *Kyklos* 46 (1993): fasc 3, pp.337–62.

5 A. Wood, "Deceleration of Inflation with Acceleration of Price Reform: Vietnam's Remarkable Recent Experience", *Cambridge Journal of Economics* 13 (1989): 571.

6 For expanded arguments on this topic, see Carolyn L. Gates and David H. D. Truong, *Foreign Direct Investment and Economic Change in Vietnam: Trends, Causes and Effects* (NIAS Report no.20 Copenhagen, 1994).

7 Information from a senior Vietnamese policy maker.

8 Ibid.

9 Before the collapse of the CMEA and the former Soviet Union, TR 1=US$1. As the rouble has been devalued greatly since that time, Vietnam and Russia are now negotiating an acceptable exchange rate for debt repayment purposes.

10 See William Easterly and Klaus Schmidt-Hebbel, "Fiscal Deficits and Macroeconomic Performance in Developing Countries", *The World Bank Research Observer* 8, no.2 (July 1993): 211–37.

11 See H. Chenery and L. Taylor; "Development Patterns: Among Countries and Over Time", *Review of Economics and Statistics* (November 1968). Late industries comprise apparel, paper and printing, basic metals, metal products, industrial machinery, electrical machinery, transport equipment, and other manufacturing.

12 This high rate of growth was possible without high levels of investment because of the great amount of slack in the economy—typical of centrally-managed economies. While efficiency measures were mainly responsible for increased output, new investment (especially private investment) is probably underestimated.

13 Estimates of Vietnam's ICOR in 1988–1992 are in a lower range of 1.15–2.14; see Le Dang Doanh and Adam McCarty, "Economic Reform in Vietnam: Achievements and Prospects", draft country report for ISEAS-ICEG Transitional Economies Project, June 1994. However, with the pressing requirements of infrastructural development and replacement of depreciated equipment, the ICOR will rise.

14 For more on this topic, see Dani Rodrik, "Conceptual Issues in the Design of Trade Policy for Industrialization", *World Deoelopnent* 20, no.3: 309–20.

15 Information based on discussions with senior policy makers and advisers. However, whether these policies are actually performing in the desired ways cannot yet be assessed because of the time lag and data issues. At this point, we can merely state that annual output in industry has grown on average by about 9 per cent since 1988 (General Statistical Office, *Nien Giam Thong Ke* [Statistical Yearbook], 1993, p. 30); and by March 1994, foreign investment in manufacturing comprised almost 42 per cent of the total stock of foreign capital and 55 per cent of total FDI projects.

16 Kwang W. Jun, Frank Sader, Haruo Horaguchi, and Hyuntai Kwak, "Japanese Foreign Direct Investment: Recent Trends, Determinants, and Prospects", IECDI, Policy Research Working Paper 1213, 1992, pp. 23–4.

17 Tran Van Tho, "Foreign Direct Investment in the Asian Pacific Region: Implications for Vietnam", *World Economic Problems*, no. 2 June 1993): 3–4.

18 See Mitsubishi Corporation, Motor Vehicle Department C, *Master Plan for the Automobile Industry in the Socialist Republic of Vietnam. Basic Concept* (Revised Version), June 1992.

19 See Kwang et. al. (1992), op. cit., and Tran Van Tho (1993), op. cit. For example, Mitsubishi might integrate Vietnam into a very simple regional network by importing Vietnamese oil (it has invested very large sums for exploration and exploitation), exporting capital goods and automobile parts to be assembled in Vietnam and marketed in Vietnam, Indochina and southern China. In reality, the strategy is likely to be much more complex than this sketch.

20 Tran Van Tho, op. cit., p. 8.

21 Ibid.

22 The main investing firms were headquartered in France, Belgium, the Netherlands and Britain.

13

JAPANESE INDUSTRIAL INVESTMENTS AND TECHNOLOGY TRANSFER IN MALAYSIA

Anuwar Ali

This chapter will examine the impact of Japanese foreign direct investments (FDI) and technology transfer in Malaysia's industrialization. Given that Japan has been one of the major players in the industrial development of the country, right from the import-substitution phase beginning in the late 1950s right through until the current export-oriented phase, there have been many expectations of its role in technology transfer to domestic industries. Since Malaysia needs to upgrade its industrial base and technological capability, the extent of technology absorption and assimilation is indeed critical. Further, the Japanese industrial experience itself has often been looked upon to be emulated by Malaysia.

In the following section, the importance of FDI in Malaysia's industrial expansion will be highlighted; FDI is sought with the expectation that it will expand employment opportunities in the manufacturing sector and enhance the country's technological capability. While the issues pertinent to both FDI inflows and technology transfer from Japanese companies will be the main theme, the nature of technology transfer into domestic enterprises in Malaysia as well as the technology absorptive capacity through human resource development will also be dealt with.

Since an important aspect of this transfer involves formal agreements between domestic licensees and Japanese technology licensors, the institutional framework within which the Malaysian government tries to ensure that such transfer will benefit domestic industries will also be highlighted. The last section of the chapter will highlight some policy initiatives to enable Malaysia to benefit more fully from rapid industrial expansion.

Technology transfer into an economy like Malaysia generally involves the transfer of written information, human-embodied skills, know-how and the adaptation of production processes by technology suppliers. Such transfers involve a variety of different modes, the principal being the purchase of

Source: *Japan and Malaysian Development: In the Shadow of the Rising Sun*, Jomo K.S. (Editor), London: Routledge, 1994, pp. 102–26.

technology through licensing agreements, imports of machinery and equipment, technical assistance contracts and turn-key arrangements. While options chosen vary from industry to industry and from firm to firm, choices are generally influenced by the objectives and capacities of users as well as the desire of the supplier to extract maximum rent from the provision of its technology.

One can also distinguish between what has generally been referred to as 'packaged' technology transfer on the one hand and 'unpackaged' technology transfer on the other. The former refers to an arrangement whereby technology is purchased as an important component of an investment package to be complemented by management, marketing services and equity participation. However, the drawback of this approach is that it tends to perpetuate technology dependency upon industrial countries and creates bottlenecks which can hamper the pace of industrial growth in a developing economy. Depending on their respective technological capabilities, many developing countries try to 'unbundle' technology packages to facilitate separate treatment of the different components offered such as management, production methods, marketing strategies and control systems.

The other common method of technology acquisition is through licensing, involving 'pure technical collaboration agreements' which exclude foreign equity participation. In fact, Japan's early industrial development and South Korea's experience since the 1960s have mainly been explained by their respective technological capabilities in acquiring and adapting technologies from more industrialized countries in this way. However, the effectiveness of this approach greatly depends upon both the industrial infrastructure and science and technology capabilities in the national economy.

Malaysian manufacturing enterprises have resorted to most of the above methods to acquire technologies from more industrialized countries. However, given the country's narrow industrial base and the dominance of FDI in key industries, technology acquisition and assimilation has been all the more difficult. A number of other factors have to be considered when a domestic industry acquires technology, including the willingness of foreign investors, mainly multinational companies (MNCs), to transfer their technologies, the appropriate price of such technologies as well as domestic absorptive capacity.

INDUSTRIAL GROWTH AND FOREIGN DIRECT INVESTMENT SINCE THE MID-1980s

Foreign direct investment inflows into Malaysia have grown markedly since the 1985–86 economic recession, after which, according to the Sixth Malaysia Plan, 'there was a remarkable increase in proposed foreign capital investment from about RM1,000 million (Malaysian ringgits) in 1985 to more than RM18,000 million in 1990. Apart from efforts by the government to enhance greater FDI, the nation has also benefited from the relocation of industries from the industrialized countries, notably Japan, South Korea and Taiwan as a result of rising costs of production and appreciation of currencies in these countries. Malaysia has, therefore, positioned itself favourably to take advantage of these opportunities' (Malaysia, 1991: 132).

In approved projects during the 1985–90 period FDI amounted to RM34,908 million, out of which Japan's share was highest with 25.7 per cent of the total. During the Sixth Malaysia Plan period (1991–95), it is projected that RM80,000 million will be invested in the manufacturing sector, of which RM33,000 million will be FDI. The government has long encouraged as much FDI inflow as possible. This thrust seems to be fully supported by the Federation of Malaysian Manufacturers (FMM), which represents most of the large manufacturing firms in the country. As emphasized by the FMM, 'a liberal policy which will encourage greater inflow of foreign capital, technology and expertise, and more reinvestments on the part of existing investors, will enable the country to be better prepared to face any economic conditions and situations arising from the current global restructuring' (Federation of Malaysian Manufacturers, 1990: 3–11).

Since the late 1950s, when Malaysia initiated its industrialization programme, imported technologies from industrial countries, including Japan, have been dominant, the consequence of FDI inflows. When export-oriented industrialization became the policy objective from the early 1970s, the importation of technologies was as important as in the preceding import-substitution phase, but more selectively, depending on the needs of the industries promoted, while a few indigenous technologies appeared in some established industries. During this phase, Free Trade Zones (FTZs) were established to encourage the relocation in Malaysia of MNC activities, particularly in electronics and textiles.

Since then, FDI has been dominant in export-oriented activities. Since 1989, for instance, foreign-controlled firms have accounted for more than 90 per cent of the export sales of the electronics industry and the machinery and electrical appliances industry. They also dominated the export of rubber products, basic metals and metal products, textiles and garments, and food, beverages and tobacco. Overall, they account for nearly 55 per cent of manufactured exports in 1989 (Bank Negara Malaysia, 1991: 51). Such foreign domination also prevails in some other countries in this part of the world, especially Singapore, where FDI participation is regarded as critical for the establishment of high-technology industries as well as for market penetration of the industrial countries (Parry, 1988: 95–128). Malaysia has also been dependent on industrial countries including Japan for international demand for manufactured exports such as electronics and textiles. In fact, the success of export-led growth in newly industrializing countries depends on the capacity of industrial countries to absorb imports from countries such as Malaysia (Thurow, 1992: 62).

As implied above, Malaysia's industrialization programme has been dominated by FDI, right from the early import-substitution phase up to the current export-oriented phase. Since 1987, the FDI presence has become more apparent, especially as a consequence of the liberalization measures to encourage foreign equity participation in 1986 with the Promotion of Investment Act. As indicated in Table 13.1, the share of proposed foreign capital investment in newly approved manufacturing projects increased substantially after 1986, reaching a peak in 1989, with 70.8 per cent of total proposed capital investment.

Apart from responding to the more open and liberal investment climate in Malaysia, the recent substantial investment inflows are also a reflection of the changing pattern of investments by firms in Japan and the East Asian newly industrialized countries (NICs). In view of their changing comparative advantage, the NICs, especially Taiwan and South Korea, have been forced to relocate industries in lower labour-cost countries such as Malaysia and its neighbours (Chen and Wong, 1989: 204–39; Tsuruoka, 1990: 87–8). In addition to the increasing domestic labour costs in Taiwan and South Korea, exacerbated by the appreciation of their currencies, such relocation has also been driven by their desire to upgrade domestic production into higher value-added and knowledge-intensive industries, especially in electronics (see Organisation for Economic Cooperation and Development, 1988: 82).

During the 1985–91 period, Japanese FDI flow has been a major source of capital for Malaysia's domestic industries. Table 13.2 shows that Japan's significance in this respect and its share of total FDI has always been very high, surpassing all other investing countries, except in 1986, 1990 and 1991. In 1986, Malaysia was experiencing an economic recession while in 1990 and 1991 Taiwanese investments overtook Japanese inflows as the latter directed greater investments to North America and Europe in anticipation of greater protection there.

Table 13.1 Proposed capital investment in approved manufacturing projects, 1985–90 (RM million)

	1985	*1986*	*1987*	*1988*	*1989*	*1990*
No. of projects	625	447	333	732	792	906
Potential employment	53,597	40,230	60,068	142,875	176,628	169,764
Malaysian capital investment	4,727.6 (83.1)	3,475.3 (67.3)	1,873.9 (47.6)	4,215.9 (46.4)	3,562.7 (29.2)	10,539.0 (37.4)
Foreign capital investment	959.3 (16.9)	1,687.9 (32.7)	2,060.0 (52.4)	4,878.0 (53.6)	8,652.7 (70.8)	17,629.1 (62.6)
Total	5,686.9	5,163.2	3,933.9	9,093.9	12,215.4	28,168.1

Note: Figures in parentheses are percentages of total capital investment in that year.

Source: Malaysian Industrial Development Authority (MIDA).

Table 13.2 Major sources of foreign investment in approved projects, 1985–91 (RM million)

	1985	*1986*	*1987*	*1988*	*1989*	*1990*	*1991*
Japan	264.4	116.3	715.1	1,222.0	2,690.4	4,212.6	3,157.7
	(27.6)	(6.9)	(34.7)	(25.1)	(31.1)	(23.9)	(19.8)
Taiwan	31.9	10.8	243.0	829.6	2,159.9	6,339.1	3,548.4
	(3.3)	(0.6)	(11.8)	(17.0)	(25.0)	(36.0)	(22.2)
Singapore	100.2	183.7	258.5	419.6	914.7	895.3	1,026.9
	(10.4)	(10.9)	(12.5)	(8.6)	(10.6)	(5.1)	(6.4)
UK	26.9	49.5	76.8	196.5	764.1	867.2	538.4
	(2.8)	(2.9)	(3.7)	(4.0)	(8.8)	(4.9)	(3.4)
USA	11.9	53.6	162.7	535.1	320.8	567.3	1,724.3
	(1.2)	(3.2)	(7.9)	(11.0)	(3.7)	(3.2)	(10.8)

Note: Figures in parentheses are percentages of total investment in that year, including other unlisted countries of origin.

Source: Malaysian Industrial Development Authority (MIDA).

Total foreign investment (RM million): 1985 – 959.3, 1986 – 1,687.9, 1987 – 2,060.0, 1988 – 4,878.0, 1989 – 8,652.7, 1990 – 17,629.1, 1991 – 15,956.0.

Despite the recent significance of Taiwanese investments, Japanese FDI undoubtedly still has the biggest cumulative impact on the country's industrialization. This is illustrated in Table 13.3, which shows proposed capital investments in approved projects during the 1980–92 period. Japanese FDI was most dominant in the electrical and electronics industry, which accounted for 43.7 per cent of the total, followed by the chemical and chemical product industries with only 13.8 per cent. Other relatively important industries in terms of, Japanese FDI include the non-metallic and basic metal products, the machinery industry, and transport equipment.

Substantial Japanese participation in these industries is largely an extension of its comparative advantage in these areas. Increasing Japanese FDI by major manufacturing firms dominance has been reinforced by the inflow of investments by Japanese small and medium-scale industries, to supply and support their larger counterparts. This has also been a consequence of increasing production (1abour and inventory) costs in Japanese industry and yen appreciation, forcing such industries to relocate their manufacturing facilities in lower wage economies such as Malaysia (George, 1988: 84–6; Kosaka, 1989: 52).

While FDI inflow has contributed to relatively more rapid growth of the manufacturing sector, such inflow provides substantial opportunities for Japanese industries to increase their exports of intermediate and capital goods to Malaysia (Nakanishi, 1990: 49–53). At the same time, they also encourage greater investments by related Japanese industries, particularly by supporting or small and medium-scale enterprises. The close links between these industries and their parent industries in Japan via sub-assembly and subcontracting systems have encouraged them to expand their activities to overseas

Table 13.3 Proposed Japanese capital investment in approved projects, 1980–92 (RM million)

Industry	*Number of projects*	*Potential employment*	*Capital investment*	*% of total*
Food manufacturing	27	3,165	112.6	1.8
Textiles	33	5,059	51.4	0.8
Leather products	3	650	1.9	—
Wood products	46	15,267	186.7	3.0
Furniture and fixtures	12	1,771	30.5	0.5
Paper and printing	15	1,139	26.5	0.4
Chemicals	63	4,239	848.4	13.8
Petroleum	5	302	15.4	0.3
Rubber products	31	3,152	48.6	0.3
Plastic products	54	4,039	251.7	4.1
Non-metallic products	77	10,719	458.1	7.5
Basic metal products	75	6,687	414.8	6.8
Fabricated metal products	62	5,267	165.0	2.7
Machinery	60	10,100	292.7	4.8
Electrical and electronics	373	114,740	2,680.8	43.7
Transport equipment	86	13,658	253.7	4.1
Scientific equipment	15	4,032	134.8	2.2
Miscellaneous	21	1,822	31.7	0.5
Natural gas	1	570	126.4	2.0
Total	1,059	206,378	6,130.7	100

Source: Malaysian Industrial Development Authority (MIDA).

locations more effectively to supply and support their parent or core companies' requirements (Go Iwaki, 1992: 309–51). Thus, according to Masayoshi Ikeda (1991: 132–47), 'while the production processes are conducted outside, they work as one synchronisation as exemplified by the processes which are interlinked with the parent company'.

While the Malaysian government is promoting the development of small and medium-scale enterprises as supporting industries, Takeshi Aoki (1992: 73–110), in his study of Japanese investment in Malaysia, concludes that 'the enterprises that have contributed to this most effectively are affiliates of Japanese firms that have shifted their production facilities and established factories in Malaysia'. This, of course, has important implications for long-term industrial expansion as such a phenomenon will inevitably stifle domestic entrepreneurship and enterprises and the potential for inter-firm linkages involving Malaysian industries.

TECHNOLOGY TRANSFER AND HUMAN RESOURCE DEVELOPMENT

Industrial progress would inevitably require the promotion of high-technology or knowledge-based industries. However, the development of such industries ought to be initiated by domestic capital, supported by an abundant supply of highly skilled labour as well as substantial increases in research and development (R&D) and technical training expenditure. With both R&D and in-service training, it is equally important to stress the role of the private sector. It is therefore crucial that human resource development be focused to develop both the critical skills needed by industry and, more important, labour's capacity to innovate. There is little doubt, as suggested by the experience of industrial countries as well as newly industrialized countries, that innovative capacities will ultimately determine the economy's competitiveness.

Basically, existing human resource development does not really emphasize the capacity to innovate. The lack of funds for R&D purposes is indeed an important constraint in this respect, while domestic industries are too reluctant to allocate substantial funds for this purpose in view of the high risks involved. Furthermore, the development of local venture capital to encourage such activities is still in its infancy in Malaysia. But equally important, FDI preferences and existing investment incentives generally encourage the importation and adoption of highly capital-intensive equipment and technology packages from the industrial countries. This not only discourages the adoption of more appropriate and indigenously developed technologies, but also undermines the capacity to innovate as the dependence on imported technologies is perpetuated.

Foreign direct investment in general thus tends to discourage meaningful technology transfer and development of domestic innovative capacity. Furthermore, most foreign-owned firms, particularly Japanese companies, do not view technology transfer as a priority in choosing to locate their manufacturing facilities in Malaysia, since their main rationale for establishing such facilities is to take advantage of cheap labour in the country (Fong Chan Onn, 1992: 193–217).

If there is any transfer at all, it is normally between the principal licensor or investor and its subsidiary or affiliate established in Malaysia. Technology transfer is thus internalized within the context of the transnational foreign firm's global production system. There is also a general reluctance on the part of most foreign firms to allocate R&D funds to their overseas subsidiaries, let alone affiliates, since most of these activities are controlled by their head offices in the industrial countries where R&D facilities have already been established in close consultation. As such, the technology linkages between FDI and locally owned enterprises are not as fully developed as in Japan (see Anuwar Ali and Muhd. Anuar Adnan, 1990: 151–71; Fong Chan Onn, 1990: 254–84; Ozawa, 1982: 7–53).

The availability of qualified and technically experienced scientists and engineers is an important determinant of the establishment of R&D facilities. As these personnel are scarce in Malaysia, the top management of foreign MNCs tends to perform mainly managerial and organizational, rather than innovative functions, unlike their counterparts in Japan or other industrialized countries. This has a stifling effect on the development of domestic entrepreneurship. Nevertheless, in an industrializing economy, it is vital for domestic entrepreneurship to take initiatives which will ensure that capital formation is directed to manufacturing activities.

However, this situation creates an industrial structure which leaves domestic entrepreneurship in areas such as services, including finance, trading, and small-scale manufacturing utilizing low-level technologies which contribute little towards a more independent industrializing process. This tendency is reinforced by other structural features characteristic of skewed, open economies like Malaysia, where high demand for luxury consumer goods tends to ensure that the most profitable areas of economic activity, to which domestic entrepreneurs are attracted, are commercial activities related to consumption. At the same time, the recent influx of FDI, including small and medium-scale Japanese enterprises, puts considerable pressure on domestic capital, crowding out enterprises, especially the weaker ones (Lim, 1990: 39–46).

In theory, technology transfer basically involves the purchase of technology from another country based on the mutuality of interests. For the importing country, there is a price to be paid for the technology import; hence, domestic industries need to assess whether the technology transferred is suitable in relation to their own technological capability and the actual technology components made available. The other costs of such transfers, including the indirect costs imposed by the technology supplier and opportunity costs, also need to be considered.

As mentioned earlier, an important rationale for encouraging FDI is the expectation that it would facilitate technology transfer. Technology acquisition is perceived as a crucial component in ensuring rapid economic growth and industrial progress, especially for the transformation of the economy into one with a larger industrial base. The flow of technology to domestic industries, as measured by the number of formal contractual agreements, has increased rapidly in recent years. However, one must note that these numbers are but a crude indicator of technology transfer, and may not reflect the actual extent of technology acquisition within domestic industries. It is difficult to measure with any certainty the complex nature of technology transfer. The increase in technology contracts may also reflect the strengthening of intellectual property rights in the last decade and greater attempts at enforcement as well as the increased significance of rent outflows in this connection.

During the 1980–92 period, the Ministry of International Trade and Industry (MITI) scrutinized and approved a total of 1,655 agreements. The number of such agreements averaged more than a hundred annually, except in 1982 and 1985; it reached a peak of 198 agreements in 1989. The trend suggests increasing reliance on foreign technology and FDI inflows into the manufacturing sector.

Slightly over half of all agreements approved since 1980 were in the form of technical assistance and know-how agreements, and another 17.0 per cent involved management and joint venture arrangements (see Table 13.4). While this suggests that considerable technology imports were needed by manufacturing enterprises, it also shows a shift away from the 'packaged' type of FDI and technology acquisition process, particularly apparent after 1985 when the number of trademarks and patents agreements increased substantially so that the share of such agreements was 17.2 per cent of the total by mid-1992.

Japan has contributed significantly to FDI inflow into Malaysia, accounting for the highest proportion (39.0 per cent) of all agreements signed during the 1985–92 period. In fact, the numbers increased substantially after 1987, partly owing to greater relocation of Japanese small and medium-scale enterprises. The other countries that were relatively important were the United Kingdom and the United States, accounting for 11.3 per cent and 10.8 per cent of the total respectively (see Table 13.5). The importance of Japan as a technology supplier is further reflected in the import of capital equipment or machinery. Since the mid-1970s, between 35 and 40 per cent of local machinery needs have originated from Japan. Only the United States appears to challenge the position of Japan in this respect. Even then, its share has been well below that of Japan. However, capital equipment or machinery alone does not constitute technology, representing as it does only that part of a technology embodied in hardware, while the remainder comprises disembodied knowledge which should best be acquired through enhancing indigenous technological capability.

Most of the agreements approved during 1980–92 were in the electronics and electrical industries (20.2 per cent), chemical industries (13.8 per cent) and transport equipment industry (10.6 per cent). Japanese investments in the transport equipment industry have been more visible during the last few years, growing in tandem with the ancillary industries stimulated by the national car project. These three industries account for more than 40 per cent of all agreements approved, thus reflecting the great need for technology transfer in these industries (see Table 13.6).

Under the Industrial Coordination Act of 1975, all manufacturing firms requiring project approval by the Ministry of International Trade and Industry (MITI) are also required to submit any agreement signed with any foreign company for approval. The main objectives of MITI are: first, to ensure that the agreements will not be prejudicial to the national interest; second, to ensure that the agreement will not impose unfair and unjustifiable restrictions on the Malaysian party; third, to ensure that the payments of fees, wherever applicable, will be commensurate with the level of technology to be transferred and will not have adverse effects on Malaysia's balance of payments; and last, to ensure a meaningful transfer of technology.

Even if the direct costs of technology transfer were not excessive,

Table 13.4 Types of technology agreements approved, 1980–92

Type of technology agreements	*1980*	*1981*	*1982*	*1983*	*1984*	*1985*	*1986*	*1987*	*1988*	*1989*	*1990*	*1991*	*1992*[b]	*Total*	*%*
Technical assistance and know-how	57	64	48	61	71	51	50	53	67	77	84	103	54	840	50.8
Management	13	6	10	13	10	6	10	5	7	12	5	6	1	104	6.3
Joint venture	14	22	14	14	17	9	19	11	11	15	15	11	5	177	10.7
Services	6	7	2	7	2	1	1	1	2	12	6	4	4	55	3.3
Trademarks and patents	4	8	8	7	1	19	33	30	44	53	36	37	5	285	17.2
Turn-key and engineering	5	5	4	4	6	—	1	—	1	—	1	1	—	28	1.7
Others[a]	15	19	8	25	12	10	9	10	18	29	8	3	—	166	10.0
Total	114	131	94	131	119	96	123	110	150	198	155	165	69	1,655	100.0

Note:

[a] Others include supply and purchase, sales, marketing and distribution.

[b] Figures for 1992 are for January–July only.

Source: Malaysian Industrial Development Authority (MIDA).

Table 13.5 Technology agreements by country of origin, 1980–92

Country	*1980*	*1981*	*1982*	*1983*	*1984*	*1985*	*1986*	*1987*	*1988*	*1989*	*1990*	*1991*	*1992*[a]	*Total*	*%*
Japan	32	35	33	46	39	33	38	37	54	87	82	92	37	645	39.0
UK	20	17	6	19	11	14	21	17	17	21	8	14	2	187	11.3
USA	11	14	10	18	12	13	12	12	22	23	10	18	4	179	10.8
India	5	4	4	4	2	6	1	—	2	2	1	1	1	33	2.0
West Germany	9	11	10	2	2	3	2	5	5	6	8	5	4	72	4.4
Australia	10	5	6	2	5	3	9	3	16	2	7	4	1	73	4.4
Hong Kong	9	2	3	2	7	4	7	7	5	9	3	6	2	66	4.0
Singapore	4	7	5	3	8	2	3	4	4	3	6	4	1	54	3.3
France	—	7	—	4	1	—	4	3	2	4	—	6	1	32	1.9
Italy	2	—	—	—	—	2	1	1	—	3	3	—	1	13	0.8
Panama	1	—	1	—	—	—	5	1	—	—	—	—	—	8	0.5
Switzerland	—	3	1	2	2	1	1	1	3	2	1	1	1	19	1.1
Norway	1	—	2	1	2	5	—	2	1	—	1	1	2	18	1.1
South Korea	—	—	2	4	6	1	3	1	—	3	10	2	7	39	2.3
Others	10	26	11	24	22	9	16	16	19	33	15	11	5	217	13.1
Total	114	131	94	131	119	96	123	110	150	198	155	165	69	1,655	100

Note:
[a] Figures for 1992 are forJanuary–July only.

Source: Malaysian Industrial Development Authority (MIDA).

Table 13.6 Technology agreements by industry groups, 1980–92

Industry	*1980*	*1981*	*1982*	*1983*	*1984*	*1985*	*1986*	*1987*	*1988*	*1989*	*1990*	*1991*	*1992*[a]	*Total*	*%*
Electronics and electrical	19	16	19	15	21	20	12	29	37	40	41	45	20	334	20.2
Fabricated metal	6	14	7	12	3	9	22	21	17	7	4	13	1	136	8.3
Chemical	11	21	5	15	17	16	15	18	29	27	24	21	10	229	13.8
Transport equipment	10	11	11	22	17	20	15	4	1	15	18	16	16	176	10.6
Food	14	15	4	21	6	10	8	8	16	21	4	6	1	134	8.1
Textiles	8	5	2	5	6	1	7	2	6	4	7	6	3	62	3.7
Basic metal	7	10	13	5	5	1	1	2	—	6	4	7	—	61	3.7
Wood and wood product	—	—	4	1	6	—	4	1	—	—	6	5	—	27	1.6
Pulp, paper, printing and publishing	—	—	—	—	—	3	4	1	3	—	4	4	—	19	1.1
Rubber and rubber products	8	14	2	7	5	4	13	8	22	18	8	10	4	123	7.4
Non-metallic mineral products	5	4	16	9	17	7	7	12	4	10	7	7	3	108	6.5
Hotel & tourist complex	4	2	4	8	7	4	4	1	2	6	3	8	1	54	3.3
Plastic	5	6	1	2	7	—	4	—	2	6	5	6	5	49	3.0
Others	17	13	6	9	2	1	7	3	11	38	20	11	5	143	8.6
Total	114	131	94	131	119	96	123	110	150	198	155	165	69	1,655	100.0

Note:
[a] Figures for 1992 are forJanuary–July only.

Source: Malaysian Industrial Development Authority (MIDA).

Malaysian-owned or managed firms might still be disadvantaged substantially if restrictive conditions are imposed by their technology suppliers. Restrictions on export outlets, the level of technology transferred, and domestic R&D activities are often observed. In view of the negative impact of such restrictions, MITI tries to minimize them to allow domestic manufacturers flexibility to expand their operations and become less dependent on their technology suppliers in the long run. For instance, if the licensors insist on export restrictions, MITI will demand that consent for sales outside the restricted territories should not be unreasonably withheld.

There have been cases in which the technology licensors insist on fixing the prices of the licensed products, while others insist that the local licensees purchase all material inputs and components from them at prices fixed by them. The second restriction appears to be more common. Such tie-in purchases undoubtedly strengthen the position of the technology suppliers, enabling them to maximize their gains by selling overpriced components, intermediate inputs, capital equipment and spare parts, thus creating opportunities for transfer pricing. Additionally, the obligation to purchase key inputs from the technology licensor enables the latter to monitor the activities of the local licensee, by constantly checking the production volume of the licensee, mainly for the purpose of determining royalty or technical fees.

In order to minimize both direct and indirect costs to local licensees, MITI has laid down a number of guidelines for the purchase of components or intermediate inputs. First, wherever possible, the licensee should determine alternative sources of supply, which obviously requires a reasonably high level of technology competence within domestic industries, to he acquired through more in-service training and R&D allocations. Second, any clause binding the licensee to purchase all imported components and supply through the technology supplier should be avoided. Third, if such a provision cannot be avoided, the licensee should stipulate that the prices are to be based on internationally competitive prices.

Despite all the above stipulations, MITI's experience suggests that it is difficult to ensure effective technology transfer given the Ministry's lack of experience, expertise and capacity to assess the 'technology content' imparted to domestic licensees or local personnel, not to mention the meticulous task of trying to keep track of the increasing number of technical assistance or joint venture agreements submitted for approval.

As in most developing countries, technology transfer regulations in Malaysia have not been utilized to screen for more 'appropriate technologies', partly because technology transfer arrangements are monitored and processed by administrators lacking the necessary technology background (also see Segal, 1987: 1–32). Nevertheless, even if the authorities are able to minimize the imposition of formal controls by the technology supplier, the latter may still be able to enforce restrictions under informal agreements with the local licensee (see MacBean and Balasubramanyam, 1978: 224). It is therefore critical that the country's technology assessment capability be upgraded to ensure that the negative effects of technology transfer arrangements can be minimized (Malaysia, 1991: 193).

The extent of technology transfer to domestic industries is largely influenced by the bargaining strengths of the foreign technology licensor and the local company or subsidiary or joint venture partner, and to a certain extent, MITI. Each of these parties has its own perception of the value of the technology and the method of transfer. MITI, reflecting the government's intention to ensure effective technology transfer to local companies, is desirous that technology be acquired at the lowest possible cost, basing its calculations on its perception of the long-term national interests, rather than immediate returns to either firm. Such calculations consider the social costs and benefits of each technology, linkages with other industries, use of domestic resources, the direct costs of technology (for example, royalties) as well as hidden costs, such as possible over-pricing by the technology licensor to the local licensee.

While this is the stated objective of the government, in practice, it invariably has to balance the desire for technology acquisition at the lowest possible cost and the need to attract FDI into the country. This has been the dilemma of many developing countries, where options are really limited. To a large degree, the fixing of royalty payments by MITI has been flexible in its attempt to encourage FDI into domestic industries and to accommodate the increasingly technological needs of these industries in the form of machinery, equipment and processes as well as managerial expertise and marketing know-how. With growing industrialization, this is inevitable because of the need for economic diversification and production of more technologically advanced products, for which the availability of technology is relatively scarce and costly. In such cases, technology suppliers are generally quite reluctant to transfer their technology under the recipient country's terms of technology regulations, particularly if they are accompanied by controls over FDI, including local equity conditions.

Technology payments required for new and increasingly complex technologies may have to be significantly higher than the maximum rates generally approved by MITI. The effective absorption of more complex technologies may also require longer periods, which may exceed the durations prescribed in the MITI guidelines. While regulatory controls continue to be applied for relatively mature and standardized technologies, the acquisition of the latest techniques in high-technology areas and special priority sectors is increasingly being encouraged and promoted through various incentives, including exemptions from regulatory norms and guidelines.

ANUWAR ALI

JAPANESE FOREIGN DIRECT INVESTMENT AND TECHNOLOGY TRANSFER

Despite the rapid pace of technological progress and global commercialization of technologies since the early 1970s, the actual choices open to locally owned enterprises as far as applied technologies are concerned may be rather limited. The bulk of imported technologies has its origins in large firms in a relatively small number of industrial countries, including Japan, which claim proprietary rights, and thus can impose obligations and restrictions upon locally owned and managed firms that utilize these technologies.

Such a high concentration of technology-generating capacity exists because most R&D activities are being undertaken by large firms in the industrial countries. Japan is one of those countries which has advanced rapidly in this regard during the last two decades. Although the international patent system was intended to protect inventors and thus encourage innovations, the system seems to work against the interests of firms in developing countries (see World Bank, 1979: 65–6). In such a scenario, it is certainly difficult for domestic industries in Malaysia to catch up with their counterparts in the industrial countries on the technological ladder. Most domestic firms have instead become increasingly dependent upon technology suppliers in the industrial countries for the supply of both mature and new technologies and technological enhancement, for both product and process development.

It must also be noted that technology transfer transactions, which take place under very imperfect market conditions, generally favour the technology suppliers of the industrial countries. This is even more true of transactions between the MNC technology supplier and its subsidiary or joint venture partner in Malaysia. This has become even more significant since 1986, with the increased pace of Japanese FDI flows, including those related to Japanese small and medium-scale industries. Apart from the oligopolistic nature of technology supply, the ability to assess the appropriateness of technology and assimilate imported technologies has generally been constrained by the lack of indigenous technological capability, particularly in locally owned or managed firms.

With a few exceptions, most domestic manufacturing firms lack sufficient knowledge of the technologies they hope to acquire from their potential suppliers because of the limited pool of suitably skilled personnel or expertise available. Furthermore, this has been complicated by the fact that the demand for highly skilled manpower in recent years has put the generally smaller, locally owned firms at an added disadvantage. Technology suppliers are reluctant to disclose full information about their products or processes to potential buyers until all transactions are completed to protect their proprietary value. Valuable technological knowledge is therefore not readily given away, but has to be purchased at a cost. Thus, local firms lacking technical expertise will generally agree to purchase technology without sufficient knowledge of its eventual functional value and actual performance.

The cost of purchasing a particular technology may also reflect the lack of the technical, legal and commercial expertise required to acquire relevant information on the technology and for evaluating the various options which may exist. This disadvantage is particularly felt by small and medium-scale enterprises, although their larger counterparts tend to have greater access, either because of their better organizational capacity or because they are in better bargaining positions *vis-à-vis* their technology suppliers.

The terms and conditions attached to a particular acquisition of technology are generally restrictive to local licensees on matters pertaining to export outlets, purchasing and pricing policies, technology diffusion and in-house R&D. One of the most common restrictions is prohibiting exports of goods produced under licensing or technical assistance agreements. There are also cases where licensees are prohibited from producing competitive products. Usually, they are required to secure prior approval from their Japanese licensors before they can sell intermediate products also covered under such agreements. There are cases where the licensees are required to sell their products only through marketing firms appointed by the licensors.

As indicated earlier, domestic firms are often also required to purchase materials from the licensors, which has significant implications for efforts to broaden the country's industrial base. According to the central bank's Survey of Private Investment in 1989, on average, 65 per cent of the total expenditure of manufacturing firms was incurred on the purchase of raw materials. Of this, a high proportion, averaging 53 per cent, represented imported materials (Bank Negara Malaysia, 1991: 47). For several industries, the import content of their raw material requirements was even higher, reaching 97 per cent for the electronics industry, 82 per cent for the paper products and printing industry, and 63 per cent for the transport equipment industry.

This is also a reflection of the fact that very few inter-firm linkages have developed between the FTZs and the rest of the national economy. Another consequence is that the possibilities for transfer pricing are great, thus negating the positive impact of FDI inflows (Bank Negara Malaysia, 1992: 60). In this regard, Takeshi Aoki (1992: 73–110) noted that:

> Foreign-owned firms operating in FTZs originally procured almost all their parts and materials from abroad. The ratio of local content in the electronics and electrical equipment industry was only 2 per cent, and in the textile industry only 0.5 per cent. Although FTZ firms contributed to the Malaysian economy in terms of expanded production, exports and job creation, they had almost no linkage with local firms in terms of procurement. FTZs were sometimes referred to as 'export-enclaves' or 'tenant industries'. From the standpoint of the input-output structure, firms in FTZs were independent, which means that

they did not procure materials from other firms. This situation changed rapidly in the latter half of the 1980s, when more foreign-owned firms established operations in Malaysia.

The supplier-buyer relationship in international technology purchases can also be viewed as a 'bilateral monopoly', where the price is largely determined through a series of negotiations between the two parties assumed to be of equal strength. If this is true, then the final negotiated price should be reflective of a price in a competitive market. However, if one party is in a weaker bargaining position, as is often the case for Malaysian firms, the final negotiated price would deviate from the competitive one in favour of the stronger party. Thus, where a licensee has less than sufficient mastery of and knowledge about the technology, the licensor is usually able to extract larger economic rents from the technology transaction.

In Malaysia, the largest proportion of technology transfer payments made by firms involves payments for new machinery and equipment. These purchases are normally made through the parent companies of foreign-controlled firms. While royalties are a popular mode of payment for contracts involving continuing technical assistance or the use of patents and trademarks, they are generally fixed within a range from 1 to 5 per cent of net sales. Lump-sum payments are also utilized for the payment of technology purchases, although this has not been encouraged by MITI. Another expense for technology transfer among Malaysian firms is the cost of overseas training for local staff, found to be common among Japanese firms.

In the event that a Malaysian firm lacks the necessary technical, financial and commercial expertise in technology transfer negotiations, it can be subjected to very disadvantageous terms or may pay unreasonably high prices. This appears to be the case among many small and medium-scale firms in Malaysia known to pay royalties even for expired patents. Thus, there is a clear need for programmes to educate small firms on various aspects of technology sourcing, purchase and negotiation. Although the recent launch of the Industrial Technical Assistance Fund (ITAF) to upgrade technological capabilities within domestic small and medium-scale enterprises is a step in the right direction, this fund has not been fully utilized by such firms.

The constraints faced by local firms are reinforced by other factors such as the Japanese companies' inherent strengths and their considerable negotiating and bargaining skills built up through extensive experience in selling technology. Hence, the bargaining position of Japanese companies tends to be greater at the beginning of a relationship, when the need for their resources and expertise is most critical. Once the manufacturing facilities are established, the recipient enterprise becomes more adept, while the services of the Japanese counterpart then become less indispensable. In such a situation, there could be a shift in the relationship in favour of the local enterprise. Even then, when Japanese interests maintain equity and management control, the relationship may not be so straightforward, as Japanese companies generally tend to have a higher proportion of Japanese personnel working in Malaysia relative to other comparable foreign companies.

Equity ownership by local capital in companies where FDI participates does not necessarily mean management control. With few exceptions, most FDI operations appear to be effectively controlled by the expatriate personnel from the parent companies. This is particularly apparent in companies dependent on foreign partners to provide technical know-how as well as market access. Thus, modest foreign equity participation may not fully reflect actual foreign control of and influence over domestic industries.

The indigenization of management, particularly at the second echelon, in some companies involving foreign FDI has been observed. Although most key posts are still usually held by expatriates, efforts have been made to Malaysianize the next most senior positions. However, this process is generally more advanced among US and European-based foreign firms, perhaps to minimize the costs of employing expatriates. In contrast, there is a tendency among Japanese companies to retain a higher proportion of expatriates at the senior level, partly to ensure that technological processes originating from the parent companies are well guarded (Fong Chan Onn, 1992: 193–217).

This can also be related to the extent of local decision-making autonomy *vis-à-vis* the global strategic framework of FDI operations generally. This issue has a crucial bearing on FDI investment and operating behaviour. Obviously, FDI with relatively centralized systems of decision-making will be less susceptible to leverage by local factors than those which practise mote decentralized styles of management.

Parent companies generally make decisions or give technical advice to local operations on matters of technology identification and the sourcing of capital equipment and machinery. It is obviously in the interest of parent companies to maintain this type of relationship, as in some cases, the parent companies are also the technology suppliers. This situation may also apply to local subsidiaries at the initial stage, when they still lack the expertise to determine their need for technology, capital equipment and machinery.

Also, a very significant proportion of international trade is intra-firm, where technology transfer offers more opportunities for transfer pricing manipulations. Vertically integrated firms (i.e. where the various stages of production from raw materials into finished goods are undertaken by the same firm or its subsidiaries) relocate their profits internationally by using transfer pricing, i.e. underpricing goods for export while selling them at market prices in foreign markets. Such behaviour seeks to minimize global tax burdens and avoid political risks. Thus, although technology may be transferable to a domestic enterprise, the costs can be very substantial. Such costs will, to a large extent, be determined by the technological gap between the foreign technology supplier and the domestic enterprise, and the socio-economic environment in the receiving country.

In such a situation, the pricing of the technology, or its components and peripherals, may not reflect competitive market prices, but may instead be dictated by transfer pricing considerations to minimize taxation on corporate income. Thus, in a country like Malaysia, where the withholding tax rate on repatriation of royalty payments under technical or licensing agreements is lower than the corporate profit tax rate, technology transfer may be over-priced to reduce such tax liabilities.

Malaysian firms' bargaining positions *vis-à-vis* Japanese technology suppliers with respect to technology transfer have tended to weaken in recent years due to intensifying competition among developing countries for FDI in general and 'high-tech' investments in particular (Djeflat, 1988: 149–65). In addition, 'sun-rise' industries characterized by rapid technological changes are unable to catch up, and as such, are much more vulnerable and dependent upon the Japanese MNCs to provide the latest improvements.

The existence of in-house R&D activities, as an indicator of a firm's technological capability, also presents one of the most effective opportunities for upgrading technical skills within such a firm. Generally, subsidiaries of foreign MNCs, including Japanese ones, which benefit directly from R&D conducted at parent companies, do not initiate substantial R&D locally. The subsidiaries simply took whatever product specifications and technology that were felt to be appropriate by the parent company. Most basic research, product design, product development and process development are conducted by the parent companies. One can only observe some product adaptation activity in some local subsidiaries. Local firms have also been lacking in R&D resources, although a few of the larger ones have small R&D units engaged in quality control or product and process adaptation.

In Malaysia, Japanese firms tend to rely more than their non-Japanese counterparts, on their parent companies for basic research and new product designs. Possible explanations for the lack of R&D in the Malaysian electronics industry (especially in the semiconductor industry), for example, are the following: the short product life-cycle, the high costs and economies of scale required for R&D, highly competitive prices, and the small domestic market. However, in domestically oriented firms, the Japanese companies have tried to diversify their R&D activities through process alteration, raw materials substitution, marketing research and product design. Although this is by no means conclusive, it seems that the R&D activities of domestically oriented import-substituting firms may, in the long term, contribute to technological independence.

ENHANCING DOMESTIC TECHNOLOGICAL CAPABILITY

The above observations suggest that Japanese FDI control production methods, leaving local subsidiaries or joint venture partners very limited control over technology. Most Japanese subsidiaries are technologically dependent on their parent companies for their requirements such as machinery, equipment, parts and components. Expenditures for such purchases usually constitute a large proportion of the costs of technology transfer, apart from other payments such as royalties and fees for foreign technical assistance and expertise.

Very little R&D is carried out by local subsidiaries as such activities are usually only conducted by parent companies, ostensibly to avoid duplication and to ensure economies of scale. Consequently, parent companies are usually the major, if not exclusive source of technical information and assistance. Such technological dependence is believed to be more pronounced among the subsidiaries or affiliates of Japanese MNCs compared with, say, American companies, e.g. in the electronics industry.

Given the increasing assymetric dependence of the ASEAN economies in general, and the Malaysian economy in particular, on Japan, it is in the long-term interest of Japan to create an environment that would make Japanese firms more responsive to the needs of Malaysian firms by enhancing the latter's capacity to absorb Japanese technology and by ensuring that technology transfer from Japan is less restrictive.

Domestic industries, on the other hand, must play an important complementary role, providing a more conducive environment for effective technology transfer. Another bottleneck is the relatively under-developed science and technology (S&T) infrastructure in Malaysia. For example, there is generally little interaction between industry and the universities and research institutes. Improved relations leading to a more productive, interdependent system require substantial planning and government initiative, involving the creation of a more supportive environment for creativity and innovation, making possible greater interaction among industrial entrepreneurs, scientists, technologists and researchers.

In Malaysia, policies on technology transfer, adaptation and development, especially in relation to FDI, are vague, involving exhortation, rather than implementation. Specific guidelines should be formulated to reduce ambiguity and to facilitate the concentration of scarce resources in priority areas of technology development. Technology agreements must be closely scrutinized to minimize restrictive clauses and to induce technology licensors to develop real technological capacities. Such capacity is indeed crucial to enhance the industrial base of the economy, and will require more positive contributions from Japanese and other foreign technology licensors.

Relevant policy-makers must specify priority industries and even types of firms for technological upgrading and development. Scarce resources cannot be spread too thin over too many sectors. Implementation of the Action Plan on Industrial Technology Development should concentrate efforts on target sectors, especially industries with potential comparative advantage. Focus must shift to potentially internationally competitive industries even if only of medium or small-scale and still domestic market-oriented, especially if resource-based. This should include specific measures to enhance development of new-technology based firms.

The weakness of the existing education system is considered a primary factor contributing to low technological capability in domestic industries. It has long been recognized that the constraints related to technology absorption capacity stem from this weakness as well as the limited in-house training available to Malaysian industrial labour (Svennilson, 1964: 405–28; Edwards, 1992). The reorientation of technical and vocational schools as well as university curricula and training are urgent necessities as industry needs have changed and become more complex with rapid technological progress. There is also a significant shortage of skilled middle-level human resources, requiring major reforms in Malaysian schooling to reduce the supply gap. A key problem has been the poor linkages between various academic institutions and local firms, although there seem to be numerous obvious opportunities for mutually beneficial collaboration. The government should therefore encourage such linkages by inducing joint ventures between private firms and state institutions involved in training and R&D.

Alternative schemes for expanding technical training must also be promoted. This may include provision of incentives, and perhaps even subsidies for training programmes in priority industries, besides expanding the supply of qualified personnel to disseminate skills to the industrial work force. Additionally, there must be more publication and wider dissemination of technical textbooks, handbooks and manuals, which can be important components of skill development and technology transfer processes.

Malaysian enterprises may initially have to depend on imported technologies, rather than be expected to develop their own know-how, but can subsequently proceed to develop appropriate adaptations. Adaptive activity may in turn encourage enterprises to establish in-house R&D facilities, thus generating their own technological capabilities. Technical progress can thus be either externally induced or achieved through 'learning by doing', which involves labour accumulating experience at the firm level. This process already takes place in Malaysian industries, although it is not widespread, and mainly involves the technically skilled. However, the occupational structure of the manufacturing sector hinders such technical progress since the semi-skilled and unskilled account for a large proportion of the Malaysian manufacturing labour force (Anuwar Ali, 1984: 44–59).

On-the-job training must therefore be emphasized as the primary mode for building a firm's capacity to apply new technologies. Foreign firms should also try to run their training programmes in Malaysia rather than at their parent-company headquarters as having such training on-site encourages testing and adaptation of the technologies to suit local requirements.

Fiscal incentives should be provided and improved to encourage technology transfer and R&D activities in Malaysia. These may include: special promotional incentives for foreign firms to be tied to a definite plan for technical human resource manpower development and skills upgrading; government subsidy for R&D projects on condition that the beneficiary firms initiate the projects, specify their needs and contribute a portion of the investment required for the R&D project; reduction of import duties on laboratory equipment and offering tax credits for investments or expenditure for R&D work in Malaysia; and to establish common user R&D facilities which firms in Malaysia could use. Such a facility would even permit small firms to use equipment which would normally be beyond their means, paying according to the extent of their usage.

It will be critical for Malaysian manufacturing enterprises to catch up with their counterparts in the more industrialized economies. This will pose a formidable challenge in the years ahead as, according to Freeman (1988: 67–84):

> Catching up and overtaking established technological leaders could pose formidable problems for imitators and aspirants for leadership, since they must aim at a moving target. It is no use simply importing today's technology from the leading countries, for by the time it has been introduced and efficiently assimilated the leaders have moved on and the relative position of the various countries may be unchanged or even worsened from the stand point of the followers.

CONCLUDING REMARKS

This chapter has identified and highlighted the major issues relating to FDI flows and technology transfer by Japanese firms in Malaysia. However, it is important to emphasize that, though the problems are due to the country's nascent industrial and technological base and the under-development of its human resources, they are also related to factors associated with the behaviour of capital and technology-exporting firms and countries. After spending substantial effort and investment on R&D and technology improvements, manufacturing enterprises expect to more than recover their costs to capture a certain economic rent. In this sense, the activities of Japanese FDI in Malaysia, or for that matter elsewhere, are logical extensions of their long-term strategic objectives to maximize profits and expand market control.

While it is crucial for Malaysia to try to reduce such problems with appropriate strategies as well as effective policy planning and implementation, it is equally important that advanced industrial countries like Japan also appreciate aspirations for technological enhancement. While the amount of FDI may be important to induce economic growth in the short term, the quality, type or nature of foreign investments will be crucial from a long-term perspective. This means that investments made by Japanese firms, for instance, must be viewed in terms of their impact on Malaysian technology acquisition and enhancement as well as inter-industry linkages within the domestic economy.

This would also mean that FDI must be selectively encouraged so that it will not stifle domestic investments or enterprises. The experiences of Japan and South Korea, for example, suggest that FDI was discouraged in favour of licensing arrangements for the purpose of domestic technological enhancement, as domination by foreign capital would have been detrimental for the development of domestic industrial enterprise (see Wade, 1988: 129–63; Amsden, 1989: 20–2).

REFERENCES

Amsden, A.H. (1989) *Asia's Next Giant: South Korea and Late Industrialization*, Oxford University Press, New York.

Anuwar Ali (1984) 'The Need for Technical Skills and Innovative Capacity: The Case of Manufacturing Industries in Malaysia', *Akademika*, 25.

Anuwar Ali and Muhd Anuar Adnan (1990) 'Technological Acquisition and Absorption Via Multinational Companies: The Malaysian Experience', *Jurnal Fakulti Ekonomi* 21, 22.

Aoki, T. (1992) 'Japanese FDI and the Forming of Networks in the Asia-Pacific Region: Experience in Malaysia and Its Implications', in Shojiro Tokunaga (ed.), *Japan's Foreign Investment and Asian Economic Interdependence*, University of Tokyo Press, Tokyo.

Bank Negara Malaysia (1991) *Quarterly Bulletin*, Vol. 6, No. 1, March–June.

Bank Negara Malaysia (1992) *Annual Report, 1991*, BNM, Kuala Lumpur.

Chen, E.K.Y and Wong, T. (1989) 'The Future Direction of Industrial Development in the Asian Newly Industrialized Economies', in Suh Jang-Won (ed.), *Strategies for Industrial Development: Concept and Policy Issues*, Asian and Pacific Development Centre, Kuala Lumpur and Korea Development Institute, Seoul.

Djeflat, A. (1988) 'The Management of Technology Transfer: Views and Experiences of Developing Countries', *International Journal of Technology Development*, Vol. 3, Issue 23.

Edwards, C. (1992) 'Foreign Investment and Industrialization in Malaysia', Paper presented at ISIS-HIID Conference on the Malaysian Economy, Kuala Lumpur, 1–3 June.

Federation of Malaysian Manufacturers (1990) 'Memorandum on National Economic Policy After 1990', *Forum 1990*, The Annual Economic and Business Journal of the Federation of Malaysian Manufacturers, Kuala Lumpur.

Fong Chan Onn (1990) 'Multinational Corporations in ASEAN: Technology Transfer and Linkages with Host Countries', in Soon Lee Ying (ed.), *Japan's Foreign Investment and Asian Economic Interdependence*, University of Tokyo Press, Tokyo.

Fong Chan Onn (1992) 'Foreign Direct Investment in Malaysia: Technology Transfer and Linkages by Japan and Asian NIEs', in Shojiro Tokunaga (ed.), *Japan's Foreign Investment and Asian Economic Interdependence*, University of Tokyo Press, Tokyo.

Freeman, C. (1988) 'Technology Gaps, International Trade and the Problems of Smaller and Less Developed Economies', in C. Freeman and B.A. Lundvall (eds.), *Small Countries Facing the Technological Revolution*, Pinter, London.

George, R.L. (1988) 'Potential NICs Move Upmarket', *Asian Finance*, Vol. 14, No. 11, 15 November.

Go Iwaki (1992) 'SMI Development and the Sub-Contracting System in Japan', in

Kim Seung Jin and Suh Jang-Won (eds), *Co-operation in Small and Medium-Scale Industries in ASEAN*, Asian and Pacific Development Centre, Kuala Lumpur.

Ikeda, M. (1991) 'A Comparative Study of International Subcontracting Systems: The Automative Parts Industries of the USA, the UK, France and Japan', in K.Shibagaki, M. Trevor and T. Abo (eds), *Japanese and European Management: Their International Adaptability*, University of Tokyo Press, Tokyo.

Kosaka, M. (1989) *Japan's Choices: New Globalism and Cultural Orientation in an Industrial State*, Pinter, London.

Lim Imran (1990) 'A Domestic Investment Initiative: Justifications and Strategies', *Forum 1990*, The Annual Economic and Business Journal of the Federation of Malaysian Manufacturers, Kuala Lumpur.

MacBean, A.I. and Balasubramanyam, VN. (1978) *Meeting the Third World Challenge*, Macmillan, London.

Malaysia (1991) *Sixth Malaysia Plan, 1991–1995*, Government Printers, Kuala Lumpur.

Nakanishi, H. (1990) 'Japan's Trade in the Asia Pacific Region', in Susumu Awanohara (ed.), *Japan's Economic Role in the Asia Pacific Region*, Centre for Asian Pacific Studies, Hong Kong.

Organisation for Economic Cooperation and Development (1988) *The Newly Industrializing Countries: Challenge and Opportunity for OECD Countries*, OECD, Paris.

Ozawa, T. (1982) 'The Role of Transnational Corporations in the Economic Development of the ESCAP Region: Some Available Evidence from Recent Experience', in ESCAP/UNCTC Publication Series B, No. 2, United Nations, Bangkok.

Parry, T.G. (1988) 'The Role of Foreign Capital in East Asian Industrialization, Growth and Development', in H. Hughes (ed.), *Achieving Industrialization in East Asia*, Cambridge University Press, Cambridge.

Segal, A. (1987) 'Learning by Doing', in A. Segal (ed.), *Learning by Doing: Science and Technology in the Developing World*, Westview Press, Boulder, Colorado.

Svennilson, I. (1964) 'The Transfer of Industrial Know-How to Non-Industrialized Countries', in K. Berril (ed.), *Economic Development: With Special Reference to East Asia*, Macmillan, London.

Thurow, L. (1992) *Head to Head: The Coming Economic Battle Among Japan, Europe and America*, Nicholas Brealey, London.

Tsuraoka, D. (1990) 'Taiwanese Investors Flock to Low-Wage Neighbours', *Far Eastern Economic Review*, 19 April.

Wade, R. (1988) 'The Role of Government in Overcoming Market Failure: Taiwan, Republic of Korea and Japan', in H. Hughes (ed.), *Achieving Industrialization in East Asia*, Cambridge University Press, Cambridge.

World Bank (1979) 'International Technology Transfer: Issues and Policy Options', Staff Working Paper No. 344, July, Washington DC.

14

INDONESIA'S GREAT LEAP FORWARD?

Technology Development and Policy Issues

Hal Hill

Technological development and technology policy are vital to Indonesian development in the 1990s and beyond. They are the subject of much public commentary and debate, there are major analytical and policy questions to be resolved, and the Indonesian government already allocates considerable resources to these activities. The purpose of this paper is to survey and assess Indonesia's industrial technological capability, and to highlight key policy issues, in the context of the large analytical and empirical literature on this subject for developing countries. Indonesia is a latecomer by East Asian industrial standards, and this is reflected in various technology indicators The paper suggests directions for effective technology policy.

INTRODUCTION

Technology policy, in all its dimensions, is one of the most debated topics in Indonesia. Much of its prominence is the result of the high public profile of the Minister of State for Research and Technology, Professor B. J. Habibie. After the President, he is Indonesia's longest-serving Cabinet member, and in the past decade he has launched several widely publicised initiatives designed to accelerate the country's acquisition of advanced technology and scientific know-how. The Minister has clearly enunciated his impatience with more orthodox approaches to economic development, espousing instead the case for an explicitly interventionist technology policy (Habibie 1986). Especially since the appointment of the current Cabinet, the Indonesian media has highlighted alleged differences in approach between the Minister and the group of economists who have dominated economic policy making since 1966.[1] Many argue that the Minister's approach is in the political ascendancy and will have a strong impact on future economic policy.

Beyond these political economy considerations, there are economic reasons

Source: *Bulletin of Indonesian Economic Studies*, Vol. 31(2), August 1995, pp. 83–124.

why technology policy and development are important. First, while Indonesia will continue to be a net technology importer for the foreseeable future, some basic technological competence is necessary simply to assess, assimilate and diffuse imported technology. Certain segments of the international market for technology are inherently imperfect, and informed choices require a measure of know-how. Second, Indonesia is entering a new phase of its export-oriented strategy in which it must establish a niche between the advanced NIEs, rapidly growing in technological sophistication, and the lower-income economies of China, South Asia, Vietnam, and others. If it is not to compete primarily on the basis of wage levels for unskilled labour, it must develop more efficient and sophisticated supply-side capabilities, among which is a stronger technology base. Third, there are long lead times in the establishment of broad-based technological capacity, both in the training phase and in the acquisition of industrial experience. Decisions about the appropriate levels of skill and technology to support a large and sophisticated industrial structure next century need to be taken a decade or more in advance. Finally, it is likely that the government will have to play the major role in technological upgrading, for reasons to be explained shortly. The state budget for research and technology is already sizeable, and there are choices to be made about the allocation of these resources. For these reasons, both economic and political, technology policy will continue to be an important topic of public debate during Repelita VI and beyond.

The literature on this subject, small but expanding, has not always focused on these central questions. The purpose of this article is to survey that literature, to sketch Indonesia's technology capabilities using scant empirical data,[2] and to offer some prognostications on policy options. The topic is large: a single article can only hope to introduce some of its dimensions and complexities, both analytical and policy-related, and to highlight some of the principal issues. Detailed research is needed on many of these. The paper's focus is restricted to the manufacturing sector. Indonesia has of course a long tradition of agricultural research,[3] and there has been some examination of technology issues in the services sector (see especially McKendrick 1992b on financial services).

The next section of the paper adumbrates some of the analytical and conceptual issues and briefly surveys a portion of the international literature on the subject. Some indicators of Indonesia's technological capability are presented, followed by a review of the limited case study literature on the subject, a discussion of the policy framework and an elaboration of policy issues. The final section summarises the conclusions of the paper.

CONCEPTUAL ISSUES AND LITERATURE REVIEW

The principal economic rationale for government intervention to develop a country's technological capability has to do with the latter's 'public good' characteristics (Lall 1992; Pack and Westphal 1986). Left to the market, there is likely to be under-investment in activities for which private agents are unable to appropriate fully the returns from their investments. Such investments tend to enter the public domain quickly, a process facilitated in part by classic 'free-rider' problems (Krugman 1990). The returns are diluted especially in developing countries by a weak legal system, which is unable to protect intellectual property rights. High inter-firm worker mobility, particularly for those whose skills are in short supply, exacerbates the problem, since firms are reluctant to invest in R&D programs if staff embodying these investments are likely to quit before returns can be appropriated. These problems are the more serious in an economic and political environment characterised by uncertainty. In the best of environments, investments in R&D are highly uncertain and generally slow-yielding. Where private agents heavily discount future earnings, owing, for example, to high real interest rates, lack of credible macroeconomic management, or political uncertainty, the incentives to invest will be weaker still. Thus, while reported rates of return on industrial R&D in the few studies to investigate the subject in developing countries (some of which are summarised in Evenson and Westphal 1994, p. 89) are generally high, these factors probably explain the limited scale of investment. In addition, the inability of firms to appropriate fully the returns on these investments results in social rates exceeding the private rates.

The literature on technological development draws on a variety of disciplines and approaches. Institutional economics is useful for its explanation of the role of government policies in promoting, and shaping the pattern of, R&D expenditures. Defence, higher education, science, and health programs are particularly significant in this regard. Business economics and business history shed much light on the development of a country's industrial technology base, particularly among major corporations. Industrial structure may be influential, to the extent that larger firms are more likely to invest in R&D. Foreign investment policy is important in shaping international technology flows.

The new growth theories, with their emphasis on the determinants of long-term growth, have revived interest in technological change and technology policy.[4] 'The suspicion that [growth differentials among countries] may have something to do with technology has been around for a long time', as Fagerberg (1994, p. 1,147) observes. But the new theories have shifted attention away from the approach of the earlier neoclassical modelling. Although these theories have yet to develop powerful policy relevance, empirical refinement is pushing in this direction, examining for example the relative growth-stimulating effects of investments in R&D versus schooling, and measuring the R&D spillovers from international trade and investment, especially that with a 'north-south dimension' (Coe, Helpman and Hoffmaister 1994).

In its simplest formulation, neoclassical growth theory provides little assistance in understanding the process of technological acquisition, innovation and dissemination. As Lall (1990, 1992) observes, this literature tends to assume away the most interesting questions: in reality, technology does not fall like 'manna from heaven'. Not all firms in a given industry are on the same production function. Adaptation and assimilation are not costless exercises, especially when they occur across international boundaries.

Neoclassical theory performs better, however, in shedding light on the course of technological development. For example, evolutionary models, generally Hecksher–Ohlin–Samuelson in orientation, stress changing comparative advantage under the impetus of growth and capital accumulation. These models trace the evolution of an economy from a reliance on natural resource-based and labour-intensive activities to development of more skill and technology-intensive industries.[5] A refinement of this genre of evolutionary models was introduced by Vernon (1966), whose product life cycle hypothesis defines more precisely the technology component in the evolutionary process. Nevertheless, this body of literature does not consider many of the fundamental technology questions to be addressed in this paper. For these we need to draw on more detailed country and firm-level studies, many of which employ intensive field research.[6]

Two related strands of the technology literature as it applies to developing countries deserve emphasis. The first is that these countries rarely sponsor and initiate 'fundamental' research, in the sense of inventing products and processes. Their principal concern is the acquisition of technology, and its modification and adaptation to the local environment. The 'D' is typically far more important than the 'R' in this context (Dahlman, Ross-Larson and Westphal 1987, p. 774). Even in the USA, it is estimated that just 8% of the country's R&D expenditure is allocated to 'basic research', a far smaller share than that of 'applied research' (25%) or 'development' activities (67%) (Rosenberg 1994, p.13). For developing countries the proportion allocated to development activity would be higher still.

Second, as a corollary, since about 96% of the global R&D effort is concentrated in OECD economies, all developing countries are large net technology importers. Indeed, notwithstanding the recent emergence of new sources of technology exports (for example, the Asian NIEs), one might be tempted to add 'importers from the G7 countries', since the latter are estimated to account for 92% of R&D within the OECD group (Coe, Helpman and Hoffmaister 1994, p. 1). The issues then are to select among different channels of technology imports, and to devise the most appropriate strategy to maximise technology imports, consistent also with the development of local absorptive, adaptive and screening capacities.[7]

Technology policy needs to be assessed as part of a country's broader socio-economic policy regime. The link to education and training policy is clear enough. There are also important connections to the trade and incentive regime. Import protection is sometimes viewed as a prerequisite for the development of local technology capacity. This argument overlooks the fact that externalities are best promoted at their source, and through subsidy rather than protection. Protection is just as likely to lead to inefficiency and a failure to innovate.[8] A strategy of self-sufficiency in goods or services may prove costly, especially if it is durable and is applied indiscriminately.[9] A third connection is that between macroeconomic management and technological effort. A predictable economic policy environment and conservative macroeconomic management will almost certainly be conducive to technological development. Low inflation, internationally competitive real interest rates, credible macroeconomic policies, and secure property rights, are the foundation on which the private sector can plan long-term, risky investments which include a significant technological component.

Other historical and institutional factors are important in shaping a country's technological evolution. A long and early commitment to extensive public education is one such factor: its presence in South Korea has arguably enabled that country to pursue somewhat more 'autarchic' policies towards foreign investment and technology than other countries at similar levels of development. Past investments may influence current technology choices. Both India and China embarked on costly heavy industry programs in the post-independence era. These investments were uneconomic, but they represent sunk costs and both countries now possess some technological advantage as a result. A third factor of relevance is size. There are scale economies and complementarities in the R&D effort, so that large countries might be expected to be able to support a more extensive R&D infrastructure than smaller ones. Fourth, it has been demonstrated that defence expenditure is generally R&D intensive, particularly if it involves the development of a local manufacturing capacity. Countries which have allocated above average support to defence might, other things being equal, have a stronger technological base, albeit one developed at considerable cost. Finally, countries which display a high propensity to save are more likely to be technologically progressive, to the extent that the resulting high levels of capital accumulation embody larger quantities of recent technology in the capital stock; in the case of the NIEs, high savings rates have been associated recently with significant instances of overseas investments in high income countries motivated by 'reverse engineering' considerations.[10]

It might be noted in passing that only one (or at most two) of these factors—size (and perhaps the savings rate)—might be regarded as predisposing Indonesia towards an advanced state of technology development relative to its per capita income. We shall return shortly to this question in assessing the country in comparative technological perspective.

There is no single 'path' to technological development. Within Asia, for example, the policy experiences have differed markedly. The Korean regime is distinctive for its huge investments in education, its large, heavily promoted business conglomerates (the *chaebol*), its open policy towards technology imports, but its restrictive policy (until recently) towards both foreign ownership and merchandise imports.[11] Its R&D expenditure as a percentage of GDP has consistently been higher than that of the other Asian NIEs, and rose sharply from 0.6% to 2% over the course of the 1980s. Reverse engineering has been important in certain industries, both through imitation and direct investment abroad. India too has placed high priority on R&D, in the context of a restrictive trade and investment regime (Lall 1987). However, its experience differs from Korea's in several respects: there has been little emphasis on export orientation until the 1990s; it has a large, poorly performing state enterprise sector; barriers to domestic competition have been intense, through a variety of reservation and protection schemes; and for most of its independence period the major international supplier of technology was Russia. As a result of this promotional effort, and the country's size, it possesses pockets of international excellence. But much of its technological base is outmoded, slow to innovate, and uncompetitive internationally.

The Indonesian experience more closely resembles that of Thailand.[12] The two are latecomers as industrialising nations, the national technological effort is small, and private sector R&D is minuscule. Thailand is more open to international investment and trade, and therefore to new technologies. The more recent studies concur that Thai manufacturing firms have generally mastered operational technologies, for example, while its strength in agribusiness is acknowledged. Yet in other respects the country's technological capability, in areas such as assimilation, adaptation and innovation, may be little ahead of Indonesia's, especially given its lower secondary education enrolment ratio and its smaller state enterprise sector. Some of the Thai literature concludes that the spillover benefits from foreign investment are inhibited by the weak domestic technology base.

INDICATORS OF INDONESIA'S TECHNOLOGICAL CAPABILITY

This section provides an overview of Indonesia's technology base, drawing on a range of secondary data sources. It is difficult to define precisely, much less measure, a country's technological effort and capability. This is especially so in Indonesia where the relevant data base is rudimentary. Until the appearance of *Scientific and Technology Indicators of Indonesia 1993*, for example, there was no collection of basic indicators, and even this publication, welcome though it is, offers little more than a preliminary sketch. Government expenditures in this area are not decomposed into analytically useful categories. Moreover, international comparisons are fraught with danger. Nevertheless, it is possible to provide a general picture of trends, and some international comparisons, for a range of crude 'input' and 'output' indicators.

First, some international comparisons (Table 14.1). As would be expected,

Table 14.1 Education and scientific indicators, selected Asian countries, *c.* 1990[a]

	Indonesia	*India*	*Korea*	*Malaysia*	*Philippines*	*Singapore*	*Thailand*
R&D indicators							
R&D expenditure as % of GNP	0.2	0.9	1.9	0.1	0.1	0.9	0.2
R&D expenditure per capita, $	0.9	2.7	75.2	2.1	0.7	68.1	1.9
Scientific publications in English[b]	60	n.a.	490	163	n.a.	315	206
Patent applications, 1980–91[c]	12	n.a.	6,629	406	141	812	144
Scientific personnel							
Scientists & engineers in R&D:							
Number ('000)	32	85	57	n.a.	5	3	n.a.
Index, 1970 = 100	185	177	1,005	n.a.	89	411	n.a.
Total personnel in R&D, 1984 ('000)	36	222	74	n.a.	10	5	n.a.
Scientists & engineers/ million population							
Total	1,280	3,329	2,426	1,801	36,649	15,849	491
Engaged in R&D	183	109	1,325	n.a.	90	1,287	104
Public expenditure on education							
% of GNP, 1992	1.9	n.a.	2.9	5.8	2.9	5.2	3.2
% of govt. expenditure, 1992	9.8	n.a.	16.2	19.6	15.0	22.9	21.1
% on tertiary sector	27.4	18.0	9.9	16.5	17.1	32.0	12.5
Tertiary education							
Enrolments as % of age group, 1991	10	n.a.	40	7	28	n.a.	16
% in science & technology, 1987[d]	14.0	27.6	21.3	13.0	22.6	51.4	n.a.
% of 22/23-year-olds with science-engineering degree, 1990	0.4	1.1	6.0	n.a.	n.a.	4.2	n.a.

Notes:
[a] Unless otherwise indicated, most data refer to a year within the period 1987–90. Where a year is indicated in the row heading, for some countries the data refer to one year before or after the specified year.
[b] Published in internationally recognised outlets.
[c] As reported to the World Intellectual Property Organization.
[d] Includes enrolments in engineering, mathematics, computer science, and natural sciences.

Sources: UNESCO, *Statistical Yearbook*, Paris, various issues: World Bank, *World Development Report*, Washington DC, various issues: STAID (nd).

Indonesia's technological and educational indicators generally lag behind those of its neighbours. Nevertheless, owing to its size, its scientific and industrial infrastructure is larger than that of some smaller countries in the comparison. Its R&D expenditures, as a percentage of GDP, are much below those of the NIEs and India, although comparable to shares in ASEAN excluding Singapore. Per capita, they are the lowest among the seven countries, except the Philippines. Complementing these 'input' indicators in the table are two 'output' indicators: in both scientific publications and patent applications, Indonesia ranks far lower than the other countries for which data are available. These indicators are crude,[13] but there is little doubt that the rankings are broadly accurate.[14]

Indonesia's stock of scientific personnel engaged in R&D is larger by regional standards, and has been growing quite quickly. However, its research establishment is much smaller than those of Korea and India, and the rate of increase since 1970 in part reflects catch-up by a latecomer. Adjusted for population size, Indonesia's pool of skilled personnel is larger only than that of Thailand in the comparison, although the numbers actively engaged in R&D (another empirically slippery concept) compare favourably to those of India and the other lower income ASEAN countries.

Indonesia's expenditure on public education appears surprisingly small in view of the major achievements since 1970.[15] Its expenditure as a percentage of both GDP and the budget is significantly below that of the other countries. Low teacher salaries—the major component of the education budget—may be part of the explanation; some educational expenditures may be excluded from the data, such as those through the Inpres schemes or the Department of Religion,[16] and the large and rapidly expanding private education sector is of course not included. Nevertheless, the figures do support the widespread view that educational expansion under the New Order has tended to be a low-cost, low-quality process. Tertiary enrolments are far below those of Korea and the Philippines; the latter's definition of 'tertiary' is, however, somewhat elastic, and the Indonesian figure is not too different from those of its other ASEAN neighbours. Perhaps more disturbing is the lower proportion of Indonesians enrolled in, or graduating from, science and technology courses. These figures confirm the popular perception that much of the expansion in Indonesian tertiary education has occurred in courses of low vocational content, such as Sospol (social and political science) and *sastra* (humanities) courses. According to data cited by Thee (1994a, pp. 26–7), the proportion of Indonesian students enrolled in science-engineering degrees in the US is also comparatively low.

Tables 14.2 and 14.3 illustrate in more detail Indonesian government priorities in science, technology and research. Since 1975 these expenditures have generally been within the range 0.9–1.3% and 0.2–0.3% of total government expenditure and GDP respectively (Table 14.2). The figures refute the perception that there has been a pronounced shift in emphasis

Table 14.2 Indonesian government expenditure on science, technology and research, 1975–92

	Expenditure (Rp billion, current prices)				*(3) as % of total government expenditure*	*(3) as % of GDP*	*(1) as % of total development expenditure*
	Development (1)	*Routine (2)*	*Total (3)*	*Total at 1985 prices*[a] *(4)*	*(5)*	*(6)*	*(7)*
1975	21	4	25	99	0.9	.21	1.6
1976	28	7	35	117	1.0	.23	1.4
1977	38	9	47	138	1.1	.26	1.7
1978	42	12	54	144	0.9	.25	1.7
1979	58	14	72	144	0.9	.24	1.7
1980	87	21	108	182	0.9	.25	1.7
1981	95	28	123	188	0.9	.22	1.4
1982	128	31	159	225	1.1	.26	1.7
1983	303	34	337	397	1.8	.45	3.1
1984	190	37	227	237	1.2	.26	1.9
1985	274	47	321	321	1.4	.33	2.5
1986	181	59	240	221	1.1	.23	2.2
1987	178	61	239	192	0.9	.19	1.9
1988	721	72	793	576	2.4	.56	5.9
1989	334	81	415	282	1.1	.24	2.4
1990	554	96	650	418	1.3	.33	2.8
1991	431	115	546	331	1.1	.24	2.0
1992	586	145	731	405	1.3	.28	2.4

Note:
[a] Deflated by the wholesale price index, excluding petroleum.

Source: *Lampiran Pidato Kenegaraan*, various issues.

towards technology projects over this period: science, technology and research expenditure as a proportion of both GDP and the budget was almost identical in 1991 to that in 1976 and 1977. The major part of official expenditure in this area occurs in the development budget. Both routine and development components grew steadily from the mid 1970s, the process of real increases being interrupted only during the recession and fiscal austerity of the mid 1980s. The routine budget, comprising mainly salaries, continued to grow in nominal terms through this period. Most of the fluctuations occurred in the development budget, with the peaks in 1983 and 1988 being the result of 'lumpy' aid projects. During the mid to late 1980s in particular, the share of expenditure on these items which was rupiah-funded fell sharply. In part this reflected general trends in the budget. But it is also indicative of donor priorities.

The Repelita (Five Year Plan) documents reveal a major shift in emphasis within the sector since the mid 1970s (Table 14.3). From Repelita II to Repelita V the share of 'science and technology' increased sharply at the expense of

Table 14.3 Science, technology and research expenditure, Repelita II–VI (% of total planned development expenditure)

Sector	*Repelita* II 1974/5–78/9	*Repelita* III 1979/80–83/4	*Repelita* IV 1984/5–88/9	*Repelita* V 1989/90–93/4		*Repelita* VI 1994/5–98/9
Science & technology	10.5	12.8	43.4	57.1		
Research	89.5	87.2	56.6	42.9		
Agriculture & irrigation	34.2	24.7	17.3	17.7	Production technology	27.2
Industry & mining	13.3	6.6	5.7	3.3	Basic & applied science	14.7
Communication & transport	10.9	3.5	7.2	1.1	Institutional infrastructure	20.2
General	8.3	21.8	10.4	9.1	Statistics & information	16.8
Statistics	11.4	6.3	10.2	7.9	Shipping	15.9
Other	11.4	24.3	5.8	3.8	Aerospace	5.2
Total	100	100	100	100		100
(Rp billion)	(101.3)	(477.6)	(1,757.7)	(2,634.2)		(3,627.1)

Source: Repelita II–VI.

'research'. The large increase in the 'science' share during the 1980s is principally the result of the government's infrastructure construction program, in particular laboratory facilities at Puspiptek (The Center for Science and Technology Development) in 1987–89. Although these categories (science, technology and research) are not easily separable analytically, the figures do reveal the growing impact of Professor Habibie as Minister for Research and Technology, and a contrast with the approach of his predecessor, Professor Sumitro. Within the shrinking research component, agriculture has always received the highest priority. For Repelita VI the subsector's categories have been altered, and are no longer consistent with the earlier series. Reflecting the Minister's priorities, transport and telecommunications now receive a higher share.

The data in Tables 14.2 and 14.3 are at best illustrative for a number of reasons. An unknown, almost certainly substantial, volume of expenditure occurs off-budget, that is, it is not recorded in the government's budget statement. This applies particularly to the 'strategic industry' investments,[17] where expenditure is understated further by numerous implicit subsidies. Moreover, the data almost certainly do not record the extent of R&D activity in government departments, state enterprises and universities. STAID (nd, p. 46) cites estimates that perhaps only 60% of the government's science and technology expenditure is recorded formally in this category.

Within the government's budget there are separate allocations for its six major research institutions: Batan (National Atomic Energy Agency), Bakosurtanal (National Coordinating Agency for Survey and Mapping), BPPT, BPS (Central Bureau of Statistics), Lapan (National Institute of Aeronautics and Space) and LIPI (Indonesian Institute of Sciences).[18] The allocations across agencies vary over time, but reflecting its political and strategic importance, BPPT is the major recipient: in 1991/92, of a total agency budget of Rp 386 billion, it received Rp 242 billion (63%). The next largest recipient was Batan (12%). No other agency received more than 10%. Significantly, BPPT captured about 87% of the total foreign aid funding for these institutions.

A disaggregation of the BPPT budget sheds further light on the government's priorities. The Agency's development budget for 1991/92 was allocated across research and development (50.2%), human resource development (34.4%), construction (10.9%) and institution building (4.5%). Over 91% of the R&D budget was funded by foreign aid, and these funds were allocated exclusively to energy and defence research. Much of the human resource development budget was devoted to training programs abroad. The 'institution building' component consists of grants to research projects. Its total budget of Rp 12 billion was stretched across approximately 100 small research projects, resulting in an average grant of $60,000 per project, and about $3,000 per scientist involved; this amount covers not only salaries, but also equipment and supplies, transportation, and other expenses (Bishry

Table 14.4 Government contribution to R&D, 1990 (%of total)

	Japan	*Korea*	*Singapore*	*Taiwan*	*India*	*Indonesia*[a]
Source	16	16	46	45	77	80
Performer	8	4	25	17	77	62

Note:
[a] 1991.

Source: STAID (nd).

1992, pp. 14–16). The equivalent expenditure in Korea at around this time was estimated to be about $50,000 per scientist. Clearly the current budget is inadequate and spread too thinly across projects.

The data in Tables 14.2 and 14.3 also exclude private sector R&D activity. This is known to be small, a conclusion confirmed empirically for the first time by the STAID survey. The Indonesian government contribution to R&D activity was the highest among the six countries compared, marginally exceeding even that of India, although as 'performer' the Indian figure was higher (Table 14.4). These figures are not surprising: in the early stages of development, governments have a large role to play in initiating R&D activities, a point emphasised in the Evenson and Westphal typology (1994, p. 44). Indonesia's private sector, still in its infancy and dominated by a short-term investment mentality, could hardly be expected to be a major investor in R&D, although there are signs that this is changing. An important characteristic of all three NIEs in the Table 14.4 sample is the much lower share of the government as performer than as funder. It is in this area that Indonesia has made less progress, although its 'performer' share is also lower.

An important explanation for the large government role is that most science graduates find employment in the public sector, reflecting a more general pattern in which graduates tend to seek public sector employment (Jones 1994). According to STAID estimates, only 13% and 15% of science diplomates and graduates respectively were employed in the private sector (excluding higher education) in 1991 (Table 14.5). The proportion is smaller still for advanced graduates (Masters and Doctorates), among whom the major R&D effort is likely to be concentrated. For these groups, the private sector (again excluding higher education) employed just 5–6% of the total. By far the largest proportion of science graduates (71% of the total) and diplomates (87%) are employed directly in the government sector. Yet the percentage of both groups engaged in R&D activity is very low, much lower than the shares in the private sector and in higher education (Table 14.6).

What other indicators shed light on trends in Indonesia's technological capabilities? The core data base above is so weak that it is useful briefly to survey a number of indirect, 'revealed' yardsticks. Each provides at best only circumstantial evidence, but together they offer a somewhat richer picture of

Table 14.5 Employment of science personnel[a] by sector, 1991[b]

Education level[c]	*Sector (% of total)* *Govt.*	*Private*	*Higher education*	*Total* *%*	*('000)*
Diplomates	87	13	n	100	(114.5)
S1	71	15	13	100	(113.8)
S2	61	6	33	100	(7.2)
S3	76	5	18	100	(4.2)
Graduates (S1 + S2 + S3)	71	15	15	100	
('000)	(88.5)	(18.3)	(18.4)		(125.2)
Graduates + diplomates	78	14	8	100	
('000)	(187.6)	(33.7)	(18.5)		(239.7)

Note:
[a] Includes graduates in natural sciences and engineering.
[b] Figures may not sum to 100 owing to rounding: 'n' indicates negligible, less than 1%.
[c] Diploma refers (in most cases) to 3-year post-secondary courses, S1 to undergraduate university degrees, S2 to masters degrees (2 years full-time study beyond S1), and S3 to doctorates.

Source: As for Table 14.4.

Table 14.6 Employment of science graduates[a] by sector and activity, 1991[b] (% of total)

Activity	*Sector (% of total)* *Govt.*	*Private*	*Higher education*	*Total* *%*	*('000)*
Graduates (S1 + S2 + S3)[c]					
R&D	6	20	42	14	(16.9)
Production engineering	0	59	0	9	(10.8)
Other	94	21	58	78	(97.6)
Total	100	100	100	100	(125.2)
Diplomats[c]					
R&D	1	13	33	3	(3.4)
Production engineering	0	73	0	10	(11.2)
Other	99	15	67	87	(100.0)
Total	100	100	100	100	(114.5)

Source and notes: As for Table 14.5.

the trends. The first is trends in manufacturing productivity. Real labour productivity, that is, manufacturing value added per worker deflated by the relevant wholesale price index series, has risen appreciably (Hill 1995, ch. 8; Szirmai 1994). This is at least a crude indicator of rising industrial competence. Over the period 1975–90 it rose by approximately 250% for non-oil manufacturing. For each 2-digit ISIC group there was at least a doubling, while in a few industries the increases were much larger. Some of these reflect fundamental transformations in the industry. Examples include basic metals, where new steel and aluminium facilities completely transformed the industrial landscape. In others, such as textiles, the increases reflected major technological innovation, in this instance the substitution of mechanised for hand technology and the introduction of new synthetic fibre manufacturing capacity.[19] Productivity has risen more slowly in the chemicals and non-metallic mineral industries, at least during the 1980s. Much of the increase in these industries occurred in the 1970s under the impetus of state-led industrialisation.[20]

A second broad indicator is direct foreign investment (DFI), an important channel for the introduction of new equipment, processes, products and management skills from abroad. Indonesia's more liberal DFI policy from the mid 1980s, combined with strong growth, resulted in a sharp increase in DFI flows. In regional terms, however, Indonesia has adopted an intermediate position as a DFI recipient (figure 14.1). As a share of capital formation and GDP, the inflows into Indonesia have been much smaller than in the traditionally open Malaysian and Singaporean economies, and closer to those of the Philippines, Thailand and Korea. However, DFI in Thailand was relatively much larger than in Indonesia during the strong economic recovery in both countries from the mid 1980s. Indonesia's restrictive policies reflect the interplay between economic and political imperatives: they have inhibited the inflow of new technologies, but perhaps the delicate political economy equation dictated such a choice.[12]

The third and fourth sets of indicators shed light on Indonesia's evolution towards an export-oriented strategy, emphasising its latecomer status and its comparative advantage in labour and resource-intensive manufactures. In its manufactured exports, Indonesia exhibits a strong specialisation in the latter two categories, as indicated by the so-called indices of revealed comparative advantage (figure 14.2). The high figures for resource-based manufactures are primarily the result of the log export ban—plywood dominates this group—although they also underline Indonesia's relatively strong natural resource base in the region. The country's specialisation in labour-intensive manufactures rose sharply during the 1980s, but remains quite low by regional standards. As would be expected, Indonesia's index for capital-intensive goods is the lowest in the comparison, indicating the country's very limited export specialisation in these products.

Another widely used indicator of the extent of technological upgrading is unit values of selected exports. The data need to be used very carefully, as they also reflect the effects of business cycles and international demand conditions. Nevertheless, for finely disaggregated categories, these are a reasonably robust indicator of quality in cross-country comparisons, while trends over time are indicative of the extent of a country's industrial upgrading. They are well suited, especially, to reasonably undifferentiated manufactures. A case in point is selected textile and garment products, the principal 'footloose'

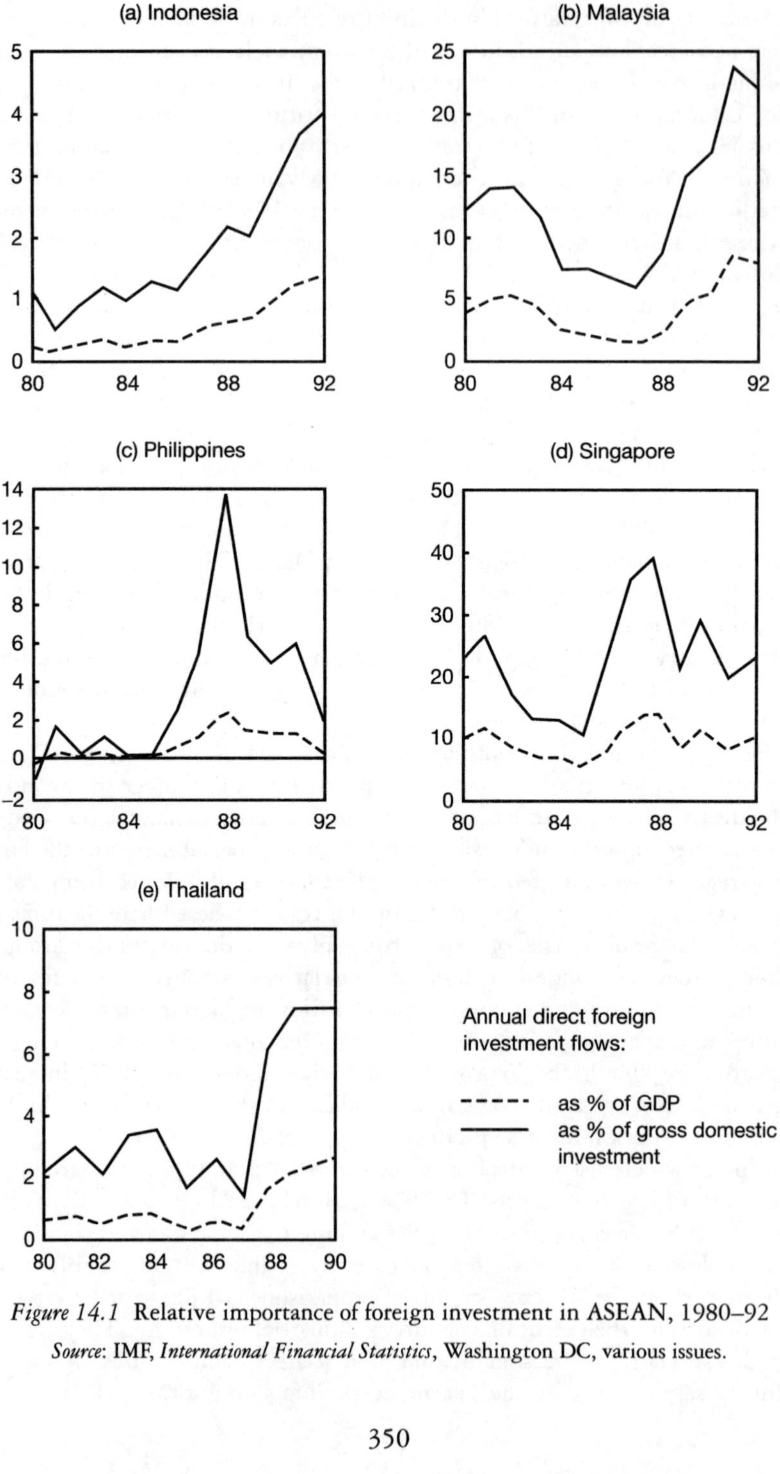

Figure 14.1 Relative importance of foreign investment in ASEAN, 1980–92

Source: IMF, *International Financial Statistics*, Washington DC, various issues.

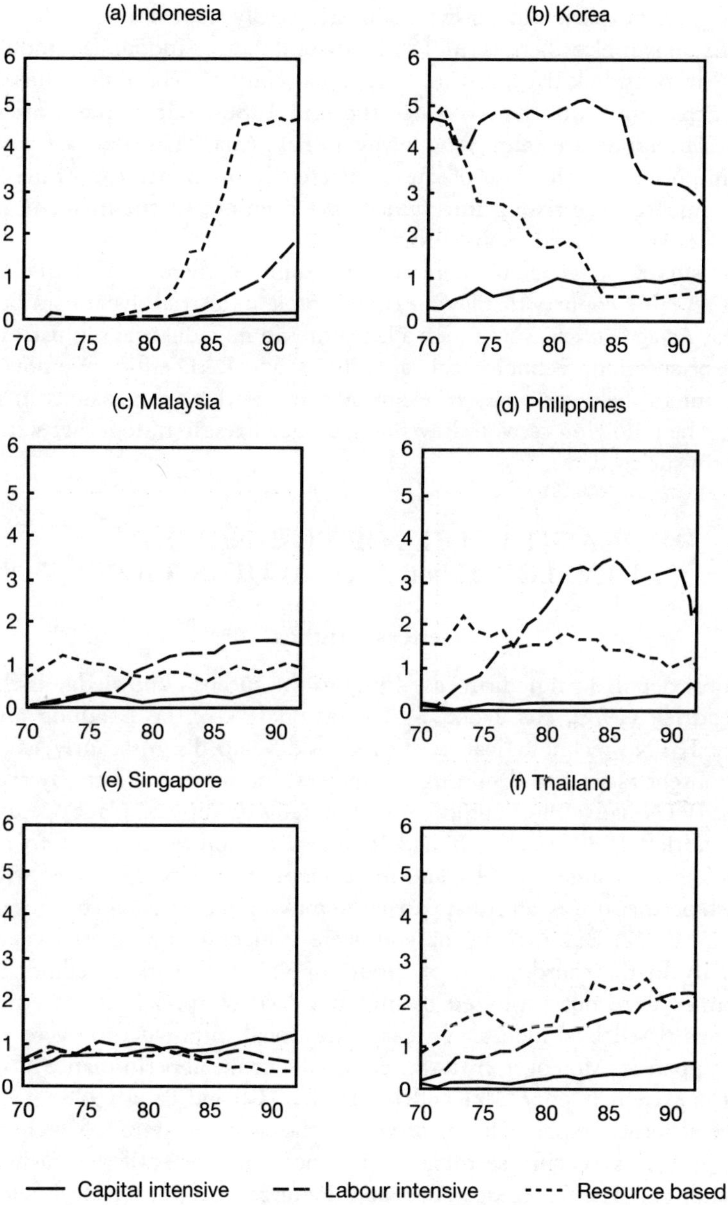

Figure 14.2 RCA indices for East Asian manufacturing, 1970–92[a]

Note: [a] RCA = revealed comparative advantage.

Source: International Economic Data Bank, ANU.

manufactured exports during most countries' early stage of outward orientation. As shown elsewhere (Hill 1992), these data put Indonesia's industrial export drive and skill capacities in regional context. The unit values have been increasing quite quickly since the mid 1980s, but in most cases the Indonesian figures are among the lowest in East Asia. These data are particularly important in the case of quota-affected items under the Multi-Fibre Arrangement, since rising unit values have been one of the main means of evading quantity-based export restrictions.

This survey of secondary data sources, some of them admittedly rather crude, reveals a country displaying considerable industrial dynamism but, in the East Asian context, very much a latecomer in its industrial sophistication, export orientation, technological capabilities, and R&D effort. We now turn to the micro, fieldwork data to examine some of these dimensions in more detail. The following section draws on a range of research, together with our own firm survey data.

CASE STUDIES OF TECHNOLOGY DEVELOPMENT AND ACQUISITION

General studies

The most detailed single firm case study to the author's knowledge is that of McKendrick (1989, chs 2 and 3; 1992a) on IPTN, the Bandung aircraft factory. IPTN's technological capability has developed significantly, as rising local content ratios and declining foreign staff numbers indicate. By the late 1980s, IPTN had 'almost completely mastered start-up and plant operations' (McKendrick 1989, p. 89), it had 'acquired an ability to adjust to minor technological changes' (p. 90), and in developing the CN-235 plane with its Spanish partner it was 'an equal partner in making incremental changes to the aircraft' (p. 92) But major problems were evident in managerial capacity, especially in the coordination of input supplies and work schedules. Scale economies were not exploited owing to a lack of specialisation. And the problems posed by Indonesia's weak educational infrastructure were everywhere apparent. Moreover, by any measure the financial performance of IPTN has been extremely poor (McKendrick 1992a; Hill and Pang 1988).

Several other reports have surveyed the general state of technology development is specific sectors, though none in as detailed a fashion as McKendrick. They include Thee and Pangestu (1994) on technological development in Indonesia's manufactured export industries, UNIDO (1984) on Indonesia's capital goods industries, SRI International (1991) on the electronics industry, Rice (1990) on technology policy in general, and various case studies commissioned by the Department of Industry and the World Bank.

Firm-level training

Given that the government's educational resources are limited, and only weakly oriented towards vocational sectors, private training activities can generate significant externalities, especially where employees transfer to other firms or establish their own business. Most firm surveys report substantial investments in training for senior employees of large corporations, much of it undertaken abroad through the foreign partner in the case of joint ventures. Formal private sector training outside this very small group appears to be extremely limited. Production workers and middle-level supervisors in large plants generally receive some instruction, mostly context-specific. For the remainder of the workforce in small and medium firms training normally takes the form of informal on-the-job education.

The most detailed survey of training was conducted in 1989/90 by a World Bank team which sampled 142 manufacturing establishments in several locations. It concluded that training was limited, and confined mainly to on-the-job arrangements. Over half (51%) of a sample of 1,985 recent recruits at skilled and supervisory levels reported no training. On-the-job 'watching' or 'teaching' constituted 88% of the cases where training was reported (Table 14.7). Just 2% of these recruits had received off-plant training. Indeed, only 16% of establishments reported some form of off-plant training for their skilled workforce. These averages conceal considerable inter-firm differences. Foreign-owned firms devoted relatively more staff and other resources to training functions. Firms which were 'high technology', government-owned, and export-oriented were also generally above average in their training effort.

Table 14.7 Training of skilled and supervisory recruits in manufacturing firms, 1989–90 (%)

		In-plant training[a]				
	No training	*On-job watching*	*On-job taught*	*Off-job*	*Off plant*	*Total*
Skilled operator (n = 847)	44.4	7.3	42.3	4.6	1.4	100
Skilled tradesperson (n = 435)	70.6	5.7	20.7	1.6	1.4	100
Supervisor/technician (n = 703)	47.7	11.5	33.9	4.1	2.8	100
Total (n = 1,985)	51.3	8.5	34.6	3.8	1.9	100

Note:
[a] Those trained included a total of 17 who reported their training was unrelated to their present work.

Source: World Bank (1991), p. 32.

Most other studies confirm these general conclusions, of limited training for unskilled and semi-skilled staff, but more extensive efforts for senior personnel, especially among large, foreign-owned concerns. Thee (1990) documents the latter, pointing to frequent instances of employment in the MNCs' plants abroad. Several studies conducted during the 1970s, when the domestic skill base was weaker, reached similar conclusions.[22] Our own field research highlighted inter-industry differences in training programs. In the automotive industry, firms have little choice but to undertake some training, given the poor state of technical education in the country: one large progressive manufacturer allocates some 1.5–2% of its total expenditure to training, while another has established an in-house training school for mechanics. By contrast, in labour-intensive industries such as garments and footwear the training effort is minimal. Anecdotal evidence suggests that rising levels of labour turnover discourage firms from undertaking extensive in-house training. The absence of a national apprenticeship system is a major deterrent to such training, an issue to which we return below.

Firm-level R&D, transfers, and technology adaptation

While firms in Indonesia have neither the capacity nor the incentive to undertake much R&D activity in the formal sense, there is some effort in the areas of product and process modification and development. Thee (1990) and Thee and Pangestu (1994) point to instances of minor product development, of a capacity to develop 'problem-solving' skills in-plant, and of laboratories with some capacity to innovate. Some quality improvement in the textile and garments industries has been noted above, and firms are now beginning to experiment with original design. In the automotive industry, 3–4% of firms' expenditure is commonly allocated to R&D. Most of this goes to the foreign licensor, but up to 0.5% of it is spent on domestic R&D effort. A major incentive is import substitution in the area of components manufacture, driven by currency appreciations in Northeast Asia. For this type of import substitution to be economic, and to receive approval from the foreign licensor, the establishment of testing, calibration, and development facilities is essential.

Simple modifications are more common. For example, one automotive firm found it necessary to develop stronger shock absorbers to suit local road conditions and overloading. Electronics manufacturers must manufacture appliances with a stronger resistance to voltage fluctuations. Firms often introduce more labour-intensive technologies in peripheral activities than would be the case in the parent plant. Bottled drinks and processed foods are modified to suit local tastes. While these changes are generally minor, they are important in the evolution towards a stronger technological base.

There have been no really detailed longitudinal case studies of technology transfer through foreign investment in Indonesia. But a number of informative micro-level studies (for example, those cited in footnotes 21 and 22) have found that foreign firms do provide limited training for senior employees, generally on a larger scale than do comparable domestic firms. They also point to informal 'spillovers', such as (limited) subcontracting relationships, and former employees establishing their own enterprises, often in an arms-length relationship with the parent corporation. Where these technology flows have been disappointing in their volume and intensity, the domestic absorptive capacity (managerial and technical skills) of the local partner appears to have been at least as important a constraint as any concerted effort by the headquarters to restrict the flows. Another important determinant of technology flows found in many studies has been the nature of the inter-affiliate relationship. Foreign firms are more willing to transfer technology to subsidiaries which are majority-owned and not at risk of sudden localisation, a point emphasised recently in the Indonesian context by Harianto (1995a, 1995b).

Subcontracting networks

The notion of subcontracting has great appeal in Indonesia. Vertical inter-firm linkages are regarded variously in policy circles—especially the Department of Industry—as a means of promoting small industry, fostering *pribumi* enterprise, achieving industrial deepening, and facilitating technical transfers from MNCs. Thus a number of (largely unsuccessful) initiatives have been introduced, including mandatory deletion programs, specific requirements aimed at state enterprises, and the *bapak angkat* (foster parent) scheme. Yet most studies of subcontracting networks in Indonesia point to weak and sporadic linkages. Certainly there are no instances which parallel the intense and durable relationships observed in the past in Japan (Odaka, Ono and Adachi 1988), nor even those evident in India (Lall 1980).

The most detailed research on this topic has been undertaken by Thee Kian Wie and colleagues (e.g. Thee 1985, 1990). From field research covering several industries in the mid 1980s, he concluded that '. . . only the firms in the automotive industry, which is engaged in implementing an official "deletion program", have been increasing the local content of the final goods through the mandatory increase of purchases of locally made parts and components' (Thee 1990, p. 231). Earlier research by Witoelar (1983) pointed to similar conclusions, arguing that in the automotive industry '. . . almost none of the subcontractors derives their technology from local assemblers'.

There is some evidence that these subcontracting networks may be strengthening over time. Large firms are under pressure from the government to expand their subcontracting, and financial incentives to enter such arrangements are intensifying. On the supply side, the base of suitable supplier firms is increasing as the country's general level of industrial competence improves. Intense competition in international markets, and even domestically, adds to this pressure. Large increases in minimum wages will also constitute an incentive to subcontract, in this instance to benefit from lower labour costs in the less regulated small-medium firm sector.

Harianto (1993), in his study of firms in the bicycle, engineering and trading industries, found cases of 'low and medium intensity' technical linkages between firms and their suppliers, although none of 'high intensity', such as joint design and development. In the bicycle industry he found close coordination between the assembler and its suppliers, including flows of technological know-how. In the author's own firm interviews, too, such cases were increasingly common. One automotive firm, for example, had about 150 regular suppliers. It now offers them training programs and assists in securing finance. Another firm in the same industry has introduced a number of its suppliers to export markets through its parent company, thus facilitating these firms' growing outward orientation. Thee and Pangestu (1994) emphasise this market connection; for example, in textiles Japanese trading houses have played a useful role in providing specialist technical inputs, while Hong Kong and Taiwanese suppliers have been a significant source of marketing and technical expertise in the garments industry. The role of buying agents was found to be important in the three-industry (garments and rattan and wooden furniture) study of small-medium scale exporters by Berry and Levy (1994), although they stressed that '. . .so far there is only limited evidence of subcontractors graduating to become fully-fledged exporters'. The phenomenon of subcontracting is still in its infancy, but at least it is expanding.

POLICY ISSUES

Indonesia does not have a 'technology policy'. As in all countries, technology policy—and industry policy more generally—is the sum of a range of macro and microeconomic interventions. Some have technological objectives, while others have incidental and often unintended effects on technological development.

It must be stressed again here that the general economic policy framework is the most important factor in the development of technological capability. That is, factors which influence a country's rate of economic growth, its investment rate, its degree of international orientation, and its stock of skilled labour are likely to be the major determinants of the pace of technology progress. All major studies of technological development (e.g. Evenson and Westphal 1994; Lall 1992; Nelson 1993a) emphasise the importance of an effective incentives regime, well developed infrastructure, sound macroeconomic management, and an open posture towards technology imports (including those embodied in foreign direct investment and skilled labour). The rest of this section examines a range of specific technology policy issues. These micro-level interventions can influence the pace and nature of technology development, but they are subordinate to the broader macro issues listed above.

Education and training

It is no exaggeration to state that education is at the heart of technology strategy. High levels of education achievement have been central to the success of East Asian economic development (World Bank 1993). The quality of education is emphasised as a key factor in building technological capability in all major studies of this issue (e.g. Nelson 1993a; Lall 1992). It is also a crucial determinant of the speed of technology transfer. Foreign firms are generally more willing to transfer their know-how if the local partner's absorption costs are small. The weak domestic skills base in Indonesia is perhaps the single most important deterrent to technology transfer by foreign firms (Thee and Pangestu 1993, 1994).

This is not the place to examine Indonesian education issues in any depth.[23] There has been tremendous expansion in education quantity since the late 1960s, but education policy makers face several pressing problems. The mix of tertiary output appears to be biased towards low cost humanities programs, to the detriment of science and technology-based courses. Vocational and technical education at the secondary level is still poorly developed. Educational curricula and pedagogic techniques at all levels do not appear to encourage curiosity and individual initiative sufficiently. Student/staff ratios are high, and educational support resources are limited. Remuneration throughout the system is generally insufficient to attract and retain quality teaching staff. At the tertiary level, there is little inducement for staff to devote attention to teaching and research. Private tertiary institutions offer considerable flexibility and innovative capacity, but their development is stifled by complex bureaucratic controls.

A related issue is government encouragement to firms to undertake training. As we have seen, most firms engage in little formal training, because of appropriability problems and short time horizons. To stimulate more training the government could impose some kind of 'training levy', as countries such as Australia, Singapore and Korea have done, and as the World Bank (1991) report recommended. It could allow such training to be tax deductible, as it has partially since 1990. It could also encourage such training at an industry level, to avoid 'free-rider' problems. All three sets of proposals have distinct advantages and drawbacks. The levy scheme requires efficient and honest bureaucratic enforcement, while industry-based schemes are predicated on the assumption that industry associations are sufficiently well developed to implement them. Neither prerequisite appears to be fulfilled in Indonesia at present.[24] Therefore, by default, the current scheme of partial tax deductions for training costs is probably the most appropriate strategy. It has the attraction of simplicity, and it implicitly provides public subsidies, and therefore incentives, for firms willing to undertake such training. Obviously the program needs to be monitored carefully, to ensure that accurate estimates of foregone tax revenue are maintained, and that its provisions are not abused.

Table 14.8 International patent and licence payments, 1990 (non-oil manufacturing)

Industry	*Payments (% of total)*	*% of value added*
Chemicals	37.1	0.2
Pharmaceuticals 55.9	32.3	
Radio, TV, communication	4.8	0.3
Electronics	1.5	0.1
Other	0.6	n
Total	100 ($11.0 million)	n

Note:
n = negligible (less than 1%).

Source: Calculated from STAID (nd).

The regulation of international technology flows

The Indonesian government has eschewed any formal controls over, or monitoring of, technology imports. BKPM does in principle have the authority to negotiate on any issue related to an investment proposal. But reportedly it rarely delves into technology questions.[25] There have been frequent suggestions that the government introduce formal screening procedures for technology agreements, as apply in Malaysia and the Philippines with their Technology Transfer Boards.

The principal rationale for such initiatives is that international technology markets are imperfect, that foreign licensors may impose 'unfair' restrictions and conditions in such agreements, and that Indonesian firms lack commercial experience in negotiating with MNCs on these matters. However, the arguments against this form of intervention are persuasive.

It is true that royalty payments in some instances are apparently quite high. Very scant information, presented in Table 14.8, suggests, as would be expected, that they are concentrated in internationally oligopolistic industries where brand names are an important component of the licensor's competitive advantage. Over half the payments in non-oil manufacturing in 1990 were in pharmaceuticals, and these were equivalent to almost one-third of value added. In all other industries, the payments were a very small proportion of value added. A study of 20 firms in the electronics, machinery and automotive industries, conducted by researchers at the Institut Teknologi Bandung (ITB 1987, cited in Muchtar 1990), did find quite extensive restrictions. The most frequent were those related to secrecy provisions following the termination of the agreement (63% of cases) and the requirement that the licensor agree to any product modification (59%).

Our own firm surveys found similar types of restrictions, and several clear conclusions emerged from our interviews. First, restrictions and royalty payments depend fundamentally on the relative bargaining strengths of the two parties. In cases of proprietary, firm-specific technology, royalty payments were invariably higher than when 'off-the-shelf' technology was being purchased. Second, such payments are sensitive to domestic market structures—the more competitive these markets, the more powerful the incentive for the domestic licensee to seek out alternative sources. Third, for many forms of close inter-affiliate transactions, government regulations on royalty payments would probably have little effect, because the MNC partner can appropriate technology rents through a variety of channels, of which direct licensing payments is only one. Finally, market forces do impinge on internal, intra-MNC markets in several ways. In the automotive industry, for example, as their technology capacity has developed, Indonesian firms no longer make payments for products and processes in which they have achieved technical proficiency. Moreover, while notional global market divisions apply, the fundamental determinant of intra-firm export sales appears to be comparative cost.

The policy implication, unpopular though it may be in certain quarters in Indonesia, is that there is no strong economic argument for intervention in technology markets. Such intervention would add an additional layer in the bureaucratic entry process for firms, thus rendering less attractive the commercial environment in Indonesia's attempt to attract scarce foreign capital. In addition, government officials rarely possess the commercial experience and technological know-how to make informed judgements about appropriate levels and forms of royalty payments, to take one of the most frequently discussed aspects of technology agreements. Moreover, where technology and product markets are competitive and open, it is the responsibility of the local partner to secure the most attractive arrangement, just as it is for any other commercial transaction. The government may play a role here, perhaps through industry associations, in providing access to international data bases and other forms of commercial information, to enable local firms to bargain effectively. In the less common cases of uncompetitive technology markets—that is, few sellers—it is doubtful that government intervention could alter fundamentally the supply price of the technology. In Indonesia the greater danger would appear to be the government supporting 'high technology' initiatives through direct public subsidy (such as the aircraft industry) or implicit subsidy (such as protection for the petrochemical industry), rather than private firms paying excessive royalties for such technology.

Other policy issues

Public funding of R&D activities

Whereas public funding of education and training tends to be universal and non-selective, R&D funding inevitably entails greater selectivity. The government's budget is rather small (Table 14.2), and its scope for influencing technology development therefore limited. The principal question is how to allocate these funds in a manner that overcomes bottlenecks and acts as a catalyst in inducing the private sector to invest.

Clearly, most of the funds will be allocated to developmental work, rather than fundamental research. As noted above, this is the case even for high income countries, and it certainly applies to developing countries. The principal focus for countries such as Indonesia will therefore be on the effective absorption, use and modification of imported technologies, on ensuring that local companies make the most effective selection from the global 'technology shelf' and that these technologies are diffused quickly. The public R&D effort is likely to have maximum impact in supporting activities which are currently beyond the technological competence of firms, or in demonstrating that investments in R&D can be economically viable. Examples might include the development of laboratory testing and calibration facilities, the introduction of new products and processes on a subsidised trial basis, and innovations in minor technical modification.

A high policy priority is a systematic evaluation of the government's current R&D expenditures. Much of this expenditure is undertaken by BPFT, but the author is unaware of any detailed review of the Agency's effectiveness. There are also various government research and training centres designed to support particular industries, such as textiles. Most anecdotal evidence suggests that these centres play a very minor role in industry promotion. The case for transforming them, and for developing stronger public-private sector cooperation,[26] is a powerful one, especially in industries such as textiles and garments, which will be a major component of Indonesian manufacturing for the foreseeable future. There is also considerable scope for the government to subcontract some of these R&D functions, possibly through open tendering arrangements, given its comparatively high share as a 'performer' of R&D activities (Table 14.4).

Patents

The number of patents issued in Indonesia is very small (Table 14.1). It might be argued that the country, as a net technology importer for the foreseeable future, has little interest in the protection of intellectual property rights. However, such an argument is overruled by three considerations. The first is the trend among industrialised economies, particularly the USA, to link international market access to the observance of such rights. Unhindered market access is critical to Indonesia's export-oriented industrialisation, and the benefits of this access far outweigh those deriving from patent evasion. Second, the observance of patent laws provides a measure of security to international (and domestic) businesses operating in Indonesia. The country still lacks a clear, simple and predictable legal and commercial code, of which patents are necessarily a component. Third, as Indonesia's industrial sophistication grows, firms are likely to extend their R&D effort. The initiatives will initially be modest, but they are an essential part of the process of technological evolution. Patent laws will encourage firms to move down this path. Indonesia's Patent Act of 1989 came into force in August 1991. The Department of Justice still lacks the technical expertise to implement the new regulations fully. But there is a strong case for them, and for continuing to observe property rights internationally.[27]

Foreign investment policy

The case for an open technology policy applies equally to direct foreign investment (DFI), as the major channel for the introduction of new technology, subject of course to the usual caveat that foreign firms must comply fully with all relevant government policies. The government's attitude towards DFI has swung sharply over the course of the New Order, from liberalism, to tight regulation, and back to a more open regime from the late 1980s (see the references in footnote 21 for discussion of this point). There are now relatively few impediments to equity capital inflows, and only a small number of outstanding policy issues of concern. One is the link between DFI and the trade regime, and the propensity of foreign investors to employ 'tariff bargaining' as a means of entry. Another is that there appears to be a case for continuing reform of BKPM, to ensure it becomes a more effective tool of investment promotion and to reduce bureaucratic barriers to new investors. This comment applies both to BKPM's own procedures and to areas beyond its jurisdiction (such as the line departments and subnational tiers of government), where apparently it has little influence.[28] Other major problems encountered by foreign investors are apparently outside the BKPM's jurisdiction.

Foreign labour policy

Indonesia maintains a broadly open policy towards the employment of expatriate workers. This is an appropriate response to the acute shortages of technical and managerial labour in some sectors. Expatriate workers may be employed as part of a foreign-owned firm, with the initial agreement of BKPM. Independent arrangements are possible through the Department of Labour. Illegal labour entry for middle and senior-level positions is widespread, as are payments to secure and extend work permits.[29] Employment of foreign labour, especially ethnic Chinese, is a sensitive issue. However the economic case for maintaining such restrictions is weak. Expatriate packages in Indonesia are high by international standards, and so market signals provide a sufficient inducement for firms to economise on the use of foreign labour. But even in cases where foreign labour might be cheaper—as seems to be the case for Filipino and Sri Lankan professionals and middle-level managers, for example—it would make sense for Indonesian firms to be able to enhance their competitive advantage by this means. Thus there is a strong case for Indonesia to liberalise its foreign labour provisions as quickly as is politically feasible.

Data base

It is appropriate to conclude this section with a plea for a much improved data base. While the recent STAID publication is greatly welcome, the data base remains very weak. There are no systematic data on the sources, channels and costs of technology. Nor is there information on the extent of, and trends in, firm-level technological capabilities. Public R&D expenditures are not reported in a disaggregated, analytically relevant form. Detailed firm-level case studies, of the type undertaken on India by Lall (1987), are not available. A good deal of the required data could be obtained economically by BPS in the course of its regular industrial surveys, with more complex issues addressed in the course of the decennial Economic Census.

CONCLUSION

Indonesia's rapid industrialisation has been accompanied by equally rapid structural change. Yet the country's latecomer industrial status is reflected in its levels of technological development which, despite significant progress, are among the lowest in East Asia. There is scope for greater government involvement in the promotion of broad-based technological development. The principal mechanism would appear to be a much stronger emphasis on education and training, broadly defined to include middle-level vocational programs, more intensive scientific effort at all levels, and specialised industry-based training and extension institutes. Government-funded research institutes have an important role to play in this process. However, it is doubtful whether ambitious 'high-tech' investment projects contribute significantly to efficient, broad-based technology development, particularly when the underlying research and education infrastructure is still rather weak. An element of selectivity is inevitable in this intervention, but at Indonesia's stage of industrialisation it would seem preferable to favour the general over the specific wherever possible. Finally, it needs to be emphasised that the data base is extremely weak, and that these conclusions have empirically flimsy foundations.

ACKNOWLEDGMENT

This paper draws on field research conducted in the early 1990s. I am particularly grateful to Thee Kian Wie for his assistance with the research and for permission to draw on his extensive writings on the subject, to Rony Bishry for much help with data and publications, and to H. W. Arndt, Rony Bishry, Sanjaya Lall, David McKendrick, Chris Manning, Robert Rice, Henry Sandee, Thee Kian Wie, Larry Westphal, and a *Bulletin* reader for helpful comments on an earlier draft The staff of the International Economic Data Bank, ANU, and Neng Hartono kindly supplied graph data. The usual disclaimer applies.

NOTES

1 In current political jargon, the contest is portrayed as 'technocrats vs technologs'. McLeod (1993) summarises public reaction to the appointment of the current Cabinet, and the Minister's statements immediately beforehand.

2 The first concerted attempt to sketch empirically Indonesia's technological capability is contained in *Science and Technology Indicators of Indonesia 1993, 1st Edition* (STAID nd), a report prepared under the Science and Technology for Industrial Development (STAID) project funded by the World Bank. The domestic implementing agencies were the Agency for the Assessment and Application of Technology (BPPT), headed by Minister Habibie, and the Centre for Analysis of Science and Technology Development at the Indonesian Institute of Sciences (Papiptek-LIPI). It is hoped that, as its title implies, the report will be the first of a regular statistical series on the subject, especially since recent editions of the principal source of comparative international statistics, the annual *Statistical Yearbook* of UNESCO, are seriously dated and incomplete.

3 There are significant differences in the commercial and R&D environment of agriculture and industry. In food crop agriculture especially, where 'non-rivalry' is a characteristic of household-based economic activity, R&D is often publicly funded and its results freely transmitted to researchers in other locations. Industrial sector R&D is more usually undertaken in the private sector, and research findings are often a closely guarded secret, protected by patent (Evenson and Westphal 1994).

4 The key early references in this field included Romer (1990) and Grossman and Helpman (1991). A recent accessible discussion is provided in the symposium on 'New Growth Theory' in the *Journal of Economic Perspectives*, Winter 1994.

5 Balassa (1979) was a pioneer in this research. Empirical applications for the East Asian region include those of Gamaut and Anderson (1950) and Ariff and Hill (1985).

6 In addition to the country studies, some of which are referred to below, these works include: two recent and comprehensive literature surveys by Evenson and Westphal (1994) and Fagerberg (1994); a large World Bank project, the key results of which are summarised in Dahlman, Ross-Larson, and Westphal (1987); the proceedings of the 17th PAFTAD conference (Soesastro and Pangestu 1990); a comparative study of national innovation systems, which includes East Asian case studies (Nelson 1993a); a cross-country study conducted under the auspices of the OECD (Lall 1990, 1992); and an extensive literature review of technology issues in East Asia by Enos (1989).

7 See Dahlman, Ross-Larson and Westphal (1987) and Enos (1989) for extensive discussion of alternative channels of technology imports, including foreign investment, licensing arrangements, turnkey projects, imports of capital equipment (and, related to this, 'reverse engineering'), and the purchase of foreign technical expertise.

8 An econometric study by Katrak (1990), one of many on this question, found that the technology effort of local licensees in India was likely to be diluted in

instances where these enterprises obtained an exclusive right of sale in the domestic market.

9 The observations of Lall (1987, p. 240) on the Indian attempt to develop domestic technological capability are worth quoting at length, especially as their author has been sympathetic to certain forms of selective policy intervention: 'The dangers inherent in such policy interventions . . . are great . . . Over-protection calls forth the wrong types of TC [technological capability] and perpetuates inefficiencies which should have been temporary. It breeds sloth in the exercise of existing TC. . . and, by slowing down the growth of the whole industrial sector, retards the pace of learning. Other forms of intervention can also have deleterious effects in the development and exploitation of TC. In India, the setting up of a large [science and technology] infrastructure divorced from production, the reservation of large chunks of industry for a poorly-managed public sector, the imposition of price controls, the virtual halting of new direct foreign investments, through regulation of licensing and so on, have all taken their toll on the process of healthy industrial growth.'

10 See Nelson (1993b) for an illuminating discussion of institutional factors in his summing up of the 15-country study of national innovations systems.

11 The literature on Korea's industrial strategy, and its technology component, is very large. Important studies include Amsden (1989); Enos and Park (1987); Kim (1990); Kim (1993); Park (1991); and Westphal; Kim and Dahlman (1985); and those cited above.

12 See for example Sumeth (1992); Santikarn (1981, 1987); and Sripaipan (1990). World Bank (1987) provides a detailed picture of technology development in the Philippines, a slower growth economy but one with a stronger educational base.

13 For example: scientific publications would exclude the (limited) scientific literature in *bahasa Indonesia;* and until 1991 Indonesia did not have a domestic patents law, unlike some of the higher income East Asian countries.

14 Indonesia's 'R&D intensity' (R&D expenditure as a percentage of GDP) is rather low in the comparative typologies presented by Evenson and Westphal (1994, p. 44), which classify Indonesia as a 'level 2' developing country, the lower ranks of which spend 0.45–0.8% of GDP on R&D.

15 see Jones (1994) for a detailed review. Pernia (1991) assesses higher education in comparative ASEAN perspective.

16 Some international data sources, for example the UNESCO *Yearbook*, report still lower expenditure as a percentage of GDP for Indonesia, as little as 1%. These figures apparently include only *development* expenditures, an error due to routine expenditures by department not commonly being reported in the budget. The World Bank data cited in Table 14.1 do not appear to suffer from this deficiency, though there may still be understatement for reasons mentioned in the text.

17 BPIS (Badan Pengelola Industri Strategis, Agency for Strategic Industries) comprises 10 state-owned industrial enterprises, including the aircraft manufacturer (IPTN), the steel factory (Krakatau), and shipbuilding, telecommunications, engineering, munitions and other factories. The Agency is governed by a Ministerial Council chaired by Professor Habibie. Its mission, in the words of the Minister for Education and Culture, is '. . . to function as the "spearhead" in the efforts to accelerate Indonesia's industrial development, both technologically as well as commercially' (Wardiman 1990, p. 12). Its establishment in 1989 was widely seen as an attempt by the Minister to protect these enterprises from the Department of Finance's state enterprise reform and privatisation program.

18 This and the following paragraph draw on an informative unpublished paper by Bishry (1992).

19 Much 1970s research highlighted these transformations, as the antiquated technology that had survived during the low investment era before 1966 began to disappear quickly when commercial conditions were normalised after 1966 (Nelson 1986; Timmer 1973; Hill 1983).

20 Of course these series relate only to labour productivity, and not total factor productivity (TFP). The latter has been growing much more slowly, especially in the era of subsidised capital up to the mid 1980s, when there was little incentive for firms to economise on the use of this input. Aswicahyono (forthcoming) provides the first comprehensive set of estimates of TFP for Indonesian manufacturing since 1975.

21 These issues are examined in more detail in Pangestu (1991); Thee (1994b); Wells (1994); and Hill (1988).

22 Studies of firm-level training over this period include Manning (1979); Rice (1974); Siahaan, Thee *et al*. (1978); and Tsurami (1980).

23 For a detailed review of education achievement and issues during the New Order, see Jones (1994); see also World Bank (1991) and Hill (1991), on vocational training and higher education respectively.

24 Recent experience in the key textile and garment industries illustrates the weakness of industry associations. There was a bitter dispute between two rival industry associations in the late 1980s (Madntyre 1991, ch. 4). One of the issues was an export levy to be used to finance export promotion activities. The levy was later dropped after it was demonstrated that there had been financial misappropriation.

25 A minor indirect control which applied through to 1984 was that royalty payments could not exceed 2.5% of net sales for the purpose of company tax deductions.

26 The observation of Evenson and Westphal (1994, p. 111) is highly apposite: 'To be productive, industrial research must be conducted in close proximity to experience gained in production. . . . [T]he good ideas for implementable adaptive innovation come largely from production experience.'

27 A reader of an earlier draft of this paper pointed to the success of Taiwan's 'mini patents' scheme in encouraging small-medium firms to innovate. This suggests that the Patent Act needs to be implemented flexibly and with a minimum of bureaucratic regulation, with the possibility of additional simplifications for very small applicants.

28 See Encarnation and Wells (1985) and Wells and Wint (1991) for assessments of the performance of BKPM in comparative perspective. In neither study did the Board compare favourably, although its procedures have been reformed in the past few years. A recent assessment of the foreign investment climate, based on extensive firm interviews, is provided by FIAS (1994). Conducted after most of the deregulation packages had been introduced, the report nevertheless found considerable dissatisfaction with the regulatory environment, and in several respects Indonesia's ranking was rather low in East Asian comparisons.

29 The usual process is for the firm wishing to employ a foreign worker to obtain a statement from the relevant department that no local skills are available; the application is then forwarded to the Department of Labour for further evaluation and recommendation to the Immigration Office if approved. Given the complexity of this procedure, it is not surprising that 'facilitation payments' are reportedly common and substantial.

REFERENCES

Amsden, A. H. (1989), *Asia's Next Giant: South Korea and Late Industrialization*, Oxford University Press, New York.

Ariff, M., and H. Hill (1985), *Export Oriented Industrialisation: The ASEAN Experience*, Allen and Unwin, Sydney.

Aswicahyono, H. H. (forthcoming), PhD dissertation on the growth of total factor productivity in Indonesian manufacturing since 1975, ANU, Canberra.

Balassa, B. (1979), 'A "Stages Approach" to Comparative Advantage', in I. Adelman (ed.), *Economic Growth and Resources*, Macmillan, London, pp. 121–56.

Berry, A., and B. Levy (1994), Indonesia's Small and Medium Industrial Exporters and their Support Systems, Paper presented to the conference 'Can Intervention Work? The Role of Government in SME Success', World Bank, Washington DC.

Bishry, R. (1992), An Overview of a Government Research Institute in Indonesia: BPP Teknologi, Unpublished paper, Jakarta.

Coe, D. T., E. Helpman and A. W. Hoffmaister (1994), 'North-South R&D Spillovers', IMF Working Paper WP/94/144, International Monetary Fund, Washington DC.

Dahlman, C. J., B. Ross-Larson and L. E. Westphal (1987), 'Managing Technological Development: Lessons from the Newly Industrialising Countries', *World Development*, 15(6), pp. 759–75.

Encarnation, D. J., and L. T. Wells, Jr (1985), 'Sovereignty en Garde: Negotiating with Foreign Investors', *International Organization*, 39(1), pp. 47–78.

Enos, J. L. (1989), 'Transfer of Technology', *Asian-Pacjfic Economic Literature* 3(1), pp. 3–37.

Enos, J. L., and Park W-H. (1987), *The Adoption and Diffusion of Imported Technology in the Case of Korea*, Croom Helm, London.

Evenson, R. E., and L. E. Westphal (1994), 'Technological Change and Technology Strategy', Economic Growth Center, Yale University, New Haven, Center Discussion Paper No.709; forthcoming in *Handbook of Development Economics*, vol 3.

Fagerberg, 1 (1994), 'Technology and International Differences in Growth Rates, *Journal of Economic Literature* 32, pp. 1,147–75.

FIAS (Foreign Investment Advisory Service) (1994), *An Investment Promotion Strategy for Indonesia*, International Finance Corporation, Washington DC.

Garnaut, R., and K. Anderson (1980), 'ASEAN Export Specialisation and the Evolution of Comparative Advantage in the Western Pacific Region', in R. Garnaut (ed.), *ASEAN in a Changing Pacific and World Economy*, Australian National University Press, Canberra, pp. 374–413.

Grossman, G. M., and E. Helpman (1991), *Innovation and Growth in the Global Economy*, MIT Press, Carnbridge MA.

Habibie, B. J. (1986), *Habibie dan Pare-Pare Lewat Aachen, dan Tulisan-Tulisan Lain* [Habibie from Pare-Pare via Aachen, and Other Writings], Gapura Media, Jakarta.

Harianto, F. (1993), 'Study on Subcontracting in Indonesian Domestic Firms', *Indonesian Quarterly* 21(3), pp. 331–43.

—— (1995a), 'The Indonesian Electronics Industry', Paper presented to the conference 'Building on Success: Maximizing the Gains from Deregulation', Jakarta, April.

—— (1995b), 'Technology Policy: A Southeast Asian Experience', Paper presented to the conference 'Building on Success: Maximizing the Gains from Deregulation', Jakarta, April.

Hill, H. (1983), 'Choice of Technique in the Indonesian Weaving Industry', *Economic Development and Cultural Change* 31(2), pp. 337–53.

—— (1988), *Foreign Investment and Industrialization in Indonesia*, Oxford University Press, Singapore.

—— (ed.) (1991), *Indonesia Assessment 1991*, Political and Social Change Monograph 14, Department of Political and Social Change, Australian National University, Canberra.

—— (1992), 'Indonesia's Textile and Garment Industries: Developments in an Asian Perspective', Occasional Paper 87, Institute of Southeast Asian Studies, Singapore.

—— 1995), *The Indonesian Economy since 1965: Southeast Asia's Emerging Giant*, Cambridge University Press, Cambridge.

Hill, H., and Pang E. F. (1988), 'The State and Industrial Restructuring: A Comparison of the Aerospace Industry in Indonesia and Singapore', *ASEAN Economic Bulletin* 5(2), pp. 152–68.

ITB (Institut Teknologi Bandung) (1987), 'Hubungan Ketergantungan antara Sistem Teknologi Industri Nasional dan Sistem Produksi Luar Negeri Berkenaan dengan Lisensinya' [The Interdependence between the National Industrial Technology System and the System of Foreign Production under License], Lembaga Penelitian ITB, Bandung.

Jones, G. W. (1994), 'Labour Force and Education', in H. Hill (ed.), *Indonesia's New Order: The Dynamics of Socio-Economic Transformation*, Allen and Unwin, Sydney, pp. 145–78.

Katrak, H. (1990), 'Imports of Technology and the Technological Effort of Indian Enterprises', *World Development* 18(3), pp. 371–81.

Kim, L. (1990), 'Korea: The Acquisition of Technology', in Soesastro and Pangestu (eds), pp 145–57.

—— (1993), 'National Systems of Industrial Innovation: Dynamics of Capability Building in Korea', in Nelson (ed.), pp. 357–83.

Krugman, P. (1990), 'Technology and Changing Comparative Advantage in the Pacific Region', in Soesastro and Pangestu (eds), pp. 25–37.

Lall, S. (1980), 'Vertical Inter-Firm Linkages in LDCs: An Empirical Study', *Oxford Bulletin of Economics and Statistics* 42(3), pp. 203–26.

—— (1987), *Learning to Industrialize: The Acquisition of Technological Capability by India*, Macmillan, London.

—— (1990), *Building Industrial Competitiveness in Developing Countries*, Development Centre Studies, OECD, Paris.

—— (1992), 'Technological Capabilities and Industrialization', *World Development* 20(2), pp. 165–86.

MacIntyre, A. (1991), *Business and Politics in Indonesia*, Allen and Unwin, Sydney.

McKendrick, D.G. (1989), Acquiring Technological Capabilities: Aircraft and Commercial Banking in Indonesia, Unpublished PhD dissertation, University of California, Berkeley.

—— (1992a), 'Obstacles to "Catch-Up": The Case of the Indonesian Aircraft Industry', *Bulletin of Indonesian Economic Studies* 28(1), pp. 39–66.

—— (1992b), 'Use and Impact of Information Technology in Indonesian Commercial Banks', *World Development* 20(12), pp. 1,753–68.

McLeod, R. H. (1993), 'Survey of Recent Developments', *Bulletin of Indonesian Economic Studies* 29(2), pp. 3–42.

Manning, C. G. (1979), Wage Differentials and Labour Market Segmentation in Indonesian Manufacturing, Unpublished PhD dissertation, ANU, Canberra.

Muchtar, I. P. (1990), Technological Change: Government Policies and Development with Special Reference to Indonesia, Unpublished Masters thesis, Flinders University, Adelaide.

Nelson, G. C. (1986), 'Labor Intensity, Employment Growth and Technical Change: An Example from Starch Processing in Indonesia', *Journal of Development Economics* 24, pp. 111–17.

Nelson, R. R. (ed.) (1993a), *National Innovation Systems: A Comparative Analysis*, Oxford University Press, Oxford.

—— (1993b), 'A Retrospective', in Nelson (ed.) (1993a), pp. 505–23.

Ng C. Y. *et al.* (eds) (1986), *Technology and Skills in ASEAN: An Overview*, Institute of Southeast Asian Studies, Singapore.

Odaka, K., K. Ono, and F. Adachi (1988), *The Automobile Industry in Japan: A Study of Ancillary Firm Development*, Kinokuniya Coy Ltd, Oxford University Press, for the Institute of Economic Research, Hitotsubashi University, Tokyo.

Pack, H., and L.E. Westphal (1986), 'Industrial Strategy and Technological Change: Theory versus Reality', *Journal of Development Economics 22*, pp. 87–128.

Pangestu, M. (1991), 'Foreign Firms and Structural Change in the Indonesian Manufacturing Sector, in E. D. Ramstetter (ed.), *Direct Foreign Investment in Asia's Developing Economies and Structural Change in the Asia-Pacific Region*, Westview Press, Boulder, pp. 35–64.

Park, E. Y. (1991), Foreign Trade, Foreign Direct Investment and the Industrialization Strategy of Korea, Unpublished paper, Korea Development Institute, Seoul.

Pernia, E. M. (1991), 'Higher Education in Asia: Indonesia in Comparative Perspective', in Hill (ed.), pp. 135–50.

Rath, A. (ed.) (1990), 'Science and Technology: Issues from the Periphery', special issue of *World Development* 18(11).

Rice, R.C. (1974), 'The Interfirm Externalities of Foreign Investment in Manufacturing in Indonesia', *Ekonomi dan Keuangan Indonesia* 22(2), pp. 127–53.

——, (1990), 'Indonesian Approaches to Technology Policy during the Soeharto Era: Habibie, Sumitro and Others, in R. C. Rice (ed.), *Indonesian Economic Development: Approaches, Technology, Small-Scale Textiles, Urban Infrastructure and NGOs*, Centre of Southeast Asian Studies, Monash University, Clayton, pp. 53–66.

Romer, P. M. (1990), 'Endogenous Technological Change', *Journal of Political Economy* 98, pp. S71–102.

Rosenberg, N. (1994), *Exploring the Black Box: Technology, Economics, and History*, Cambridge University Press, Cambridge.

Santikarn, M. (1981), *Technology Transfer: A Case Study*, Singapore University Press, Singapore.

—— (1987), 'Technology Acquisition under Alternative Arrangements with Transnational Corporations: Selected Industrial Case Studies in Thailand', in *Technology Transfer under Alternative Arrangements with Transnational Corporations*, United Nations ESCAP/UNCTC Joint Unit of TNCS, Bangkok, pp. 240–90.

STAID (nd), *Science and Technology Indicators of Indonesia 1993*, 1st Edition, Science and Technology for Industrial Development, and Badan Pengkajian dan Penerapan Teknologi, Jakarta.

Siahaan, L., Thee K. W. *et al.* (1978), *Japanese Direct Investment in Indonesia: Findings of an Experimental Survey*, Joint Research Program Series No. 9, Institute of Developing Economies, Tokyo.

Soesastro, H., and M. Pangestu (eds) (1990), *Technological Challenge in the Asia-Pacific Economy*, Allen and Unwin, Sydney.

SRI International (1991), Industrial Restructuring of the Electronics Subsector in Indonesia, Report prepared for the Department of Industry, Jakarta.

Sripaipan, C. (1990), 'Constraints to Technology Development in a Rapidly Growing Economy: The Case of Thailand', *TDRI Quarterly Newsletter* 5(3), pp. 6–11.

Sumeth Vongpanitlerd (ed.) (1992), *The Development of Thailand's Technological*

Capability in Industry, Research Monograph No. 9, Thailand Development Research Institute, Bangkok.

Szirmai, A. E. (1994), 'Real Output and Labour Productivity in Indonesian Manufacturing, 1975–90', *Bulletin of Indonesian Economic Studies* 30(2), pp. 49–90.

Thee K. W. (ed.) (1985), *Kaitan-Kaitan Vertikal Antarperusahaan dan Pengembangan Sistem Subkontraktor di Indonesia: Berberapa Studi Kasus* [Vertical Interfirm Linkages and the Development of the Subcontracting System in Indonesia: Several Case Studies], special issue of *Masyarakat Indonesia* 12(3).

—— (1990), 'Indonesia: Technology Transfer in the Manufacturing Industry', in Soesastro and Pangestu (eds), pp. 200–32.

—— (1994a), Developing Industrial Technological Capabilities in Indonesia, Unpublished paper, Economic Development Institute, Washington DC.

—— (1994b), *Industrialisasi di Indonesia: Beberapa Kajian* [Industrialization in Indonesia: Selected Essays], LP3ES, Jakarta.

Thee K. W. and M. Pangestu (1993), 'Technological Dynamism in Indonesia's Exports of Electronic Products', in *Dialog Teknologi dan Industri* (Industrial and Technological Dialogue], BPP Teknologi, Jakarta, pp. 125–48.

—— (1994), Technological Capabilities and Indonesia's Manufactured Exports, Unpublished report prepared for UNCTAD, Geneva.

Timmer, C. P. (1973), 'Choice of Technique in Rice Milling in Java', *Bulletin of Indonesian Economic Studies* 9(2), pp. 57–76.

Tsurumi, Y. (1980), 'Japanese Investment in Indonesia: Ownership, Technology Transfer, and Political Conflict', in G. Papanek (ed.), *The Indonesian Economy*, Praeger, New York, pp. 295–323.

UNIDO (1984), *Prospects for Industrial Development and for a Capital Goods Industry in Indonesia*, Volumes I–III, Regional and Country Studies Branch, Vienna.

Vernon, R. (1966), 'International Investment and International Trade in the Product Cycle', *Journal of Political Economy* 80, pp. 190–207.

Wardiman Djojonegoro (1990), Comprehensive 'Catch-up' S&T Development Strategies: An Indonesian Perspective, Paper presented to a conference on 'Keys to Asian Renaissance of the 1990s: Science and Technology for Development', Bangkok, August.

Wells, L. T. Jr (1994), 'Mobile Exporters: New Foreign Investors in East Asia', in K. A. Froot (ed.), *Foreign Direct Investment*, University of Chicago Press, Chicago, for the NBER, pp. 173–91.

Wells, L. T. Jr, and A. G. Wint (1991), 'The Public-Private Choice: The Case of Marketing a Country to Investors', *World Development* 19(7), pp. 749–61.

Westphal L. E., L. Kim, and C. J. Dahlman (1985), 'Reflections on the Republic of Korea's Acquisition of Technological Capability', in N. Rosenberg and C. Frischtak (eds), *International Technology Transfer: Concepts, Measures, and Comparisons*, Praeger Press, New York, pp. 167–221.

Witoelar, W. (1983), 'Ancillary Firm Development in the Motor Vehicle Industry in Indonesia', in K. Odaka (ed.), *The Motor Vehicle Industry in Asia: A Study of Ancillary Firm Development*, Singapore University Press, Singapore, pp. 17–84.

World Bank (1987), 'Technology Development', ch. 6, Volume III of *The Philippines: Issues and Policies in the Industrial Sector*, Washington DC.

—— (1991), *Indonesia: Employment and Training: Foundations for Industrialization in the 1990s*, Washington DC.

—— (1992), *World Bank Support for Industrialization in Korea, India and Indonesia*, Operations Evaluation Department, Washington DC.

—— (1993), *The East Asian Miracle: Economic Growth and Public Policy*, Washington DC.

15

EXPORT PROCESSING ZONES

The Economics of Enclave Manufacturing

Peter G. Warr

Since the mid 1960s, many developing countries have tried to stimulate exports of nontraditional manufactures. One form this effort has taken is the establishment of export processing zones (EPZs). Many EPZs were set up in the early 1970s; by the early 1980s around thirty-five existed in Asia alone, with an aggregate employment of at least 250,000 (United Nations 1985). Globally, their importance was probably more than twice as great.

EPZs are special enclaves, outside a nation's normal customs barriers. The firms inside them are mostly foreign and enjoy favored treatment with respect to imports of intermediate goods, taxation, and infrastructure. They are also free from industrial regulations applying elsewhere in the country. These privileges are subject to the conditions that almost all of the output is exported and that all imported intermediate goods are used within the zones or else re-exported.

Despite the heavy state investment involved, perusal of government documents on EPZs invariably reveals confusion about the economic and welfare effects of the zones. Similar confusion is also present in the economic literature on EPZs. This article tries to clarify the issues and to draw out the crucial relationship between the benefits and costs of establishing EPZs and the overall trading regime of the host country. The frame of reference is the economic welfare of citizens of the host country. The article starts with a simple theoretical analysis, which is then illustrated by case studies from four East Asian countries.

The most common activities in EPZs have been labor-intensive light manufacturing processes: electronics assembly, garment production, assembly of light electrical goods, and so forth. A notable feature of the firms in the zones is their international mobility. Firms leaving an EPZ in one country often migrate to an EPZ in another, in which conditions are more favorable.

The "footloose" character of EPZ firms has been overlooked in most of the small amount of theoretical work that has appeared. This literature has drawn upon the classical Heckscher-Ohlin model of production.[1] Insofar as the

Source: *World Bank Research Observer*, Vol. 4, 1989, pp. 65–88.

model treats capital as being internationally mobile, it fails to capture the international mobility of *capital goods*—which is central to the functioning of EPZs. The main conclusion of most of the literature—that EPZs necessarily reduce the welfare of the host countries—is thus largely irrelevant for EPZs as they actually operate.

Empirical work on EPZs has also tended to overlook the footloose character of EPZ firms. It has therefore had a misplaced preoccupation with the factor intensity of production within the zones. In an otherwise useful descriptive study of EPZs, Spinanger claims that they tend to produce welfare benefits analogous to those resulting from a movement toward free trade, because the elimination of tariffs and other distortions causes factor intensities of production "to correspond more closely with the factor endowment of the host country" (1985, p. 65). This conception of an EPZ rests on the traditional assumption that capital is internationally immobile. It assumes implicitly that the capital used in the EPZ is domestic capital in fixed supply, which has moved there from elsewhere in the host country. Once this assumption is discarded, the factor intensity of production within EPZs is of limited relevance for an assessment of their welfare impact.

Although most of the literature on EPZs has been concerned with their benefits and costs, it has stopped short of formal benefit-cost analysis. The explanation is usually that the data are inadequate. In fact, EPZs are closely monitored by host governments; compared with the data available for other public projects in developing countries, the statistical information on EPZs is unusually complete. It includes detailed time series of exports, imports, employment, use of utilities, infrastructure, and administrative costs. What the empirical studies have lacked has been an analytical framework, so that the benefits and costs of EPZs can be identified conceptually and quantified empirically.

This article describes the footloose character of EPZ firms and the incentives and other facilities in a "typical" EPZ. It then looks at the economic performance of EPZs in four Asian countries: Indonesia, the Republic of Korea, Malaysia, and the Philippines. Using a simple conceptual framework—the "enclave model"—the article analyzes the benefits and costs of the four Asian EPZs. Finally, it discusses the relationship between EPZs and trade policy in general.

THE FOOTLOOSE MANUFACTURER

In its standard forms, international trade theory treats factors of production—capital, labor, land—as immobile internationally but mobile domestically. In contrast, commodities are considered mobile across, as well as within, international boundaries. EPZs exploit the international mobility of capital goods owned by a "footloose" manufacturing firm, combine them with domestic labor (relatively immobile internationally), and produce traded goods which the firm exports. The firm tries to move its capital equipment to countries in which it can earn the highest rate of return

This process can be viewed as an indirect form of exporting labor. The foreign firm producing within the EPZ receives the services of domestic labor. In return the workers receive wages and some training. Not surprisingly, many of the countries establishing EPZs have also engaged in the direct export of temporary labor, to the Middle East and elsewhere.[2] In the case of EPZs the capital goods move to where the labor is; with labor export, the movements are reversed.

A simple model to represent the international mobility of capital goods has been developed by Jones (1980) and Caves and Jones (1985). This article uses an amended version of the Caves and Jones model to bring out the essential economic features of EPZs.

The processing activity within the zone produces final traded goods using three kinds of inputs: traded intermediate inputs, capital goods, and labor. The traded intermediate inputs include the electronic components, plastic casings, electrical circuitry, and so forth used in producing electronic goods, and the textiles, buttons, cotton thread, and so forth used in producing garments. The prices of these goods, the wages paid, and the return to the capital goods used are formally related by

$$P_j = \Sigma_i a_{ij} P_i + a_{Kj} R_j + a_{Lj} w \quad (1)$$

where P_j is the price of the final goods j; P_i is the price of the intermediate input i; a_{ij}, a_{Kj} and a_{Lj} are the amounts of intermediate good i, capital goods, and labor, respectively, required to produce a unit of good j; and w is the wage rate. These variables determine R_j, the rate of return to capital goods resulting from the production of good j in an EPZ.

It is convenient to define the value added per unit of production of good j, V_j, by

$$V_j = P_j - \Sigma_i a_{ij} P_i \quad (2)$$

and (1) now becomes

$$V_j = a_{Kj} R_j + a_{Lj} w. \quad (3)$$

Figure 15.1 represents equation 3 for two countries, labeled “poor” and “rich.” In the rich country unit labor costs, a_{Lj}w, are higher than in the pour country, but unit requirements of capital goods, a_{kj}, are lower. The rich country’s schedule thus has a higher vertical intercept (unit labor costs)—that is, point B lies above point C—and a lower slope (unit capital good requirement) than the poor country’s.

A footloose manufacturer moves to the country where the highest value of

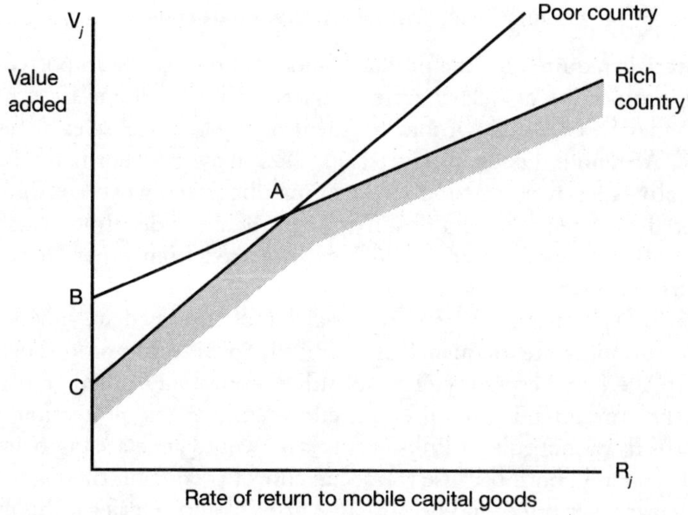

Figure 15.1

R_j, can be realized. This is represented by the shaded surface in the diagram. When unit value added is high, implying high returns to the capital goods specific to commodity *j*, the rich country is able to attract the processing activity. The rich country uses the scarce capital goods more efficiently—its unit capital good requirements per unit of output are lower—and in this case unit labor costs are relatively unimportant. But if unit value added falls, implying a squeeze (on returns to its capital goods, unit labor costs become relatively more important. Below point A, the process moves to the poor country.

This analysis is consistent with the "product cycle" process identified by Vernon (1966). It suggests a gradual migration of newly developed manufacturing processes from rich countries (where scarce capital goods are used more efficiently) to poor countries (where unit labor costs are lower) as international competition forces down the unit value added generated by these processes.

THE ECONOMIC ENVIRONMENT OF THE EPZ

In the early 1970s, after Japan had relaxed restrictions on investment abroad, other Asian countries competed to attract these and similar foreign investments. Light manufacturing, intensive in the use of unskilled or semi-skilled labor, was identified as a target: it was well suited to EPZs. The zones appeared to offer the advantages of export promotion without threatening the position of indigenous manufacturers. The "typical" EPZ had four characteristics:

Duty-free import of raw materials

Raw materials required for the production of exports may be imported duty-free and irrespective of quantitative restrictions in the domestic economy. Products may be exported without payment of export taxes, sales duties, and so forth. Although goods produced in EPZs may not normally be sold domestically, special permission to do so may be given when consignments are rejected by foreign buyers or fail to meet delivery deadlines. Such sales simply displace imports that would have occurred from other sources and usually attract normal customs duties.

EPZ firms' purchases of raw materials and intermediate goods from domestic suppliers are frequently subsidized, in an attempt to encourage links with the home economy. The subsidies, commonly called "rebates" or "drawbacks," are intended to offset the effects of domestic protection. In the early 1970s it was hoped that links of this kind would generate big benefits to the local economy, both because the social cost of producing these goods was below their market prices and because EPZ firms would transfer technology to domestic suppliers.

Tax holidays

Firms in an EPZ are often exempted from normal income tax provisions for three to ten years. The firms often negotiate successfully to extend these tax holidays by threatening to move to another country. Once relocated, the firm's tax-free holiday begins again.

The Philippines offers a generous schedule of deductions instead of tax holidays. Very little tax revenue has been raised from its EPZs, because most firms declare overall trading losses.[3] Some firms have declared losses every year for more than a decade, while still producing and even expanding. Vertically integrated firms use transfer pricing to relocate their profits internationally, thereby minimizing their global tax burdens. The Philippines experience suggests that efforts to monitor transfer pricing are ineffective and that tax holidays are less important than they may appear.

Streamlined administration

EPZ firms usually have to conform to simplified administrative requirements, which often deal with a special government agency. They are exempted from many national rules, such as restrictions on foreign ownership of firms (EPZ firms are usually allowed to be fully foreign-owned), restrictions on repatriation of profits, restrictions on the employment of foreign nationals, and requirements for special approval for importing capital equipment. EPZ firms may also obtain a share of the host country's allocation of import quotas—vital for garment producers wishing to export to the European Economic Community.

Infrastructure and utilities

An EPZ consists of a heavily fenced area policed by customs officials to prevent duty-free materials from being smuggled into the domestic economy. Its infrastructure and telecommunications are normally superior to those in the host economy, but not as good as those in industrial countries.

Utilities are often subsidized. Electricity tariffs are especially important, because light manufacturing firms are heavy users of electrical power. The rates charged in EPZs are frequently below, and never above, industrial rates elsewhere in the host country. The same applies to rental rates. Some firms rent buildings from a government agency; others lease land within the zone and construct their own buildings.

THE ECONOMIC RECORD IN FOUR ASIAN COUNTRIES

This section summarizes the results of detailed studies of EPZs in four Asian countries:

- Indonesia: The Jakarta Export Processing Zone
- The Republic of Korea: The Masan Free Export Zone
- Malaysia: The Penang Free Trade Zone
- The Philippines: The Bataan Export Processing Zone.

All four began operations in the early 1970s. Each is the largest and oldest EPZ in the country concerned. The Indonesian zone is less typical of EPZs than the other three. It is small and has a number of unusual characteristics but is worthy of examination because it began as an experimental project and, partly on the basis of its performance, the Indonesian government has decided to establish several more EPZs. Detailed case studies of these four zones have been conducted by the present author.[4] Tables 15.1 to 15.4 summarize the economic performance of these four zones through 1982. Altogether, they employed roughly 90,000 people in 1982.

A feature of the zones not revealed by the tables is their industrial composition. Garment production initially dominates, then electronics assembly becomes more important. Indonesia and Malaysia are exceptions to this pattern, in that garments have always been the dominant industry in the former and electronics in the latter. The two industries are quite different. Garment production is generally far more labor-intensive, and its technology has changed little in years.

The data in Tables 15.1 to 15.4 also fail to reveal the footloose character of EPZ firms. The case of the Philippines' Bataan EPZ provides a good example. In Table 15.4, the number of firms barely changed between 1979 and 1982. But during 1979, four firms entered the zone and four others left. In 1980, five entered and four left; in 1981, three entered and three left; and in 1982, two entered and four left.

Table 15.1 Indonesia: aggregate economic performance of Jakarta EPZ

Indicator	*1977*	*1978*	*1979*	*1980*	*1981*	*1982*
Number of firms	4	7	15	18	18	18
Number of persons employed	773	1,653	4,317	6,174	7,520	7,742
Value (millions of U.S. dollars)						
Exports	0.9	12.8	5.9	18.7	28.7	37.5
Imports of raw materials	1.2	11.8	6.4	13.0	13.5	13.8
Local raw materials	0	0.01	0.6	1.9	5.2	9.5
Imports of capital goods	0.1	1.0	1.0	1.2	0.8	0.3
Local capital goods	0	0	0.03	0.01	0.03	0.01
Total official taxes	0.01	0.15	0.33	0.40	0.56	0.56
Estimated unofficial taxes	0.23	3.11	1.32	2.76	3.60	3.60
Percentage						
Local to total raw materials	0	0.80	9	13	28	41
Local to total capital goods	0	0	2.9	0.8	4.6	3.2

Note: All monetary quantities are in current prices.

Sources: Bonded Warehouses Indonesia, Jakarta; International Monetary Fund, *International Financial Statistics*, various issues; and Warr 1983.

Aggregate data on export volumes and employment also disguise annual volatility for individual EPZ firms. Table 15.4 shows that, between 1981 and 1982, total exports from the Bataan EPZ rose by 19 percent. For individual firms, however, exports rose in only twenty-nine of the fifty-two that were present at the beginning of 1981 and declined in twenty-six (including the three that left the zone during that year). In the first group, the average increase in firm-level exports, weighted by exports in 1981, was 42 percent; in the second group (excluding the three which left the zone) the weighted average decline was 29 percent. These large variations in output partly reflect the adjustments made by the headquarters of the large corporations to which EPZ firms belong, in response to perceived changes in market demand. They also reflect the way that such corporations relocate their activities when the profitability of their firms changes.

Raw materials and technology transfer

Two of the anticipated benefits of EPZs were that firms would buy more local raw materials and that such links transfer technology to domestic firms. In reality, local raw materials make up no more than a third of the total purchases of raw materials. The exception is Indonesia, where local textiles are purchased significantly by the zone's garment producers. In Malaysia, local raw materials constitute only a small percentage of the total. Purchases of raw materials and intermediate goods produced by *other* EPZ firms are more than

Table 15.2 Korea: aggregate economic performance of Masan EPZ

Indicator	*1972*	*1973*	*1974*	*1975*	*1976*	*1977*	*1978*	*1979*	*1980*	*1981*	*1982*
Number of firms	70	115	110	105	99	99	97	94	88	89	83
Number of persons employed	7,072	21,240	20,822	22,248	29,615	28,401	30,960	31,153	28,532	28,016	26,012
Value (millions of U.S. dollars)											
Exports	23.9	145.5	298.0	257.1	441.0	496.5	579.2	621.7	577.3	664.4	601.3
Local sales	0	0	6.2	7.9	25.2	28.1	81.7	90.7	82.5	99.0	92.1
Imports of raw materials	16.5	91.7	176.7	137.8	216.7	239.3	270.7	293.0	266.2	295.9	281.7
Local raw materials	1.0	23.1	48.6	44.6	92.7	120.0	130.0	149.4	131.3	144.0	142.7
Total wages and equipment	5.9	17.9	18.9	23.2	36.2	41.4	47.5	51.5	49.4	59.0	59.6
Total electricity used	0.2	1.3	2.3	2.0	3.4	3.8	4.5	4.8	4.5	5.1	5.3
Total taxes	0	1.44	1.79	1.55	1.71	1.50	1.85	1.78	1.74	2.31	2.17
Percentage of local to total raw materials	6	20	22	24	30	33	32	34	33	33	34

Note: All monetary quantities are in current prices.

Sources: Administration office, Mason Free Export Zone, Masan; International Monetary Fund, *Financial Statistics*, various issues; and Warr 1984.

Table 15.3 Malaysia: aggregate economic performance of Penang EPZ

Indicator	*1972*	*1973*	*1974*	*1975*	*1976*	*1977*	*1978*	*1979*	*1980*	*1981*	*1982*
Number of firms	10	21	31	32	33	34	35	35	41	49	50
Number of persons employed	—	15,627	18,569	22,412	25,780	27,895	30,372	35,379	38,355	38,078	36,298
Value (millions of U.S. dollars)											
Exports	2.1	53.6	94.2	192.2	274.3	226.1	591.5	1,085.2	972.9	717.5	714.9
Local sales	—	0.1	2.3	1.7	6.9	4.6	9.4	2.6	0.06	14.5	47.1
Imported raw materials	1.3	55.0	127.8	185.1	237.2	193.6	425.6	492.4	707.0	523.1	520.6
Local raw materials	0.07	0.9	2.8	7.1	6.7	10.5	13.3	14.5	14.5	16.9	22.8
Raw material from EPZs	—	—	—	5.8	12.0	13.1	40.3	64.5	76.6	48.9	82.3
Imported capital goods	0.4	13.4	54.7	29.7	9.5	15.2	120.0	53.9	36.6	36.7	36.6
Local capital goods	0	1.8	18.9	27.0	2.2	3.6	2.6	21.7	3.3	4.0	3.9
Total wages paid	0.9	6.3	5.2	14.0	17.4	25.0	43.2	56.6	72.3	80.5	83.4
Total electricity used	0.4	0.7	1.7	5.7	6.9	.0	8.6	12.1	17.8	23.5	23.2
Total taxes paid	0	0	0	0	0	0	0.14	0.15	0.09	0.74	1.29
Percentage											
Local to total raw materials	5	2	2	4	3	5	3	3	2	3	4
Local to total capital equipment	0	12	26	48	19	19	18	29	8	10	10

— Not available.

Note: All monetary quantities are in current prices.

Sources: Penang Development Corporation, Penang; International Monetary Fund, *International Financial Statistics*, various issues; and Warr 1987b.

Table 15.4 The Philippines: aggregate economic performance of Bataan EPZ

Indicator	*1972*	*1973*	*1974*	*1975*	*1976*	*1977*	*1978*	*1979*	*1980*	*1981*	*1982*
Number of firms	1	5	14	16	39	38	47	51	51	52	52
Number of persons employed	—	1,298	3,321	5,502	8,962	12,821	17,495	18,877	19,204	19,858	19,410
Value (millions of U.S. dollars)											
Exports	0.4	0.9	2.1	7.3	22.4	39.7	73.1	98.2	122.7	134.0	159.6
Local sales	—	3.9	6.8	4.3	11.7	13.6	14.8	16.5	13.3	8.2	5.0
Imports of raw materials	0.2	0.5	2.9	7.8	15.8	38.5	47.3	66.4	77.3	81.2	122.3
Local raw materials	0.07	0.2	0.3	0.8	4.2	9.9	3.8	7.9	9.5	7.4	8.5
Total wages paid	—	0.6	1.5	2.5	4.3	6.6	9.3	14.4	20.4	22.4	21.8
Total electricity used	—	0.1	0.3	0.5	0.7	0.9	1.2	1.6	1.5	1.7	1.6
Total taxes paid	—	—	0.07	0	0.4	0.6	1.5	2.2	1.9	1.7	1.4
Total domestic borrowings	1.8	22.8	61.4	117.8	85.9	89.4	3.3	2.8	2.3	1.9	1.5
Percentage of local to total raw materials	30	30	8	10	21	20	7	11	14	9	6

— Not available.

Note: All monetary quantities are in current prices.

Sources: Export Processing Zone Authority, Manila: International Monetary Fund, *International Financial Statistics* various issues; and Warr 1985.

three times greater. In the Philippines, the share of local raw materials had declined to less than 10 percent by 1982.

Managers of EPZ firms report that the main obstacle to buying local raw materials is their low and unreliable quality. Entire shipments of finished goods may be rejected if the raw materials or intermediate goods used were inferior. The changing industrial composition of the EPZs is also a factor: garment and footwear manufacture uses a much higher proportion of local raw materials than electronics assembly. And a third factor is the global strategies of the corporations involved. Parent firms wish to preserve the international mobility of their processing operations; developing long-term relations with local suppliers does not serve this goal. If the corporation wishes to retain the capacity to relocate its activities at short notice, it is better to buy these inputs from the cheapest reliable international source.

As for the transfer of technology, the initial hopes have not been fulfilled. Many EPZ industries use technology that is universally available: labor-intensive garment production is a good example. Those that do have special information—electronics firms are the best example—guard it carefully, even from their own workers. To hand technical know-how to the locals is thought to be equivalent to handing it to one's competitors. It is hardly surprising that know-how is not readily given away; it has to be purchased.

Working conditions and wages

Working conditions in EPZs have been widely criticized by writers from industrial countries. This perspective is often combined with the claim that EPZ firms "exploit" their workers and enjoy big profits, at the expense of jobs back home in the industrial countries. Such arguments have usually reflected a lack of familiarity with the conditions and wages in developing countries; unless workers were better off being "exploited" in an EPZ, EPZ firms would find it impossible to hire.

Useful information on the Philippines was provided by Castro (1982). In the Bataan EPZ, 74 percent of workers were female; two-thirds were with no previous factory experience; and most were between the ages of seventeen and twenty-four. Turnover rates were high; the average duration of zone employment was around three years. Most of the workers in Castro's sample were members of larger households (the average size was six members); incomes represented roughly half the combined cash incomes of these house-holds. Almost half of all zone workers worked overtime. The average working week was fifty-four hours. Of those who had previously had paid employment, their average earnings in the EPZ were 35 percent higher than these previous earnings. Castro concludes that there was a clear income gain from moving to the EPZ.

Data provided in a survey conducted by the Philippines' Ministry of Trade and Industry suggest that—allowing for differences in living costs—real wages of unskilled workers were roughly the same in the EPZ as in similar employment in the capital city (Warr 1985). Real wages for skilled workers were somewhat higher in the EPZ. Whereas unskilled workers may be drawn from any part of the country, including rural areas, skilled workers must be recruited from the capital city, requiring a premium to attract them.

EPZ firms appear generally to adhere to minimum wage laws, where these exist. Firms operating within the domestic manufacturing sector may often avoid these regulations, but the greater visibility of EPZs and their politically sensitive position make violations of minimum wage restrictions more difficult.

THE WELFARE ECONOMICS OF EPZS

This section considers the benefits and costs of an EPZ, as experienced by citizens of the host country by comparing the observed situation with the hypothetical results of not having a zone.[5] The foreign ownership of firms and the "offshore" nature of the zones themselves suggest a simple framework for analyzing their impact on the domestic economy. This framework can be termed the "enclave approach," following Corden (1974 and 1985). It is shown in Figure 15.2.

Consider (a) the flows of goods and services and the financial flows between the EPZ and the rest of the world and (b) the flows between the EPZ and the host country. The essence of the enclave approach is that the flows in (b) are relevant for evaluating the welfare impact of the zone, but that the flows in (a) are not.

EPZ firms purchase intermediate and capital goods from abroad, which results in outflows of foreign currency.[6] In vertically integrated firms these transactions occur within the firm, giving rise to questions of transfer pricing. The firm may also repatriate profits to its parent abroad. These transactions are irrelevant for an evaluation of the welfare effects of the zone, except insofar as they affect the domestic economy.

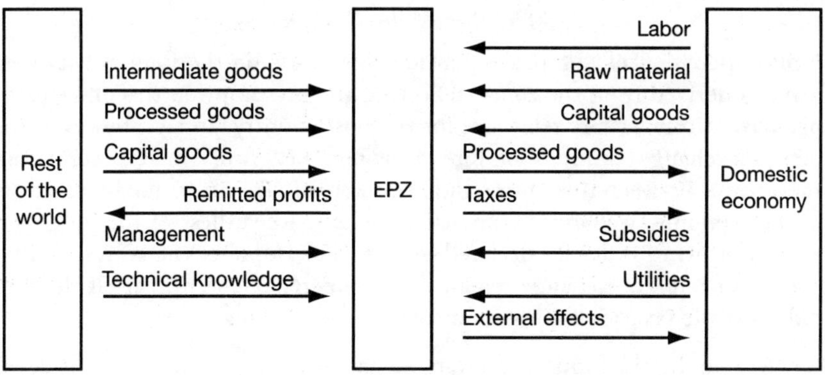

Figure 15.2

The issue of transfer pricing provides a good illustration. Suppose that (as is often the case) there is no profits tax on EPZ firms. Transfer pricing influences whether a firm's profits will be recorded in the host country or elsewhere. But, so long as these profits are earned by the EPZ firm, whether they are realized in the host country or abroad and whether they are repatriated or retained by the EPZ firm are irrelevant for economic welfare in the host country. But if profits are taxed within the host country, transfer pricing affects the size of these taxes and becomes highly relevant.

Economic conditions in an EPZ are generally less distorted than those elsewhere in the domestic economy. Nevertheless, this does not imply that the net outcome of the real and financial flows in figure 2 necessarily raises welfare in the host country. Only a detailed examination of the benefits and costs can resolve this question. The next section looks at each of the main links between EPZ firms and the domestic economy and its welfare significance.

Components of a benefit-cost analysis of EPZs

Profits and losses

Most EPZ firms are foreign-owned. Their profits or losses, to the extent that they are retained or incurred by the firms themselves, do not enter our calculations directly. The *domestically* owned profits and losses (if any) properly belong in an evaluation of the zone, but they can seldom be estimated satisfactorily from the available data. To the extent that such data are collected, they are unreliable, but they do suggest that the profits of domestic firms are only a minuscule proportion of the overall benefits from EPZs. So, for the purposes of this study, the profits of domestically owned firms will be omitted.

Foreign exchange earnings

Public discussion of EPZ places considerable stress on the foreign exchange earnings derived from the zones, reflecting the presumption that these earnings have direct welfare relevance for the host country. In fact, however, the foreign exchange earnings of foreign-owned EPZ firms merely constitute transactions between these firms and firms abroad. They have no direct effects on the economic welfare of domestic nationals. Regardless of the difference between a firm's officially declared exports and imports, the corresponding amount of foreign exchange remains the property of the firm itself (leaving aside possible taxation for the moment). The money may be:

(*a*) held in liquid form in foreign exchange accounts, whether inside or outside the host country

(*b*) used to buy imported capital equipment
(*c*) converted into the domestic currency to be spent on wages and purchases from the local economy.

Item (*a*) is of little welfare importance and reduces to a decision as to where the firm chooses to do its banking. Item (*b*) can also be disregarded if the imported capital equipment is ultimately disposed of abroad or scrapped. Only item (*c*) has welfare importance, because there may be a net benefit to the host country from these purchases.

To purchase raw materials and services from the domestic economy and to hire local workers, EPZ firms must convert their foreign exchange into domestic currency. This is done through the central bank at the official exchange rate. The question is therefore whether the social value of the foreign exchange received by the host country's central bank exceeds the value of the domestic currency the firms obtain in return. The value of the foreign exchange means the domestic value of the extra traded goods and services the host country may absorb as a result of its extra foreign exchange holdings. The value of the domestic currency given to EPZ firms means the domestic value (opportunity cost) of the domestic factors of production and intermediate goods and services purchased by EPZ firms with the money. When exchange controls and domestic protection imply that the social value of foreign exchange in terms of the domestic currency exceeds the official exchange rate, the requirement that these conversions must be made through the central bank at the official exchange rate constitutes, in effect, a form of taxation.

The firm's true foreign exchange earnings will presumably differ from their conversion of foreign exchange into domestic currency. Transfer pricing may be one mechanism by which this profit is realized, but to measure the host country's actual gains, the firm's actual foreign exchange conversion is the relevant statistic.

Employment

The concern that host country governments have for the jobs created by an EPZ presumably reflects their view that the social benefits derived from generating an additional job outweigh the costs. In other words, the wage received by a worker is considered to exceed the social opportunity cost of employment in the zone. However, it is difficult to measure the relevant opportunity cost. Wages in the zones are normally equal to, or slightly above, wages in comparable employment outside the EPZ. Nevertheless, estimates of the social opportunity cost (the shadow price) of unskilled and semiskilled labor commonly suggest that it is less than wages paid in manufacturing.

A difficulty in applying these estimates arises in relation to the transfer of skills to EPZ employees. The estimated value of such skills could in principle be incorporated either by reducing the parameter of the estimated opportunity costs of labor or by increasing appropriately the parameter of the wage received. But, lacking detailed estimates of the value of these transfers, there is no solid basis for making such an adjustment. Consequently, some arbitrariness cannot be avoided.

Technology transfer

Administrators of EPZs agree that there have been few significant transfers of technology and skills from EPZ firms to the domestic economy. Those firms with the technical knowledge from which local firms could benefit (most notably electronics and electrical companies) have been isolated from the domestic economy. Little of their raw materials and capital equipment has come from local suppliers. In retrospect, the early expectations that much technology would be transferred were naive. To the extent that intermediate products are internationally traded, EPZ firms will buy from the cheapest reliable source.

Managerial practices and notions of quality control are inevitably transferred to the local middle managers whom EPZ firms employ. These managers can eventually obtain significantly higher salaries in domestic industry than they could after a similar period of employment elsewhere. This suggests that the training they receive confers a benefit to the domestic economy, which may not be fully captured in the wages they receive in the EPZs. One way of treating this issue is to say that the social opportunity cost of the employment of these workers in the EPZ is lowered by such training. These externality effects can be incorporated in principle by lowering the parameter of the opportunity cost of labor.

Domestic sales

Almost all of the output of EPZs must be sold abroad, but domestic sales are permitted when, for example, finished consumer goods are rejected by foreign buyers. Such sales are typically treated as imports, and duty must be paid at the normal rate. The net value to the host country of the goods consumed is the value at c.i.f. prices of the imports which would otherwise have occurred, which is also the net price actually paid to the EPZ firm. Thus, as these sales have no net welfare effects, they can be ignored in the benefit-cost analysis.

Purchase of domestic raw materials and capital goods

Governments typically encourage EPZ firms to use domestic raw materials, intermediate inputs, and capital goods. This can be interpreted to mean that governments believe that the prices paid by firms for these materials exceed the marginal social costs of supplying them. Local raw materials and capital goods generally compete with imported substitutes, and the duty applied to these imports provides the basis for estimating the difference between the social opportunity cost of providing these imports (their border c.i.f. prices) and the prices paid (tariff inclusive). When EPZ firms receive a rebate from the host government equivalent to the duty that would have been paid on these imported inputs, there is no net welfare effect from their purchase by EPZ firms.

Use of electricity

EPZ firms, especially garment and textile prducers, are big users of electricity. The benefit-cost analysis must compare the tariff rates paid with estimates of the long-run marginal cost (LRMC) of supplying extra power. If the average tariff exceeded the LRMC, the electricity used by EPZ firms would entail a net tax—or, in the reverse case, a net subsidy.

Domestic borrowing

Foreign investors are sometimes allowed to borrow on local capital market, perhaps with a government guarantee. This arrangement would be unimportant if the local capital markets was open to international capital flows: borrowing by EPZ firms would then simply induce inflows of private capital from abroad and would not displace local investment. However, when local capital markets are closed and interest rates suppressed—a combination present in Latin America (Diaz-Alexandro 1970) and the Philippines—the analysis is different. The implication is that the domestic output forgone as a result of additional borrowings by (foreign) EPZ firms exceeds the compensation received from them in interest and principal repayments. To put it another way, the shadow price of capital exceeds its market price.

Taxes

Although taxes raised from EPZ firms are generally small, they are a clear benefit for the domestic economy: without the zone, there would be no taxes. Firms that move to a zone from elsewhere in the host country or foreign firms that would have entered even without a zone are exceptions, but unimportant ones. Most firms are foreign and, according to managers, few would have invested in the host countries without the EPZ incentives. Taxes are therefore counted as a net benefit to the host country.

The low rates of company income tax offered by host country governments to attract foreign firms into the EPZs sometimes achieve this goal. Some foreign investors legally reside in countries that allow their firms to credit taxes paid abroad against taxes due at home. The United States is such a home country. In these cases, a tax holiday for firms investing in the EPZ may merely transfer revenue from the treasury of the EPZ country to that of the investor's home country.

Development and recurrent costs

The establishment of the zone site, its maintenance, and administration all represent economic costs—and in principle should be evaluated at shadow prices. In the absence of disaggregated data, however, it is necessary to rely on financial costs. Against these costs are the rents and other charges received from EPZ firms, not counted elsewhere in the analysis.

EVIDENCE FROM FOUR ASIAN COUNTRIES

Estimates of the shadow prices of labor, foreign exchange, capital, and so forth are available for most developing counties. Their quality varies widely, but the best estimates for each country were:

- Indonesia: Hughes (1983), Pitt (1981), and Munasinghe (1980)
- The Republic of Korea: Koo (1981) and Nam (1981a and 1981b)
- Malaysia: Veitch (1977, 1979, and 1984)
- The Philippines: Medalla and Power (1984) and Manalaysay (1979).

These studies provided the basis for the shadow prices, but they were sometimes updated, corrected, or amended to a form more suitable for evaluating EPZs. Table 15.5 summarizes the information as ratios of the estimated shadow prices to market prices.

Table 15.6 shows the contributions of each of the major benefit cost categories to the aggregate net present value (NPV) of the EPZs. Costs appear as

Table 15.5 Estimated ratios of shadow prices to market prices

Category	*Indonesia*	*Korea*	*Malaysia*	*Philippines*
Labor	0.75	0.91	0.83	0.64
Foreign exchange	1.00[a]	1.08	1.11	1.25
Domestic raw material	0.85	0.92	0.90	0.96
Domestic capital equipment	0.85	0.98	0.91	0.96
Electricity	1.05	1.33	0.93	1.30
Domestic financial capital	n.a.	n.a.	n.a.	1.58

Notes: n.a. Not applicable.

[a] Hughes 1983 concluded that the effects of Indonesia's import barriers (tariffs and quotas), which raise domestic prices above border prices, and subsidies on the consumption of traded goods (such as rice and petroleum products) roughly cancelled, implying that the shadow price of foreign exchange was approximately equal to the official rate.

Sources: Indonesia: Hughes 1983, Pitt 1981 and Munasinghe 1980, Korea: Koo 1981 and Nam 1981a and 1981b. Malaysia: Veitch 1977, 1979, and 1984. Philippines: Medalla and Power 1984 and Manalaysay 1979.

Table 15.6 Welfare impact of EPZs: net present value (millions of 1982 U.S. dollars)

Category	*Indonesia*	*Korea*	*Malaysia*	*Philippines*
Employment	4	39	111	59
Foreign exchange earnings	0	65	94	72
Local raw materials	5	16	18	3
Local capital equipment	0	0	10	0
Taxes and other revenue	23	18	10	11
Electricity use	−1	−13	−53	−4
Administrative costs	−13	−17	−4	−23
Infrastructure costs and subsidies	−3	−68	−43	−196
Domestic borrowing	0	0	0	−147
Total net present value	15	40	143	−225
Internal rate of return (percent)	26	15	28	−3

negative items. For consistency, the calculations assume a real discount rate of 7.5 percent and a life for the EPZ of twenty-five years. The final row of Table 15.6 displays the calculated internal rate of return for each of the EPZs. Table 15.7 presents the NPV computations in more convenient form, by expressing the various components as a percentage of the *gross* benefits of the EPZ (the sum of all positive NPV items appearing in Table 15.6).

Before discussing the results in detail, it is necessary to focus on a methodological point: the distinction between the benefits from "foreign exchange earnings" and those from other sources. As explained earlier, the benefits attributed to foreign exchange earnings arise because EPZ firms must convert foreign exchange into domestic currency to meet their domestic costs. It is analytically possible to separate the net gains from the currency conversion from those arising from the subsequent domestic payments, as reflected in tables 15.6 and 15.7. Alternatively, the two can be combined—and it makes economic sense to do so. Indirectly, foreign exchange is being paid to local workers, suppliers, and so forth.

Consider a hypothetical example: the conversion of $1,000 into Philippine

Table 15.7 Composition of net present value (percent of gross benefits)

Category	*Indonesia*	*Korea*	*Malaysia*	*Philippines*
Employment	13	28	46	41
Foreign exchange earnings	0	47	39	50
Local raw materials	16	12	7	2
Local capital equipment	0	0	4	0
Taxes and other revenue	72	13	4	8
Electricity use	−3	−9	−22	−3
Administrative costs	−41	−12	−2	−16
Infrastructure costs and subsidies	−9	−49	−18	−135
Domestic borrowing	0	0	0	−101
Total	47	29	59	−155

pesos at the official 1982 exchange rate of P9.17 = US$1 for the payment of local wages. When the $1,000 is converted into pesos, there is a net gain to the Philippines arising from the difference between the official exchange rate and the shadow price of foreign exchange. Since the ratio of the shadow price to the official rate was an estimated 1.25, this implies a net gain of P2,290. When the P9,170 is paid to Philippine workers, there is a second net gain—from the difference between the social opportunity cost of labor and the market wage. The estimated value of 0.64 for the ratio of these two sources of gain arises from the way our shadow prices have been defined. But the two are aspects of the same phenomenon: the (indirect) payment of $1,000 to hire domestic workers. Philippine workers are indirectly earning for the Philippines $1,000 in foreign exchange, generating a net gain to the Philippines of P4,590.[7]

Table 15.8 incorporates this analysis and shows the re-estimated distribution of net benefits, substituting for the first five rows of Table 15.7. The gains from "foreign exchange earnings" have been redistributed among the other benefit-cost categories. The results for Indonesia are unchanged from Table 15.7, because the estimated net gains from foreign exchange earnings were zero (see note a to Table 15.5). The percentage totals do not add to 100 because only part of the firms' foreign exchange conversions can be attributed to the four categories in the table.

Benefits

Table 15.7 shows that the big gains in Korea, Malaysia, and the Philippines come from employment and foreign exchange earnings. With the gain from foreign exchange earnings distributed as in table 15.8, employment accounts for more than half the gross benefits. Local suppliers and tax revenue are much less important. For these three countries, the EPZs are in effect a form of indirect labor export.

For Indonesia, two unusual features must be stressed. First, an unusually high proportion of raw materials is obtained within Indonesia: primarily textiles used in garments. By 1982 more than 40 percent of all raw materials used were bought in Indonesia. The estimated net gains from this source outweigh the estimated net gains from job creation. The second unusual

Table 15.8 Composition of net present value with foreign exchange earnings distributed (percent of gross benefits)

Category	*Indonesia*	*Korea*	*Malaysia*	*Philippines*
Employment	13	55	68	69
Local raw materials	16	14	15	3
Local capital equipment	0	0	8	0
Taxes and other revenue	72	14	5	9

feature is the importance of the "taxes and other revenue" category. Of the $22.6 million shown in table 15.6, property tax accounted for $2.9 million; other official taxes $0.9 million; "unofficial" taxes $25.9 million; and expenditure on the drawback scheme $7,100.[8]

The "unofficial" tax item, discussed in detail in Warr (1983) and Gray (1979), represents the outcome of rent-seeking behavior by government officials. This reveals much about the way the net benefits from the zone are distributed among individuals and also shows that these are collected at considerable social cost. If these revenues are excluded from the benefit-cost analysis, the NPV of $15,000 shown in table 15.6 becomes $11,000, and the internal rate of return also turns negative (Wart 1983).

The $7,100 spent on the drawback scheme is a subsidy to the use of domestic raw materials. It is intended to counteract the effects of protection on the costs of the imports used in producing these raw materials. Since the estimated net gain from the use of these raw materials is only $4,900, the drawback provisions are costing Indonesia more than they are worth.

Costs

The costs of achieving the benefits are summarized by the negative items in Tables 15.6 and 15.7. In Table 15.7 they are expressed as a percentage of the sum of all net benefits. The striking features of this table both involve the Philippines: (a) the enormous infrastructure cost of the Bataan EPZ and (b) the heavy cost of giving EPZ firms (subsidized) access to the local capital market. Each of these items is itself large enough to outweigh the sum of all benefits derived by the Philippines from its EPZ.

Another feature is the low administrative and infrastructure cost of Malaysia's Penang Free Trade Zone. However, the cost of Malaysia's subsidization of electricity outweighs the combined benefits from the use of local raw materials and local capital equipment and all tax revenues raised from EPZ firms.

THE POLICY IMPLICATIONS OF EPZS

Any cost-benefit analysis of EPZs is bound to ignore a deeper question: would it be possible to achieve the benefits available from EPZs in another, more cost-effective way? For governments considering the merits of EPZs this fundamental issue needs to be addressed directly.

In recent years, several of the countries that established EPZs in the 1970s have extended the right to import free of duty to firms producing for export but located outside EPZs. The duty-free raw materials are held in bond on the factory site until required for production. This change of policy—in the Philippines, Malaysia, and Korea—undermined the advantages of EPZs and showed that expensive special zones were not really necessary.

The same applies to other attractions of EPZs: the simplification of customs procedures, the clarification or elimination of regulations, and the upgrading of industrial infrastructure—each could be achieved for the whole economy. And, as foreign firms frequently attest, countries need stable and clear policies to attract foreign investment. This obviously applies as much outside the EPZs as within. Most of the features that have enabled EPZs to attract foreign investment could be applied outside the zones, with similar effectiveness, and without establishing special enclaves.

The features of the domestic economy that impede foreign investment and that EPZs are intended partly to counteract also impede the development of efficient domestic industries. If a liberalized environment within the EPZs deflects attention from these matters, the net outcome could be worse than what would have occurred in the absence of the zones.

The benefits from EPZs are limited. They are definitely not "engines of development." For countries in the early stages of development, zones can be an efficient and productive means of absorbing surplus labor. Even then, they will never be more than a modest part of the solution to the vast employment problems of these countries. EPZs also expose domestic businesses to examples of internationally competitive enterprises; this demonstration effect is undoubtedly valuable, especially in the early stages of industrialization, as is the on-the-job training of local managers. Even so, such benefits should not be exaggerated.

As industrial development proceeds, interest in EPZs tends to wane. Taiwan and Korea, having been pioneers in the establishment of EPZs in the late 1960s and early 1970s, are now much less interested in this type of enclave development. In the next couple of decades a similar change of attitude may occur in many of the countries now actively promoting EPZs.

ACKNOWLEDGMENTS

This paper has benefited from the comments of W. M. Corden, Demetrios Papageorgiou, and Marcelo Selowsky. The author is responsible for the views presented and any errors.

NOTES

1 See Hamada 1974, Rodriguez 1976, and Hamilton and Svensson 1982. Hamilton and Svensson 1983 is a partial exception to this description. See also Balasubramanyam 1988 for a useful discussion of this literature.

2 Examples in East and Southeast Asia include the Republic of Korea, the Philippines, Thailand, and Indonesia.

3 For example, the proportions of firms in the Philippines' Bataan EPZ (discussed later) that declared overall trading losses in their annual financial statements were: 1980, 58 percent; 1981, 81 percent; 1982, 75 percent; and 1983, 64 percent (Warr 1985, p. 12).

4 These case studies are: Indonesia, Warr 1983; Korea, Warr 1984; Malaysia, Warr 1987b; and the Philippines, Warr 1985 and 1987a.

5 Our discussion will disregard income distribution within the host country.

6 To keep figure 15.2 simple these financial flows are not indicated in the diagram. Most of the flows shown in the diagram are accompanied by financial flows in the opposite direction, but exceptions are taxes and subsidies and external effects such as transfers of managerial and technical knowledge.

7 The aggregate welfare outcome for the Philippines would have been essentially no different if the $1,000 had been paid directly to Philippine workers who then converted it into the domestic currency through the central bank.

8 The negative sign draws attention to the fact that this item is a revenue outlay—a subsidy—rather than a tax receipt.

REFERENCES

Balasubramanyam, V. N. 1988. "Export Processing Zones in Developing Countries: Theory and Empirical Evidence." In D. Greenaway, ed. *Economic Development and International Trade.* London: Macmillan.

Castro, J. S. 1982. "The Bataan Export Processing Zone." ILO-ARTEP, Bangkok.

Caves, R. E., and R. W. Jones. 1985. *World Trade and Payments: An Introduction*, 4th ed. Boston: Little, Brown.

Corden, W. M. 1974. "The Theory of International Trade." In J. H. Dunning, ed. *Economic Analysis and the Multinational Enterprise.* London: Allen and Unwin.

——. 1985. *Protection, Growth and Trade: Essays in International Economics.*. Oxford: Basil Blackwell.

Datta-Chaudhuri, M. 1980. "The Role of Free Trade Zones in the Creation of Employment and Industrial Growth in Malaysia." ILO-ARTEP, Bangkok.

Diaz-Alejandro, C. F. 1970. "Direct Foreign Development in Latin America." In C. P. Kindleberger, ed. *The Multinational Corporation.* Cambridge, Mass.: MIT Press.

Edgren, G. 1982. "Spearheads of Industrialization or Sweatshops in the Sun?: A Critical Appraisal of Labour Conditions in Asian Export Processing Zones." ILO-ARTEP, Bangkok.

Gray, C. 1979. "Civil Service Compensation in Indonesia." *Bulletin of Indonesian Economic Studies 15: 85–113.*

Grubel, H. C. 1982. "Towards a Theory of Free Economic Zones." *Weltwirtshaftliches Archiv* 118, no.l.

Hamada, K. 1974. "An Economic Analysis of the Duty-Free Zones." *Journal of International Economics* 4: 225–41.

Hamilton, C., and L. E. O. Svensson 1982 "On the Welfare Economics of a Duty Free Zone." *Journal of International Economics* 13: 45–64.

——. 1983."On the Choice between Capital Import and Labor Export" *European Economic Review* 20: 167–92.

Hughes, G. A. 1983. "Shadow Prices and Economic Policy in Indonesia." Faculty of Economics and Politics, University of Cambridge.

Jones, R. W. 1980. "Comparative and Absolute Advantage" *Swiss Journal of Economics and Statistics* 3: 235–60.

Koo Bohn-Young. 1981. "A Preliminary Estimate of Shadow Price Parameters in Korea" (in Korean). *Hankuk Kaebal Yongu* 3: 40–50.

Manalaysay, C. P. 1979. "Estimating the Shadow Price of Capital." In R. M. Bautista, J. H. Power, and associates. *Industrial Promotion Policies in the Philippines.* Manila: Philippine Institute for Development Studies.

Medalla, E. A., and J. H. Power. 1984 "Estimating the Shadow Exchange Rate, the Shadow Wage Rate and the Social Rate of Discount for the Philippines." Staff Paper 84–03. Philippine Intstitute for Development Studies, Manila.

Munasinghe, M. 1980. "Energy Pricing Policy: The Case of Electricity." World Bank, Washington, D.C.

Nam Chang Hyun. 1981. "Trade and Industrial Policies, and the Structure of Protection in Korea." In W. Hong and L. B. Kraust, eds. *Trade and Growth of the Advanced Developing Counties in the Pacific Basin*. Seoul: Korea Development Institute.

——. 1981b. "The Industrial Incentives and Structure of Protection in Korea" (in Korean). Korea Development Institute Seoul.

Pitt, M. M. 1981. "Alternative Trade Strategies and Employment in Indonesia." In Anne O. Krueger and others, eds. *Trade and Employment in Developing Countries*, vol.1: *Individual Studies*. Chicago: University of Chicago Press.

Spinanger. D. 1984. "Objectives and Impact of Economic Activity Zones—Some Evidence from Asia." *Weltwirtschaftliches Archiv* 120: 64–89.

Rodriguez, C. A. 1976. "A Note on the Economics of the Duty-Free Zone." *Journal of International Economics* 6: 385–88.

United Nations. 1985. *An Evaluation of Export Processing Zones in Selected Asian Countries.* ESCAP/UNCTC Publication Series B, No. 8 (ST/ESCAP/395). Bangkok.

Veitch, M. 1977, 1979. and 1984. "National Parameters for Project Evaluation in Malaysia." United Nations Development programme/World Bank State and Rural Development Project, Kuala Lumpur.

Vernon, R. 1966. "International Investment and International Trade in the Product Cycle." *Quarterly Journal of Economics* 80: 190–207.

Wall, D. 1976. "Export Processing Zones." *Journal of World Trade Law* 10: 478–89.

Warr, P. G. 1983. "The Jakarta Export Processing Zone: Benefits and Costs." *Bulletin of Indonesian Economic Studies* 19, no.3: 28–49.

——. 1984. "Korea's Masan Free Export Zone: Benefits and Costs." *Developing Economies* 22: 167–84.

——. 1985. "Export Processing Zones in the Philippines." ASEAN-Australia Economic Papers 20. Australian National University, Canberra.

——. 1987a. "Export Promotion via Industrial Enclaves: The Philippines Bataan Export Processing Zone." *Journal of Development Studies* 23: 220–41.

——. 1987b. "Malaysia's Industrial Enclaves: Benefits and Costs." *Developing Economies* 25: 30–55.

Part V

CHANGING LABOUR CONDITIONS

16

APPROACHING THE TURNING POINT?

Labour Market Change under Indonesia's New Order

Chris Manning

I INTRODUCTION

In August 1991 a violent labor dispute broke out over wages and working conditions in the multiplant enterprise Gadjah Tunggal in Tangerang, west of Jakarta. The strike was unprecedented in the new order period in terms of the number of workers involved and its media coverage. By all reports, a significant proportion of the 12,000 strong work force of Gadjah Tunggal were actively involved, the dispute lasted over a month, resulted in considerable damage to property and a strong military involvement in its resolution.

This strike, like many other well publicized labor disputes which occurred in 1991–92, might be seen as symptomatic of the emergence of a new era for labor in Indonesia. It could be argued that Indonesia had entered a new phase of capitalist development in which labor was an increasing force to be reckoned with, both politically and on the factory floor. Parallels could be drawn with neighboring countries and in particular the Republic of Korea, where several years earlier sustained economic growth and labor shortages in the context of a repressive military regime had spilt over into substantial labor unrest. In the Korean case, labor action in 1987–88 had forced the military government to make major concessions to organized labor in terms of labor freedoms, social security, and industrial relations processes [6] [46].

In this paper, it is argued that although the industrial relations climate has changed in Indonesia since the late 1980s, there has not been any change in fundamental labor market circumstances which might sustain a greater role for organized labor. Economic conditions are much less favorable to a change in the relative bargaining power of labor than in Malaysia and even Thailand, much less than in emerging industrialized countries such as Korea and Taiwan. By most criteria, it has still not reached the "turning point" in economic development which might be viewed as marking an important transition from a labor surplus to a labor scarce economy.

Source: *Developing Economies*, Vol. XXXIII(1), March 1995, pp. 52–81.

Why has Indonesia been slower in achieving a transition in labor markets than several of these other countries? Part of the difference in experience with these other countries can be attributed to different initial starting conditions in the early postwar era and the demise of organized labor as a political force in the early new order period. But it shall also be argued that Indonesia's rather unique mix of abundant natural resources and high levels of rural population pressure and poverty have brought about different policy responses and outcomes. Unlike the NIEs, which had no choice but to base their drive for economic development on the cost advantages of labor-intensive industries, economic development in Indonesia has been strongly supported by the rents from natural resource exploitation.

Development programs, especially during the oil boom period, have contributed to different outcomes for labor and have proved a mixed blessing for Indonesian workers. While it can be argued that investment of some of the rents on infrastructure, agriculture, and human resources has been beneficial to unskilled labor, investment in relatively capital-intensive industries has not. These investments tended to favor the creation of a small elite group of highly skilled workers and widening differentials between wage workers. Manufacturing labor absorption has been relatively slow until very recently, although indirect evidence suggests that manufacturing exports have made an important contribution to income growth among the poor in the past decade.

The paper is divided into four major sections. In the second, I deal with the notion of the turning point and its significance for unskilled labor, income distribution, and general economic development. The third section examines the structure of Indonesian labor markets around 1990, the fourth looks at the changing structure of labor markets, and the fifth at labor standards, unions, and the welfare of wage workers.

One point of clarification is warranted. The paper focuses on the fortunes of relatively unskilled labor both absolutely and relative to skilled workers. While developments for more skilled and professional workers are also of relevance—especially to discussions of emerging class structure and the growth of the "middle class"—the paper is primarily concerned with unskilled labor. The main question which is posed is the extent to which labor market developments among the unskilled, from the bottom rather than from the middle or top, have or are likely to become a force for economic and political change.

Unlike many approaches to labor issues which tend to focus either on rural workers in the context of agricultural development and class formation or urban workers in the context of industrialization, I am interested in both rural and urban workers as a group which is linked within a general labor market for unskilled labor. The multiplicity of jobs held by rural workers in particular and high levels of rural-urban mobility justify such an approach. More importantly, an assessment of the prospects for economic and political change depends not only on the conditions experienced by industrial workers but also in the villages from where they come and in services and related industries where they might seek alternative employment.

II LABOR MARKET TRANSITIONS: THEORY AND PRACTICE

In this paper, I will adopt the well-known notions of labor surplus and labor scarce economies and the "turning point" in labor markets as a framework for analyzing labor developments in Indonesia. These constructs are helpful for an understanding of the relative bargaining power of labor, patterns of income distribution, and potential changes in industry structure and technology associated with economic development.[1] Both are useful for an understanding of labor market changes and their broader implications in Indonesia over the past twenty-five years. The basic idea is that in the early stages of development real wages of unskilled labor are held down by an abundant supply of labor in agriculture.[2] They begin to rise only after this surplus is absorbed in the modern (industrial) sector.

During the surplus labor phase, cheap labor is the main basis for capital accumulation, the profits share rises, and income disparities increase between capitalists and skilled labor on the one hand unskilled labor on the other. Only when labor becomes scarce in agriculture and the modern sector begins to absorb a significant share of the work force do real wages begin to rise. Market forces then dictate a shift toward more capital- and skill-intensive industries, skill differentials in wages begin to narrow, and the shares of profits fall and wages rise relative to GDP.

Several of the main ideas underpinning Lewis's theory were quite justifiably criticized at the time. But the central notion of constant or even declining real wages in the early stages of economic development, followed by a fairly clearly defined turning point (in countries which have experienced sustained high rates of economic growth), has been empirically vindicated by the experience of East Asian countries in particular.[3]

The basic model needs to be modified in two important respects, however. First, rapid population growth rather than surplus (underemployed) labor in agriculture has been the main labor market factor contributing to excess labor supply and stagnant wages in many countries.[4] It is worth bearing in mind that labor force growth rates in developing countries have been 3–4 times more rapid since the 1950s than was the case in the western industrialized countries in the latter half of the nineteenth century and 2–3 times as rapid as in Japan during the same period.[5] Indonesian labor supply growth has been similar to other developing countries since the 1960s.

Second, the basic dichotomy in intersectoral analysis of the labor surplus economy is not between agriculture and industry as many earlier authors have emphasized. Rather it is between high- and low-productivity jobs or more loosely defined "modern" and "traditional" sectors.[6] The former represent greater inputs of capital, skill, and management in the deployment of unskilled labor, whereas the latter are frequently created partly in response to labor supply pressures. Self-employment in the "fungible" informal sector is one example.

Thus, movements of labor out of agriculture to industry or services may not represent a positive sign. This would be true if people are leaving higher productivity jobs in agriculture or, alternatively, they are being pushed out of agricultural employment into low-paid informal activities. As will be seen below, the significance of intersectoral labor shifts in Indonesia has been one important issue of controversy, especially in the interpretation of national labor force trends.

A The East Asian experience

What has been the experience of East Asian countries (excluding China) in the transition from a labor surplus economy?[7] In the case of Japan, it is now generally accepted that the turning point did not occur until after World War II, more than half a century after Japan began to industrialize [41] [43]. In contrast, the transition occurred much more rapidly in the NIEs. In all these countries real wages began to grow rapidly within the space of approximately one decade after these countries instituted major programs of economic reform and began their outward-oriented programs of industrialization.[8] In Malaysia and Thailand, sustained real wage growth appears to have occurred from around the mid-1980s, also approximately a decade—slightly less in Malaysia and slightly more in Thailand—after these countries began a major push into manufacturing exports (Table 16.1).[9]

A range of factors seem to have played an important role in bringing about a much more rapid transition in the East Asian economies compared with Japan. The dual labor market, relative insulation of large-scale firms with permanent employment systems from pressures of surplus labor in traditional

Table 16.1 Growth in real earnings per employee in manufacturing in selected East Asian countries (% p.a.)

	1970–80	*1980–88*
Taiwan	6.2	6.3
Korea	8.4	5.3
Malaysia	1.8	3.6
Thailand	1.9	6.5
Philippines	–4.1	0.6

Sources: [52, 1989/90 and 1991/92]. For Taiwan, from [16, Table 4.2]. For the Philippines (1980–88), from [26].

sectors, has not been as strong in these countries as it was in Japan. Several other factors delayed the turning point in Japan: relatively capital-intensive investments in heavy industry early in the industrialization process, a much larger economy, slower rates of economic growth, and a less favorable international trading environment for labor-intensive export growth in the first half of this century.

Available wage data need to be interpreted carefully, however, especially bearing in mind that they deal primarily with average earnings rather than wage rates. At least in the early stages of real wage growth, wages increased not because the lowest paid workers were being paid more for the same job. Rather, many workers changed jobs and sectors, worked more intensively than previously, and employees in new sectors were more skilled and educated. The classic example is Korea which for some time has had the dubious honor of recording the longest average working hours in manufacturing in the world: transfer of relatively underemployed labor in agriculture to manufacturing alone appears to account for a substantial share of record rates of real wage growth in the early stages of industrialization in Korea [10] [2]

Aside from real wage trends, two other important indicators which have been used to help identify the timing of the turning point have been trends in the absolute number of persons engaged in agriculture and skill differentials. Although in Japan the size of the agricultural work force had already begun to stabilize in the 1930s, it began to decline steeply in the 1950s, as did skill differentials in wages. Similariy the agricultural labor force began to decline absolutely in Korea from the early 1980s and in Taiwan somewhat earlier, and wage differentials by skill and industry appear to have begun to narrow in Korea since the mid-1970s [3] [2].

The experience of Malaysia and Thailand with regard to agricultural employment bas been somewhat different. Although the relative share of employment in agriculture has declined, absolute levels of employment have continued to increase in this sector despite reported shortages of labor and real wage growth. A more extensive land frontier, albeit now much more limited than in the immediate postwar period, more favorable climatic conditions, and richer agricultural resources per capita help explain this rather different pattern of development compared with Japan, Korea, or Taiwan.[10]

The patterns of development associated with these labor market transitions are well known. In the literature, the move toward export-oriented industrialization and rapid employment growth in manufacturing has been identified as the major stimulus. Less emphasized is the growth of agricultural output, employment, and incomes in the early stages of growth, partly supported by macroeconomic policies which supported agriculture (Oshima [44]). Oshima also emphasizes investment in rural infrastructure and human capital as key factors behind the success of the NIEs.

B Labor market processes and labor repression

The labor surplus model and notion of a turning point assume that wage and employment trends are determined entirely through the market. East Asia has been held up by some observers as a successful example of market-determined processes in labor allocation: outcomes have been favorable to labor precisely because governments have played a minimum role in wage fixing (or enforcement) and trade unions have been weak or tightly controlled by governments [15] [16]. In contrast, others have contended that government repressive actions have limited the gains made by labor through adopting policies which maximize employment growth and tightly control worker welfare and wages [12].

From the standpoint of welfare gains, the former view is more in accordance with the facts. By almost any indicator of labor welfare: wage and income growth, poverty decline, and social indicators such as health and education, workers and their families have done remarkably well in general in the rapidly growing East Asian countries, and better than anywhere else in the developing world [51, 1990] [40].[11]

However, in contrast to the view of some neoclassical economists (for example, [15] [14]), East Asian governments have by no means been noninterventionist in the field of labor, although some have intervened more than others (Korea and Singapore versus Taiwan and Hong Kong). Control and repression of trade union activities and activists has been common throughout the region.[12] Some countries, especially Singapore and to a lesser extent Korea, also attempted to control wage growth to ensure a steady inflow of investment in labor intensive industries (Deyo [12]). The latter policies have been far less successful than Deyo and others suggest however: the Singapore policy of encouraging immigrant labor came to a halt in the late 1970s; the indirect guidelines for minimum wage growth appear to have had little impact on wage growth in Korea, especially in the 1980s.

How much does the story of labor gains through rapid employment growth, which facilitated a transition beyond the turning point, need to be qualified by the emergence of a "hyperproletariat" identified by Heyzer [19], Deyo [12], and many others. This term refers to low wage, predominantly young, and unmarried female labor which has dominated the labor-intensive export-oriented industries in most countries. The argument is that new investors, especially multinationals, chose young female labor because they were willing to accept lower wages, manipulated easily, and replaced by a surplus of workers coming from the countryside.

In one sense the claims of the labor exploitation theorists are correct. Unmarried female labor appear to have been more willing to work for low wages, and were less likely to organize and protest against onerous labor standards than males. In many cases they worked for target incomes over a limited number of years before quitting the work force to marry (or being fired once they married) or seek employment in less difficult work. Wages were generally lower and working conditions often worse among these workers than male counterparts in more capital-intensive industries.[13]

Nevertheless, in my view, the labor exploitation argument has been overstated and to some extent misses the central point if we are interested in improvements in labor welfare. First, while labor standards have been very poor compared with developed countries, wage rates were generally not lower in new industries than in alternative traditional agriculture, small-scale industry, and informal sector work. Labor incomes were frequently higher because of more intensive and regular work.[14] Second, as shortages of labor began to emerge, wages did not stagnate in industries like textiles and footwear, despite the attempts of governments to maintain a cheap labor policy in some countries. While a gap in average wages with more capital intensive activities persisted for some time, frequently rose more rapidly in the labor-intensive industries (and in agriculture) as countries approached the turning point [41] [3].

Finally, dramatic increases in female labor force participation in full time work have been a powerful force toward overall poverty decline throughout the region, a point which is rarely mentioned in the literature. While women worked extremely long hours under sweat labor conditions which have long been outlawed in most developed countries, household incomes rose quite dramatically among the poor households from which these women have come in all the NIEs, especially as countries approached the turning point.

There are difficult moral issues involved in the assessment of the welfare gains of the "hyperproletariat" in the context of relative deprivation between first and third world countries, and MNCs operating in both.[15] Nevertheless, unqualified, pious condemnation of both national enterprises and MNCs for employing young women of their own volition in low-wage jobs which delivered incomes often far higher than they could have earned elsewhere (given the greater intensity of work effort in new jobs) is misplaced in the context of individual and household welfare. Further, it is patronizing to the individual workers who, for the most part, made the difficult decision themselves to leave their villages and engage in factory work.

III LABOR MARKET STRUCTURE IN INDONESIA CIRCA 1990

How does the Indonesian case fit in with this general picture of labor market transitions in the East Asian region? In this section, I will discuss labor market structure around 1990 and compare it with other selected countries in the region. The subsequent section will examine labor market change.

The Indonesian employment structure has several characteristics which are common to labor surplus economies, although it is quite segmented by occupation, gender, and region. Four characteristics are worthy of mention. First, a high proportion of persons were engaged in sell-employed and informal sector jobs (around two-thirds of the total), mainly in agriculture and to a lesser extent in trade, services, and manufacturing (Table 16.2). This contrasts with other countries in the region where wage work was much more common, especially among females engaged in nonagricultural work (Table 16.3). Although this is not a definitive indicator of labor surplus conditions, it implies that modern sector employment was relatively small nationally, and rapid growth in this sector alone would be unlikely to substantially affect the labor market in general.

This "informal" nature of the labor market is further indicated by the concentration of work in a few traditional sector occupations. For example, self-employed and family workers in petty trade alone were reported to account for approximately 40 per cent of all employment in services in 1985.[16] Although this share has almost certainly fallen since then, it indicates the continuing dominance of small-scale self-employment in total employment.

Second, the agricultural sector still employed around half of the total work force, a much higher share than countries like Korea and Malaysia, higher

Table 16.2 Structure of employment of selected regions in Indonesia, 1990 (%)

	Region						
	Urban				*Rural*		
	Jakarta	*West Java*	*Other Java*	*Outer islands*	*Java*	*Outer islands*	*Indonesia*
Sector of employment:							
Agriculture	1.1	7.1	12.9	11.6	58.3	71.8	50.4
Manufacturing	20.5	24.3	18.8	10.2	11.3	6.1	11.5
Government & other services	36.3	27.8	28.9	33.3	8.5	6.9	14.1
Other[a]	42.1	40.8	39.4	44.9	21.9	15.2	24.0
Total	100	100	100	100	100	100	100
Employment status:							
Self-employed/family workers	25.6	36.4	41.4	41.0	67.3	80.2	63.5
Employees	72.2	61.4	56.7	56.2	31.4	18.1	34.9
Occupation:							
Professionals	6.7	6.1	6.1	8.3	2.1	3.0	3.7
White-collar workers[b]	25.4	18.5	16.1	24.4	4.1	5.1	8.9

Note:
[a] Includes mining, public utilities, construction, trade, and transport/communications.
[b] Professional, managerial, and clerical workers.

Source: [22, 1990 (series S2)].

Table 16.3 Employment structure in selected Asian Countries circa 1990 (%)

	Korea (1991)	*Malaysia (1988)*	*Thailand (1988)*	*Philippines (1990)*	*Pakistan (1990/91)*	*Indonesia (1990)*
Employment by major sector:						
Agriculture	16.3	30.6	64.4	41.5	44.5	50.4
Manufacturing	27.0	16.0	8.1	8.9	9.9	11.5
Government & other services	14.6	20.6	9.9	17.2	12.4	14.1
Other	42.1	32.8	17.6	32.4	32.9	26.0
Total	100	100	100	100	100	100
% of females in total manufacturing employment	41.7	45.5	45.3	40.7	15.9	44.9
Work status:						
Employees as % of agricultural employment	7.4	28.8	10.6	20.4	9.5	11.5
Self-employed/family workers as % of nonagricultural employment:						
Males	26.0	22.7	31.4	23.1	39.6	42.6
Females	30.5	25.2	41.8	35.6	25.7	62.7
Occupation:						
White-collar workers as % of total employment	22.0	18.8	5.0	10.8	9.9	8.9
% of nonagricultural employment:						
Professionals	8.9	10.6	6.4	9.8	8.3	7.3
White-collar workers[a]	26.3	27.1	14.1	18.5	17.8	17.6

Note:
[a] Professional, managerial, and clerical workers.

Sources: [26]. For Indonesia, [22, 1990 (series S2)]. Except for Indonesia, all data from national labor force surveys.

than in the Philippines and Pakistan, but lower than in Thailand. Insofar as underemployment on a regular and seasonal basis is more marked in agriculture, this also implies a considerable supply of unskilled labor available for work in growing sectors such as manufacturing.[17]

Third, whereas wage earners were concentrated on Java, in urban Java and especially in JABOTABEK region (in and around Jakarta) where recent manufacturing growth has been most rapid, small farmers, who are generally most associated with problems of underemployment, were concentrated outside Java. Although surplus labor in the Indonesian context has long been associated with the "lilliputian" farms on Java [17], greater employment opportunities might well have turned the balance in favor of Java in recent years.

A fourth factor which points to continuing labor surplus conditions is low absolute level of wages. Even by regional standards, they were quite skewed by region within Indonesia and on average much higher in urban than in rural areas. Monthly wage incomes (including overtime and second jobs) reported in the *National Labor Force Survey* (SAKERNAS) averaged Rp90,000 or approximately Rp3,000–3,500 (around U.S.$1.50) per day (Table 16.4).[18] These labor incomes, however, were substantially higher than minimum wage rates set by provincial governments and the Department of Manpower which were highest in DKI Jakarta at Rp2,100 in 1990 and a much lower Rp750 in Central Java.[19]

In U.S. dollar terms, Jakarta minimum rates were less than half those in Thailand (Bangkok) and less than a quarter of laborer's wages in Malaysia, and they were also substantially below minimum wage rates in the Philippines in 1990.[20] These differentials, especially with Malaysia, have probably widened in the past few years; unskilled wage rates in Kuala Lumpur had risen to around 15 ringgit (U.S.$6) per day, and average wages of semiskilled workers to around 30–50 ringgit (U.S.$12–15) by 1992.

Surveys of wages and working conditions in large-scale manufacturing establishments in 1989–90 indicate that many firms still paid wage rates below the minimum in the JABOTABEK region, especially in the footwear and garments industries oriented toward export [49]. It is likely that this situation has changed during the past few years as the government, NGOs, and labor organizations increased pressure on larger firms to at least meet minimum wage standards in this region [37].

Nevertheless, as in other countries in the region, the new labor-intensive industries and firms, including those from Korea and Taiwan, are paying

Table 16.4 Wage income in Indonesia by major regions, 1990

	% of wage earners		*Mean earnings (Rp) (month)*	*% of all wage earners*
	Under Rp 50,000 (month)	*Over Rp 200,000 (month)*		
Urban;				
Jakarta	12.9	23.4	151,000	9.5
West Java	22.9	11.7	114,000	9.5
Other Java	37.6	6.1	92,000	17.0
Outer islands	12.5	13.9	125,000	11.1
Rural:				
West Java	45.5	2.9	67,000	13.0
Other Java	61.1	1.6	53,000	25.5
Outer Islands	24.7	4.3	89,000	14.4
Indonesia	36.3	7.3	90,000	100

Source: [23].

wage rates which are closely aligned to market rates in agriculture and the informal sector. Among foreign investors, this contrasts with the quite high wages paid by more established firms in metals and machinery industries where minimum wages of regular employees are frequently well above Rp100,000 per month, 2–3 times the minimum wage.[21]

Low absolute wage levels are, not surprisingly, associated with a quite skewed distribution of wage incomes. Over one-third of all wage workers made less than Rp50,000 with a high proportion of low-income workers being concentrated in rural Java. At the other end of the distribution, nearly 25 per cent of wage workers in Jakarta earned Rp200,000 or more and average wage earnings per month were more than three times higher in Jakarta compared with rural Central and East Java. Also in accordance with expectations, average wages were lowest in agriculture and highest in mining, public utilities, and finance and banking among the major sectors of the economy (not shown in the table).

In terms of educational status, national labor force data suggest that university graduates earned approximately five times the salary of primary school graduates in 1990, a differential which would probably be much larger if data could be assembled for university graduates in the private sector alone. Of course, these differentials do not capture the quite extreme differentials within the modern sector in particular, where it is not uncommon for foreign trained managers, accountants, and engineers to earn Rp10–20 million (around U.S.$5,000–10,000) or more per month.

IV LABOR MARKET CHANGE

Rapid economic growth for most of the new order period has been accompanied by structural change similar to that experienced by several other developing countries in the region. This includes a substantial rise in industry's share of GDP offset by steep decline in the agricultural share, the steady growth of services, and the extension of new infrastructure, transport, and construction activities throughout the archipelago.

Indonesia has at the same time experienced its own unique blend of outcomes related to resource endowments and international developments: especially the natural resource, predominantly oil, boom of the 1970s, rapid agricultural growth, and import-substitution-oriented manufacturing development, all ahead of a rather late shift toward export-oriented manufacturing.

A Employment trends by major sector

Overall, employment growth has been rapid, mirroring the growth of the labor force.[22] There has been quite a substantial shift of labor out of agriculture into industry and services (Table 16.5). These shifts have not been as

Table 16.5 Employment, value added, and labor productivity by major sector, Indonesia, 1971–90

	Year	*Agriculture*	*Industry*	*Services*	*All sectors*
Employment:[a]					
Total (1,000)	1990	36,113	12,048	23,409	71,570
Distribution (%)	1971	66.0	10.0	24.0	100
	1990	50.5	16.8	32.7	100
Growth (% p.a.)	1971–80	1.17	6.00	5.69	2.93
	1980–90	2.16	5.65	3.97	3.26
	1971–90	1.69	5.82	4.74	3.10
Distribution of increment (%)	1971–80	24.2	23.8	52.0	100
	1980–90	35.2	26.2	38.6	100
	1971–90	31.1	25.3	43.6	100
Value added and labor productivity:[b]					
Growth of value added (% p.a.)	1971–80	4.16	14.23	7.41	7.48
	1980–90	3.17	8.36	8.04	6.78
	1971–90	3.63	11.13	7.73	7.11
Labor productivity indices (1980 = 100)[c]	1971	77	46	86	66
	1980	100	100	100	100
	1990	110	131	150	142
Labor productivity increase (% p.a.)	1971–90	1.9	5.5	2.9	4.0

Note:
[a] All employment data adjusted for exclusion of rural Irian Jaya and East Timor from the 1971 census. Owing to lack of data on hours worked in 1971, no adjustments are made for underemployment in different sectors in the data on employment trends over time.
[b] Constant 1983 prices, excludes oil and mining.
[c] Productivity measured by value added per employed worker per year.

Sources: [22, 1971 (Series C)] [22, 1980 (Series S2)] [22, 1990 (Series S2)] and National Accounts (various years).

rapid as in Korea and Taiwan but they have been on a par with similar shifts in Malaysia, Thailand, and other rapidly growing LDCs.

Three important aspects of labor absorption will be highlighted in the context of the shift toward the turning point. There are the continued importance of labor absorption in agriculture, the relatively high rate of growth of labor productivity in manufacturing, and the important role of services in absorbing surplus labor.

Despite the decline in the agricultural share in employment from around two-thirds to half, this sector has continued to account for a major share of jobs created: approximately 30 per cent of new jobs over the period 1971–90.[23] Even on densely populated Java there has been some growth in agricultural employment and even during the past decade when there has been increasing concern regarding the encroachment of new residential and commercial buildings on scarce agricultural land.

As might be expected, growth in agricultural employment has been much more rapid in the relatively land-abundant regions of the outer islands of Indonesia than on Java (Table 16.6). The agricultural sector in the outer islands of Indonesia was by far the largest creator of jobs over the period 1971–90, accounting for almost twice the increment in employment in each of the major sectors (manufacturing, trade, and services) on Java over the period 1971–90.

Also, perhaps surprising, employment in agriculture in the outer islands appears to have accelerated during the past decade, rising to close to 3.5 per cent per annum for the decade as a whole. Transmigration based on land settlement, which reached a peak in the early 1980s, and associated and other movement of workers into new agricultural areas probably had an important influence on these figures.[24]

Even on Java agricultural employment continued to increase during these two decades. This was despite the common belief that the densely populated island had long reached a stage when a large pool of surplus labor desperately needed to be directed elsewhere. Although the intensity of employment in agriculture may not have been high—indeed official data suggest that a large proportion of persons (48 per cent nationally) employed in agriculture worked fewer than thirty-five hours—Java had not begun to experience an absolute decline in its agricultural work force.[25]

A second important trend has been rapid growth in value added and labor productivity in industry and especially in manufacturing. Employment

Table 16.6 Employment distribution and growth by major sector, Indonesia

	Distribution (%)				*Growth rate (1971–90, % p.a.)*	
	Java		*Outer islands*			
	1971	*1990*	*1971*	*1990*	*Java*	*Outer islands*
Agriculture	60.9	42.5	75.2	62.4	0.9	2.7
Industry:						
Manufacturing	9.3	14.3	5.1	7.3	5.1	5.5
Construction	2.0	4.8	1.7	3.1	7.3	6.7
Other	0.2	1.2	0.6	1.3	11.1	7.6
Services:						
Trade & commerce	13.3	17.6	6.6	10.7	4.3	6.2
Transport	2.6	4.3	2.1	2.9	5.4	5.3
Other services	11.7	15.4	8.7	12.3	4.3	5.5
All sectors	100	100	100	100	2.8	3.6

Sources: [22, 1971 (Series C)] [22, 1990 (Series S2)].

growth has not been particularly high when compared with the growth of value added which averaged over 10 per cent in the period 1971–90 and was one of the most rapid in the world over this period (Table 16.5). Labor productivity also rose steeply, over 5 per cent per annum on average (outside oil and mining). This was well above that recorded for the other two major sectors and the country as a whole (3–4 per cent).

This is not to say that employment growth in industry has been particularly disappointing compared with the experience of many other Third World countries. Employment grew on average by just under 6 per cent from a very low base (10 per cent in 1971) and new jobs in this sector accounted for around 25 per cent of all employment growth from 1971. The share of industrial sector employment increased more rapidly than in lower income and lower middle income LDCs (7–11 and 11–16 per cent respectively, 1960–80).[26] However, employment growth in manufacturing has not been nearly as rapid as that which has occurred in the NIEs, especially Korea and Taiwan, where annual rates of growth of 10 per cent per annum were recorded frequently in the 1970s and 1980s [32] [31].

A major contribution to national productivity growth has come from the changing structure of the manufacturing sector. One might expect a substantial share of "surplus" labor in agriculture to flow into low-wage and relatively low-productivity manufacturing employment in the early stages of industrialization. Relatively capital-intensive investments, both resource and skill intensive [20], made during the oil boom period and backwash effects on the large, low-productivity manufacturing sector especially contributed to slower employment growth but a rapid increase in labor productivity.[27]

The third important development has been the important role which services rather than manufacturing have played in absorbing new job entrants and labor from the countryside. Services have accounted for the largest share (44 per cent) of all new jobs created in the period 1971–90, and over half in the 1970s.

Although services labor productivity grew more rapidly than in "agriculture," the gap in labor productivity with "manufacturing" has narrowed substantially. Labor productivity in services exceeded that in manufacturing by approximately 15 per cent in 1971. However productivity in the former grew much more slowly than in manufacturing and was around 25 per cent lower in 1990. It seems that while manufacturing shed a considerable amount of low-productivity labor, the opposite was true in the case of services: many workers moved into low-wage segments of this sector.

There is an important regional dimension to these developments. Despite the resources boom and associated protection afforded domestic industry, a quite high proportion of all manufacturing development and employment has continued to be concentrated on Java (see Table 16.6). This has occurred principally because there is a more abundant supply of unskilled and skilled labor and infrastructure is more developed on Java.

Within Java manufacturing employment growth has been heavily concentrated around the capital Jakarta in the west and to a lesser extent Surabaya in the east, and away from traditional towns, small cities, and rural Central Java in particular. This applies to some products using outer island natural resources such as rubber, timber, and rattan, consumer goods products for the domestic market, and, more recently, labor-intensive exports.

Unlike in manufacturing, the growth in service sector employment has not been heavily concentrated on Java. Government, community, and personal services in particular contributed to a significant share of total employment and employment growth in the outer islands. As noted, growth in employment in this subsector can be especially attributed to the spread of government administration, health and education services throughout the archipelago. This is in contrast to the plethora of low-wage services which are more common and likely to be related to greater labor supply pressures on Java.

B Employment growth in the 1970s versus the 1980s

The above-mentioned general trends in employment growth during the new order period hide an important contrast in the experience of the 1970s compared with the 1980s. Whereas growth in most of the former period was dominated by the dispersal of economic rents acquired by government from the oil boom, the 1980s was marked much greater diversity in economic performance and the forces driving economic growth: economic slowdown in the early 1980s, deregulation and the takeoff of non-oil exports from the middle of the decade.

These macroeconomic developments were reflected in the changing employment structure. In the 1970s, the service sector—especially other services mainly comprising government administration and public-sector-supported community services—and the smaller construction and mining industries grew more rapidly than manufacturing employment. The situation was reversed in the 1980s. Manufacturing employment increased more quickly than services and accounted for just under 20 per cent of all new jobs created.

This shift toward much greater labor absorption in manufacturing took place mainly in the latter half of the decade as the size of non-oil exports began to impact on the labor market.[28] On the other hand employment in the service sector (including trade, transport, and other services) slowed considerably. In particular, employment growth in other services halved as did the contribution of this sector to employment growth.

As noted, the slow rate of manufacturing employment growth during the 1970s in particular can be partly attributed to investment in relatively capital-intensive industries. This is reflected in the more rapid increase in labor productivity in the industrial sector during the 1970s. In part, this was induced by government policies, but in part it was the consequence of exchange rate outcomes and a surplus of foreign exchange accumulated as a result of the oil boom.

In contrast, in the 1980s when the oil prices slumped, the government was forced to look elsewhere for foreign exchange. Deregulation contributed to the rapid growth of labor-intensive exports especially from 1986 when the first major reform package was introduced and Indonesia devalued the rupiah. Greater fiscal stringency, on the other hand, meant that government-supported service sectors no longer played such a dominant role in overall employment growth. All these policies contributed to a real depreciation of the rupiah against the U.S. dollar through to the early 1990s, and provided a major stimulus to exports [18] [21].

C Occupation, gender, and skill

There have also been significant changes in the structure of employment in terms of location, education, skill, and gender (Table 16.7). These changes appear to have been most marked in the manufacturing sector in which changes in the size distribution and technological profile of enterprises has probably been most intense. Thus, for example, the percentages of secondary educated and white-collar workers increased by more than fivefold and by over 50 per cent respectively since 1971. The manufacturing work force became much more urbanized and its share of wage workers also increased quite significantly.[29]

Similar changes occurred in other sectors but at a slower pace. It is instructive, for example, that in the large trade sector the proportion of white-collar

Table 16.7 Some characteristics of employed persons in major sectors, Indonesia, 1990

	Agriculture	*Manufacturing*	*Trade*	*Government & other services*	*All sectors*
Characteristics of the work force (%):					
Urban	5	42	47	58	27
Senior high school & above	3	15	13	49	14
White-collar	1	5	1	52	9
Family workers	32	11	12	3	20
Female	24	37	44	40	36
Index of worker characteristics (1971 = 100)					
Urban	204	179	141	125	183
Senior high school & above	1,000	585	420	293	472
White-collar	400	155	87	118	154
Family workers	97	76	91	68	84
Female	107	91	109	138	128

Source: The same as Table 16.6.

workers and wage employees actually appears to have declined over the period 1971–90, and similar trends were apparent in transport and construction.[30] Despite a fall in the share of family workers, the proportion of relatively poor "informal sector" workers (family workers plus self-employed) has probably increased in trade.[31]

How has structural change affected the involvement of females in employment? Higher participation rates among females has led to an increase in their share of work in trade and especially service sectors. However, perhaps surprising to some in light of the heavy involvement of females in low-wage industries in the region, there has been a fall in the proportion of females employed in manufacturing where female participation was relatively high in 1971. There are two possible explanations for this development. First, the demise of many traditional cottage industries which tended to employ a high proportion of females. Second, low-wage, export-oriented industries have only became prominent in Indonesia from the mid-1980s and many of the new industries (which produce mainly for the domestic market) have tended to employ a high proportion of males.

Even more than males, female workers have experienced a substantial improvement in education, the proportion of female white-collar workers has increased in all sectors, and the proportion of female employees has increased more rapidly, except for manufacturing. The higher rate of increase in skilled and educated workers can partly be attributed to the much smaller base share among females in 1971—even in 1990 less than 10 per cent of all female employees had a senior high school education, and the share of white-collar workers was still very low except in other services (chiefly school teachers, health care workers, and clerical workers). Nevertheless, greater female labor force participation does appear to be associated with a qualitative as well as a quantitative improvement in women's involvement in the work force.

D Wage growth

The rapid transformation of the labor market described above might be expected to be associated with significant increases in wages. Wage incomes increased quite markedly. But growth in wage rates of unskilled and semi-skilled labor was generally sporadic. With the exception of the traditional rice sector, real wage rates of unskilled labor rose during the oil boom period but have stagnated since then in most sectors. This contrast in trends in wage rates and productivity is at odds with the experience of the NIEs where labor productivity and wage growth are reported to have gone hand in hand in the early stages of rapid industrialization'[32]

Data on wage trends in selected activities (hoeing in rice, all activities on estates, unskilled labor in construction, minimum negotiated wages in textiles, and a lower echelon civil servant salary level) in each of these segments of the labor market are presented in Figure 16.1 and Table 16.8. Although

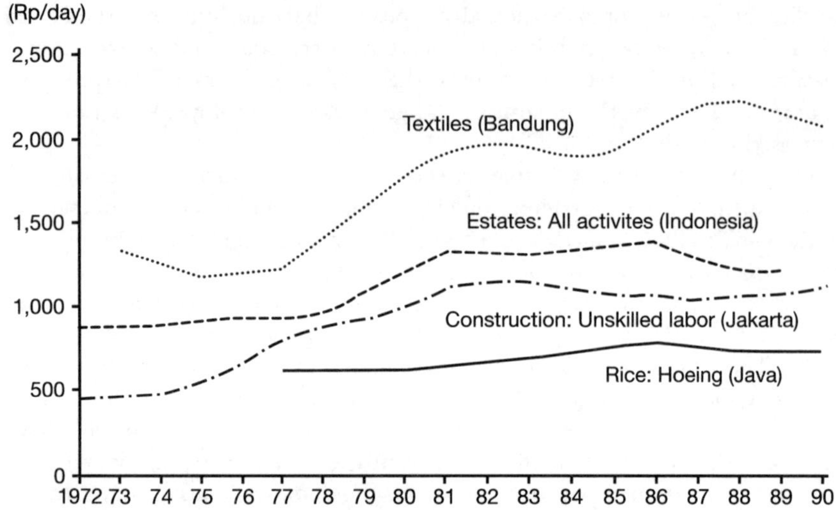

Figure 16.1 Real Daily Wages in Selected Activities in Indonesia, 1972–90

Note: 1. See Table 16.8 for explanation and sources. 2. Three-year moving averages.

wages have grown over the entire period in all series, growth rates have been very much higher in the "modern" sector and in nonagricultural activities than in agriculture. Thus textile and public sector wages grew most rapidly—impressively at an annual rate of around 5 per cent per annum from the early 1970s, whereas wages were recorded as rising at only around 1 per cent per annum in the two agricultural wage series; wages of casual labor on construction sites increased by an intermediate amount of around 3 per cent per annum.

At the same time, there are very clear contrasts in the behavior of wages during different periods. Real wage rates hardly rose in all sectors in the early 1970s. They then increased much more rapidly in the oil boom years from around the middle of the decade to the early 1980s when they began to stagnate. The exception was the rice sector. In rice on Java, real wage growth began later and lasted until the mid-1980s before leveling off in line with the other series.

What factors lie behind these patterns of real wage growth? Nominal wage growth was more rapid in the 1970s than in the 1980s, which might partly be attributed to price expectations forged by the experience of rapid inflation during the previous decade [45]. But as the rate of inflation stabilized during the 1970s, it is clear that wage growth was driven by excess labor demand during the oil boom years, especially as government spending programs expanded and non- tradable sectors grew rapidly during the second half of the 1970s and early 1980s [9] [27].

Conversely, from the early to mid-1980s economic growth slowed as

Table 16.8 Rate of growth in real wage rates of unskilled/ semiskilled labor, selected sectors, 1972–90 (three-year moving average)

	Rice[a]	*Estates*[b]	*Construction*[c]	*Textiles*[d]	*Civil Service*[e]
Activity	Hoeing	All field & processing	Unskilled	Unskilled (minimum)	Grade Ib Level 9
Location	All Java	Indonesia	Jakarta	Bandung	Indonesia
Gender	Male	Both sexes	Male	Both sexes	Both sexes
Deflator	Rural COL (9 commodities)	Rural COL (9 commodities)	Jakarta COL (9 commodities)	Bandung COL (9 commodities)	Indonesia CPI
Annual growth rates (% p.a.):					
1972–80	−0.3[f]	3.8	4.1[g]	9.7	11.9
1980–85	4.3	2.8	1.7	1.6	1.4
1885–90	−0.8	−3.4[h]	1.6	0.6	−2.1
1972–90	1.3	1.8	2.6	5.0	5.1

Note: COL = cost of living index.

[a] Average of monthly data collected 1976 onwards; unweighted mean of daily wage rates for West, Central, and East Java.

[b] Average of half yearly data for permanent employees.

[c] Average of monthly data.

[d] Minimum wage for unskilled labor based on annual agreements between the association of textile producers (PERTEKSI) and the labor union (SPSI).

[e] Basic salary only; generally included in the budget beginning in April.

[f] 1977–80.

[g] 1972–80.

[h] 1985–89.

Sources: Unpublished data from Central Bureau of Statistics (CBS), Department of Public Workers (Jakarta), and Department of Finance; CBS, *Average Wages on Estates* (various years); PERTEKSI, *Annual Agreements on Wages* (various years).

Indonesia reached the limits of the easy phase of import-substitution industrialization. In part, general macroeconomic and stabilization policy also put a damper on labor demand in this period. Government expenditure was pruned for several years in the mid-1980s, and this further slowed down public sector and construction wage growth. In textiles and other labor-intensive sectors of manufacturing, much slower nominal and real wage growth can be partly attributed to relative stagnation of domestic demand which had grown so rapidly during the previous decade.

It is of some interest, despite the quite quick revival of Indonesia's economic fortunes and economic deregulation after 1986, that real wage rates remained flat through to the end of the decade. While manufacturing export growth has been rapid, this sector was not large enough to significantly affect real wage growth, even in the economic boom years of 1989–90. Further, largely due to the transport "revolution," improved communications, and knowledge of job opportunities among more educated young people, interprovincial and interdistrict mobility has probably increased substantially. In recent years, there appears to have been a greater flow of workers from poorer regions to compete for jobs in the centers of manufacturing growth, most notably from the Priangan region of West Java and southern Central and East Java to the JABOTABEK area [47] [49].[33]

Thus, it seems that excess labor supply continued to influence wage growth and that despite the apparent tightening of labor markets in the previous period, the country had not yet made a clear transition to a labor scarce economy. It appears that movements in wage rates have been relatively uniform by region, sector, and gender, although wage adjustments were affected by specific regional circumstances, and also differed between different sectors and segments of the economy [39].

V LABOR STANDARDS, UNIONS, AND WELFARE

So far the discussion has assumed implicitly that, as in other East Asian countries, developments in wages and labor welfare have been largely determined by economic changes irrespective of government and union intervention in labor market processes. Such a conclusion would seem to be warranted in the case of Indonesia, given the relatively minor role which the government has played in promoting labor standards, especially minimum wages, and the tight controls imposed over union organizations [37]. An alternative viewpoint, and one which has gained increased popularity in Indonesia in recent years, is that low wages and poor working conditions are the result of government neglect of labor standards and repressive policies toward unions. There is widespread concern that while Indonesia has made considerable progress in a range of welfare indicators (education and health in particular), conditions among wage workers have lagged and the imbalance needs to be addressed.

Our analysis of labor market conditions and change has stressed the fact that by a range of indicators—the size and growth of agricultural employment, the pervasive influence of the informal sector, and growth in wage rates—Indonesia in the early 1990s is still most aptly described as a labor surplus economy. Although the "modern" wage employment sector outside government employment has grown rapidly, it is still too small to significantly affect wages and working conditions of the majority of the work force.

Has suppression of independent union activity in Indonesia significantly affected wage and labor welfare outcomes? The above analysis suggests no, if one is talking about labor incomes of the large majority of unskilled and semiskilled workers. In two respects in particular, however, employee welfare could have been greater. First, active unions in larger scale firms and especially in public sector enterprises might have driven harder wage bargains. Second, stronger unions, either enterprise, occupation, or industry based, would have prevented many of the abuses of the labor law which have become the focus of labor unrest in recent years.[34] Arbitrary dismissal, forced overtime, cramped and unhealthy work environments would all have been contested by a stronger union movement. At the same time, there may well have emerged a greater gap between "elite" workers in modern sector firms and the mass of employees in smaller establishments and casual employment which tend to be beyond the influence of union activities.

As noted, non-oil manufacturing export growth has been rapid and has given a major stimulus to employment from the mid-1980s. At the same time this has been accompanied by increasing labor unrest in the industrial belt in the BOTABEK region close to Jakarta, in particular. Why has labor unrest emerged at this time and what are the implications for labor's role in economic and political processes? One possible interpretation is that the poor labor conditions among heavily "exploited" wage workers in the new export factories has contributed to strikes and labor unrest. This would suggest a growing awareness of worker rights and possibly the beginnings of worker organization and activism in the face of poor labor standards.

Although these issues are not dealt with in detail in this paper, it has been suggested that labor conditions are not necessarily worse, in general, in the export factories than in alternative employment opportunities in agriculture or self-employed work from which some of the workers come and their families continue to earn a living. There is frequently illegal but officially sanctioned abuse of labor rights and freedoms. In addition, labor conditions are poor in many of the new factories in terms of international labor standards [47] [49]. However, while the former can be addressed by political and government action, the latter are related to broader labor market structure. It is important to bear in mind the unpalatable fact that wages are low primarily because Indonesian workers are still poor, in general, rather than because of repressive activities of the export- oriented factories.

In this context, it seems worthwhile to distinguish between four aspects of labor rights and welfare: basic worker rights, working conditions, worker incomes, and finally the incomes of wage workers relative to other groups in society. Many of the strikes have been focussed on the first and second of these issues: the right to organize and make claims to employers, and the right to negotiate improvements in basic working conditions (food, transport, systems of overtime payments, and bonuses). The first issue in particular has important political implications and involves a wider set of human rights issues. The prerogative of local authorities in particular to intervene in labor disputes and detain local labor leaders—a pattern which has been common in most major strike and labor dispute cases in Indonesia over the past two decades—is increasingly being challenged by political and social groups as no longer acceptable.[35] Conditions of work which are out of step with national standards are similarly receiving considerable attention from both the state and labor activists.

Greater recent political openness (*keterbukaan*), action programs of NGOs, and greater focus on labor issues by international agencies should encourage progress in both of these areas. I have argued, however, that improvements in labor incomes and in the wages of unskilled laborers relative to those of skilled and professional manpower are still heavily dependent on overcoming general conditions of labor surplus in the labor market. Implicitly, it is also argued that attempts to raise wages, through government or union intervention, significantly above what people can earn elsewhere in the economy is unlikely to be successful. Moreover, premature efforts in this area are likely to be harmful to the longer term interests of labor. General improvements in labor incomes are heavily dependent on rapid employment growth outside agriculture and rapid progress toward achievement of the turning point.[36]

Thus, the political agenda of labor activists and concerns regarding the abuse of labor standards and rights by individual employers need to be separated from policies directed to raising the welfare of wage labor in general. The sustained increases in employment in labor-intensive manufacturing export industries is an important element in achieving the goal of increased labor welfare.

A Wage stagnation and poverty decline: a paradox?

Although wage rates (and the price of labor) have not risen markedly for the majority of Indonesian workers in the past decade, average income growth has been rapid and poverty has declined substantially, even by East Asian standards. According to Central Bureau of Statistics figures, the incidence of both rural and urban poverty declined from around 40 per cent in the mid-1970s to around 15 per cent in 1990.[37]

How do we reconcile this apparent paradox? The answer is crucial to an understanding of the relationship between economic change and labor processes in a labor surplus economy. Four major factors related to labor markets would seem to have influenced the result. First, workers moved out of highly labor-intensive, low-earning jobs outside agriculture into which they had been pushed in order to survive into higher earning jobs.[38] Second, workers moving out of agriculture and traditional industries have been engaged in longer hours of work in new jobs: the long hours worked by those employed in new export-oriented industries is a prime example of this process in Indonesia as it has been in other East Asian countries.

Third, new entrants into the labor force are better educated on average and command higher wages than those entering employment years ago. While Indonesian enrollment rates are still lower than in Northeast Asia, they have increased very substantially in the 1980s at both secondary and tertiary levels (Table 16.9). Whereas the average wage worker entering wage employment outside agriculture in the early 1970s was only primary educated or less, by the early 1980s most had secondary education and earned more than twice as much as those with only completed primary education (according to the national labor force surveys).

Finally, already mentioned above, female labor force participation rates have risen quite markedly (by around 20 per cent between 1971 and 1990) and this must have made a major contribution to total household incomes of the poor. In particular, young females have experienced all of the above gains from economic transformation: in the early 1970s they were typically

Table 16.9 Educational enrollment ratios (selected Asian countries)

	Secondary		*Tertiary*	
	1968	*1989*	*1965*	*1989*
Asian NIEs:				
Taiwan	66	82[a]	11	26[a]
Korea	35	86	6	38
Singapore	45	69	10	12[a]
Hong Kong	29	73	26	29[b]
ASEAN:				
Malaysia	28	59	2	7
Philippines	41	73	19	28
Thailand	14	28	2	16
Indonesia	12	47	1	8
South Asia:				
Sri Lanka	35	74	2	4
India	27	43	5	—
Pakistan	12	20	2	5
Bangladesh	13	17	1	4

Note:
[a] 1987.
[b] 1986.

Source: [51, 1992 (Development Indicators)].

concentrated in underemployed or low-income earnings activities, such as part-time work in agriculture, or weaving and food processing, which featured very low returns per hour worked, and also had much lower levels of schooling compared with males.

These changes are reflected in trends in average earnings in large and medium-sized firms in manufacturing according to the annual survey of manufacturing. These suggest a more than doubling in real average earnings both for all manufacturing and for textile, clothing, and footwear workers over the eighteen-year period. Growth in real manufacturing wages was, moreover, sustained over the entire period, with the partial exception of the early mid-1980s, and has continued up to recent years. The SAKERNAS data, broken down by major sectors and computed only for primary graduates, imply less sustained wage growth than the manufacturing wage series. Nevertheless, here too real wages appear to have increased quite significantly, especially during the late 1970s and late 1980s.

Modernization of industry and the relative capital-intensive orientation of manufacturing growth in particular imply greater application of skilled manpower and capacity utilization. Even in the textile industry, which has undergone substantial structural change during the new other period, the same effects could be expected to apply. The shift away from labor-intensive to more capital-intensive production implies a higher share of employment in more stable and skilled occupations in which average wage rates are likely to be significantly higher than in the past.[39]

B Income distribution

This different pattern of manufacturing growth has had implications not only for employment growth but also for income distribution. The more capital-intensive and resource-based industries require a higher share of highly skilled and professional manpower. A priori, one would expect this to contribute to less equal income distribution in Indonesia than the East Asian NIEs. This pattern is confirmed by available secondary data. The gini ratio and other indicators of inequality do not show much change in Indonesia over the 1970s and 1980s [8]. This is in contrast to the gini ratios in both Taiwan and Korea which declined substantially during modernization and are relatively low by third world standards.[40]

In addition, the important role of foreign investment in economic development in Indonesia (like the other "ersatz" economies of Southeast Asia) may also contribute to worse income distribution through the effects of international standard wage rates paid to foreign professionals on the Indonesian labor market. The high salaries (U.S.$ 10,000–20,000 a month, excluding housing and other fringe benefits) paid to expatriate technical staff in foreign oil and other mining companies are well known in Jakarta, and undoubtedly have had an impact on domestic managerial and professional manpower in that industry. Also, returns to domestic participants in the "foreign affected" segment of the labor market are likely to be very high, partly because of the country's shortage of highly skilled and professional manpower and its need to import persons to fill many of these posts.

VI CONCLUSIONS

This paper has examined labor market developments during the Suharto era in the context of transitions toward the "turning point" in other countries in the East Asian region. It has been argued that although there have been some substantial changes in the Indonesian labor market over the last twenty years, it is still basically characterized by labor surplus conditions. An excess supply of labor to the modern sector continues to depress wage rates and make it difficult to sustain impiovements in working conditions for industrial workers.

In light of the experience of relatively rapid transformation in labor markets in the NIEs, it might be asked why there does not appear to have been a more rapid transition toward the turning point in Indonesia? Two factors help explain the difference. The first would be the much greater rural "surplus population," in particular the higher proportion of rural landless in Java—a feature of labor markets stretching back to the nineteenth century—when Indonesia began to industrialize rapidly in the 1970s.[41]

The second is the different nature of the industrialization process in Indonesia compared with other countries which were less well endowed with natural resources. Relatively captial-intensive industry was encouraged in many sectors during the oil boom years—partly for import substitution, and paffly to take advantage of high-value-added exports in resource-based industries. The exchange rate reflected the latter in particular—to some extent in the form of "Dutch disease" effects during the oil boom—and gave less encouragement to labor-intensive, non-oil exports than might have been the case if Indonesia had not had access to oil and minerals to generate foreign exchange.

Thus, in resource abundant countries like Indonesia, the shift to export-oriented industry is likely to be delayed. This contributes to slower rates of labor absorption outside agriculture and hence a delay in the progression toward the turning point. The period of import-substitution industrialization could be sustained longer because processing of natural resources for the domestic market, which typically absorbs much less labor, was viewed as a national priority. With similar commitment to rapid economic growth, Korea and Taiwan had no choice but to go into labor-intensive industries to earn foreign exchange, and benefited in terms of employment growth.[42] Even when Indonesia did make the switch, in addition to more labor-intensive activities it specialized in industries such as rubber, tires, timber, palm oil, and sugar processing which use less labor per unit of output.

With the formation of the new cabinet in Indonesia in 1993, there has been increasing debate regarding economic strategy to be adopted over the next twenty-five years. One important choice is between greater emphasis on self-reliant, high-tech, and more capital-intensive projects sponsored by Minister Habibie versus continuation of policies of the economic "technocrats" which reportedly favor an industrial policy based on comparative advantage. The latter policy emphasizes the central role of labor-intensive exports at the present stage in Indonesia's development.

The debate has implications for labor as well as for macroeconomic and general development strategy. As we have seen from the experience of the oil boom period, high-tech, more capital-intensive investments are likely to limit employment growth and promote a more differentiated work force in terms of skill and income. It also places greater strains on the supply of skilled and professional manpower, increasing foreign participation in the short run, and absorbing resources in training and skill formation in the medium term.[43]

I have argued that a strategy broadly based on comparative advantage will provide more employment growth and more equitable outcomes for labor in Indonesia in the 1990s. It supports a move to more capital-intensive areas only once the labor market reaches the turning point and the real price of unskilled labor begins to rise. Such an approach has become much less attractive to many community and political leaders and engineers (and even some economists) who are impatient with slow progress in raising living standards, and many of whom are especially interested in national symbols and concrete displays of development achievements.

Some persons have quite incorrectly attributed slow growth in living standards to technocrat policies which have encouraged comparative advantage in the past. One implication of developments discussed in this paper, in the broader context of East Asian development, is that it is precisely because Indonesia has chosen greater liberalization (deregulation) so late—and has encouraged resource allocation which does not follow the country's comparative advantage—that labor incomes have not risen as quickly as they might have.

Thus our analysis of the labor market suggests that the welfare of poorer workers and potential job seekers, and their families, is at risk in any program which favors high-tech projects at the expense of labor-intensive activities at this stage in Indonesia's development. Prior to achievement of the turning point, equity and welfare are both likely to be best served by policies which continue to encourage an allocation of resources to areas of rapid labor absorption.

ACKNOWLEDGMENTS

An earlier version of this paper was given at the conference "Indonesia: Paradigms for the Future," Asia Research Centre, Murdoch University, July 22–23, 1993. The author is grateful for comments on the paper from Hal Hill and an anonymous referee, and for research assistant and typing help from Mr. Abrar Yusuf, Ms. Sonya Bodger, and Ms. Jesmin Fernando. The normal disclaimers apply.

NOTES

1 The idea of a clearly defined turning point had its origins in early postwar theories of economic development and especially in the work of Lewis [33] and his theory of the labor surplus economy. Lewis wrote of classical and neoclassical phases of economic development before and after the turning point. Fei and Ranis developed a more rigorous model of labor dynamics in a labor surplus economy and preconditions for achievement of a turning point [13].

2 Throughout, the term real wages refers to money wages adjusted for changes in the cost of living.

3 See especially [16] [25].

4 The major criticisms of the Lewis model were directed at his notion of disguised unemployment in agriculture and in particular at the idea that the marginal productivity of labor might be zero.

5 The figure for the industrialized countries is around 0.5 per cent per annum and Japan around 1 per cent per annum compared with 2–3 per cent per annum in most LDCs. Labor force growth rates in Indonesia have been close to 3 per cent since the 1960s.

6 Lewis himself was not guilty of this mistake—he first conceived of the basic idea of the labor surplus economy while walking in the streets of Bangkok.

7 Since both Hong Kong and Singapore hardly have any agricultural work force to draw on, only fleeting reference is made to the experience of these countries.

8 Real wage rates had begun to rise in Taiwan and Republic of Korea by the early 1970s: in Taiwan the turning point is estimated to have occurred around 1970 and in Korea around 1975 [32] [3].

9 Several authors have suggested that real wages had begun to rise much earlier (around the mid-1970s) both in the agricultural and nonagricultural sectors in Malaysia—a development which is more consistent with its much higher level of economic achievement on a range of criteria [4]. However real wages during this period in Malaysia are a matter of controversy.

10 Some country-specific factors have also been important. In the case of Malaysia, the availability of a relatively cheap supply of Indonesian immigrant workers has undoubtedly influenced both wage and employment adjustment. In Thailand the highly seasonal patterns of labor demand in the north and northeast in particular may be an important factor affecting the reported absolute size of the agricultural work force.

11 Among the countries mentioned above, Thailand is the exception. While real wages have begun to rise quite rapidly, the gains to wage labor seem to have been spread quite unevenly and the welfare of wage workers (housing, health standards, etc.) would appear to be far below that of workers in Malaysia and the NIEs. Of course, in the Philippines real wages have declined since the early 1970s.

12 By far the most extreme cases have been in Korea where the military-backed security organization frequently intervened in labor affairs [42].
13 See especially [34] [1] [12].
14 Precisely the same processes occurred in Britain close to two centuries earlier as peasants moved out of underemployed activities in agriculture to factory work [11].
15 Of course, in both Korea and Taiwan MNCs have played a relatively minor role in investment in labor-intensive export industries. The MNC labor exploitation story which has been developed to describe developments in Malaysia and Thailand, in particular, is not relevant to these countries.
16 This figure is taken from the 1985 Intercensal Survey (Central Bureau of Statistics, *SUPAS*, Series S2, 1987). Other prominent low-wage occupations included household servants, *becak* (trishaw) drivers, traditional healers, masseurs, and barbers. The major "formal sector" occupation was teachers which accounted for 10 per cent of all service sector employment followed by government officials (3 per cent).
17 Overall, around 25 per cent of persons are recorded as working less than twenty-five hours a week in agriculture according to the *1990 Population Census* [22]. It must be borne in mind however that these figures almost certainly quite substantially overstate the extent of underemployment and understate the share of individual households engaged in nonagricultural activities especially on Java: the true figure is probably closer to around 75 per cent in Java and probably slightly less in the outer islands.
18 The SAKERNAS data are only a crude indication of wage incomes but they are the only national source of wages across sectors and regions in Indonesia. Almost certainly they understate wage incomes at the upper end of the earnings scale.
19 By 1993 the Jakarta minimum wage had risen to Rp3,000 (approximately $1.50), the BOTABEK (Bogor-Tangerang-Bekasi) minimum was Rp2,600 and the Central Java minimum was Rp1,600.
20 In 1990 the Bangkok minimum was 90 baht per day (about $3.50), laborers wages were 160–200 ringgit per month in Malaysia ($6–7 per day) and the minimum wage in the Philippines was 89 pesos per day ($3–4). See [48]. Owing to international differences in purchasing power, these are only crude comparisons of real differences in wages.
21 Data based on information provided by firms in the Jakarta region during visits by the author to several automotive, established textile and pharmaceutical plants in 1989.
22 Labor force growth rates appear to have exceeded growth of employment in the 1980s and, consequently, official estimates suggest that unemployment rates rose, although not substantially.
23 As in other developing countries, trends in agricultural employment are most difficult to measure because of the high proportion of part-time female and other family workers, substantial underemployment, and seasonality. The absolute number of persons engaged is likely to fluctuate substantially according to the definition adopted. Nevertheless, given that basic definitions of employment have not changed in censuses conducted in Indonesia since 1971, and that the censuses were all conducted at approximately the same time of the year, we have no reason to doubt the validity of the general trends suggested.
24 See especially [50].
25 Remember that an absolute decline in the agricultural labor forces is one of the criteria suggested by Minami [41] as evidence of achievement of the "turning point."

26 These data were taken from Bloom and Freeman [5, p. 399].
27 In 1971 Indonesia had one of the largest traditional manufacturing sectors in the Third World in terms of the share of rural employment in manufacturing and the low level of productivity of most manufacturing activities. It was dominated by food processing, basket weaving, batik and traditional textiles concentrated on Java [35] [28].
28 Problems of comparability of national force data from various sources make it hard to establish a figure on the impact of manufacturing exports on employment; one source suggests, however, that the share of employment in the textiles, clothing, and footwear industry (the major manufacturing export industry), and other labor-intensive industries rose quite sharply in the second half of the 1980s [36].
29 It is worth noting that despite these changes, the proportion of educated and white-collar workers was quite small by international standards in manufacturing in 1990, and the majority of workers in the sector were still employed in rural areas.
30 The decline in the proportion of white-collar workers suggested in Table 16.7 especially in the trade sector, may be partly due to our definition of white-collar workers (professionals, managers, and clerical employees) based on occupational classifications. The occupational classification also has a category of sales workers and some white-collar workers in sales may be recorded in this category.
31 The census data imply that the share of family workers has tended to decline in most sectors, and this is consistent with what might be expected in a country experiencing such rapid rates of economic growth (although the enumeration of family workers in censuses and national labor force surveys show such wide variations that one should be wary of reading too much into these figures). See [29] [30].
32 In part the difference is due to the measure of wage growth used: most international wage series use average earnings as a basis for computing trend wages, thus ignoring compositional effects of changes in the nature of jobs and worker characteristics.
33 I have also argued elsewhere that a much more cost concious attitude among businessmen who had begun to enter the export market also probably influenced wages in these sectors [37].
34 See especially [24] for documentation of many of these abuses.
35 See [37] for an elaboration on some of these points.
36 Direct intervention in the labor market should, of course, be distinguished from government involvement in programs to help the poor—education, health, and housing—which are of very great importance for poverty alleviation, equity, and labor welfare (and also, in th longer term, for labor productivity).
37 Booth shows that the extent of the decline depends on the measure of poverty adopted but nevertheless concludes that ". . . whatever the poverty line used . . . there seems to be little doubt that the proportion of the population living below the poverty line has declined in both urban and rural areas" [7, p. 69].
38 These processes are now documented in a wide range of village and macro studies conducted in the 1980s. See especially [27] [20].
39 See [38] for a discussion of the link between capital intensity and earnings in the textile industry.
40 One should interpret international comparisons of income distribution with care, however, given large differences in sampling and concepts used.
41 Remember that both Korea and Taiwan instituted land reform in the early 1950s and landlessness has historically been relatively small in both Thailand and

Malaysia compared with Java. The situation in parts of the Philippines fits Indonesia somewhat better.

42 Thus employment growth in these two countries, often averaging close to 10 per cent per annum, was twice as rapid as in Indonesia during the 1970s and 1980s [30].

43 These effects on resource allocation are not insiguificant if one bears in mind that it costs approximately 50–100 times more to produce one graduate from tertiary schooling than it costs to produce a primary graduate.

REFERENCES

1 Addison, T., and Demery, L. "Wages and Labour Conditions in East Asia: A Review of Case-Study Evidence," *Development Policy Review*, Vol. 6, No. 4 (December 1988).

2 Amsden, A. H. *Asia's Next Giant: South Korea and Late Industrialization* (New York: Oxford University Press, 1989).

3 Bai Moo Ki. "The Turning Point in the Korean Economy," *Developing Economies*, Vol. 20, No. 2 (June 1982).

4 Barlow, C. "Changes in the Economic Position of Workers on Rubber Estates and Smallholdings in Peninsular Malaysia, 1910–85," Working Papers in Trade and Development No. 86/7 (Canberra: Division of Economics, Research School of Pacific Studies, Australian National University, 1985).

5 Bloom, D., and Freeman, R. "The Effects of Rapid Population Growth on Labor Supply and Employment in Developing Countries," *Population and Development Review*, Vol. 12, No. 3 (September 1986).

6 Bongnanno, M. "Korea's Industrial Relations at the Turning Point," KDI Working Paper No. 8816 (Seoul: Korean Development Institute, 1988).

7 Booth, A. "Counting the Poor in Indonesia," *Bulletin of Indonesian Economic Studies*, Vol. 29, No. 1 (April 1993).

8 ——. "Income Distribution and Poverty," in *The Oil Boom and After: Indonesian Economic Policy and Performance in the Soeharto Era*, ed. A. Booth (Singapore: Oxford University Press, 1992).

9 Booth, A., and McCawley, P. "The Indonesian Economy since the Mid-Sixties," in *The Indonesian Economy during the Soeharto Era*, ed. A. Booth and P. McCawley (Kuala Lumpur: Oxford University Press, 1981).

10 Cho Yong Sam. *Disguised Unemployment in Underdeveloped Areas with Special Reference to South Korean Agriculture* (Berkeley, Calif.: University of California Press, 1963).

11 Deane, P. *The First Industrial Revolution* (Cambridge: Cambridge University Press, 1965).

12 Deyo, F. C. *Beneath the Miracle: Labor Subordination in the New Asian Industrialism* (Berkeley, Calif.: University of California Press, 1989).

13 Fei, J. C. H., and Ranis, G. *Development of the Labor Surplus Economy: Theory and Policy* (Homewood, Ill.: Richard D. Irwin, 1964).

14 Fields, G. S. "Labor Standards, Economic Development and International Trade," in *Labor Standards and Development in the Global Economy*, ed. S. Herzenberg and J. F. Perez-Lopez (Washington, D.C.: Bureau of International Labor Affairs, U.S. Department of Labor, 1990).

15 Fields, G. S., and Wan, H., Jr. "Wage-Setting Institutions and Economic Growth," *World Development*, Vol. 17, No. 9 (September 1989).

16 Galenson, W. *Labor and Economic Growth in Five Asian Countries: South Korea, Malaysia, Taiwan, Thailand and the Philippines* (New York: Praeger, 1992).

17 Geertz, C. *Agricultural Involution* (Berkeley, Calif.: University of California Press, 1963).
18 Godfrey, M. *Labour Monitoring and Employment Policy in a Developing Economy: A Study of Indonesia* (New Delhi: International Labour Organisation, 1993).
19 Heyzer, N. *Women Workers in Southeast Asia: Problems and Strategies* (Kuala Lumpur: Asian and Pacific Development Centre, 1987).
20 Hill, H. "Indonesia's Industrial Transformation," *Bulletin of Indonesian Economic Studies*, Vol. 26, No. 2 (August 1990) and Vol. 26, No. 3 (December 1990).
21 ——. "The Economy," in *Indonesia's New Order: The Dynamics of SocioEconomic Transformation*, ed. H. Hill (Sydney: Allen and Unwin, 1994).
22 Indonesia, Central Bureau of Statistics. *Population Census*.
23 ——. *National Labour Force Survey 1990*.
24 INDOC (Indonesian Documentation and Information Centre). *Indonesian Workers and Their Right to Organise* (Leiden, 1981, 82, 83, 84, 85, 86, 87/88).
25 International Labour Organisation. *World Labour Report*, Vols. 1–7 (Geneva, 1987–93).
26 ——. *Yearbook of Labour Statistics 1992* (Geneva, 1993).
27 Jayasuriya, S., and Manning, C, "Agricultural Wage Growth and Rural Labour Market Adjustment: The Case of Java 1970–1988," Working Papers in Trade and Development No. 90/2 (Canberra: Australian National University, 1990).
28 Jones, G. "Structural Change and Prospects for Urbanization in Asian Countries," Papers of the East-West Population Institute No. 88 (Honolulu: East-West Center, 1983).
29 ——. "What Do We Know about the Labour Force in Indonesia," *Majalah Demografi Indonesia*, Vol. 1, No. 2 (1974).
30 Jones, G., and Manning, C. "Labour Force and Employment during the 1990s," in *The Oil Boom and After: Indonesian Economic Policy and Performance in the Soeharto Era*, ed. A. Booth (Singapore: Oxford University Press, 1992).
31 Kim Jang Ho. *Wages, Employment and Income Distribution in South Korea: 1960–83 (New Delhi: International Labour Organisation, 1986).*
32 Kuo, S. *The Taiwan Economy in Transition* (Boulder, Colo.: Westview Press, 1983).
33 Lewis, W. A. "Economic Development with Unlimited Supplies of Labour," *Manchester School of Economics and Social Studies*, Vol. 22, No. 2 (May 1954).
34 Lim, L. Y. C. "Women Workers in Multinational Corporations: The Case of the Electronics Industry in Malaysia and Singapore," Michigan Occasional Paper No. 9 (Ann Arbor, Mich.: University of Michigan, 1978).
35 McCawley, P. "Industrialisation in Indonesia: Developments and Prospects," Occasional Paper No. 13 (Canberra: Development Studies Centre, Australian National University, 1979).
36 Manning, C. "Examining Both Sides of the Ledger: Employment and Wages during the New Order," in *Indonesia Assessment 1993—Labour: Sharing in the Benefits of Growth?* ed. C. Manning and J. Hardjono, Political and Social Change Monograph (Canberra: Research School of Pacific Studies, Australian National University, 1993).
37 ——. "Structural Change and Industrial Relations during the Soeharto Period: An Approaching Crisis?" *Bulletin of Indonesian Economic Studies*, Vol. 29, No. 2 (August 1993).
38 ——. "Wage Differentials and Labour Market Segmentation in Indonesia Manufacturing" (Ph.D. diss., Research School of Pacific Studies, Australian National University, 1979).

39 ——. "What Has Happened to Wages in the New Order," *Bulletin of Indonesian Economic Studies*, Vol. 30, No. 3 (December 1994).
40 Manning, C., and Pang Eng Fong. "Labour Market Trends and Structures in ASEAN and the East Asian NIEs," *Asian-Pacific Economic Literature*, Vol. 4, No. 2 (September 1990).
41 Minami, R. *The Turning Point in Economic Development: Japan's Experience* (Tokyo: Kinokuniya Co., 1973).
42 Ogle, G. *South Korea: Dissent within the Economic Miracle* (London: Zed Books, 1990).
43 Ohkawa, K. *Differential Structure and Growth* (Tokyo: Kinokuniya Co., 1972).
44 Oshima, H. T. *Economic Growth in Monsoon Asia: A Comparative Survey* (Tokyo: University of Tokyo Press, 1988).
45 Papanek, G. F. "The Effect of Economic Growth and Inflation on Workers' Income," in *The Indonesian Economy*, ed. G. F. Papanek (New York: Praeger, 1980).
46 Park Fun-koo. "Emerging Issues of Industrial Relations and Labor Markets in Korea," in *Emerging Labor Issues in Developing Asia*, ed; Lee Chung-hoo and Park Fun-koo (Seoul: Korea Development Institute, 1991).
47 Tjandraningsih, I., et al. *Tenaga kerja pedesaan pada industri besar sepatu olahraga untuk exspor* [Rural workers in large-scale export-oriented firms in the footwear industry], West Java Rural Nonfarm Sector Research Project, Working Paper Series No. B-20 (Bandung: Institute of Social Studies, 1991).
48 U.S. Department of Labor. *Foreign Labor Reports*, various years.
49 White, B., et al. "Workshops and Factories: Dynamics of Production Organisation and Employment in West Java's Rural Footwear Industries," Paper presented at the Ninth Biennial Conference of the Australian Asian Studies Association, Armidale, July 6–9, 1992.
50 World Bank. *Transmigration in Indonesia* (Washington, D.C., 1986).
51 ——. World Development Report.
52 ——. World Tables.

17

LABOUR FLEXIBILITY IN THE MALAYSIAN MANUFACTURING SECTOR

Guy Standing

Malaysia may be one of those countries in which there is successful industrialisation without there ever being a period in which manufacturing accounted for anything like a majority of total employment. Policymakers and social scientists in the 1990s may also look back on the growth of labour flexibility in the manufacturing labour market of the late 1980s as not just a response to the international economic crisis of the early and mid-1980s but a critical phase in the emergence of a modern society and economic structure.

This is not to suggest that the phase is desirable in itself, or even necessary. It does, however, pose considerable dilemmas for those who will have to shape labour market policy in the era following the end of the New Economic Policy (NEP) in 1990. As will be suggested in this chapter – albeit tentatively and partially – a more flexible labour market will place a far greater onus on labour policy to provide protection against abuse and insecurity and to provide an environment in which the interests of equity and efficiency are jointly served.

This chapter is based in part on the analysis of a survey of over 2,600 manufacturing establishments across Peninsular Malaysia carried out in 1988. The context of the study was particularly intriguing, for the 1988 Manufacturing Labour Flexibility Survey (MLFS) came at the mid-point between the end of the crisis that hit the economy in the early 1980s and the beginning of the post-NEP era. In a sense, the survey was designed to tell a story about what had happened, was happening and was likely to happen between 1985 and 1990. The story may be deficient in details and unclear in some respects, but it had been hoped that it would establish a national benchmark for economists and policymakers inside and outside Malaysia to examine subsequent labour market changes in an era of structural adjustment and accelerated industrialisation. As a detailed analysis has been presented to

Source: *Industrialising Malaysia: Policy, Performance, Prospects*, K. Jomo (Editor), London: Routledge 1993, pp. 40–76.

the Economic Planning Unit (EPU) in the Prime Minister's Department, this chapter will only review the principal findings.

Any study of the manufacturing labour market in Malaysia has to be placed very firmly in the historical context of the objectives and evolution of the NEP and the underlying development goals of successive governments since Independence in 1957. To put the story in context, it is worth reminding ourselves of the main macro-policy changes influencing Malaysian industrialisation.

Malaysian industrial policy has passed through four distinctive phases. The first was one of import substitution, which lasted from Independence in 1957 until 1968; the second was what might be called selective export-led industrialisation, from 1968 until the early 1980s; the third was a phase of crisis and retrenchment, from 1983 until 1986; and the fourth could be described as liberalised export-led industrialisation, which began in late 1986.

From 1958 until 1968 the most symbolic policy instrument for manufacturing investment and employment was the Pioneer Industries Ordinance, which provided fiscal incentives to production rather than tariff protection; this was supplemented by the Tariff Advisory Board, set up to promote 'infant industries' through the granting of selective protection. It was a decade in which capital-intensive industries flourished, partly because tax exemptions were linked to capital expenditure. Total manufacturing employment grew, but only slowly.

In 1968 there was a marked shift to export-led industrialisation with the introduction of the Investment Incentives Act, drafted in the face of chronically high unemployment and growing racial tensions. The latter were associated with the labour market stagnation and growing inequalities that had accompanied the pattern of economic development. The Investment Incentives Act boosted export-oriented industrialisation by providing tax relief for export-oriented firms, investment tax credits, accelerated depreciation allowances, export incentives, tariff protection for new manufacturing establishments and exemption from import duty and surtax. These were complemented by the establishment in July 1971 of the Labour Utilisation Relief, which granted tax relief to companies based on the number of workers employed, and by the abolition of the 2 per cent payroll tax so as to encourage labour-intensive industries. But this second phase of export-led industrialisation was also marked by the strong direct involvement of government, in that industrial growth was made dependent on the restructuring objectives of the NEP. Public enterprises spread, as did public investment in private industrial enterprises, while government regulations played an important role in shaping the emerging pattern of employment.

From then until the early 1980s the growth of manufacturing output, exports and employment was spectacular, far faster than the equivalent for the whole economy. Between 1970 and 1980 the value of manufacturing exports almost doubled in real terms, and as a share of total exports rose from under

12 per cent to 22 per cent. The manufacturing employment growth rate was double that of the whole economy, while its share of total employment rose from 11.4 per cent in 1970 to 15.8 per cent in 1980. Most of that growth came in export-oriented sectors and most of that in the free trade zones. Most spectacular of all was the expansion of the electrical components and electronics sector, mainly through electronic component assembly.[1] Overall, manufacturing employment more than quadrupled between 1968 and 1980, reaching 802,000 in 1980 (Department of Statistics, various years). By the early 1980s it was not just the estate and construction industries that were complaining of labour shortage, for by then there was a tight labour market in many parts of the country.

In 1983 the international recession and the collapse of commodity prices began to bite. For a while total manufacturing employment stabilised, with falls in key export sectors such as textiles and rubber products. Then in 1985–6 a severe recession – the worst since Independence – shook manufacturing, obliging managements to focus on their labour policy and resulting in widespread retrenchments in wood products, electrical goods, electronics, textiles and many other industries. To a certain extent it was the responses to this upheaval – which in later times may be seen as a hiccough in the country's industrialisation – that formed the context of the MLFS.

One can identify 1986 as the beginning of a fourth distinctive phase, that of liberalised export-led industrialisation. Its key features have been a relaxation of the NEP in the interest of boosting industrial investment, exports and employment, with the intention of attracting more foreign investment, coupled with a reversal of the longstanding policy of promoting industrialisation through investment in publicly owned enterprises.[2] In particular, there has been a drive to create 'Malaysia Inc.' via privatisation. There has been the much-discussed *Industrial Master Plan 1986–95*, which *inter alia* identified twelve industrial sectors for special expansionary treatment in the early 1990s. More immediately, the 30 per cent foreign equity restriction on foreign investment was dropped; since 1986 foreign investors have been able to hold up to 100 per cent of the equity as long as the company exported at least 80 per cent of its production, and could hold up to 51 per cent if more than 51 per cent of its production was exported or if the output consisted of high-technology products. New investment applications received from October 1986 until 1990 were allowed to have any level of foreign equity as long as the company agreed to export more than 50 per cent of its product or if it employed more than 350 Malaysians.

This fourth phase has involved a macroeconomic policy shift within the NEP away from restructuring towards boosting economic growth, primarily through its focus on market liberalisation. This is not to suggest that policy-makers abandoned the one, or had formerly given the other no attention, merely that there has been a perceptible reorientation. It seems, for example, that there has been a shift from income redistribution, via the expansion of public non-financial enterprises, the public sector and tax-financed subsidies to Bumiputra interests, to capital redistribution, via privatisation and a more concerted policy of subsidising export-oriented enterprises. Probably, a policy of market liberalisation means that micro-level policies will have to bear more responsibility for social restructuring, not lust in the conventional Malaysian sense but in terms of protecting all vulnerable groups in the labour market.

Although unemployment rose to over 10 per cent in 1987 and 1988, by then industrial expansion was once again impressive. The ideas of supply-side structural adjustment were being promoted in an international atmosphere favouring labour and capital market 'deregulation', including the wholesale privatisation of economic and social activities. Industrial policy has shifted towards a more market-oriented, outward-oriented strategy that favours multinational capital and more management control of their establishments. By 1988, with privatisation in full swing, the industrial structure seemed set for a period of profound change.

That reorientation made it important to take stock of how manufacturing firms had responded to the shocks of the mid-1980s and to obtain an impression of how the further influx of foreign and export-oriented firms could be expected to tilt subsequent labour market developments.

Our core hypotheses can be stated quite clearly. In the second half of the 1980s a more sharply defined industrial dualism had been emerging: large establishments had been growing and strengthening their position relative to small ones, while within establishments of almost all sizes and in all industries a labour flexibilisation process had been gaining strength, involving a shift away from employment security and a shift of employment risk from companies to workers.

If these trends were supported by the data, then policymakers might be advised to address both questions with some urgency in the post-NEP era, particularly as the most disadvantaged groups tend to be crowded into more precarious forms of employment. It would be in nobody's interest for industrial fragmentation to undermine the considerable social achievements of the past two decades. Yet it will be argued that certain long-term trends in the labour market that were expected to accompany industrialisation, including the 'formalisation' of employment, have been checked if not reversed. This partly reflects adoption of trends from highly industrialised economies and partly arises because manufacturing enterprises in Malaysia have realised the advantages of alternative employment relations.

SUPPLY-SIDE VERSUS SOCIAL ADJUSTMENT LABOUR MARKET POLICIES

At this point it might be useful to step out of the Malaysian scene to consider the swirl of international debate surrounding the two vogue notions of 'structural adjustment' and 'labour market flexibility', the latter being seen by many as a necessity for the former, which in turn is seen as necessary for successful industrialisation and development.

For a long period the dominant mode of economic thinking about the medium and long term was what might be called 'social adjustment'. In essence, its underlying model is Keynesian, with a social-democratic ethos and a belief that markets could and should be circumvented or moderated by institutional and other regulatory devices in the interest of both equity and long-run economic growth.

For well-known reasons, this model was put on the defensive by the economic upheavals of the 1970s and 1980s and the pressure for rapid and extensive adjustments to internationally transmitted economic shocks and instability. The pursuit of outward-oriented development became a global panacea, with earnest economists everywhere diligently searching for 'rigidities' – particularly associated with trade unions and labour regulations – that were alleged to be raising production costs and undermining the international competitiveness of country X or Y. There re-emerged an overwhelming faith in markets untramelled by regulations, collective organisations or other institutional interventions. This supply-side critique has been pervasively influential during the past decade, becoming the conventional wisdom of the era. In Malaysia, as elsewhere, it can be predicted that the next few years will witness a critical debate between this supply-side model of structural adjustment and a re-emerging social adjustment model that is more concerned with distributional issues.

One can juxtapose, necessarily rather crudely in the interest of brevity, the two perspectives as they relate to labour market policy and the pursuit of labour flexibility. In doing so, we may be able to highlight some of the critical dilemmas facing economists and planners considering the next phase of Malaysia's economic development. As for the notion of labour flexibility, it has been used as a euphemism for many changes but ultimately refers to the responsiveness of the labour market, the ease and cost with which labour mobility of various types can be achieved, and the ease with which the workforce can be adjusted to achieve rapid productivity growth. For unions and workers, flexibility has suggested insecurity; for employers, it has suggested efficiency and adaptability. In a sense, both sides are correct.

In recent years the pressure for adjustment to external shocks and the belief in outward-oriented development have led to a sustained 'supply-side' critique of many labour market policies that had been perceived as desirable attributes of socioeconomic development. One is therefore obliged to consider this critique, and the appeal of alternatives that they wish to put in its place, dwelling rather more on those that might have resonances to Malaysian debates.

Price versus social distortions

The essence of a social adjustment strategy is 'growth with social protection'. Among its elements are the following labour-related aspects. First, to ameliorate poverty of the most basic kind, there are usually food subsidies and price support systems to encourage the production of domestically consumed food. Critics say this is a 'market distortion'. Second, there is usually some minimum wage protection machinery, designed ostensibly to reduce exploitation and alleviate poverty. Critics say that this amounts to a market distortion, raising wages above the market-clearing, equilibrium level, deterring employment by favouring capital–labour substitution and increasing 'inequalities between the formal and informal sectors'. Third, there are institutional forms of labour security protection – safety-and-health standards, employment security regulations (preventing arbitrary dismissal, for example), limits on working time, overtime, etc. These are also intended to protect workers from exploitation and, by ameliorating working conditions, enhance productivity. Critics say these amount to market distortions since they represent non-wage labour costs and rigidities that impede labour mobility and thus the efficient allocation of resources.

Fourth, the social adjustment school believes in promoting freedom of association and that participatory collective organisations, notably trade unions, should be given an active role, to encourage dynamic efficiency, to strengthen democratic tendencies, to ensure more equitable income distribution and to restrict discrimination. Again, critics see such organisations as market distortions in that they limit the ability of firms to react to market forces and limit the realisation of high profits that could boost investment. Fifth, the social adjustment school sees public expenditure as complementing private expenditure, as potentially productive and as a means of mobilising and retaining resources for national development. Critics say this too is a market distortion, arguing that it results in 'financial crowding out' of private investment and growth, while being unproductive, unresponsive to market forces and an inappropriate standard-setter for wages and conditions of employment.

By contrast, the labour-related policies that characterise the supply-side strategy focus on price mechanisms and overcoming price distortions. Its approach to structural adjustment combines a 'stabilisation' policy and a development policy, for which a set of microeconomic reforms are perceived as necessary for macroeconomic success. Stabilisation essentially means a deflationary monetary policy to hold down domestic demand – so limiting imports – and combat inflation. That means temporarily lowering consumption and employment. This is complemented by an 'outward-looking' development strategy, involving 'trade liberalisation', nominal and real exchange rate devaluation and a shift in relative prices between tradable and non-tradable goods and services. Governments should cut subsidies to basic consuinption goods, thereby raising the relative return to investment in tradable goods and services. The social adjustment school might say that this results in 'social distortion' and that subsidies on non-tradables promote productivity of the current and future workforce while lowering the efficiency wage in the sectors. The evidence is far from conclusive that cutting such subsidies is unequivocably beneficial for development.

Minimum wages and relative wages

The supply-side strategy puts overwhelming emphasis on 'competitiveness', which *inter alia* means reducing labour costs and making them more flexible. Statutory minimum wages are opposed on the grounds that they price goods out of the market that would be produced by low-paid, low-productivity workers, thus causing unemployment. Critics of that view refer to the multiple functions of minimum wages. They note that very low wages encourage low productivity and favour unscrupulous employers over those more concerned for long-term stability and community development. Perhaps most importantly, although minimum wages may be above the average or marginal income of those outside modern, export-oriented industrial enterprises, or above the 'aspiration wage' of unemployed job-seekers, it cannot be presumed that they exceed the optimum 'efficiency wage', the wage at which the average worker works with optimal effort. Finally, critics of a policy of wage reduction claim that lowering unit labour costs can be achieved either by lowering wages with constant productivity (or with a lower decline in the latter) or by raising productivity with constant wages (or with a rise in the latter, if they rise less than productivity).

Those advocating a supply-side approach also press for relative wage changes or adjustment in the 'equilibrium' structure of wages. Supposedly, wages of skilled workers in consumer goods industries have to decline, to encourage them to shift to export industries, while wages in the latter should stabilise, or rise *if* inter-sectoral labour mobility is slow or limited. They also contend that reducing wage differentials by minimum wage regulations or other mechanisms reduces the return to education and training to the point that the incentive to invest in them is insufficient. This is further reason, in their view, to avoid minimum wage machinery.

This too is not clearcut. At the micro-level, real wages may fall below the efficiency wage level, so resulting in poor or stagnant productivity. At the macro-level, it is too easy to assert that high unemployment (in whatever form) is 'classical', due to excessive real wages. It may be more 'Keynesian' in nature, even in low-income countries and even where there is high inflation. In that case, the critics would say, if real wages rose, not only would there be efficiency gains in tradable industries, but demand for wage goods produced outside the export-oriented sectors would grow. Structural adjustment could be aided because the demand for such goods would stimulate small-scale, informal businesses. If so, higher real wages would not 'crowd out' investment in tradable sectors, but could create a virtuous process of accumulation in low-income sectors.

As for securing labour mobility into the tradable sectors, the supply-side school, recognising that relative wages are 'sticky', argues that, as most governments have little control over private sector wages, they should concentrate on reducing public sector wages. They should also restrict wage indexation, and wage subsidies designed to limit unemployment resulting from structural changes are opposed on the grounds that they would slow the shift of resources into export industries from those supposedly with low to those with high social marginal product.

However, do wages in non-tradable sectors have to fall? The social adjustment side would argue that labour market policies, notably those associated with (re-)training and mobility, could avoid the need for wider wage differentials. Some argue that by *reducing* wage differentials, labour mobility from low- to high-productivity sectors would be accelerated, rather than slowed, if only because that would raise the relative and absolute return to high-productivity sector investment, while high costs in low-productivity industries would squeeze firms out of business. They also argue that it is too facile to claim that, by narrowing wage differentials, minimum wages deter skill acquisition by reducing the return to education. There are many non-wage benefits of education, and as in any case schooling is a job screening device, it is the enhanced access to job opportunities that maintains high individual economic returns to education and training. In sum, low wages plus wider differentials are not a panacea for labour market adjustment.

Public versus private sector employment

As for reducing public sector wages, this may or may not make sense. In many countries, just as it has been too easily presumed that the public sector is 'bloated' and that it is socially unproductive, it has become almost an article of faith that public sector wages and fringe benefits are excessive. It may be that wages should be reduced; or it may be that they should be maintained while public employment is cut to raise efficiency; or it may be that wages and employment should be cut relative to expenditure on other inputs involved in social service provision. All these responses are possible. But the necessary analysis rarely precedes the action taken.

Similarly, one should be wary about justifying wage cuts by reference to higher productivity in the private sector. That might be valid. But *if* high profits in some private sectors were the result of wages and working conditions that were so poor that workers could be productive only for a while before having to leave or before reaching the point where employers sought their replacement, then a policy of cutting public sector wages could compound an overall problem of stagnant labour productivity. Again, one cannot presume that if relative prices are in imbalance the higher one should be lowered.

Another aspect of public sector wage and employment policy is that, while salaries, benefits and employment security of a core of public sector employees may be advantaged in many countries, there are many whose wages are low by comparison with many private sector workers and whose security of employment is minimal. In the face of public expenditure cuts those workers are the first to suffer. Yet they are often the least skilled and thus the least able to transfer from non-tradable to tradable sectors. In short, the role of the public sector in labour market adjustment is a major unresolved issue.

Unemployment policies for structural adjustment

The structural adjustment model expects a period of resource reallocation – through trade liberalisation, market deregulation, etc. – to lead to a transitional period of high unemployment. Advocates and critics alike agree that this should be minimised. But supply-side economists would leave that largely to market forces, and would explain prolonged high unemployment as due to 'market failure' or even 'voluntary unemployment', whereas social adjustment proponents call for institutional mechanisms to secure labour reallocation, and thus would attribute high unemployment to inadequate labour market policies.

Conceptually there are four modes of labour (market) adjustment: (i) external (mid-career) labour market; (ii) inter-generational; (iii) internal labour market; (iv) redeployment.

The first can be painful, since it means existing workers being retrenched in some sectors and competing for jobs in others, during which overall and relative wages are expected to adjust in response to labour market disequilibria. With the second, most of the existing workforce does not engage in mid-career job changes, but labour force entrants, mainly youth, are channelled into tradable rather than non-tradable sectors; in a period of structural adjustment, this mode can result in high youth unemployment, and possibly accelerated 'early retirement'. With the third mode, workers change jobs within enterprises, corresponding to product or technological changes or job restructuring. There is certainly scope for more resort to this form of adjustment, a point that we will take up later with regard to Malaysian developments. Finally, the redeployment mode relies more on the state or some institutional mechanism to direct labour mobility, perhaps on a subsidised basis or with retraining.

The more inter-sectoral and other labour mobility can be achieved by the third and fourth modes of adjustment, the less likely that structural change will result in high unemployment. As that would also mean less reliance on relative wage rate changes, the more policymakers can rely on modes (iii) and (iv), the less the need to widen wage differentials.

In discussing adjustment and employment, Streeten (1988: 27) recently concluded:

> There is one good aspect in conducting adjustment policies in the current environment of unemployment. It is easier to move unemployed workers into the right industries than to shift workers from one job to another. Redeployment and restructuring out of unemployment should be the programme for both developing and advanced countries.

No doubt that was drawing small comfort from adverse realities. But it is far from self-evidently true. Workers are rarely made more productive by experience of unemployment, especially if that is prolonged, while unemployed, impoverished workers are scarcely able to indulge in optimal labour market mobility in response to job restructuring. There is little evidence that high unemployment is either necessary for structural change or preferable to other forms of labour market adjustment, and a number of countries have shown that structural change can be achieved without any period of high unemployment.

Labour regulations and labour market fragmentation

Both the supply-side and social adjustment perspectives give a pivotal role to labour market 'dualism'. According to the former, excessive regulations and minimum wages are shown by the growth of the 'informal sector' and the non-growth of the 'formal', tradable sector. They advocate dismantling regulations so that more of the 'informal' can become 'formal' and so that employment can rise. The social adjustment school retorts that the long-term objective should be the extension of social protection to those currently uncovered and surviving in petty units of production or in other peripheral activities, whether productive or merely survival oriented. In particular, the social adjustment model would give high priority to anti-discrimination and protective regulations designed to reduce the marginalisation of socially vulnerable groups, notably women, children, migrants and ethnic minorities.

To be fair, the debate about the role and impact of labour regulations is unresolved. What we do know is that there has been an enormous growth in so-called informal economic activities all over the world. Part of that has been due to the international recession and so on, whereby the unemployed have taken up petty production and the like, or whereby those whose regular earnings have fallen have supplemented them with secondary activities. Partly it reflects a growth of sub-contracting by large enterprises to reduce costs, or as an aspect of privatisation or in response to the increased uncertainty and risk in times of recession and structural adjustment. And partly it reflects resort to more informal, unprotected types of worker to bypass regulations or reduce costs.

Considering such developments, statements about the supposedly adverse effects of labour market regulations on employment *levels* should be treated with reservation. This is important to stress, for a key theme of the supply-side perspective is that 'fewer labour market regulations . . . would promote labour market flexibility and higher employment' in developing countries, and that 'rules on job security . . . distort the labour market in ways that reduce employment and overall living standards' (World Bank, 1987: 32, 9). Yet labour regulations may have more impact on the *types* of employment rather than on the level and have positive effects on living standards by setting guidelines, which may not be met everywhere but which help to reduce the prevalence of poor working conditions, exploitation and oppression. Once again, these are empirical matters on which it is too easy to reach conclusions in the absence of real data.

The key theme is worker security, of which there are various forms. Unfortunately, some economists lump them together, thus blurring analysis and policy debates. One should distinguish between: (i) labour market security; (ii) employment security; (iii) job security; (iv) work security; and (v) income security. Labour market security is high when job changing involves only moderate personal costs and reasonable prospects of subsequent benefits, and is typically inversely related to the level of unemployment. Employment security is high when workers cannot be dismissed without either costs to employers or the satisfaction of pre-specified conditions. Job security is high when workers have rights to particular niches within enterprises, and where unions or other institutions safeguard craft barriers or skills. Work security is high when working conditions are safe and so on. Finally, income security is high when workers have their wages or earnings protected from income fluctuations, through indexation, collective bargaining or other forms of institutional protection.

All five forms of security have potential costs and potential benefits for enterprises. Because there has been overwhelming stress on their alleged costs in recent international debates, it may be appropriate to stress the potential benefits, bearing in mind that ultimately these too are empirical matters.

Take, for example, job security. Many firms have introduced job security arrangements precisely because they were perceived as conducive to productivity growth; this was the essence of Taylorist management, since narrowly defined job classifications were seen as enabling employers to have control over output, work input and labour costs. Accordingly, one should not presume that the erosion of job security is always desirable even on efficiency grounds. Moreover, job security surely encourages the development of technical skill within jobs, because workers can expect a return to training and informal learning. Against that, if job demarcation results in workers resisting technological change and redeployment, then regulations or union agreements protecting job security could hinder structural adjustment and thus impair economic growth.

However, it is employment security that most critics have in mind when castigating 'regulations', claiming that workers in secure employment have less incentive to be productive, are immobile in the face of a need for structural adjustment, or have to be compensated so much that the potential benefits of resource reallocation are lost. It is also argued that employment protection discourages firms from hiring and encourages them to opt for more capital-intensive techniques. Unfortunately, there is little evidence to support or refute such arguments. Moreover, employment security regulations also have potential benefits, as follows:

(a) they can improve workers' commitment to the enterprise and thus raise work motivation and productivity;
(b) they may reduce the 'transaction costs' of employment by reducing labour turnover, especially important where productivity rises with on-the-job learning;
(c) they may encourage worker acceptance of productivity-raising rationalisation and other modernisation measures;
(d) they may improve job and work flexibility, that is, improve the willingness of workers to accept occupational and work environment changes;
(e) they may induce greater acceptance of work disciplinary measures;
(f) they may improve 'dynamic efficiency', by obliging management to become more efficient and competitive by means other than by laying off workers;
(g) they may induce workers to accept lower wage rises in return for the employment security;
(h) they may reduce the probability of frictional unemployment by enabling workers to have adequate notice of impending job loss to seek out alternative employment.

In sum, the benefits of employment security may well offset the costs. But one should not stop there, for what is needed are forms of employment security that promote flexibility and productivity. That is the challenge that comes to the fore in the context of structural adjustment rather than stable development. Advocates of social adjustment would argue that only if workers could share in the decisions and in the benefits of investment could this issue be resolved.

Wage flexibility

As for income security, the supply-side view is that wages should be allowed to fluctuate and that, if they were tied more to economic performance and profits, not only would employment be stabilised cyclically, but it would do so at higher levels than with fixed wages. Critics of this view would argue that, as long as workers do not at least share in decisions over investment or productive strategy, it would be unjust for them to have to bear the risk. Moreover, if payment systems were made more flexible – as is happening in some countries where adjustment strategies are being implemented – then earnings differentials will grow between those in high-tech sectors and those outside them. This has been a feature of such systems. For some economists, that is perfectly acceptable, but from a social equity point of view it may be undesirable, leading to active discontent among those unable to share in the benefits. Furthermore, flexible payment systems may result in extremely low and uncertain earnings for low-productivity workers and may slow structural change rather than accelerate it, to the extent that capital could be tied up in inefficient, low-productivity production.

Again, there are pros and cons about more flexible payment systems. The challenge is to move towards systems that promote adjustment, productivity and flexibility while maintaining rather than disrupting progress towards social equity.

Education and training for adjustment

Both the social adjustment and supply-side models favour increased education and training to promote flexibility and adjustment. But there is a difference of emphasis. The supply-siders stress that schooling and training should be geared to the needs of export-oriented industries, and take an economic rate of return approach to investment in education and training. By contrast, the social adjustment adherents see education as more of a social end in itself, as well as a means of promoting development.

There is no space here for an extended discussion but, given the emphasis on education and training, a few words of caution are in order. It is conventional to argue that the economic rate of return to investment in schooling is higher than that in 'physical capital'. This is comforting. However, the utilisation of educated or trained workers may be very sub-optimal, since access to many jobs may require an excessive level of schooling, simply because schooling attainment is a convenient low-cost 'screening' device in recruitment. Far more attention should be given to the effective deployment of educated workers. The sub-employment of educated and technically proficient workers in large corporations, as well as in the public sector, is a phenomenon found in many countries.

We should be wary too about the potential abuse of the system for short-term efficiency purposes. It is no coincidence that the word 'schooling' means both taming and liberating. If used to produce docile, disciplined workers (as many stress as a primary objective; World Bank, 1987: 63), then it may actually hinder the workforce's mobility and relearning potential in future eras of adjustment. This is a reason for having reservations about policies based on short-term economic rates of return.

Similar problems arise in assessing the extent to which governments should invest in training, making it hard to accept that 'some developing country governments have tended to expand higher-level vocational training too fast' (World Bank, 1987: 63). The difficulty is to identify appropriate criteria for reaching such conclusions.

Training policy can facilitate structural adjustment by raising the productivity of workers in existing jobs, by raising the overall productivity of the labour force, and by facilitating labour mobility as job structures change with technological and productive restructuring. Also, policy can be oriented towards either vocational (or craft) training or job training. The former puts emphasis on developing all-round capabilities, whether through prolonged apprenticeship or institutional courses. The latter means workers being trained solely for jobs they are required to perform in the immediate future. That is cheaper and has involved schemes that impart 'modules of employable skill'; as such, it may make fewer demands on trainee and trainer alike, requiring less formal schooling and work commitment. However, it probably also leaves the worker less adaptable and less equipped to shift jobs or work status in times of industrial restructuring. In effect, a low-cost option with a higher short-term return may yield a lower longer-term social return.

Similarly, training policy should not be divorced from job structures. If those are highly stratified, such that there is a limited internal labour market, the required amount of more costly off-the-job training will rise. To reduce the need for public investment in training schemes, policymakers could explore ways of promoting internal labour adjustment, through on-the-job learning, incentive structures, anti-discrimination regulations, etc.

Too often, a perceived shortage of skilled labour is *presumed* to mean that the appropriate policy is more schooling or training. It is conceivable that a more appropriate and cost-effective approach would be a policy to alter job structures rather than the attributes of people required to fill them. It is technologically deterministic to focus exclusively on training.

Finally, there is the form of training. Many economists favour government labour market training schemes as a way of easing labour force adjustments. Undoubtedly, such schemes have a role to play. But they do have drawbacks. If governments subsidise the training of the unemployed, firms may simply substitute those trainees for others already trained or partially trained, implying a 'substitution effect'. Or the subsidy may result in workers being trained who would have been trained anyway, resulting in a 'deadweight effect'. Or the trainees may be hired to do jobs for which their training is not really required, because the cost of the training is underpriced. Or, as a result of altering the effective 'price' of technically skilled workers, enterprises may alter job structures to increase the relative demand for workers with those skills, thereby contributing to a persistent 'shortage' of such workers. In sum, because labour market training schemes are very rarely evaluated, they tend to be overvalued as a means of promoting labour market adjustment. An alternative policy to facilitate labour mobility and adjustment is 'in-plant' training. If, as is common, this involves the use of subsidies, the same problems arise, perhaps in more acute form since employers receive the subsidy directly, even though the public cost of this form of training may be lower because part of it may be borne by employers.[3] Here, too, the challenge is to minimise substitution and deadweight effects.

These notes of caution should not be construed as dismissive of training policy per se. They do suggest that, in encouraging firms to train more extensively, other policies are worth more active consideration, such as anti-poaching regulations – preventing other enterprises attracting newly trained workers without bearing the costs of training – and statutory obligations on firms to train a stipulated percentage of their workforce, perhaps distributed across the range of skills normally required. Such proposals would have to be carefully considered so as to minimise costs and to maximise efficiency and dynamic flexibility. But they may be critical for successful labour force adjustment.

LABOUR FLEXIBILITY IN MALAYSIAN MANUFACTURING

The preceding may seem to have been a protracted theoretical discussion of little relevance to current developments in the Malaysian economy. It is hoped that is not the case, though by international standards the Malaysian labour market has been fairly deregulated in that there has been no minimum wage, no effective system of employment security, and so on. However, we turn now to a few aspects of the labour market that seem likely to emerge as more critical issues in the post-NEP era. The discussion will skirt the paramount issue of the NEP, if only because it is implicit in every labour market policy question and because others are much better equipped to deal with it. As the following highlights a few points from the 1988 MLFS, the focus is on manufacturing, which should not be taken to imply that this is seen as the only important sector. Indeed, the transition to a high-technology service-oriented economy will be a major challenge for Malaysia in the 1990s.

Labour absorption in manufacturing: recent trends and prospects

Overall changes, 1985–90

The manufacturing sector has long been regarded as a primary source of employment expansion in the country, especially considering the long-term labour displacement in agriculture and mining and the desired shift of the rural workforce into modern, urban-based industries. However, in the 1980s economists became less sanguine about the ability of manufacturing to provide large numbers of new jobs. Despite the unprecedented surge of manufacturing in 1989, a big question is whether or not the employment elasticity has shrunk to the point where reasonable output expansion could be achieved with little impact on employment. The cause could be technological or the result of a shift towards more capital-intensive industries and types of establishment or because companies are more inclined to pursue a labour-shedding and labour-avoiding policy in the wake of the recent recession.

Employment expansion in manufacturing slowed sharply in the mid-1980s when, as the MLFS shows, there were far more widespread labour surplus conditions than were implied by the level of retrenchments, conditions which persisted after 1985. Yet, according to retrospective data from the survey between mid-1985 and mid-1988 a majority of manufacturing establishments in the country expanded employment. Export-oriented industries such as textiles and electronics, and to a lesser extent chemicals and wood products, recovered most robustly. But in such large employment-generating sectors as food, beverages and tobacco, non-metallic mineral products, basic metals and fabricated metals, machinery and equipment, only a minority of establishments expanded in the three years covered by the data (Table 17.1). Foreign establishments were far more likely to have expanded than were their Malaysian counterparts (Table 17.2).

Table 17.1 Change in manufacturing employment by industry, 1985–8 (percentage of establishments)

	Fell			*Rose*			
Industry	>25%	0–25%	*No change*	0–10%	10–25%	>25%	Total
Food	7.8	28.0	21.7	13.0	11.9	17.6	100
Textiles	10.5	21.0	8.8	9.7	15.5	34.4	100
Wood	8.7	22.6	12.6	13.7	12.6	29.9	100
Paper	6.7	27.9	8.5	9.1	12.1	35.8	100
Chemical	7.8	26.5	8.7	13.0	12.4	31.8	100
Non-metal	21.1	28.5	18.8	9.7	7.9	13.9	100
Basic metal	14.5	28.9	10.5	14.5	10.5	21.0	100
Fabricated metal	18.7	20.1	12.2	6.6	11.6	30.7	100
Electronic	17.2	19.0	3.4	8.6	13.8	37.9	100
Other manufacture	11.8	15.6	21.6	7.8	15.7	27.4	100

Source: MLFS, 1988.

Table 17.2 Change in employment, by ownership, 1985–8 (percentage of establishments)

	Fell				*Rose*			
Ownership	>25%	10–25%	0–20%	*No change*	0–10%	10–25%	>25%	Total
Foreign	9.1	14.9	11.7	6.4	13.9	10.7	33.3	100
Chinese Malaysians	10.7	12.2	8.5	17.2	9.5	13.6	28.3	100
Other Malaysians	14.6	15.6	15.7	10.0	12.1	10.3	21.6	100

Source: MLFS, 1988.

The MLFS also revealed that only a minority of employment establishments expected to expand employment in the following two years. No doubt this partly reflected a lack of *planning* at the firm level, which is surely worth encouraging in the interest of promoting an orderly, efficient labour market and of helping planners formulate labour market policies. However, although the number of firms that expected to expand employment was much greater than the number that expected to cut it, the largest group by far consisted of those that expected no change (Table 17.3).

A further substantial minority were uncertain. The net expected expansion corresponded to the bullish sentiments in mid-1988. Even so, only in the electronics industry did a majority expect to increase employment. If one excludes those without employees at the time and counts those under receivership or closing as expecting employment to fall, then over 7 per cent of all establishments were ready to admit that they expected employment to decline, whereas about a third expected it to grow. These figures have to be seen in the context of what was a booming economy when a strong expansionary sentiment could have been expected.

Establishments in export-oriented industries were most likely to be expecting to expand their employment. Even so, one can only be struck by the widespread caution, or pessimism, shown among firms manufacturing non-metallic mineral products, wood products and basic metal products.

One potential tool for employment planning policy is identification of what management perceive to be the main factors affecting their employment *change*. Normally, one would expect that the main factor would be the level of

Table 17.3 Expected/planned employment change in next two years, by industry, 1988 (%)

	Expected change				
Industry	*Rise*	*Fall*[a]	*No change*	*Don't know*	*Total*
Food, etc.	18.7	8.2	68.5	4.5	100
Textiles	47.3	7.0	41.9	3.7	100
Wood, etc.	30.5	6.9	57.7	4.9	100
Paper, etc.	39.9	8.3	49.4	2.4	100
Chemical, etc.	41.4	7.0	47.5	4.1	100
Non-metal	25.6	8.3	60.7	5.4	100
Basic metal	26.6	5.1	64.6	3.8	100
Fabricated metal	37.1	5.5	50.9	6.5	100
Electronics	51.7	13.8	34.5	—	100
Other manufacture	43.1	7.8	45.1	3.9	100

Note:
[a] Closing establishments and those under receivership included as expected 'falls'. 'Closing' includes those already closed, those not having any workers at the time of the survey and those planning to close or under receivership.

Source: MLFS, 1988.

demand for their final product. But that cannot be presumed in any specific period. Accordingly, respondents were asked to identify the principal and second most important factors influencing their employment, and were asked separately about the past two years, the present (i.e. mid-1988) and the expected factors in the next two years.

Over the previous two years, from mid-1986 to mid-1988 (Table 17.4), the major factor besides overall demand was business uncertainty, which was scarcely surprising in the wake of the recession. This factor was particularly prominent in industries dealing with basic metals, non-metallic mineral products and wood products. It shows just how important the creation of an economic environment of stability and *steady* growth is to employment creation.

The second most cited factor was new technology, notably in electronics, followed by plant capacity, implying that a fairly large number of establishments could not expand employment without first expanding their productive investment. This raises questions about the extent to which financial and other encouragement is given to expansion of existing enterprises rather than new ones – a crucial policy issue for the 1990s.

A key point about Table 17.4 is the rarity with which labour-related factors were cited as having influenced employment, although some did report as their main or second most important consideration the desire for a *stable* workforce, presumably because either cutting or expanding the workforce could affect morale, productivity, training and supervision costs.

Wage costs were scarcely mentioned in any industry or size category of establishment, and nor were non-wage labour costs. As for the much-discussed labour shortage factor, a mere 1.5 per cent of all establishments mentioned a shortage of qualified labour as having had an adverse effect. Finally, at a time when some commentators were calling for reform of labour regulations to promote industrial employment, it is instructive that on the ground, as it were, employers did not see labour laws as having had any substantial effect. This is strong evidence from a large survey and should be recalled in the event of further calls for 'deregulation'.

As for what firms expected to be the major influences on employment in the next two years, much the same pattern emerged, with labour-related factors being remarkable for their insignificance, even as a secondary factor. Abstracting from the demand influence, Table 17.5 shows that new technology and business uncertainty were expected to be the main factors, followed by plant capacity and new products. Neither labour costs nor labour shortage nor labour laws were perceived as very significant at all. In sum, as employers saw it, it is market stability and technology that most influence plans and changes in employment.

Table 17.4 Main factor besides demand affecting employment, by industry, 1986–8 (%)

Factor	Industry								
	Food	*Textiles*	*Wood*	*Paper*	*Chemicals*	*Non-metal*	*Basic metal*	*Fabricated metal*	*Electrical*
None	54.3	43.0	46.4	50.9	50.6	47.6	43.0	48.4	24.1
Work reorganisation	4.0	4.5	3.0	3.5	6.5	5.9	5.1	4.7	1.7
New technology	5.9	8.3	2.7	6.4	7.0	3.6	1.3	3.7	27.6
New products	1.8	3.3	3.8	2.9	5.5	2.4	6.3	5.5	8.6
Shortage of qualified labour	1.3	2.9	1.9	2.9	0.7	0.6	2.5	1.2	—
Firm restructuring	1.2	1.2	1.1	1.2	2.4	0.6	—	2.2	6.9
Wage rise	1.7	2.9	2.5	2.9	1.7	2.4	—	1.8	3.4
Export quota	0.3	4.5	1.1	1.2	0.2	—	—	0.6	1.7
Desire for stable workforce	3.7	3.3	3.8	4.1	5.1	3.0	5.1	3.5	3.4
Plant capacity	5.9	5.8	9.6	5.8	6.7	4.8	5.1	5.5	5.2
Non-wage labour costs	0.7	0.8	0.3	0.6	0.2	1.2	1.3	0.4	—
Business uncertainty	11.1	8.7	16.9	9.4	7.2	20.8	24.0	12.5	8.6
Labour laws	—	—	0.3	—	—	0.6	—	—	—
Other	8.1	10.7	6.6	8.2	6.0	6.5	6.3	10.0	8.6
Total	100	100	100	100	100	100	100	100	100

Source: MLFS, 1988.

Table 17.5 Main factor besides demand expected to affect employment in next two years, by industry, 1988 (%)

	Industry								
Factor	*Food*	*Textiles*	*Wood*	*Paper*	*Chemicals*	*Non-metal*	*Basic metal*	*Fabricated metal*	*Electrical*
None	42.3	35.1	29.5	40.9	36.9	39.3	35.4	40.0	27.6
Work reorganisation	2.0	1.6	6.0	8.2	4.6	5.4	2.5	3.9	1.7
New technology	11.6	8.7	6.6	11.1	10.6	8.3	7.6	6.5	19.0
New products	6.7	4.1	6.0	5.3	11.6	1.8	7.6	8.8	24.1
Shortage of qualified labour	0.7	2.9	1.6	1.7	0.7	—	2.5	0.8	—
Company restructuring	1.7	2.1	1.9	1.2	1.2	3.0	1.3	2.2	3.4
Rising wages	1.2	2.5	2.5	1.7	1.7	0.6	1.3	2.2	1.7
Export quota	0.2	6.6	4.4	0.6	1.4	—	—	2.3	1.7
Desire for stable labour force	2.3	2.5	3.8	1.2	2.2	3.6	3.8	2.7	—
Plant capacity	7.6	7.8	9.0	7.6	11.3	7.7	6.3	7.1	5.2
Rising non-wage labour costs	0.2	0.8	—	—	1.0	0.6	—	0.2	—
Business uncertainty	16.3	14.9	18.8	10.5	11.1	22.6	29.1	17.1	6.9
Labour laws	—	0.4	—	—	—	1.2	—	—	—
Other	6.5	9.5	8.2	9.4	5.5	4.8	2.5	5.7	8.6
Total	100	100	100	100	100	100	100	100	100

Source: MLFS, 1988.

Industrial relocation and employment mobility: a new geographical divide?

Labour mobility and enterprise mobility may have a growing impact on restructuring in the 1990s. For years Penang and the Klang Valley have been the industrial hubs of the Malaysian economy, drawing capital and labour from the rest of the country and from abroad. In the late 1980s that began to change fairly dramatically, although it has probably been insufficiently absorbed into policy debates.

There has been a drift of manufacturing establishments and employment 'southwards', which other secondary evidence suggests has been a more general trend. Thus, as Table 17.6 shows, manufacturing establishments were far more likely to have expanded employment in southern states than elsewhere, except in Penang. For example, in Johore and Malacca nearly a third of all establishments had expanded their employment by more than 25 per cent between 1985 and 1988, and a further one in four had expanded by up to 25 per cent. By contrast, only a minority of establishments had expanded at all in Trengganu, Kelantan, Perak, Selangor and Kuala Lumpur, and hardly any in Perlis. Other states had modest expansion in net terms, though one should note the stronger growth in Kedah, as well as Penang, as moderating the 'southern' trend. There are various reasons for a southern drift, among which of course is the proximity of Singapore, with its tight labour market, rising labour costs and the desire of Singapore-based companies to set up factories close to where there is a more ample and lower-cost labour supply (Salem, 1988).

It is expected that Johore and Malacca will become the next industrial growth centres in the Malaysian economy, and these data lend support to that belief. Already Johore Bahru is closely linked to Singapore and the state government has made 'economic twinning' with Singapore one of the four

Table 17.6 Change in employment by state, 1985–8 (%)

State	*Fell* >25%	*Fell* 0–25%	No change	*Rose* 0–25%	*Rose* >25%	Total
Johore	10.5	22.2	11.0	23.4	32.8	100
Kedah	8.1	21.6	15.3	27.9	27.0	100
Kelantan	15.0	15.0	28.3	23.3	18.3	100
Malacca	11.8	15.3	16.5	25.9	30.6	100
N. Sembilan	5.7	25.3	17.2	27.6	24.1	100
Pahang	6.7	31.7	11.5	29.8	20.2	100
Penang	8.8	24.2	15.4	20.5	31.1	100
Perak	9.7	26.4	17.0	24.1	22.7	100
Selangor	14.0	28.2	8.0	22.8	27.0	100
Trengganu	14.5	34.5	20.0	18.2	12.7	100
Kuala Lumpur	15.4	21.1	15.2	21.4	26.9	100

Source: MLFS, 1988

components of its Development Strategy. But the drift southwards seems set to continue (Table 17.7). Establishments in Malacca, Johore and Negri Sembilan were the most inclined to expect employment expansion. Conversely, the limited growth in the least-industrialised states should be a worry for those concerned with formulating post-NEP policies.

The intensification of establishment dualism?

Another crucial feature of recent changes in employment is that, while there was an overall stability in the size distribution of establishments, with a large majority remaining approximately the same size in 1988 as in 1985, only a very small proportion of establishments with less than five employees expanded. Employment growth was concentrated in establishments that were already large in 1985.

As Table 17.8 shows, a majority of very large firms with over 500 workers in 1985 had grown over the three years from 1985 to 1988, whereas only a minority of those with 1–4, 5–20 and 21–50 workers had grown. It appears that small firms were not a good source of new jobs in the late 1980s, which should be borne in mind in formulating policies for the post-NEP era.

Moreover, on balance only large firms with more than 250 workers expected to expand in the next two years; most other size groups tended to expect no change, although on average the smallest firms actually expected to shrink still further (Table 17.9). That surely is a signal of immense signifi-

Table 17.7 Expected/planned employment change in next two years, by state, 1988 (%)

	Expected change				
State	*Rise*	*Fall*[a]	*No change*	*Don't know*	*Total*
Johore	44.5	5.5	45.4	4.6	100
Kedah	42.7	6.8	47.0	3.4	100
Kelantan	21.3	3.3	73.8	1.6	100
Malacca	47.7	1.2	50.0	1.2	100
N. Sembilan	44.2	4.6	45.3	5.8	100
Pahang	26.5	2.9	68.6	2.0	100
Penang	40.2	2.6	53.6	3.7	100
Perak	27.7	3.7	63.4	5.2	100
Perlis	(40.0)	—	(40.0)	(20.0)	100
Selangor	32.0	7.4	55.0	5.3	100
Trengganu	12.7	1.8	78.2	7.3	100
Kuala Lumpur	23.9	5.4	64.3	6.4	100

Note: Figures in parentheses indicate that there were too few observations to justify confidence in the data.

Source: MLFS, 1988.

Table 17.8 Change in employment, by establishment size in 1985, 1985–8 (%)

Change in employment	*Employment size in 1985* 1–4	5–20	21–50	51–100	101–250	251–500	501+
Fell							
Over 25	3.6	10.0	12.1	10.5	12.6	15.6	17.0
10.1–25	—	12.6	13.5	10.5	16.2	20.8	18.9
0.1–10	—	4.0	10.2	13.3	16.8	7.8	7.5
No change	57.1	30.1	14.1	6.8	5.6	—	1.9
Rose							
0.1–10	—	3.8	10.1	16.4	13.3	7.8	18.9
10.1–25	3.6	11.0	10.2	14.1	13.8	16.9	7.5
25.1–50	10.7	9.8	12.7	13.1	10.1	13.0	15.1
Over 50	25.0	18.6	16.9	15.4	11.6	18.2	13.2
Total	100	100	100	100	100	100	100

Source: MLFS, 1988.

Table 17.9 Expected/planned employment change in next two years, by establishment size, 1988 (%)

Employment size	*Expected change* *Rise*	*Fall*[a]	*No change*	*Don't know*	*Total*
1–4	2.9	17.1	71.4	8.6	100
5–20	20.0	5.5	68.0	6.5	100
21–50	30.2	6.2	59.5	4.0	100
51–100	34.3	7.8	53.2	4.7	100
101–250	38.6	7.7	50.1	3.7	100
251–500	50.8	8.6	35.8	4.8	100
501–1000	54.6	10.5	33.7	1.2	100
1001+	56.2	10.9	29.7	3.1	100

Note:
[a] Includes closing concerns, etc.

Source: MLFS, 1988.

cance. It scarcely suggests that small is very beautiful, and probably partly reflects a realistic expectation among small-scale concerns that they may go out of business.

As many believe that small-scale enterprises have a great potential for generating employment, this point should be stressed. As research has shown elsewhere, the vast majority of small concerns begin and stay small and do not operate on the basis of expected expansion into corporate giants. They seek a niche of security. What this means is that those who push for deregulation and hefty subsidies, etc., for small-scale 'informal' firms, on the grounds that they could increase labour absorption, are effectively proposing an increase in the *number* of such concerns, not in their average size. The implications of that are not usually well articulated; one is inclined to believe that there is a distinct chance (to put it no stronger than that) that this strategy would merely force down average incomes and the 'survival probability' of any small-scale establishment – at least, of those not tightly linked to one or more larger-scale companies. That in turn would inhibit risk-taking investment, in-plant training, and so on.

Some economists have claimed that small firms in Malaysia are relatively efficient because they are subject to a higher degree of competition as a result of unrestricted entry into the industry. The only reason why they have not been able to hold their own is that the fiscal incentives are heavily biased against them. There would be widespread agreement that fiscal policy has favoured large, export-oriented companies, but there is little reason to suppose that an even more competitive environment, in which mere survival for small firms would have to be a very high priority objective, would be conducive to productive efficiency. In sum, manufacturing employment growth is likely to come from large firms rather more than from existing small-scale establishments.

The feeling that undue emphasis has been laid on the creation of new establishments is given added weight by the fact that most very small-scale firms could give no identifiable factor for not changing employment, further supporting the view that most small establishments do not actively contemplate expansion or, therefore, the constraints to it. They react, not plan – and they ought to be helped to do the latter. Scarcely any factor other than demand and business uncertainty was cited as influencing employment changes in small-scale establishments, whereas technological change and new products were the main factors in large firms. This pattern also applied to their future expectations. In an economic climate of more intense competition, such patterns suggest that small firms would be less inclined to expand employment than in more stable periods and be less able to take advantage of employment-enhancing technological change.

In the late 1980s, export-oriented firms expanded their employment, whereas import-substituting firms did not. As small firms scarcely export, whereas over half of all manufacturing establishments with over 500 workers export over three-quarters of all their output, this has been a major cause of the strengthening of large establishments and the weakening of small-scale units. Indeed, the close relationship between size, export orientation and employment expansion is an increasingly strong feature of the Malaysian economy.

There is little evidence that small-scale manufacturing firms could be the major source of labour absorption in the next few years. They are also relatively unlikely to be generators of new technology. Almost certainly, workers and others connected with such firms will also be subject to more income insecurity, as well as lower incomes. Such uncomfortable realities will need to be taken into account.

Sales and employment changes

Ignoring the (probably unsustainable) recent surge in manufacturing output, there is reason to be cautious about labour absorption. Nearly two-thirds of all firms increased the value of their sales in 1986–8. Yet only a little over half of those reported that they had increased employment as a result; for most of the remainder it had made no difference (Table 17.10).

This corresponds to the view that employers were reluctant to hire labour in the late 1980s, even when business was picking up, because of the lasting effect of the crisis of the mid-1980s. This leads one to ask whether manufacturing can be expected to be a major source of new jobs in the next few years. Will increased demand for the product be met by only limited labour absorption as firms either limit their output to 'plant capacity', introduce labour-saving technological change or turn to 'outsourcing'? These may become major questions for the post-NEP era and for industrial policy. And, although one should treat such qualitative data with due caution, Table 17.11 suggests that it was the larger firms that were relatively likely to expand

Table 17.10 Change in value of sales in past two years and the perceived impact on employment, 1988 (%)

Employment effect	*Value of sales*	
	Risen	*Fallen*
Increased	52.2	2.9
Decreased	3.7	41.0
No change	43.6	54.6
Don't know	0.4	1.5

Source: MLFS, 1988.

Table 17.11 Establishments whose increased sales had 'increased employment', by establishment size, 1988 (%)

Employment size	%
1–20	25.3
21–50	42.1
51–100	54.5
101–250	54.6
251–500	73.5
501+	78.7

Source: MLFS, 1988.

employment in response to sales increases. So, a disturbing point for those who believe small-scale firms are the potential source of labour absorption is that the likelihood of increased sales leading to increased employment was positively related to the size of the establishment. The measure is crude, in that the scale of the rise in sales would have varied considerably. Nevertheless, the sample was large and the relationship quite strong. Moreover, of those whose sales had fallen, the larger the firm the less likely it was to have cut employment as a result (Table 17.12).

The growth of external labour flexibility

Industrial enterprises across the world have been responding to economic instability and international competition by making the level and structure of employment more flexible. In that regard Malaysian enterprises have been no exception.

In recent years, as noted above, there has been a fierce debate over the links between employment security and the level and growth of employment. Many economists argue that employment protection regulations and non-wage labour costs hinder employment growth. An alternative hypothesis that guided this study is that, faced with uncertainty and the need for labour flexibility, enterprises in Malaysia and elsewhere respond by trying to *bypass* (not evade) such regulations as well as social security contributions and other institutional 'rigidities' such as collective agreements. Firms find ways of containing wage and non-wage labour costs, while regulations and 'rigidities' act not so much on the level as on the nature of employment.

What seems to have happened is this. Nearly one in five manufacturing establishments suffered from surplus labour in the mid-1980s, and to increase their employment flexibility many reduced the fixed core of their workforces. Many retrenched only to rehire the same workers, often on lower wage rates and usually with less employment security. Very small-scale firms tended to replace wage workers with family, unpaid workers, or relied on them more

Table 17.12 Establishments whose reduced sales had 'decreased employment', by establishment size, 1988 (%)

Employment size	%
1–20	41.0
21–50	35.8
51–100	41.3
101–250	53.1
251–500	29.6
501+	36.4

Source: MLFS, 1988.

exclusively. More importantly, very many firms resorted more to temporary or casual labour. In every manufacturing industry the number of firms resorting more to such workers relative to regular full-time workers increased, while firms that expanded total employment were the most likely to have expanded the proportion that were in temporary or casual work statuses.

In principle, there is no such category as temporary worker in Malaysian labour law. Its prevalence reflects labour market reality and the difficulty of enforcing the labour laws in circumstances where the major reason cited by respondents for hiring temporary and casual labour was either fluctuating demand or market uncertainty, followed by the ability to pay lower wages. The authorities would be concerned by widespread casualisation, and if it is accepted that casual workers need employment protection by enforcement of the labour laws, then it is important to know where in the country and in what types of establishment casual forms of employment have been spreading. This is particularly important given the limited number of labour law officers employed by the Ministry of Labour – some 200 in the whole country.

All this begs a number of questions. In what respects is temporary, casual employment precarious for the workers concerned, putting them in need of legislative and administrative protection? A lack of employment security is one major characteristic, but there one finds wide variation. Some temporary workers have the most precarious contractual relationship, that is, a casual work status involving an oral understanding that can be modified from day to day or week to week. Others have a written contract for some short-term period, such as three months or a month. In mid-1988 temporary workers in small-scale establishments tended to be in the most precarious, casual relationships (Tables 17.13 and 17.14), giving further cause for reflection about labour in small firms.

One feels that the Ministry of Labour should be enabled to ensure that temporary workers be given the minimal protection of written contracts of employment. Labour Inspectors could perhaps concentrate more on

Table 17.13 Main form of temporary work arrangement, by establishment size, 1988 (%)

	Employment size						
Work arrangement	*1–4*	*5–20*	*21–50*	*51–100*	*101–250*	*251–500*	*501+*
Short-term, specific:							
written contract	—	10.5	23.5	40.2	66.4	81.0	72.1
oral contract	(66.7)	52.6	55.1	29.5	20.3	10.3	13.1
Continuing, casual	(11.1)	33.7	19.4	23.2	12.6	8.6	11.5
Other	(22.2)	3.2	2.0	3.6	0.7	—	3.3
Total	100	100	100	100	100	100	100

Source: MLFS, 1988.

Table 17.14 Whether or not temporary workers given new contracts, by employment size, 1988 (%)

Employment size	*New, temporary contract*	*Regular contract*	*No new contract*
1–4	(22.2)	—	(77.8)
5–20	30.9	9.6	59.6
21–50	38.1	13.4	48.5
51–100	47.7	17.8	34.6
101–250	47.9	18.7	33.3
251–500	46.6	25.9	27.6
501–1000	32.1	28.6	39.3
1001 +	27.3	39.4	33.3

Source: MLFS, 1988.

small-scale establishments, because it is there that temporary workers are most vulnerable to the absence of a protective contract. That conclusion follows unless, perhaps, those who favour labour market deregulation could show realistically that such protection would harm the employment prospects of the workers involved. That seems unlikely.

Casual workers also have little prospect of moving from temporary to regular or quasi-permanent status, particularly in smaller establishments. They are in effect used as a buffer or labour reserve, bearing the risks of cyclical fluctuations in demand. Is temporary employment a major form of labour stratification emerging in Malaysian industry, just as it is elsewhere? It was scarcely surprising that those employed as temporary workers were not compensated by higher wage rates, the reverse being the case, again most of all in small-scale firms. And they had much less access to fringe benefits than regular workers. In short, the lot of a temporary worker is not an enviable one. Moreover, not only had casualisation grown but overall firms expected to increase the share of total employment in temporary work statuses.

Contracting out employment has also been spreading, notably in larger companies and in Japanese companies most of all. But the trend has been fairly widespread. Again, this is symptomatic of a downloading of employment risk. However, in terms of employment flexibility the outstanding development has been a growth, or regrowth, of *contract labour*. In Malaysia this was a traditional feature of the wood products industry, but it grew between 1985 and 1988 in practically all industries. Firms also expected it to continue to grow relative to regular employment, particularly in the wood products, textiles and non-metallic mineral products industries.

In some respects contract workers are in a less precarious position than casual or temporary workers, and were less likely to be among the low paid. Often they have skills in demand. What they lack is employment security. Also, one suspects that a long-term cost of reliance on contract labour is that such workers have skills that do not evolve with technological change, if only because there may be a lack of pressure to innovate when production work is fragmented into contract labour. This need not be the case, but is a hypothesis that deserves to be pursued, especially given the spread of managerial models of decentralisation. Short-term expediency may have long-term costs in terms of lost dynamic efficiency, involving an atrophy of manual skills at a time when the need for higher-level skills is growing.

In sum, although there has been only a modest spread of part-time working, there has been a fairly substantial shift from regular, full-time wage and salaried employment to various forms of non-regular work status, particularly in the lower end of the labour market. This trend was widely expected to persist into the early 1990s, at least. It may have been started as a short-run response to the recession of the mid-1980s. That it was expected to continue suggests that it is a longer-term trend that will need to be addressed by policymakers in the post-NEP era. What sort of protection do such non-regular workers receive? For temporary and casual labour, the primary need is for income protection and contractual security, or at least knowledge of where they stand. For contract labour, the primary need is access to training and some mechanisms for reducing income fluctuations.

There is another type of employment flexibility that also needs to be monitored in the next few years. Many workers are put on probationary status for some months, during which they have no employment security and can be laid off at any time. Employers have good reasons for using this device. But there has been a tendency for the probation period to grow and for more workers to be in that insecure status. The most likely reasons are that such workers can be easily laid off and be paid lower wages and benefits. *If* probationary employment were abused, it could erode the already vulnerable position of those who have only a foothold on the labour market ladder. Tighter regulation of the probationary worker status seems desirable, so that it corresponds more closely to reasonable criteria, such as the time required to learn the skills required for the job.

As for the role of labour regulations on these trends, it is worth reiterating that they did not appear to have a negative effect on the level of employment. When asked whether the provisions of the Employment Act on termination of employment had affected their employment policy in any way, nearly 94 per cent of manufacturing firms said that it had not had any effect; only a little over 2 per cent said that it had affected the level of employment, and 1.6 per cent said that it had encouraged them to resort more to contract labour rather than direct labour. One must be wary about drawing too much from such figures, because the Act may have conditioned behaviour and was only one of various factors having an influence. Nevertheless, the responses do not indicate pressure or need for reform on employment grounds.

With the growing employment flexibility, there does not seem to be any need. It is not labour regulations that dictate employment levels but market influences such as cyclical fluctuations in demand, structures of production, technological options and the need for a flexible labour force. There is no evidence that labour regulations have affected those issues, so that one can conclude that there is no *prima facie* case for weakening existing regulations. Conversely, one might also be inclined to conclude that strengthening them or their implementation would have little effect on employment per se but may have a beneficial effect in encouraging good employment practices. In general, for both welfare and dynamic efficiency reasons, in the 1990s policymakers may be concerned to see that labour flexibility is achieved in a context of growing labour market and employment security, not the reverse.

Internal labour flexibility

We have been looking also at how firms have been adjusting 'internal labour market' practices, including many aspects of recruitment, training, retraining, mobility and retrenchment that may preoccupy policymakers in the next few years. Here there is only time to highlight one or two trends, which are elaborated elsewhere.

Preliminary analysis indicates that both labour turnover and internal labour mobility are low in manufacturing. The latter may be related to the growth of something like skill polarisation of employment, corresponding to what has been happening in some industrialised economies. This has implications for labour market and training policy. Technological and other changes have been increasing the demand for technicians and diminishing that for skilled manual workers. And large-scale establishments, which have been growing relative to smaller firms, have higher ratios of technical and semi-skilled workers to other categories than was found in small-scale firms. These combined shifts imply a reduced scope for internal labour markets, whereby workers who enter on lower rungs could expect to climb occupationally through on-the-job experience or training. If so, off-the-job training and qualifications will become more important for labour mobility and for overall labour efficiency. That will probably mean that government will have to assume a greater role in the provision or organisation of technical training. And if there is a further growth in demand for technicians, the fact that only larger and more profitable companies could afford to pay for training courses will surely mean that the government will have to strengthen 'anti-poaching' measures. Otherwise many firms will find that the prospective return to training such workers will be insufficient to justify the cost. Already small firms do little training and have faced difficulties in retaining those they have trained. The four modes of labour adjustment were discussed above. The data show that the least developed in Malaysia are the third and fourth modes, which happen to be the least painful for the workforce. In-the-job *retraining*, both to replace obsolescent skills and to augment those workers have absorbed, must play a greater role in the post-NEP era. And the Ministry of Labour will surely have to develop a more complex and multi-layered employment exchange service, to reduce frictional unemployment and help make the labour reallocation process more efficient.

The feminisation of labour

In many parts of the world, the growth of external and internal labour flexibility has led to a rapid growth in female employment (see, e.g. Standing, 1989). Of course, that was a feature of the second and third phases of Malaysia's industrialisation, involving an influx of young girls to carry out semi-skilled jobs in the main export industries. Some fears have been expressed about a reversal of that trend, through automation and declines in 'direct labour'. Yet in the late 1980s female employment grew across the board. A large number of establishments in the 1988 MLFS had increased their female employment share and reported that they expected to increase it further in the next two years. Moreover, the nature of the demand has been changing, since proportionately fewer women workers seem to be hired on the expectation that they would work for two or three years and then withdraw in their early twenties to have families. The Malaysian economy in the 1990s will have passed the stage when it could rely on low-paid, young female labour. Women have been gaining shares of skilled, technical and administrative employment.

The authorities may have to consider refining family policy to correspond to such changes in the labour market. More women should be enabled, if they choose, to remain in the labour force to pursue an uninterrupted 'career', which means that government and employers may have to give more attention to the provision of childcare facilities. Labour policy may have to shift from the point of labour market entry, since it is apparent that women have been gaining access to a broad range of jobs, towards measures to facilitate subsequent labour mobility. Other studies have found that women workers, unlike men, have had no discernible income return to labour market experience. In future, the discouragement of discrimination against women in the internal labour market of enterprises will be more important than at the enterprise entry point. This will have a triple purpose. It could reduce sex-related inequality in the labour market. It could reduce inter-household inequality – since almost certainly it is women from lower-income households who most suffer from discriminatory barriers, and it is they who provide a substantial share of their family income. And it could reduce ethnic inequality – since Malay women in particular will need to be assisted in obtaining upward occupational and income mobility. This issue will be made all the more critical if privatisation and cutbacks of the public sector continue, since the public sector has been a major source of upward labour mobility for Malay women under the NEP.

Wage flexibility and inequality

Income inequality has diminished in Malaysia according to official statistics. If so, whatever the causes, then the emergence of more flexible labour markets suggests that several specific forms of wage inequality may grow. Probably a growing proportion of the labour force in manufacturing is not having access to fringe benefits because of their work status; these nowadays have considerable financial value for many workers, and their exclusion from measures of earnings results in an understatement of earnings inequality, because it tends to be the lower-paid who do not have access to such benefits. There is also an international trend whereby management and white-collar workers are receiving larger shares of their incomes in the form of bonuses, shares and perks that lower-paid blue-collar workers do without. There is some evidence that this divergence has been growing in Malaysia too.

As for pay flexibility, efforts to promote 'profit-sharing pay' systems are in their early days in Malaysia, although of course traditional forms have characterised many small, family businesses. We found that only about 3 per cent of manufacturing establishments were operating a profit-related pay system, but various observers believe that this practice will spread as a means of imparting wage flexibility. If so, it can be predicted that it will contribute to income inequality, between those in large, profitable, export-oriented enterprises and those outside them, and between privileged insiders in such enterprises and others. Finally, if there is a skill polarisation of sorts in progress, that in itself could widen earnings inequality, enabling a small core of technicians and upper-level management to strengthen their position at the expense of middle-level supervision labour (which, quite clearly, has been shrinking) and skilled manual workers. This will pose policymakers with various dilemmas connected with tax policy and redistribution, in particular. It will also pose a challenge for trade unions, since bargaining only for 'insiders' may become increasingly difficult, especially if employers can effectively play off one group against another, if only by the threat of turning to more flexible worker categories. This is going to be a major dilemma for trade unions everywhere, and nowhere more so than in Malaysia where unions are facing a painful phase of adjustment.

Some concluding points: the danger of beggar-my-neighbour 'competitiveness'

The Malaysian economy has rebounded from the traumas of the mid-1980s, and industry surely faces the post-NEP era with justifiable confidence. The NEP has been a success by many yardsticks. But what we have called the fourth phase of the country's industrialisation strategy raises new types of challenge for policymakers.

One issue that must be reconsidered is the headlong pursuit of 'competitiveness' based on measures and pressures to lower labour costs, symbolised by amendments to the labour laws, hostility towards industrial trade unions, and so on. It is understandable that cost cutting should be a response to a recession, but already labour costs are only a small proportion of total production costs, while such a strategy is inherently unstable and inequitable. The call to pare labour costs usually means lowering the wages and benefits of low-wage production workers relative to those earning their income from profits or those in salaried employment whose incomes are tied to levels prevailing in other typically higher-income countries. That aside, the concern to cut labour costs in this way to match those of other economies is likely to be more than matched elsewhere, whether it be in Thailand or Indonesia tomorrow or some other countries shortly afterwards. 'Beggar-my-neighbour' wage cutting is simply not a realistic or desirable option. The emergence of a more flexible labour market may make wage and other labour cost cutting more feasible in the short run, but, as labour costs are probably only about 15 per cent of total production costs, there is not much to be gained by that route anyway.

It is the alternative strategy that deserves to be pursued more vigorously and single-mindedly, that of providing a regulatory framework coupling worker security with labour flexibility in which the overall utilisation, development and replenishment of skills can be ensured. A basic issue for Malaysia in the post-NEP era will be the awkward transition from an economy geared to exports based on low-cost, semi-skilled labour to one based on dynamic efficiency and technical skills. This in a sense is what lies behind many of the current traumas in the South Korean labour market. And this is what is meant by a Human Resource Development Strategy. As part of that strategy one could envisage a Set of policies to promote the model of human-resource-oriented enterprises (HRE), firms that pursue active labour policies to upgrade their workforces through work design, training, retraining and negotiated flexibility.

Seeing the future labour policy framework in this way may not seem very novel. But being quite clear about it does alter one's sense of priorities and concerns. It implies a more systematic recognition that workers are more than factors of production. It will mean that very long workweeks of 60 hours or suchlike will be regarded as alien to dynamic efficiency, to be curtailed or discouraged as incompatible with the refinement of real technical skills. It will mean giving contractual security in which workers are encouraged to feel the dignity of work, which should not be seen as the right of a minority and which will be essential for effective labour utilisation in an era when 'flexible specialisation' of various kinds will be a key to long-term development success. It will mean creating a framework in which organisations genuinely representing the interests of workers will be integrated into the production process, where employers and government can recognise that this could be a vital source of pressure on industrial enterprises to achieve dynamic efficiency in the work process.

Such conclusions may seem to relate to some distant future. However, Malaysia's successful development owes a great deal to a correspondence between its industrial strategy and the character of its labour supply. The post-NEP era will see an evolution of that industrial strategy, to higher-technology, higher value-added production and more complex production and work processes. To be truly successful, the labour supply and the labour policies that shape it will have to evolve accordingly.

NOTES

1 One is tempted to call this phase assembly-led industrialisation, so prominent was this aspect of the process.

2 In an earlier survey done for the EPU in 1982, we showed how upward socio-economic mobility in the labour market – a critical aspect of the NEP – had been achieved predominantly through public sector employment.

3 It is probably not uncommon for the 'subsidy' to exceed the cost of training.

REFERENCES

Department of Statistics (various years) *Industrial Survey*, Government of Malaysia, Kuala Lumpur.

Salem, E. (1988) 'Twinned Hinterlands', *Far Eastern Economic Review*, 18 August.

Standing, G. (1989) *Labour Flexibility and Global Feminisation*, ILO, Geneva.

Streeten, P. (1988) 'Employment and Macro-economic Policies', paper prepared for the UNDP, July, mimeo.

World Bank (1987), *World Development Report 1987*, The World Bank, Washington, DC.

18

THAILAND'S INDUSTRIALIZATION
Implications for Health, Education, and Science and Technology

Sirilaksana Khoman

18.1 INTRODUCTION

Thailand's economic growth during the past decade is often cited as a success story, the result of years of industrialization, structural shifts in production and significant advances in real incomes. From an economy dominated by agriculture, Thailand has been so transformed that in 1991 the share of GDP from agriculture registered a mere 12 per cent. Manufactured exports and tourism are clearly responsible for much of the growth, and indeed industry and services have become major sources of employment and income.

At the same time significant strides have been made in health and education. Severe malnutrition has been eliminated, average life expectancy increased from 60 to 65 years between 1980 and 1990, mean caloric consumption has equalled caloric requirements, and population growth has slowed to a rate of 1.3 per cent per annum. With respect to education, expansion of school enrolment has been rapid, and literacy rates are among the highest in the region.

Yet amidst the affluence generated by industrialization, complex problems have emerged. Thailand is currently plagued with infrastructure bottlenecks, environmental degradation, occupational health hazards, widening disparities between urban and rural areas, and the inequitable distribution of wealth. Income distribution has not improved, despite achievements in the provision of social services. Pockets of poverty and inaccessibility to basic services remain. All this points to underlying problems capable of derailing the buoyant economy.

The favourable world environment that allowed high growth in the late 1980s began to falter in 1990 and continues to deteriorate. The year 1992 was a particularly sobering one for Thailand, with political upheavals that required a rethinking of policy and an overhauling of power structures. More

Source: *Thailand's Industrialization and its Consequences*, Medhi Krongkaew (Editor), London: Macmillan, 1995, pp. 289–323.

imperative than at any other time in recent history is the need to counterbalance the drive towards high growth with the need for sustainability and a more equitable distribution of wealth and opportunity. In this process, human-resource development can be singled out for its crucial contribution to economic and social development and Thailand's capacity to adjust to rapid changes. The quality of the workforce will determine the economy's future competitiveness. Greater equity in human development will affect the social structure, improve income distribution, and enhance the overall quality of life.

The objective of this chapter is to provide a cursory view of the main issues and problems in health and education that have arisen with Thailand's industrial progress, and the situation in terms of manpower for science and technology (S&T). The chapter also explores mechanisms for the development of human resources as users and generators of technological progress for the purpose of achieving sustained and balanced economic and social development. Emphasis is placed on correcting market failures in the economy to encourage those industries that are 'environmentally friendly' and 'health-friendly', and instituting the minimum amount of regulatory machinery that would encourage suitable human-resource training in industry as well as awareness and accountability for health and environmental impacts. The chapter does not claim to be exhaustive, and is necessarily selective in emphasis due to its wide-ranging scope.

18.2 INDUSTRIALIZATION AND HEALTH

Industrialization and high income growth have no doubt made possible the substantial health improvements that Thailand has seen over the last three decades. Better sanitation, better nutrition and improved medical care are the obvious products of higher incomes. The standard of medical care is indeed one of the highest in the region, and the Ministry of Public Health has ensured a fair amount of equity in the distribution of services and health personnel in the rural areas. However specific problems arise with the rapid growth of industries.

That industrial expansion and heavy concentration in Bangkok have taken a heavy toll in terms of pollution and traffic congestion is clearly evident in Thailand's capital city. Less obvious however is the inexorable toll on health and well-being. Bangkok and its satellite provinces account for over 50 per cent of the 52 000 factories and 23 industrial estates in the country, generating three quarters of manufacturing GDP and industrial waste. Although heavy concentration of industry also implies heavy concentration of industry-related health problems, certain environmental consequences have far-reaching implications for the rest of the country.

Three major health concerns can be identified: environment-related health, occupational health hazards, and health problems related to the service sector, particularly tourism.

18.2.1 Environment-related health problems

The benefits of industrialization, in terms of employment opportunities, increased incomes, consumption, and higher living standards, are largely private; the costs, on the other hand, in terms of congestion, pollution and waste, are largely social. The lack of a system of 'environmental accountability', whereby generators of the negative spillover effects of industrialization are made to bear those costs directly or proportionately, means that such costs do not enter into profit calculations and no incentive exists to minimize them.

Thailand's industrial-promotion policies have further encouraged the accelerated introduction of technology-based industries. A wide range of privileges and incentives are given to attract foreign investors, but pollution intensity per unit of GDP has not been included among the selection criteria. The generation of industrial waste and the environmental impact has therefore not been kept in check. Like the NICs until recently, the regulatory framework to safeguard the environment and ensure safe waste disposal is weak or non-existent.

An important concern is over hazardous industrial waste. Analysis of promoted industries shows that the share of hazardous-waste-generating industries increased from 25 per cent in 1987 to almost 60 per cent in 1990. The largest quantity of hazardous waste originates from the manufacturing sector, which accounts for 90 per cent of all such waste in the country. Industrial hazardous waste was estimated to be about two million tons in the early 1990s and is projected to grow to six million tons by the year 2000 (Dhira and Panayotou, 1990).

The basic metals industry generates two-thirds of the hazardous waste, with small amounts being produced by various industries such as fabricated products, transport equipment, electrical machinery, chemical products, textiles, and printing and publishing (Table 18.1). With the exception of a pilot treatment facility for the electroplating industry, which treats about 40 000 tons of waste a year, industrial waste is dumped freely and often haphazardly into rivers and landfills or stored in drums on site with little or no treatment.

Heavy metal sludges and solids, followed by acid waste, pose the greatest environmental risks to humans, fish and wildlife. Harmful effects can spread through direct contact, fire and explosion, ground-water pollution, surface-water pollution through run-off, air pollution through combustion, evaporation, sublimation and erosion by winds, as well as intoxication through the food chain (Kasemsri *et al.*, 1991).

With respect to biodegradable waste, the bulk of it is generated by sugar factories (29 per cent), pulp and paper industries (20 per cent) and the rubber industry (18 per cent). The rest emanates from the beverage industry, tapioca mills, slaughterhouses, canneries and tanneries. Current biochemical oxygen demand (BOD) from industrial sources is estimated at 0.5 million tons and is

Table 18.1 Hazardous waste quantity, 1986

Industry	*Oil*	*Liquid organic*	*Organic sludge*	*Inorganic sludge*	*Heavy metal sludge*	*Solvent*	*Acid waste*	*Alkaline waste*	*Off spec. prod.*	*PCB*	*Aqueous organic residues*	*Photo waste*	*Total*
Basic metal industry	—	—	—	—	732 508	—	—	—	—	—	—	—	732 508
Fabricated products	1303	—	—	4116	55 854	760	56 272	14 563	—	—	—	—	132 868
Transport equipment	58 509	—	—	1078	3521	501	384	—	—	—	—	—	63 993
Electrical machinery	701	—	—	1491	20 096	591	20 407	5246	—	2458	—	—	50 990
Chemical products	15 455	187	2751	1003	10 034	3250	3266	1843	12	—	116	—	37 916
Machinery	25 150	—	—	132	—	4715	3	158	—	—	—	—	30 158
Textiles	17 362	—	—	—	—	—	—	—	—	—	—	—	17 362
Printing, publishing, allied	—	—	642	—	—	5405	—	—	—	—	—	8820	14 867
Rubber and rubber products	3823	—	—	—	—	4350	—	—	—	—	—	—	8273
Paper and paper products	1325	—	42	1370	—	—	—	—	—	—	—	—	2737
Petroleum products	454	—	302	509	508	205	—	—	—	—	—	—	1978
Miscellaneous nec.	12	—	—	393	549	7	719	142	—	—	—	—	1821
Furniture and fixtures	—	—	2	1092	—	—	—	—	—	—	—	—	1092
Wood and cork	—	—	—	515	—	—	—	—	—	—	—	—	515
Non-metallic minerals	—	—	—	—	—	—	—	—	—	—	—	—	—
Tobacco	—	—	—	—	—	—	—	—	—	—	—	—	—
Leather prod. and footwear	—	—	—	—	—	—	—	—	—	—	—	—	—
Beverages	—	—	—	—	—	—	—	—	—	—	—	—	—
Food	—	—	—	—	—	—	—	—	—	—	—	—	—
Clothing	—	—	—	—	—	—	—	—	—	—	—	—	—
	—	—	—	—	—	—	—	—	—	—	—	—	—
Total	124 194	187	3737	11 698	823 070	19 783	81 051	21 952	12	2458	116	8820	1097 078

Source: Engineering Science *et al.*, 1989.

expected to reach two million tons by the year 2010 (Dhira and Panayotou, 1990). The projections are presented in Table 18.2. Most of this waste is discharged untreated in the form of effluent into public water bodies, where it combines with waste water from households to reduce the dissolved oxygen (DO) in rivers below acceptable standards in many of the canals and tributaries. The main rivers are currently at risk of becoming anaerobic in certain sections at certain times of the year. Biodegradable waste can cause ailments ranging from digestive disorders to neurological problems, and can be fatal to marine life.

Other pollutants in the form of air pollutants, gas emissions, noise levels, dust and particles have localized effects, but these can become quite serious. A high concentration of lead in the air, for example, can pose considerable health dangers. The latest figures obtained by the Ministry of Public Health (MOPH, 1992) show that at three monitoring stations the worst cases of lead concentration in the air were measured as being between 0.29 and 0.40 mg/cu.m, which is well above Thailand's standard of 0.10 mg/cu.m, and far exceeds the US standard of 0.05 mg/cu.m.

As for noise pollution, all 14 MOPH monitoring stations in Bangkok recorded decibel levels that exceeded the limit of 70 decibels in the course of 24 hours, ranging from 79.6–82.9 decibels (MOPH, 1992).

On the other hand recorded levels of nitrogen dioxide, sulphur dioxide, and carbon monoxide in the air were generally found not to exceed danger levels (MOPH, 1992). However recent sulphur-dioxide emissions from a lignite-fuelled electricity generating plant in the north became a major health hazard – causing sickness and damaging crops and livestock – and has been dubbed a 'mini-Chernobyl'. Lignite-fuelled power has increased from 9 per cent to 27 per cent between 1980 and 1992 and the possibility of leakages of toxic fumes has not been adequately attended to, or even admitted.

In terms of dust particles, the severest incidence (1137 mg/cu.m) was found to be in Saraburi province (north of Bangkok), with the eastern province of Chon Buri experiencing the greatest exposure to lead (0.15–0.20 mg./cu.m on average).

The kind of industrialization that seeks to upgrade agriculture through agro-industries also leads to dangers from productivity-augmenting chemicals. A survey by the Agriculture Toxicology Division in 1982–5 found that out of 606 rice and cereal specimens on the market, 90 per cent contained organochlorins – chemicals that cannot be broken down or digested. Large build-ups in the human body can cause cancer. Statistics from the Ministry of Agriculture also link illnesses and even death among farmers to heavy use of chemical pesticides and herbicides.

Further, with structural changes in industry and changes in production materials, there is an increasing shift away from traditional pollutants, such as waste-water pollution in the form of BOD, to more complex toxic forms including heavy metals, toxic air and water pollutants, and hazardous wastes.

Table 18.2 Projection of industrial biochemical oxygen demand (BOD), 1990–2010

	BOD load (thousand tons)										
Industry	*1990*	*1991*	*1992*	*1993*	*1994*	*1995*	*1996*	*1997*	*1998*	*1999*	*2000*
Sugar	140.7	153.7	168.2	183.3	199.2	215.6	232.4	249.5	266.7	284.2	302.2
Pulp and paper	93.2	102.7	113.3	124.6	136.5	149.0	162.0	175.4	189.1	203.2	217.9
Rubber[1]	89.7	96.5	104.4	112.5	120.8	129.2	137.5	145.7	153.8	161.6	169.6
Beverages[2]	84.0	91.3	99.0	106.7	114.7	122.8	130.9	139.0	147.0	155.0	163.0
Tapioca	36.7	40.2	44.2	48.3	52.6	57.1	61.8	66.5	71.3	76.2	81.3
Slaughterhouses[3]	14.9	15.5	16.1	16.7	17.3	17.8	18.2	18.6	18.9	19.2	19.4
Canned fish and crustaceans[4]	10.1	10.9	11.8	12.7	13.7	14.6	15.6	16.6	17.5	18.5	19.4
Tannery	9.6	10.6	12.0	13.8	15.8	18.2	20.9	23.9	27.3	31.1	35.4
Canned pineapple[5]	3.5	3.7	3.9	4.1	4.3	4.5	4.6	4.8	4.9	5.1	5.2
Total	482.5	525.2	573.0	622.7	674.8	728.8	784.0	840.0	896.6	954.0	1013.4

Industry	*2001*	*2002*	*2003*	*2004*	*2005*	*2006*	*2007*	*2008*	*2009*	*2010*
Sugar	321.1	341.1	362.4	358.2	409.9	436.4	465.2	496.2	529.7	565.8
Pulp and paper	233.5	250.1	268.0	287.3	308.3	331.1	355.9	382.8	412.1	444.0
Rubber[1]	177.7	186.1	195.0	204.4	214.5	225.2	236.7	248.9	262.0	276.0
Beverages[2]	171.3	180.0	189.2	198.9	209.4	220.5	232.5	245.3	259.0	273.7
Tapioca	86.7	92.3	98.4	104.9	112.0	119.6	127.9	136.8	146.5	157.0
Slaughterhouses[3]	19.6	19.8	20.0	20.2	20.4	20.7	21.0	21.3	21.6	22.0
Canned fish and crustaceans[4]	20.4	21.5	22.6	23.7	25.0	26.3	27.7	29.3	30.9	32.6
Tannery	40.3	46.0	52.4	59.9	68.4	78.4	89.8	103.1	118.5	136.3
Canned pineapple[5]	5.3	5.4	5.5	5.7	5.8	6.0	6.1	6.3	6.4	6.6
Total	1075.8	1142.3	1213.5	1290.2	1373.7	1464.1	1562.8	1670.1	1786.8	1913.9

Notes:
1. Rubber sheet processing only.
2. Beer, distillery and soft drink processing.
3. Beef and pork only.
4. Exported products only.
5. Exported products only.

Source: Dhira and Panayotou, 1990.

The share of factories generating hazardous waste increased from 29 per cent in 1979 to 60 per cent in 1990, and the trend is expected to continue. Tables 18.3 and 18.4 show that major generators of hazardous waste are in fact among the fastest-growing industries, so that their share is inevitably increasing.

What is important for policy is that waste treatment is possible, based on the principle that the polluter should pay. It is estimated that treatment of all treatable hazardous waste from all industries except the basic metal industry would cost about 600 million baht annually, or 0.3 per cent of the GDP produced by these industries (Table 18.5). Seventy per cent treatment of the current level of BOD would cost about 1 per cent of the GDP generated by the BOD-generating industries (Table 18.6). These are all affordable costs requiring only the necessary machinery to be put in place. Industrial estates also have a potential for pollution control. Currently, while all 23 estates have waste-water-treatment facilities, not one operates facilities to treat hazardous waste.

As for the use of chemicals in agriculture to feed agro-industries, organic production or 'alternative agriculture' has been proposed. If consumer knowledge about the relative merits of organic and chemical production becomes more widespread, the health benefits and dangers would be reflected in market prices, so that environmentally friendly and health-friendly products could also become profitable to produce. Government intervention here could take the form of information dissemination, product grading, testing and certification, as well as fiscal incentives.

18.2.2 Occupational Health Hazards

Industrial development has brought into use several newly synthesized chemicals and industrial processes. Workers are thus subject to ever-increasing exposure to toxic chemicals and unfamiliar production routines. In addition, working conditions may be poor and workers may be forced to endure dust and particles, poor ventilation, inadequate lighting and squalid living conditions at factory sites.

An increasing proportion of poisoning incidences is found to be occupation-related, and the incidence of industrial accidents and injury, though underreported, has shown a marked upward trend. Table 18.7 shows that reported cases of industrial injury increased in total by almost three times between 1981 and 1990, with the largest percentage increases in the chemicals-related industries and in textiles, wood and wood products, where the number of injuries have more than doubled. Table 18.8 also shows a substantial increase in the incidence of occupational health problems – from two to nine per 100 000 people between 1978 and 1987.

One of the most important occupational ailments is lead poisoning. It causes neuro-physiological diseases whose incidence may soon reach alarming

Table 18.3 Manufacturing industry: GDP share and growth, 1960–89

	1960–5		*1970–4*		*1975–9*		*1980–4*		*1985–9*	
Industry group	*Share*	*Growth*	*Share*	*Growth*	*Share*	*Growth*	*Share*	*Growth*	*Share*	*Growth*
Food	34.5	25.7	15.3	8.2	15.6	10.0	15.4	8.8	14.9	9.0
Beverages	10.6	10.6	9.4	8.0	10.2	17.4	10.3	9.3	9.5	9.6
Tobacco	13.0	12.1	7.7	7.0	6.4	4.6	5.6	–1.3	4.2	6.7
Textiles *	5.2	10.6	11.5	18.5	13.6	12.4	14.0	4.4	14.1	12.7
Clothing	8.0	5.5	9.2	11.5	8.7	7.2	9.3	7.1	10.9	15.8
Leather products and footwear	0.7	0.6	2.1	4.6	1.9	0.8	2.2	11.9	2.8	19.3
Wood and cork	4.8	5.2	3.6	6.9	2.9	3.2	1.7	–1.4	1.2	–1.4
Furniture and fixtures	1.2	1.4	1.6	0.7	1.3	7.6	1.2	4.4	1.2	14.1
Paper and paper products	0.2	0.4	1.4	10.9	1.3	24.8	1.7	3.1	1.6	11.0
Printing and publishing *	3.2	2.6	1.4	10.8	1.5	10.8	1.7	8.6	1.5	3.2
Chemical products *	6.8	5.8	3.6	8.7	3.6	13.6	4.2	7.3	4.4	9.7
Petroleum products	0.0	4.5	7.5	17.5	6.7	4.9	5.1	2.8	4.3	7.3
Rubber and plastic products *	0.6	0.7	2.6	11.2	2.7	11.4	2.5	1.6	2.6	15.4
Non-metal products	2.9	4.0	4.0	10.5	3.7	9.3	3.8	9.0	4.1	15.1
Basic metal industries *	0.4	0.5	2.3	1.4	1.7	13.4	1.4	–4.7	1.4	4.3
Fabricated products *	0.4	0.7	2.7	3.5	2.0	6.4	1.8	5.3	1.9	13.8
Machinery *	0.6	1.3	2.8	7.6	1.9	10.2	4.2	12.5	3.7	14.7
Electrical machinery *	0.6	0.8	1.8	8.9	2.4	18.7	3.0	9.0	3.3	18.4
Transport equipment *	5.4	5.9	7.2	19.7	7.9	16.3	6.5	–1.3	5.7	26.8
Miscellaneous	0.9	1.1	2.3	25.0	2.9	15.1	4.6	11.3	6.6	22.3
Average		5.0		10.1		10.9		5.4		12.4

Notes: Growth rates are computed as follows: growth rate = l/t *ln(Yn/Yo)* 100.
* = Top generator of hazardous waste.

Source: National Economic and Social Development Board (new series).

Table 18.4 Major industries registered with the Department of Industrial Works

Major industry group	*End 1969*	*End 1979*	*End 1989*
Food[1]	112	4200	10 099
Beverages	3	60	232
Tobacco[2]	0	146	108
Textiles[3]	30	764	1793
Wearing apparel	4	226	1989
Leather products and footwear	5	97	771
Wood and cork	59	1713	3353
Furniture and fixtures	11	405	1586
Paper and paper products	7	162	537
Printing, publishing and allied[3]	21	817	1674
Chemical products[3]	38	632	1061
Petroleum products	2	21	32
Rubber and rubber products[3]	35	1089	2643
Non-metallic mineral products	20	635	2798
Basic metal industries[3]	6	347	530
Fabricated products[3]	98	2859	6107
Machinery[3]	69	2422	6141
Electrical machinery[3]	9	409	1121
Transport equipment[3]	30	1028	6553
Miscellaneous nec.	72	1659	2370
Total	631	19 691	51 500

Notes:
1. These figures are an analysis of data from the Department of Industrial Works.
2. Tobacco factories at that time registered under the Department of Excise, Ministry of Finance.
3. Top generators of hazardous waste.

Source: Dhira and Panayotou, 1990.

proportions. Even data from several years ago showed that the lead-in-blood level had reached as high as 48 mg/100 ml among some workers in battery plants, which was much higher than the International Labour Organisation standard of 25–30 mg/l00 ml. A later study by the Ministry of Public Health (MOPH, 1987) showed that more than 14 per cent of cases of occupational exposure to lead recorded lead-in-blood levels exceeding 60 mg/l00 ml, with 0.5 per cent of the sample reaching the critical risk level of more than 100 mg/l00 ml. As for concentration of lead in urine samples, a staggering 20 per cent of the sampled workers in lead-associated plants registered above-normal concentration levels.

This points to the need for greater selectiveness in industrial promotion and a more developed information and institutional infrastructure to manage the undesirable effects of an expanding industrial sector with its health effects and ecologically disruptive by-products. In practice this would mean taxing the polluters in proportion to their waste generation, and expanding the

Table 18.5 Cost of treatment at 70 per cent level (million baht)

Industry	*1991*	*1996*	*2001*	*2006*	*2010*
Sugar	107.6	162.7	224.8	305.5	396.1
Pulp and paper	71.9	113.4	163.4	231.7	310.8
Rubber	67.6	96.3	124.4	157.6	193.2
Beverages	63.9	91.7	119.9	154.3	191.6
Tapioca	28.2	43.2	60.7	83.7	109.9
Slaughterhouses	10.8	12.7	13.7	14.5	15.4
Canned fish and crustaceans	7.6	10.9	14.3	18.4	22.8
Tannery	7.4	14.6	28.2	54.8	95.4
Canned pineapple	2.6	3.2	3.7	4.2	4.6
Total	367.7	548.8	753.1	1024.8	1339.7

Source: see text.

Table 18.6 Cost of treatment per industrial GDP (per cent)

Industry	*1991*	*1996*	*2001*	*2006*	*2010*
Sugar	3.33	3.35	3.37	3.39	3.40
Pulp and paper	2.82	2.82	2.82	2.82	2.82
Rubber	1.42	1.23	1.06	0.91	0.81
Beverages	0.44	0.44	0.44	0.44	0.44
Tapioca	5.29	5.29	5.29	5.29	5.29
Slaughterhouses	0.60	0.60	0.60	0.60	0.60
Canned fish and crustaceans	0.12	0.12	0.12	0.12	0.12
Tannery	0.57	0.57	0.57	0.57	0.57
Canned pineapple	0.17	0.17	0.17	0.17	0.17
Average	1.05	1.05	1.04	1.03	1.02

Note: Assuming that a waste stabilization pond system is employed with a cost of 1000 baht/ton BOD.

Sources: Table 18.5 and industrial GDP from NESDB (new series).

health-insurance aspect of the Social Security Fund through increased premiums and increased compensation in high-risk industries.

18.2.3 Service-industry health problems

The most important health problem relating to the service sector and the tourism industry in particular is the AIDS nightmare. The link between AIDS and industrialization has not been clearly investigated, but it is certainly believed that the spread of this disease in Thailand started with the tourist industry.

AIDS may be but one of the many diseases with potentially significant economic effects, but its impact is likely to be greater than that of other (more prevalent) diseases. The ultimate outcome of the HIV virus (or full-blown

Table 18.7 Occupational injuries in whole kingdom by industry, 1981–90

Industry	*1981*	*1982*	*1983*	*1984*	*1985*	*1986*	*1987**	*1988*	*1989*	*1990*
Agriculture	85	49	67	25	106	29	24	155	—	5
Mining	399	532	565	594	623	605	15	438	489	678
Manufacturing	21 642	22 370	27 124	31 200	31 099	30 045	10 450	40 418	51 700	62 145
Manufacture of food, beverages and tobacco	—	—	6174	7596	7303	6428	1140	8394	10 001	10 415
Textiles, clothing	—	—	3435	4150	4291	4197	1313	5345	6604	8302
Wood and wood products including furniture	—	—	2203	2857	3026	3535	1655	4932	5602	5814
Paper and paper products, printing and publishing	—	—	791	700	816	767	297	953	999	1266
Chemicals, petroleum, coal, rubber and plastic products	—	—	2091	2376	2688	2544	1073	3455	4752	6189
Non-metallic mineral product except petroleum and coal	—	—	2245	2372	2015	1960	395	2003	2276	3183
Basic metal industries	—	—	1997	2336	2181	2322	530	2730	3244	3318
Fabricated metal products, machinery and equipment	—	—	8105	8691	8693	8124	3946	12 377	17 710	15 334
Other manufacturing industries	—	—	83	122	86	168	101	229	512	8324
Electricity, gas and water	401	408	729	982	591	367	325	361	547	635
Construction	3008	3560	2948	4086	3881	2889	1820	3451	4925	8403
Wholesale and retail trade, restaurants and hotels	1210	1408	1716	1946	1958	2297	1510	2561	3205	3868
Transport, storage and communication	1051	991	968	1230	1208	1083	757	1212	1408	1679
Services	686	671	811	1024	955	1095	724	1278	1583	2374
Total	28 482	29 989	34 928	41 087	40 421	38 410	15 625	49 874	63 857	79 787

Note:
* Incomplete information due to reclassification into occupational injuries under Workmen's Compensation Law in whole kingdom and in Bangkok by industry, and unavailability of some data.

Source: Labour Studies and Planning Division, Department of Labour.

Table 18.8 Incidence of occupational diseases, 1978–87 (per 100 000 population)

Type	*1978*	*1979*	*1980*	*1981*	*1982*	*1983*	*1984*	*1985*	*1986*	*1987*
Insecticide poisoning	1.970	4.040	3.980	4.550	4.510	4.76	6.37	5.03	5.90	8.64
Lead poisoning	0.013	0.020	0.020	0.040	0.020	0.03	0.07	0.03	0.10	0.10
Manganese, mercury and arsenic poisoning	0.009	0.002	0.020	0.008	0.006	0.02	0.02	0.02	0.02	0.04
Petroleum products poisoning	—	—	0.004	—	—	—	0.03	0.01	0.01	0.02
Gas, vapour poisoning	0.005	0.020	0.013	—	0.010	0.02	0.04	0.09	0.05	0.06
Caisson's disease	—	0.070	0.070	0.070	0.030	0.01	0.008	0.02	0.02	0.01
Silicosis	0.002	0.013	—	—	—	—	—	—	—	—
Total	2.00	4.14	4.11	4.66	4.58	4.84	6.55	5.21	6.10	8.88

Source: Ministry of Public Health, 1990.

AIDS) is certain death, given existing medical knowledge. The incubation period ranges from one to twenty years, so that fatality and the duration of illness combine to raise the impact per case relative to other causes of morbidity. The impact of existing levels of infection will be felt far into the future even if all infection ceased today. Studies in Africa show that the benefits of averting one case of HIV in terms of discounted healthy life years ranks second only to neonatal tetanus (Ainsworth and Over, 1992). AIDS may also have a greater economic impact than other diseases because it primarily affects adults in their economically most productive years. Weighting the benefits of averting a case by the productivity of years lost would result in AIDS being ranked highest among all the diseases in terms of the value of preventing a case (Over and Piot, 1992).

A conservative estimate is that by the year 2000 at least two million Thais will be infected with HIV if the annual rate of increase can be slowed by 1994. However if slowing down does not occur until 1996, about 3.4 million Thais can be expected to be infected by the year 2000 (Population and Community Development Association, 1990). The cost in terms of lost productivity is estimated at US$5 billion by the year 2000 if infection peaks in 1992 and US$8 billion if the peak occurs in 1994. Additional costs take the form of health-care costs and macroeconomic impacts such as a decline in tourism, reduced income from labour exports, a decline in foreign investment and so on. The looming threat of an AIDS epidemic requires concerted efforts in information dissemination and direct preventive methods. If unsuccessful, the momentum towards 'fifth-tiger' status will certainly be checked.

18.3 INDUSTRIALIZATION AND EDUCATION

The link between industrialization and education in Thailand seems to be a rather unusual one. Industrialization and higher incomes have made expansion of education possible, and indeed enrolments at all levels have increased manifold during the course of industrial development. The occupational distribution of the labour force has undergone significant change, and this distribution, broken down by educational attainment, clearly attests to the correlation between pay, status and education. The educated, on average, have better jobs, and the share of this group has increased over time. In fact studies invariably show that education is the single most important determinant of income and social mobility.

However the general observation that education augments income and that average educational attainment has increased in the general population does not mean that all segments of the population have benefited from educational expansion. In spite of three decades of rapid expansion of education, the quality of education remains a key concern and improper targeting of beneficiaries has led to problems of regional disparity, inequality of access and inefficiency of resource use. Out of the total number of children and youths not attending school, more than 60 per cent live in rural areas (NSO, 1987), reflecting selective migration in response to the urban bias in school location, and the conditions of production in the rural and urban areas.

The notion that expanded education is both a cause and consequence of economic development only has weak support from the evidence for Thailand. The industrial policy that initially pursued import substitution in earnest had little direct effect on upgrading the skills and capabilities of the general workforce due to the inherent bias in favour of utilizing imported capital. The reversal of policy in the 1970s towards export promotion, on the other hand, hinged upon the ability to utilize the vast supply of low-cost labour, largely with low education.

Thailand's high growth is all the more amazing when international comparisons of enrolment ratios, educational attainments and sectoral employment are made. More than 60 per cent of the labour force is still in the agricultural sector as opposed to 40 per cent in the Philippines or 55 per cent for the Republic of Korea as early as 1965. Almost half of the children who complete primary school do not go on to receive secondary education. In 1990, 83 per cent of Thai workers had completed only primary school or less, compared with 49 per cent and 44 per cent for the Republic of Korea and Taiwan, respectively, even ten years earlier (Table 18.9). The secondary-enrolment ratio is the lowest of all the ASEAN countries, and well below that of the Republic of Korea a decade ago (Table 18.10). Educational inequities abound, with huge regional disparities and differential access based on socio-economic status. And income distribution has deteriorated. Thus Thailand's statistics can either inspire awe or induce nervous tension.

18.3.1 Industrialization and low secondary enrolment

The first decade of industrialization (1960–70) saw enrolments doubling at the lower-secondary level and tripling at the upper-secondary level, with secondary enrolment as a whole growing at an annual rate of 12 per cent. However secondary gross enrolment ratios have remained low. It was estimated that the enrolment ratios for lower and upper secondary in 1986 were 41 per cent of those aged 14–16 and 28 per cent of those aged 17–18 (NEC, 1986). This implies that more than half of the Thai children in the age group 14–18 were not attending school. Statistics on continuation rates by cohort show that, while the percentage of students moving on to the next grade is high (85–98 per cent) in the primary grades, the percentage of those continuing on to secondary school after completion of the final primary grade drops dramatically to around 40–50 per cent. In 1990 this rate was 39 per cent for government schools and 60 per cent for private schools.

Low secondary enrolments are partly due to expansion of primary enrolment; transition rates tend to increase at lower levels first as schooling becomes more universal. But a more important factor is the low continuation

Table 18.9 Shares of workforce with primary education or less: selected countries

	Percent of work force
Thailand (1990)	83.0
Republic of Korea (1980)	49.1
Taiwan (1980)	44.0
Singapore (1980)	62.7
China (1982)	71.3
Malaysia (1980)	58.4
Philippines (1980)	56.5

Sources: For Thailand, unpublished data; for other countries, Psacharapoulos and Arriagada, 1986, cited in Pernia, 1990.

Table 18.10 Gross enrolment ratios for selected Asian countries, 1988

	Primary	*Secondary*	*Tertiary*
Thailand (1990)	95	29	10
Republic of Korea	104	87	37
Singapore	111	69	12
Hong Kong	106	74	13
Indonesia	119	48	7
Malaysia	102	57	7
Philippines	110	71	28

Note: Data for Indonesia, Singapore and Hong Kong for the tertiary level is for 1985.

Sources: For Thailand, unpublished data; for other countries, World Bank, *World Development Report*, 1991.

rates among children from socially and economically disadvantaged backgrounds. About 88 per cent of youths aged 12–14 are still in school in urban areas, whereas the corresponding figure for rural youths in the same age group is a mere 68 per cent (NSO, 1987). This pattern has remained unchanged throughout the years.

The low secondary enrolment and the high share of the labour force with primary education may be the key constraints to achieving sustained growth and better income distribution in the future. With the economy's dependence on manufactured exports and the need to remain competitive in the world market, there is an additional need to equip the workforce with appropriate skills and capability in science and technology (S&T). The ability of the labour force to adapt to rapidly changing skill requirements becomes more and more crucial as technologically sophisticated sectors play a more and more prominent role. The low continuation rates into secondary school will be a major hindrance in the production of a skilled and adaptable labour force, not to mention the creation of scientific, engineering and technical manpower to enhance Thailand's technological capability.

Low secondary enrolment can be attributed to factors on both the demand and supply side, as well as their interaction. On the demand side several studies have shown that socioeconomic status appreciably affects the probability of continuation to a higher level of education. Tan and Wannasiri (1980) found from their analysis of the Children and Youth Surveys of 1975 and 1976, that for the lowest SES group the probability of continuing on to secondary school was found to be only 14 per cent, while the corresponding probability for the highest SES group was as high as 97 per cent. Supang (1979) also reports that the opportunity to move on to secondary level among the children of farmers and labourers was much lower than for the children of businessmen and government officials. Analysis of the 1981 Socioeconomic Survey (Chalongphob *et al*., 1988) further confirms that parents' education, household income and wealth are important determinants of continuation to secondary school.

In addition the expected returns to additional schooling depend on the student's eventual occupation. If the prospect of being employed in the formal sector is believed to be low, many children of poor rural families choose not to attend secondary schools because of the high cost and low perceived returns. Members of farm households and labourer households have lower expected returns from schooling and consequently drop out at a younger age.

Various studies also show that a large number of siblings also depresses the chances of a child continuing on to secondary school (for example, Chalongphob *et al*., 1988). This finding brings out the link between fertility and the demand for education that has been found in other countries. In addition, even when remaining in school is an option and educational opportunities are available, children from poor, large families do not perform as well as other children. High birth-order has been found to have an independent negative effect on school performance and possibly the ability to learn, which further reduces the chance of continuation (Sirilaksana, 1986).

On the supply side, geographically unequal distribution is one of the main causes of non-continuation among disadvantaged groups. Some regions have virtually no upper-level schools or persons educated beyond primary level. Except for the primary schools run by provincial authorities, which are evenly located in the rural areas, a disproportionate number of schools are situated in towns and cities. And of these urban schools a disproportionate number are located in Bangkok. Out of the 2923 private secondary schools in the country, almost half (that is, 1046) are located in Bangkok, and none in the villages (MOE, 1989). For municipal schools, 427 out of a total of 894 schools are situated in Bangkok, with enrolment of 233 321 as opposed to an almost equal number – that is, 238 620 – for the rest of the country. Distance from school means longer travelling times and higher money costs, as well as forgone contributions to family production. For some, such costs can be prohibitive.

Part of the low secondary enrolment also stems from quality variations among primary schools. 'Input' measures such as the availability of textbooks, instructional materials and laboratory equipment, as well as teachers' qualifications show that large differences in quality exist between schools. High continuation rates have been attributed to such variables as the high ratio of teachers holding higher teaching certificates or above, a large educational budget (staff salaries) and low land rents in the provinces (Supang, 1979). Sukanya (1988), using different sources of data, also reports a positive relationship between provincial education budgets and the provincial rate of continuation to secondary level. Low perceived quality no doubt interacts with the expected return on continued education and the added cost of sending children to better schools elsewhere. Chalongphob *et al.* (1988) also find that the lower the student/teacher ratio at the primary and secondary levels in the community, the more likely are the children to continue.

The problem of access to secondary education (and above) is compounded by the financing problem. The education system limits access to all but favoured segments of the population and may, through public financing, tax some groups of the population more heavily to subsidize the education of others. The direct cost of many kinds of public education in Thailand is almost entirely borne by the government. Fees charged, as a percentage of costs, vary from level to level and within levels: ranging from 1.6–21.8 per cent for secondary schools, from 3.3–36.6 per cent in vocational education, from 28.1–41.7 per cent in teacher training and from 7–12 per cent in public, closed-access universities. Consequently all calculations of the rate of return on investment in education have invariably shown private rates of return exceeding social rates at all levels. Tuition fees at the tertiary level on average amount to only 2.5 per cent of the annual family income of the university students.

At the secondary level, the low fees in (heavily subsidized) public schools and the fee controls imposed on private schools prevent school expansion, quality improvements and quality-enhancing competition. The highest fees charged by public schools are usually less than 20 per cent of the maximum fees allowable at the corresponding levels in private schools. Such controls limit the ability of the private sector to expand. The share of private enrolment at most levels below higher education has declined, especially at lower-secondary level and the academic stream of upper-secondary level (Table 18.11). Studies comparing public and private schools show that private schools are more cost effective, but no less effective and no more inequitable than public schools (Jimenez *et al.*, 1988). Expansion of private schools in urban areas would therefore not produce inefficiencies or inequity if it allows more public resources to be devoted to promoting and subsidising secondary enrolment and improving quality in rural areas.

Table 18.11 Percentage of public and private-school students in Bangkok metropolitan area and other provinces

	1978						*1988*					
	Total		*BMA*		*Other provinces*		*Total*		*BMA*		*Other provinces*	
Level of education	*Public*	*Private*	*Public*	*Private*	*Public*	*Private*	*Public*	*Private*	*Public*	*Private*	*Public*	*Private*
Pre-primary education	40	60	4	96	51	49	76	24	14	86	82	18
Prim ary education	91	9	48	52	94	6	91	9	52	48	94	6
Lower-secondary education	78	22	66	34	80	20	88	12	78	22	91	9
Academic	77	23	66	34	80	20	88	12	78	22	91	9
Vocational	100	0	100	0	100	0	100	0	100	0	100	0
Upper-secondary education	64	36	48	52	72	28	78	22	55	45	86	14
Academic	77	23	82	18	76	24	92	8	86	14	94	6
Vocational	51	49	28	72	67	33	57	43	28	72	71	29
Higher education	81	19	76	24	93	7	64	36	60	40	72	28
Vocational	87	13	78	22	100	0	64	36	54	46	71	29
Undergraduate and higher	78	22	75	25	85	15	65	35	63	37	73	27

Source: Educational Planning Division, Office of the Permanent Secretary, Ministry of Education.

The government is currently conducting pilot projects that offer lower-secondary education in some of the rural primary schools that have excess classroom and teacher capacity, charging no fees or tuition, and issuing free uniforms and textbooks. Experiments with new curricula based on the concept that education should be student-centred rather than teacher-centred, have also begun in the hope of enhancing quality. But the success of this approach hinges on high teacher quality and motivation, and strong teacher-student and school-community relations.

18.3.2 Industrialization and S&T requirements

Technical human-resource development is seen as a key factor underlying the economic success of the newly industrialized economies of East Asia. All the NICs, except possibly Hong Kong, started massive technical-education programmes in the early 1970s. Technically sophisticated sectors are playing an increasingly important role, and the need to master technology is critical if Thailand is to remain competitive in a world where protectionist sentiment, however veiled, is on the increase. S&T manpower is important for the productivity and competitiveness of services and agriculture, and is vital for Thailand's export industries, which will face increasing competition from developed countries using automated techniques to regain competitiveness in labour-intensive products, and from developing countries with lower labour costs. The ability to compete depends on the availability of (1) a skilled and adaptable workforce and (2) scientific and technological manpower capable of linking Thailand to international technology and generating modifications to suit local conditions.

However, while there is general consensus on the need to develop human resources for technological development, the *kind* of human capital development advocated seems to fall into two extreme, alternative directions. Those concerned with competitiveness and productivity increases in line with modern industrialized economies consider that absorption and adaptation of 'mainstream' technology is crucial to sustained growth. Those concerned with human development, on the other hand, view sustainability as conditional upon social coherence and avoidance of further environmental degradation. Perhaps as technologies become more and more science and knowledge-based and less craft-based, an attempt can be made to honour the principles inherent in both views. The generation and creation of technology, and the ability to incorporate traditional technology into modern processes, calls for high levels of scientific and technological education and specialization, and for special skills in managing creative human resources and institutions.

Some form of S&T development can be seen as crucial for increasing the productivity and competitiveness of services, agriculture, and manufacturing alike. Thus the problem lies in three main areas: (1) inadequate local supplies of appropriate S&T manpower by educational institutions, (2) inadequate research and development (R&D) activity for industrial use, and (3) inadequate upgrading of skills through training and continuing education.

Inadequate local supply of S&T manpower

All projections of supply and demand, for example that by the Human Resources Institute and the Ministry of Science, Technology and Energy (HRI/MOSTE, 1986), point to the imbalance between demand and supply. Analyses of Thailand's development pattern indicate a persistent underinvestment in human-capital development. A common complaint is that there are insufficient linkages and information flows between the predominantly private-sector users and the predominantly public-sector producers of S&T manpower, both quantitatively and qualitatively. Consequently there are serious manpower shortages, especially in the areas of skilled technicians and engineers.

It can be seen from Table 18.12 that although the overall distribution of S&T manpower by degree level has been fairly stable, usage by the private sector has increased. Although the data are not strictly comparable due to some differences in definitions, the trend towards greater employment of S&T manpower in private industry is clear. Use of 44 per cent of the S&T manpower by the private sector in 1986 as opposed to 6 per cent in 1979, points to increasing sophistication in private industry. Moreover if employee qualifications are broken down by field of study, employment of engineers dominate in the private sector, especially below Bachelor level (Table 18.13). The fastest growing industries (see Table 18.3 above), such as textiles, machinery, transport equipment and so on, tend to be large users of S&T manpower, as shown by the coefficients in Table 18.14.

The greater demand by private industry for S&T manpower and concern about imbalances have been expressed since the early 1980s. MOSTE (1981) indicated a shortage of about 3500 graduate engineers, but an oversupply of technicians and craftsmen (36 082 persons in engineering and 13 358 in agriculture).

A rough international comparison of S&T manpower in Table 18.15 shows that the number of scientists and engineers per 10 000 population for Thailand is among the lowest among middle-income Asian countries. And when S&T manpower is broken down by field, a KMIT study (1984) shows the lowest proportions of S&T manpower in total employment even in comparison with economies such as Taiwan a decade earlier. A comparison between the S&T manpower structure of Thailand in 1984 and the Republic of Korea in 1981 (Table 18.16) shows that, while the number of scientists and engineers in Korea was almost double that of Thailand, the number of Korean technicians was larger by more than 700 per cent. Per 10 000 people the number for Thailand was only 69 compared with 584 for Korea. In fact, since 1962 when the education system in Korea was not responding fast enough to

Table 18.12 S&T manpower by employer status and degree level

	Bachelor		*Master*		*Doctorate*		*Total*	
	No. of persons	%	*No. of persons*	%	*No. of persons*	%	*No. of persons*	%
1979 (NRC):	10 025	47.6	1796	28.9	173	18.8	11 994	42.5
Government	5446	25.8	3875	62.3	693	75.4	10 014	35.5
Education	4084	19.4	355	5.7	32	3.5	4471	15.8
State enterprises	1519	7.2	194	3.1	21	2.3	1734	6.1
Private enterprises	21 074	100.0	6220	100.0	919	100.0	28 213	99.9
Total	(74.7%)		(22.0%)		(3.3%)		(100%)	
1986 (HRI/MOSTE):								
Public sector	33 137	74.1	9726	91.2	1687	91.5	44 550	55.5
Private sector	11 577	25.9	934	8.8	156	8.5	12 667	44.2
Total	44 714	100.0	10 660	100.0	1843	100.0	57 217	100.0
	(78.2%)		(18.6%)		(3.2%)		(100.%)	

Sources: National Research Council (NRC), 1979 and HRI/MOSTE, 1986.

Table 18.13 S&T manpower by employer status, field of study and degree level

	Agriculture	%	*Science*	%	*Engineering*	%	*Total*	%
Below bachelor	17 003 (17.5%)	100.0	6181 (6.4%)	100.0	73 991 (76.1%)	100.0	97 175	100.0
Public	14 403 (34.6%)	84.7	2212 (5.3%)	35.8	25 055 (60.1%)	33.9	41 670 (100%)	42.9
Private	2600 (4.7%)	15.3	3969 (7.2%)	64.2	48 936 (88.2%)	66.1	55 505 (100%)	57.1
Bachelor degree	16 217 (36.3%)	100.0	9144 (20.4%)	100.0	19 353 (43.3%)	100.0	44 714 (100%)	100.0
Public	15 187 (45.8%)	93.6	5948 (17.9%)	65.0	12 002 (36.2%)	62.0	33 137 (100%)	74.1
Private	1030 (8.9%)	6.4	3196 (27.6%)	35.0	7351 (63.5%)	38.0	11 577 (100%)	25.9
Master degree	3945 (37.0%)	100.0	3570 (33.5%)	100.0	3145 (29.5%)	100.0	10 660 (100%)	100.0
Public	3922 (40.3%)	99.4	3381 (34.8%)	94.7	2423 (24.9%)	77.0	9726 (100%)	91.2
Private	23 (2.5%)	0.6	189 (20.2%)	5.3	722 (77.3%)	23.0	934 (100%)	8.8
Doctoral degree	653 (35.4%)	100.0	735 (39.9%)	100.0	455 (24.7%)	100.0	1843 (100%)	100.0
Public	651 (38.6%)	99.7	730 (43.3%)	99.3	306 (18.1%)	67.3	1687 (100%)	91.5
Private	2 (1.3%)	0.3	5 (3.2%)	0.7	149 (95.5%)	32.7	156 (100%)	8.5
Total	37 818 (24.5%)	100.0	19 630 (12.7%)	100.0	96 944 (62.8%)	100.0	154 392 (100%)	100.0
Public	34 163 (39.6%)	90.3	12 721 (14.2%)	62.5	39 786 (46.1%)	41.0	86 220 (100%)	55.8
Private	3655 (5.4%)	9.7	7359 (10.8%)	37.5	57 158 (83.8%)	59.0	68 172 (100%)	44.2

Note: Percentages in parentheses show the distribution across three fields of study of employers with different levels of education.

Source: HRI/MOSTE, 1986.

Table 18.14 S&T coefficient and total S&T manpower by type of industry and employer status

Type of industry	Government and state enterprises		Private sector		Total	
	Coefficient	No.	Coefficient	No.	Coefficient	No.
Agriculture	27.52	6797	0.79	282	1.72	7079
Mining	—	—	1.68	2512	1.68	2512
Manufacturing	15.73	6743	4.75	48 666	5.19	55 409
Food	12.12	311	3.03	5927	3.15	6238
Beverage	5.13	589	1.06	1849	1.31	2438
Tobacco and snuff	32.95	5574	0.58	267	9.28	5841
Textiles	0.22	16	2.23	2926	2.12	2942
Wearing apparel (excluding footwear)	—	—	1.78	271	1.78	271
Leather and leather products	—	—	2.14	276	2.14	276
Wood and cork	—	—	12.62	3339	12.62	3339
Furniture and fixtures	—	—	8.74	4234	8.74	4234
Paper and paper products	—	—	5.31	176	5.31	176
Printing and publishing	—	—	8.71	153	8.71	153
Chemicals and chemical products	1.81	29	7.28	5010	7.16	5039
Petroleum refining	—	—	4.43	176	4.43	176
Rubber and rubber products	—	—	3.94	946	3.94	946
Non-metallic mineral products	—	—	3.67	1838	3.67	1838
Basic metal industries	—	—	14.94	8467	14.94	8467
Metal products	7.04	224	0.36	30	2.21	254

Table 18.14 (Cont.)

	Government and state enterprises		*Private sector*		*Total*	
Type of industry	*Coefficient*	*No.*	*Coefficient*	*No.*	*Coefficient*	*No.*
Machinery	—	—	16.97	4549	16.97	4549
Electrical machinery and supplies	—	—	2.72	1455	2.72	1455
Transport equipment	—	—	9.48	6733	9.48	6733
Other industries	—	—	0.89	44	0.89	44
Construction	4.12	253	17.03	9265	15.72	9518
Electricity, gas and water supply	15.47	10 033	11.17	64	15.43	10 097
Wholesale and retail trade	7.36	525	4.48	1437	5.00	1962
Transportation and communications	1.27	2181	5.80	405	1.45	2586
Service	14.38	46 383	7.60	5122	13.21	51 505
Banking and insurance	23.64	10 720	1.29	840	10.47	11 560
Total	9.99	83 635	4.81	68 593	6.73	152 228

Note: S&T coefficient equals the ratio of S&T employees to total employment, which amounted to about 2.2 million persons.

Source: HRI/MOSTE, 1986.

Table 18.15 Relative position of technological personnel in selected countries

		Total scientists and engineers		*Scientists and engineers engaged in research and development*	
Country	*Year*	*Per 10 000 population*	*Per 10 000 labour force*	*Per 10 000 population*	*Per 10 000 labour force*
Bangladesh	1979	8.5	15.2	0.2	0.4
China	1979	48.5	85.4	20.6	36.2
India	1979	11.6	21.0	0.4	0.6
Indonesia	1976	7.3	13.8	0.6	1.1
Japan	1979	49.6	77.6	29.4	46.0
Korea	1978	24.4	40.5	5.3	7.1
Malaysia	1978	17.5	28.0	0.6	1.0
Nepal	1979	1.8	3.4	0.4	0.8
Pakistan	1979	15.5	30.2	0.6	1.3
Philippines	1979	26.9	50.5	8.4	15.9
Sri Lanka	1983	5.8	10.0	1.0	1.7
Thailand	1975	4.8	9.1	1.4	2.7

Source: APCTT, 1986a, as derived from UN-ESCAP, 1986.

the demands created by rapidly changing productive structures, the Korean government promptly instituted various legal, financial and administrative steps to address the problem, ranging from laws to promote S&T manpower development and improve the status of subprofessional manpower, to the establishment of research institutes, vocational institutes, mission-oriented graduate schools to serve the needs of industry, and fiscal incentives for in-house training programmes. The concept of 'relevance' was stressed rather than academic excellence, to ensure linkage with the industrialization process. Kim (1987) however argues that insufficient effort to improve the functioning of the labour market limited the effectiveness of these programmes.

In Thailand there are currently acute shortages in some fields, such as metallurgy and material sciences, electronics and information technology (Yongyuth *et al.*, 1985), and a serious lack of experts (Harit, 1987). However there are excess supplies of some types of technicians due to mismatches, the high expectations of job seekers, imperfect labour markets and inadequate on-the-job training to compensate for the inability of educational institutions to supply S&T manpower in sufficient quantities and skills.

In the educational institutions, there is also a higher proportion of students in non-S&T fields, as compared with the Republic of Korea, pointing to the need to allow market factors to play a greater role in setting tuition fees, incentives and patterns of remuneration.

Though few would support economic planning as a method of resource allocation, education is an area where market failures abound due to the presence of externalities and the long gestation period that would be required for market adjustment.

Both producers and users of S&T manpower in Thailand were found to have a myopic view on education and training. The TDRI survey observed that feedback responses (such as short-term signals in the form of wage rates and unemployment rates, applications and completion rates) were the most common. 'Feed-forward' medium-term consideration and incorporation of macroeconomic forecasts and investment trends into planned allocation of resources for S&T manpower development was hardly observed, and 'foresight', or the long-term vision of 'what technologies the future will hold and what S&T manpower resources will best position the economy to react most effectively to changing technical requirements', was virtually non-existent (see TDRI, 1989).

The educational institutions producing S&T manpower remain severely constrained in terms of the resources needed to keep up with advances in knowledge and maintain modern facilities, and in terms of retaining quality staff. The high cost of operating and keeping up with new technologies (new equipment, materials and so on) and the much higher salaries offered to S&T personnel in private industry, thus drawing in qualified educational staff, add to the difficulty experienced by public educational institutions in producing adequate S&T manpower supplies. In general private-sector producers, when unconstrained by regulations and tuition ceilings, are seen to respond fairly well to short-term signals. However the large investments required to implement a long-term S&T manpower production strategy require a clearly committed public sector. The financing of higher education needs to be overhauled so that social benefits and costs are more closely aligned. This would mean a whole package of differential fee structures to reflect social costs and benefits, deregulation, and student loans taking the place of current government control and subsidy.

Inadequate R&D activity

In the area of R&D, the UNESCO/MOSTE survey (1983) showed that only a very small number of S&T employees (approximately 5.6 per cent) were engaged in R&D activities, with the highest percentage share of R&D manpower working in the rubber and rubber products, machinery, chemicals, agricultural products and food industries. In comparison with other countries Thailand's figures are dismal, even taking into account differences in production structures and requirements.

Inadequate R&D activity is limiting the nation's access to inventions, technology and innovations developed worldwide. It is limiting the country's ability to adapt technologies, to draw upon and assimilate the world's scientific and technological resources, to provide support for new productive activities and upgrade the old, and to accumulate the kind of knowledge that will

Table 18.16 S&T manpower and labour force by industry for Korea (1981) and Thailand (1984)

Industry	*Scientists and engineers*	*Technicians*	*Total S&T*	*Total labour force*	*S&T manpower per 10 000 labour force*
Korea					
Agriculture, forestry and fishing	1404	1797	3201	4 806 000	6.7
Mining	2467	2823	5290	124 000	426.6
Manufacturing	47 893	60 461	108 354	2 873 000	377.1
Electricity, gas and water	2385	3746	6131	70 000	875.9
Construction	33 886	15 411	49 297	875 000	563.4
Wholesale and retail trade	267	17 620	17 887	2 151 000	83.2
Transport, communication and storage	2189	27 296	29 485	649 000	454.3
Finance, insurance and real estate	4257	25 073	29 330	498 000	589.0
Other services	12 566	558 602	571 168	2 003 000	2851.6
Total	107 314	712 829	820 143	14 049 000	583.8
Thailand					
Agriculture, forestry and fishing	6408	767	7175	13 398 600	5.4
Mining	935	1579	25141	100 200	250.9
Manufacturing	7836	47 420	55 256	2 283 900	241.9
Electricity, gas and water	946	9151	10 097	119 600	844.2
Construction	1938	7349	9287	755 100	123.0
Wholesale and retail trade	594	1379	1973	2 468 400	8.0
Transport, communication and storage	683	1903	2586	577 900	44.7
Finance, insurance and real estate	5074	6495	11 569	2 556 300	256.3
Other services	32 805	21 132	53 937		
Total	52 219	97 175	154 394	22 302 500	69.2

Sources: (Korea) Lo, 1985; (Thailand) HRI/MOSTE, 1986; NSO, Labour Force Survey, 1984 (round 1).

lead to sustained increases in productivity and international competitiveness. Even advocates of 'appropriate technology' would concede that such capability is essential for the process of drawing upon indigenous knowledge, local materials, processes and know-how. Because the educational institutions are not able to produce an adequate supply of researchers and scientists, the ability to build up an expanding capacity for R&D within the institutions as well as in industry is limited.

In developed countries most of the R&D that results in the generation of technology takes place within industrial enterprises. Only some of the more highly specialized work is undertaken by independent research institutes. In developing countries, however, most R&D activity takes place in nationally funded research institutes and laboratories. The utilization of technologies thus generated has therefore been rather limited. Attention is now being given to the commercialization of such technologies and linkage with industry. Home-grown technology, however, has to confront many problems. A survey by TDRI in 1990 encountered complaints from technology users that indigenously produced technologies in most cases do not fit their needs and are not available when required. The user is also concerned about the risk associated with first use of indigenously produced technologies, and often prefer brand name imports or even non-brand-name imports because of the lower risks involved. There is thus a valid infant-industry-type argument for government incentives (credit, subsidies and so on) to motivate local production units towards greater use of domestically produced technologies, but only where efficient production is envisaged in the long run.

Inadequate upgrading of skills

Data from several employer associations have shown that formal training or the upgrading of workers' skills is rather limited, that most of the formal training undertaken by private industry is confined to larger-sized firms, and that scattered, more intensive, formal training is offered mainly to new workers. Most training is informal and given on the job, as high labour mobility, labour poaching and high costs act as disincentives, especially to small firms. There is therefore less training in industry than is socially optimal.

18.3.3 Industrialization and labour force upgrading

The overall fit between the education and training system and the economy is weak and not improving: secondary enrolment remains low, vocational-school graduates do not have the skills employers seek, worker training and upgrading in industry, services and agriculture is much less than is needed, and the university system cannot produce sufficient numbers of people in the fields the private sector demands. The formal public education system needs to be more flexible and responsive to users (students and employers); private schools need to be less controlled and constrained; intensive worker upgrading needs to be accelerated since increased enrolment at the secondary level, even if successful, will affect the economy only after a lag.

Given this situation, what has been proposed is a conversion of the labour force currently with primary education or less into the equivalent of secondary-school graduates in agriculture as well as in industry, to provide a human-resource base for specialized training. There are new training and information needs in agriculture due to structural changes in the rural economy, including crop diversification, increased mechanization and the use of agro-chemicals. System-based rather than crop-based extension work by the public sector is needed, and should include training that relates to machine maintenance and safety in the application of agro-chemicals, through the use of the mass media in combination with existing training programmes and site visits.

Intensive worker training is needed to upgrade workers with primary education to lower-secondary level so that they become more attractive to the industrial sector and able to benefit from additional training in industry. A minimum level of general and technical education is considered a prerequisite for the development of human resources and for the acquisition of skills for employment or self-employment. This minimum level needs urgently to be attained. For the proportion with only primary education to be reduced to 55 per cent by the year 2000, the upgrading of 7.4 million workers over the next eight years will be required. Research on training in industry, services and agriculture suggests that currently about 300 000 are upgraded per year, meaning that the effort needed is 2.5 to 3.0 times the current level. The estimated total cost of the strategy to the year 2000 is about 42 000 billion baht, but the gains in real GDP will be three times the cost, and there will be significant improvements in income distribution as well (Chalongphob, 1991).

While educational planning by the government is not advocated, government incentives could be provided for training programmes to produce not only high-level scientists, technologists and engineers, but also shop-floor workers, foremen, first-level supervisors, maintenance personnel, electricians, mechanics and technicians at all levels. Otherwise technology options may be overlooked, and many may be prevented from locating in rural settings, for example, despite overwhelming agricultural and rural applications.

Strategies for the development of technological human resources must also emphasize special skill-development programmes for rural and urban informal sectors, small-scale industrial enterprises, women and youth. Biomass and solar energy (in preserving and processing agro-products and meeting energy needs) are of increasing importance to agricultural communities. The use of simple technologies and simple equipment made out of locally available materials has to be explored. In the process, local communities can be involved. Maintenance and repair of simple agricultural equipment, for example, can be the vehicle through which technology is transferred, thereby allowing use of equipment that would otherwise be idle as well as providing opportunities for off-farm employment and management of facilities. Merely making primary and secondary education science-oriented is by itself ineffective, unless students are exposed to a scientific, technological environment, and to the products of applied science and technology. Thus special projects need to be developed such as technology parks that display various scientific and technological devices for the benefit of young minds.

Human settlements provide a wide range of technological possibilities, from the provision of shelter and basic infrastructure, to the construction of complex structures to the installation of transport systems for the movement of people, goods and services. The construction industry alone absorbs workers with different levels of skill and professional know-how. Training is possible in the production, testing and use of building materials, backed by research into improved traditional materials and techniques, as well as materials from agricultural and industrial wastes. The construction sector already employs a large number of workers with primary education. Training could involve participation in activities that range from the provision of shelter to the formulation of legislation, involving practitioners in infrastructure, architecture, planning, project management and investment, and the administration of public and private agencies. What is needed is a policy environment – including a policy framework, a planning apparatus and institutions and mechanisms involved in implementing policies – that provides incentives for such training. The institutional infrastructure needs to be strengthened to support technological generation and application, such as standards institutions, development-finance institutions, consultancy and engineering organizations, industrial-safety institutions and so on, in both private and public sectors.

The whole range of activities and events from inception to use of technology needs to be integrated, and a close link developed between the science and technology systems and the productive sectors. Taking part in the technological decision-making process is an integral part of technological capacity, and the ability to make such decisions has to be enhanced in government, in private production units, and in the scientific and technological community. Involvement in the decision-making process is also conducive to selective use of technology that could stem the adverse environmental and health effects. Many applications of biotechnology and genetic engineering, microelectronics and material sciences are scale-independent and may provide opportunities for more humanized work environments, and training could run the full spectrum from training to operate machinery to taking part in complex processes.

18.4 CONCLUSIONS

The accelerated pace of industrial development in Thailand has so far been unimpeded by human-resource constraints, with demands being met through imported manpower, technology and materials. Having originally followed an import-substitution strategy, for years a large part of the industrial sector was isolated from the international mainstream of technological advance, and the need to upgrade skills did not arise. On the other hand, industries producing for export have generally incorporated technologies that have enabled them to produce goods of an internationally acceptable quality, though much of the technology and personnel were non-indigenous.

However the situation cannot continue. As production technology becomes increasingly more complex and as employment shifts increasingly out of agriculture and into industry, low secondary-school enrolment will become increasingly more problematic. Workers require ever more basic education, technological know-how and specialized skills. There is no way of overcoming disparity in economic status without overcoming disparity in education. Education and technology should go hand in hand; where shortages of qualified teachers occur, distance-education through satellite relays can now be used. Computers will be able to act as tutor and library, interacting with students individually. Education's formal rigidity needs to be broken down to allow students to learn at their own pace. The concept of apprenticeship could be revived to allow young people to divide their time between school and training, with provision for adult education to allow workers to retrain for new jobs, keep up with developments in fast-moving fields and learn new skills.

As long as production for export remains essential to the country's economic viability, it will be vital to develop capabilities for technology assimilation and adaptation, better management of export production units, strict quality control, product design, packaging, finance, credit and export risk guarantees, after-sales service and supply of spare parts. Knowledge of available technology also needs to be improved: often technology is purchased without prior evaluation of available alternatives, or is dictated by donor countries, and acquired technology is frequently transplanted without modification. Competition will increasingly lie in the field of technology, making it imperative to develop local skills for managing technology, to move from purchasing turn-key projects to selecting appropriate plant designs and modifications to suit local conditions. Education and training have to include both 'know-how' and 'know-why'.

The institutional infrastructure for managing technology – providing incentives to use indigenous technology, upgrade skills and produce S&T manpower – needs to be strengthened. This would involve enlisting the greater participation of the private sector and substantial deregulation. Thus tackling the problem calls for three types of public-finance reform:

redirecting spending towards activities in which government participation is most critical, increasing reliance on user and other benefit-related charges to finance such spending, and decentralizing some public responsibilities to those in closer touch with industrial needs and conditions.

Public investment and intervention are urgently required to encourage and develop activities and programmes that the market will not undertake. Such intervention should include incentives to retrain and upgrade rural primary-school teachers and rural primary schools; experiments with curricula and teaching methods to promote critical thinking and learning skills; promotion of enrolment of rural children in good-quality secondary schools; incentives to increase private-sector training in industry and services; support for training and information dissemination to farmers; support for a programme to upgrade the productivity and learning skills of workers with only primary education; and measures to increase the incentives for environmental and health consciousness of industry and households.

Whether the issue is fostering environmental awareness, accountability for workers' health or skill upgrading in industry, a common theme can be found. Health, education and skill upgrading contain significant public-goods elements, offering spillover effects to the rest of the community in a way that private benefit calculations tend to ignore. The role of economic policy is to provide systems of incentives – where market failures exist – to internalize both positive and negative externalities, and to reduce knowledge imperfections through information-dissemination regarding product, industrial and input safety, so as to induce socially desirable behaviour in these areas.

This poses a complex challenge for Thailand. The ability of Thailand to replicate the experience of the four Asian NICs to become the so-called fifth tiger is not as straightforward as it may seem. The four Asian NICs achieved accelerated growth through the use of autocratic rule and national discipline to an extent that would not be easily accepted or easily accomplished in Thai society. That path is therefore not a desirable one. On the other hand, the path of development that Thailand has chosen cannot be further pursued without encountering severe stumbling blocks, and appropriate policy directives are now vital.

BIBLIOGRAPHY

Ainsworth, Martha and Mead Over (1992) 'The Economic Impact of AIDS: Shocks, Responses and Outcomes', technical working paper no.1, World Bank, Population, Health and Nutrition Division, June.

APCTT (1986a) Technology *Policies and Planning: Regional Report* (Bangalore: Asian and Pacific Centre for Transfer of Technology).

ACPTT (1986b) Technology *Policies and Planning: Republic of Korea* (Bangalore: Asian and Pacific Centre for Transfer of Technology).

APCTT (1986c) Technology *Policies and Planning: Thailand* (Bangalore: Asian and Pacific Centre for Transfer of Technology).

Chalongphob Sussangkarn (1991) 'Education, Labor Markets, and Economic Development: Policy Simulations', paper presented at the 1991 TDRI Year-End Conference, December.

Chalongphob Sussangkarn *et al.* (1988) 'The Long-Term View on Growth and Income Distribution', paper presented at the 1988 TDRI Year-End Conference on Income Distribution and Long-term Development, December.

Dhira Phantumvanit and Theodore Panayotou (1990) 'Industrialization and Environmental Quality: Paying the Price', synthesis paper no. 3, the 1990 TDRI Year-End Conference, Chon Buri, 8–9 December.

Engineering Science, Inc., Thai DCI Co. Ltd. and System Engineering Co. Ltd. (1989) Main Report: 'National Hazardous Waste Management, vol. 2', report submitted to Office of the National Environmental Board.

Harit Sutabutr (1987) 'Science and Technology Manpower for Development: The Thai Way', paper presented at the Seminar on Technological Considerations in the Development of Thailand, Pattaya, April.

Human Resource Institute 9hri) and Ministry of Science and Technology and Energy (MOSTE) (1986) *Manpower planning and Survey for Scientists and Technologists*, (Human Resources Institute, Thammasat University, and Ministry of Science Technology and Energy).

Jiminez, Emmanuel, Marlaine Lockheed and Nongnuch Wattanawaha (1988) 'The Relative Effectiveness of Private and Public Schools in Enhancing Achievement: The Case of Thailand', mimeo (Washington, DC: World Bank).

Kasemsri Homchuen, Boonchong Kaositthiwong and Bandid Tantien (1991) 'Preliminary Review of Potential Health Hazards from Industrial Activity, Technical Report' (Bangkok: National Epidemiology Board of Thailand) (in Thai).

Kim, Y.B. (1987) 'Evaluation of Manpower Policies in the Republic of Korea', in R. Amjad (ed.) *Human Resource Planning: The Asian Experience* (International Labour Organization, Asian Employment Programme).

King Mongkut Institute of Technology (KMIT) (1984) 'Status of Science and Technology in Thailand', report submitted to USAID, Thailand, by the Center for Operation for research and Development, King Mongkut Institute of Technology, Thon Burl Campus.

Lo, S. Y. (1985) 'Industrial Technology Development in the Republic of Korea', Asian Development Bank Economic Staff Paper no 27.

Ministry of Education (MOE) (1989) *Education Statistics* (Bangkok).

Ministry of Public Health (MOPH) (1987) Department of Health, 'Survey of concentration of Lead in Blood and Urine', (Bangkok) (in Thai).

Ministry of Public Health (MOPH) (1990) Department of Health, Division of Occupational Health, 'Review of the Occupational Health Status and Problems in Thailand' (Bangkok) (in Thai).

Ministry of Public Health (MOPH) (1992) Department of Health, 'Report from Air Pollution Monitoring Stations', mimeo (Bangkok) (in Thai).

Ministry of Science, Technology and Energy (MOSTE) (1981) *Survey of Science and Technology Manpower: 1981* (Bangkok) (in Thai).

National Educational Council (NEC) (1986) *Education in Thailand* (Bangkok).

National Research Council (NRC) (1979) *Survey on University Graduate Manpower in Thailand:* 1979 (Bangkok).

NESDB (various issues) *National Income of Thailand* (Bangkok).

NSO (1987) *The Children and Youth Survey* (Bangkok).

Over, Mead and P. Poit (1992) 'HIV Infection and Sexually transmitted Diseases', in D. Jaison and H. Mosely (eds.) *Disease Control Priorities in Developing Countries* (New York: Oxford University Press).

Pernia, Ernesto (ed.) (1990) *Human Resource Development in Asia* (Manila: Asian Development Bank).

Population and Community Development Association (1990) 'HIV and Its Economic Impact', paper presented at the Chulabhorn Research Institute International Congress on AIDS, Bangkok, 17–21 December.

Sirilaksana Chutikul (1986) 'Malnourished Children: An Economic Approach to the Causes and consequences in Northeastern Thailand', East-West Population Institute, paper series no, 102 (Honolulu: East–West Center).

Sirilaksana Chutikul (1987a) 'The Economics of Education Subsidies and the Effect of Fee Increases: A Case Study, discussion paper series, no. 93, Faculty of Economics, Thammasat University.

Sirilaksana Chutikul (1987b) 'Education Policy in Thailand: Promises and Problems', paper presented at the International Conference on Thai Studies at the Australian National University, July.

Sukanya Mitungkorn (1988) 'The Problems of Secondary Education Expansion in Thailand', *Journal of Southeast Asian Studies*, vol. 26, no. 1 (June), pp. 24–1.

Supang Chantavanich (1979) 'Equality of Opportunity of Continuation to Secondary Education', *Journal of National Education*, vol. 14, no. 1 (in Thai).

Tan, Edita A. and Wannasiris Naiyavitit (1984) 'The Distribution Flow of Education in the Formal School System: An Analysis on Distribution of Educational Attainment', *Journal of the National Research Council of Thailand*, vol. 16, no. 2 (July–December).

TDRI (1989) 'The Development, of the Thailand technical Capability in Industry: Overview and recommendation, STD Project.

UN-ESCAP (1986) *Human Resources Development: Its Technological Dimensions* (Bangkok).

UNESCO/MOSTE (1983) *Survey of Science and Technology Manpower and Research and Development* (R&D) *in the Private Sector in Thailand* (Bangkok: Ministry of Science, Technology and Energy and the Science Committee of the Thailand National Commission for UNESCO).

Yongyuth Yuthavongs *et al.* (1985) 'Key Problems in Science and Technology in Thailand', *Science*, vol. 227.

Part VI

THE CHANGING NATURE OF SOUTH EAST ASIAN CAPITALISM

19

CHANGING PATTERNS OF CHINESE BIG BUSINESS IN SOUTHEAST ASIA

J. A. C. Mackie

Over the last twenty years or so, more than seventy very large corporate conglomerates have emerged in Southeast Asia, several of them owned or controlled by men who are in or close to the billionaire category in US dollar terms.[1] Some of these conglomerates have become transnational; nearly all of them are linked with multinational corporations (MNCs) in various ways, and all but a handful of them are owned or controlled by ethnic Chinese.[2] Many of these new conglomerates have become larger than all but the biggest local branches of the global MNCs which proliferated throughout the region in this period.[3]

There is nothing unique about such large-scale enterprises in a developing region: similar organizations can be found in India, the Middle East, Latin America, in the Northeast Asian newly industrializing countries (NICs), and even a few in Africa. What is distinctive in Southeast Asia is that postcolonial business leadership has been in the hands of the domestic Chinese minority, and that indigenous entrepreneurs have lagged far behind them, both as private businessmen and as successful managers of state enterprises, despite massive government help in the form of protectionist and discriminatory regulations.

I take it as axiomatic that certain cultural characteristics of the Southeast Asian Chinese, relating in particular to their family firms and clan or *pang* (speech group) networks, were highly conducive to economic success at the elementary stages of commercial activity on which the region's entrepreneurs operated prior to the 1960s.[4] Whether these features are still helpful in the very different circumstances of present-day, large-scale corporate activity is less certain. As the studies in this volume have shown, the Chinese big businesses are all essentially "family firms," in the sense that ultimate control is exercised by one man or one family, rather than joint-stock companies with widely dispersed shareholdings. This has not prevented their growth into giant conglomerates (as some analysts once predicted it would); but we will also note from the essays here that there have been increasing efforts to

Source: *Southeast Asian Capitalists*, Ruth McVey (Editor), Cornell University Southeast Asia Program, Studies on Southeast Asia, 1992, pp. 161–90.

modernize management and to broaden the bases of control. Will this succeed? Is it a response to a recognized need or an imitation, for political or public relations purposes, of what is supposed to be "modern"? We should be careful about assuming that what made for success at one point is always a positive feature, or that changing business arrangements necessarily reflect fundamental changes in business culture.

We should also bear in mind that Chinese businessmen have not "made" the recent Southeast Asian capitalist upsurge in the same way that the entrepreneurial bourgeoisie of nineteenth century Europe or the USA created capitalism there. Rather, as the studies here have made clear, the state has been central to change. The political-economic "growth coalitions" that lie behind state power have ensured that advantage has been taken of the unusual opportunities for sustained and rapid growth which confronted Southeast as well as East Asia from the 1960s through the 1980s. Expanding markets, foreign capital inflows, new technologies, and the growth of urban, educated middle classes—all factors involving but not determined by the Chinese entrepreneurs—created the environment in which business could take off.[5]

Before discussing the recent development of Southeast Asian Chinese business, some general background may be helpful, particularly for those not familiar with the region's development. The total Chinese population of the region was about 4 million in 1931 and almost 17 million by 1981, despite the cessation of large-scale immigration after the 1930s (see Table 19.1).

The Chinese businessmen who are prominent in Southeast Asia today are mostly the descendants of poor immigrants from Fujian and Guangdong, who came to the region as coolie laborers, mainly between the 1860s and the 1930s, or of long-established communities of Chinese traders, tax farmers,

Table 19.1 Ethnic Chinese in Southeast Asia, 1931/1981 in millions (approx. estimates)

	Total Chinese population		*Chinese percentage of Total population (1981)*
	1931	*1981*	
Indonesia	1.2	4.1	3
Malaysia	1.7	4.2	33
Philippines	0.1	0.7	1.5
Singapore	*	1.8	77
Thailand	0.5	6.0	13

Note:
* Singapore included in Malaysia total for 1931; its Chinese population was then approx. 0.5 million.

Source: For 1931, Purcell, *The Chinese in Southeast Asia*, p. 3; for 1981, Leo Suryadinata, 'Ethnic Chinese in Southeast Asia: Problems and Prospects,' *Journal of International Affairs* 41, 1 (1987).

miners, or agriculturalists which were scattered throughout the region.[6] The favored position the Chinese had already achieved in what Wertheim has aptly called the "colonial caste structure"[7] was one factor that enabled them to move progressively into more desirable economic roles in the early twentieth century as tradesmen, artisans, and the embryonic mercantile class in all these countries. In general they occupied far more lucrative commercial positions than the local people. That early advantage was one of the principal reasons why the foremost Chinese have been better placed than others to seize the business opportunities that have arisen in the boom conditions of recent years throughout most of Southeast Asia, although it is not the whole explanation.[8] They were constrained by the dominance of the European colonial overlords until the 1950s–1960s, but have been able since then to diversify their occupations and economic strength, although along different lines in each country.

Since the ending of colonial rule in Southeast Asia, the economic roles of the Chinese have been changing, gradually at first, but very dramatically over the last twenty years as economic growth has picked up momentum throughout the region. Chinese commercial middlemen, often characterized as "compradors," used to occupy a position subordinate to the big European companies of the colonial era—trading houses, banks, shipping and plantation companies, and so on. The estimates made by Callis of the total amount of capital invested in Southeast Asia in 1937, the only reasonably precise set of figures available to us, showed a total of about US$670 million of Chinese capital in the region (excluding Burma and Brunei) as against about $2,750 million of European capital, about a fifth of the total (Table 19.2). The greatest amount of Chinese capital was in Malaya, where it totaled nearly half the European sum, whereas in the Netherlands East Indies a slightly smaller amount reached only about 10 percent of the vastly greater European investment. In Thailand, Chinese and European capital were roughly similar in amount, there being relatively little of the latter at that time, whereas in both the Philippines and Indo-China the Chinese proportion, although lower in absolute terms, was of the order of 20 to 25 percent of the European stake.

Since that time, the amount of Southeast Asian Chinese capital in these

Table 19.2 Chinese and European Capital in Southeast Asia; 1937

	Chinese	*European*	*Chinese proportion of total*
Malaya–Singapore	US$ 200m	US$ 455m	30%
NEI	150m	1411m	10%
Thailand	120–140m	124m	ca. 50%
Philippines	100m	376m	21%
Indo-China	80m	384m	17%

Source: H. G. Callis, *Foreign Capital in Southeast Asia* (New York: Institute of Pacific Relations, 1942), p. 109.

countries must have increased enormously, while there has been considerable disinvestment of British, Dutch, US, and French capital, followed by new, very different, and larger MNC investment, especially in mining ventures.[9] A very rough set of estimates of Southeast Asian Chinese capital in 1975 by Wu and Wu[10] resulted in US$10–16 billion, which in real terms would amount to at least two or three times the 1937 figure. There has undoubtedly been a considerable increase since, quite possibly a doubling of the total, in spite of the fact that a good deal of Chinese capital was liquidated in Vietnam and Cambodia. Whether or not the total amount of Chinese capital now exceeds European capital invested in Southeast Asia, it is certainly no longer subordinate to it in the way it was only twenty or so years ago.[11] The prevalence of joint ventures in which Chinese firms are the most favored partners or agents of foreign companies—and frequently their competitors—testifies to the great shift that has taken place in the bargaining strength of the two sides. Increasingly, it is the foreigners who most need the domestic Chinese in order to get access to Southeast Asian markets, whereas the big Chinese corporations are increasingly able to pick and choose worldwide in obtaining the capital and technology they need from foreign companies. The globalization of capitalism over the last thirty years has worked very much to their advantage.

The efforts made by economic nationalists in the various Southeast Asian governments in the 1950s and 1960s to break what they saw as "the economic stranglehold of the Overseas Chinese" excluded them altogether from certain lines of business, put entire sectors under state enterprises, or gave indigenous businessmen favored conditions of access to licenses, contracts, subsidized credits, and joint ventures with foreign companies; but none of these mechanisms achieved its objective, except partially in Malaysia and at a high cost in economic disruption.[12] Most Chinese businessmen proved extremely resourceful in getting around such measures or finding opportunities which proved even more profitable in the fast-changing economic conditions of the last thirty years, when adaptability has been at a premium. Economic nationalism has subsequently fallen out of favor with the more technocratic policy makers, although not yet entirely amongst the politicians.

It is generally the Chinese firms rather than the financially weaker indigenous ones that are able to survive the cut and thrust of competition when controls are lifted and markets deregulated so that a "level playing field" is made accessible to them. The reasons for that are well known. The Chinese firms generally have access to well-established networks of credit, market information, and domestic and overseas trading contacts, which enable the stronger among them to ride out the fluctuations of business cycles. Most also have to rely on political connections, bribes, and pay-offs to ensure immunity from arbitrary imposts. It is generally the larger Chinese corporations which can do this; not enough is known about the myriad small Chinese firms to generalize about how they cope with adverse political conditions.

Because the degree of assimilation or integration into local society that has been achieved in Thailand and the Philippines is much greater than in either Indonesia or Malaysia, impediments to Chinese business have been considerably less there.[13] This has been profoundly important in setting the sociocultural, political, and economic parameters within which the economic roles of the local Chinese have developed. Little discrimination has been applied against the Chinese in Thailand since the mid 1950s, and the distinction between Sino-Thais and full-blood ethnic Thais is commonly said to be no longer a particularly important one in respect of their economic roles. There has been virtually no significant indigenous business class in Thailand in competition with the Chinese—many of the emerging Thai businessmen have been coopted into partnerships with the Chinese on advantageous terms—in contrast to both Indonesia and Malaysia, where attempts have been made to build up a class of indigenous businessmen.[14]

The reasons why assimilation of the Chinese has proceeded so much more smoothly and steadily in Thailand than in Indonesia have previously been clarified[15] and need be mentioned only briefly here. Religion (i.e., the fact that Islam seems to pose a barrier to acculturation and assimilation, whereas Buddhism attracted Chinese adherents very easily) is probably less salient than it is often thought to be, although it is clearly not irrelevant. More important is the fact that for several generations the leaders of the Sino-Thai communities have been moving toward integration into the Thai social hierarchy; and as role models to other Sino-Thai they have led the way toward a general assimilation and social acceptance. That did not happen in Indonesia until very recently (some would say it has not yet happened at all), for in colonial times the Chinese were more inclined to identify with the Dutch than the Indonesians and only in the 1950s began to shift toward full identification with the latter.[16] In Malaysia the prospects of ultimate assimilation are even less promising, because the Chinese are so numerous and their economic power seems so overwhelming. The strong drive to advance the Malays under the New Economic Policy sharpened the ethnic division and heightened racial antagonisms. Malaysia is the classic case of a "plural society" and likely to remain so for a long time to come.

In considering the recent developments of Southeast Asian Chinese entrepreneurs, we will concentrate on the very largest private businesses in the three countries of the region which can be most profitably compared in this regard—Malaysia, Thailand and Indonesia. The names and certain characteristics of their major conglomerates are set out in the appendix to this essay. Being the largest and wealthiest Chinese corporations in the region, they are obviously not typical of Chinese business in general and should not be taken to reflect more than a limited if powerful segment of Chinese entrepreneurial experience. They are also strikingly diverse among themselves, in spite of the many characteristics they share. Of their common features, the most noteworthy is perhaps the fact that they nearly all represent "new money" rather than "old wealth."[17] Only a handful of the biggest family firms of the early twentieth century flourished into the 1980s, mainly in Malaysia, not at all in Indonesia, and only to a small extent in Thailand. Why these survival rates differed was, as we shall see, related less to the firms' characters than to the very different socio-political environments these countries presented Chinese businessmen.

The failure of old money to thrive raises the question whether the traditional (and still prevalent) Southeast Asian Chinese family firm has adapted to a modern business world in which impersonal corporate enterprise predominates.[18] Are the old-style *towkay* businessmen changing into new-style tycoons or *taipan* as Southeast Asia is drawn ever further into the cosmopolitan network of worldwide capitalist enterprise?[19] As we shall see, this is no easy question to answer, with much depending on the specifics of time and place; but we will attempt some general conclusions at the end of the paper.

MALAYSIA

We shall begin our consideration of Chinese business experience in individual countries with Malaysia, for there it is easier to document the processes of change from old-style family firms based on commodity production and trading towards modernized corporations with increasingly wide international connections. These transformations have also gone further in Malaysia than in the other two countries, partly because its Chinese population is much larger and its educational system and economic structures are more highly developed, but also because its stock exchange has been longer established and has hastened the process of corporatization. By the same token, the Malaysian experience may provide clues to the future direction of change elsewhere in the region. Moreover, Malaysia illustrates in a particularly poignant manner how much the fortunes and even the character of Southeast Asian Chinese big business is affected by the need to adapt to the local politico-economic environment.

Chinese business firms have played a leading part in the economic life of Malaya/Malaysia and Singapore since the late colonial era, assuming roles more prominent than their counterparts in Indonesia and more diverse than those in Thailand at that time.[20] A greater degree of continuity from old wealth to new is discernible among the leading Chinese firms in Malaysia-Singapore than in the two other countries, although since the early 1970s "new men" have been coming to the fore and most of the old-established firms seem to have been slowly declining. In this respect, we can posit a tendency toward convergence in the patterns of development of Chinese big business in all these countries.

Chinese *kongsi* (multi-member business partnerships, or firms) pioneered the tin-mining industry in Malaya in the mid-nineteenth century, long before the British became involved in it, while Straits Settlements Chinese became extensively engaged in shipping, commodity trading, money-lending and the rudimentary financial services appropriate to a pre-banking era, gambir and pepper cultivation and other agricultural pursuits, mostly on a very small scale.[21] As elsewhere in Southeast Asia, the many Chinese business enterprises that rose and fell in the course of the nineteenth and early twentieth centuries were family firms, sometimes quite large and complex ones in their prime, but none of them enduring for more than the legendary three generations from rags to riches to ruin. British capital began to supersede Chinese in the last decades of the nineteenth century, particularly after large-scale mechanized tin mining became more profitable than the labor-intensive methods of the small Chinese firms, while the development of vast British-owned rubber estates on a corporate basis around 1910 brought about a new wave in British investment in the colony. The Chinese businessmen could not match the huge amounts of capital brought in by the British, but they were able to benefit from such ancillary activities as rubber dealing and, some time later, small-scale banking services. They were never as remorselessly excluded from modern, corporate-sector activities as were the Indonesian Chinese (mainly because Dutchmen were involved much more deeply and broadly throughout the modern, commercial sector than the British were), with the result that by the 1930s at least half-a-dozen famous Chinese towkays had emerged with substantial investments in various fields of activity, including rubber plantations and tin. On the other hand, British capital remained the dominant force within the Malaysian economy until well into the 1970s, far longer than Western capital prevailed in the other countries[22]

The foremost of these early businessmen was Tan Kah Kee, an unusually single-minded man who made a fortune in the early years of the century, lost it in the 1920s, and then made another. With his extensive holdings in pineapple cultivation and canning, then in rubber plantations and remilling, he was renowned throughout both Southeast Asia and in his home province of Fujian for his munificence in building schools and other educational institutions, long before he returned to China after the Communist revolution in 1949.[23] Tan was an archetypal old-style towkay, very autocratic and austere in his life-style, yet forward-looking in his belief in education and business practices. Among the others of his ilk to emerge in prewar Malaya-Singapore were the redoubtable Lee Kong Chian, founder of a vast business empire which eventually embraced, inter alia, the plantation interests of Lee Rubber Company and the Overseas Chinese Banking Corporation (OCBC), still one of the biggest as well as the oldest of the big Malaysia-Singapore corporate conglomerates; Tan Lark Sye, whose fortune was based on rubber trading; and Aw Boon Haw, the Tiger Balm king, who later diversified into newspapers, banking, and other fields. Some of the firms they established have survived into the postwar era, more of them proportionately than in Thailand and far more than in Indonesia.

We can most easily discern the changes occurring in the patterns of business enterprise in Malaysia from 1957 on by comparing the picture given on the eve of independence by James Puthucheary in his account, *Ownership and Control in the Malayan Economy*,[24] with later studies of the subject in the mid-1970s by Lim Mah Hui and Tan Tat Wai, and of the mid-1980s by Ranjit Gill, Bruce Gale, and others.[25] Puthucheary rejected the commonly held view that "the Chinese dominate the economy," describing the part they played as still very limited: "Even the most developed Chinese capitalist organization has not gone very far in taking over 'European' concerns" he noted; it could only be said that "Chinese capital has gone into partnership with British capital." Even that degree of partnership did not go beyond locally floated companies, however, for there had been very little Chinese penetration into the ownership structures of the big British corporate enterprises, based in London, which dealt mainly in rubber and tin. The Singapore and Malayan stock exchanges were still very rudimentary arrangements, little more than personal networks of brokers, and local share trading was extremely limited. But Puthucheary also remarked on "the growing maturity of [the] Chinese compradors," some of whom had recently "gathered momentum" although only in one case could it be said that "in their process of evolution from comprador to partner [they] have gone on to become the senior partner." In other words, they were then just beginning to challenge the dominance of the British.

Puthucheary noted also that "Chinese capital is not concentrated to the same extent as European capital," but tended to be very fragmented even in the secondary industry sector, where the Chinese then predominated, and in tin mining. A few important clusters of Chinese ownership and control of large companies were becoming discernible in the 1950s, mostly around the Lee-OCBC group of interests, interlocked by a network of common directors. However, Chinese businessmen generally still preferred to run their own private companies or partnerships rather than to invest in public firms over which they might lose control. Chinese small savers did not yet regard shares as a safe or attractive way to invest their money; hence only the well-off were willing to put funds into public companies at that time, and even they preferred real estate as a safer investment. There was very little mobility of Chinese-owned capital from industry to industry at the end of the 1950s, except in such cases as the long-established Lee Rubber-OCBC group, the Aw Boon Haw interests (manufacturing, banking, insurance, and newspapers), the Loke group (tin-mining, real estate, mining insurance, and entertainments) and the Eu Tong Sen group of tin-mining, plantation, real estate, and importing interests. These forerunners of today's conglomerates were still on a very small scale, and only the first would be regarded today as a significant force in the Malaysian business world.

The Chinese business role in Malaya and Singapore changed remarkably in less than fifteen years after Puthucheary's account. They did not long remain mere "partners" of the British in locally floated companies, but soon emerged as aggressive competitors to them in various fields, displacing British capital altogether, even from London-based companies. The British continued to hold the lion's share of tin-mining, rubber, and palm-oil investments, fields into which not much Chinese money has flowed in recent times. But in the manufacturing sector, property development, and to an increasing extent in banking, Chinese capital has become generally dominant, frequently in conjunction with foreign capital, Japanese and American as well as British. It prevails in spite of the fact that under the New Economic Policy inaugurated after the May 1969 race riots the Malaysian state's share in these sectors has also been increasing.[26] Equally important to Chinese business growth has been the gradual diversification of ownership of much of the corporate sector in both Malaysia and Singapore since the development of the stock market there in the early 1960s.[27] This not only drew scores of thousands of small, middle-class investors into the capital market, but made it much easier for larger Chinese companies to advance beyond the single-family firm toward more complex patterns of interlocking share ownership and control, bringing very large sums of capital within the grasp of a single group through takeovers, capital issues, and share swaps. They rarely advanced much more than one step, to be sure, for few family firms were willing to risk losing control to outsider shareholders, as happened increasingly to smaller and more vulnerable corporations in the 1970s and 1980s. Though the family firm remains the rule, ownership patterns in Malaysia are undoubtedly much more diversified, with family members frequently holding no more than enough shares to maintain control. Moreover, this share-dealing activity contributed to the emergence in Malaysia and Singapore of several large corporations headed by "stock-market millionaires," of a kind familiar enough in Hong Kong and other advanced capitalist countries but still barely known in Indonesia or Thailand.

The changes in ownership patterns were well depicted in Lim Mah Hui's mid-1970s survey of one hundred of the largest corporate enterprises in Malaysia.[28] He identified eight major "cliques," of which four were still based on the old British companies and the other four were essentially Malaysian Chinese. All of the latter could still be called "old money" (my term, not his)—with the possible exception of the Kuok group, which began to emerge only in the 1950s–1960s—in contrast to the "new money" that came to the fore in both Malaysia and Singapore in the 1970s. Those four locally owned conglomerates consisted of two large and well-established clusters, the OCBC-Sime Darby and Kuok groups, and the smaller but long-established Lee Loy Seng and Sung Chi Fang groups of plantation companies. With their diversified financial and property interests and more complex interlocking share holdings, they displayed some of the features of the new-style Nanyang conglomerates. But even the largest and most modernized of them still kept control securely in the hands of one family, unless straitened circumstances or political pressures forced them to include outsiders.

The changes discernible between the time of Puthucheary's study in the late 1950s and Lim's in the mid-1970s were hardly greater, however, than those which have occurred between the latter date and now. The big British companies have largely been taken over or broken up, mainly as a consequence of the Malaysian government's drive under the New Economic Policy to achieve by 1990 a 30 percent share of corporate wealth for the "*Bumiputera*" (i.e., the Malaysian government and private Malay businessmen). Many Chinese also benefitted greatly from this policy, having been able to collect good pickings as the British sold up. Whereas between 1970 and 1985 the "foreign" (i.e., British) share of corporate wealth in West Malaysia fell from 62 to 30 percent, the Chinese share rose from about 37 to 48 percent, while the Bumiputera share is estimated to have increased from about 2 to 22 percent.[29]

Another major change during these years was wrought by the tremendous surge of activity on the Malaysian and Singapore stock exchanges during the relatively prosperous period between the early 1970s and 1984–1985. The fortunes made and lost then resulted in the emergence of at least a dozen new multi-millionaires, some of them Malays, whose businesses tended to be of a very different character from the "old money" firms established before 1970. Many of the new ventures were little more than "paper" companies, built around highly leveraged share dealings and speculative transactions in property companies or finance, and these often experienced difficulties in the more austere environment of the mid-1980s. The most successful of the new "paper millionaires" were Khoo Kay Peng (MUI group) and Vincent Tan (Berjaya group), whose rapid rise was due largely to the backing of influential Malay political leaders.[30]

The rise of these new-style tycoons has coincided with a decline in the prominence of the older towkays. The Lee Loy Seng, Loke Yew, and Eu Tong Sen plantation-mining groups no longer rank amongst the largest conglomerates, although they too diversified into new and more lucrative fields of investment or shifted part of their capital off-shore. On the other hand, several other "old money" groups benefitted from the post-NEP expansion of the economy, notably the OCBC-Lee Rubber-Sime Darby empire, the Hong Leong group, and the Kuok conglomerate. Significantly, the first and last of these developed around basic core groups of enterprises—rubber and banking in the former; sugar, shipping, shipbuilding, and metal industries in the latter—while Hong Leong built up a solid reputation in the property and financial fields.

The big Chinese firms in Malaysia appear to have moved a good deal further than their counterparts in Thailand or Indonesia in the direction of modern-style managerial techniques and structures, with OCBC, the Kuok empire, and several other older firms leading the way. There has been some tendency towards diversification and interlocking of shareholdings, although not yet enough to imperil the dominance of the family-based group. Old-style autocratic towkays like Tan Kah Kee or Tan Chin Chuan of OCBC are rarely prominent in the larger companies. The smaller corporations are likely to follow in the footsteps of the larger ones in the adoption of modern structures, despite (or perhaps because of) the more difficult political environment confronting them.

Whereas political connections were not crucially important to Chinese businessmen in Malaya during the late colonial era or the early years of independence, they became quite essential from the 1970s. As is richly illustrated by the studies on Malaysia in this volume, all the leading towkays who did well under the NEP had close personal connections with particular government ministers or key Malay political figures. Concomitantly, major business leaders no longer tried to utilize the Malaysian Chinese Association (MCA) as a source of political influence and connections, for it no longer had great clout; government decisions could best be influenced through direct relations with the Malays who made them. Political patronage was now essential if one wanted access to contracts and licenses; moreover, the government itself became heavily engaged in business activities through large public-sector investments, while increasing numbers of Malay politicians and officials became shareholders in a wide range of businesses and thus had entrepreneurial interests of their own to defend.

Malaysia's political circumstances have forced Chinese businessmen into dependency relationships akin in kind if not degree to Riggs' "pariah entrepreneurship." Will this trap Malaysian capitalists into a subordination to bureaucrats and politicians which they had hitherto been spared? In this regard, it is worth reflecting on the career of the country's greatest capitalist success, Robert Kuok. Having come from a moderately well-off Johore family, he obtained a good education at Raffles College and in Britain, along with Lee Kuan Yew, Goh Keng Swee, and several Malays who were later to become leading UMNO politicians—Datuk Razak, Datuk Ismail, and Husein Onn. These political contacts were undoubtedly helpful to him later as he expanded and diversified his Malaysian interests beyond sugar trading and planting into flour milling, shipbuilding and shipping, and manufacturing.[31] He was thus well placed to take advantage of the political patronage central to success under the NEP. But instead of cherishing his political links, he began to de-emphasize them and to extend his Hong Kong and China interests, eventually himself moving to Hong Kong. This did not reduce his standing in Malaysia, however. On the contrary, his off-shore investments, together with his great financial strength and industrial expertise, have given him considerable leverage with the Malay political leadership.

No other Malaysian Chinese businessman has Kuok's strengths, but the implications are clear. The wider network of overseas Chinese investment is a source of support for those powerful enough to have access to it It also serves as a haven for flight capital for those less sanguine of their ability to reconcile their interests with the ambitions of the Malaysian regime. As international

Chinese investment is increasingly important in Southeast Asian economies, Malaysia's in particular, this is something which political leaders must bear in mind when seeking to apply the screws to local entrepreneurs.

THAILAND

Thailand's commercial and industrial activity is dominated by about thirty large conglomerates of which all but two (the Crown Property Bureau and the military-owned Krung Thai Bank) are owned by Sino-Thai.[32] In spite of their size they are all in family hands, and in their business arrangements none has moved very far across the spectrum from traditional Chinese family firm to modern-style corporate organization. A few of them developed from businesses founded in the early years of this century, but most have come to the fore since the 1960s, when the Thai economy began its great leap forward. "New money" is even more characteristic of Thai capitalism than of Malaysian.

Most Chinese immigrants to Thailand arrived at about the same time in the late nineteenth and early twentieth centuries as their counterparts in Malaysia and Indonesia.[33] I shall not discuss the historical development of their business involvement, as Suehiro has done so in this volume. It is worth noting, though, the relatively strong positions of the Thai Chinese: in the 1930s the amount of their capital was roughly comparable to European capital invested in the country.[34] In spite of this relative equality and the absence of colonialism, we do not find wealthy towkays in pre-war Thailand, as we do in Malaya-Singapore. Most likely this was because the economy of Thailand did not experience the rapid economic growth which rubber brought to the Malayan peninsula early in the century, which made fortunes for Chinese as well as Europeans. The leading Thai capitalists were in the rice trade, a highly competitive and speculative business, and the hazards of this specialization were no doubt one reason why few of the firms they founded rank among the leading businesses in Thailand today.

In spite of Thailand's formal independence, the scope for Chinese businesses in Thailand was limited by the fact that foreign banks and trading firms dominated commercial life. The Great Depression and World War II loosened the foreign grip, only to be followed by the intense nationalism and anti-Sinic policies of Phibun Songkhram's regime.[35] This caused Chinese businessmen to increase their reliance on financial deals with political leaders to ensure protection and access, providing the model for Riggs' "pariah entrepreneurship" discussed earlier in this volume. A less celebrated but at least equally significant effect was that it compelled community leaders to decide once and for all whether they wished to be accepted as citizens of Thailand or would identify with China under its new and strong Communist regime.[36] The firm commitment to assimilation which resulted from the crisis was later strengthened by increasingly close social relations and intermarriage.

The subsequent transformation of Thai business-political relations may be illustrated by the adventures of the Bangkok Bank and its leader Chin Sophonphanich.[37] In the bureaucratic polity of the 1950s the bank had invited General Phao Sriyanon, a key figure in the Phibun regime, to be chairman of the corporate group to which the bank belonged. When the regime was overthrown in 1957, Chin deemed it prudent to withdraw for a time to Hong Kong, where he occupied himself by drumming up overseas business for the bank. As the new Sarit regime abandoned parasitization for the promotion of private business and encouraged foreign investment, Chin was able to return under favorable circumstances for himself and his bank.

This did not mean an end to the bank's involvement with political leadership. Indeed, the prominence of former Bangkok Bank executives in high government offices reached a point where they came to be known as "the Bangkok Bank Mafia."[38] But political connections were not, as Suehiro points out, the critical factor behind the bank's success.[39] They were now a way of increasing leverage over politics, not of sheltering under a patron; and growing pluralism in Thai politics has required that business establish links with a range of bureaucrats and parties rather than one or two powerful protectors.[40] Not only is political connection no longer central to business success, but the most "political" of the big conglomerates are not the most successful or the most modernized. On the whole they are those which continue to operate in the manner of earlier towkays, in areas which are highly dependent on bureaucratic or political contacts or which rely on corruption for their success.

The new independence and the publicly wielded political influence of Thai businesses, particularly the banks, have led some analysts to return to Marxist models based on European capitalist development to explain the Thai system. Thus Hewison has characterized Thailand's bank-based conglomerates as the core of the country's "financial bourgeosie," unified by marriage and interlocking ownership and directorships. They are, he argued, able to monopolize the capital market, since "their investments have penetrated into every sector of the Thai economy."[41] While it is true there are many elements of oligopoly and market distortion in the Thai economy from which those corporations have been able to benefit, the bank-based groups have nothing like monopoly control. As Suehiro has pointed out above, the leading industrial capitalists have neither derived from nor depended on the "old money" of the Thai banking groups; rather, they have looked to foreign joint venture partners as sources of both capital and access to new technologies. The model of finance capital giving rise to industrial capital does not work in the Thai case, the more so since the main stimulus to the country's post-1960 economic growth has been the remarkable increase in and diversification of agricultural production and exports. This gave impetus to the commercial sector and the tertiary services generally, as well as to government revenues, all of which helped generate a rising demand for the goods and services to which the great financial and industrial conglomerates could respond.[42] More than elsewhere in

Southeast Asia, the rise of big Chinese-owned conglomerates seems to have been a product rather than the producer of national economic growth.

Though, as we have noted, Thai business groups have not yet moved far from their origins as old-style Chinese family firms toward modern, impersonal corporate entities, the trend is clear enough. At the traditional end of the spectrum are one-man autocracies like Sukree's textile empire or Saworn's Siam Motors group. At the modernizing pole are groups like the Lamsam-Thai Farmers Bank conglomerate, the agribusiness giant Charoen Pokphand, and the Bangkok Bank—this last especially since Chartri Sophonphanich took over in 1983. The modernizers are adopting new managerial techniques from the international business schools and going beyond the family circle to hire the best executives they can find, though not (yet) to the point that family control of the core companies is endangered. Some groups have compromised, conducting their commodity trading very much along traditional lines but modernizing in sectors such as banking and finance (e.g the Wanglee group, Saha Union, Hong Yiah Seng).

In the trend toward more expert and impersonal management the Sino-Thai conglomerates are not very different from their Malaysian and Singapore counterparts, but the latter have gone much further in using the stock exchange to raise capital and diversify their holdings across a range of business interests while retaining control of the core holding company. Thailand did not have a stock exchange at all until the Securities Exchange of Thailand (SET) was established in 1975, long after Malaysia and Singapore but several years ahead of Indonesia. Even today the SET's significance as a vehicle for share transactions and transfers of ownership in the major public companies is very slight.[43] The volume of daily turnover on the Bangkok exchange in June 1988, about US$8 billion, was only about one-fifth of the combined Singapore-Kuala Lumpur turnover and one-tenth that of Taipei's stock exchange. Trading in the shares of the big conglomerates is marginal and there have so far been no major changes of ownership or takeover battles via the exchange.

It is worth noting, with regard to the modernization of Thai Chinese entrepreneurial values, that the prestige of business leaders within the Chinese community rests on "old money" rather than current wealth. At the same time, it is accorded to businessmen of standing in either Thai or Chinese social systems. Thus the Lamsam family, highly assimilated into Thai society, is regarded almost as "aristocratic" in the Thai sense, while equal admiration is accorded the related Wanglee clan, which stresses its Chinese heritage and remains closely connected with the country's network of rice traders. In this mixture of old money and new, modernization and tradition, there is much similarity between the Chinese leadership of Thailand and Malaysia. It is very different from the new, socially unprestigious wealth of the Chinese in present-day Indonesia and the Philippines.

INDONESIA

The term "pariah entrepreneur" has become generally inappropriate to describe Chinese businessmen in Thailand, but it is not yet entirely so in Indonesia. Indonesian Chinese still have to take great care to maintain cordial relations with both civilian and military authorities, operating as they do in a highly centralized, authoritarian, and strongly patrimonialist political system. Whereas the families controlling the big Sino-Thai conglomerates are now very firmly entrenched near the heart of the economy and class structure of Thailand, the Indonesian Chinese are far more marginal, the super-rich as well as the middle-class and the poor.

One result of this vulnerability is that Indonesian Chinese businessmen have a strong interest in the status quo, for (as Robison's essay has elaborated) they have grown rich under the Suharto regime, with whose leadership they have a symbiotic relationship. They have had a harder and longer struggle to get to their precarious eminence than the Sino-Thai businessmen. Whereas ethnic origins and identities are fast becoming of little consequence in Thai social and economic life, that is far from the case in Indonesia. It is hardly surprising, therefore, that most of the leading Sino-Indonesian businessmen have short investment time-horizons, put a premium on security, accept the need to make pay-offs for political protection on a patron-client basis, and play no part in efforts to expand civil rights. We cannot, therefore, interpret their economic role solely in class or structural terms,[44] nor should we take their short-term perspectives and political dependency to mean that they are not real capitalists at all.[45]

The economic roles of the Chinese in Indonesia were already changing quite considerably in the last twenty years before World War II, as many Chinese moved into a wider range of commercial and some rudimentary industrial activities throughout the archipelago. However, they were still constrained by the dominance of Dutch capital in all the modern sectors of the economy, and only the Oei Tiong Ham Concern and a handful of others were able to make any inroads there. The 1930s depression, World War II, and the Indonesian struggle for independence opened up a wider range of opportunities.[46] The early post-revolutionary period was one of expanding but still strictly limited economic opportunities for the Chinese, as the Dutch retained control of the commanding heights until their assets were nationalized in 1957–1958. No Chinese business firms became as prominent during that period as Oei Tiong Ham in colonial days. On the other hand, some newcomers who had learnt how to cut deals with Indonesian officials and military officers during the struggle for independence began to take advantage of the new opportunities, particularly members of two very small Chinese sub-groups, the Hok Chia and the Hin Hua, of whom the most famous representatives are Liem Sioe Liong and Mochtar Riady, today the leading taipan and top banker in the country.[47]

After the nationalization of Dutch investments and their incorporation into the now huge state sector under President Sukarno's "Guided Economy," a new phase of business activity began to unfold for the Indonesian Chinese. This was at first a very difficult period for them, for the official ideology was strongly antagonistic to private business in general, and intense anti-Chinese sentiment was stirred up by right-wing elements as a means of attacking Sukarno and the left.[48] Yet it was in the chaotic and highly inflationary conditions of the Guided Democracy years that Chinese businessmen proved themselves indispensable, for the cumbrous state enterprises and distribution networks were incapable of operating effectively in those circumstances except with the assistance of Chinese as fixers (*tukang catut*, in Indonesian terminology).[49] Apart from a few of those, not many Chinese businessmen grew rich in those years, since there was little money to be made. But in general they survived better than their indigenous competitors, private as well as public, and so were well placed to take advantage of the improved economic climate and openness to private enterprise of Suharto's New Order.

The prosperity of Chinese businessmen under the post-1965 regime has often been attributed to their political connections as *cukong* to the New Order powerholders.[50] The term came into currency around 1970 to denote a close relationship between a Chinese who knew how to raise money and an Indonesian official (often an army officer) who could provide protection and influence. During the early years of the regime the government budget was quite inadequate to fund more than a small part of the routine expenditures of the armed forces and the regional civilian administration. "Unconventional finances" had to be raised by any means whatever, at both the local and national levels. For this purpose, recourse was made to Chinese financiers and business advisers—in return, of course, for protection from harassment from other military or civilian marauders and access to scarce goods, bank credits, licenses, and government contracts. There was thus a massive expansion of a relationship which had already existed for some time between certain army officers and Chinese businessmen.

By 1970/71 about a dozen of the *cukong* became notorious because of their very close relations to the president and members of his family. Of these the foremost was Liem Sioe Liong, an associate of Suharto since very early in his career and today Indonesia's leading entrepreneur. But almost every provincial governor and military cornmander was said to have developed similar relationships with the wealthiest local Chinese, and the system was perpetuated on a lesser scale at lower administrative levels, so that it became a highly visible characteristic of relations between Chinese businessmen and Indonesian authorities. By the 1980s it could be said that "the economic fortunes of the Indonesian ruling class are firmly intertwined with those of the Chinese."[51] When we recall the intensity of anti-Chinese sentiment amongst many of the New Order anti-Communist activists in 1965–1967,[52] the anti-Chinese riots of 1959 and 1963, and sporadic outbreaks under the

New Order itself, we can appreciate both the distance that Chinese businessmen have traveled and the fragility and dependence of their position.

Even so, the balance between political and business power has been changing. It began to do so with the economic improvement of the 1970s, and by the early 1980s the word *cukong* itself came to be heard far less frequently. A crucial juncture was the 1973/74 oil boom, which vastly increased the decision-making authority of the government and the financial resources at its disposal. This strengthening of the bureaucracy paradoxically freed businessmen of their close dependence on one or two powerful government patrons, as it released officialdom from its dependence on "unconventional financing." By the late 1980s several of the top ten businessmen—those who had most profited from the system—relied far less than before on political connections. Of course, it has remained important for Chinese businessmen to maintain good connections with the relevant authorities and to be able to "lubricate" them with occasional bribes, sweeteners, and "administration costs"—a common enough phenomenon in countries where the government intervenes extensively in economic life. But these days that may mean little more than keeping on the right side of the Directorate of Industry, or the Ministry of Public Works, or the Forestry Department; it does not necessarily mean establishing the same sort of symbiotic linkage with top-level government officials as in the classical *cukong* relationship.

Leading Chinese businessmen of today exhibit varying degrees of political involvement.[53] Among the more highly "political" of the original group of *cukong* might be included, in addition to well-known names like Liem Sioe Liong and Bob Hasan, the late Ong Seng Keng (one of the earliest and most controversial of them all); Hendra Rahardja; Cokrosaputra of the "Batik Kris" organization; Goh Swie Kie, the "Bulog *cukong*"; Ir. Ciputra, associated initially with the Jakarta municipal government and later directly with Liem Sioe Liong and the palace circle; and Liem Bian Koen. But since the 1980s there have been notable businessmen who were less directly "political," such as William Soerjadjaja and Tan Siong Kee, who head the large Astra and Roda Mas groups respectively, Go Ka Him of the fast-rising Dharmala group, the late Suryo Wonowijoyo of the giant Gudang Garam cigarette company, and Adil Nurimba, a leading shipping magnate. All of these seem to have built up their wealth more by carefully nurturing their businesses than by wheeling and dealing, although most have judged it expedient to cut in members of the Suharto family or their circle as shareholders or functionaries. None entirely neglect the cultivation of political connections. Lacking institutionalized mechanisms for exerting influence over the government's economic policies through pressure group mechanisms of the kind we see in more advanced industrial economies, they have to rely on personal ties to bend public policies or obtain dispensation from them.[54] In general this has meant achieving special privileges and exemptions (e.g. Liem Sioe Liong's monopoly rights over steel imports for tin-plate [a quid pro quo for bailing out the state's loss-making Krakatau Steel plant in 1983} and the exclusion of Bob Hasan's rattan-processing monopoly from the 1988 trade deregulation package). However, at the level of general economic policy making, these businessmen do not have anything approaching the influence of the technocrats in the bureaucracy.

All Indonesia's major private corporations are owned and controlled by what are essentially family firms. Although most of the twenty-odd largest corporations have connections with business groups involving the presidential family and Liem Sioe Liong, there has otherwise been very little interlocking of shareholdings and directorships. The interlocking process has not yet gone as far as in Malaysia or Thailand, where it is also quite rudimentary compared with the NICs and other capitalist economies. In a handful of Indonesian family firms, most notably Astra, there has been some progress toward modern-style managerial structures and the employment of well-trained executives from outside the family circle, although here again this has occurred far less than in Malaysia or Thailand. Most heads of Indonesian conglomerates are no longer old-style towkays, but only a few have moved far toward modern business practices.

Most Indonesian conglomerates are highly diversified. This makes good sense in an uncertain economic or political environment, as a means of spreading risks, but it has hindered serious industrial commitment and long-term investment strategy. Liem Sioe Liong may be richer than was his friend Chin Sophonphanich, and he controls a vast and heterogeneous business empire, including the fast-growing Bank Central Asia (BCA) group, but he rules over a much more rambling collection of enterprises. Cash flow and control of assets seem to be his primary aims, not corporate strategy or market dominance, and this is true of the other Indonesian conglomerate heads.

The main exceptions to the disinterest in concentrated investment are the Astra International corporation (mainly involved in motor-vehicle assembling and manufacture), Sinar Mas (cooking oil and oil-palm plantations), and Gudang Garam (*kretek* cigarettes), although all of these also have property divisions and minor investments in other lines of business. A few business leaders have concentrated predominantly in one field of activity: thus we find a "textile king" (The Nien King), a "timber king" (Jos Sutomo), a "sewing machine king," and even a "prawn king." To them we might add Adil Nurimba, owner of the largest inter-island shipping fleet by the early 1980s; Mochtar Riady, Liem Sioe Liong's right-hand man in charge of Bank Central Asia; and the Director of PT Kalbe Farme, Dr. Bunyamin Setiawan, who made a fortune in pharmaceuticals. Like all the leading Indonesian Chinese businessmen, theirs is new money; Adil Nurimba, for example, started life on a river boat in the east Sumatra fishing port of Bagan Siapiapi.

The fact that the risks of specialization began to recede much earlier in Thailand than in Indonesia is one reason for the latter's failure to produce industrial leaders. In addition, the larger role of foreign capital in manufacturing has probably had a more inhibiting effect on Indonesian industrial entrepreneurship than in Thailand or Malaysia.[55] Moreover, investment in real estate has been a highly attractive alternative. A prime focus of Chinese business investment in all these countries, it has been particularly important in Indonesia. Because of the country's rudimentary property markets prior to the 1970s, there were huge windfall gains to be made as land values and rents rose rapidly during the boom years. As in most countries, political connections and back-door pay-offs are essential in that line of business; this reinforced the need for political patronage, and gave men close to the inner circle of the presidential palace the inside running. Property development became one of the easiest means of accumulating capital during the boom phase of New Order growth, with extensive financial leverage being assured by easy access to bank credit on subsidized terms.[56]

Few of the big Indonesian firms have been able to call on private commercial bank connections in the manner of their Thai equivalents. Indonesia has nothing comparable to the Bangkok Bank, nor any big banking-based conglomerates like Thailand's "Big Four." Because the lucrative field of deposit banking is dominated by the state banks, which are also the major source of subsidized credit, only a few of the sixty or so private banks with which many of the big corporations are associated had reached any significant size prior to the deregulation of the banking industry in 1988–1989.[57] In 1983, only two of them ranked among the top ten Indonesian banks, BCA and its main rival Panin (Pan Indonesia Bank); another seven, all considerably smaller, were in the top thirty. Most private banks existed mainly to transact the business of the companies that owned them. Throughout the 1980s the private financial sector in Indonesia was still extremely rudimentary in all respects, apart from informal-sector credit transactions.[58] The stock exchange only began to play a significant role as part of the capital market in late 1989, and only a few small parts of the largest conglomerates are as yet registered there for share transactions. Much more important as a source of finance has been (and still was at the end of the decade) the state banking system, which made cheap credit easily available to the politically well-connected. Needless to say, this reinforced the dependency of businessmen on political patronage.

The Indonesian conglomerates have, however, been able to call on foreign sources of capital to varying degrees. Many are associated on a joint-venture basis with Japanese companies; others have connections with Hong Kong, Taiwan, and, increasingly, South Korean capital. European industrial firms seeking access to the Indonesian market through joint ventures are also sources of finance, but relatively few conglomerates have ties with US capital, which is mainly invested in oil and minerals, where the Indonesian Chinese have little involvement. In a few cases the Indonesian companies have been able to emulate their Thai counterparts in achieving substantial bargaining leverage vis-a-vis their joint-venture partners. In general, though, they have been less independent. A key factor in this has been the changing attractiveness to foreign investors of the Indonesian economy: this looked good during part of the 1970s, but seemed far less so after 1983, causing the foreign investors to drive much harder bargains. By the end of the decade, however, Indonesia was regaining its appeal and hence, perhaps, increased leverage. Moreover, the fact that several of the big conglomerates have a variety of foreign partners and are thus not dependent on any one has changed their negotiating strength considerably. In short, it seems likely that the link with foreign capital is less a source of national economic dependency, as was feared in the early 1970s, than a potential mitigator of business dependency on domestic political patronage.

CONCLUSION

These accounts reveal that, in spite of the great variety of Southeast Asian Chinese business experience, there are significant similarities in business leaders' sources of wealth, the predominance of "new money" and the relative decline of old entrepreneurial families, the importance of property dealings and of political connections. Foreign capital has not determined their role. In spite of the importance of joint ventures, few big corporations seem to be fronts for MNCs, while several Southeast Asian business groups are aggressively moving into the international commercial arena themselves. If anything, foreign capital has served to decrease Chinese business dependence on local sources of support, and thus to increase its political and financial leeway. Nor has finance capital played a central role in business development: only in Thailand is banking capital a main base for business development, and even here the major banking conglomerates appear to be quite distinct from the industrial groups.

We have seen that virtually all the large conglomerates are still owned or controlled by family firms, and that relatively few have moved noticeably toward more modern corporate organization. Nor is there much sign of movement toward the separation of ownership from managerial control.[59] We can, however, see some movement, and corporatization has gone further in Malaysia (and Singapore and the Philippines) than in Indonesia or Thailand. We must bear in mind that the very newness of most big Southeast Asian businesses means that we are talking about change within one generation, and it is very hard to expect men who rose from nothing to head great corporations to relinquish the methods that were their key to success and remain the basis for their current power.

It is also notable that the wealthiest businessmen of the 1980s engaged primarily in financial and commercial activities rather than in manufacturing.[60] This is not because, as has sometimes been suggested, Southeast Asian Chinese have no stomach for manufacturing. We need only remember that they pioneered many manufactures all over Southeast Asia, in products like food processing, soap, cooking oil, matches, cigarettes, and biscuits. To be sure, these were small-scale ventures, requiring none of the financial and organizational inputs of today's large industries. Perhaps even more significantly, the really big money-makers of recent decades have been commercial activities and property deals with short turnover times, or financial operations, banking, insurance, and building construction. Capital tends to flow into those spheres of activity where the rate of return is highest, and in the economic circumstances of the last decades manufacturing industry has often not provided very high rates of return. Nevertheless, there are signs that the long-term advantages of a manufacturing base are making themselves felt, aided by foreign investors' willingness to provide finance. Domestic industrial groups are now a marked feature of the Thai economy, and even in Indonesia exports of manufactured gcods are becoming significant.

We have noted the connection of major Southeast Asian business leaders with overseas Chinese capital, centering on the greater Nanyang (southern seas) area. Only half-a-dozen are yet operating transnationally on a large scale, although many businessmen have moved part of their capital abroad and many more have minor business connections in other countries. In one sense this is not new: late-colonial tycoons such as Tan Kah Kee, Aw Boon Haw, and Oei Tiong Ham had overseas connections, but the internationally active Southeast Asian Chinese businessmen of the present day are making much larger investments throughout the region. Many have links with Hong Kong, as a source of finance, an investment nest egg, or a trade connection looking to the China market.[61] The volume of Chinese money moving around Southeast Asia has increased enormously over the last thirty years, and we have noted the leverage which this mobility gives businessmen against local government pressure. Regionally active Chinese capital is also being invested differently: instead of the old commercial emphasis on rubber, copra, rice, and other commodities, it now concentrates on international financial and property transactions. New types of skills and connections are required to make large profits in these new fields, and one might assume (though so far there is not much evidence) that this will have an impact on Southeast Asian Chinese ways of doing business.

While Southeast Asian businessmen are becoming more integrated with capital in the greater Nanyang region, they are detaching themselves from Chinese communities in their own countries. The successful tycoons of the present day do not provide social leadership in the same way as the great *siang hwee* (chamber of commerce) leaders of the last colonial century. They may command a great deal of respect and influence among other Chinese merchants, but, as Heng's essay points out for the case of Malaysia, they have avoided formal leadership responsibilities within their communities. Indeed, the Chinese communities themselves have changed profoundly, and non-communal types of social organization are meeting the needs that Chinese institutions used to address. Save in the Philippines, the *siang hwee* have disappeared, and the traditional community associations are atrophying.

Increasingly, though slowly and at different speeds, the Southeast Asian Chinese are identifying as Thais, Indonesians, or Malaysians, and so, too, are Southeast Asian Chinese businessmen.

NOTES

1 The foremost of these men have been Liem Sioe Liong of Indonesia, the late Chin Sophonphanich of Thailand (who died in 1988), and Robert Kuok, whose fortune originated in Malaysia and Singapore. Several other conglomerates are owned or controlled by multi-millionaires who rank well above the hundred-million dollar level in net worth, like the Lee Rubber-OCBC (Overseas Chinese Banking Corporation) group and the Kwek family's Hong Leong group in Singapore-Malaysia, William Soeryadjaya's Astra International group in Indonesia and the Thai Farmers Bank/Lamsam group in Thailand. For details, see the appendix, below, pp. 185–90. The estimates of net worth given here are taken from the periodic estimates in *Forbes, Fortune*, and *South* of the world's biggest corporations and richest millionaires. All such figures raise major problems of categorization and measurement (aggravated by the natural reticence of their subjects); however, they serve as rough indicators of rankings and orders of magnitude. All the groups mentioned, except the Lamsams, now the second largest of the Thai conglomerates, were listed in a survey of "The Super-Duper Rich" by Ranjit Gill, *Insight* (December 1983): 9–22.

2 The word "Chinese" is used here to refer to people of ethnic Chinese descent, regardless of their citizenship status, even though this fails to distinguish between the vast majority of Chinese who have adopted the nationality of those countries and the relatively few who have retained PRC or Taiwan nationality. It also implies a more significant distinction than one would wish between the ethnic Chinese and the indigenous citizens of those countries. Law and administrative practice take no cognizance of this difference in theory, although in practice they often do. Prior to 1941, many of the Chinese in Southeast Asia were mere sojourners and remained Chinese citizens. Since World War II the nationality issue has been very complex, and I will not deal with it here. Increasingly Southeast Asian Chinese businessmen are locally born, but this has only been common in the last generation of big business leaders.

3 This paper does not touch on the large indigenous private corporations or big state enterprises that exist alongside the Chinese conglomerates, mainly in Indonesia and Malaysia. Nor does it do more than refer incidentally to the Philippines and Singapore, the latter an essentially Chinese city-state, the former a country whose capitalist class is centered on a large indigenous property-owning elite (many of its families having Sino-mestizo ancestors from the eighteenth or nineteenth century). The Philippines has several large, old-established family-controlled corporate conglomerates, such as San Miguel and the Ayala Corporation, of a kind we do not find elsewhere in the region. Like Thailand, it has also had a high degree of assimilation of its ethnic Chinese immigrants over the centuries. See Edgar Wickberg, *The Chinese in Philippine Life* (New Haven: Yale University Press, 1965). The distinctive features of both the Philippines and Singapore make comparisons with the other three countries not very fruitful.

4 On the importance of *pang* groups or organizations, usually referring to dialect groups, see Yen Ching-hwang, *A Social History of the Chinese in Singapore and Malaysia 1800–1911* (Singapore: Oxford University Press, 1986), pp. 177–83; on trust, *shinyung*, in a Vietnamese context, see Clifton Barton, "Trust and Credit:

Some Observations Regarding Business Strategies of Overseas Chinese Traders in South Vietnam" In *The Chinese in Southeast Asia*, ed. Linda Lim and J. A. Peter Gosling (Singapore: Maruzen Asia, 1983). The significance of such networks is stressed as an important structural advantage for the Chinese businessmen in Southeast Asia by Yoshihara Kunio, The *Rise of Ersatz Capitalism in South-East Asia* (Singapore: Oxford University Press, 1988), pp. 53–55, and, as a mechanism for reducing transaction costs, particularly in large-scale organizations, by Nathaniel H. Leff, "Capital Markets in Developing Countries: the Group Principle," in *Money and Finance in Economic Growth and Development*, ed. Ronald I. McKinnon (New York: M. Dekker, 1976).

5 Harold Crouch and James Morley, "The Dynamics of Political Change," in *Economic Growth and Political Change in East Asia*, ed. James Morley (forthcoming).

6 The best synoptic account of the economic roles of the Southeast Asian Chinese is given by Mary Somers-Heidhues, *Southeast Asia's Chinese Minorities* (Melbourne: Longman, 1976), pp. 8–29; for a longer but largely anecdotal and not very coherent story, see Victor Purcell, *The Chinese in Southeast Asia* (London: Oxford University Press, 1965). G. W. Sinner's, *Chinese Society in Thailand: an Analytical History* (Ithaca, NY: Cornell University Press, 1957), is still the model comprehensive account of Chinese contributions to a Southeast Asian country's development.

7 W. F. Wertheim, *Indonesian Society in Transition* (The Hague: van Hoeve, 1956), p. 136.

8 No thorough analysis of the reasons for the remarkable business success of the Chinese in Southeast Asia has yet been attempted, but for some suggestive ideas see Wang Gungwu, *Trade and Cultural Values: Australia and the Four Dragons* (Sydney: Asian Studies Association of Australia, 1988). The perennial question of whether these should be attributed mostly to values (hard work, frugality, enterprise, etc.) or to structural factors (the corporate character of the family firm and its property, the various types of socio-economic networking mechanisms, such as the *pang* or *siang hwee*, with their benefits in providing better access to credit, market information, and sanctions ensuring payment of debts) have direct relevance to our concerns here, but are too complex to unravel thoroughly. One of the earliest and best treatments of the problem was that of Maurice Freedman, "The Handling of Money; A Note on the Background of the Sophistication of Overseas Chinese," *Man* 59 (1959): 64–65, who observed that they prospered "not simply because they were energetic immigrants, but more fundamentally because they knew how to handle money and organize men in relation to money," which in turn was because their "shrewdness in handling money was an important part of the equipment which ordinary Chinese took with them when they went overseas in search of a livelihood." He was referring to the first-generation Chinese immigrants who became small-scale traders, but we lack any comparable analytical treatment of the economic skills of the Southeast Asian Chinese at much higher levels of commercial, financial, and organizational activity thirty years later.

9 The total inflow of foreign capital into the ASEAN countries between 1970–1984 is estimated by Hal Hill, *Foreign Investment and Industrialization in Indonesia* (Singapore: Oxford University Press, 1988), p. 48, to have been around US$27 billion, including oil investments; but figures such as these are not much more than guesstimates, because of the inadequacy of the statistics. Very little private foreign capital was invested in any part of Asia between 1945–1970.

10 Wu Yuan Li and Wu Chun-hsi, *Economic Development in Southeast Asia* (Stanford: Hoover Institute, 1980).

11 Yoshihara, *Rise of Ersatz Capitalism*, pp. 16–19; Hill, *Foreign Investment*, p. 48.

12 Frank Golay et. al., *Underdevelopment and Economic Nationalism in Southeast Asia* (Ithaca, NY: Cornell University Press, 1969); Somers-Heidhues, *Southeast Asia's Chinese Minorities*; Wu and Wu, *Economic Development*; and Lim and Gosling, *Chinese in Southeast Asia*.

13 The word assimilation implies something very like "becoming similar," hence indistinguishable—the ideal of the old "melting pot" theory, whereas integration implies retention of the cultural and social characteristics of various immigrant ethnic groups as in the United States; my own views on this are set out more fully in J. A. C. Mackie, "Changing Economic Roles and Ethnic Identities of the Southeast Asian Chinese: A Comparison of Indonesia and Thailand," in *Changing Ethnic Identities of the Southeast Asian Chinese since World War II*, ed. Jennifer Cushman and Wang Gungwu (Hong Kong: University of Hong Kong Press, 1988), pp. 225–33.

14 Golay, *Underdevelopment*; Mackie, "Changing Economic Roles."

15 G. W. Skinner, "Change and Persistence in Chinese Culture Overseas; A Comparison of Thailand and Java" *Journal of the South Seas Society* 16, 1–2 (1960): 86–100.

16 Somers-Heidues, *Southeast Asia's Chinese Minorities*; Leo Suryadinata, *Pribumi Indonesians, the Chinese Minority and China* (Singapore and Hong Kong: Heinemann Educational Books (Asia) Ltd., 1978); Charles Coppel, *Indonesia's Chinese in Crisis* (Kuala Lumpur: Oxford University Press, 1983).

17 Terms like "old wealth" and "new money" are, of course, relative: I include in the former category all family firms that were well-established before World War II (e.g. the OCBC-Lee Rubber empire in Malaysia-Singapore, the Tan Cheng Lock rubber interests, the Lamsam and Wanglee family companies in Thailand, the Oei Tiong Ham Concern in Indonesia), or are today second-generation firms (such as the H. S. Lee-Alex Lee family interests in Malaysia). The latter category would include those which have come to prominence over the last twenty or thirty years. This leaves an intermediate group of those that emerged in the 1950s, of which the Kuok, Hong Leong and perhaps the Sophonphanich groups might be included, i.e. those that are not really in the "new money" category, but are not very old, either.

18 The traditional Chinese family firm is well described by Linda Lim, "Chinese Economic Activity in Southeast Asia: An Introductory Review," in *Chinese in Southeast Asia*, pp. 245–46, as family-owned rather than a joint stock company, usually employing a mix of unpaid family labor and wage labor, small in size and scale of operations, concentrated in commercial-sector activities (rural and urban retailing, crop brokerage, market gardening, money lending, simple processing, etc.) and performing "middlemen functions" between the indigenous and the modern economy. Maintenance of family control and ownership is the key consideration, even when such firms grow into large corporate empires and become joint stock companies. See also John T. Omohondro, *Chinese Merchant Families in Iloilo: Commerce and Kin in a Central Philippine City* (Athens: Ohio University Press, 1981), for a fine picture of the commercial culture of such family firms in Iloilo. The emergence of a new and different type of family-firm activity over recent years, modern manufacturing for export markets, is dealt with by Lim, "Chinese Economic Activity," pp. 1, 245–75.

19 On the origin of the words *towkay*, tycoon, and *taipan*, Mary Somers-Heidhues (*Southeast Asia's Chinese Minorities*, p. 114) refers to the former as "widely used to refer to a Chinese big businessman." According to Yen Chin-hwang, *Social History of the Chinese*, pp. 53–55, 154, citing Vaughan, it derives from *t'ou-chia*, a title bestowed on the leader of a dialect association (*luchou*) "owner of the incense

burner" which only a wealthy Chinese could afford; Vaughan says it was applied in early British Malaya to a leader of a dialect *kongsi* of that name. There were no rules about who could become a *lu-chou* or *t'ou-chia*, but it was necessary to have a house or shop with the proper place for the incense-burner, hence only a few wealthier merchants were qualified. The term came to be applied also to leaders of *pang* (speech-group) and clan organizations; since they were expected to donate to festivals and group functions: "a charitable spirit, education and charisma had their role in determining the leadership of Chinese dialect organizations." Edwin Lee, The *Towkays of Sabah* (Singapore: Singapore University Press, 1976), p.1, says the word means "head of either the household, community or business, and worthy was he who could discharge the duties of all three. . . . "—but also that he often "earned the Chinese the reputation for rapacity and aggrandizement. But equally he came forth to lead the Chinese from a base in the Chamber of Commerce. He organized the social and educational institutions that so distinguished the overseas Chinese and sustained them with such munificence. This, at any rate, was the image of the ideal towkay." The word tycoon is defined in Webster's Collegiate Dictionary, 1985, as from the Japanese "*taikun* fr Chin (Pek) *ta* (great) + *chun* (ruler) 1858; 1. Shogun; 2 a. a top leader (as in politics) b: a businessman of exceptional wealth and power: Magnate. ibid." Likewise, taipan means "a powerful businessman and especially a foreigner living and operating in China"—Chinese *tai pan* (ca. 1898). It seems no longer to be confined to foreigners, however.

20 Singapore was incorporated into Malaysia briefly between September 1963 and August 1965, when it was expelled and became an independent state. In the colonial era, it was administered as part of the British Straits Settlements, along with Malacca and Penang. Its economic links with its Malayan hinterland were always very close until 1965 and many business firms still operate in both, the OCBC-Lee Rubber, Hong Leong, and Kuok groups being the most substantial.

21 The word *kongsi* (Mandarin, *kung-ssu*) means, literally, a company (Somers-Heidhues, *Southeast Asia's Chinese Minorities*, p. 114), but was commonly used to designate the semi-cooperative mining and agricultural enterprises of Borneo and the Malayan peninsula. On the general character of early Chinese businesses in Malaysia, see Purcell, *Chinese in Southeast Asia;* Wong Lin Ken, *The Malayan Tin Industry* (Tucson: University of Arizona Press, 1965); James C. Jackson, *Planters and Speculators: Chinese and European Agricultural Enterprise in Malaya 1786–1921* (Kuala Lumpur: University of Malaya Press, 1968); and Yen Ching-hwang, *Social History of the Chinese.*

22 Jomo K. Sundaram, *A Question of Class: Capital, the State and Uneven Development in Malaya* (New York: Monthly Review Press, 1982).

23 For an informative life of Tan Kah Kee, see C. F. Yong, *Tan Kah Kee. The Making of an Overseas Chinese Legend* (Singapore: Oxford University Press, 1986). The huge monument erected by the seashore at Xiamen after his death in 1961 to celebrate this great capitalist's contributions to his Communist homeland was a notable oddity of People's China of that day.

24 James Puthucheary, *Ownership and Control in the Malayan Economy* (Singapore: Eastern University Press, 1959), pp. 123–40.

25 Lim Mah Hui, *Ownership and Control of the One Hundred Largest Corporations in Malaysia* (Kuala Lumpur: Oxford University Press, 1981); Tan Tat Wai, *Income Distribution and Determination in Malaysia* (Kuala Lumpur: Oxford University Press, 1982); Ranjit Gill, *The Making of Malaysia Inc.* (Petaling Jaya: Pelanduk, 1985); and Bruce Gale, *Politics and Business: A Study of Multi-Purpose Holdings Berhad* (Singapore: Eastern Universities Press, 1986).

26 The Second Malaysia Plan (1971–1975) incorporated a two-pronged New Economic Policy for development, intended, first, to reduce poverty and increase employment opportunities for all Malaysians, ostensibly regardless of race; second, to bring about the restructuring of Malaysian society to redress the economic imbalances and eventually eliminate the identification of race with economic function. Special rights for Malays were to be extended into the private economy and the ambitious goal set for the achievement of 30 percent Malay ownership of all corporate assets by 1990. The principal means of achieving this has been through the acquisition of the share capital of British-owned companies. For the best recent account of Malaysian politics since 1969, see Zakariah Haji Ahmad, ed., *Government and Politics in Malaysia* (Singapore: Oxford University Press, 1987) and, on the socio-economic situation, the fine studies by Tan Tat Wai, *Income Distribution*, and E. K. Fisk and H. Osman Rani, eds., *The Political Economy of Malaysia* (Kuala Lumpur: Oxford University Press, 1982).

27 A colorful journalistic account of the development of the stock markets of Malaysia and Singapore is given in Ranjit Gill, *The Making of Malaysia Inc.;* see also Michael Skully, *Financial Institutions and Markets in Southeast Asia* (London: Macmillan, 1984), chap. 3.

28 Lim Mah Hui, *Ownership and Control.*

29 The figures are from Gill *The Making of Malaysia Inc.*, p. 94, based on the *Mid-Term Review of the Fourth Malaysia Plan 1981–1985.* These figures have been criticized for faulty categorization and inconsistencies, resulting in an under-estimate of the Malay share, although it is unlikely that the figures are very wide of the mark.

30 Khoo Kay Peng, Vincent Tan, and Alex Lee all benefitted from their close personal and business connections with Daim Zainuddin or Tunku Razaleigh. Other leading Chinese who did well in the boom conditions of the 1970s were Teng Hong Pow (Public Bank), Tan Koon Swan (Magnum and Multi-Purpose Holdings), Chong Kok Lim (Landmark Holdings), Loy Hean Heong, Wong Kee Tat, Lim Goh Tong, Loh Boon Siew, and Teo Soo Chuan. Some of these came to grief later in the 1980s. I am much indebted to Peter Searle for his assistance and much of the information contained here, although responsibility for its presentation and interpretation rests solely with me.

31 Kuok's "blue-chip background" is regarded as one of his particular strengths and "his connections with government and business figures . . . cut across national, racial and party lines," according to Robert Cottrell, *Far Eastern Economic Review* (hereafter *FEER*), October 30, 1986. He was a founder-director of Bank Bumiputera and a partner with Daim Zainuddin in the Malaysia-French Bank; yet he also led a syndicate that assisted Tan Koon Swan, the MCA Secretary, when he was imprisoned in Singapore on breach of trust charges.

32 Details on the twenty largest Sino-Thai conglomerates in Thailand in 1979 are given in Krirkiat Phipatseritham and Kunio Yoshihara, *Business Groups in Thailand* (Singapore: ISEAS Research Notes and Discussions, 1983), pp. 3–9, and Suehiro Akira, *Capital Accumulation in Thailand 1855–1985* (Tokyo: The Center for East Asian Cultural Studies, Toyo Bunko, 1989), who lists about twenty additional industrial conglomerates prominent in the 1980s; see also Suehiro in this volume. For other information on these firms, I am indebted to Dr Ammar Siamwallah, Anek Laothamatas, M. R. Prudhisan Jumbala, the late Jennifer Cushman, Kevin Hewison, John Girling, Bob Muscat, and Marcel Barang. The Crown Property Bureau is described in the *FEER*, June 30, 1988, pp. 60–63, as "perhaps the wealthiest institution in Thailand," with shares in more than forty companies, but its status is anomalous, being "neither public nor private."

33 Skinner, *Chinese Society*, pp. 80–118, 213–27.
34 Callis, *Foreign Capital in Southeast Asia*, p. 109.
35 Skinner, *Chinese Society*, pp. 353–65.
36 E. B. Ayal, "Thailand," in Golay et al., *Underdevelopment and Economic Nationalism*, pp. 299–329.
37 For good accounts of the rise of Chin Sophonphanich and the Bangkok Bank, see Suehiro, *Capital Accumulation.*, pp. 158–60, 253–56 and *Insight* (June 1978): 8–18, *The Institutional Investor* (November 1981): 136–44, *FEER*, July 28, 1983, pp. 52–8 and April 13, 1989, pp. 52–7.
38 Skully, *Financial Institutions*, p. 309.
39 See Suehiro's paper in this volume, and his *Capital Accumulation*, pp. 4–77.
40 When civilian politicians and political parties became active to an unprecedented degree during the "democratic interlude" (1973–1976), many Chinese capitalists became involved in the iounding or funding of parties. Business-party identification was especially close in the main provincial towns, the Bangkok-based corporations preferring instead to spread their risks by making contributions to several political organizations. See Benedict Anderson, "Withdrawal Symptons; Social and Cultural Aspects of the October 6 Coup," *Bulletin of Concerned Asian Scholars* 93, 3 (1977): 13–30.
41 Kevin Hewison, "The Financial Bourgeoisie in Thailand," *Journal of Contemporary Asia*, 11 (1981): 401, 409.
42 E. C. Chapman, "Thailand's Recent Economic Growth," in *Economic Development in East and Southeast Asia: Implications for Australian Agriculture in the 1980s*, ed. M. G. Adams (Canberra: Australian Government Printing Service, 1984), pp. 205–17; Peter Warr, *The Thai Economy* (Cambridge: Cambridge University Press, forthcoming); Suehiro, this volume.
43 Regulations intended to guard against the use of the Stock Exchange by the big conglomerates to enhance the concentration of ownership of Thai industries had the effect of discouraging them from going public in the early 1980s; for details see Skully, *Financial Institutions*.
44 Robison, *Indonesia*.
45 Yoshihara, *Rise of Ersatz Capitalism*.
46 Many of the more solidly established firms which were linked into Dutch business networks failed to survive the disruptions of the 1930s and 1940s because they were unable to adjust to the changed conditions. See Twang Peck-yang, "The Transformation of the Trading Minorities in Indonesia, 1940–50" (Ph.D. diss., Australian National University, 1988).
47 Ibid. I am much indebted to Twang for drawing my attention to the extraordinary prominence of the Hok Cia among the top businessmen in Indonesia since World War II.
48 The government regulation PP X/1959, banning trade-stores owned by aliens from rural areas, caused a great deal of racial tension in the early 1960s and there were several outbreaks of anti-Chinese violence between 1959–1965. See J. A. C. Mackie, ed., *The Chinese in Indonesia: Five Essays* (Melboume: Thomas Nelson, 1976).
49 At a time when most channels of trade were clogged by the tangle of government regulations in the name of Sukarno's "Guided Economy," the Chinese were the only group sufficiently adaptable to be able to keep at least minimal flows of goods and services. See Lance Castles, "Socialism and Private Business: The Latest Phase," *Bulletin of Indonesian Economic Studies* 1(1965): 13–45, and J. A. C. Mackie, *Problems of the Indonesian Inflation* (Ithaca, NY: Cornell Modern Indonesia Project, 1967).

50 The word *cukong* is of Hokkien derivation and literally means "master" (Leo Suryadinata, "Chinese Economic Elites in Indonesia: a Preliminary Study' in *Changing Ethnic Identities*, p. 266). More broadly, it signifies something between "boss" and "grandfather," referring originally to a kinsman who was both a patron-adviser and backer to a businessman, although in the Indonesian context the *cukong* is much more subordinate to his political protector (Coppel, *Indonesia's Chinese*, p. 212). The first article published on the *cukong* phenomenon, by Frank Hawkins in the *Bangkok Post*, January 28, 1971, named four major *cukong;* Liem Sioe Liong, Yap Swie Kie, Njoo Han Siang, and Harjyanto Lim, and referred to a group of about twenty in all who had a "steady and inside track to government contracts, investment credits and other funds" (Suryadinata, "Chinese Economic Elites," p. 267). Interestingly, quite a few of these are no longer prominent today. Several later lists of leading Chinese businessmen in Indonesia in the years 1973, 1979, and 1984 are published by Suryadinata in ibid., pp. 282–88). A useful list of the forty major Chinese business groups in the 1980s is given in Richard Robison, *Indonesia: The Rise of Capital* (Sydney: Allen and Unwin, 1986), pp. 278–88.

51 Robison, *Indonesia*, p. 317.

52 Coppel, *Indonesia's Chinese*.

53 Most of the information about the leading Indonesian Chinese capitalists in the following section is based on material compiled by Dorodjatun Kuntjorojakti, who generously allowed me access to it; and from P. N. Sondang, "100 Tokoh Milyarder Indonesia: Apa dan Siapa Mereka?" *Expo*, nos. 1,2, 4, and 18, 1984, *Fokus* (1984), and Robison, *Indonesia*.

54 The formal channels for business interaction with government on policy matters have been rudimentary in New Order Indonesia; the extent of informal pressures by big business leaders cannot be gauged, but has on some issues been substantial. Andrew Maclntyre, "Politics, Policy, and Participation: Business-Government Relations in Indonesia" (Ph.D. diss., Australian National University, 1988) discussed several cases where private business interests in the late 1980s were able to exert some influence through official channels. He expects the process to go further, but, given the opacity of Indonesian policy making, the evidence is unclear.

55 Thee Kian Wie and Yoshihara Kunio, "Foreign and Domestic Capital in Indonesian Industrialization," *Southeast Asian Studies* 24, 4 (1987): 327–50; Hill, *Foreign Investment*.

56 A few corporations have specialized in property dealings, displaying, apart from small banking connections, few other interests. These include the Pembangunan Jaya group, led by Ir. Ciputra, the "Medan group" of Ongko Kaharuddin and Lembana Ali, and the Tripoda group. It should be remembered that the activities of the great property developers in Jakarta, Medan, and Surabaya are replicated on smaller scales in hundreds of cities and towns throughout the archipelago, as urban growth pushes up land values. Thus it has been a source of capital accumulation not only for major *cukong* but also for thousands of smaller Chinese businessmen.

57 J. A. C. Mackie and Sjahrir, "Survey of Recent Developments," *Bulletin of Indonesian Economic Studies* 25, 3 (1989).

58 Skully, *Financial Institutions*.

59 It is possible, of course, to introduce managerial and administrative techniques of the business-school variety that should result in better allocation of resources without losing overall control of the firm. Many new Chinese corporations, particularly in Malaysia, seem to be moving in this direction. In Indonesia, William

Soerjadjaja's Astra group has long been seen as the paragon of a new breed of local business; and in Thailand, the Lamsam, Charoen Pokphand, and Saha Union groups illustrate the trend.

60 This is particularly noticeable in Thailand, where the three largest conglomerates are bank- based (the fourth is the Crown Property Bureau, which has the large Siam Cement Co. and various other industrial investments, as well as the Siam Commercial Bank). The more exclusively industrial corporations are a good deal smaller. See Krirkiat and Yoshihara, *Business Groups*, p. 29. In Malaysia, Robert Kuok is the sole tycoon with big manufacturing investments, and these form only a small part of his highly diversified empire. In Indonesia, the Liem Sioe Liong and Astra groups are both among the largest conglomerates and have major industrial interests, though Liem's fortune was made on non-manufacturing investments.

61 The most dramatic internationalization has been that of Liem Sioe Liong, who moved into Hong Kong with the establishment of the First Pacific group in the early 1980s and subsequently acquired companies in the USA and the Netherlands; he was also making major investments in Singapore (and minor ones in Thailand) in 1990–1991. Dozens of smaller Chinese business leaders in Singapore, Malaysia, and Indonesia have financial investments in at least two of these countries, as do various shipping and commodity trading companies. Since the 1960s, the Bangkok Bank has steadily extended its network of branches throughout Southeast Asia (but not in the Philippines or Hong Kong) in order to service Chinese business requirements in the region, particularly those involving international linkages; however, it does not appear to have made investments or equity acquisitions outside Thailand.

APPENDIX
MAJOR CHINESE CONGLOMERATES IN THAILAND, INDONESIA AND MALAYSIA

This table lists leaders and names of about twenty of the largest Chinese conglomerates of the 1970s–1980s in each of the three countries, including a handful, marked *, which subsequently collapsed or their founders died. For Malaysia, it also lists some of the older colonial-era firms.

Family and group	*Major activities*	*Date of origin*	*Other*
THAILAND			
Group 1: "The Big Four" in banking			
Sophonphanich – Bangkok Bank	Banking, investments.	1930s Chin Sophonphanich	Relatively concentrated. Major bank in region.
		1944 Bangkok Bank	Strong pol. connections initially, later more diffuse. Modernizing in the 1980s.
Lamsam – Thai Farmers Bank	Banking, manufacturing, investments.	1900–10 1945 Thai Farmers Bank	Diverse but strong modern corporate structure: close ties with other leading groups, relatively non-political.
Techaphaibun – Bangkok Metropolitan Bank	Whisky, banking, etc.	1910–30 Tae Tsu Ping	Diversified around liquor-banking core. Highly political.
		1950 Bkk. Metro. Bank	
		1959 Mahaguna Distillery	
Ratanarak – Bank Ayudhya	Lighterage, banking, manufacturing.	1950 Bankok Lighters	Relatively concentrated initially, diversifying later. Strong political links early.
		1958 Chuan R – Bank of Ayudhya	

Group 2: Rice, sugar, and agribusiness groups			
Wanglee Bank	Rice milling, banking, property development.[a]	1874–1910	Diversified.
Hong Yiah Seng – Betagro	Rice trading, textiles, importing, and manufacturing.	1946	Diversifying.
Thai Roong Ruang	Sugar and related business.	1946	Concentrated. Political ties crucial.
Mitr-Pol – Kwang Soong Lee	Sugar and related business.	1950s (?)	Concentrated. Political ties crucial.
Yongsak Kanathanavanich – Laem Thong	Rice & jute export, animal feed etc.	1960s–70s	Diversifying into agribusiness generally.
Chia Bros. – Charoen Pokphand	Chickens, animal feed, agribusiness, telecommunications.	1940s	Started in agribusiness, diversifying in 1980s: joint venture links with various MNCs. Overseas branches in several countries.
Prasert Tangtrongsakdi – Metro	Fertilizer importer & manufacturing, flour mill.	1966	Several families involved. Diversified.
Group 3: Industry-based groups			
Boonsong	Auto importing, and manufacturing.	Early 1900s	Concentrated. Dominant position in the industry. US & Japan joint venture links in autos and manufacturing.
Chirathiwat – Central Dept. Stores	Retail trade, property development.	1940s–50s	Relatively concentrated. Business links with other large groups.
Taworn Pornprapha – Siam Motors	Motor distribution & assembly (Nissan), property development.	1930s Taworn's firm est. 1950s Siam Motars founded	Concentrated. Strong pol. connections early. Old style autocratic management until 1985 business downturn leads to bank intervention.
*U Chu Liang – Bangkok Metropolitan Bank	Importing, banking, misc.	1920s 1950 Bangkok Metro Bank	Diversified: Leader of Teochiu community: died 1976.

APPENDIX (Cont.)

Family and group	*Major activities*	*Date of origin*	*Other*
Damri Darakanda – Saha Union	Wholesale trade, manufacturing (household goods).	1960s	Diversified.
Sukree Phothirattanangkun – Thai Wuthipat	Manufacturing (textiles).	1949s–50s	Concentrated.
Osathanukroh – Osothsapha	Pharmaceuticals (importing and manufacturing), property development.	1940s–50s	Diversified.
Srifuengfung – Cathay	Trade, banking, finance, manufacturing	1940s–50s	Diversified.
* Sithi-Amnuay – PSA	Finance, insurance, tourism.	1970s	Substantially diversified. Collapsed mid-1980s.
* Tarnvanichkul – Asia Trust Bank	Banking, finance, property development.	1965	Collapsed early 1980s.
	INDONESIA		
Liem Sioe Liong – SEDC (Salim Economic Development Co.)	Trading, cement, steel, autos, property development.	1938–40s 1967–70 big expansion	Joint ownership with Suharto family in various firms. Links with foreign capital diversified. Large off-shore arm in First Pacific Holdings. Highly diversified group.
William Soerjadjaja – ASTRA	Auto importing and manufacturing, property development, agribusiness	1950s 1968 auto business	Relatively concentrated group, but diversifying. Joint venture with Toyota Corp. Political connections important initially, less significant later. Strong corporate structure.
Indra Wijaya – Sinar Mas	Cooking oil manufacturing and distribution.	1950s	Concentrated. Business associate Liem Sioe Liong in 1980s.

Gondokusuma – Dharmala	Commodities trading, manufacturing, finance, property development.	1950s	Initially concentrated, latterly diversifying. Non-political.
Goh Swie Kie – Gunung Sewu	Rice, sugar, commodities distribution.	1960s ??	Diversified. Close connections with BULOG.
Yap Swie Kie – Berkat	Trade, manufacturing, timber.	1960s	Concentrated. Close political connections.
Mochtar Riady – Lippo	Banking (Lippobank and BCA), finance, etc.	1960s	Concentrated. BCA part of Liem empire.
Gunawan Gunadi – Panin Bank	Banking, finance, etc.	1950s–60s ??	Concentrated. Main rival to BCA.
Ciputra – Pembangunan Jaya	Construction, property development	late 1960s	Diversified. Strong in real estate and construction: close to Jakarta City administration and latterly to Palace group.
Bob Hasan	Shipping, timber, property development, misc.	late 1960s	Diversified. Highly political with close Palace connections.
*Ong Seng Heng – Bank Ramayana/Coopa	Trading, banking.	1960s	Close to Gen. Suryo, the most notorious of early *cukong*; died 1976.
*Hendra Rahardja – Harapan	Motorcycles (Yamaha), property development, finance.	1970s	Diversified. Collapsed 1983–84, bailed out by Liem Sioe Liong.
Agus Nursalim – Kedaung	Manufacturing (glass, cooking oil).	1960s	Concentrated; Suharto's brother Probosutedjo a shareholder.
The Nien King – Damatex	Textile manufacturing.	1970s	Relatively concentrated. "Textile king" in 1980s. Strong political connections.
Tan Siong Kie – Roda Mas	Glass and electrical goods importing and manufacturing.	1950s	Relatively concentrated. Limited political connections.
Ongko Kaharuddin – Arya Upaya	Real estate, banking, manufacuring.	1970s	Diversified. Strong Medan connections.

APPENDIX (Cont.)

Family and group	*Major activities*	*Date of origin*	*Other*
Adil Nurimba – Gesuri Lloyd	Shipping.	1950s	Concentrated. Biggest shipping group by 1970s; in difficulties mid-1980s. No longer appears very political.
MALAYSIA			
Group 1: "Old Wealth"			
Kuok Bros – Perlis Plantations	Sugar trading, flour, shipping, manufacturing, property development, finance, investments.	1950s	Largest Malaysian conglomerate, with many overseas affiliates: close links with UMNO leadership since 1960. Relatively modern corporate structure.
Kwek Bros – Hong Leong	Finance, investments, construction, manufacturing.	1950s (Singapore)	Originally Singapore-based group, Malaysian arm now significant in its own right. Close UMNO connections.
Lee Seng Wee – OCBC/Lee Rubber[b]	Banking, plantations (rubber, palm oil), investments, property development.	1930s	The oldest large corporation, Singapore-based: founded by Lee Kong Chian in 1930, now dominates rubber trade. Unpolitical and fairly corporatized.
Loke Yew – Cathay Group	Tin, plantations (rubber), property development, banking, finance.	1860s	Initially tin, later diversified.
Eu Tong Sen	Tin, rubber, banking, finance.	1890–1910	Ditto.
Lee Loy Seng – Austral Amalg. Tin	Rubber, plantations, investments, banking.	1930s	Fairly concentrated: founder was MCA Senator, broad political and business links.
Group 2A: 'New Wealth' (pre-1980s)			
Loh Boon Siew – Oriental Holdings	Investments, motorcycle distribution (Honda), property development.	1960	Relatively diversified; modest political links.

*Chang Min Tien	Banking (UMBC), property development, manufacturing, plantations, investments.	1960s	Diversified, loose group; modest political links; leader moved offshore to Hong Kong 1981, died soon after.
Khoo Teck Puat[c]	Banking, real estate (hotels), investments.	1960	Founded Malayan Banking Bhd., later forced out, then diversified; frail political links.
Lim Goh Tong – Genting	Casino, plantations, property development.	1960s	Initially concentrated, later diversified; broad links with various UMNO leaders.
Chong Kok Lim – Landmarks	Tin, property development.	1960	Concentrated (tin, then real estate); political links with Perak royalty, then MCA and UMNO leaders in 1960s.
Teh Hong Piow – Public Bank	Banking, finance.	1965	Concentrated' links with UMNO leaders.
Group 2B: "New Wealth, post-NEP"			
Khoo Kay Peng – MUI	Property development, banking, finance, manufacturing (cement).	1976	Diversified; links with Razaleigh, then other Malays.
Vincent Tan – Berjaya	Manufacturing, property development, investments, Sports Toto lottery.	1982	Diversified; wide political links, especially to Daim Zainuddin.
Chan Teik Huat – Metroplex			Diversifying; links with UMNO leaders and Fleet Group.
Yap Lim Sen – Ipoh Garden Bhd.	Property development, construction, investments, manufacturing.	1970s	Diversified. Significant international operations and investments.
Lim Thian Kiat – Kamunting	Toll road concession, plantations, manufacturing, trading.	1987	Previously linked to brother and nephew of Daim Zainuddin in Seri Angkasa.
Loy Hean Heong – MBF Finance	Financial services.	1970s	Concentrated. Links to Negri Sembilan royalty.

APPENDIX (Cont.)

Family and group	*Major activities*	*Date of origin*	*Other*
Alex Lee – Roxy	Banking (D&C Bank), property development, manufacturing (electrical goods).	inherited wealth	Diversified; founder is son of Col. H. S. Lee, extensive political links to Daim, Mahathir, etc.
* Tan Koon Swan – GUH/MPH	Investments, tin, property development.	1976	Diversified; founder had a unique political career in MCA; jailed in 1987 in Singapore on breach of trust charges.
Teo Soo Chuan – Paramount	Property development, investments, plantations (palm oil).	1960s	
Group 3: Major Colonial-era groups (Malaya–Singapore)			
Tan Kah Kee	Rubber (plantations, processing, and trading), pineapples, rice trading.	1900–1910	Wealthiest colonial-era Chinese businessman in Malaya–Singapore for thirty years. Strong KMT supporter and active community leader and educational benefactor.
Lee Kong Chian	Rubber (founder of Lee Rubber), banking (OCBC)	1920s	Son-in-law of Tan Kah Kee, father of Lee Weng See. Close links with British authorities.
Aw Boon Haw	Chinese medicines ("Tiger Balm"), newspapers, banking.	1920s	Wealthy Singapore firm to 1960s.
Tang Cheng Lock – Unitac Plantations	Shipping, rubber plantations.	1880s	From old-established Malacca family; prominent in MCA politics 1940s–50s; son, Tan Siew Sin, was long-time finance minister in 1960s–70s.
Tan Lark Sye	Rubber trading, misc.	1920s	Leading Singapore community leader in late colonial era; prominent in 1950s; later deprived of citizenship by PAP for alleged pro-Communist sympathies.

Col. H. S. Lee	Tin, banking, misc.	1920s–1930s	Major tin interests in 1920s–30s; leading MCA-Alliance minister; first finance minister of Malaya.

Note:
[a] The term property development also embraces hotels and real estate.
[b] OCBC is Singapore-based, as also Lee Rubber, although the main plantations and other assets of the latter are in Malaysia.
[c] Khoo Tek Puat was active in business in Malaysia in 1960s–70s but is now based mainly in Singapore and elsewhere.

Sources: For Thailand, Krirkiat and Yoshihara, *Business Groups in Thailand*, Yoshihara, *Rise of Ersatz Capitalism*, Suehiro, *Capital Accumulation in Thailand*; for Indonesia, Sondang, "100 Toko Milyarder Indonesia," *Fokus*, May 10, 1984, Robison, *Indonesia*; for Malaysia, Lim, *Ownership and Control*, Tan, *Income Distribution*, Searle "Changing Character of the Malaysian Elite."

20

THE TRANSFORMATION OF MALAYSIAN BUSINESS GROUPS

Sieh Lee Mei Ling

Malaysia's New Economic Policy (NEP), introduced in 1971, has been widely regarded as a unique and bold attempt in social engineering by a young developing country. Prompted by the racial riots of 1969, which marked a watershed for the country's social and economic development, the NEP replaced policies which since independence in 1957 had emphasized growth from private sector investment, supplied primarily by foreigners and non-indigenous races. Despite early attempts to promote Bumiputera (Malays and other indigenous) participation in commerce and industry through opening up new land for rubber and oil palm, and through education, financial assistance, and business projects, it was evident that the Bumiputera, who were concentrated in the backward rural economy, needed far more stimulus if they were to play a substantial part in the modern sectors thus far dominated by non-Bumiputera.

The NEP, as set down in the Second Malaysia Plan (1971–1975), had two main objectives. First, it aimed to eradicate poverty irrespective of race; second, it intended to restructure Malaysian society so as to reduce and eventually eliminate the identification of race with economic function. Occupational division along racial lines was believed to be a root cause of economic inequality and social discontent, and the ultimate goal was to foster national unity through economic redistribution so as to reduce inter-racial imbalances in all spheres including income and wealth.[1] As a prime means to this end, the policy makers sought to develop a Bumiputera business middle class over a twenty-year period.

One clear result of the NEP's implementation is that the free enterprise philosophy which Malaysian governments had previously endorsed was discarded in favor of massive direct state intervention aimed at creating a Malay capitalist class. In the early 1970s numerous and diverse public enterprises were established in pursuit of the grand goals of restructuring society, correcting economic imbalances, bridging disparities between Bumiputera and non-Bumiputera, developing and providing employment in rural areas,

Source: *Southeast Asian Capitalists*, Ruth McVey (editor), Cornell University Southeast Asia Program, Studies on Southeast Asia,1992, pp. 103–26.

decentralizing industrial growth, eliminating poverty, and creating far more opportunities for Malays in the commercial and industrial sectors.

Fueled by the high rates of growth of the 1970s, the NEP booked considerable success in its first decade. Poverty eradication efforts such as new land schemes, education and training institutions, and loan facilities for housing and small businesses benefitted the Bumiputera population to such an extent that non-Malays felt hard done by. The NEP demanded that by 1990 Bumiputera own and manage at least 30 percent of the country's commerce and industry in all sectors, and that employment by occupational categories should reflect the country's racial composition. Efforts to document the achievement of these goals have been hampered by such problems as inconsistent definitions for classifying statistics and the use of nominees in stock ownership; but data by sectors from the Fifth Malaysia Plan (1986–1990) indicate that already by mid-1985 Bumiputera owned 69 percent of domestic banking and financial institutions and at least 32 percent of the plantations.

Undoubtedly, then, the NEP brought about major structural changes that affect the way Malaysians live, and the consequences of this have already been the subject of much study.[2] Some of the intentional results of these changes, such as the rise of a new breed of business elite with close state and political connections, have had other and unforeseen socio-economic consequences. This article will focus on the major socio-economic and political changes that have begun since the NEP's inauguration and will look in particular at the evolution of Malaysia's business elites. It will attempt to analyze the trends underlying corporate transformation by comparing the relatively new business groups formed after the NEP with the ones that existed before. These changes will then be illuminated by examining the bases on which the entrepreneurs formed their initial ties as well as the manner in which their affiliations have given rise to present business networks. Finally, the implications of these findings will be explored, with an eye to their socio-political relevance.

IMPORTANT CHANGES IN BUSINESS CHARACTERISTICS

It is already possible to see major transformations which the NEP has brought about in the way in which Malaysian business is carried on. Among these are: changes in the social sources of entrepreneurship, a shift in emphasis from single line of business to multi-industry conglomerates, a tendency for leadership to move from individual tycoons to professional management teams, a decline in growth through greenfield investment in favor of growth through acquisitions, a movement from reliance on internally generated funds to external borrowings or sale of shares, increasing dependence on public or state funds rather than private sources, a growing involvement of bureaucrats as businessmen, and the emergence of corporations whose goals are sociopolitical rather than purely a matter of business. In this section, we will give a brief description of these developments.

To consider first the changing character of the Malaysian business elite, we should note that prior to NEP the Malaysian economy was largely controlled by two main categories of businessmen, primarily foreigners (mainly European) and secondarily Chinese Malaysians. For a decade or so after independence in 1957, foreign investors maintained extensive control over a large part of the production of primary commodities, especially rubber and tin, as well as commerce through agency houses. The latter were large firms that specialized either in managing rubber or tin companies belonging to foreign investors or in acting as import-selling or export-purchasing agents for foreign manufacturers, or both—that is, being full-service agents that managed estates or mines and simultaneously acted as merchants. Among the well-known agency houses were Boustead & Company, Harrison and Crosfield, Sime Darby, Guthrie, and Harper Gilfillan. Agency houses constituted the major link between local raw material producers and Western markets for commodities on the one hand, and between Western manufacturers and the domestic market for manufactured imports on the other. This was made possible by factors that included the availability of a large supply of European capital, political control which facilitated the virtually unconditional entry of foreign investment, ease of contact with Western buyers of primary produce and with domestic buyers of finished goods, and knowledge-cum-technical expertise for managing large plantation and mining enterprises.

Local Chinese entrepreneurs also featured importantly as owners of rubber estates and tin mines, either as wealthy individuals, as partners, or as families or clans. Good examples of tycoons in the earlier part of the century were Tan Cheng Lock for rubber and Eu Tong Sen for tin. Around the time of independence prominent Chinese business family groups included those of Lee Kong Chian of Lee Rubber, and Heah Joo Siang of Heah Estate Ltd. But the more visible role of Chinese businessmen was that of intermediary at all levels between the producer and exporter for primary commodities and between the importer and consumer for manufactured goods. Chinese merchants operating as middlemen, wholesalers, and shopkeepers formed a substantial part of the economy's collection and distribution network. However, despite the Chinese' apparent dominance over domestic trade, it was foreign interests which held the real grip over the economy.

After the launch of the NEP in 1971, this dichotomy of foreign versus Malaysian business became less central than one involving Bumiputera interests on the one hand and non-Bumiputera, mainly Malaysians of Chinese and Indian origin, on the other. (Recent studies have concentrated on this latter contrast, foreign interests receiving relatively little attention despite their changing manner of involvement. We will deal here with all three major business categories—foreign, Bumiputera, and non-Bumiputera—but will give more attention to Malaysian groups.)

Business leaders before the NEP were easily identified with particular industries as their core economic activity. For example, individuals were labelled "sugar king" or "rice king" for their close association with those commodities and their leading position in the respective industries. Business expansion was usually within related industries, through either forward or backward linkages with the mother firm. Investment across sectors occurred, but it was not common or sizeable.

Under the NEP, business groups may not be readily identified with any specific industrial focus. Instead of a high degree of concentration within a particular sector, recent business leaders invest in divergent fields, priding themselves as builders of conglomerates with interests in a number of industries that may not be closely related. The Antah group and the Pernas group are examples of this tendency, which implies that the analysis of business groups can no longer be confined to a single sector.

The manner in which emerging corporate groups have accumulated wealth and economic power also appears different from that of older business groups. Although documentation of such processes is difficult, inferences can be drawn from media reports and general observation. It appears that whereas businesses previously tended to develop around a highly motivated entrepreneur, who built with pioneering and authoritarian leadership, this pattern is being replaced by investment-oriented management groups or cliques who rely on teams of professional, knowledgeable subordinates to suggest new directions.

Under the NEP, the manner of business expansion is also different. Former growth through real investment ventures into new industries, opening of markets, and expansion into vertically related fields at a relatively slow pace to allow steady consolidation is being replaced by financial takeovers, shifts into established and proven industries, rapid acquisition of franchise and marketing systems, and fast growth not only vertically or horizontally but also crosswise into totally unrelated areas of business. In other words, greenfield entrepreneurship has been virtually replaced by the acquisition of proven businesses.

Business groups in the earlier period depended heavily on funds generated internally for reinvestment and growth whilst striving for larger-scale operations which would improve efficiency and profitability. New business groups, however, turn to external sources of finance, either through borrowing or through stock floatation to the investing public. It is not uncommon to find takeovers of substantial corporate equity financed by loans advanced to businessmen. In fact, budding groups place particular emphasis on gaining control of a "listed vehicle," which will attract funds from small investors and thus enrich those at the center of the group. It is clear that, as far as finance is concerned, the older groups were more risk-averse than the newer ones. The latter, however, rely on business heterogeneity through diversified lines to dilute the financial risks they bear.

Another crucial difference between pre-NEP and post-NEP business lies in the source of their funds. Prior to the NEP, business capital had nearly always originated in the private sector, irrespective of whether it was foreign or local. Under the NEP, however, the scope of sourcing widened to include substantial public-sector funds as well as investment from cooperatives and such traditionally non-profit organizations as religious institutions.

State enterprises have existed since colonial days, when enterprises in the form of statutory corporations were employed to perform special activities thought best handled by organizations that were independent of the regular bureaucracy, for such reasons as administrative flexibility and economic expediency. For example, the Malayan Railway and the Central Electricity Board (now National Electricity Board), both established in 1949, supplanted government departments in control of the country's rail and power networks. In this period, negligible use was made of public enterprises for achieving economic development, a role left mainly to the private sector. Two notable exceptions were RIDA (Rural and Industrial Development Authority), established in 1953 and later replaced by MARA (Majlis Amanah Rakyat), and Felda (Federal Land Development Authority), which was started in 1956 to benefit the poorer peasantry.

In the period after independence but before the NEP (1957–1971), public enterprises were still seldom used as tools for national development, investment, and industrialization. Reliance continued to be placed on private-sector investment to mobilize resources for growth. New public enterprises set up in the period, such as MIDF (Malaysian Industrial Development Finance), NISIR (National Institute of Scientific and Industrial Research), FIDA (Federal Industrial Development Authority), Bank Bumiputera, and FAMA (Federal Agricultural Marketing Authority), were engaged in facilitative activities such as providing credit, coordinating, promoting, and advising industrial projects, as well as in regulatory tasks. Again, Felda and MARA were exceptions in being directly involved in business enterprises. The former provided capital for opening up new land for rubber and oil palm estates, while the latter, besides promoting Malay participation in commerce and industry via education, training, and financial assistance, ventured directly into such business enterprises as running a bus service and printing and selling batik.

Under the NEP, however, public sector or state capital has been liberally utilized to achieve the goals of redressing economic imbalances among the races and regions and of eradicating poverty. The Second Malaysia Plan categorically stated that the public sector "would participate more directly in the establishment and operation of a wide range of productive enterprises," admitting that "direct participation by the Government in commercial and industrial undertaking represents a significant departure from past practice."[3]

It is not uncommon to find such publicly funded business enterprises incorporated under the Companies Act and operating along the usual commercial lines, thus giving rise to state capitalism. This takes us to another fundamental difference before and after NEP, the involvement of bureaucrats as businessmen.

It is clear that the Malaysian government assumed a radically different economic role with the takeoff of the NEP. Between 1969 and 1972, no fewer than sixty-seven new public enterprises were created, the majority of them concerned with the NEP, and in the next few years the number increased to well over a hundred. Such "departmental enterprises" of "public corporations" served a host of socio-economic objectives, including the almost sacrosanct target that by 1990 "the Malays and other indigenous people will manage and own at least 30% of the total commercial and industrial activities in all categories and scales of operation." Following from this new approach of direct involvement in business, either in the name of the government itself or in trust for the Bumiputera, the role of bureaucrats was dramatically widened to include the management of capital, investment, production, marketing, and so on. Civil servants are no longer confined to administration concerning public services, provision of general infrastructural facilities, and planning and enforcing regulatory activities. Bureaucrats not only deal with businessmen and their problems across the counter but experience business problems themselves in running state enterprises. At the same time, with their established contacts within, and knowledge of the government machinery, many have become very successful businessmen upon their departure from the civil service, as we shall see later.

We have noted that the new, state-generated enterprises were largely created to serve the NEP's socio-political goals. This involvement of noneconomic purposes has been true also of nongovernmental business enterprise set up since the NEP began. Of course, business groups still seek to amass wealth and generate income, but there exists a distinction between older Malaysian business leaders and emerging ones in their motivation for coming together to undertake profit-making enterprises. Partly as a response to the NEP's effort to restructure society and create a Bumiputera business community, other groups (organized as political parties, cooperatives, or pressure groups for specific social causes such as education) have pulled together resources as capital for business ventures, the gains from which are to be channeled ultimately toward nonbusiness goals. In short, businesses are employed to champion social and even political causes rather than for the sole purpose of economic gain. The very existence of the large number of criteria for business association which we shall find in the next section, particularly those unrelated to traditional linkages such as family, clan, friendship, or fraternity, testifies to the prevalence of nonbusiness objectives.

THE EVOLUTION OF CORPORATE GROUPS

A close examination of secondary data, company reports, and newspaper accounts of business and corporate developments, together with discussions with relevant authorities and knowledgeable individuals, has revealed that dramatic changes have begun to take place in the linkages that give rise to business ties and affiliations and the motivations for the growth of strong business networks. At the risk of artificial segregation, this section attempts to discuss the transformation process under categories that range the historical forms of big foreign business and Chinese family enterprises through the new politically driven and state-backed businesses of the Malay elite, to recent business groups spawned as a response to the changing political-economic situation.

FOREIGN-OWNED ENTERPRISES

In spite of successful attempts to Malaysianize foreign holdings since the NEP, foreigners have continued to form business ties on the basis of their historical role and linkages. In the modern agricultural sector they have remained important as managers of rubber and oil palm estates and as large trading agents. In the manufacturing sector, companies established by foreign direct investment before and after independence persist, although many are increasingly sharing management control with Malaysians who have taken up equity and board positions.

We should bear in mind that the influence of the older foreign-owned companies is not restricted to the continuing presence of non-Malaysian personnel. The contribution of prominent pre-NEP business groups, most of which were composed of foreigners, lies not only in the capital that is still retained in the economy, but more importantly in the management systems, organizational skills, corporate behavior, and philosophies that they implanted as models for big business. For example, despite Sime Darby's "bringing home to Malaysia" its headquarters, Guthrie's well-known "dawn raid" at the London Stock Exchange to ensure Malaysian command, and Harrisons and Crosfield's major restructuring to transfer control of large tracts of rubber estates into the hands of locals, their new managements have built on the foundations and traditions that each corporation already possessed.

After substantial equity control over such large, long-established business groups (largely British and in plantations or mining) had passed into Malaysian hands, often in the form of state agencies in trust for Bumiputera, the Malaysian government directly or indirectly played a major role in guiding them. This oversight has often been achieved by placing a prominent political or bureaucratic figure in a commanding position in the company. It is not by accident that from the 1970s the chairmanship of the Sime Darby conglomerate was held by Tun Tan Siew Sin, a former minister of finance who remained a financial consultant to the government. (Tun Tan was simultaneously the chairman of ten other companies and a director of another six.) Also on the board of Sime Darby is Tun Ismail bin Mohamad Ali, who has impeccable civil service credentials, topped by being governor of the Bank Negara, Malaysia's central bank. Tun Ismail is also close to the center of political power, since he is a brother-in-law of the prime minister. The chief executive of Sime Darby, Tunku Dato' Ahmad bin Tunku Yahya, a prominent Malay executive of aristocratic descent, is also a director of the Bank Negara.

But apart from the older pattern of foreign direct investment, many new forms of foreign involvement appeared not long after independence. Foreigners, particularly American and Japanese multinationals, responded well to the government's drive towards industrialization. Japanese subsidiaries have been active in a range of manufacturing industries: iron and steel (Malayawata, Federal Iron Works), car assembly, and electrical appliances (Sanyo, Matsushita, Toshiba). American investments tended to be concentrated in petroleum and chemicals (Esso Malaysia) and later in the electronics industry. Japanese firms have been mostly joint ventures with local Malay, non-Malay, or government partners, while the Americans have by and large preferred to keep their companies wholly owned. Even so, many US companies have been allowed the advantages of pioneer status, preferential equity ratios, and benefits of locating in free trade zones.

Foreign investors have not relied wholly on this tolerance for non-Malaysian ownership, however. Partly in response to more stringent equity conditions under the NEP, especially after the Industrial Coordination Act of 1975, foreign investors, including transnational corporations, began to employ other devices for exerting control over their business interests. Management contracts, licensing agreements, royalty payments, and contracts for technology are particularly widely used. A good example is the set of agreements drawn up between Heavy Industries Corporation (Hicom), a Malaysian government company, and Mitsubishi Motor Corporation of Japan for the national car and other industrial projects.[4]

We can see in Hicom's leadership a pattern of political-bureaucratic involvement similar to that marking the indigenization of the older foreign-owned companies. The corporation is currently under the chairmanship of Tan Sri Jamil Mohamad Jan, who is the former chairman of the Malaysian Industrial Development Authority (MIDA).[5] He is also involved in the management of other business organizations with state interests, such as Kontena Nasional and the Armed Forces Fund. A number of other individuals close to political and government leaders are in direct control over growing corporations, the majority of them acting as directors in several companies. They thus not only interlock firm to firm but also link economic power in the private sector, including foreign sources, with political power in the public sector.

CHINESE FAMILY BUSINESS

The other major source of pre-NEP entrepreneurship were Chinese tycoons and family businesses. Family has traditionally been a significant force that spurred Chinese entrepreneurs and united them around common business goals; even before Malaysian independence there were large enterprises that originated in a Chinese family or group of closely related families. Among the well known longer-established groups are those of the Lee family (Lee Rubber, Lee Pineapple, Lee Biscuit, and the Lee Foundation); the family of Tan Chin Tuan (Overseas Chinese Banking Corporation), which works closely with the Lee family in Singapore and in Malaysia; the Yeo family (Yeo Hiap Seng); and the Kwek family (the Hong Leong Group). There are also less widely publicized families with substantial business interests, such as the Teo family of Paramount Malaysia, which developed the large housing estates of Paramount Garden, Damansara Utama, and Damansara Jaya; the Teh family of Malayan Flour Mills; the Kuok family of Kuok Brothers and the Kuok Foundation; and the Lim family of the Genting group.

The equity requirements of the NEP have meant that family business control, which was for so long jealously guarded through marriages, adoption, and other means, has had to adapt to the new socio-political environment. We can see the results of this in the business networks of the Kuok brothers, who rose meteorically to become owners of one of the largest and richest plantation, mining, and hotel conglomerates in the region. They have gone into joint ventures with other Chinese families, such as the Chan and Teh families in Selangor Dredging Bhd., and also with non-Chinese businessmen such as Datuk Ibrahim of Associated Plastic Industries, with state governments such as Selangor SEDC and Johore SEDC in property development projects, and with foreign groups in shipping and hotel ventures[6].

The need to rely on non-family linkages is also illustrated in a venture of recent vintage that is becoming one of Malaysia's largest corporations, Genting Bhd. Incorporated in 1968 with an authorized capital of M$800 million, of which slightly over a quarter is paid-up,[7] the company operates a tourist resort at Genting Highlands along with land and real-estate development, transportation services, tour promotion, recreation and amusement services, and recently agricultural activities. Genting Bhd.'s chairman and managing director is Tan Sri Lim Goh Tong, and the business centers on his family. However, it is important to observe that the management includes highly influential political-bureaucratic figures. On the board of directors are Tan Sri Haji Mohamad Noah bin Omar, the former speaker of the lower house of parliament (he is also the father-in-law of two former prime ministers, the late Tun Razak and Tun Datuk Hussein Onn); Tan Sri Haji Abdul Kadir bin Yusof, a former minister of law and attorney general; Nik Hashim bin Nik Yusof, a prominent lawyer-banker; and Tan Sri Chong Hon Yan, a former minister of health and secretary-general of the Malayan Chinese Association (MCA).

POLITICALLY CONNECTED NON-BUMIPUTERA ENTERPRISES

The adaptability of Chinese businessmen has been demonstrated not only by this opening up of family-controlled companies but also by the parallel emergence of entrepreneurs who have specifically concentrated on exploiting political connections to achieve business objectives. Under the NEP many Malaysians, including those of Chinese descent, have recognized that wealth may come from the pursuit of political positions as well as through the more orthodox capitalist pattern of political power proceeding from the acquisition of wealth.

Amongst the Chinese, the most visible expression of politically based entrepreneurship was Multi-Purpose Holdings Bhd., a public listed company incorporated in 1975 with a paid-up capital of M$450,616,949.[8] Its largest shareholder, owning 40.9 percent of the equity, was the Koperatif Serbaguna Malaysia (KSM), one of the country's biggest cooperatives with membership approaching a quarter of a million individuals. (Subsequently, the KSM was among twenty-three cooperatives whose activities were frozen by the Bank Negara for dubious collection of deposits from the public.) Commonly referred to as the "business arm" of the MCA, Multi-Purpose was supported by a host of Chinese guilds and associations. Initially, its numerous subsidiaries operated under the chairmanship of Datuk Lee San Choon, a past president of the party, and its managing directorship was held by Tan Koon Swan during the time he was MCA president.

The nearly forty companies in the MPH group have engaged in the cultivation of oil palm, rubber, and cocoa; in processing and marketing these and other crops; importing and distributing consumer goods, fertilizers, chemicals, building materials, and engineering equipment; general engineering and contracting; manufacture of scientific instruments and electrical goods; general insurance; and shipping. The most well-known subsidiary, listed on the Kuala Lumpur Stock Exchange, is Mulpha International Trading Corporation Bhd. As we might expect, both Multi-Purpose and Mulpha share several common board members drawn from the upper echelons of the MCA party hierarchy. Until 1988, boards of the two conglomerates included Senator Kee Yong Wee, Senator Datuk Loh Fook Yen, Senator Datuk Choo Ching Hwa, and several other prominent politico-businessmen.

The entrepreneurial genius of Multi-Purpose Holdings, Tan Koon Swan, had been actively involved in the corporate scene since the early 1970s, controlling several large companies under the Supreme Corporation (former Sungei Way Dredging) group. Through an intricate merger scheme with Textile Corporation and Grand Ocean Development, the former became the controlling shareholder of Supreme, with 49.8 percent of the equity, and was renamed Grand United Holdings (GUH).[9] Subsidiaries of the group engaged in licensed finance operations, credit and leasing, general insurance, property development, property investment, and agro-based industries. Tan Koon Swan had a personal stake of 30.6 percent in GUH, while his family-owned companies held an additional 29.6 percent.[10] In 1985, GUH acquired 22.3 percent in Pan-Electric Industries (Pan-El) and subsequently became entangled in that firm's financial disaster.[11] As part of a rescue scheme, shares in GUH were bought up by UNICO Holdings Bhd., whose directors were prominent Chinese businessmen involved in both Multi-Purpose and Mulpha, among them Senator Kee Yong Wee; Tan Sri Wee Boon Ping (acting as chairman), who is the president of the Associated Chinese Chamber of Commerce and Industry; Datuk Wong Tok Chai, business advisor to the Standard Chartered Bank and managing director of the Amoy Canning Corporation;[12] and Datuk Koh Pen Ting, chairman of Allied Malayan Development.[13] As we can see, the wielding of political influence for business opportunities, profits, and as a defense against business failure is not confined to Bumiputera.

Political connection is not a guarantee of success, however. In 1986 Multi-Purpose reported a loss of nearly M$200 million, of which M$131 million was attributed to Promptship Holdings, a shipbuilding subsidiary.[14] Tan Koon Swan found himself convicted of Criminal Breach of Trust (CBT) by a Singapore court, several other politico-entrepreneurs found it necessary to depart the leadership of Multi-Purpose, and, to ensure the conglomerate's survival, it was placed under the management of a new board headed by a non-politician, Robert Kuok Hock Nien (of the Kuok Brothers).

The Indian community has produced an equivalent political-business organization, Maika Holdings Bhd. This is the chief corporate vehicle of the Malaysian Indian Congress (MIC), the Indian faction of the ruling Barisan Nasional government, and is under the chairmanship of Senator D.P. Vijandran, a lawyer who is the vice-president of the MIC and chairman of MIC Youth.[15] Also on its board are such prominent Indian political figures as Tan Sri G.K. Rama Iyer, secretary-general of the Ministry of Primary Industries. Maika is envisaged as a symbol of Indian socio-economic progress and a means of developing Indian corporate management personnel and entrepreneurs. An example of this ambition is its attempt to establish itself in the banking industry. The president of the MIC, Datuk Samy Velu, tried —unsuccessfully—to negotiate on its behalf the purchase of the Indian government's one-third stake in the United Asian Bank (UAB).[16] In the plantation sector Maika was more successful, expanding by acquiring Tumbuk Estates, a 386–hectare oil palm estate, for M$13 million.[17] As it had become "fashionable" to dabble in property development, Maika participated in a low-cost housing project, and it owns a 10 percent interest in the Fleet Group's Sistem Televisyen Malaysia Bhd.(STMB).

MALAY FAMILY BUSINESSES

The most interesting of the new sources of entrepreneurial activity are perhaps those which have emerged among the Bumiputera. Here family businesses have been much less important than among the Chinese; they have mostly developed under the NEP and have centered on that segment of the indigenous population with greatest access to resources: the royal families. In the post-independence period the sultans of Malaysia's nine royally ruled states have been sufficiently powerful to affect decisions in their territories, especially those pertaining to land. Moreover, the royal privilege of awarding highly valued titles, such as *datuk*ships, to deserving subjects—including successful businessmen—ensures the perpetuation of a patronage system centering on the royal households. The prestige conferred by a title is much sought after as a source of influence, connections, privileged access to information, and advantage in obtaining permits and licenses and winning government contracts. Moreover, some corporations use the appointment of royalty to their boards as a token of compliance with the NEP desideratum of Malay participation—after all, members of the ruling families are no less Bumiputera than their subjects. Under these social and political circumstances, high-born Malays can profit greatly by playing the role of businessmen. Several corporate groups based on royal families have been founded, and more will doubtless evolve. Time will be the best test of their viability, but we might look at a few of the more prominent in order to get an idea of their character and substance.

Among the best known is Antah Holdings, an investment holding and management company belonging to the royal family of Negri Sembilan. It was first incorporated in 1976 as a joint venture between Syarikat Pesaka Antah, the family's investment company, and the Hong Kong firm, Jardine Matheson. From the start the royal participants ensured their domination, first by owning 54 percent of the equity through Pesaka Antah, and secondly by placing immediate family members in major board and management positions—all this despite the fact that Jardine Matheson, with 46 percent of equity, provided the capital, technical know-how, and executive input for actual operation. Antah Holdings turned public in 1983 and obtained listing on the Kuala Lumpur Stock Exchange three months later, thus gaining access to external funds. With Tuanku Naquiyuddin ibni Tuanku Ja'afar, eldest son of the current ruler, as chairman, the company expanded rapidly into many fields, with thirty subsidiaries and associate companies. The managing director of Antah Holdings, Tuanku Imran, is a brother of Tuanku Naquiyuddin; also active in the business is Tuanku Dara Naquirah, the sultan's daughter.[18] The business activities of its subsidiaries include the marketing and distribution of consumer products, building materials, hardware, technical products, electrical and office equipment, computer services and equipment, engineering contracting and equipment, aircraft and aviation equipment, medical supplies and equipment, industrial security, publication of telephone directories, oilfield equipment supplies and services, dental supplies, water-treatment engineering, advertising agency, insurance claims and settlements, shipping agency, equipment leasing, safes and security-equipment manufacturing, travel and tourism, car-park management, reinsurance brokerage, air freight forwarders, color television rental, and engineering design and project management.

Antah Holdings is not the only corporate group to have been spawned by Negri Sembilan royalty. Another fast emerging force is the Melewar group, controlled by Tunku Abdullah ibni Almarhum Tuanku Abdul Rahman (Tunku Panglima Besar), brother of the state ruler. Although some of the businesses in the group commenced more than twenty years ago, Melewar Corporation Sdn. Bhd. was incorporated only in November 1981, with a paid-up capital of M$35 million. Day-to-day decisions are made by the group's managing director, Tunku Iskandar, son of Tunku Abdullah. Its subsidiaries are engaged in investment, general trading, design engineering, real-property development, manufacturing, and services, particularly transport and tourism. In 1986 Melewar expanded into insurance, acquiring a stake of 60 percent in the Malaysian American Assurance Bhd. (now known as Malaysian Assurance Alliance Bhd.),[19] and plans were made to inject Melewar's holding of 20 percent of MBF Finance Bhd., a public listed finance company, into the new venture. In general, Melewar seems to adopt a consolidating approach, strengthening existing businesses rather than moving into new areas.[20] For instance, the group's 32 percent interest in TDM Bhd., a public listed company involved in the cultivation, processing, and trading of palm oil and rubber, was sold off in 1986 to Terengganu state agencies.[21] Its purchase of 10 percent of Sports Toto, a betting company, is another example of the formation of royalty-bureaucratic-political business linkages, as 30 percent of Sports Toto is held by Makuwasa Securities, a company owned by the Ministry of Finance.[22]

Another well-known royally sponsored group, TAB Holdings Sdn. Bhd., was established in 1978 under the chairmanship of Tengku Tan Sri Ibrahim ibni Almarhum Sultan Sir Abu Bakar, better known as Tengku Ariff Bendahara of Pahang, brother of the sultan of that state.[23] The TAB group got started when Tengku Ariff Bendahara secured a large timber concession—not a difficult acquisition given royalty's authority over state lands. It grew rapidly on log extraction, sawmilling, timber impregnation, and the import and export of timber and wood-based products, carried out by TAB Timber Traders and Mentiga Forest Products. In addition, TAB Holdings moved into the construction industry with the formation of TAB FAIYIN Construction Sdn. Bhd., and diversified through joint ventures into related industries such as drilling and engineering. In the industrial sector, TAB controls 70 percent of TATAB Industries Sdn. Bhd. through its subsidiary TAB General Agencies Sdn. Bhd. The remaining 30 percent is held by TATA Industries of India.

TAB is also making inroads into the services sector, as exemplified by its control of the Kuantan Beach Hotel and its interest in United Asian Bank Bhd.[24] Nonetheless, since the death of its founding chairman in June 1987, the group's future appears uncertain.

Malay family participation in business has not been limited to royalty. There have long been smaller-scale family enterprises organized around a key proprietor or several partners, but large Malay family-based business groups organized along modern corporate lines are something new. Given the NEP's incentives for Malays to involve themselves in business, one would expect many families to take advantage of the opportunities available, but it is not as easy to find good examples of Malay family business as it is to find Malay directors, executives, and managers in groups based on other kinds of association—particularly those connected with military, government, and government-related corporations. Nevertheless, two family companies deserve mention. Unsurprisingly, they have strong political connections.

One is Bidara Holdings, 51 percent owned by Mazlan Harun, son of Datuk Harun Idris, former chief minister of Selangor. His younger sons, Ramlan Harun and Azman Harun, have 20 percent each, while Mazlan's wife accounts for the remaining 9 percent. With a paid-up capital of M$1 million, Bidara has interests in electrical goods assembly and retailing, brickmaking, property development, and motorcycle servicing, carried out by a battery of twenty-four companies.[25] In the mid-1980s Bidara diversified into feedmilling and soon appeared likely to emerge as the country's largest operator in that sector.

Another prominent Malay family-based corporate body is the Safuan Group. Its chief executive, Haji Mat Shah Safuan,[26] is also the executive of Konsortium Putra (M) Sdn. Bhd., and chairman of the Malay Housing Developers Association. A businessman in his own right, he is also a member of the UMNO Setapak division and chairman of UMNO Kampung Pindah division,[27] and hence he enjoys the advantages of political connection. The Safuan group has done well in property and housing development, with projects implemented through four main subsidiaries.

MALAY POLITICO-ENTREPRENEURS

As we have seen, politically connected business groups have sprung up rapidly in the NEP period, resulting in large conglomerates which blur the distinction between business and politics. They are visible as Bumiputera-based or non-Bumiputera based companies, under the patronage of political parties organized primarily along racial lines. The Malays have been uniquely well placed to take advantage of political connections, and it is this kind of business that has been the main fount of Malay entrepreneurship under the NEP.

Perhaps the most notable example of Malay politico-business enterprise is the Fleet Group Sdn. Bhd., established in 1976 with a paid-up capital of M$55,699,805.[28] Representing the interests of the ruling Malay component of the National Front government, the UMNO party, the Fleet Group acquired control of the country's major newspaper-publishing company, the New Straits Times (M) Bhd. But UMNO did not stop with this politically important asset, for the group has moved into several service industries, especially within the financial sector. It participates in insurance, commercial banking, leasing, car rental, and travel,[29] and, under the leadership of its former chairman, Daim Zainuddin (minister of finance until 1991 and a close friend of the prime minister), it also bought up shares in the corporate sector. In 1983, the Fleet Group ventured into an entirely new business through the formation of Sistem Televisyen Malaysia Bhd. (STMB, widely known as TV3), with an issued share capital of M$10 million.[30] As with other companies in the group, the STMB'S board comprises UMNO politicians and persons close to those at the pinnacle of political power. One is Datuk Syed Kechik, a lawyer turned businessman whose career started in the Kedah UMNO with the first prime minister, Tengku Abdul Rahman Putra Al-Haj, and who later became the right-hand man of Tun Mustapha, former chief minister of Sabah, heading the resource-rich Sabah Foundation.[31] Another distinguished STMB director—and its current chairman, replacing Daim Zainuddin—is Mohamad Taufik bin Tun Dr. Ismail, son of the late, highly regarded deputy prime minister.

Daim Zainuddin's astounding business success has been widely attributed to his close association with the prime minister. He conducts his businesses through two family-owned companies, Daan Sdn. Bhd. and Dani Sdn. Bhd., both of which are under the management of Daza Holdings. Until the mid-1980s both these companies were controlled by Daim's brother, Abdul Hamid Zainuddin, together with close business associates such as Low Chan Tian, Zain Azhari (the present secretary-general of the Ministry of Finance), and Azmi Wan Hamzah (who was later appointed chief executive of Malayan Banking Bhd.). Daan and Dani also successfully acquired a 40.7 percent stake in UMBC (United Malayan Banking Corporation) in exchange for Daim's 51 percent interest in Malaysian French Bank Bhd.[32]—a deal finalized just a week before Daim was appointed finance minister and before the Bank Negara announced a policy forbidding individuals or family-owned companies from owning more than 10 percent of the equity in a local bank or finance company.

Another Malay, politically based business group is Syarikat Permodalan Kebangsaan (SPK), sometimes referred to as the "pnvate sector investment arm" of the government. SPK has diversified into various business activities, such as transport (S.J. Kumpulan Bhd., Nakufreight (M) Sdn. Bhd.), property (Bandar Raya Development Bhd.), manufacturing, finance, plantations, and mining. Under the leadership of its current chairman, Datuk Abdullah Ahmad, a politician turned businessman, SPK has succeeded in acquiring large shareholdings in several financial institutions. Datuk Abdullah, the current chairman of UMNO's Kok Lanas division in Kelantan, was a deputy minister in the Prime Minister's Department in the 1970s, but then served five years as a political detainee under the Internal Security Act. Other members of the SPK board include Tuan Haji Annuar bin Jaffar, a director of Bank Rakyat First Merchant Bankers and former financial controller of Kumpulan Perangsang Selangor Bhd.; Tuan Haji Mat Sari bin Haji Hamin, managing director of Sarikon Sdn. Bhd., Dato' Mohamad Tahir bin Haji Abdul Rahim, and Ahmad bin Abdul Rahman.[33]

BUREAUCRATIC ENTREPRENEURS

In addition to politicians who have used their connections as a basis for business enterprises, Malays have become businessmen by virtue of their role as civil servants. The entry of bureaucrats onto the Malaysian business and commercial scene was not entirely unknown before the NEP, for even prior to independence government funds had been utilized for operating commercial enterprises, with the ultimate objective of achieving social goals. For instance, the Malaysian Building Society Ltd. and its predecessor, the Malaya Borneo Building Society Ltd., was an important financier of housing projects and rental schemes, particularly for much-needed low-cost housing. In 1953, the Majlis Amanah Rakyat (MARA) was established, initially as the Rural Industrial Development Authority (RIDA), to assist the economic development of the Malay community in diverse fields, including the nurturing of small Malay entrepreneurs. Thus the way was paved for public enterprises to enter into what was otherwise seen as the private sector. Despite the overall success of MARA in the economic uplift of the Malays, certain MARA businesses have tended to operate like government departments—not a surprising outcome when business' financial objectives are tempered with social goals, when executives are bent towards public administration procedures rather than normal business practices, and when managers tend to be plucked off the senior ranks of the civil service rather than recruited from the relevant market. It is therefore not difficult to understand how the MARA group of companies suffered a loss of M$8 million in 1982.[34]

Examples of the infusion of bureaucrats may be seen from the leadership of MARA: Tan Sri Abdul Aziz bin Yeop, MARA's chairman in 1976/77, boasted an impressive string of political and civil-service credentials, having been a member of Parliament for Padang Rengas, served as high commissioner to the United Kingdom, and was permanent secretary to the Ministry of Agriculture.[35] Similarly, MARA's current chairman, Datuk Abdul Rahim bin Abu Bakar, is a former Menteri Besar (state chief minister) of Pahang and deputy chairman of the state UMNO liaison committee. As Pahang's chief minister, Datuk Rahim also headed its State Economic Development Corporation (SEDC), a state-owned enterprise.

Two other pre-NEP groups of state companies should be mentioned, for they were of immense significance in introducing bureaucrats into powerful corporate circles. Both the Bank Bumiputera and Pernas (Permodalan

Nasional, National Corporation) were founded much later than the MARA and have differed from it in that, notwithstanding their origin and connections, their executives and managers strive towards financial objectives, with economic efficiency as a major (though not sole) consideration. They employ modern business methods for analysis and decision making, and are oriented towards market competition. As players in the private sector, they are subject to fewer bureaucratic constraints, to the extent that their power has been abused—notoriously so in the corruption-ridden Bumiputera Malaysian Finance (BMF) scandal in Hong Kong, which underlined the need to temper the management power of such enterprises with public accountability.[36]

Bank Bumiputera was established in October 1965 as a wholly government-owned bank; within ten years it had become the second largest bank in the country. Its first chairman was Tengku Razaleigh Hamzah, then a rising star in UMNO and highly favored for the top political leadership; subsequently, he became the first Malay finance minister and then minister of trade and industry. His successor at Bank Bumiputera, Senator Tan Sri Kamarul Ariffin, was simultaneously president of the National Chamber of Commerce and Industry of Malaysia. The third chairman, Dr. Nawawi bin Mat Awin, a former chairman of MARA, was appointed amidst the BMF crisis in mid-1982; he has since become chairman of the Malaysian Chamber of Commerce. With well over 5,000 employees in the bank, not counting those engaged in its many subsidiaries, the Bank Bumiputera certainly provided an opportunity for Malays to gain business experience. But the lack of effective control over the way it handled its government capital, aggravated by opportunities arising from access to information and to networks created by the presence of multiple directorships within the group of companies, gave rise to unethical practices which culminated in a crisis within its Hong Kong subsidiary, Bumiputera Malaysia Finance. With losses amounting to M$25 billion, the government was forced to intervene, replacing the BMF board with a new one headed by Tan Sri Basir bin Ismail.[37] The bank was bailed out by Petronas, the state oil company, which took over the entire equity of the PNB (the national investment company, of which more later).

The Pernas (National Corporation) group has had a less chequered career. Established in late 1969, it deals with direct and indirect investment in general trading, plantations, shipping, hotels, real estate, engineering, construction, manufacturing, and financial services. Heading the group is Tunku Dato' Shahriman, a former chairman of United Malayan Banking Corporation (UMBC).[38] Its managing director, Datuk Abdul Rahman bin Hamidon, was an assistant district officer of Kota Tinggi, then an assistant secretary in the Ministry of Commerce and Industry, and finally served in the Ministry of Agriculture prior to his appointment with Pernas. The degree to which Pernas has been successful in the development of entrepreneurship, investment, and management skills is discernible from its positive public image, attributable to the professionalism and integrity of those at its helm.

However, its financial performance cannot be meaningfully gauged, due to the fact that there has been an intermittent equity transfer of its subsidiaries to other government investment corporations such as the PNB. What is perhaps most important to bear in mind from the viewpoint of this paper is the great power which Pernas and other state enterprises have given to their "new princes," officials who control vast assets although they own no shares in the group. Many of these bureaucatic entrepreneurs obtained their formative business experience in the boom period of the 1970s, and it has not always been easy for them to adapt to less expansive times.

These examples notwithstanding, direct government participation in business before the NEP was limited in scope if not in depth. The new policy changed this, bringing a proliferation of government-owned and -controlled private limited companies. For instance, under the Ministry of Land and Regional Development alone, eighty-one subsidiaries, corporations, and joint ventures have been set up by the ministry's eleven agencies.[39] Although the exact number of government-owned companies is not easy to ascertain via public records, Minister of Finance Daim Zainuddin gave an idea of their significance when, admonishing ineffective directors serving on their boards, he referred to the existence of more than 900 government companies and statutory organizations involved in business activities. The government has provided loans worth M$2.5 billion to government-owned companies and M$14 billion to statutory organizations; in addition, it has stood guarantee for loans amounting to M$12 billion taken out by such bodies.[40]

Despite the fact that many of these companies are far from doing well—a statement by former Auditor-General Tan Sri Ahmad Noordin bin Zakaria revealed that 350 of them were suffering continuous losses[41]—many of Malaysia's top firms are government controlled. They include six out of the top ten tax-paying companies and seven out of the top ten employers; among them are Petronas, Harrison Malaysia Plantation Bhd., Malaysian Airlines System (MAS), and Malayan Banking Bhd. Through these, too, a new business elite is being spawned from among the bureaucrats. The common practice of secondment or transfer of civil servants to government-owned companies appears likely to accelerate the intermingling of bureaucrats and business. Let us look somewhat more closely at two instances of this, the well-known National Equity Corporation or Permodalan Nasional Berhad (PNB) and the rather more mysterious investment arm of the government, Makuwasa Securities Sdn. Bhd.

The PNB was incorporated in 1978 with an authorized capital of M$200 million, of which half was paid up two months later. Its main function was to acquire a portfolio of shares in limited companies to be held in trust for subsequent sale to individual Bumiputera investors through Amanah Saham Nasional (ASN), the national unit trust scheme.[42] Although the PNB is intended to be totally commercial in its manner of operation, its leadership is saturated with staunch government loyalists who are powerful, well-connected senior bureaucrats, military, and political veterans. The chairman of PNB's seven-man board, Tun Ismail bin Mohamad Ali, brother-in-law of the current prime minister, is the former governor of the Bank Negara and the strongman of the country's banking and financial system. Unsurprisingly, Tun Ismail also presides over the boards of other large companies controlled by the PNB, such as the ASN (the national trust, mentioned above) and Harrison Malaysia Plantation Bhd. Also on the PNB board is Dato Jaffar bin Hussain, the chairman of the Malayan Banking Corporation, the largest, government-owned local bank. So, too, is the former chief of staff of the armed forces, General Tan Sri Ibrahim bin Ismail—an example of the evolving close affiliation between military and bureaucratic managerial elites, of which more later. Needless to say, the presence of the secretary-general of the Ministry of Trade and Industry and the governor of the Bank Negara on the PNB board facilitates the allotment of new company shares and the provision of financial resources to acquire them.

The immense economic power vested in these few men is best measured by the assets accumulated by the PNB and ASN. In the first quarter of 1986 their total investments in the corporate sector amounted to over M$6 billion at cost.[43] Of this, M$2.8 billion was transferred to the ASN to be distributed as trust units for ASN investors, who have virtually no control over the assets they own. As a group, PNB-ASN holdings represent approximately 45 percent of the M$13.5 billion worth of Bumiputera shares in the corporate sector. The intense concentration of power is further seen in the fact that decisions by the few persons constituting the board are made on behalf of over two million Bumiputera (representing about 43 percent of eligible investors), whose interests they are supposed to safeguard.[44] Further, policy directions set by the board members influence not only subsidiaries where the PNB-ASN hold a controlling interest but all the 140-odd companies whose stocks appear in their portfolios. With such vast financial resources firmly held in the hands of a government-backed elite, it is no wonder that PNB investments have grown at such a phenomenal pace as to enable its wholly owned subsidiary ASN to boast of being the largest unit trust scheme in the world.[45]

A closer examination of the relationship between the PNB and ASN shows that the latter is buffered from poor results or losses by the policy of having only good performers transferred to it. In turn, political interests protect the PNB's viability. This was demonstrated by the scheme whereby the Bank Bumiputera was saved from the BMF loans scandal in Hong Kong. As we have seen, the state oil company Petronas had to put out M$2.2 billion[46] in a rescue package which effectively transferred ownership of Bank Bumiputera from PNB to the resource-rich Petronas. The bail-out met with strong criticisms, including those from the then auditor-general, Tan Sri Ahmad Noordin bin Haji Zakaria.[47] The affair clearly showed that the basis of power for bureaucratic business groups (and this is true of all vintages and types) rests ultimately with their political masters. The vital question, therefore, is the effect political changes may have on the strength and continuity of such business leadership.

If the PNB illustrates the vast scope and resources of bureaucratic capitalism, Makuwasa demonstrates the opportunity for anonymous activity that the bureaucratic-political business network provides. Makuwasa Securities Sdn. Bhd., a wholly government-owned private limited company,[48] was incorporated in June 1984 with an initial paid-up capital of M$2 increased to M$10 million two months later.[49] The company aroused curiosity because it used Ministry of Finance officials as nominees, called on the funds of the National Employees Provident Fund (EPF) to finance its stock-purchasing activities, and most of all because the reason for its existence was far from clear. Shares in thirteen companies that made new issues between June 1984 and April 1985 were acquired by the EPF; 70 percent of these were transferred to Makuwasa at the subscription price—below the market price—thus enabling Makuwasa to reap almost immediate gains by trading on the open market. In return, the EPF was to receive 10 percent per annum interest and handling costs when the advances were reimbursed and the right to 30 percent of its original investment. Trade unions were especially upset to discover the M$141 million paper loss suffered by the EPF in stock transactions over the one and a half years since the beginning of 1985. Reportedly Tan Sri Thong Yaw Hong, who had recently retired as chairman of EPF and secretary-general of the Ministry of Finance, was the head of Makuwasa. His position as the chairman of the Capital Issues Committee, which approves all new issues, is another illustration of the manner in which multiple appointments of certain individuals to key government positions concentrate power in the hands of a few.

It is evident that government-sponsored companies and public enterprises have succeeded in creating an elite that straddles business and government. This is true at the state as well as the federal level. The State Development Corporations (SEDCs) engage in a wide range of business enterprises. For example, the Selangor SEDC has extensive investment ventures in the field of mining, shipping, banking and finance, construction and engineering, transport, and property development. These activities are carried out through numerous subsidiaries, such as Kumpulan Perangsang Selangor Bhd. and Shah Alam Properties Sdn. Bhd. SEDCs are usually managed by highly experienced civil servants, who serve on boards chaired by the chief ministers themselves. Board members are often drawn from various federal government departments, thus forging extremely close ties between state and central administrators.

Clearly, the involvement of numerous—mostly Malay—civil servants in business through state-sponsored corporations, the government's encouragement of Malays to develop themselves as entrepreneurs, and the shortage of Bumiputera qualified for management positions in private corporations have placed civil servants at an advantage for entry into the business community upon retirement. Indeed, many resign prematurely from government service to benefit from more lucrative job offers in the private sector. From the viewpoint of the firms they join, their intimate knowledge of government machinery and close personal contacts with officials are valuable assets for winning public-sector contracts and avoiding red tape.

Let us illustrate this by tracing the career of one official who became a leading Malay businessman. Datuk Azman Hashim began his career as a chartered accountant with the Bank Negara in 1960. Six years later, he was appointed to the board of Malayan Banking, becoming its full-time executive director in 1971. He also started one of the first Bumiputera-owned audit firms, Azman and Company (subsequently renamed Azman, Wong, Salleh and Co.), which has a staff of about one hundred. Besides serving in various corporations in the public and private sectors, such as Pernas Securities, Malaysian Airlines System, Credit Guarantee Corporation, Tabung Haji Investment Panel, Malayawata Steel, Kompleks Kewangan Malaysia, and the Advisory Council of Bandaraya, Datuk Azman is active in professional bodies. He chaired the Malaysian Institute of Chartered Administrators and Secretaries and the Association of Borrowing Companies. In the banking sphere he also once headed Kwong Yik Bank and Finance, besides being a director of Malayan Finance, Mayban-Phoenix Insurance, and Aseambankers. Datuk Azman is currently the chairman and largest shareholder of Arab Malaysian Development Bhd., with a holding of 22.8 percent. His subsidiaries are engaged in merchant banking, finance, credit, and insurance in the financial sector; in property development in the construction sector; and in the production and export of cotton, polyester, viscose yarn, and finished fabrics in the manufacturing sector.

OTHER BASES FOR ASSOCIATION

The NEP-inspired businesses which we have so far considered have been based on the family, politics, or the state (and frequently all three). However, we must bear in mind that this is not the only source of local entrepreneurship, and we should consider some of the other bases for business association before we conclude. Most of them involve groups brought together by some perceived common interest. Such associations existed before the NEP, primarily in the Chinese community, where they were mostly oriented around clan and dialect groups, common trading interests, and school ties. The clan and dialect networks central to the Malaysian Chinese cultural heritage are often the nuclei from which other social, professional, and economic activities grow. Only since the NEP, however, have they been used for large-scale business purposes. This may be seen as part of the Chinese reaction to the threat which the NEP is perceived as posing to traditional businesses, a strategy to overcome government-sponsored business restrictions and communal discrimination. It also appears as part of a general trend towards the "corporatization" of Chinese business, for which an example was set by the MCA with its Multi-Purpose Holdings endeavor.

Most of the corporations based on clan and dialect ties are involved in property development, credit, lending, finance, and trading; they prefer low-risk projects that bring fast payback and constant profit. For example, Hok Lian Holdings Bhd, a company of the Hokkien community incorporated in 1981 with an authorized capital of M$100 million, of which M$12.5 million was paid-up, is engaged in housing development, plantations, credit, and leasing. Similarly, the Hakkas' Ka Yin Association established Ka Yin Holdings Bhd. in 1980 with M$10 million paid-up capital for ventures in property development and hire purchase. Fui Lian Holdings Bhd., started in 1982 with over $411 million capital paid in by members of the Fui Chew Association, is involved in credit and leasing, jewelry trading, and housing development. The Hainanese community's Kheng Chew Association launched Koperasi Mewah in 1978, a cooperative with total assets amounting to M$25 million and investments mainly related to housing development, credit, leasing, and insurance. Similar companies include Heng Ann Enterprise (M) Bhd. of the Heng Ann Association, Taipu Holdings Bhd. of the Taipu (Cha Yong) Association, the Holian Holdings Bhd. of the Hopo Association, and Koperasi Jasa Rakyat Bhd., a cooperative movement started by the Hokkien Association.

Another basis for Chinese entrepreneurial association has been common trade, both for the purpose of furthering the business sector concerned and for spreading members' risks through investment in other fields. Many small businessmen, believing that they have no access to official help, are very conscious of the need to make provisions of their own. Thus car dealers and car-financing companies, acting through their trade association, set up the Cafina Corporation Bhd. in 1978, with M$1.4 million paid-up capital; it is active in automobile insurance and related businesses, and also has property development as one of its objectives.

It is common for such groups to have investments managed by a board comprising prominent businessmen, not necessarily in the same field and sometimes including politically connected Malays. Thus the Selangor Hawkers and Petty Traders Cooperative Society Ltd. (Sakkap) has a strong team to oversee its members' funds of M$30 to M$40 million: its chairman is Tan Sri Wee Boon Ping, a timber tycoon and president of the Associated Chinese Chambers of Commerce and Industry of Malaysia; and Haji Mat Shah Safuan, chairman of the Malay Housing Developers Association, is deputy chairman. Other prominent directors include Datuk Loy Hean Heang, the chief executive of the Malaysia Borneo Finance group, and the lawyer Joseph Tan Boon Heng.[50]

Chinese chambers of commerce have long been focal points for Chinese businesses, but they have not usually gone directly into business themselves. Under the NEP they have begun to do so, however. The most prominent of these enterprises is Unico Holdings Bhd., a project of the Associated Chinese Chambers of Commerce and Industry of Malaysia. Formed in 1981, Unico has an authorized capital of M$100million, of which half is paid-up.

The company is in plantation, property, credit, leasing, and other minor lines.

Business association based on the "old school tie" is common to many countries, but in terms of Malaysian entrepreneurial development it is primarily a post-NEP development. Such groups provide a broader basis than the family in terms of resources and talent, and sometimes they also provide an opportunity for inter-racial participation. A notable example is Pilecon Engineering Bhd., which was formed by several engineering graduates of the University of Malaya and soon grew from a small bored-piling firm into a well-known construction company, undertaking major building and civil engineering projects in Malaysia, Singapore, and Brunei. With Datuk Abdul Rahim bin Haji Abdul Rahman as chairman of the board and Chong Kok Keong and Dr. Lim Yit Chow as directors, the company has ventured into condominium development projects, computer consultance for building-maintenance services (through a later-acquired subsidiary), and, with French collaboration, into international markets. A more modest specimen is Chung Ling Holdings Bhd., founded by the Chung Ling Old Boys Association of Penang to invest in credit, leasing, property, and housing-development businesses.[51]

Malay business associations based on group interests are new, linked to politics and the state, and highly geared to the NEP. Let us look briefly at two of the most interesting, identified with the military and religion. While these could be seen simply as part of the state capitalist apparatus, the fact that they represent groups which are highly conscious of their special interests, and that they dispose of considerable funds and political influence, makes it worth noting them separately.

The Armed Forces Provident Fund (Lembaga Tabung Angkatan Tentera or LTAT), established under the Tabung Angkatan Tentera Act 1973, is a source of great economic power for the military elite. Servicemen contribute 10 percent of their monthly wage, to which the government adds another 15 percent, for the purpose of providing superannuation benefits. The fund's portfolio of assets is distributed as follows:

Assets of the Armed Forces Provident Fund

	Amount invested (million ringgit)	*Percentage*
Corporate securities	416.7	45.1
Loans to private sector	29.6	3.1
Federal government securities	34.6	3.7
Cash and fixed deposit with domestic financial institutions	328.2	35.5
Other liquid and fixed assets	115.9	12.6
Total	924.4	100.0

Source: Bank Negara Malaysia, *Money and Banking* (Kuala Lumpur: Economics Department Bank Negara Malaysia, 1984).

It is interesting that as much as 45 percent is invested in corporate securities, while another 3 percent is extended as loans to the private sector. Obviously, this gives the fund's leadership considerable influence in the business world. An examination of LTAT's portfolio reveals that the fund managers have been investing in the plantation sector (Boustead Holdings), in manufacturing industries (Ericsson Telecommunications and Perwira Ericsson), and in banking and other service activities (Perwira Habib Bank, Chartered Merchant Bankers).

Until the mid-1980s LTAT board members were often related to the national political leadership, but later appointments have favored retired generals and other senior military or military-related officials. Chairman Tan Sri Zain Mahmud Hashim and his predecessor, Tan Sri Ibrahim Ismail, are retired generals,[52] while the earlier chairman (and still executive director) Datuk Salleh bin Yusof is a former director of Bank Rakyat and a partner of Azman, Wong, Salleh, and Co. Similarly, Tan Sri Abu Bakar Samad, the former secretary-general of the Ministry of Defense and later treasurer of the Ministry of Finance, was given a board position in Boustead and Ericsson upon his retirement in 1977.

Through its provident investment fund, the military leadership not only marshals considerable financial power but provides senior officers with the opportunity to gain expertise that will enable them to move rapidly into the business world upon retirement. It is therefore not suprising to find that business leaders derived from the military elite have been making an impact on the Malaysian business scene.

The other interesting category of Malay interest-based business association, religion, may seem incongruous given Islam's restriction of interest and profit making, but the Lembaga Urusan dan Tabung Haji (LUTH) has had some prominence as an investor on the corporate scene. A statutory body established by an Act of Parliament, LUTH is basically a trust fund for collecting and managing Malay savings to facilitate the pilgrimage to Mecca. Deposits in the fund, amounting to nearly M$200 million from well over 609 thousand savers,[53] have been invested in corporate securities. As an institutional investor, LUTH participates in the equity of no less than twenty-seven public companies listed on the Kuala Lumpur Stock Exchange.[54] An example is LUTH's share of Nestle Malaysia Holdings Sdn. Bhd.'s issued capital allocated to Bumiputera after Nestle's restructuring. To show how this feeds into and confirms the political-bureaucratic nexus, we might note that another 3 percent is owned by Toh Puan Norashikin, widow of the late deputy prime minister, Tun Dr. Ismail.[55] Her son, Taufik bin Tun Dr. Ismail, is one of the company's directors, thus forming a link with the UMNO-controlled Fleet Group, on whose board he sits.

IMPLICATIONS AND CONCLUSIONS

We have seen that the corporate vehicle has been used extensively under the NEP as a tool for social restructuring. The corporation as an institution has played a role in propelling Malays into the business world. Directors of different races do sit on the same corporate boards, and most large industries have workers of various races working side by side. At the same time, it is also clear that Bumiputera business endeavor remains heavily dependent on the government, and it would appear that considerably more business training and management skills are needed if Malays are to compete on their own.

Although the NEP has brought a narrowing of economic differences between races, it is no secret that there has been a significant increase in intra-racial inequality, as evidenced in income levels and asset ownership. Moreover, as a reaction to the NEP's emphasis on Malay welfare, non-Bumiputera have formed a large number of self-help institutions in the form of cooperatives, education funds, and community-based corporations. These have been on a much smaller scale than the government-backed Bumiputera institutions, and they have been notably unstable. In the mid-1980s the financial insolvency of many deposit-taking businesses, including cooperatives, further shook the confidence of non-Bumiputera in their ability to withstand the pressures of the NEP. This, together with capital flight by better-off Chinese, was an expensive lesson in the limits of employing the corporate form for social objectives.

We have seen that, rather than rely on nationalization to secure local command of resources, Malaysia has taken the more acceptable path of public issues of stocks and the acquisiton of corporate control, as exemplified in its buying-up of Guthrie stocks in the London markets. Such massive purchases cannot be conducted without full government support, and the consequence has been companies with substantial bureaucratic connections. Indeed, we have observed throughout this article the strong linkage of politics with business in Malaysia. This in itself casts doubt on the stability, performance, and future of the many new, politically connected business groups. We will only really be able to judge their viability when, over time, their particular political shelters are removed.

Perhaps the single most critical issue in the present-day corporate sector of Malaysia is that of control: internal business control over the deployment of assets by management, internal corporate control of management by shareholders, and external control by relevant sectors and authorities to ensure the acceptability of enterprises within the larger socio-economic system. We have seen that enormous economic power is wielded by corporate heads, regardless of the basis on which they first grouped together. To what extent does this power meet the essential criterion of being seen as legitimate, responsible, and accountable? Speculation and peculation marked Malaysian corporate development in the 1980s and have done much to dis-credit the corporation as an institution in the public's eye. A remedy is the more elusive because the government itself has become a business partner rather than keeping to its earlier claims to be impartial guardian of social equity and justice.

What are the reins available to check the phenomenal economic power concentrated in the hands of corporate leadership? Market forces, which are inextricably related to technological and organizational capabilities, do serve to check on efficiency and the achievement of corporate goals. But they usually come into play only when it is too late for them to be a means of controlling corporate behavior. Besides, there exist too many artificial obstacles, such as government intervention, for them to function effectively for this purpose. Nor does legal regulation offer great promise, however well it may serve elsewhere. In Malaysia the lawmakers have gotten too involved in the game themselves, and few officials have the courage and independence to enforce the controls that do exist. This is particularly so because the government has utilized corporations not only as a means of getting things done but also as an extended arm of bureaucratic power. Officials thus have an institutional interest in preserving corporate freedom from public scrutiny.

Self-regulation, widely employed in developed economies, has been attempted in Malaysia, for example in the early days of the securities industry. However, its success is highly dependent on the values of big-business leaders, and we find little consensus on standards of behavior among Malaysian entrepreneurs, or indeed within the society as a whole. So far, relevant business knowledge has been seen in terms of command over information and the ability to turn a profit, to the exclusion of ethics, social obligation, and responsible administration.

Social control of business behavior did not seem a critical issue as long as Malaysia's economic growth rate remained high. For one thing, the NEP was based on the assumption of a continually expanding economy. This depended on increased productivity and the efficient allocation and utilization of resources, hence on buoyant business activity. Besides, in a developing economy incentives for new industries and entrepreneurial endeavor generally were perceived as essential, and not too many questions were asked about how success was achieved. But, as we have seen, the bases for new business ventures in Malaysia have tended to be political and speculative rather than economically rational and productive. Can corporations based on elite political connections be useful for the reduction of poverty, income redistribution, and economic prosperity at large?

The prolonged recession of the 1980s, which witnessed heavy business losses, retrenchments, and failures, contraction of productive capacity, and a high rate of bankruptcies, resulted in a shrinkage of the economic pie. Even state and politically backed enterprises were not spared. The result was to expose some of the weaknesses of corporate development under the NEP, for the government could no longer ignore economic realities in favor of political connections. The misadventures of Tan Koon Swan and his stable of companies in the Pan-Electric group, the Makuwasa furore, the Multi-Purpose shakeout, the Bumiputera Malaysian Finance scandal (triggered by the collapse of the property market in Hong Kong), and the woes of many state-owned companies were all products not simply of hard times but of the inability of the government to camouflage the problems.

Compared to the family-owned businesses and partnerships of earlier years, the corporate form is a particularly powerful way of pooling capital and other resources. It offers greater scope for vision, the possibility of overcoming communal demarcations, and a way of integrating state and business interests. But if the interests of corporate profit are allowed to reign unchecked, without reference to social values, and if cooperation between government and business serves not to facilitate genuine enterprise but to shield the privileged from the consequences of mismanagement, then the ultimate consequences of the new form will be negative and divisive. As Adolf A. Berle Jr. aptly described, the corporation is "a commercial instrument of formidable effectiveness, feared because of its power, hated because of the excesses with which that power was used, suspect because of the extent of its political manipulations within the political state, admired because of its capacity to get things done."[56]

NOTES

1 Federation of Malaysia, *Second Malaysia Plan 1971–1975* (Kuala Lumpur: Government Printer, 1971).
2 See, for example, Sieh Lee Mei Ling, *Ownership and Control of Malaysian Manufacturing Corporations* (Kuala Lumpur: UMCB Publications, 1982); Tan Tat Wai, *Income Distribution and Determination in West Malaysia* (Kuala Lumpur: Oxford University Press, 1982); Lim Mah Hui, *Ownership and Control of the One Hundred Largest Corporations in Malaysia* (Singapore: Oxford University Press, 1981).
3 *Second Malaysia Plan*, p. 7.
4 Jomo Kwame Sundaram, ed., *The Sun Also Sets* (Petallng Jaya: INSAN Publications, 1983).
5 *Who's Who in Malaysia and Singapore 1983–84*, 15th ed., vol. 1 (Kuala Lumpur: Who's Who Publications Sdn. Bhd., 1983).
6 *Kuala Lumpur Stock Exchange Annual Companies Handbook*, vol. 10 (Kuala Lumpur: Kuala Lumpur Stock Exchange Press, 1984).
7 *New Straits Times*, February 14, 1986.
8 *Kuala Lumpur Stock Exchange Annual Companies Handbook*, vol. 10 (1984).
9 *The Star* January 25, 1986.
10 Ibid., February 18, 1986.
11 *New Straits Times*, January 18, 1986. The Pan-El crisis brought about a historic closure of both the Singapore and Kuala Lumpur stock exchanges for two days, resulting in a loss of confidence by bankers and investors. Pan-El was reported to be struggling with a debt of nearly 400 million Singapore dollars.
12 *Business Times*, July 15, 1985.
13 Ibid., December 6, 1985.
14 Ibid., June 13, 1986.

15 lbid., July 16, 1986.

16 *New Straits Times*, August 14, 1985. The attempt failed due to strong objections by the UAB's then chairman, Tengku Ariff Bendahara.

17 *Business Times*, July 30, 1985.

18 *Business Times*, August 14,1985. By 1985 members of the Negri Sembilan royal family directly commanded at least 31 percent of Antah's M$25 million paid-up capital, Jardine Matheson controlled 15 percent, Merchant Nominees 7.3 percent, Bapema Corporation 2.6 percent (Bapema is a subsidiary of the state investment corporation PNB; thus this links royal and government enterprises), and the Negri Sembilan Foundation 2 percent.

19 Ibid., March 5, 1986.

20 Ibid.

21 *The Star*, July 1, 1986.

22 Ibid., August 23, 1986.

23 *Kompass Buku Merah 1984–5* (Kuala Lumpur: Berita Kompass SIn. Bhd., 1984).

24 Tan Tat Wai, *Income Distribution*, p. 189.

25 *Business Times*, July 24, 1985.

26 *Who's Who in Malaysia and Singapore 1983–84*.

27 *Kuala Lumpur Stock Exchange Annual Companies Handbook*, 1985, vol. 2.

28 *Kompass Buku Merah 1985–86*, p. 182.

29 Ibid.

30 Ibid.

31 *Who's Who in Malaysia and Singapore 1983–84*, p. 309.

32. *Asian Wall Street Journal*, July 10, 1986.

33 *New Straits Times*, March 1, 1986.

34 *Business Times*, June 17, 1986.

35 *Who's Who in Malaysia and Singapore 1978–79*, p. 4.

36 See Jomo Kwame Sundaram, *BMF: The People's Black Paper* (Petaling Jaya: Insan Publication, 1986).

37 *Business Times*, February 19, 1986.

38 *Kompass Ruku Merah 1985–6*, p. 288.

39 *The Star*, July 2, 1986.

40 *Business Times*, July 25, 1986.

41 *The Star*, July 2, 1986.

42 Sieh Lee Mei Ling and Chew Kwee Lyn, "Redistribution of Malaysia's Corporate Ownership in the New Economic Policy," in *Southeast Asian Affairs 1985*, ed., Lim Joo Jock (Singapore: Institute of Southeast Asian Studies, 1985), p. 236.

43 *New Straits Times*, June 17, 1986.

44 *Business Times*, August 8, 1985.

45 Ibid., May 14, 1985.

46 *New Straits Times*, May 8, 1985.

47 *Business Times*, January 1, 1986.

48 *The Star*, July 29, 1986.

49 *Asian Wall Street Journal*, July 10, 1986.

50 *The Star*, July 29, 1986.

51 Chung Ling Holdings Bhd. was registered in 1974 with authorized capital of M$10 million, of which over $3 million is paid-up.

52 *The Star*, July 17, 1985.

53 *lnformation Malaysia 1986 Year Book* (Kuala Lumpur: Berita Publishing Sdn. Bhd., 1986).

54 Ozay Mehmet, *Development in Malaysia: Poverty, Wealth and Trusteeship* (London: Croom Helm, 1986), p.108.

55 *New Straits Times*, September 23, 1983.
56 A. A. Berle Jr., foreword in *The Corporation in Modern Society*, ed. Edward Mason (Cambridge, Massachusetts: Harvard University Press, 1961), p. x.

21

THE CHINESE IN BUSINESS

Yoshihara Kunio

POPULATION SIZE

The Chinese in South-East Asia were an easily identifiable group in the pre-war period. Most were immigrants from China, all spoke Chinese and had Chinese surnames. They did not speak Mandarin, though; instead, coming from southern China, they spoke Cantonese, Hokkien, Hakka, Teochew, or Hainanese. In the Philippines, the Hokkien accounted for about 80 per cent of the Chinese population, and the Cantonese the remaining 20 per cent. In Thailand, the Teochew were the dominant group, followed by the Hakka, Hainanese, Cantonese, and Hokkien.[1] If their mothers were local women, many Chinese children born locally lost their 'Chineseness' because they did not learn to speak Chinese, and were integrated into the local community. (In the Philippines, they were called Chinese mestizos.) Especially before the First World War, very few Chinese women migrated, thus many of the children born to Chinese fathers were 'lost' in that way. The children who were identified as Chinese spoke Chinese, retained Chinese surnames, and belonged to the Chinese community.

In the post-war period, the Chinese became a less easily identifiable group. Many were naturalized. In Thailand, locally born Chinese were entitled to citizenship. A large number of them localized their names. Because of the forced localization of Chinese schools, Chinese children could barely speak Chinese, and became socially integrated into the local community. Conceptually, it may be said that one is Chinese if he thinks that he is Chinese, but this does not serve as an objective criteria for counting the number of Chinese. In arriving at the size of the Chinese population, there was a data problem even for the pre-war period, but post-war, the conceptual problem became an additional complication.

There is, however, a consensus that there were—and still are—many more Chinese in Thailand than in the Philippines. The question is how many more. According to the Overseas Chinese Affairs Commission of the Nationalist Government in Taiwan, the Chinese population in 1950 was 3.5 million in Thailand and 180,000 in the Philippines.[2] Since the total population of

Source: *The Nation and Economic Growth: The Philippines and Thailand*, Singapore: Oxford University Press 1994, pp. 15–27.

Thailand was about 18 million and of the Philippines about 19 million (both countries had roughly the same population throughout the 40-year period), the Chinese proportion of the population in Thailand in that year was almost 20 per cent and that in the Philippines a little less than 1 per cent. There is no knowing, however, how reliable these figures are.

The most often quoted figures are Victor Purcell's and G. William Skinner's. Purcell's estimates for 1947 are 2.5 million (14.4 per cent of the total population) for Thailand and 120,000 (0.6 per cent) for the Philippines.[3] Skinner's estimates for 1950 are 3 million (16.7 per cent of the total population) for Thailand and 230,000 (1.2 per cent) for the Philippines. The discrepancy was unlikely to be due to the different years of estimation. It was mostly likely due to the different data sources used.

Purcell also gives estimates for 1960. The Chinese population in Thailand increased to only 2.7 million (possibly because Chinese immigration stopped due to severe government restriction and because of fewer new marriages, there was little natural growth), while the total population grew at a little over 3 per cent per annum between 1947 and 1960. As a result, the proportion of the Chinese population fell to 10.2 per cent. In the Philippines, the Chinese population increased from 120,000 to 181,000 over the same period, and the proportion of the Chinese increased slightly to 0.67 per cent in 1960. Estimates for later years are also available, but their reliability becomes more questionable. For example, one Chinese-Filipino organization maintains that there were 800,000–900,000 ethnic Chinese in the Philippines in the late 1980s, or about 1.5 per cent of the total population.[4] However, based on the estimates of early years when the Chinese were more identifiable, this author considers the Chinese population in the Philippines to have been a little less than 1 per cent, and in Thailand to be at least 10 per cent, so that in the period under consideration, Thailand had at least 10 times more Chinese than the Philippines in percentage terms as well as in absolute numbers.

A large Chinese population was a favourable factor for economic growth. This might appear to be a simplistic proposition, but there is supporting evidence for it. This assertion, however, presupposes that the Chinese did not pose a social problem for the country concerned. In fact, they did in both Thailand and the Philippines, and how and to what extent this was overcome will be considered in the next section. This chapter is concerned with why the Chinese were a greater propelling force of economic changes than the indigenous population, and the concrete ways in which they contributed to economic growth.

WORK ETHIC

To make a general statement about an ethnic group is dangerous, because there are always people who do not fit into it. For example, if one says that the Chinese are diligent, one is bound to encounter a number of Chinese who are not. But a comparative statement can be made of an average Chinese with an average indigene (and this average reflects the majority of the group). It is in this sense that the statement that the Chinese have a stronger work ethic than the indigene should be understood.

The immigrants, who made up the bulk of the Chinese population in the pre-war period, are thought to have had a stronger work ethic than the indigenes because most of them had experienced poverty in southern China where the population density was high and the economic reality harsh. Although they left their homes to escape poverty, they did not lose the work ethic required for survival at home. On the other hand, historically, the population density of South-East Asia was low, and nature was bountiful, so that there was no need for the indigenes to work hard for a living. As a result, their value orientation was more towards leisure and the adaptation of man to nature.

King Chulalongkorn's statement 'I regard them [the Chinese] not as foreigners but as component parts of the kingdom' was possibly made because he needed Chinese labour.[5] Economic modernization in Thailand required a number of tasks the Thais were not able to do, or if they could, they were reluctant to perform. For instance, when the king wanted to build a railway system for reasons of national security, it was the Chinese who supplied the coolie labour for this task. In addition, they were needed as workers in new processing industries such as rice and sawmills; as stevedores in the Bangkok port; as coolies for building canals in the Bangkok area; as tin miners in southern Thailand; as artisans and mechanics; and as traders handling new exports and imports. From the king's point of view, the Chinese who were willing to offer the labour he needed were welcome.

In the Philippines also, American businessmen demanded the importation of Chinese coolies because they believed that the Chinese were more hard-working than the Filipinos. But the American administration did not allow the Chinese into the country as coolies. Those who came did so as traders, and despite their small number, they achieved control of the greater bulk of retail and wholesale trade. How can this phenomenon be explained? Victor Purcell attributed their success in business to their 'patience in adversity, adaptability, determination and good humored resilience'. The German geographer, Albert Kolb, put it down to their ingenuity and 'satisfaction with small things'.[6] The political scientist Joseph Hayden, who was Vice-Governor of the Philippines in the mid-1930s, ascribed it to 'energy, thrift, self-control, physical and spiritual endurance, cheerfulness, infinite capacity for hard work'. Hayden elaborated:

> these qualities mean that while he is struggling to establish himself the Chinese will work sixteen hours per day. So will the members of his family. He and they will live with appalling frugality in order to put every penny back into the business. No economy is too petty to be practiced; no transaction or profit too small to be sought. Small wonder that such a people have dominated the economic life of the tropical, more easy-going Philippines.[7]

It was not only foreign observers who recognized the personal qualities which made the Chinese successful in business in the Philippines. Tomas Confesor, Filipino director of the Bureau of Commerce, told local businessmen in 1933 that if they wanted to supplant the Chinese, they must develop the economic efficiency of the Chinese and perform for the community the same services performed by the Chinese. He told Filipino businessmen that they should not use political means to supplant the Chinese, for that would not serve national interests.[8] For his pains, a storm of Filipino indignation broke over his head.

BUSINESS NETWORKS

In the viewpoint of a Filipino businessman, the system was loaded against him. He was excluded from a Chinese network because he was not Chinese, and the reason that he could not succeed was not a matter of his personal qualities but an unfair system that shut him out. As early as 1900, the Philippine Commission set up by President McKinley in 1899 (one of its functions was to investigate conditions in the Philippines) attributed the success of the Chinese to their in-group co-operation.

> They [the Chinese] succeeded everywhere in obtaining a monopoly of wholesale and retail trade, becoming, by the unity of purpose which they possess, the proprietors of mechanical arts and trades in the country. They lend each other cooperative aid, and all work together for the same end, thus forming a vast commercial society with which it is impossible for other merchants, who work separately, to compete.[9]

It should not be assumed that the Chinese community had one integrated network. The fact is there were numerous networks, which sometimes had connections with each other, especially when one network did not serve the purpose of a group member who wanted to expand his trading; but usually the networks were independent of each other. It was essentially a co-operative business group. Those who belonged to the group could buy goods on credit, receive special price discounts from other members, and (when they got together) exchange business as well as social information. It was not a fixed group as some were brought in by the introduction of a member, and others were expelled for cheating or failing members in various ways. It was an exclusive group in that the non-Chinese, or even the Chinese who belonged to other dialect groups or had other cultural attributes, were excluded.

The network was also a performance-based group. Trustworthiness had to be maintained in order to remain in the network. Those who could not be trusted were left out, and those who were thought untrustworthy were not allowed in. It was a way to reduce risk in doing business in an uncertain world—a world where there were frequent cheatings and unkept promises arising from human frailties. A network evolved in a dynamic world. Those who could not grow with others fell behind and were marginalized, if not left out entirely. There was, therefore, pressure on members to be adaptable to new economic opportunities.

Thailand did not break up the Chinese networks, which turned out to be a blessing to the economy. The Philippines, however, did great damage to them by discriminating against the Chinese in foreign exchange allocation in the 1950s and passing the Retail Trade Nationalization Law and other measures (for example, in the nationalization of the trading and processing of rice and corn). The Philippine government used legal measures to break up the Chinese trading networks and relied on government corporations such as the Philippine National Bank to help Filipinos develop alternative networks. But this strategy did not work very well because a workable network required time, experience, and connections to build. An artificially created network was a poor substitute for one which had evolved over time, for—trust being weak among its members—it did not function well in facilitating transactions. In addition, it could not be easily connected with networks outside the country, at least not as well as a Chinese network could be with those in Hong Kong, Taiwan, or South-East Asian trading centres.

Economically, Bangkok can be regarded as a Chinese city. Half its population in 1947 was Chinese.[10] There were many Chinese traders in Thai regional cities and market towns as well (about half the Chinese population lived in the provinces).[11] They gave advances to peasants, bought their crops, and introduced them to new crops. It was through these networks that rice was brought to Bangkok for export. Later, cassava and corn were exported in the same way. As the government built more highways, Chinese trading networks expanded and, at the same time, were strengthened. Since the mid-1980s, pineapples, asparagus, bamboo shoots, mushrooms, young corn, and canned tomatoes have been exported through these networks.

Chinese networks for commercial crops were greatly helped by their connections with those in Taiwan. Many of these recent agricultural exports were what Taiwan used to export, but because the cost of production increased as the economy grew, Taiwan lost its competitiveness in agricultural products. Taiwanese exporters tied up with Thai traders in introducing the necessary capital and technology to rural areas in Thailand. Numerous Thai-Taiwanese joint ventures were set up in the North and North-east in the 1980s. In a number of other cases, however, the initiative came from the Thais, and what was obtained from Taiwan was primarily technology. A typical case was the entry of the Charoen Pokphand group (popularly known as the CP group) into shrimp culture. The group, which had grown large as a chicken processor and trader, had enough capital to diversify into new fields.

Thailand's connections with Taiwan were not restricted to agribusiness. In the 3-year period after mid-1985, the Taiwanese currency appreciated from about NT$40-to NT$26 per dollar, and many of its labour-intensive products ceased to be competitive in the export market. Consequently, some Taiwanese producers shifted their production to Thailand. In a few years, in the late 1980s, Thailand became a major producer of toys, rubber shoes and gloves, tennis rackets, and other labour-intensive products. Thai traders and manufacturers formed joint ventures with Taiwanese investors, or became their subcontractors. During 1987-May 1990, Taiwan invested about $2 billion in Thailand, about five times more than it did in the Philippines.[12]

Thai Chinese networks were also connected to neighbouring countries. Thai Chinese traders sought out their counterparts in Laos, Cambodia, Vietnam, and Burma (now Myanmar) for business dealings. In the past, political instability in these countries caused some Chinese traders and skilled workers to move to Thailand. In particular, the coming of gem traders and manufacturers from Burma in the mid-1960s (as a result of Ne Win's anti-Chinese policy) boosted the fledgeling jewellery industry, which became a leading export industry two decades later. Another helpful factor in the growth of this industry was the availability of rubies in Thailand (which has provided about 80 per cent of the world's gem-quality rubies).[13] Many of these were apparently brought in from neighbouring countries through Chinese networks.

Many Chinese traders and producers went to some length to be independent. For example, they worked hard at absorbing technology from abroad. If necessary, they formed joint ventures with foreign companies, and then eased them out when they were no longer useful. (The textile-based conglomerate, Saha Union, absorbed technology in this manner from its Japanese partners in its early years.) Traders often tried to reduce the number of foreign intermediaries to reach final purchasers as directly as possible. In many industries, since distribution channels had been firmly established (especially in selling to the Japanese), they did not succeed, but in others (for example, textiles), they did. Foreign buyers were more willing to accept the Chinese because they could meet internationally accepted business standards as their business tradition had prepared them for internationally shared business practices. Many, of course, behaved unscrupulously, but many more imbibed the business values which brought about long-term success.

CHINESE DOMINANCE IN THAILAND

The Chinese population was large enough to dominate practically all business fields in Thailand. Among the large businesses, non-Chinese ones are mostly government-related, such as the government-owned public utility companies like Thai Airways International. There is also a government bank (Krung Thai Bank) and government bodies such as the Petroleum Authority of Thailand which owns petrol stations and oil refineries. There are no reasons why these had to be government-owned, but they are kept as such, possibly to keep lucrative posts for bureaucrats (military as well as civilian). In addition, there are two major companies controlled by the Crown Property Bureau: Siam Commercial Bank and Siam Cement. These were originally set up to counter the British (not the Chinese) who dominated business in the pre-war period.

Large Thai entrepreneurs are few in number. There is the Bhirom-bhakdi family which owns Boon Rawd, known for its Singha beer, the most popular brew in Thailand. The founder, Phya Bhirombhakdi, was a Thai of Chinese ancestry who worked as a bureaucrat for the King (rising eventually to the rank of Phya, the second highest rank conferred on bureaucrats and soldiers before the Revolution of 1932). Another Thai entrepreneur is Chaijudh Karnasuta, who controls Italian-Thai Development Corp., a major construction company set up jointly with Giorgio Berlingieri. At first, the Italian ran the company, but after his death in 1981, Chaijudh took over and managed it with the assistance of his children and sons-in-law.

Practically all other large private companies are controlled by the Chinese. The most often mentioned Chinese companies are Bangkok Bank, the largest commercial bank not only in Thailand but also in South-East Asia; the textile-based conglomerate, Saha Union; and the agri-business group, Charoen Pokphand. A recent entrant to the 'big league' is the Karnchanapas family who has moved back from Hong Kong. Mongkol Karnchanapas made money in Bangkok as the distributor of Seiko watches, and probably because in the mid-1970s Thai security was threatened by the Communist victory in Indo-China, Mongkol moved the centre of his business to Hong Kong. Having become even more successful there, the family returned to Thailand as a big real estate developer. They were the developers of two large real estate projects, Muang Thong and Thana City. They have also won a bid for an elevated mass transit system in Bangkok.

According to Board of Investment (BOI) data, Hong Kong was the largest foreign investor in Thailand in 1991. Because there has been a great deal of anxiety among Hong Kong businessmen about the status of Hong Kong after it reverts to China in 1997, there has been a large outflow of capital, and some has come to Thailand. In the late 1980s, BOI-approved investments went to such labour-intensive industries as toys, plastic products, and electronics. In addition, there must have been a large financial investment from Hong Kong.

Hong Kong–Bangkok connections are close. Many Chinese companies in Thailand have offices and subsidiaries in Hong Kong, and there is a lot of travelling between the two cities. In the late 1980s, there were over a dozen flights each way daily, and the flight time was less than three hours. It was possible to go from Bangkok to Hong Kong in the morning, do business there, and come back in the evening of the same day.

A NEW ENVIRONMENT UNDER MARCOS

In the Philippines, the Chinese were less dominant. This could be seen from the existence of many big Filipino (non-Chinese) companies. Some of the best-known were the Ayala group, inclusive of the Ayala Corp. (which developed Makati), the Bank of Philippine Islands, and Insular Life Insurance; San Miguel Corp., the food conglomerate; the Lopez group, which controlled the power company Meralco and the Philippine Commercial & Industrial Bank; the Republic Flour Mills controlled by Jose Concepcion (former Secretary of Trade and Industry), and Concepcion Industries by his brother, Raul; the Cebu-based Aboitiz family engaged in shipping and trading; the engineering company A G & P headed by Roberto Villanueva; and Dante Santos's Philippine Appliance Corp. During the period of martial law, President Ferdinand Marcos's Filipino cronies wielded great power. His best-known associates were Eduardo 'Danding' Cojuangco, Roberto Benedicto, Rodolfo Cuenca, Herminio Disini, Antonio Floirendo, Ricardo Silverio, and Bienvenido Tantoco. In addition, there were a large number of sugar-based Filipino business families, such as the Cojuangcos (from which President Corazon Aquino comes), the Elizaldes, the Aranetas, the de Leons, and the Montelibanos. By the late 1970s, the Filipinos had become a more dominant group than the Chinese.

The situation, however, began to change in the 1980s. The Chinese became more visible, and the Filipinos began losing influence. The first change came about following Marcos's measures in 1975 and 1976 to make naturalization easier for the Chinese. Prior to this, naturalization was difficult, and the large majority of Chinese immigrants did not have Philippine citizenship. Since *jus soli* was not the citizenship criteria, the children also remained Chinese. These non-Filipino Chinese were discriminated against under nationalistic measures such as import control and retail trade nationalization. But thanks to Marcos's measures, a large number of them (one source cites a figure of about 160,000) obtained citizenship.'[14] Marcos believed that by raising the economic position of the Chinese, he could counter the power of the old rich who were critical of him.

More immediate reasons for the rise of the Chinese in the 1980s were the collapse of sugar prices and the fall of Marcos and his cronies. Under free trade with the United States, sugar became the major export crop of the Philippines in the pre-war period, and remained so until the late 1970s. Unlike other colonies, in the Philippines, little foreign capital went into sugar production. It was Filipinos, especially mestizos, who took advantage of new economic opportunities and organized sugar production. Many of them became large sugar planters or owners of sugar mills (called centrals in the Philippines). In the post-war period, with government encouragement, some of these people diversified into banking, trading, and industry.

The sugar industry started facing problems in the 1970s. With the expiration of the Laurel-Langley Treaty in 1974, the Philippines lost its quotas in the US market which paid higher prices than the international market. But in the mid-1970s, sugar prices were good, and the loss of the American market was not felt immediately. In the second half of the 1970s, prices started to go down, but in 1980, they increased again, almost to the 1974 level of 65 cents per kilogram, the highest level recorded thus far. However, sugar prices began plummeting in 1982, and hit the bottom in 1985 when prices were down to about 9 cents per kilogram. In the late 1980s, prices recovered somewhat, but most Filipino sugar producers could not continue production with such low sugar prices, and sugar became a depressed industry in the Philippines.

The mismanagement of the National Sugar Trading Corp., which was given a monopoly on sugar trading during the martial law period, contributed to the depressed state of the sugar industry, but a more fundamental reason was change in the international market. In Europe, the supply increased as a result of government subsidies to sugar beet producers, whereas the demand declined because a cheaper corn-based sweetener became available. Moreover, public concern over the health effects of sugar reduced per capita consumption in sugar-importing countries.[15] Furthermore, the cost of sugar production in the Philippines tended to be high. In earlier years, Filipino producers had done well because they were given preferential treatment in the American market, without which many of them could not have competed.

Among Marcos's cronies were a few who 'made it big' during martial law and fell together with Marcos (or a little earlier when the economy began stagnating and Marcos was forced by international lending agencies to rationalize his economic policy). A typical example was Herminio Disini, who was little known in business before martial law. But a number of others were well known before martial law. For example, Ricardo Silverio was an assembler of Toyota cars, and Rodolfo Cuenca was the largest constructor (he owned the Construction & Development Corp. of the Philippines). These people started using their connections with Marcos for quick profits or aggressive expansion. When the economy faced a financial crisis in the early 1980s, they got into trouble too, but Marcos could not help them out because international lending agencies pressured him to impose greater rationality on government policy. Their companies were taken over by the government, or liquidated. Some left the country with Marcos because they feared that the new Aquino government would prosecute them for collaborating with Marcos in plundering the country.

Although most of Marcos's cronies were Filipinos, there were a few Chinese among them. They were Ralph Nubla, Jose Campos, and Lucio Tan. Nubla did not go into business in a big way during the martial law period. Having been Marcos's classmate at the University of the Philippines and as President of the Federation of Filipino–Chinese Chambers of Commerce and Industry, he served as a liaison between Marcos and the Chinese community. Campos (also known as Jose C. Yao) owned the largest drug company in the Philippines, United Laboratories, and used his government connections for the benefit of his business (for example, by selling his drugs to government hospitals), but the company was well managed before martial law and remained so even after it. He co-operated with the Aquino government by disclosing Marcos's assets which he had been holding, and thus survived the transition.

Lucio Tan's ties with Marcos were much closer. Before martial law, he had a small foothold in the cigarette business. It was after he went into banking in 1977 that he joined the big business league. According to a government committee, Marcos was behind his venture into banking. In that year, he took over a small bank (General Banking and Trust) and changed its name to Allied Banking Corp. In the following few years, it became a leading bank, with a large infusion of low-interest loans from the Central Bank and a rapid increase in branches. The Aquino government tried to prosecute him for his collaboration with Marcos, but he was still untouched in 1991.

THE RISE OF CHINESE BUSINESSES IN THE PHILIPPINES

With the collapse of the sugar industry and the disappearance of the cronies, the Philippine business leadership changed greatly. Chinese businessmen became more successful and visible. The most dramatic change came about in department stores. Until the early 1980s, the most prestigious department store was Rustan's, set up in the Makati Commercial Center in 1971 by Bienvenido Tantoco, who later became a close associate of Marcos. In the mid-1970s, Tantoco set up another store in Cubao. But he became more interested in making quick profits under Marcos, for example, by operating duty-free shops. While he was doing this, some Chinese ventured into the large-scale retail business. In particular, Henry Sy's Shoe Mart and John Gokongwei's Robinson's began competing with Rustan's.

Then with the fall of Marcos, Tantoco lost the monopoly on duty-free shops and sought political asylum in the Vatican where he had been serving as ambassador since 1983. He was granted asylum, but the Vatican court soon sentenced him to 3 years' imprisonment on an arms conviction. Rustan's was, however, kept open by his children, though the Makati store was burnt down and closed for renovation for over a year. In 1992, Rustan's opened a new store (Rustan's Tower) in the Shangri-la Plaza in Mandaluyong. But it was surpassed by Robinson's and Shoe Mart (SM) which had aggressively expanded while Tantoco was engaged in a 'monopoly game' or while his children were busy adjusting to the post-Marcos period. The shopping malls, Robinson's Galleria and SM Megamall, are the most recent additions to their sprawling retail empires.

The retail business is competitive. Shoe Mart is planning to set up a large shopping complex in Cebu to challenge the Gaisano family's firm foothold there. Not to be outdone by Shoe Mart's challenge, the Gaisanos built the Gaisano Country Mall, a large leisure and shopping complex. They have also diversified into Metro Manila and set up Isetan Department Stores in Quiapo and Cubao.

Henry Sy's rise was the most dramatic. He was born in Fukien around 1925. His father was probably a 'commuter' Chinese in the Philippines who had a family in China, and Henry probably came to join him when he was still a boy. It is known that his father was operating a *sari-sari* (sundry goods) store when he set up a shoe store in downtown Manila shortly after the Pacific War at the age of about 20. It is not clear how he managed to survive the Retail Trade Nationalization Law, but he probably succeeded in getting naturalized. Naturalization was a slow and expensive process, but it was not an insurmountable obstacle for those who had money and determination to go through with it. His dream was to become rich by selling a pair of shoes to all Filipinos (about 19 million of them in 1948). In the following years, he became modestly successful, but it was not until 1975 that he became prominent. In that year, he set up a large department store in the Ayala Center in Makati. However, it was only in 1985 when he set up SM City at the end of the EDSA highway that a spectacular expansion began. In 1991, his SM chain held the premier place in the Philippine retail trade, and his business empire which included banking, real estate, and aquaculture (shrimps) was probably the largest Chinese business group in the country.[16]

There are a number of other visible Chinese entrepreneurs. There is the flamboyant Tan Yu who ventured into Taiwan and came back with Taiwanese money in the early 1980s, investing it in hotels and other projects. George Ty is probably the biggest banker among the Chinese; his Metropolitan Bank challenged the Bank of Philippine Islands, the largest private bank, in the early 1990s. In terms of total assets, it became slightly larger than the Bank of Philippine Islands in the second quarter of 1992. William Gatchalian became big in the plastics industry in a relatively short time. A couple of other recent stars are William Ley in construction and the Ang brothers in the fast-food business. In addition, though in a less dramatic way, a number of other Chinese became successful by exporting labour-intensive products such as garments. When these new stars were combined with the long-established Chinese companies, such as the China Banking Corp. and the Equitable Banking Corp., the Chinese business community became a formidable force in the Philippine economy in the late 1980s.

There was some residual anti-Chinese feeling in the Philippines as late as 1990. Some so-called nationalist journalists and intellectuals were trying to foment it by essentially repeating the theme nationalist Filipinos had used in the 1950s: they asked whether or not the country was really independent with the Chinese controlling the economy, or attributed the rise of basic commodity prices to the hoarding and manipulation of Chinese merchants. But they were fighting a lost cause. In the 1950s, people had faith in the potential of Filipino entrepreneurs, and were willing to accept government intervention in promoting them. However, it turned out that many Filipino entrepreneurs were better as political entrepreneurs than as business entrepreneurs, and though not all the blame could be placed on them, they were at least partly responsible for the miserable economic condition the country was mired in the 1980s.

Since the mid-1980s, the trend of economic thought has been in favour of competition and an open economy. People are less willing to accept the protectionist recipe of the 1950s, for the chances are that it will make the already weak economy worse. The public has become more tolerant towards the ethnic Chinese. Several of them participated in the SEA Games in 1991 and won gold medals for the Philippines; this was a big change compared with the early years when there had been a feeling against ethnic Chinese representing the Philippines in international sports events. President Aquino's pride in her Chinese lineage is also a reflection of the people's increased tolerance.

CHINESE NETWORKS: CONTRASTS

The resilience of Chinese businesses is a bright side of the Philippine economy today. When the economy becomes more open and peace and order prevails, these businesses can act as a catalyst for economic rejuvenation. But they cannot be so powerful a force as their counterparts in Thailand for two reasons. First, their number is limited. Even economically, Manila is not a Chinese city, unlike Bangkok. Secondly, Chinese networks in the Philippines are not as strongly established as those in Thailand. Discrimination against the Chinese in the 1950s and 1960s did great damage to these networks. In the 1970s, the monopolies set up in grain, sugar, and coconut oil trading destroyed the Chinese networks in these commodities which had survived the discrimination of the earlier decades. Government intervention, which prevailed throughout the period, affected Filipino as well as Chinese entrepreneurs. Many of the former developed political entrepreneurship to the detriment of business entrepreneurship. These legacies act as a brake on the Philippines when Hong Kong, Taiwan, and South-East Asian Chinese networks try to connect with the country.

It is true that Chinese networks in Thailand face some of the same problems of the Philippine networks. In general, however, they work better than those in the Philippines. In Thailand, the period of Chinese discrimination was short; the level of discrimination was lower; and government intervention was less. Chinese businesses and networks evolved more naturally under a freer and more competitive business environment. Unlike in the Philippines, they did not have to go through a turbulent period in which many businesses declined and some rose for non-business reasons. Thus, traditional practices could adjust to new ones more or less at their own speed to produce a workable business system.

The tragedy of the discrimination against the Chinese and of other government intervention measures in the Philippines was not only that less efficient Filipino businesses replaced more efficient Chinese ones, but also that when Chinese businesses became important in the region, Philippine Chinese networks were so weak that they could not easily connect with Chinese businesses overseas. This became a serious disadvantage to the Philippines in the 1980s when Taiwan and Hong Kong became important foreign investors.

NOTES

1 The percentage distribution of the Chinese by dialect group was as follows: Teochew, 56; Hakka, 16; Hainanese, 12; Cantonese, 7; Hokken 7; and others, 2. Richard J. Coughlin, *Double Identity: The Chinese in Modern Thailand*, Hong Kong: University of Hong Kong Press, 1960, pp. 6–7. Quoted in Likhit Dhiravegin, *Thai Politics: Selected Aspects of Development and Change*, Bangkok: Tri-Sciences Publishing House, 1985, p. 363

2 *Far Eastern Economic Review*, 3 July 1952: 13.

3 Victor Purcell, *The Chinese in Southeast Asia*, reprinted Kuala Lumpur: Oxford University Press, 1980, p. 3.

4 Teresita Ang See, *The Chinese in the Philippines: Problems and Perspectives*, Manila: Kaisa Para Sa Kaurnaran, 1990, p. 1.

5 D. J. M. Tate, *The Making of Modern South-East Asia*, Kuala Lumpur: Oxford University Press, 1979, Vol. 2, p. 545.

6 George Weightman, 'The Philippine Chinese: A Cultural History of a Marginal Trading Community', Ph.D. thesis, Cornell University, 1959, p. 141.

7 Joseph Ralston Hayden, *The Philippines: A Study in National Development*, New York: Macmillan Co., 1942, p. 700.

8 Ibid.

9 Quoted in Jacques Amyot, *The Manila Chinese: Familism in the Philippine Environment*, IPC Monographs No. 2, Quezon City: Ateneo de Manila University, 1973, p. 65.

10 Wendell Blanchard, *Thailand: Its People, Its Society, Its Culture*, New Haven: HRAF Press, 1958, p. 66.

11 *Far Eastern Economic Review*, 21 November 1957: 663.

12 Samart Chiasakul and Koji Taniguchi, *The Role of Foreign Capital in the Manufacturers Market Development in Thailand*, Joint Research Programme Series No. 89, Tokyo: Institute of Developing Economies, 1991, p. 32.

13 *Far Eastern Economic Review*, 9 May 1991.

14 *Far Eastern Economic Review*, 15 February 1990. This article also reports that one of the papers Marcos took to Hawaii when he fled the country shows that he

received a contribution [or bribe] of $12 million from the Chinese community for these measures.

15 For changes in the international sugar market which affect the Philippines, see Joop Theunissen, 'Litskage and Alternatives: The Philippine Sugar Industry in the 1990s', Discussion paper, Tilburg University, July 1989.

16 There is not much information on Henry Sy. The most detailed and readily available write-up on him appeared in *Asiaweek*, 25 March 1988. Though less detailed, see also *Far Eastern Economic Review*, 22 December 1988 and *Asahi Shinbun* (a Japanese newspaper), 28 June 1989. This paragraph is partly based on these sources.

22

FAMILY BUSINESS REASSESSED

Corporate Structure and Late-starting Industrialization in Thailand

Akira Suehiro

I THE FAMILY BUSINESS, ZAIBATSU, AND THE BUSINESS GROUP

A What is a family business?

In the present paper the term "family business" will be defined as a form of enterprise in which both ownership and management are controlled by a family kinship group, either nuclear or extended, and the fruits of which remain inside that group, being distributed in some way among its members.[1] However, businesses formed through affiliation like a family and their friends or persons sharing the same place of origin may be defined as family businesses in the broadest sense of the term.

In the case of a family business that has expanded and diversified the scale, scope, and composition of its business activities, we will refer to it as a zaibatsu. That is to say, a zaibatsu is formed when (1) a specific family exercises exclusive control over its ownership and management, (2) its business endeavors extend across a number of industries and/or economic sectors, and (3) the group thus formed shares oligopolistic market control over at least one of those industries or sectors.[2] Therefore, despite the Japanese origin of the word, as long as a business satisfies the above three conditions, it may be defined as a zaibatsu, no matter in what region of the world it may be located.

On the other hand, economic associations that satisfy conditions (2) and (3), but are not limited in terms of their ownership and managerial control to a specific kinship group, are, generally speaking, "business groups." Such groups may be formed via personal relationships, such as friendship, academic affiliation, similar place of origin, etc., through legal incorporation without exclusive family control, or under the direction of an overriding financial institution. What has become known as *kigyō shūdan* in postwar Japan no doubt comes under this more universal category of "business group."[3]

Source: Developing Economies, Vol, XXXI(4), December 1993, pp. 378–407.

Therefore, the term business group as defined in this paper takes on a broader meaning than such concepts as the family-controlled zaibatsu group, the partnership-type business group, or the commercial-bank-centered business group.

B Management control and the affiliation network

The body of research to date confronting directly the phenomenon referred to as the "family business" is surprisingly small in quantity and rather shallow in its theoretical consideration of the subject matter. Of the few publications that include the term in their titles, there is the collection of papers edited by Okochi and Yasuoka [26]; but even there we find a mere introduction of family business and zaibatsu groups in various countries around the world with no real attempt to analyze them theoretically.

Two approaches dominate the research literature. The first is a business science (including business history) approach developed within American scholars, which discusses the issue from the standpoint of "corporate control." The second is a sociological approach, which attempts to understand business management from the aspects of social relationships and family structure indigenous to each region where the family business is found.

The former "corporate control" approach was conceptualized by A. A. Berle, Jr. and G. C. Means [3] under the notion of "a separation of ownership from management control in the modern corporation." This approach then evolved around a discussion of the question, "who controls the business?" and concluded with a scheme describing the modern corporation as the result of a transition process from "ownership control" to "management control."

The work of E. S. Herman [11] is probably the most representative of what this type of approach has contributed to our knowledge of the family business. Utilizing a methodology similar to Berle and Means, Herman surveyed in great detail 200 nonfinancial American corporations during tlte mid-1970s and found a deconcentration of family ownership and domination of management control in comparison with the situation in the 1930s. That is to say, Herman concludes that "the decline of family control appears to be an unassailable historical fact" [11, p. 79], given (1) the diffusion of corporate stock ownership as the business expands, (2) capital concentration through mergers and acquisitions, and (3) a deconcentration of holdings through diffusion of the founding family members themselves.

It should be pointed out that the "corporate control" approach has come under attack from the Marxian viewpoint of financial capital domination since the publication of Baran and Sweezy's *Monopoly Capital* [2] in 1966. In addition, the fundamental ownership to management control transition scheme has been called into question by Burch [4], who found to the contrary a continuation of family control from a study of American big business through an unique investigation of corporate data.

However, what should be emphasized here is not whether or not one should support the idea of a transition to "management control," but rather the fact that the whole discussion about family business has put stress on stockholding patterns. Under this type of preconception it is almost impossible to come up with more sophisticated theory about how family businesses continue to expand intact generation after generation.

Along this vein we find the research carried out by T. Hattori [9], which empirically takes up the zaibatsu in the Republic of Korea (called there *chaebol*) and shows paradoxically that as the economic scale of these groups increased, the ownership control exercised by their core families tended to be further solidified. Furthermore, the research conducted by this author on financial conglomerates in Thailand [33, pp. 251–65] describes how financial and insurance groups fonned by coalitions of a number of families and their friends actually moved in a direction towards exclusive control by one particular family within the process of enterprise expansion.

In explaining why family control has continued to dominate the business communities of the developing nations, scholars have conventionally turned to the underdevelopment of capital markets as the major reason. However, looking at the unique development of zaibatstu in the developing nations, underdevelopment of a system supporting joint-stock companies in itself is insufficient to explain fully what actually is happening there.

In this respect there is one more viewpoint that has appeared in an attempt to explain the growth and strength of zaibatsu and business groups in the developing nations, especially of Asia by focusing on family structure and affiliation networks in Japan, Korea, and China (including locally born citizens of Chinese descent in other countries). Representative of this approach is the research done by such scholars as Yu Chunghsun [41], who attempts to understand Chinese outside of China as "a networking economic nation," a group led by G. Hamilton, who looked at East Asian enterprise groups from the aspect of social organization [6], and T. Hattori in a study of management development in Korea [10].

What this latter approach attempts to accomplish is to oppose the joint-stock company control concept (which presumes a linear-type growth and expansion of enterprise organization) by attempting to explain through relationships to family structure the management organizations of large businesses which dominate the economies in the developing nations. At least in the case of the family business, this approach insists that it is not an early capitalist management form that will necessarily wither away in the midst of the advance of a modern joint-stock company system. Rather, this approach insists, the family business has a rationality all its own.

C Objectives of the study

In Thailand, the majority of large businesses are controlled either by foreign capital (especially multinational enterprises) or family-run business groups (i.e, zaibatsu groups) [35]. The aim of this paper is to investigate the characteristic features of this latter form of enterprise management.

In Thailand the business group is usually called the *klum* (group), but it has also been referred to as *thurakun-yai* (big family) and *thurakit khrop-khrua* (family-run business) [15] [16]. In other words, the business group is generally equated with a family business that has expanded to a scale of huge proportions.[4]

First, let us reexamine why within Thai big business the family business form of management has continued intact and developed in many cases into a conglomerate-type group of companies. The objective here is to investigate the rationality of family business growth by considering (1) the various economic conditions of Thailand as a late-starting industrializer or late comer, and (2) the social background of the Chinese business community in Thailand.

II THE RESEARCH TO DATE

A Family capitalism

A major proponent of the idea of a transition from family capitalism to managerial capitalism is Alfred Chandler, Jr., who argued that together with expanded enterprise scale due to mass production mass marketing, and mass transportation, the family business gives way to the modern business enterprise run by managerial experts. This transition marks what Chandler terms the "managerial revolution" [5, p. 10].

In asking the question, "who rules American society?," M. Useem, a supporter of Chandler's theory, boldly focused on the developmental stages of capitalism via the concept of "the inner circle" [38]. Useem divides the history of capitalism to date into three distinct stages: family capitalism, managerial capitalism, and institutional capitalism. Each of these stages is characterized by a certain principle of social organization: family capitalism is based on "upper class" principles; managerial capitalism on "corporate" principles; and institutional capitalism on "classwide" principles [38, pp. 13–18].

According to Useem, family capitalism equates kinship relations with the control and ownership of a business enterprise and is a system consisting of business mergers via descent and marriage. The overriding organizational principle of this system is upper-class coalition, which often results in the creation of a landed aristocracy as seen in the United Kingdom, which, according to Useem, assumes the character of an "anti-industrial culture" [38, p. 184].

However, with the expansion of enterprise scale, the advent of specialized business managers and the formation of complex occupational stratification, control over both day-to-day, as well as final, decision making is transferred from the founding families to professional managers, a state of affairs which marks the stage of managerial capitalism. At the corporate level this stage is one in which

> the guiding concern is no longer preservation of the fortunes of the upper class families who once built and controlled the firms, but preservation of the profits of the enterprises that now control the families' economic destinies. Rather than the firm serving as an instrument for the accumulation of family wealth, the manager has come to be the instrument for the accumulation of company wealth. [38, p. 177]

Furthermore, as capitalism becomes more "institutionalized," it enters upon a new stage in its development based on an organizational principle which abandons reliance on individual managers to control the business in favor of management via intra-corporate networks (interlocking directorates, etc.). The groups that are supported and selected by these networks constitute what Useem terms the "inner circle" that rules contemporary American society.

What is interesting about Useem's theory is that he understands the characteristic feature or motivation of family capitalism as the preservation of the "fortunes" or the family. It is this point that seems to be a common feature of family businesses in the developing nations, as well. On the other hand, Useem's understanding of family capitalism as "culturally anti-industrial" is not indicative of the social role or position of family businesses in the developing nations today. That is to say, the existing research on developing economies strongly indicates that family businesses and zaibatsu in these countries are the most active economic actors promoting industrialization.

In any case, we should not forget that Useem's thinking clearly falls within the context of "who controls the modern corporation," which regards family business as the precursor or initial stage to the "managerial revolution." Therefore, Useem's concept is extremely economically deterministic in the conceptualization of organizational principles of various stages of capitalism determining the forms which the general social structure takes. This is in clear opposition to the sociological approach, which attempts to understand the problem in terms of social relations influencing and promoting the expansion of family management.

B The sociological approach

Within the research based on the sociological approach, we find in general two viewpoints concerning the family business. One is called the "affiliation network model," the other looks at family business expansion as determined by indigenous kinship relations.

The "affiliation network model," which is often utilized when discussing Chinese-run business groups in Taiwan or the countries of Southeast Asia, attempts in concrete terms to discover the origins of business group formation not only in kinship and marriage, but also through a wide range of interpersonal relationships based on similar ancestry, similar place of birth, similar academic background, as well as friendship. The proponents of this model point to a much looser business coalition, different from the prewar Japanese "zaibatsu." This form of business organization has been described by Hamilton et al. as "*guanxi* capitalism" [7] and by Numazaki as *guanxiqiye* (related enterprises) or the "banana-bunch-shaped partnership" [25, Chap. 5].[5]

Here is what Numazaki has to say about this kind of business group organization.

> If we shift our focus from a single firm to a larger network of firms, we gain a different picture of Chinese business organization. Instead of "centralized" narrowly confined family firms, we find out a loosely connected set of firms, all of which are partnerships. [25, p. 360]

Therefore, according to this view, the dominant form of business group in Taiwan should be defined as a loosely connected set of partnerships.

One more approach considers the business group in Asia as an extended form of family management originally determined by the principle of kinship, as in China and Korea. Unlike the affiliation network model, this approach puts more emphasis on the vertical = centripetal aspects than the horizontal = diffused aspects of business groups.

Take, for example, the empirical work of Tong Chee Kiong on business groups in Singapore. Chinese family firms are an important ingredient within Singapore's large business groups, like the Hong Leon group, meaning exclusionary family control over stock ownership and a concentration of authority over decision making is the personage of one certain individual, the owner-family patriarch [37].

The Hong Leon group was founded in 1941 as a machinery shop, and over the past half century has expanded from this base into a classic case of the conglomerate-type business group with interests in the finance, construction, manufacturing, and real estate sectors. As of the mid-1980s Hong Leon has amassed ninety-one subsidiaries in Singapore and another seventy-three in Malaysia. Tong has documented in detail the design by which the founder, Kwek Hong Png, and his family members exclusively control the group's enormous enterprises by means of family-owned stockholding companies and interlocking directorates [37, pp. 23–26]. While at first glance the corporate organization of this group seems quite Western in appearance, with respect to the aspects of control over ownership and management, Hong Leon is, according to Tong, concentrated within a small circle of Kwek family members.

The above two sociological approaches to business group organization may seem to be proceeding in opposite directions at first glance, but kinship and affiliation may just be two sides of the same coin. Even Tong's work on the Hong Leon group, which puts a lot of emphasis on the patriarchal and centripetal aspects of ownership and management, also indicates an interpersonal network within the group that has been built on a foundation of trust (*xiyong*). On the other hand, in the research done by Hattori, which stresses a "network of human relationships" among the business elite of Korea, we observe Korean zaibatsu groups that are operated through a concentrated, top-down decision-making process within core families [10, p. 128]. The difference between these two approaches therefore arises only when the discussion turns to the aspect of corporate expansion.

C Traditional enterprise structure in China: Hegu and Hehuo

One issue that cannot be overlooked when studying family businesses, especially those of overseas and local-born Chinese residing in the countries of Southeast Asia, involves the Chinese traditional enterprise management forms of *hegu* and *hehuo*.

The character *gu* (literally the thigh portion of the leg) in the compound *hegu* indicates the portion of a divided family inheritance that a particular heir receives. The term *hegu* at the same time indicates a Chinese form of partnership in which the participants pool (*he*) their resources (*gu*) to start a joint-management enterprise.

Generally speaking, the Chinese family is based on a system of communal fortune, with the head of the family, the patriarch, holding managerial control over it. When the patriarch dies, the family fortune is transferred to the group of heirs, but in practice comes under the managerial control of the new patriarch, the eldest male heir, or in his absence, the eldest member of the collateral family. However, situations do arise in which the heirs choose to divide the family fortune between them and go their separate ways. In this case, the division is made in principle with equal portions going to each male member of the same generation. We see here that under the traditional Chinese family system, the two contrasting aspects of managerial (vertical) control by the patriarch over the family fortune and equal (horizontal) division of the inheritance coexist side by side [24, Chap. 13].

Negishi argues that the original meaning of *hegu*, therefore, is a re-pooling of the divided inheritance, in order to maintain and/or expand the family fortune; but this meaning, or at least the principle involved, was adopted by not only families, but also groups of friends or "hometowners" in forming *hegu* business enterprises. Legally or institutionally speaking, Negishi puts these business organizations in the corporate category of "ordinary partnership," and also distinguishes them from the joint-stock company forms that have emerged in Europe. He claims that the joint-stock company could never have developed in any sense in premodern China [23, pp. 553–55].[6]

In studies of the subject published in postwar Japan, we find a lot of the research equating the institution of *hegu* with feudalistic commercial organizations and practices. One aspect that has received much discussion is the question of why *hegu* did not develop into modern corporations. For example, M. Yamana argues that whenever capital mobilization is made into the nucleus of *hegu*, capital accumulates there under the presumption of some confederacy or partnership based on shared kinship ties, geographical origin, or occupation. However, if the investors form the nucleus of *hegu*, each individual or family becomes a party to financing a number of *hegu*. Figure 22.1 illustrates this arrangement, which promises to diffuse investment risk, utilize investment funds to their fullest extent, and insure safety in capital increases through personal bonding. For this reason, *hegu* functioned only as a temporary organization for making profits and did not develop into a rational, permanent form of capitalistic enterprise management [40, p. 258] It was Yamana's ideas that precluded and stimulated the formation of the partnership models, which have been employed in the study of business groups in contemporary East Asia.

One more viewpoint is represented by the research of S. Imabori into the

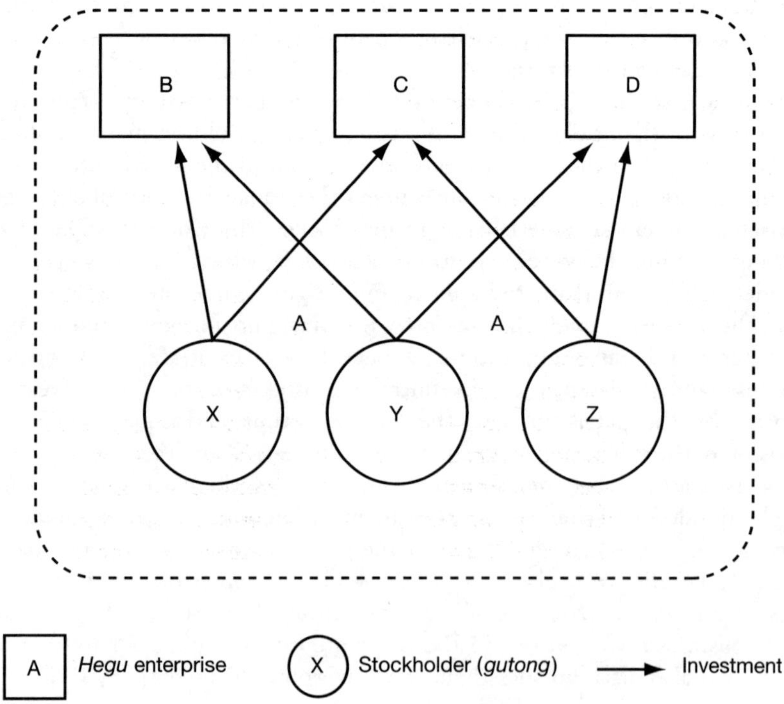

Figure 22.1 Model of *Hegu* Enterprises

historical development of *hehuo* (an organization similar to *hegu*) from the Ming period up to the end of the Qing period. Imabori noticed a change in *hehuo* as the institution entered the Qing period. What happened was that investors *cum* managers characteristic of the original form of *hehuo* became divided into two major groups of mere investors (*pudung*), on the one hand, and investors who took on managerial duties (*puhuo*). This amounted to a separation of ownership (*gu*) from management (*zhang*). Therefore, if a situation had developed in which *puhuo* assumed unlimited responsibility for the enterprise, while *pudung* were relegated only limited liability, Imabori argued that the joint-stock company would be been born in China.

What came about in reality was a clear differentiation between the character of the investment shares of the *pudung* investors and the investment shares of the *puhuo* investor-managers. For example, in the case of a 70–30 capitalization ratio between the two groups, the profit sharing ratio would be set at 50–50, resulting in far higher evaluation of the capital contributed made by the *puhuo* investor-managers. This evaluation method was not intended to compensate *puhuo* with a salary for managerial services rendered, but was rather an attempt to put a higher value on their share of the profits. As a result, Imabori argued, shares of stock could not be divided evenly over the whole *hehuo* enterprise, thus preventing the transformation of capital into a joint-stock form.

As to the reason why joint-stock companies did not develop in China, Imabori concluded that being determined by human relationships, *puhuo* was supported by a communal, confederate structure which rested on the foundations of family organization inherent to Asia [12, p. 45].

The research on *hegu*, and *hehuo* has continued to point to the strong influence exercised by these institutions even today on the organizational patterns of Chinese-run business enterprises in Southeast Asia. That is to say, such characteristic features of the family business as the importance of interpersonal networks in their founding, diversification motivated by family fortune expansion and risk diffusion, as well as joint appointments to directorships and corporate executive positions can all be traced back to the customs and practices characterizing *hegu* and *hehuo*.

On the other hand, the notion that these indigenous enterprise forms by their very nature-lacked continuity or permanency certainly does not jibe with the well-documented continuation of the family business in the developing nations. In order to explain why family businesses have not only survived, but also expanded, we will have to approach the subject matter from a different viewpoint.

D The family business and late-starting industrialization

In answer to the query, why does the family business remain so deeply rooted in the developing nations, the work of K. Nakagawa on economic development and family enterprise management offers some very suggestive arguments [20] [21] [22]. As far as this author is aware, Nakagawa's work is the pioneering effort in directly examining the relationship between the family business and developing (or "late-starting") economies.

To begin with, Nakagawa describes modern capitalism as characterized generally by a clear separation of the corporation of a production unit from the household as a consumption unit. Moreover, he understands economic activity involving both production and consumption as the family enterprise (*kagyō*), and distinguishes it from the modern business enterprise. He then compares the role that this family enterprise played in economic development in such early starters as the United Kingdom with those of the late starters (latecomers) such as the United States and Japan. Through this comparison, he finds two points on which family enterprises displayed superiority in late-starting industrial countries.

The first point may be summarized in the statement; when compared to joint-stock companies, family enterprises excel in maintaining mobility in the managerial decision-making process. For this reason, in times of both accelerated economic growth and extraordinary economic change (that the United Stales and Japan both experienced), the family enterprise form has in many cases been very effectively utilized [22, p. 249].

Together with the managerial decision-making process, the family enterprise in late-starting countries, Nakagawa insists, worked more effectively in the capital-procurement process as well. Namely, capital markets could not keep up with accelerated growth experienced in these countries, resulting in a shortage of investment funds for joint-stock companies. However, the family enterprise could expand its business by utilizing its personal networks to procure the necessary capital funds [22, p. 259].

To the contrary, Nakagawa observes, family enterprises in the early starters such as the United Kingdom had relatively stagnated vis-à-vis industrialization. They acted in extremely cautious, conservative patterns, thus having a restrictive effect on economic development. Family enterprises in these countries tended to fall to a level of activity that either emphasized real estate property as the most important form of family fortune, or became concerned with enterprises that would build a material base for upholding the family's honor and social standing [22, p. 261]. This point is on the same track as Useem's argument (discussed earlier) that British family enterprises in historical perspective have been anti-industrial in their attitudes.

Nakagawa's problematic deserves recognition on the point that the family enterprise needs to be reevaluated in a positive manner as one form of capital accumulation in late-starting industrial nations. The discussion that will follow in this paper with respect to Thailand proceeds from this very proposition. To wit, what will be presented in the following pages not only is a discussion of how family control over ownership of large corporations has managed to continue, but also is an attempt to clarify both the development patterns of the Thai family business and its mode of capital accumulation within the strictures imposes by late-starting industrialization.

III THE FAMILY BUSINESS IN THAILAND

A The ownership structure of large Thai corporations

Tables 22.1 and 22.2 on the top stockholders of large corporations in Thailand have been compiled by selecting firms whose annual sales (or revenue in

Table 22.1 Characteristics of top stockholders in large Thai corporations, 1979 and 1988 (persons, firms)

Top stockholders/equity percentage	*1979*	*%*	*1988*	*%*
(1) Individual:	72	(33.0)	74	(29.7)
1–9%	3		4	
10–29%	35		43	
30–50%	29		23	
51–100%	1		4	
Foreigner	4		0	
(2) Family investment company:	26	(11.9)	16	(6.4)
1–9%	3		5	
10–50%	17		9	
51–100%	6		2	
(3) Thai corporation:	37	(17.0)	67	(26.9)
1–9%	3		5	
10–29%	15		24	
30–50%	10		19	
51–100%	9		19	
(4) Foreign corporation:	78	(35.8)	81	(32.5)
10–48%	32		26	
49–50%	10		11	
51–98%	10		13	
99–100%	26		31	
(5) Government bureau	3	(1.4)	8	(3.2)
(6) Crown Property Bureau	2	(0.9)	3	(1.2)
Total	218	(100.0)	249	(100.0)

Notes:
1. Large corporations indicate firms with 0.3 billion baht (1979) and 1 billion baht (1988) in terms of total annual sales.
2. Public corporations have been excluded.

Sources: Calculated from the following firm directories: for 1979, Pan Siam Communication Co., *Million Baht Business Information Thailand, 1980–81* (Bangkok, 1981); for 1988, Internatinal Business Research Thailand Co., *Million Baht Business Information Thailand, 1989* (Bangkok, 1989).

Table 22.2 Top three stockholders in Thai large corporations, 1979 and 1988

Top three stockholders	*1979*	*%*	*1988*	*%*
(1) Individuals (Thai):	60	(27.5)	61	(24.5)
Belonging to the same family	21		33	
Belonging to the multiple families	39		28	
(2) Individuals plus corporations:	38	(17.4)	32	(12.9)
With group companies[a]	14		13	
With non-group companies	24		19	
(3) Thai corporations:	22	(10.1)	48	(19.3)
Belonging to the same group	4		17	
Among different groups	15		19	
Holding-company type[b]	3		12	
(4) Foreign corporations:	90	(41.3)	97	(39.0)
Exclusively foreigners[c]	33		38	
With Thai corporations	43		51	
With Thai individuals	14		8	
(5) Government bureaus	8	(3.7)	11	(4.4)
Total	218	(100.0)	249	(100.0)

Notes:
[a] Group companies are members of the group of companies that the stockholders in question own and operate.
[b] Siam Cement Co., Ltd. and Suramahakhun Co., Ltd.
[c] Includes a single firm with 100 per cent stockholdings.

Source: Same as Table 22.1.

the case of financial institutions) exceeded 0.3 billion baht (U.S.$15 million) in 1979 and 1 billion baht (U.S.$40 million) in 1988. The firms satisfying these requirements numbered 218 in 1979 and 249 in 1988 and give us a very good cross-section of the leading businesses, including foreign enterprises, in Thailand.

It should also be noted that only about 20 per cent of the firms so selected are companies listed on the Securities Exchange of Thailand (SET) and thus public limited companies. The remainder are private limited companies.[7]

Looking at the distribution of top stockholders in Table 22.1, we can discern the following characteristics.

First, the proportion of foreign firms (mostly subsidiaries of multinational corporations) is very high (36 per cent in 1979 and 33 per cent in 1988), and entirely controlled subsidiaries total twenty-six in 1979 and thirty-one in 1988 respectively.

Secondly, of the Thai companies in the sample, a large amount (about 30 per cent) are not corporate-ownership-type firms (juristic persons holding), but individual-ownership-type firms (natural persons holding). No drastic change can be seen in this tendency over the ten years between 1979 and 1988.

Thirdly, among individual-ownership-type firms, over half of the top stockholders control by themselves a very high percentage of a firm's stock (30 per cent and over), indicating that no diffusion of stockholding has accompanied the creation of these large corporations.

Fourthly, the percentage of corporate-ownership-type firms has constantly increased among large Thai corporations over the ten-year period in question.

Now, adding the number of companies with individuals as their top stockholders to the number of family-owned investment companies (A)[8] and then adjusting the total sample by subtracting the number of foreign affiliates and companies financed either by public entities or the Crown Property Bureau (B),[9] we find that A amounts to 72 per cent of B in 1979 and 57 per cent of B in 1988. These figures show the dominance of individually- or family-owned enterprises in Thai big business.

Looking at the composition of the top three stockholders for each company in the sample (Table 22.2), we find again a very high percentage (about 40 per cent) of foreign corporations participating either on their own or in the form of joint ventures. The next largest group (25 to 28 per cent) is occupied by individual-ownership-type firms in Thai-owned businesses. To the contrary, in the case of corporate-ownership-type Thai firms, joint investment among multiple Thai corporations owned by different families is observed for only fifteen companies (7 per cent of the sample) in 1979 and nineteen companies (8 per cent) in 1988.

The number of companies in which all the top stockholders were either (1) members of the same family, (2) individuals or group corporations affiliated with the same family, or (3) a corporation directly owned by the same family totaled thirty-nine in 1979 (18 per cent of the total sample; 33 per cent of B) and sixty-three in 1988 (25 per cent; 45 per cent of B). The reason for the rise in this number is a growing trend towards investment practices utilizing affiliated corporations of each business group (pattern 3).

Due to limited source materials, it is only possible to identify "same family" when checking members of direct descent with the same family name. Therefore, stockholders who may be "same family" by virtue of collateral lines of descent or affinal ties have not been included in the above calculations. If we survey this sample by expanding the definition of "family" to include affinal ties, we will find not few firms in the sample that should be reclassified as "family businesses" in terms of their ownership.

Using Tables 22.1 and 22.2, it is also possible to point out the following characteristics of large corporate ownership patterns in Thailand. Namely, the proportion of corporate-ownership-type companies in big business is on the rise, due mostly to the increasing presence of foreign enterprises.[10] On the other hand, large Thai-owned corporations still rely more heavily on individual ownership than corporate and show no notable tendency towards diffused stock ownership.

B The management structure of large Thai corporations

Next, let us examine the characteristic features of top management levels in large-scale Thai-owned corporations using our enterprise data for 1988.

First, we must exclude wholly-controlled-type foreign enterprises from the 249 companies with annual sales figures over 1 billion baht in our sample. Now looking at the enterprises for which we know who their company presidents (and/or board chairpersons: CEOs) are, we will set up four categories to describe them: (1) a member or the top stockholding family, (2) a member of the second or third largest stockholding family, (3) a Thai national other than categories (1) and (2), or (4) a foreign citizen. The purpose of this grouping is to get a general idea of to what extent ownership and management are tied together in Thai-owned businesses.

Table 22.3 summarizes the results. We were able to identify the top management of 174 companies in the sample. From this total we further subtract all the enterprises that are 100 per cent owned by a holding company like the subsidiaries of Siam Cement Co., Ltd. In this case, there is no relevance to family-ties between the top stockholders (holding companies) and the appointed CEOs. In sum, we get a 160-company sample to work with.

Taking this total as our denominator, we find that 60 per cent of the company presidents and 63 per cent of the board chairpersons are members of the top stockholding families. Particularly in cases where the top stockholding family controls over 50 per cent of the stock, it is almost assured that a family member will be appointed to at least one CEO position. If we add to this number CEOs from second and third largest stockholding families, the number of companies in which the company president is a member of a large stockholding family accounts for two-thirds of the sample.

One more point to be noticed is the "different families" category in Table 22.3, in the sense that these CEOs are not necessarily all professional or salaried managerial executives. In other words, since the only criterion we have for establishing kinship connections between CEOs and stockholders is the same family name, our results probably understate the frequency of such connections, due to the likelihood of CEOs being connected to shareholders through marriage. Moreover, among CEOs recruited from a "different family," there are also friends and business partners of stockholding family members.

These facts can only lead us to believe that there are very few CEOs in large Thai-owned corporations who have been appointed only on the basis of their specialized managerial skills.[11] Overall, what we must conclude from Table 22.3 is that the majority of large Thai-owned corporations are of the ownership-control type rather than the management-control type, and that they are, moreover, "family"-ownership-control-type businesses.

Table 22.3 Family stockholders and management control in Thai large corporations, 1988

Top management	*Equity percentage of largest stockholder* 1–9%	10–49%	50–100%	*Total*	*%*
Presidents/general managers:					
(1) Same family with the largest stockholder	3	33	55	91	59.5
(2) Same families with 2nd or 3rd stockholders	2	8	1	11	7.2
(3) Different families[a]	4	22	11	37	24.2
(4) Foreigners	2	11	1	14	9.2
Sub-total	11	74	68	153	100.0
(5) No data available	—	3	2	5	
Chairmen of board:					
(1) Same family with the largest stockholder	1	21	34	56	62.9
(2) Same families with 2nd or 3rd stockholders	1	4	—	5	5.6
(3) Different families[a]	7	13	5	25	28.1
(4) Foreigners	1	2	—	3	3.4
Sub-total	10	55	39	89	100.0
(5) No data available	1	39	31	71	
Presidents (P)/chairmen (C):					
(1) Both of P/C belonging to the same family with top three stockholders	2	14	29	45	50.0
(2) Either of P/C belonging to the same family with top three stockholders	2	19	8	29	32.2
(3) Others	6	8	2	16	17.8
Sub-total	10	57	39	90	100.0
(4) No data available	1	38	31	70	

Notes:
1. Figures cover large corporations with annual sales of 1 billion baht in 1988.
2. Foreigner 100 per cent controlled and government partially owned companies have been excluded.
3. Subsidiaries of Siam Cement group and Suramahakhun group have been excluded.

[a] Figures include non-identified presidents or chairmen.

Sources: Survey by the author: same as Table 22.1.

C Ownership and management control of Thai Zaibatsu

From the above analysis, we have seen how within the Thai-controlled big business sector of Thailand there remains a broad area of individual and family ownership, where stockholding concentrates within particular families, who at the same time exercise control over managerial affairs. In addition to this characteristic, it is also necessary to point out one more important fact; namely, that many large Thai corporations are not independent entities, but rather belong to business groups in the form of zaibatsu (as defined above) [31, pp. 6–8]. To clarify this fact, let us look at the case of the Charoen Pokphand group (known as CP group).

The CP group is an agribusiness conglomerate consisting of close to 280 member firms as of 1991. CP group's consolidated annual sales ranks second among all the business groups in Thailand. Table 22.4 has been constructed summarizing data compiled by the Ministry of Commerce related to CP group's member firms and their ownership structure in the mid-1980s.[12]

Despite a wide-ranging expansion of its business enterprises, CP group's stock-holding composition has remained quite simple. That is to say, the investors in the group's member firms may be divided into three groups, a main group and two complementary groups. The main group consists of members of the Chiarawanon family headed by the Chia brothers, Chia Ek Cheow and Chia Shiau Hui, while the two complementary groups include (1) investment companies held exclusively by the Chiarawanon family and (2) the group's major member firms. Moreover, with the exception of a joint-venture enterprise [Arbor Acres (Thailand) Co., Ltd.] financed partly by capital from the United States, about 80 per cent of the stock of just about every group member firms is held by the Chiarawanon family or its investment companies.

It is this kind of "three-group investment composition" ("four group" in the case of joint ventures with foreign capital) that forms the most fundamental pattern in the ownership structure of Thai zaibatsu. Historically speaking, the general pattern begins with initial individual investment by the founding family (together with its affines and friends); then, as enterprise expansion proceeds, such capital fund sources as family investment companies and member firms are employed.[13]

We can also observe a pattern somewhat different from the above case in the form of the founding family retaining exclusive, individual control over group ownership through its hold on the group's parent or main company. This is pattern followed by the maker of Singha beer, the Boon Rawd Brewery group, and the Central Department group.[14]

Another practice in the effort by founding families to solidify their control over their zaibatsu is to reorganize the parent or main company of the group into an enterprise management stockholding company. Siam Motors Co., Ltd. performs this type of role for the automobile manufacturing group of the

Table 22.4 Ownership structure of CP group around 1983

Company name	Year of establishment	Type of business	Stockholding (%)		
			Family members[a]	Investment companies[b]	Group companies[c]
1. Chia Tai Seeds & Agricultural	1951	Fertilizer importing	100.0		
2. Charoen Pokphand Feedmill	1967	Feed milling	60.5	27.1	
3. Charoen Pokphand Produce	1967	Broiler raising	81.9	11.7	
4. Bangkok Feedmill	1968	Feed milling	63.8	11.3	
5. Kasetphan Industry	1970	Chicken farming	35.7	12.3	7.1
6. Arbor Acres (Thailand)[d]	1971	Parent stocks			50.0
7. Advance Pharma	1971	Vaccine importing	70.0	10.0	
8. CP Textile	1973	Textiles	16.9	49.6	
9. Bangkok Farm	1973	Chicken breeding	55.8	22.5	
10. Bangkok Livestock Processing	1973	Broiler processing	57.6	22.5	
11. Bangkok Fisheries	1974	Fish-ball processing	50.0		49.7
12. J. P. & Sons	1975	Investments	75.0		
13. Montri & Sons	1975	Investments	100.0		
13. Bangkopk Im-Ex	1976	Agri. exporting		16.0	56.0
15. Charoen Pokphand Investment	1976	Investments	10.4		54.2
16. Bangkok Food Product	1977	Food processing	67.5	67.5	22.5
17. CP Feedmill	1977	Food milling	68.2	68.2	22.7
18. Sumeth Investment	1978	Investments		100.0	
19. CP Intertrade	1979	General trading		28.0	35.5
20. Bangkok Produce Merchandising	1979	Agri. exporting	56.8	22.7	11.4

Notes:
[a] Combined percentage of Chiarawanon family members.
[b] Family-owned investment companies (companies Nos. 12, 13, 15, and 18).
[c] Companies of Nos. 2, 4, and 10.
[d] Joint venture with American company.

Source: "Kan toepto khong CP: borisat kham-chat rairaek khong Thai" [The growth of CP: the first multinational enterprise in Thailand], *Young Executive*, Vol. 2, No. 12 (September 1987), pp. 76–77.

same name [33, pp. 305–7]. We also see in the case of the Saha and Saha-Union groups, their stockholding companies (Saha Pathana Inter-Holding Co., Ltd. and Saha-Union Corp., Ltd. respectively) being listed on the Thai stock market, thus putting them on the road to evolving into modernized organizations. Both of these holding companies control managerial decision making over not only investment planning, but also their respective groups' personnel, marketing strategy, and research and development affairs.[15]

However, in these latter cases, as well, the basis of group ownership structure as a whole is still the family business, and they therefore represent no diversion from the way in which expansion and group formation have resulted in the present-day Thai zaibatsu. Therefore, what is happening in Thai zaibatsu today cannot be explained by the conventional theory of the joint-stock company, which states that as the scale of each group company grows and the sphere of enterprise expands, an evolution from family control to managerial control is bound to occur.

IV DIVERSIFICATION AND INTEGRATION OF THE FAMILY BUSINESS

A The political economic aspects

Why is it that the family business not only attempts to increase the scale of its business, but also creates enterprise groups by increasing the number of firms under its control? The answer to this question suggested by the business environment in the developing nations is that group formation is advantageous with respect to taxation. In other words, by forming new companies (including dummy corporations) it is possible to retain a portion of group profits that would otherwise flow out in the form of individual income tax, etc.

We can also observe in Thailand new group firms being founded not only to take advantage of tax loopholes, but also to use tax incentives set up by the government to promote industry. Since the end of the 1950s the Thai government, as one part of its industrial promotion policy, granted to private enterprises tax incentives (e.g., exemptions from machinery and raw material import duties and corporate income tax) for periods ranging from three to six years in duration. However, these privileges could be granted to each company only once during their existence. Therefore, when expanding into any particular enterprise sector business groups prefer to establish new companies instead of expanding existing plant and equipment. The Sukree group, also known as the "King of Textiles" in Thailand, has done this very thing in establishing many new spinning and weaving companies with facilities adjacent to one another [31, pp. 15–21].

However, probably the most important reason why family businesses in general tend to form enterprise groups is because they want to diversify their business lines and products. Let us first examine the theoretical aspects of diversification from the viewpoint of the theory of the firm.

In their research on the product strategy of the modern firm, Aoki and Itami [1] theoretically examine the motivation, rationale, scope, and economic effect of diversification by any one firm. According to this discussion there are three types of motive for diversification: (1) the need to respond to changing in market conditions or technological innovation; (2) the desire to take advantage of yet-unutilized resources that have accumulated within the firm; and (3) subjective resposes on the part of management to possible future changes (i.e., entrepreneurial motivation).

There are two rationales behind diversification: (1) entrepreneurial, which stems from the entrepreneurship of the firm's managers and (2) economic, which attempts to link existing business activities with new areas of endeavor for economic gain. Aoki and Itami point to what they term "economies of scope" as the most important factor in the rationale for diversification. That is to say, the appearance of yet-unutilized resources that could be employed in a number of areas encourage firms to proceed in the direction of diversification [1, pp. 66–8]. "Yet-unutilized resources" include not only idle plant and equipment, but also intangible assets such as a marketing and sales network or trademark, as well as information resources which can be employed many times over.

Meanwhile Y. Kobayashi's study of diversification by business groups emphasizes what he calls "the principle of growth opportunity maximization," in which expansion of the group as a whole is hoped to be realized through advancing into fast-growing industries or product lines. Kobayashi argues that attempts to diffuse risk or employ internally accumulated resources more efficiently are only secondary motivational factors in any business group's decision to diversify [14, pp. 77–8].

Considering these theoretical discussions, let us examine from what standpoint to view diversification within family business groups active in the developing countries. In the following sections three points will be discussed. They may be summarized as follows.

First, does the rationale behind diversification already exist within the group? This rationale may be found in "economies of scope" for the purpose of either (1) diversifying into related production or enterprise activities (i.e., vertical integration of production processes) or (2) diversifying into related product lines or markets (i.e., horizontal integration of product mixes).

Secondly, does the rationale behind diversification stem from late-starting industrial conditions within the economy? Here fast growth business chances are offered by the narrowness of domestic markets and the compressed or telescoping nature of industrialization. At the same time, factors to be considered here are government industrial promotion policies and easy access to foreign capital and technical know-how.

Thirdly, does the rationale behind diversification stem from the nature of the family business itself or the business practices of Chinese-run enterprise groups? Here, a hypothesis concerning the maintenance and expansion of the family fortune will be discussed.

B Diversification related to economies of scope

There are many cases of group formation in Thailand that have been the result of advancing into production processes and markets that are directly related to the company's initial area of business. There are basically two ways to diversify here: (1) moves to vertically integrate through advancing into upstream areas like raw materials or downstream areas like product assembly and (2) moves to horizontally integrate through manufacturing new products under the same brand name or through previously established marketing networks. In practice, however, many groups have chosen to vertically and horizontally integrate at the same time.

The typical ease of economies-of-scope-motivated diversification in Thailand is the Boon Rawd Brewery group, which dates back to 1933 with the establishment of Boon Rawd Brewery Co., Ltd. Since that time moves to vertically integrate its main business of brewing beer can be observed in the establishment in 1968 of the crown cap maker, Crown Seal Co., Ltd., in a joint venture with Toyo Seikan Kaisha, Ltd. of Japan, the acquisition of a glass bottle company in 1982, the founding (year unknown) of a company to manufacture plastic cases for shipping bottled products, and the construction of both a barley plantation and a malt factory in 1985.

Horizontally integrated diversification has been carried out by within the Boon Rawd Brewery Co., Ltd. itself in response to the appearance of a domestic competitor and moves by the government to raise taxes on beer. Boon Rawd has begun brewing a "light," low-calorie beer and has advanced into the soda water and soft drink industry. With the exception of its real estate interests, all the companies under the Boon Rawd Brewery group are related in one way or other to the manufacture and marketing of the group's initial product, beer [35, Chap. 8].

Similar cases include the chicken broiler and shrimp breeder CP group, the Sukree textile group, the automaker Siam Motors, and the construction materials maker Siam Cement. The Siam Cement group should be noted for reorganizing its machinery repair division, which it set up in 1942, into an independent iron and steel maker (Siam Iron & Steel Co., Ltd.) in 1966 [30, p. 155] and using the technical know-how accumulated in this sector to advance into the automobile industry [34]. Here we see an example of how a business group was able to employ yet-unutilized resources accumulating internally to raise its production activities to a higher level.

The Saha group is a unique example of how diversification into various product markets gave birth to a huge manufacturing zaibatsu in the field of consumer goods. The group's founder, Thiam Chokewattana (Lee Heng

Thiam), first started out as an importer of sundries (shirts, etc.) from China. Then in 1962 he formed a detergent manufacturing and sales company in a joint venture with Lion Corporation of Japan. From that time on the Saha group expanded by leaps and bounds through a nationwide network of traveling salespeople marketing Japanese goods such as Pias brand cosmetics. The group then utilized this same network to market the Wacoal women's undergarments it began to manufacture in 1970 [35, Chap. 4].

Today, the Saha group is organized into an integrated production-marketing conglomerate of about forty manufacturing companies organized according to different fields of production technology. For example, Saha Pathanapibul Co., Ltd. handles such mass consumption items as detergent and instant noodles, while International Cosmetic Co., Ltd. deals in well-known brand products such as Wacoal undergarments and child's ware. Here we find an excellent example of a zaibatsu that has effectively utilized to the maximum intangible assets accumulating within the group enterprises.

C Diversification and late-starting industrialization

The business environment that has contributed much to making possible the diversification carried by all Thai zaibatsu is Thailand's late-starting industrialization economy. That is to say, because of the limited scale and size of domestic markets, it is impossible to take full advantage of scale merits in any industry, be it cement or automobile and home appliance assembly. It is this situation that encouraged (or forced) business groups to diversify in Thailand. Moreover, diversification was further stimulated in the cases of such industries as automobiles and home appliances where a large number of assemblers were involved in severe competition.

On the other hand, late-starting industrialization actually helped business groups to diversify successfully in a number of ways. First, there is the governmental response to the situation in granting privileges to foreign firms and making it possible for domestic companies to employ capital funds, production technology and managerial know-how via joint venture agreements. Such groups as Siam Cement, Sukree, Siam Motors, and Saha, as well as the Saha-Union textile and garment accessory group, the Metro chemical fertilizer group, and Srifuengfung plate glass and chemical group, all furthered their diversification into zaibatsu by means of joint ventures with companies in Japan and the rest of the world [33, pp. 229–32].

The second way in which late-starting industrialization has helped diversification along is the government's attempt to address the situation directly through its industrialization promotion policy, which involved granting privileges to earmarked industrial sectors. The government has positively assisted import substitution industries, especially for consumer goods, since the 1960s, and from the mid-1980s has been promoting export-oriented and heavy industries. Most noteworthy is the government's efforts to provide new business opportunities for Thai entrepreneurs through policies linked to becoming a NIEs-type of country and taking full advantage of the foreign investment rush caused by the appreciation of the yen.

The appearance of new business opportunities and the expansion of the economy as a whole is clearly enabling Thai zaibatsu to continue their diversification ways. We have already mentioned Siam Cement's automobile venture, and the CP group's advance from agribusiness into petrochemicals and telephone lines, and the Saha and Saha-Union groups' new found interests in petrochemicals and export-oriented electronics are also good examples of recent diversification trends.

D Diversification and the family business

However, "economies of scope" and late-starting industrialization are not sufficient to explain fully the reason behind the widespread existence and enterprise growth of Thai zaibatsu. That is to say, many zaibatsu in Thailand have been formed into groups by advancing (from very early on, by the way) into induatries completely unrelated to their initial business ventures.

For example, the Kamol Sukosol group, initially an importer of products manufactured by the Westinghouse Corporation of the United States, formed a joint-venture company with Toyo Kogyo Co., Ltd, (Mazda) in 1974 to begin assembling automobiles, and since then has invested in such unrelated industries as hotel management, ethyl alcohol production, stainless steel refrigerator manufacturing, recording, finance, and real estate [13]. Such a pattern of zaibatsu development cannot be thoroughly explained by the previous discussion. Figure 22.2 represents a classic case of the formation of such a conglomerate type of zaibatsu in the Osothsapha (or Premier) group.

This type of conglomerate formation has two aspects. First, generational transition within these zaibatsu tends to promote business diversification. Here we see many cases of sons (or sons-in-law) of zaibatsu owners or founders advancing into industries completely different from the initial family business enterprise. The Premier group outlined in Figure 22.2 is an excellent example of this type of enterprise diversification.

As shown by the family genealogy constructed in Figure 22.3, the Premier group finds its roots in Pe Osathanukhro, who in 1930 founded Osothsapha (Teck Heng Yoo) Co., Ltd., an importer and purveyor of medicinal Chinese herbs. Following World War II, the company advanced into the manufacture and sale of Western pharmaceuticals on the strength of a technological tie-up with Taisho Pharmaceutical Co., Ltd. of Japan in producing a vitamin elixir. The Osothsapha group was built upon this company, and then it was turned over to the founder's son, Sawat.

It was during the third generation of Sawat's sons and daughter that the group began to diversify into such unrelated industries as leasing, finance, real estate, and export-oriented manufacturing (processed food, sport shoes,

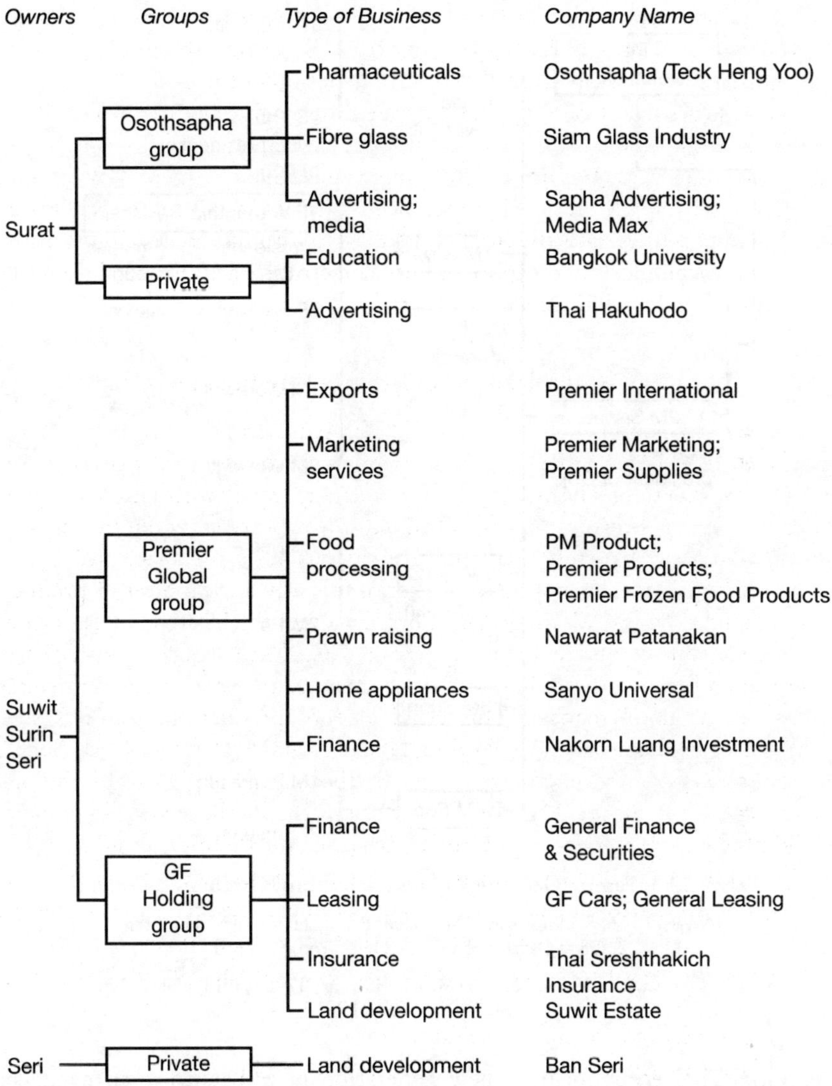

Figure 22.2 Business Diversification of Osothsapha (Premier) Group
Source: *Phu chatkan*, Vol. 7, No. 78 (March 1990), pp. 115–29.

luggage, and shrimp). While maintaining the pharmaceutical business as their main line, this new generation of owner/managers turned their investment activities mostly towards new, growth industries that were popping up in Thailand at the time [27].They also separated new businesses of the Premier group and the GF Holding group from their parents' business. This move was an attempt to respond to the quickly expanding and structurally

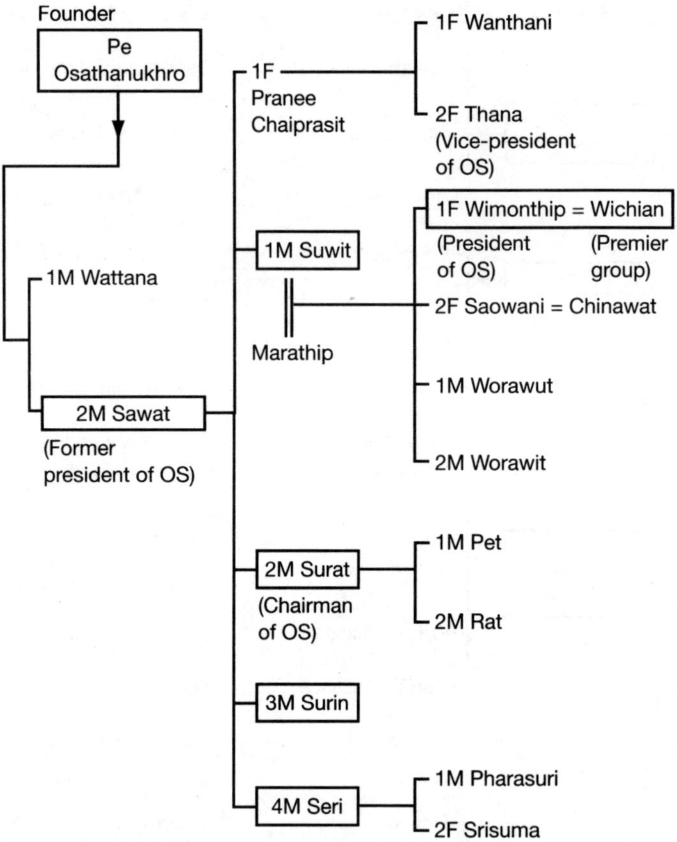

Figure 22.3 Family Genealogy of Osathanukhro (Osothsapha Group)

Notes: 1. 1M = eldest son; 2M = second son; 1F = eldest daughter.
2. OS = Osothsapha (Teck Heng Yoo) Co., Ltd.

Source: Phu chatkan, Vol 5, No. 56 (May 1988), pp. 82–83; ibid, Vol. 7, No. 78 (March 1990), p. 120.

changing Thai economy by a new generation of zaibatsu owner/managers resulting in the formation of a conglomerate.

A similar pattern can be observed in the diversification of the Shinawatra group, a nothern Thailand zaibatsu initially involved in the production and export of silk and traditional cotton clothing. This group first made advances into various non-industrial sectors around Chiang Mai, like hotel management and real estate, then during the third-generation regime of Thaksin Chinawat, the group entered the computer and telecommunications industries with an agreement in 1982 to supply the National Railway of Thailand with IBM-brand computers. Since around 1983, when Thaksin established Shinawatra Computer Co., Ltd., the Shinawatra group has added fourteen subsidiaries to its computer and telecommunications sectors, including capturing exclusive rights in 1991 to satellite broadcasting, followed by plans to advance into the telephone line and private TV broadcasting industries [17].

On the other hand, in the case of traditional Chinese family-run businesses, where the family fortune is divided equally among the heirs, generational transition brings with it a danger of enterprise diffusion and a decline of the zaibatsu's main line of business. In fact, in prewar times one can cite quite a few cases (like Kim Seng Lee and Nai Lert), in which zaibatsu with substantial business interests were led down the road to ruin by such generational transitions.

In contrast, however, there are business groups that have managed to keep the family intact through such transitions, resulting in expansion and reorganization of their enterprise bases. A classic case is the Wanglee family, which grew over five generations (over 100 years) into the largest rice miller and exporter in prewar Thailand [33, pp. 110–14]. Today this same family maintains an important place in the Thai economy as a zaibatsu active in the fields of banking and real estate.

It is not unusual to find in the Thai business community zaibatsu that have stayed intact now for three generations since their founding. We should also notice here that all of these groups have maintained their integration through family business management practices. For example, the Lamsam family-run Thai Farmers Bank group and the Taechaphaibun family-run BMB group have been centrally controlled by one dominant family figure, but at the same time other family members have been put in charge of various important group enterprises. The previously mentioned Central Department and Saha groups have been run under a similar family business system.

In sum, we can observe here a clear intent on the part of the family business to maintain intact and even expand the family's enterprises and assets over a number of generations. In the opinion of this author, such an intent represents a definite tendency towards conservation and expansion of the family fortune inherent in the business management characteristic of the family in general and the traditional Chinese-run enterprise in particular.[16] In such cases, the purpose of business endeavors is not to maximize profits and market shares of their enterprises, but rather to expand the total fortune of the family, resulting in advances into areas, such as finance and real estate, unrelated to existing enterprises. This is the second factor encouraging the formation of conglomerates by Thai zaibatsu.

Even though the above aspects can explain both the rationale and motivation for conglomerate formation, they do not necessarily explain why it is possible for zaibatsu to maintain family business organization and practices, while at the same time diversifying their enterprises. In this regard, it is necessary to add three additional points.

First, up to even the present day economically powerful Chinese businessmen in Thailand have tended to be polygamous in their relationships with women, resulting in the creation of very large families. For example, the founder of the Central Department group boasts a total of fourteen sons and twelve daughters, who in turn have produced over forty grandchildren. Moreover, there being no primogeniture rules among contemporary Chinese families, the most able member of any generation (be he or she the third eldest son, daughter, or a son-in-law) will be placed in the group's leadership role. For these reasons, even in the case of business expansion, the family is in a position to take advantage of a rich pool of human managerial resources made available by kinship and affinal ties characteristic to Thai Chinese.

Secondly, from quite early on in their histories, Thai zaibatsu have expanded their enterprises through not only kinship and regional ties, but also via a network of foreign Chinese residing throughout Asia. One case in point is the Sophonpanit family, which controls the Bangkok Bank group, advancing into the manufacturing sector in joint ventures with Chinese entrepreneurs in Hong Kong, Taiwan, and Singapore [32].

The third and final point concerns the generational transition that has continued in zaibatsu families since the 1970s. We have seen the rise of a new generation of skilled managers with high levels of education, experience abroad, and close relationships with overseas corporations.

Up to the beginning of the 1950s the Chinese business community in Thailand continued to send their young sons and daughters abroad to such places as the Chinese mainland, Hong Kong, Swatow, and Singapore, where they could learn Mandarin and English, while becoming accustomed to traditional Chinese commercial practices. While residing in these overseas localities, those generations were also able to strengthen the regional network of personal relationships first built by their fathers.

However, with the establishment of the People's Republic of China in 1949, there occurred a shift in points of destination for overseas study to such faraway places as the United States, Japan, and Australia. Instead of traditional Chinese commercial practices, this new generation was and is being exposed to modern concepts of business administration and accounting systems, new production technologies and marketing skills, as well as the inner workings of the Japanese general trading company. For this reason, the management style characterizing the first and second generations of zaibatsu managers is not being reproduced in the third and fourth generations, as a new type of Chinese businessman has appeared in Thailand emphasizing improvements in the quality of entrepreneurship and enterprises management. This shift in business practices has made possible advances into new fields of endeavor never before imagined by zaibatsu families.

V CONCLUSION

First, it should be emphasized that despite separate treatment given to the aspects of economies of scope, late-starting industrialization, and the characteristic features of Chinese family business management in this paper, all of these factors are interrelated in encouraging the formation of Thai zaibatsu groups and forming their diversification policies. In Conclusion, let us again ask the question why the family business still remains a dominate form of business group management in Thailand.

One reason is the underdevelopment of both domestic capital markets and the joint-stock company form of business organization. As of 1988, only 20 per cent of the top 250 corporations in Thailand had put their stock up for public sale. In addition, despite the establishment of a stock exchange system as early as 1975, increased stock activity resulting in the possibility of widespread equity finance transactions has only occurred since 1987.

In spite of these developments, it is still impossible to state that the managerial control hypothesis concerning the inevitable decline of the family business in the wake of capital market development and enterprise scale expansion will come true. This is because the case of Thai zaibatsu indicates a deep-rootedness and enterprise expansion capability far stronger than any family business institutions that may have existed in the industrialized countries of the world.

Therefore, it becomes necessary to search anew with a more positive attitude for the reasons why the family-business-type zaibatsu continues to exist. In this author's opinion the reasons may be found in the ability of zaibatsu to carry on internal reform, or adapt to changing business environments. In concrete terms, this means improvements in management practices, willingness to employ personnel from outside the controlling family, and forward-looking, innovational enterprise operations.[17]

The main point that should be made here is that zaibatsu which have grown and expanded in Thailand are not of the type described by such researchers as Useem; that is, they are by no means "anti-industrial" business groups concerned only with preserving their family honor and social position. To the contrary, Thai zaibatsu are interested in expanding their enterprises by means of quick responsiveness to changing economic environments both at home and abroad and with an eye to reaping profits offered by late-starting industrialization. Therefore, even though these zaibatsu are indeed family businesses just like the British groups studied by Useem, their management style is very different in their promotion of "innovation" on all the fronts of organization, production, and distribution.

This is the reason why we see contemporary Thai zaibatsu being led by owners filled with entrepreneurship and founded on very systematically organized family businesses. If these characteristics are not positively viewed and evaluated, we will never really understand what has been the keys to their growth and prosperity.

NOTES

1 Chandler defines the family business as follows.

> In some firms the entrepreneur and his close associates (and their families) who built the enterprise continued to hold the majority of stock. They maintained a close personal relationship with their managers, and they retained a major say in top management decisions, particularly those concerning financial policies, allocation of resources, and the selection of senior managers. Such a modern business enterprise may be termed an entrepreneurial or family one, and an economy or sectors of an economy dominated by such firms may be considered a system of entrepreneurial or family capitalism. [5, p. 9]

2 Morikawa [18] defines zaibatsu as "a widely diversified business enterprises under the ownership and managerial control of wealthy family group, either nuclear or extended." See also [19].

3 In fact, *kigyō shūdan* is usually translated into English as "business group." For a discussion of interrelations between prewar *zaibatsu* and postwar *kigyō shūdan*, see [8].

4 The monthly business magazine, *Phu chatkan* (The manager), featured special reports in its August and September 1988 issues on a total of twelve Thai business groups, including the Boon Rawd Brewery group, the agribusiness group Charoen Pakphand (CP), and the textile manufacturing Saha-Union and Sukree groups. The term *thurakit khrop-khrua* was used in the title of these reports. See [36].

5 See also the article by Numazaki in this special issue.

6 Negishi [23] is very helpful in studying the origins, organizational aspects and accounting practices of these traditional Chinese enterprises. The reader will also find a comparison with corporate development in Europe.

7 As of 1988, there were a total of 141 companies listed on the Securities Exchange of Thailand. Of this total, 44 companies surpassed 1 billion baht in sales, thus qualifying them under our definition of "large corporation." These listed companies come to only 18 per cent of 249 firms in our sample. Calculated from [29].

8 A "family-owned investment company" is defined here as an enterprise financed totally by the members of a particular family with the aim of investing in both its group enterprises and outside corporations. This aim is different from the "holding company," which aims to systematically keep control over ownership and management within the group. Rather, the aim in the former is to reduce the individual income-tax burden on family members. These investment companies first appeared in Chinese business groups which controlled commercial banks, and then spread to the manufacturing sector groups during the latter half of the 1960s. Groups containing such companies include Bangkok Bank group (Chatri Sophon Co., Ltd.; established 1966), BMB group (Tejapaibul Co., Ltd.; established 1967), Sukree group (Thai Wythipat Co., Ltd.; established 1969), and Saha group (Chokwatana Co., Ltd.; established 1972).

9 The Crown Property Bureau is an office set up in 1936 to control and manage the holdings accumulated by the Thai royal family over many generations. The bureau invests in many business enterprises, including Siam Cement, and in the real estate business. There is a different office, the Royal Household Bureau, that manages the financial affairs of the present king, Rama IX.

10 Pichet and Yasuda [28, pp. 235–37] have utilized corporate data for 1982 to analyze the top stockholders of the 200 largest (annual sales) companies and 62

listed companies. However, they divide these enterprises into only two categories, individual ownership (natural persons holding) and corporate ownership (juristic persons holding), resulting in far too much emphasis on the existence of corporate ownership.

11 One large business group which has clearly appointed managerial experts to the posts of CEO in its member enterprises is the Siam Cement group. For an analysis of the managerial structure of this group, see [31, p. 19, Table 8].

12 It should be mentioned, however, that CP group embarked on a restructuring of its ownership composition beginning in 1987 with the listing of a portion of its member firms on the Thai stock market [35, pp. 98–99]. Table 22.4 therefore indicates the situation before restructuring.

13 A description of changes that have occurred in the Sukree group ownership pattern may be found in [31, p. 19, Table 8].

14 On the Boon Rawd Brewery group, see "Prachaup Phiromphakdi: naenon, khon run-mai yomdi kwa khon run-kon" [Prachuap Phiromphakdi: it is natural that a successor gains more than an ancestor], *Phu-nam thurakit*, October 1987. The ownership structure of the Central Department group is outlined in [39, p. 53].

15 Securities Exchange of Thailand provides information on both Saha Pathana Inter-Holding Co., Ltd. [29, Vol. 1, pp. 781–9] and Saha-Union Corp., Ltd. [29, Vol. 1, pp. 790–801].

16 One can anticipate two possible ways of criticizing such a postition. First, there is the view that the concept of "family fortune" that existed in prewar Japanese zaibatsu does not exist in the case of Chinese-run zaibatsu, which is based on equally divided inheritance. Secondly, there is the view that Chinese family fortune should be divided into fortune held by the group and fortune held by its individuals, and it is the latter that tends to be emphasized in expansion plans.

17 Concrete examples of a variety of reforms actually carried out by zaibatsu groups in Thailand may be found in [35].

REFERENCES

1 Aoki, M., and Itami, H. *Kigyō no keizaigaku* [Economies of the firm] (Tokyo: Iwanami-shoten, 1985).

2 Baran, P. A., and Sweezey, P. M. *Monopoly Capital: An Essay on the American Economic and Social Order* (New York: Monthly Review Press, 1966).

3 Berle, A. A., Jr., and Means, G. C. *The Modern Corporation and Private Property* (New York: Macmillan, 1932).

4 Burch, P. H. *The Managerial Revolution Reassured: Family Control in America's Large Corporations* (Lexington, Mass.: Lexington Books, 1972).

5 Chandler, A. D., Jr., *The Visible Hand: The Managerial Revolution in American Business* (Cambridge, Mass.: Harvard University Press, 1977).

6 Hamilton, G. G., Orrù, M.; and Biggart, N. W. "Enterprise Groups in East Asia: An Organizational Analysis," *Shōken keizai*, No. 161 (September 1987).

7 Hamilton, G. G., Zeile, W., and Kim, W. J. "The Network Structures of East Asian Economies," in *Capitalism in Contrasting Cultures*, ed. S. R. Clegg and S. G. Redding (Berlin: Walter de Gruyter, 1990).

8 Hashimoto, J., and Takeda, H., eds. *Nihon keizai no hatten to kigyō shūdan* [Japan's economic development and business groups] (Tokyo: University of Tokyo Press, 1992).

9 Hattori, T. "Gendai Kankoku kigyō no shoyū to keiei" [Ownership and management of contemporary Korean enterprises], *Ajia keizai*, Vol. 25, Nos. 5–6 (May–June 1984).

10 ——. *Kankoku no keiei hatten* [Management development in Korea] (Tokyo: Bunshindo, 1990).
11 Herman, E. S. *Corporate Control, Corporate Power* (New York: Cambridge University Press, 1981).
12 Imabori, S. "Shindai ni okeru gōka no kindaika eno keisha" [Modernization of *hehuo* enterprises during Qing dynasty era], *Tōyōshi kenkyū* (Kyoto University), Vol. 17, No. 1 (June 1958).
13 Kamol Sukosol Group. "Kamon Sukoson: thang song phraeng khong Kamola" [Kamol Susosol Group: Mr. Kamola at the crossroads], *Setthakit kan-muang*, October 11, 1982.
14 Kobayashi, Y. *Kigyō shūdan no bunseki* [Analysis of business groups] (Sapporo: Hokkaido University Press, 1980).
15 Kroekkiat Phiphatseritham. *Wikhro laksana kan-pen-chao khrong thurakit khanat-yai nai prathet Thai* [Analysis of ownership patterns of big businesses in Thailand] (Bangkok: Thammasat University Press, 1981).
16 Mathuphum Thurakit, ed. *Klum borisat thurakit khanat-yai* [Big business groups], 2 vols. (Bangkok: Mathuphum Thurakit, 1986).
17 Matichon. *Thaksin Chinawat: asawin haeng khlun luk-thi-sam* [Thaksin Chinawat: leader of the third generation/industrial wave] (Bangkok: Matichon Co., 1993).
18 Morikawa, H. *Nihon zaibatsushi* [History of Japanese zaibatsu] (Tokyo: Kyōikusha, 1974).
19 ——. *Zaibatsu: The Rise and Fall of Family Enterprise Groups in Japan* (Tokyo: University of Tokyo Press, 1992).
20 Nakagawa, K. "Kōshinkoku kōgyōka to kigyōsha katsudō" [Indusrialization and entrepreneurs in less advanced countries], *Keizaigaku ronshū* (University of Tokyo), Vol. 28, No. 3 (November 1962).
21 ——. "Kaizai hatten to kazokuteki keiei" [Economic development and family-type business], in *Kokumin keizai no shoruikei* [Types of national economies], ed. T. Kawashima and T. Matsuda (Tokyo: Iwamami-shoten, 1968).
22 —— *Hikaku keieishi josetsu* [An introduction to comparitive business history] (Tokyo: University of Tokyo Press, 1981).
23 Neoishi, T. *Shōji ni kansuru kankō chōsa hōkokusho: gōko no kenkyū* [Research report on commercial practices: a study of *hegu*] (Tokyo: Tōa-kenkyusho, 1943).
24 Niida, N. *Chūgoku hōseishi* [History of Chinese legal institutions], rev. ed. (Tokyo: Iwanami-shoten, 1963).
25 Numazaki, I. "Networks and Partnerships: The Social Organization of the Chinese Business Elite in Taiwan" (Ph.D. diss., Michigan State University, 1992).
26 Okochi, A., and Yasuoka, S., eds. *Family Business in the Era of Industrial Growth: Its Ownership and Management* (Tokyo: University of Tokyo Press, 1984).
27 Phoemphon Phophoemhen. "Premier krup: mua Suwit-Seri Osathanukhro thot nakak na-thi-song" [The Premier group: when Suwit and Seri Osathanukhro threw off their second mask], *Phu chatkan*, Vol. 7, No. 78 (March 1990).
28 Pichet Maolanond and Yasuda, N. *Corporation and Law in ASEAN Countries: A Case Study of Thailand*, Joint Research Programme Series No. 49 (Tokyo: Institute of Developing Economies, 1985).
29 Securities Exchange of Thailand. *Sarup khu-sonthet: borisat chot-thabian borisat rapanuyat, pho. so. 2532* [Directory of registered and authorized public limited companies], 2 vols. (Bangkok, 1990).
30 Siam Cement Co., ed. *Pun-siment Thai, 2456–2526* [Siam Cement Co., Ltd., 1913–1983] (Bangkok, 1983).

31 Suehiro, A. "Tai-kei kigyō shūdan no shihon chikuseki kōzō: seizōgyō gurūpu o chūshin to shite" [Capital accumulation of Thai business groups: a case study of the industrial group], *Ajia keizai*, Vol. 25, No. 10 (October 1984).
32 ——. "Bangkok Bank: Management Reforms of a Thai Commercial Bank," *East Asian Cultural Studies*, Vol. 28, Nos. 1–4 (March 1989).
33 ——. Capital Accumulation in Thailand 1855–1985 (Tokyo: Centre for East Asian Cultural Studies, 1989).
34 ——. "Tai ni okeru sangyō konguromaritto no keiei kaikaku: Saiamu gurūpu no jirei kenkyū" [Management reforms of industrial conglomerate in Thailand: a case study of the Siam Cement group], *Kikan keizai kenkyū* (Osaka City University), Vol. 12, No. 4 (Spring 1990).
35 Suehiro, A., and Nambara, M. *Tai no zaibatsu: Jamiri bijinesu to keiei kaikaku* [Zaibatsu in Thailand: family business and management reforms] (Tokyo: Dobunkan-shuppan, 1991).
36 "Thurakit khrop-khrua" [Family-run business], Parts 1, 2, *Phu chatkan*, Vol. 6, Nos. 59, 60 (August, September 1988).
37 Tong Chee Kiong. "Centripetal Authority, Differentiated Networks: The Social Organization of Chinese Firms in Singapore," Working Paper No. 99, Department of Sociology, National University of Singapore, Kuala Lumpar, 1989.
38 Useem, M. *The Inner Circle: Large Corporations and the Rise of Business Political Activity in the U.S. and the U.K.* (New York: Oxford University Press, 1984).
39 Wirat Saengthongkham and Bunsiri Nambunsri. "Chirathiwat lae hang central kam-lang-cha phan khao-su yuk-thi sam" [The Chirathiwat family and Central Department Store enter into the third stage of its development], *Phu chatkan*, Vol. 4, No. 37 (October 1986).
40 Yamana, M. *Chūgoku keizai no kōzō teki kenkyū* [Study of economic structure in China] (Tokyo: Chuo-keizaisha, 1954).
41 Yu Chunghsun, ed. *Sekai no Chainzu: bōsōuru kakyō, kajin no keizairyoku* [Ethnic Chinese overseas: their expanding economic power] (Tokyo: Simul Press, 1991).

Part VII

TRENDS IN POVERTY

23

AGRICULTURAL GROWTH, LANDLESSNESS, OFF-FARM EMPLOYMENT AND RURAL POVERTY IN THE PHILIPPINES

Arsenio Balisacan

23.I INTRODUCTION

Rapid agricultural growth has been suggested as an alternative development strategy for less developed countries (LDCs).[1] The strategy is deemed superior to either an industry-led import substitution development strategy or to export-led growth, especially in the context of an unfavorable environment for expanded global trade and finance. Agricultural growth is considered to provide direct as well as indirect stimulus to the setting up of new activities through linkage effects, thereby facilitating industrialization in addition to directly addressing the twin problems of poverty and unemployment in LDCs.

In the Philippines, the Aquino administration's Medium-Term Philippine Development Plan (1987–92) identified agriculture and rural development as the central focus of development efforts aimed at reducing poverty. Although some earlier development plans (e.g., the Yulo Plan of 1950) and political regimes also emphasized agricultural development, none presented it as the major component of a development strategy directly aimed at alleviating poverty, particularly rural poverty, and at enhancing economic recovery. Previous plans tended to emphasize agricultural development insofar as this would enhance domestic food security and foreign exchange earnings.[2]

This article provides a critical look at the country's record with respect to agricultural growth and poverty alleviation. It argues that rapid agricultural growth, as demonstrated by the experience in the 1960s and 1970s, is not enough to pull the rural poor out of poverty as well as sustain rapid overall economic growth. Economic structures and the economic policy environment have to be conducive to the rapid growth of employment opportunities for the fast-growing labor force, particularly in the nonagriculture sector.[3] Section 23.II of the article characterizes Philippine agricultural growth in an

Source: *Economic Development and Cultural Change*, Vol. 41(3), April 1993, pp. 533–62.

international perspective. Section 23.III then examines the historical record with respect to income distribution and poverty. Section 23.IV turns to issues concerning access to land, agricultural productivity, and rural poverty. Section 23.V discusses the link between access to employment opportunities and rural poverty. Finally, Section 23.VI provides concluding comments.

23.II POSTWAR AGRICULTURAL GROWTH

The agricultural sector (comprising crops, livestock and poultry, fishery, and forestry) of the Philippine economy performed remarkably well during most of the post-World War II period. The sector posted an annual average growth rate of 3.9% from the mid-1950s to the late 1980s. The growth, however, decelerated in the 1980s. While the average annual growth rate for the period 1965–80, the height of the Green Revolution, was substantially higher than the averages for the developing Monsoon Asian countries and the middle-income developing countries, and compared favorably with those for Thailand and Indonesia, it was way below the averages for those countries in the 1980s (Table 23.1).

The changes in food production per capita depict the same pattern (Table 23.2). The increase in food production per capita in the Philippines surpassed those of the averages for the low-income economies (including India and China) and the middle-income economies in 1975–80. But by the late 1980s, food production per capita in the Philippines was 10% lower than the level prevailing at the start of the decade. In contrast, the average food production per capita for low-income economies increased by 12%, while that for middle-income economies remained nearly the same. Among ASEAN-member nations, Indonesia had a remarkable performance—food production per capita increased by 17% during the period.

Partly explaining the decline in food production per capita is the continued high growth rate of the Philippine population. The average population growth rate of 2.5% per year for the period 1980–88 was above the averages for low-income economies (2.0%), middle-income economies (2.2%), and Thailand and Indonesia (1.9% and 2.1%, respectively).

It is interesting to note that developing countries with relatively high growth rates of agricultural value added also tend to have comparatively high GDP growth rates. This observation is, of course, not surprising given that agriculture is a large fraction of the economy in a typical developing country. In the Philippine case, the remarkably robust agricultural growth for the period 1965–80 was accompanied by a GDP growth that closely matched the averages for the developing Monsoon Asian countries and the middle-income developing countries (Table 23.1).

The expansion of cultivated area (i.e., the opening up of new lands for cultivation) provided the major source of the production growth of Philippine agriculture (defined in the rest of this section to include only crops and

Table 23.1 Agricultural growth in developing monsoon Asia and middle-income developing countries

		Share of agriculture in GDP (%)		*Annual growth rate (%)*			
				GDP		*Agriculture*	
Country	*1988 Per capita GDP (US$)*	*1965*	*1988*	*1965–80*	*1980–88*	*1965–80*	*1980–88*
Developing monsoon Asia	1,019	39	28.8	5.4	5.5	2.3	2.9
Malaysia	2,052	28	21.1	7.3	4.6	...	3.7
Thailand	1,063	32	17.0	7.2	6.0	4.6	3.7
Indonesia	476	56	24.0	8.0	5.1	4.3	3.1
Philippines	655	26	23.0	5.9	0.1	4.6	1.8
Sri Lanka	386	28	26.0	4.0	4.3	2.7	2.7
Pakistan	320	40	26.0	5.1	6.5	3.3	4.3
India	292	44	32.0	3.6	5.2	2.5	2.3
Bangladesh	177	53	46.0	2.4	3.7	1.5	2.1
Nepal	159	65	56.0	1.9	4.7	1.1	4.4
China	342	44	33.0*	6.4	10.3	2.8	6.8
Burma	192*	35	37.0*	2.9†	5.3‡	...	...
Taiwan	6,113	18§	4.8	10.3‖	9.8#	...	...
Middle-income developing countries	2,061	20	12.0	6.1	2.9	3.6	2.7

Notes:
* 1985.
† 1965–73.
‡ 1973–86.
§ 1970.
‖ 1975–79.
1986–89.

Sources: Asian Development Bank, *Key Indicators of Developing Asian and Pacific Countries* (Manila, July 1990); World Bank, *World Development Report* (Washington, D.C.: World Bank, 1990).

Table 23.2 Food production per capita and population growth rate

	Index of food production per capita (1980 = 100)		*Percent change*		*Average annual growth rate of population (%)*	
	*1975**	*1987**	*1975–80*	*1980–87*	*1965–80*	*1980–88*
Low-income economies	90	112	11	12	2.3	2.0
Middle-income economies	91	99	10	−1	2.4	2.2
East Asia	...	123	...	23	2.3	1.5
South Asia	...	100	...	0	2.4	2.3
ASEAN-3:						
Philippines	79	90	27	−10	2.9	2.5
Thailand	81	101	23	1	2.9	1.9
Indonesia	84	117	19	17	2.4	2.1

Note:
* Three-year averages, centered on the year shown.

Source: World Bank, *World Development Report*, various issues.

poultry and livestock), at least up to the 1950s. Since the closure of the agricultural land frontier in the 1960s resulting from increased population pressure, the contribution of land productivity (output per hectare) growth has increasingly become the more important source of production growth.[4] Over the last 2 decades, increases in yield accounted for about 80% of total agricultural production growth. Whereas cultivated area per farm worker declined by an annual average of 2.5% during the same period, yield grew by an annual average of about 5%, enabling agricultural output per farm worker to grow by about 2% annually.[5] In contrast, the 6 decades preceding the 1960s were marked by increasing cultivated area per farm worker, decreasing output per cultivated area, and virtually unchanged per capita agricultural output.[6]

There exist, however, substantial differences among crops. Whereas yield growth from the mid-1970s to the mid-1980s contributed nearly two-thirds of the production growth of the major staple crops (palay and corn) and of banana and pineapple, area expansion largely contributed to output growth of coconut, coffee, sugarcane, abaca, tobacco, and root crops.[7] In the case of rice, the rapid diffusion of the modern-variety-fertilizer-irrigation technology beginning in the mid-1960s was largely responsible for the yield increases. By the mid-1980s, about 85% of the total rice area was planted to modern varieties, and nearly 65% of this was irrigated. Fertilizer use on rice also rose from 8 kilograms of nitrogen, phosphorus, and potassium (NPK) per hectare in the mid-1960s to 40 kilograms NPK per hectare in the mid-1980s.

23.III AGRICULTURAL GROWTH, INCOME DISTRIBUTION, AND RURAL POVERTY

The conceptual and empirical difficulties surrounding the measurement of income inequality and poverty are fairly well known. In this article, purely practical considerations, such as the availability of data and the impossibility of obtaining new data, dictated definitional and measurement choices. More important, the imposition of consistency of definition, not a mixture of definitions, became the dominant factor in the choice of one concept over another.

The statistical base for the analysis in this section is mainly the various rounds of Family Income and Expenditure Survey (FIES) conducted by the National Statistics Office based in Manila, Philippines. These surveys were undertaken in 1961, 1965, 1971, 1975, 1979, 1985, and 1988. The 1975 and 1979 surveys, however, were not published due to some technical problems, one of which was the implausibility of the data generated arising from substantial underrepresentation of certain households. Excluding 1975 and 1979, it appears that the FIES provides a reasonably good series—in fact, the only one available—for the analysis of trends in income inequality and poverty over the last 3 decades. Unfortunately, I was limited to published tabulations for 1961, 1965, and 1971 and have been able to acquire data tapes only for 1985 and 1988. Given the imprecision of the data, particularly for earlier years, the results should be interpreted as indicating trends rather than precise magnitudes.[8]

Has income distribution gotten worse with agricultural growth?

It is often desirable to use more than one summary index of inequality, since some indexes are more sensitive than others to changes in different parts of the size distribution of income. The Gini (G) index, the summary measure commonly used in the Philippines, is relatively more sensitive to changes in the middle ranges than in the extreme ranges of the size distribution of income. This is because G depends on the rank order weights of income recipients and on the number of recipients in a given range. The coefficient of variation (CV), on the other hand, is more sensitive to change in the upper ranges of the distribution, since it attaches equal weights to transfers at all levels of income. The standard deviation of logarithms (SDL), derived when incomes are expressed in logarithms, is one measure which is more sensitive to changes in the lower ranges than in the other parts of the distribution. That is, the fact that a logarithmic transformation staggers income levels tends to soften the blow in reflecting inequality. Looked at differently, each of these measures is most sensitive to a particular type of inequality: G for inequality among the less extreme incomes, the CV for inequality due to extreme wealth, and SDL for inequality due to extreme poverty.[9]

Table 23.3 shows the estimates of these measures for the five rounds of

Table 23.3 Indexes of income inequality, 1961–88

Index	*1961*	*1965*	*1971*	*1985*	*1988*
All families:					
Coefficient of variation	1.094	1.076	1.003	.963	.949
Standard deviation of logarithm	.409	.445	.436	.373	.374
Gini index	.486	.491	.478	.446	.445
Rural families:					
Coefficient of variation	.797	.797	.920	.772	.769
Standard deviation of logarithm	.318	.366	.396	.310	.310
Gini index	.386	.410	.448	.378	.378
Urban families:					
Coefficient of variation	1.116	1.129	.893	.945	.910
Standard deviation of logarithm	.462	.448	.395	.373	.363
Gini index	.506	.503	.440	.442	.431

FIES.[10] All the above measures exhibited little changes over the years. Considering that per capita GDP grew by an annual average of nearly 2% from 1961 to 1971, the relatively small change was rather unusual in relation to the growth and income distribution experience of East Asia's newly industrialized countries (NICs) where economic growth was accompanied by considerable improvement in income distribution.[11] Even the growth spell in the latter half of the 1960s when GDP grew by about 5%—although low in relation to the average for middle-income economies and ASEAN countries—and the economic recovery in the latter part of the 1980s barely improved income distribution. One may argue that this is hardly a surprise when viewed in the context of the so-called inverted U-shaped relationship between economic growth and income distribution.[12] While plausible, such a relationship has, however, received little empirical support. Gary Fields, in surveying the available evidence from the experiences of various countries, concludes "that whether inequality increases or decreases with economic growth depends on the type of growth rather than on the level of GNP or the rate of GNP growth *per se*."[13] Many others also emphasized that income inequality is determined as much or more by the type of economic development, including policies followed, as by the level of development per se.[14]

It bears noting that the inequality of income in rural areas was somewhat less than in urban areas. This difference could be larger than the figures shown in Table 23.3 when one takes into account the underrepresentation of residential enclaves of rich families, particularly in Metro Manila, in FIES rounds. Notice, however, the narrowing of the gap (e.g., the difference of the Gini index for urban and rural areas) from 1961 to 1971, and the widening of it in 1985. The trend in the first period was mostly associated with decreased income inequality in urban areas and increased inequality in rural areas. The widening of the gap in 1985 (relative to 1971) resulted largely from the improvement of income equality in rural areas.

The increase in income inequality from 1961 to 1971 in rural areas deserves a closer look. This period was characterized by fairly rapid agricultural growth, especially in the rice sector where the adoption of high-yielding modern varieties was unusually rapid vis-à-vis many other Asian countries. Indeed, the average real family income in rural areas increased by 19% from 1961 to 1965 and by another 19% from 1965 to 1971 (Table 23.4). In contrast, while average real family income in urban areas increased by 21% in the first period, it stagnated in the second period. Thus, the rural-urban income ratio increased from about 40% in 1961 and 1965 to 48% in 1971. Then, in the 1980s, when agricultural growth slowed down along with the rest of the economy, income distribution in the rural areas improved somewhat, even though the rural-urban income ratio was almost steady from 1971 to 1988. Robert Herdt and others observed that the adoption of modern technologies in the 1960s and early 1970s tended to be initially concentrated among large farmers, with small farmers catching up in later years.[15] This fact, along with the highly skewed distribution of agricultural landholdings in the Philippines, and the slow growth of more productive employment opportunities in off-farm areas in relation to the growth of the labor force, partly explains the pattern of income inequality in rural areas.

Has agricultural growth trickled down to the poor?

The identification of the poor and the attendant aggregation that combines the data on the poor into an overall measure of poverty almost always involve a construction, albeit imprecise, of a poverty line or threshold.[16] For practical purposes, I define a poverty threshold as the critical minimum amount of income below which a person cannot attain a predetermined consumption bundle of goods and services, as judged necessary for the fulfillment of certain basic consumption needs, most important (in the context of this study) adequate nutrition. I have adopted the NEDA-FNRI-NSO technical working group's estimates of poverty lines for 1985 for the country's 13 regions, subdivided into rural and urban areas.[17] I have adjusted these estimates for inflation to obtain poverty thresholds (at current prices) for 1961, 1965, 1971, and 1988. Although necessarily still imprecise, these estimates take into account regional price differences and consumption patterns (and thus avoid a major shortcoming of previous studies) as well as the desirability of imposing consistent definitions of poverty thresholds throughout the period of analysis.[18]

The commonly used summary measure of poverty in the Philippines is the head-count index, expressed as the proportionate number of households whose incomes fall below the poverty line. The drawback of this measure is that it is entirely insensitive to changes below the poverty line. A poor person may become poorer, but measured poverty will remain the same. Furthermore, an income transfer from a person below the poverty line to one above it

Table 23.4 Average real family income of urban and rural households, 1961–88

	Average family income (in 1978 pesos) *					*Percent change*			
	1961	*1965*	*1971*	*1985*	*1988*	*1961–65*	*1965–71*	*1971–85*	*1985–88*
Philippines	7,452	8,582	9,386	8,806	9,907	15.2	9.4	−6.2	12.5
Rural	4,971	5,928	7,080	6,204	6,939	19.3	19.4	−12.4	11.9
Urban	12,262	14,873	14,730	13,082	14,700	21.3	−1.0	−11.2	12.4
Rural/urban ratio	40.5	39.9	48.1	47.4	47.2	...	...	...	...

Note:
* For 1961 and 1965, average family income is deflated using the consumer price index (CPI) for Metro Manila. For all other years the CPI for the Philippines is used.

Source: Basic data are from National Statistics Office, *Family Income and Expenditure Surveys*, various issues.

does not change measured poverty—indeed an absurd property of a summary measure of poverty.

In addition to the head-count index, I have used the following summary measures.

1. The income gap is measured as the average income shortfall of the poor (expressed in proportion to the poverty line).

2. The poverty gap is measured as the arithmetic mean of the income shortfall (expressed in proportion to the poverty line) over the whole population. This measure is sensitive to both the number of the poor and to how poor they are, although the various poverty deficits of the poor are weighed equally. One objection to it, however, is that it is insensitive to redistribution of income within the poor units.

3. The FGT ($\alpha = 2$) index is measured the same way as the poverty gap except that the weights are simply the squared income shortfalls themselves.[19] Unlike in the head-count and poverty gap measures, measured poverty in FGT ($\alpha = 2$) decreases whenever a transfer of income takes place from a poor household to a poorer one.

4. The Sen index is a well-known distributionally sensitive measure that takes into account the poor's income shortfalls as well as the inequality of income among the poor.

All the poverty measures show a decline in poverty incidence from 1961 to 1988 (Table 23.5). Head-count poverty declined from 75% in 1961 to 49% in 1988. The average income shortfall of the poor was 53% of the poverty line in 1961 and 36% in 1988. Note that, although income inequality hardly changed between 1961 and 1971, the head count declined by an annual average of 1.3 percentage points.[20] This shows that the benefits of relatively modest growth of GDP per capita—averaging about 2% per year—trickled down to the poor during this period, although only minimally compared with the experience of other Asian countries.[21] Moreover, the often-asserted argument that post-World War II economic growth completely bypassed the poor[22] is not supported by the figures in Table 23.5. Note too, however, that the relatively fast growth of the population—averaging 2.9% per year from 1961 to 1971 and 2.6% per year from 1971 to 1985—meant a 57% increase in the total number of poor families from 3.3 million in 1961 to 5.2 million in 1988.

The incidence of poverty was higher in rural areas than in urban areas, although the difference has tended to narrow down since 1961. This tendency paralleled the increase in the ratio of average rural family income to average urban family income. Based on the head-count index, rural poverty accounted for the bulk of overall poverty (nearly three-fourths in 1965 and 1971 and about two-thirds in 1985 and 1988), mainly because of the greater number of families residing in rural areas. This contribution appeared to be even larger if poverty gaps were used as weights (i.e., consideration is given to poverty aversion), simply because poverty gaps were larger in rural areas than in urban areas.

Table 23.5 Indexes of poverty incidence, 1961–88 (in %, unless otherwise indicated)

Year and area	Total number of families (1,000)	Share of area in total families	Head-count index	Income gap	Poverty gap	FGT (α = 2)	Sen index	Contribution to total poverty: Head count	Poverty gap	FGT (α = 2)
Total:										
1961	4,426	100.00	75.02	52.78	39.60	25.62	...	100.00	100.00	100.00
1965	5,127	100.00	67.08	50.29	33.74	21.33	...	100.00	100.00	100.00
1971	6,348	100.00	61.63	48.81	30.08	18.29	...	100.00	100.00	100.00
1985	9,847	100.00	59.65	40.23	24.00	12.00	24.00	100.00	100.00	100.00
1988	10,533	100.00	49.52	36.35	18.00	8.00	19.00	100.00	100.00	100.00
Rural:										
1961	2,920	65.97	80.19	53.62	43.00	28.00	...	70.52	71.64	72.10
1965	3,606	70.33	71.15	52.00	37.00	24.00	...	74.60	77.13	79.13
1971	4,434	69.85	66.08	51.45	34.00	21.00	...	74.89	78.95	80.21
1985	6,121	62.16	63.30	39.49	25.00	13.00	25.00	65.97	64.75	67.34
1988	6,548	62.17	54.08	35.13	19.00	9.00	20.00	67.89	65.62	69.94
Urban:										
1961	1,506	34.03	65.00	50.77	33.00	21.00	...	29.48	28.36	27.90
1965	1,521	29.67	57.43	45.27	26.00	15.00	...	25.40	22.86	20.87
1971	1,914	30.15	51.32	40.92	21.00	12.00	...	25.11	21.05	19.79
1985	3,726	37.84	51.98	38.48	20.00	10.00	20.00	31.52	30.14	30.14
1988	3,985	37.83	39.95	35.04	14.00	6.00	14.00	30.52	29.42	28.37

It bears noting that despite the noticeable increase in income inequality in rural areas from 1961 to 1971 (see Table 23.3), all the indexes of rural poverty in Table 5 show a decline during this period, further supporting the argument that rural (mainly agricultural) growth itself, even if it initially increases income inequality, is a powerful stimulus to poverty reduction.

The vast majority (62%–68%) of the rural poor are engaged in farming (Table 23.6). About two-thirds of all farming families were considered poor in 1988; this group had an average income shortfall of about 40% of the poverty line. The incidence of poverty was equally high among families whose incomes depended mainly on fishing. Their contribution to total rural poverty, however, was much lower (11%) than that for farming families, simply because this group accounted for only 9% of all rural families. Families dependent mainly on incomes earned outside farming, fishing, and forestry constituted another single block (37%) of families in rural areas.[23] The incidence of poverty among this group was much lower—about 40% of the families were poor, and the average income shortfall for the group was 31%.

The traditional characterization of the rural poor is that the poorest of them are the landless and those dependent mainly on wage incomes.[24] Surprisingly, Table 23.6 shows that the intensity of poverty, as indicated by their income shortfalls, among the self-employed is as severe as, if not more severe than, "wage" households (although there are differences across occupations, as shown below). In agriculture, the poor self-employed heads of households include primarily lessees, tenants, and small owner-cultivators.

Within agriculture (farming, fishing, and forestry), among the poorest were (i) farm workers in sugarcane, rice, corn, coconut, and forestry, and (ii) corn and other crop farmers, coconut farmers, and fishermen (Table 23.7)[25] Rice producers had lower average income shortfall and a smaller proportion of their group below the poverty threshold, but they contributed almost one-fourth of overall poverty in agriculture owing to the large proportion (28%) of rice farmers in agriculture.

The poor families in agriculture are characterized by a high level of underemployment, inadequate access to or use of modern technology (partly because of lack of access to credit), high dependence on incomes in agriculture, and little access to social services, including health care and family planning services. The high level of underemployment in agriculture arises partly from the monsoon-dependent nature of agricultural production. The access of the poor to land is limited by the high concentration of landholdings (especially in sugarcane, coconut, and export crops such as banana and pineapple), and, ironically, by land reform programs covering only tenanted rice and corn farms.[26] For the large number of poor owner-cultivator farmers, farm size is small, and the farm is often located in unfavorable areas (e.g., outside of irrigated areas). Their ability to improve their lot is substantially limited by their low incomes and little access to credit. With the sluggish growth of productive employment opportunities outside the farm, the bulk of the

Table 23.6 Poverty incidence by industry, rural families, 1988 (in %, unless otherwise indicated)

Industry	*Total number of families (1,000)*	*Share of group in total families*	*Head-count index*	*Income gap*	*Poverty gap*	*FGT (α = 2)*	*Sen index*	*Contribution to total poverty*		
								Head count	*Poverty gap*	*FGT (α = 2)*
All rural families	6,548.1	100.00	55.03	36.84	20.27	9.41	20.00	100.00	100.00	100.00
Farming:										
Wages	614.6	9.39	69.40	38.90	27.00	13.00	27.00	11.84	12.50	12.96
Self-employed	2,853.3	43.57	63.17	39.58	25.00	12.00	25.00	50.02	53.74	55.56
Forestry	72.2	1.10	50.46	39.64	20.00	10.00	20.00	1.01	1.09	1.17
Fishing	592.5	9.05	66.77	35.94	24.00	11.00	24.00	10.98	10.71	10.58
Agricultural services	25.6	.39	52.69	37.96	20.00	10.00	20.00	.37	.39	.42
Other occupation:										
Wages	1,217.5	18.59	38.19	28.80	11.00	4.00	11.00	12.90	10.09	7.90
Self-employed	1,172.4	17.90	39.58	32.84	13.00	6.00	13.00	12.88	11.48	11.41

Table 23.7 Poverty incidence in agriculture by main occupation of household head, 1985 (in %, unless otherwise indicated)

Main occupation of household head	*Total number of families (1,000)*	*Share of group in total families*	*Head-count index*	*Income gap*	*Poverty gap*	*FGT ($\alpha = 2$)*	*Sen index*	*Contribution to total poverty*		
								Head count	*Poverty gap*	*FGT ($\alpha = 2$)*
All agricultural families	3,962.3	100.00	72.86	41.36	30.13	15.82	30.58	100.00	100.00	100.00
Rice farmers	1,103.9	27.86	66.21	39.27	26.00	13.00	26.48	25.32	24.04	22.90
Corn farmers	596.4	15.05	83.49	49.11	41.00	24.00	41.04	17.25	20.48	22.84
Sugarcane farmers	19.4	.49	60.73	29.64	18.00	7.00	18.12	.41	.29	.22
Other crop farmers	203.4	5.13	84.40	42.65	36.00	22.00	39.80	5.95	6.13	7.14
Coconut farmers	360.9	9.11	75.46	41.08	31.00	16.00	31.38	9.43	9.37	9.21
Fruit tree farmers	17.6	.44	56.29	26.65	15.00	7.00	15.30	.34	.22	.20
Livestock and poultry farmers	23.4	.59	61.38	34.21	21.00	9.00	20.98	.50	.41	.34
Other farmers	9.2	.23	73.04	38.34	28.00	13.00	28.36	.23	.22	.19
Rice and corn farm workers	215.2	5.43	81.07	44.41	36.00	20.00	36.18	6.04	6.49	6.87
Sugarcane farm workers	88.5	2.23	93.81	43.71	41.00	20.00	40.83	2.88	3.04	2.82
Other crop farm workers	16.4	.41	84.69	42.51	36.00	20.00	36.17	.48	.49	.52
Coconut farm workers	61.6	1.55	83.70	41.82	35.00	17.00	34.69	1.79	1.81	1.67
Livestock and poultry workers	13.8	.35	62.69	33.50	21.00	8.00	20.63	.30	.24	.18
Other crop and animal husbandry	80.1	2.02	51.42	35.01	18.00	9.00	18.25	1.43	1.21	1.15
Forestry workers	46.6	1.18	82.60	39.95	33.00	16.00	33.03	1.33	1.29	1.19
Fishermen	515.4	13.01	76.70	40.42	31.00	16.00	31.06	13.69	13.38	13.16
Other occupations	590.5	14.90	61.74	35.63	22.00	10.00	22.43	12.63	10.88	9.42

income of the poor in agriculture comes mainly from the agricultural sector. Their limited access to social services, however, is due to the concentration of these services in urban areas, to lack of information, to ill-designed composition of publicly provided services, or to intimidation by officials.

Rural poverty is also common in areas where agricultural productivity is low and where droughts and typhoons occur frequently (e.g., in the Bicol Region). In these areas, rural nonfarm employment forms an important source of supplementary household income. However, the poor are concentrated in traditional industries with low skill and capital requirements and very low labor productivity. Moreover, the pressure of the very rapid growth of the labor force in rural areas has led to the decline in real wages, especially for unskilled workers (see Section. 23.V below). But in areas where agricultural productivity growth is high (e.g., Central Luzon), the substantial growth of nonfarm employment slows down the fall in real wages.

23.IV LAND RESOURCES, LAND TENURE, AND POVERTY

Population growth in rural areas has outpaced the opening of new lands for cultivation, particularly since the beginning of the 1970s. Combined with the limited growth of employment opportunities in the nonagricultural sectors of the economy, population pressure has inevitably led to the continued decline in farm sizes and in cultivable land per unit of agricultural worker. For all farms, the average farm size fell from about 3.5 hectares in 1960 and 1971 to 2.8 hectares in 1980, the latest census year.

Farm size and land/labor ratio have often been associated with rural poverty, but as Table 23.8 shows, the correlation is rather weak. The Ilocos Region, Central Luzon, and Cagayan Valley had the lowest average farm sizes in 1980, but the average poverty gap in these regions was among the lowest in 1985. Similarly, in the Bicol Region and in the Northern and Western Mindanao where average farm sizes were relatively large, poverty gaps were above the national average.

The incidence of poverty in agriculture appears to have a sharper association with the size distribution of operational landholdings than with average farm size. This is, of course, not surprising considering that landlessness is highly correlated with landholding concentration and that the landless agricultural workers are among the poorest groups with little employment opportunities outside of agriculture. Southern Tagalog and Cagayan Valley do not seem to fit this generalization, but note that agriculture has been more diversified in Cagayan Valley than in most of the regions and that, for Southern Tagalog, employment opportunities outside of agriculture are available partly due to its proximity to Metro Manila.

Tenancy has also been associated with rural poverty. Indeed, an important feature of post-World War II land reform programs was the prohibition of

Table 23.8 Incidence of poverty in agriculture (1985), agricultural productivity measures (1980), and land resources by region

	Poverty incidence in agricultures		*Value aded in agriculture, fisheries, and forestry*					
	Head count (%)	*Poverty gap (%)*	*Per labor*	*Per hectare*	*% in regional GDP*	*Land/ labor ratio**	*Average farm size (ha)*	*Percent of physical area above 10 ha*
Philippines	...	...	2,705	2,697	29.18	.62	2.84	2.6
NCR †	43.9	24.0	...	...	...	.28	.73	...
Ilocos Region	53.9	18.0	2,767	4,361	46.90	.46	1.45	11.9
Cagayan Valley	56.2	19.0	2,233	2,117	57.04	.80	2.53	23.3
Central Luzon	47.0	15.0	3,160	4,439	29.07	.79	2.13	8.8
Southern Tagalog	55.8	22.0	3,936	3,100	30.29	.51	3.16	27.6
Bicol Region	72.4	31.0	1,975	1,751	58.55	.43	3.35	35.4
Western Visayas	73.8	33.0	2,462	3,620	42.17	.55	2.75	37.6
Central Visayas	68.0	30.0	1,599	2,496	23.22	.48	1.71	21.7
Eastern Visayas	70.8	31.0	1,510	1,800	59.18	.37	2.75	22.7
Western Mindanao	63.5	26.0	3,428	2,626	64.68	.77	3.73	24.6
Northern Mindanao	66.7	29.0	3,062	2,213	44,35	.93	3.66	28.4
Southern Mindanao	62.1	24.0	3,272	2,812	49.70	.63	3.96	31.9
Central Mindanao	64.3	25.0	3,714	2,412	57.65	1.05	3.30	15.7

Notes:
* Including arable land only. Labor includes only employed labor in agriculture.
† National Capital Region.

Sources: Basic data are from National Economic and Development Authority, *Philippine Statistical Yearbook* (Manila, 1986, 1989); Department of Labor and Employment, *Yearbook of Labor Statistics* (Manila, 1984); National Statistics Office. *Family Income and Expenditure Survey* (Manila, 1985).

share tenancy. The argument has been that farmers are poor because of the high incidence of tenancy (the proportion of farms under tenancy to total farms), considered one of the highest in Asia, which has changed only minimally since 1960. The census of agriculture in 1960 indicates that only about 45% of the total crop and livestock farms (and 53% of the total physical area) were fully owned by the operators themselves. In the 1980 census, this was about 59%. The proportion of rented or leased farms, on the other hand, hardly changed, from 37% in 1960 to 38% in 1980.

By systematically assessing the importance of these factors in explaining regional differences in agricultural poverty incidence, I have estimated reduced form head-count and poverty gap functions using the 1985 and 1988 FIES data. These data are supplemented by regional indicators obtained from various sources. In each function, I have included the following explanatory variables: size distribution of farms (FDIST), expressed as the ratio of physical area above 10 hectares to total area; average farm size (FSIZE); irrigation (IRRIG), expressed as the ratio of irrigated to total farm area; incidence of tenancy, alternatively defined as the ratio of the number of farms under share tenancy to total number of farms (NTENANCY) and as the ratio of area of farms under share tenancy to total area of farms (ATENANCY); level of urbanization (URBAN), expressed as the ratio of urban population to total population; and road density (ROAD), defined as the ratio of total road (in kilometers) to total harvested area (in square kilometers). The variable IRRIG is a proxy for land quality. The last two variables—URBAN and ROAD—are proxies for access to markets and off-farm employment. A dummy variable (YEARDUMMY) reflecting the macroeconomic difficulties in 1985 is also included. All the regression equations take a double-log specification. The regression results are given in Table 23.9.

The variable FDIST is consistently significant in all regressions, thereby affirming the common observation in development literature concerning the negative association between operational landholding inequality and rural poverty. The variable FSIZE is significant in half of the six estimated equations. Although IRRIG does not appear to be an important determinant of regional head count, it contributes significantly to the variation of regional poverty gaps. This suggests that, at the very least, land quality is an important factor contributing to differences in household farm incomes. Neither ROAD nor URBAN is significant. It is, however, possible that these variables could not adequately capture the influence of access to markets and off-farm employment opportunities on poverty in agriculture. Interestingly, tenancy is not significant in any of the regressions. (I will return below to the implication of this result.) Finally, I note that the severe macro-economic difficulties in the mid-1980s significantly influenced the incidence of poverty in agriculture.

What these observations, as well as many other recent empirical and theoretical studies,[27] suggest is that tenancy by itself is not as important and compelling a correlate of poverty as expected: the variation in incomes within

Table 23.9 Estimation results of agricultural poverty incidence determination functions: regional data

Explanatory variable	Head-count index			Poverty gap		
	(1)	*(2)*	*(3)*	*(4)*	*(5)*	*(6)*
Intercept	.18	.31	.18	−.66	−.50	−.92
	(.69)	(1.20)	(.83)	(−1.56)	(−1.24)	(−3.28)
FDIST	.21**	.24**	.23**	.35**	.39**	.35**
	(3.61)	(4.35)	(4.26)	(3.87)	(4.57)	(3.85)
FSIZE	−.20	−.30*	−.23*	−.27	−.40*	−.17
	(−1.56)	(−2.44)	(−2.35)	(−1.31)	(−2.10)	(−1.05)
IRRIG	−.05	−.03	−.04	−.12*	−.10	−.16**
	(−1.37)	(−.85)	(−1.18)	(−2.10)	(−1.79)	(−4.10)
ROAD	−.12	−.15	−.10	−.12	−.15	...
	(−1.32)	(−1.49)	(−1.20)	(−.81)	(−.09)	
NTENANCY	.17	...	...	.19	...	.23
	(1.45)			(1.02)		(1.29)
ATENANCY	...	.04	.08	...	.03	...
		(.51)	(1.16)		(.22)	
URBAN	.03	.05	...	.09	.11	.05
	(.67)	(.92)		(1.04)	(1.26)	(.75)
YEARDUMMY	.09**	.09**	.08**	.18**	.19**	.17**
	(2.77)	(2.70)	(2.57)	(3.52)	(3.49)	(3.46)
Adjusted R^2	.71	.68	.68	.76	.74	.76
F-value	8.97	7.82	9.07	11.17	10.39	13.19

Notes: All variables, except YEARDUMMY, are in national logarithm. Figures in parentheses are t-ratios.
* Significant at 5%.
** Significant at 1%.

tenure classes (reflecting the effect of farm size, yield, cropping intensity, land quality, etc.) has been found to be much greater than the variation between classes.

The common presumption of past land reform designs in the Philippines was that share tenancy would induce resource allocation inefficiencies. That is, since part of the tenant's output goes to the landlord, there is less incentive for the tenant to apply labor and other inputs to optimum levels. However, recent empirical and theoretical development increasingly shows that the same degree of efficiency can be achieved under the share tenancy contract as, say, under the fixed-fee contract and owner farming. The share tenancy contract also has the advantage of risk sharing and tenant-landlord credit relations. Over time and across space, however, contract choice reflects the farmer's (and the landlord's) consideration of economic, social, and sociological factors. In rural environments, for example, where production is risky (and the farmer is risk averse) and the costs of enforcing contracts are prohibitively high, both the share tenant and the landlord may find it mutually advantageous to choose the share tenancy contract. In general, in the absence of tightly enforced tenancy regulations, the efficiency of alternative contracts depends on the relative magnitudes of risk, transaction costs, and returns to entrepreneurial ability.[28]

23.V LABOR SUPPLY AND EMPLOYMENT GROWTH

The growth of the labor force, particularly from among the female population, was relatively high (averaging 3.8% annually) in the latter part of the 1970s and early part of the 1980s, although it decelerated in the latter part of the 1980s. The level of this growth closely matched the expansion of employment in the 1970s but was slightly higher than employment growth in the 1980s, particularly in the 1983–85 economic crisis. It is interesting that, while employment growth was persistently lower than output growth in the 1970s (the implicit employment elasticity with respect to output for this period was close to 0.65), this was not the case in the early part of the 1980s. Employment continued to expand at an extraordinarily high rate of 3.5% per year in 1981–85 even though GDP contracted by an annual average of 1.9%. However, the number of visibly underemployed workers (defined as those working fewer than 65 days in a quarter and reporting their willingness to work additional time) was high, averaging 25.8% of the total number of employed workers during the period, in contrast with the average of 19.7% for the period 1976–80 (Table 23.10).

The economic recovery in 1986–89 which pulled GDP growth to an annual average of 5.5% also brought with it an expansion of employment, although at a rate hardly sufficient to absorb the new entrants to the labor force. Thus, the open unemployment rate continued to increase from about 4.6% in the 1970s and 6.6% in 1983–85, to 8.6% in 1986–89. By 1989, there were 2 million unemployed individuals, more than half of them in the rural areas. Of the employed, a large number were underemployed in the urban informal sector (mostly services) and in subsistence agriculture.

The rate of unemployment in rural areas was only about one-half of that in urban areas. However, the ratio of the visibly underemployed to the total labor force was nearly twofold greater in rural areas than in urban areas, although the difference tended to diminish in the latter part of the 1980s. The seasonality and irregularity of monsoon agriculture partly explain the high underemployment in rural areas. Moreover, as shown below, average labor productivity in agriculture has been much lower than in manufacturing or urban industries.

While agriculture accounted for nearly one-half of the total employment in the late 1980s, it contributed only about one-fourth of the total national output (Table 23.11). Services, on the other hand, accounted for 40% of output and also about 40% of total employment. Although the shares of agriculture in output and employment were comparable to those of other countries of similar income levels, the same cannot be said for services. In

Table 23.10 Unemployment and underemployment rates, 1971–89*

	1971	*1972*	*1973*	*1974*	*1975*	*1976*	*1977*	*1978*	*1980*	*1981*	*1982*	*1983*	*1984*	*1985*	*1986*	*1987*	*1988*	*1989*
Unemployment rate (%)	5.3	5.3	4.8	3.2	4.2	5.2	4.5	4.1	5.0	5.3	6.0	5.4	7.3	7.1	8.0	9.5	8.3	8.4
Urban	8.7	9.8	8.0	5.7	7.8	8.5	7.2	6.0	8.2	8.3	9.8	9.3	12.2	11.8	11.5	13.8	12.3	11.7
Rural	3.7	3.3	3.3	2.0	2.6	3.5	3.1	3.2	3.7	4.0	4.2	3.7	4.4	4.4	3.9	6.8	5.9	6.4
Underemployment rate (%):																		
A†	...	...	...	...	...	25.5	17.4	19.2	20.9	23.9	25.5	29.8	36.4	22.2	28.4	23.9	23.6	22.7
Urban	...	...	...	...	...	21.6	15.2	18.9	19.9	19.5	24.0	29.9	34.0	16.9	27.7	18.1	24.1	17.3
Rural	...	...	...	...	...	27.3	18.5	19.3	21.4	25.8	26.2	29.8	37.7	25.1	28.8	27.2	23.3	25.9
B‡	...	...	...	...	...	13.8	8.1	9.0	12.0	14.5	13.9	17.2	22.5	15.3	17.8	11.1	11.4	10.9
Urban	...	...	...	...	...	7.8	5.4	5.5	7.4	7.0	8.9	8.1	8.7	16.9	13.7	6.9	6.8	6.0
Rural	...	...	...	...	...	16.6	9.5	10.6	13.9	13.1	16.9	14.4	21.3	25.2	19.9	13.5	13.9	13.7

Notes:
* No data available for 1979.
† Those who worked for the reference quarter but wanted additional work, expressed as a proportion of the employed.
‡ Those who worked less than 65 days in the quarter but wanted additional work, expressed as a proportion of the employed.

Sources: *Philippine Statistical Yearbook*, various issues; National Statistics Office, *Integrated Survey of Household Bulletin*, various issues.

Table 23.11 Sectoral composition of gross domestic product and employment, 1955–89

	1955	*1965*	*1975*	*1985*	*1989*
Gross domestic product:					
Agriculture	33.22	30.22	29.92	28.64	27.11
Industry	25.66	28.09	33.79	32.61	32.9
(Manufacturing)*	18.63	21.21	24.98	24.21	25.00
Services	41.12	41.69	39.29	38.75	39.99
Employment:					
Agriculture	60.03	57.59	54.28	49.52	45.61
Industry	15.67	14.76	14.74	14.11	15.67
(Manufacturing)*	12.37	11.31	10.97	9.59	10.46
Services	24.29	27.67	30.99	36.38	38.71

Notes: Three-year averages centered on the year shown, except for 1989 wherein the figures refer to averages for 1988 and 1989.
* Subsector of industry.

Sources: National Economic and Development Authority, *Philippine Statistical Yearbook*, various issues; National Statistics Office, *Philippine Yearbook*, 1987.

other countries, the average share of services in national output was about 45% while in total employment the average share of services was about 25%, thereby implying a much higher relative labor productivity.[29] It is apparent that a large part of employment in services (as well as in agriculture) reflects a forced adoption of redundant workers and a high degree of underemployment in the sector.

Equally disturbing is the fact that the expansion of the share of industry in GDP was not matched by an increase in its share of employment. Industrial output growth, albeit low in relation to the country's Asian neighbors, rose from about 26% in the mid-1950s to 33% in the late 1980s. The rise is, of course, expected, as this is a well-known stylized pattern in development.[30] But from the mid-1950s to the late 1980s, the industry's share in total employment remained relatively low at about 15%. Employment in this sector grew at an average of only 2.9% during the 1956–89 period. The growth of its major subsector, manufacturing, was even poorer—only 2.3% during the period. The residual labor force and the new entrants to the labor force were thus absorbed largely in agriculture and informal services sectors where self-employment was more common and wages were more flexible. This process, however, limited the growth of labor productivity and real incomes in these sectors.

The patterns of labor productivity growth and real wages are reflective of the structural bottlenecks in the economy, particularly the persistent inability to absorb the growing number of underemployed members of the labor force. Figure 23.1 shows the trends in average labor productivity in the three major sectors of the economy—agriculture, industry, and services—since the mid-1950s. At least three major observations can be made. First,

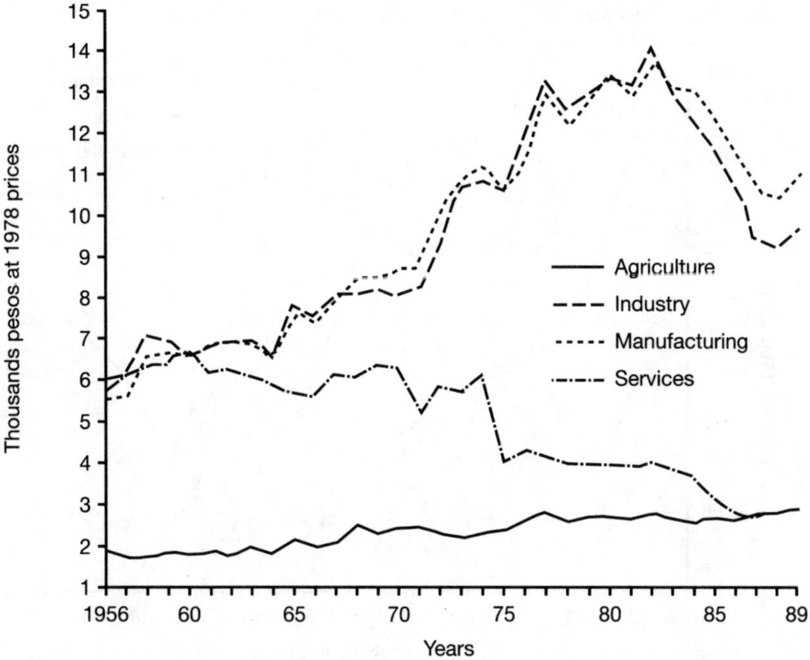

Figure 23.1 Real value added per worker, by industry of origin, 1956–89

average labor productivity in agriculture has been consistently lower than that in industry and, not until the latter part of the 1980s, in services. Second, labor productivity in the services sector was comparable to that in manufacturing in the latter part of the 1950s, remained virtually stagnant in the 1960s and early 1970s, and then dropped steadily in the latter part of the 1970s and in the 1980s. This occurred in tandem with the substantial increase in the share of the services sector in total employment—from 25% in the mid-1950s to 39% in the late 1980s. Third, although labor productivity in industry managed to rise in the 1960s and 1970s, the growth soon petered out and labor productivity fell for the most part of the 1980s. Average labor productivity in industry in 1986–89 was even lower than during the economic crisis of 1983–85. It is apparent that not only did industry fail to absorb an increasing proportion of the labor force, as was the case in other countries with similar income levels and in newly industrializing countries, but it was also unable in recent years to reverse the decline in labor productivity.

The rapid growth of the labor force and the slow pace of employment generation in productive areas combined to create a large pool of unemployed and underemployed. Because the rural sector failed to absorb the additional labor force members and to provide full employment to its workers, pressure built up for laborers to move out of the farm to rural nonfarm and to urban

(A) By type of workers

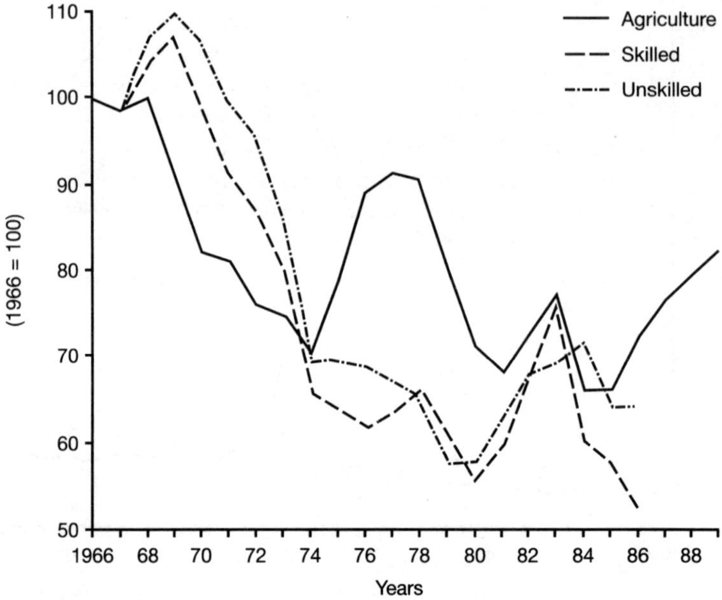

(B) By crops

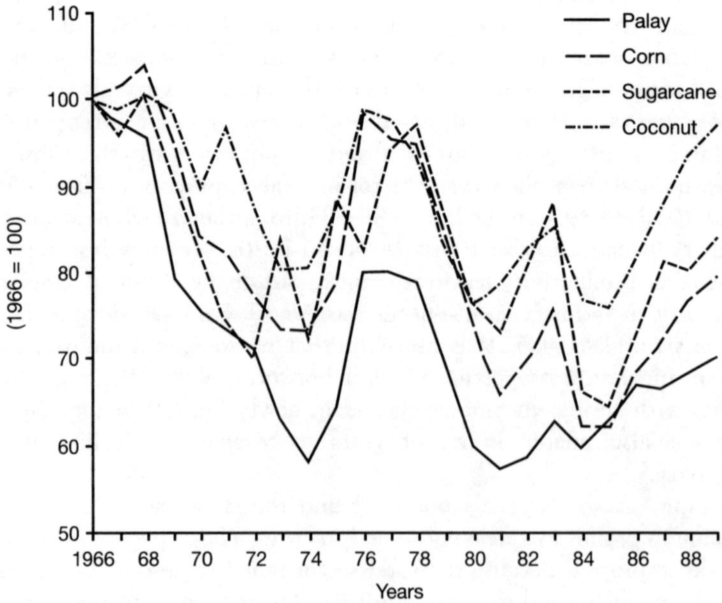

Figure 23.2 Real wage indexes. *A*, By type of workers. *B*, By crops

areas. This tended to depress real wages outside the farm, especially those of unskilled occupations (mainly in the services sector). Figure 23.2, which shows the trends in real wages for skilled, unskilled, and agricultural workers over the last 2.5 decades, lends support to this claim. The persistent fall in labor productivity in the services sector was matched by a persistent fall in real wages for both skilled and unskilled workers. Moreover, although real wages in agriculture were lower in the 1980s than in the late 1960s, the drop was not as sharp as those for skilled and unskilled workers. This implies that the unskilled and skilled occupations outside the farm might have borne the larger proportion of the adjustment on real wages.

As shown in Section 23.III, the incidence of poverty declined between 1961 and 1988 despite the overall fall in real wages. In addition to the slight reduction in income inequality in the 1980s, two other factors partly explain the decline in poverty—the increased participation rate of the labor force, particularly among women, and the substantial rise of the share of nonwage, nonentrepreneurial incomes in total household incomes. Comparable estimates of labor force participation rates rose from 60% in the mid-1970s to 65% in the late 1980s.[31] Based on the various rounds of the Family Income Expenditure Survey, the share of rent, remittances, gifts, support assistance, and relief in total household incomes swelled from only 17% in 1961 to 32% in 1985 and 27% in 1988. The proportion of households dependent mainly on these incomes rose substantially from about 5% in 1961 to 19% in 1985 and 16% in 1988. Finally, the proportion of families reporting remittances, support assistance, and relief increased from 22% in 1961 to 88% in 1985.[32]

It bears noting that persistent declines in real wages and the rise in per capita income were rather unique in the Philippines. In the postwar experience of Asia, particularly Taiwan and South Korea, growth was accompanied by rising real wages in agriculture and industry, even when there was considerable unemployment.[33] Not that these countries had effective laws on minimum wages; labor productivity growth and expansion of employment accompanied the growth of GDP per capita in these countries. Government policies in the Philippines, on the other hand, tended to undermine both productivity growth and the generation of productive employment opportunities for its expanding labor force.

Postwar government policies tended to run against the dictum of comparative advantage (although public pronouncements often called for efficient use of scarce capital resources) by unduly promoting capital-intensive, import-substituting industries and, in the process, severely penalizing labor-intensive exports and backward integration.[34] While these policies led to an initial spurt in overall economic growth (such as during the "easy import substitution" period in the early part of the 1950s), they subsequently constrained the country's capacity to earn necessary foreign exchange for the importation of capital goods for continued growth. Macro pricing policies tended to overvalue severely the exchange rate, particularly in the 1950s when import and exchange controls were the primary means of trade and payments adjustments and in the 1960s when a cascading tariff structure replaced import and exchange controls. The overvalued exchange rate depressed the relative prices of labor-intensive tradable goods and encouraged the movement of scarce resources toward less labor-intensive nontradable or home goods production, and thus put a downward pressure on real wages.[35]

Moreover, generous fiscal incentives provided a window for the development of export-oriented manufacturing establishments, but for the most part, "the new export sector functioned almost as export processing zone and bonded warehouse 'enclave' . . . which had little interaction with, and provided little benefit to, the domestic economy except primarily through the [limited] employment of labor."[36] Government interventions, especially in the 1970s and early 1980s, also tended to diminish the role of market mechanism in favor of regulations by parastatals as well as to promote a monopolistic structure in important sectors of the economy. The use of governmental functions to dispense economic privileges to some select groups close to the ruling elite was rampant. Fiscal and monetary policies thus tended to be expansionary in the 1970s and early 1980s. All told, the intermittent balance of payments crises during the postwar period (in late 1949, in the early 1960s, in 1983–85, and at the turn of the 1990s) and the persistence of widespread poverty and unemployment (and underemployment) have been a reflection of the weaknesses of the economic structure engendered by policy regimes.

23.VI CONCLUSION

Rapid agricultural growth has contributed to the reduction of measured rural poverty in the Philippines, although only minimally compared to the experience of other Asian countries. Moreover, the incidence of poverty remains high. Though the rural poor as a proportion of the total rural population diminished from 80% in 1961 to 54% in 1988, the average income shortfall for all poor rural households hovered high at 35% of the poverty threshold. Moreover, the absolute number of the rural poor, who constituted about 70% of the country's total poor population, increased from 2.9 million families in 1971 to 3.6 million in 1988.

In the rural development literature, it is common to characterize the landless and those who are dependent mainly on wage incomes as the poorest group among the rural poor. In this article I show that the intensity of poverty for self-employed households, as indicated by their average income shortfall, is as severe, if not more severe, than that for wage-dependent household. In agriculture, the poor self-employed heads of households include primarily lessees, tenants, and small owner-cultivators. This group constitutes the single largest block of the total poor, regardless of the summary measure of poverty used, in rural areas. One implication of this finding is that, from the viewpoint of poverty alleviation policies, the payoffs—in terms of the reduction in measured overall poverty per peso investment—to targeting this group appears high relative to other groups in rural areas.

I have argued that the root causes of the rural problem in the Philippines—low productivity, landlessness, high underemployment, and high incidence of rural poverty—go beyond agriculture. The economic welfare of the rural population can be secured only by a comprehensive economywide policy reform aimed at correcting the disincentives against the production (and consumption) of labor-intensive goods, particularly labor intensive exports, and at promoting backward integration. This allows the expansion of productive earning opportunities for the relatively fast-growing labor force. In particular, the reform has to allow a rapid, sustained growth of agriculture, combined with equally rapid employment growth outside of agriculture. The importance of the latter is clearly demonstrated by the country's experience in the second half of the 1960s and in the 1970s: rapid agricultural growth did occur, but the linkages of this growth with the rest of the economy were weak owing partly to the failure of economic policies and structures to allow a similarly rapid, sustained overall economic growth along the lines of the country's comparative advantage. The fact that industry's share in total employment failed to grow despite the rapid expansion of its share in GDP meant that the services and agriculture sectors were the primary sources of employment generation for the rapidly expanding labor force. In large parts of these sectors, however, labor productivity is low and underemployment is high.

Finally, I note that further investigations into why rapid agricultural growth in the Philippines in the second half of the 1960s and in the 1970s did not lead to substantial poverty reduction and sustained overall economic growth are likely to offer important lessons for development policy in the Philippines and in other less developed countries. Future research would have to look closely, for example, at the expenditure pattern of rural households, the incremental demand for nonagricultural goods generated by the increase in agricultural incomes, and the domestic supply response—particularly the rural supply response—to that demand. The recent papers of Gustav Ranis, Frances Stewart, and Edna Angeles-Reyes and of Romeo Bautista are important steps in this direction.[37] This effort could be supplemented with a systematic assessment of the relative influence of various factors, including public policies, on the observed pattern of rural growth, income distribution and poverty, and overall economic growth.

ACKNOWLEDGMENT

Earlier drafts of this article have benefited from valuable comments and criticisms by participants in the thirty-fifth annual meeting of the Australian Agricultural Economics Society and of a seminar at the Philippine Department of Agriculture. I am particularly indebted to two anonymous referees of this journal and to Keijiro Otsuka, Harry Oshima, and Romeo Bautista for comments on an earlier draft of this article.

NOTES

1 See, e.g., John W. Mellor, "Agriculture on the Road to Industrialization," in *Development Strategies Reconsidered*, ed. John P. Lewis and Valeriana Kallab (Washington, D.C.: Overseas Development Council, 1986); Irma Adelman, "Beyond Export-led Growth," *World Development* 12 (1984): 937–49; and Romeo M. Bautista, "Agricultural Growth as a Development Strategy for the Philippines," *Philippine Economic Journal* 27 (1988): 9–19.

2 For an overview of postwar development planning, objectives, and strategies, see Arsenio M. Balisacan (with the assistance of Joseph Capuno, Ruby Asuncion, and Soledad Balisacan), "Rural Poverty in the Philippines: Incidence, Issues, and Policies" (paper presented at the Finalization Symposium on Priority Issues and Policy Measures to Alleviate Rural Poverty, Asian Development Bank, Manila, November 14–16, 1990).

3 To be sure, even proponents of agriculture-led development strategy consider agricultural growth as merely a necessary, but not sufficient, element in the strategy. There is, however, a paucity of development-country experiences that can be used to illustrate the conditions required by the strategy.

4 As Yujiro Hayami et al. in "Agricultural Growth against a Land Resource Constraint: The Philippine Experience," *Australian Journal of Agricultural Economics* 20 (1976): 144–59, pointed out, population pressure pushes the cultivation frontier into marginal lands, thereby causing the marginal cost of production via expansion of cultivated area to rise relative to the marginal cost of production via more intensive land use. The intensification of irrigation and the adoption of land-saving modern rice technology can thus be seen as efforts to augment land in response to the increasing cost of land relative to labor. Cristina C. David, Randolph Barker, and Adelita Palacpac, "The Nature of Productivity Growth in Philippine Agriculture, 1948–1982" (paper presented at the Symposium on Agricultural Productivity Measurement and Analysis, Asian Productivity Organization, Tokyo, October 1–8, 1984), also noted the influence of other factors in promoting land intensification in lowland areas of the Philippines. Among the principal ones are the suitability of early modern varieties to irrigated conditions, the worsening peace-and-order situation in Mindanao and upland areas, and the economic policy bias against agriculture and labor use.

5 David, Barker, and Palacpac.

6 Richard W. Hooley, "Long-Term Growth of the Philippine Economy, 1902–1961," *Philippine Economic Journal* 7 (1968): 1–24.

7 For a decomposition of the sources of commodity production growth into yield and hectarage growth, see Balisacan.

8 See Balisacan for a detailed discussion on the limitations and comparability of the various rounds of FIES.

9 See D. G. Champernowne, "A Comparison of Measures of Inequality of Income Distribution," *Economic Journal* 84 (December 1974): 787–816, for a comparison of the various indexes typically used in measuring the inequality displayed by given frequency distributions of income. Anthony B. Atkinson "On the Measurement of Inequality," *Journal of Economic Theory* 2 (1970): 244–63; and Amartya Sen, *On Economic Inequality* (New York: Norton 1973), characterize the form of the social welfare function implicit in each of the most common measures.

10 It should be noted that since these estimates are obtained from grouped data, they tend to be less than what would be obtained from individual observations. For 1961, 1965, and 1971, grouped data are a reconstruction of published official tabulations. For 1985 and 1988, grouped data are based on FIES tapes.

11 Based on Romeo M. Bautista's compilation of Gini estimates obtained from several studies. See Romeo M. Bautista, "Poverty Alleviation, Economic Growth, and Development Policy in East Asia" (paper prepared for the Project on Poverty Alleviation and Development Policy, Australian National University, March 1990). See also the earlier comparison of Gini ratios in selected Asian countries by Harry Oshima and Bruno Barros, "Trends in Growth and Distribution of Income in Selected Asian Countries," *Philippine Economic Journal* 15 (1976): 480–521.

12 Most often associated with Simon Kuznets, the inverted U-shaped hypothesis depicts a development path whereby income inequality increases in the early stages of development and decreases in the later stages.

13 Gary S. Fields, "Income Distribution and Economic Growth," in *The State of Development Economics: Progress and Perspectives*, ed. Gustav Ranis and T. Paul Schultz (Oxford: Blackwell, 1988), p. 469.

14 See, e.g., John C. H. Fei and Gustav Ranis, *Development of the Labor Surplus Economy: Theory and Policy* (Homewood, Ill.: Irwin, 1964); and Irma Adelman and Cynthia Taft Morris, *Economic Growth and Social Equity in Developing Countries* (Stanford, Calif.: Stanford University Press, 1973).

15 Robert W. Herdt, "A Retrospective View of Technological and Other Changes in Philippine Rice Farming, 1965–82," *Economic Development and Cultural Change* 35 (January 1987): 329–49.

16 For a discussion of conceptual and empirical issues involved in poverty measurement, see T. N. Srinivasan, "Rural Poverty: Conceptual, Measurement and Policy Issues" (paper prepared for the ADB Study on Priority Issues and Policy Measures to Alleviate Rural Poverty, Manila, March 1990); Anthony B. Atkinson, "On the Measurement of Poverty," *Econometrica* 55 (July 1987): 749–64; and Aldi J. M. Hagenaars, *The Perception of Poverty* (Amsterdam: Elsevier, 1986).

17 For details on the estimation, see Balisacan (n. 2 above).

18 The poverty line can be argued to be positively related with correlates of development (e.g., urbanization). However, Martin Ravallion et al. have demonstrated in "Quantifying the Magnitude and Severity of Absolute Poverty in the Developing World in the Mid 1980s" (background paper for the World Bank's *World Development Report 1990*, Washington, D.C., 1990) that, for a large number of low-income countries, real poverty lines tend to increase with growth, but they will do so very slowly for the poorest countries.

19 The FGT index is a class of additively decomposable poverty measures (see James E. Foster, Joel Greer, and Eric Thorbecke, "A Class of Decomposable Poverty Measures," *Econometrica* 52 [May 1984]: 761–66). The head count and the poverty gap are special cases of this index, i.e., for $\alpha = 0$ and $\alpha = 1$, respectively. These measures are additively decomposable in the following sense: the aggregate (population) poverty level is simply a weighted average of the subgroup poverty levels, the weights being their population shares. Moreover, a distributionally sensitive FGT measure ($\alpha > 1$) satisfies the main axioms for a desirable summary measure of poverty. For a survey of aggregate poverty measures, see James E. Foster, "On Economic Poverty: A Survey of Aggregate Measures," *Advances in Econometrics* 3 (1984): 215–51.

20 These rates of decline were, however, lower than those for other countries of similar income levels, based on data in the World Bank's *World Development Report 1990* (pp. 45–48).

21 A referee noted that poverty trends are partly explained by changes in the relative prices of consumer goods, particularly for goods consumed by the poor. Food constitutes the bulk (about 70%) of the total expenditures of the bottom 40% of all families. Food prices, however, rose faster than nonfood prices during the periods 1961–65 and 1965–71. The annual percentage increase in food prices was 8.6% in the first period and 9.2% in the second period, while the corresponding figures for nonfood prices were only 1.4% and 4.6%. The government's rice pricing policy during these periods also tended to confer protection to producers, i.e., domestic prices tended to be higher than border prices. It thus appears that the reduction in poverty, especially in urban areas, would have been higher than that shown in Table 23.5 if food prices moved at the same rate as nonfood prices. During the succeeding periods, 1971–85 and 1985–88, both food and nonfood prices tended to increase at the same rate. As the country shifted from being a net importer of rice in the 1960s and early 1970s to a net exporter in the second half of the 1970s and early 1980s, the government's rice pricing policy tended to confer protection to consumers, i.e., domestic prices were lower than border prices. However, for livestock and poultry, the protection on producers remained. For an analysis of food pricing policies in the Philippines, see Cristina C. David, "Philippines," in *Food Trade and Food Security in ASEAN and Australia*, by Anne Booth, Cristina C. David, et al. (Canberra: ASEAN-Australia Joint Research Project, 1986).

22 See, e.g., International Labour Organisation, *Sharing in Development: A Programme of Employment, Equity and Growth for the Philippines* (Geneva: ILO, 1974); and Harry T. Oshima, "Employment Generation: The Long-Term Solution to Poverty," *Asian Development Review* 8 (1990): 44–70. It is interesting that the same basic data from the FIES series were used in these other studies. However, in contrast with this article, the other studies used a mixture of definitions with respect to poverty norms, units of analysis, and levels of aggregation, thereby making comparison of poverty estimates over time problematic.

23 There is some overrepresentation here, considering that some families whose occupations were not declared were lumped into the "other occupation" category.

24 See, e.g., Yujiro Hayami, Agnes Quisumbing, and Lourdes Adriano, *Toward an Alternative Land Reform Paradigm: A Philippine Perspective* (Quezon City: Ateneo de Manila University Press, 1990); and Mahar Mangahas, "Rural Poverty and Operation Land Transfer in the Philippines," in *Strategies for Alleviating Poverty in Rural Asia*, ed. R. Islam (Dhaka and Bangkok: Bangladesh Institute for Development Studies and ILO/Asia Employment Program, 1985).

25 Unlike the 1985 FIES, the 1988 FIES does not allow for a disaggregation of agricultural families by main occupation (i.e., self-employed rice farmers, sugarcane workers, etc.).

26 The limitation of land transfer programs to tenanted rice and corn lands encouraged eviction of tenants by landlords and the hiring of landless workers. Moreover, it induced landlords to shift to crops other than rice and corn. See Keijiro Otsuka, "Determinants and Consequences of Land Reform Implementation in the Philippines," *Journal of Development Economics* 35 (1991): 339–55, for evidence on tenant eviction in selected rice-growing villages in the Philippines.

27 For an excellent survey of the literature on share tenancy and alternative contractual arrangements, see Keijiro Otsuka and Yujiro Hayami, "Theories of Share Tenancy: A Critical Survey," *Economic Development and Cultural Change* 37 (1988): 31–68; and Keijiro Otsuka, Hiroyuki Honma, and Yujiro Hayami, "Towards a General Theory of Land and Labor Contracts in Agrarian Economies" (Tokyo, July 1989, mimeographed).

28 See Otsuka, Honma, and Hayami.
29 Based on figures from the World Bank's *World Development Report* and ILO's *International Labour Statistics* (various issues).
30 See Hollis Chenery and Moshe Syrquin, *Patterns of Development, 1950–1970* (London: Oxford University Press, 1975).
31 Harry T. Oshima, Elizabeth de Borja, and Wilhelmina Paz, in "Rising National Income per Worker and Falling Real Wages in the Philippines in the 1970s," *Philippine Review of Economics and Business* 22 (September and December 1986): 151–90, at 160, noted that the average number of earners per family rose from 1.83 to 2.0 in the 1970s. This, in turn, might have accentuated the fall in real wages as the rise in female participation increased the labor supply.
32 See Balisacan (n. 2 above) for a discussion of the trends in functional and personal distribution of income.
33 Oshima, de Borja, and Paz, p. 151.
34 Indeed, this is a common theme in the writing of serious students of Philippine development. See, e.g., John H. Power and Gerardo P. Sicat, *The Philippines: Industrialization and Trade Policies* (London: Oxford University Press, 1971); Emmanuel de Dios, ed., *An Analysis of the Philippine Economic Crisis: A Workshop Report* (Quezon City: University of the Philippines Press, 1984); Romeo M. Bautista, *Production Incentives in Philippine Agriculture: Effects of Trade and Exchange Rate Policies*, Research Report 59 (Washington, D.C.: International Food Policy Research Institute, 1987); and Manuel F. Montes and Hideyoshi Sakai, eds., *Philippine Macroeconomic Perspective: Developments and Policies* (Tokyo: Institute of Developing Economies, 1989)
35 Deepak Lal, "Stolper-Samuelson-Rybczynski in the Pacific: Real Wages and Real Exchange Rates in the Philippines, 1956–1978," *Journal of Development Economics* 21 (1986): 181–204, provides a systematic explanation of the movements of real wages in the Philippines in terms of the standard trade-theoretic Stolper-Samuelson-Rybczynski model.
36 Ponciano S. Intal, Jr., and John H. Power, "Trade, Exchange Rate, and Agricultural Pricing Policies in the Philippines" (World Bank, Washington, D.C., 1990), p. 42.
37 Gustav Ranis, Francis Stewart, and Edna Angeles-Reyes, *Linkages in Developing Economies: A Philippine Study* (San Francisco: International Center for Economic Growth, 1990); Romeo M. Bautista, "Rapid Agricultural Growth Is Not Enough: The Philippines, 1965–80" (paper prepared for the Conference on Agriculture on the Road to Industrialization, Taipei, September 4–7, 1990).

24

RAPID ECONOMIC GROWTH AND POVERTY DECLINE

A Comparison of Indonesia and Thailand 1981–1990

Anne Booth

INTRODUCTION

The purpose of this paper is twofold. First, it examines the problems and pitfalls inherent in comparing poverty incidence across countries. It is argued that meaningful international comparisons of poverty incidence depend crucially on the construction of comparable poverty lines, and that this is by no means a straightforward task. In some recent studies, international poverty lines have been set in terms of calorie equivalents, but this practice can be criticized on the grounds that poorer people tend to derive most of their calories from cheaper, lower quality foodstuffs (Ravallion, 1992, p. 28; Lipton and Ravallion, 1995, pp. 2576–7). In this paper, these problems are illustrated with reference to recent research published under the auspices of the World Bank, which compares the incidence of poverty in different parts of Asia. Particular attention is paid to the World Bank's comparison of poverty levels in Indonesia and Thailand.

The second purpose of the paper is to examine the reasons for the much more pronounced poverty decline in Indonesia than in Thailand in the 1980s, in spite of the fact the per capita GDP growth was faster in Thailand. Several reasons for the relatively poor Thai performance are put forward, which in turn throw some light on the broader international debate about the relationship between growth and equity, and the factors which assist or impede the 'trickle down' of the benefits of rapid economic growth to the poorer groups in developing countries.

THE WORLD BANK STUDIES

An important contribution to the cross-national comparison of poverty incidence was made by the World Bank in their 1990 *World Development*

Source: *Journal of International Development*, 1997, Vol. 9(2), pp. 169–87.

Report (WDR). In this report, an international poverty line of $275 (in 1985 ICP dollars) was established for the 'very poor' and $370 for the 'poor'. When the 'very poor' poverty line was applied to income distributions from different regions of the developing world, it was found that the 'headcount measure' of poverty (the proportion of the population below the poverty line) was highest for Sub-Saharan Africa and India, followed by the Middle East and North Africa, Latin America and the Caribbean, and East Asia (World Bank, 1990, p. 29). More recently the World Bank (1993, p. 6), in a monograph devoted to the rapidly growing economies of East Asia and the Pacific, compared the incidence of poverty (headcount measure) in Cambodia, China, Indonesia, Korea, Lao PDR, Malaysia, the Philippines, Thailand and Vietnam, and found it had fallen from 35 per cent of the population in 1970 to only 10 per cent in 1990. This report pointed out that the two largest countries in this group, China and Indonesia, made the most progress in reducing poverty; in the case of Indonesia the proportion of the population below the poverty line fell from 60 per cent in 1970 to just 15 per cent in 1990, while in China the proportion below the poverty line fell from 33 per cent in 1970 to 9 per cent in 1990. By 1990 the proportion of the population below the poverty line in Indonesia was lower than in Thailand (16 per cent in Thailand compared with 15 per cent in Indonesia).

These figures were, according to the World Bank study, based on 'comparable poverty lines', although the methodology used to derive the internationally comparable poverty lines was rather different from that used in the 1990 *World Development Report:*

> To achieve homogeneity in the definition of poverty and derive meaningful regional aggregates and trends, an equivalent poverty line was used across countries . . . the food budget included in that line allows for 2150 calories per day per person, with 90 per cent of the calories from grains that are the lowest-cost source of calories in East Asia (as in the official poverty lines in China and Indonesia) or other food choices costing the same (World Bank, 1993, p. 6).

The findings of this report received considerable attention in the international press.[1] Of particular interest to several commentators was the fact that there had been so little decline in the incidence of poverty in Thailand during the 1980s in spite of the fact that the country had achieved very rapid rates of growth during that decade by international standards. Indeed, according to the World Bank figures, the rate of decline in the incidence of poverty (measured as the proportion of the population under the stipulated poverty line) in Thailand over the 1980s was so slow that it did not keep up with population growth; in 1990 there were more poor people in Thailand than there had been in 1980 in spite of the fact that per capita GNP grew at 6 per cent per annum between 1981 and 1990. In Indonesia, by contrast, according to the World Bank estimates, the decade witnessed such a rapid decline in the incidence of poverty that the numbers of poor people declined from 42 million in 1980 to only 27 million in 1990 (Johansen, 1993, Table 1). This occurred in spite of the fact that the growth of both real per capita GNP and real per capita consumption expenditures were much higher in Thailand than in Indonesia, and by 1990 per capita GDP (in US$) was well over twice as high in Thailand (Table 24.1). Converting the US$ estimates to ICP$ reduced the disparity only slightly. There was an even larger disparity between average per capita consumption expenditures as measured in the national income data of both countries (Table 24.1).

But the finding that the incidence of poverty in Thailand in 1990 was higher than in Indonesia is crucially dependent on the choice of poverty line. Is the assertion that they were truly comparable indeed correct? If not, then it is far from clear that the World Bank results can be accepted as valid. And if the comparisons for 1990 are invalid, then doubt is also cast on the results for the earlier years, and the conclusions about the rate of decline in the incidence of poverty in the two countries. We must therefore begin with an

Table 24.1 Per capita GDP and per capita consumption expenditures in Indonesia and Thailand (annual data)

	US$		*ICP$* [a]	
Year	*Indonesia*	*Thailand*	*Indonesia*	*Thailand*
Per capita household expenditures				
GDP data				
1981	340	477	732	1142
1990	322	871	1196	2631
Household expenditure survey data				
1981	207	387	447	927
1990	197	579	733	1750
		Indonesia		*Thailand*
Annual average growth: 1981–1990				
Per capita GNP		3.2		6.0
Per capita household Expenditure [b]		1.8		4.5
Per capita consumption Expenditure [c]		2.8		3.1

Notes:
[a] Adjusted using the data for 1980 and 1988 respectively as reported in Summers and Heston (1988, 1991).
[b] Calculated from the GDP data.
[c] Calculated from Household Income and Expenditure survey data.

Sources: *National Income of Thailand: Rebase Series 1980–1991*, Bangkok: Office of the National Economic and Social Development Board: *Report of the 1981 Socio-economic Survey: Whole Kingdom*, Bangkok: National Statistical Office; *Statistical Yearbook of Indonesia*, Jakarta: Central Bureau of Statistics, various years.

examination of the choice of poverty line, and its implications for the poverty estimates produced in World Bank (1993).

THE CONSTRUCTION OF COMPARABLE POVERTY LINES

The estimates of poverty contained in World Bank (1993) are based on the work of Johansen (1993). She points out that the official poverty lines vary widely across various Asian countries covered in the report;[2] although most of the official poverty lines used in Asia claim to be sufficient to provide around 2,000 calories, the type of food varies considerably. In addition, although most countries adopt the procedure of marking up the food poverty line by the food/non-food expenditure ratio found among households whose food expenditure equals, or closely approximates, the food poverty line, the mark-up varies considerably across Asia (Johansen, 1993, p. 26; see also Booth, 1992a).

Given these wide variations, Johansen proposes two sets of 'standardized' poverty lines, a low one where 90 per cent of the caloric requirement is obtained from foodgrains and a higher one where only 66 per cent comes from foodgrains. Mark-ups for non-food requirements were left as in the official poverty lines, as it was not clear whether the higher non-food shares in some countries compared with others reflected different needs (depending for example on the climate), different tastes, or different relative prices. The resulting poverty lines for Thailand and Indonesia in US$ (exchange rate conversions), and in ICP$ are given in Table 24.2. It is clear that the Thai poverty line is still substantially higher than the Indonesian one, especially in rural areas.

How can such a difference be justified? Given the very similar climates in the two countries, there is no obvious reason to use a higher poverty line in Thailand in order to provide warm winter clothes or sturdier, cold-resistant housing. Thais and Indonesians have broadly similar food tastes, with the diet in each country being based on rice, vegetables, fish and modest amounts of meat. Neither can it be plausibly argued that a higher poverty line should be used in Thailand because food is more expensive. Historically, the use of the rice premium and other forms of rice export taxation had the effect of depressing foodgrain prices well below those in other parts of South-east Asia, and even after the abolition of most forms of export taxation in the 1980s, wholesale rice prices in Bangkok remain below those in Jakarta (Table 24.3). This is also true of wholesale prices of maize (not widely consumed in Thailand, but an important staple in parts of Indonesia), and of retail prices of meat, fish and eggs. Indeed only vegetable oil appears to be substantially cheaper in Indonesia than in Thailand.

There appear to be two main explanations for the difference in the Thai and Indonesian poverty lines used by Johansen. First, the basket of 'foodgrains'

Table 24.2 Poverty lines for Indonesia and Thailand

	Indonesia		*Thailand*	
	Rural	*Urban*	*Rural*	*Urban*
US$				
Official	80	125	182	272
Standardized				
Low [a]	80	125	126	158
High [b]	90	138	182	272
ICP$				
Official	320	512	582	870
Standardized				
Low [a]	320	512	403	506
High [b]	369	566	582	870

Notes:
[a] Low cost diet: 90 per cent of calories from foodgrains.
[b] Higher cost diet; 66 per cent of calories from foodgrains.

Source: Johansen (1993, p. 31).

Table 24.3 Prices of Food Staples in Bangkok and Jakarta Markets, 1990 (US$)

	Bangkok	*Jakarta*
Rice 15% broken (ton)	236.43	
Rice 25% broken (ton)	221.65	
Rice Saigon/Bandung (ton)		302.35
Maize	125.85	191.05
Beef (kg)	2.59	3.61
Duck egg (Unit)	0.07	0.12
Condensed Milk (Can)	0.49	0.69
Vegetable Oil (Bottle)	1.17	0.49
Fish (kg)	1.23	1.27

Notes: Rice and maize prices refer to wholesale data: all other prices are retail. 15 and 30 per cent broken refers to the proportion of broken grains. Saigon/Bandung is an inferior grade of Indonesian rice equivalent to 15 per cent broken or worse. Tons refer to metric tons.

Sources: *Statistical Yearbook of Indonesia 1991*, Jakarta: Central Bureau of Statistics, pp. 482ff; Bank of Thailand *Quarterly Bulletin*, December 1993; *Statistical Yearbook of Thailand, No. 39, 1992*, Bangkok: National Statistical Office.

which provides most of the calories for the Thai poverty line contains higher quality, and thus more expensive, items than in Indonesia. And second, the mark-up for non-foods used in Thailand is much higher, reflecting the higher average levels of income in Thailand and thus the higher propensity to consume both more, and higher quality, non-food items. (The rather lower cost of basic foodstuffs in Thailand is a further reason for the higher share devoted to non-food expenditures.) As far as the first explanation is concerned, it is well-known that many poorer Indonesians, especially in rural areas, consume cheaper quality rice mixed with corn. In some months of the year they also rely on cassava for part of their calories. A recent attempt to construct a poverty line for the different provinces of Indonesia, based on a food bundle yielding 2100 calories per day (which represents the food consumption patterns of a reference household typifying the poorest 15 per cent of the expenditure distribution) found that 2.2 kilograms of rice were consumed per capita per week and 0.7 kilograms of tubers (cassava).[3] The available evidence from Thailand indicates that, although maize and cassava are widely grown in some parts of the country, especially the relatively impoverished North-east, their cultivation has been entirely commercial and neither is consumed by cultivating households.[4]

As far as the mark-up for non-food consumption is concerned, it is clear that this mark-up has been much higher in the poverty lines in common use in Thailand than for those used in Indonesia. This follows from the fact that in Indonesia the food component of the total poverty line expenditures is 79 per cent, compared with only 57 per cent for Thailand (Bidani and Ravallion 1993, Table 24.2; Krongkaew, 1993, Table 24.5). The question thus arises as to whether two poverty lines for two different countries which reflect differences in aggregate consumption expenditure patterns on the part of households who happen to be procuring roughly the same number of calories (albeit from different kinds of foods) can really be considered comparable.[5] Does the difference in the two lines not reflect the fact that members of those households which are deemed 'poor' in Thailand are in real terms considerably better off than those deemed 'poor' in Indonesia?

An alternative approach is to examine the distribution of household expenditures for the two countries in terms of ICP$. The expenditure classes[6] in terms of Thai baht and Indonesian rupiah respectively are converted into ICP$ using the prevailing exchange rates adjusted by the correction factors given in Summers and Heston (1991). Once this is done it is very clear that a much higher proportion of the Indonesian population is in the lower expenditure categories than the Thai population. It follows that, if we apply a common poverty line (set in ICP$) to both these expenditure distributions, a considerably higher proportion of the Indonesian population will fall below the poverty line than will the Thai population. Table 24.4 gives the results of applying two poverty lines to the 1990 expenditure distributions, one based on the new Thai poverty line recently proposed by Krongkaew (1993)[7] and one based on the Indonesia poverty line proposed by Bidani and Ravallion (1993). For both poverty lines the proportion below the poverty line was considerably greater in Indonesia, which indeed is what would be expected given the average figures shown in Table 24.1.[8]

Table 24.4 Percentage of the population[a] below two poverty lines, Thailand and Indonesia, 1990.

	New Krongkaew	*Bidani and Ravallion*
Indonesia		
% in poverty	84.2	22.0
Numbers of poor (million)	151.0	29.4
Thailand		
% in poverty	41.5	3.2
Numbers of poor (million)	22.6	4.0

Note:
[a] Thai data refer to numbers of households.

Source: Poverty lines as given in Bidani and Ravallion (1993, Table 2) and Krongkaew (1993, Table 5). The Thai and Indonesian poverty lines were converted to rupiah and baht respectively using exchange rates and then adjusted to allow for differences in purchasing power using the ICP$ equivalents reported in Summers and Heston (1991, Table II).

Table 24.5 Changes in the incidence of poverty between 1981 and 1990, Indonesia and Thailand

	1981	*1990*
Official Indonesian poverty line		
Indonesia		
% in poverty	26.9	15.1
Numbers of poor (million)	40.6	27.2
Thailand		
% in poverty	6.5	2.1
Numbers of poor (million)	2.95	1.1
Thai poverty line		
Indonesia		
% in poverty	58.7	50.4
Numbers of poor (million)	88.3	90.4
Thailand		
% in poverty	15.2	12.5
Numbers of poor (million)	6.95	6.9

Source: Central Bureau of Statistics (1992); Krongkaew (1993).

It would thus appear that the finding reported by Johansen (1993) and reported in World Bank (1993) that the incidence of poverty in Thailand in 1990 was similar to (indeed slightly higher than) Indonesia is highly questionable. It relies on the use of two very different poverty lines for the two countries which cannot really be considered comparable. Using a common poverty line converted into ICP$ is not a perfect solution to the problem, but it is preferable to the method used by Johansen (1993).[9] Certainly such a common poverty line shows clearly that the incidence of poverty (measured using the headcount method) is considerably lower in Thailand than in Indonesia, which is indeed what would be expected given the difference in average per capita expenditures.

THE DECLINE IN INCIDENCE OF POVERTY IN THAILAND AND INDONESIA, 1981–90

But what of the other assertion made in World Bank (1993), that poverty incidence, and numbers of people below the poverty line, have declined more rapidly in Indonesia than in Thailand over the 1980s? This result is also very surprising, given the much more rapid growth of GDP and household consumption expenditures experienced in Thailand than in Indonesia during the 1980s. Indonesia indeed went through a fairly painful process of restructuring its economy as world oil prices fell between 1981 and 1986, including two large devaluations and a long period of budgetary austerity, when both current and capital expenditures were either frozen or cut. Thailand also underwent some structural adjustment in the 1980s but its problems were much less severe, as its exports were already far more diversified in the early 1980s than were Indonesia's, and being an oil importer, Thailand obviously benefited from the falling world oil price. Thus we would expect that poverty would have declined far more rapidly in the booming Thai economy than in Indonesia.

The World Bank conclusion that in fact the incidence of poverty declined only slowly in Thailand, and the numbers in poverty actually increased is again dependent on the poverty line which they used. It is however broadly confirmed by the results shown in Table 24.5 which use the lower poverty line adopted by Krongkaew in several studies of poverty trends in Thailand, and by other Thai researchers as well.[10] According to this poverty line, numbers in poverty in Thailand stayed virtually constant through the 1980s, while the incidence of poverty declined only slightly. Converting this poverty line into Indonesian rupiah, and making adjustments to allow for differences in the cost of living, we see that 58.7 per cent of the Indonesian population were below the Thai poverty line in 1981, and this declined to 50.4 per cent in 1990. The numbers in poverty in Indonesia according to this poverty line actually rose in 1990 compared with 1981.

This is a very different result from that suggested by the World Bank Study which actually used the official poverty line for Indonesia put forward by the Central Bureau of Statistics (Central Bureau of Statistics, 1992, Table 3.1). This poverty line indicates a considerably larger decline in the incidence of poverty (from 27 per cent in 1981 to 15 per cent in 1991), and also a substantial decline in the numbers of poverty (Table 24.5). Converting the CBS poverty line into Thai baht and adjusting for differences in purchasing power, it is clear that the incidence of poverty as measured by this poverty line also declined in Thailand, although from a very low initial level (only 6.5

per cent of the population) in 1981. There was also quite a sharp decline in the numbers of poor, although again from a very low level in 1981.

Obviously the conclusions to be drawn about the rate of poverty decline in the two countries over the 1980s depends crucially on the poverty line chosen, a point which has been made in other recent poverty studies. In fact it is much more revealing to examine the change in the frequency distribution of people (or households) according to consumption expenditure per capita, and how these distributions have changed between 1981 and 1990 in the two countries. Figures 24.1 and 24.2 plot the relevant data for Indonesia and Thailand respectively (in each case the 1981 data have been inflated to 1990 prices using the private consumption expenditure component of the GDP deflator). These two figures allow us to understand why such different results were derived for different poverty lines, as shown in Table 24.5.[11] At the lower levels of expenditure the gap between the two distributions is quite high in the Indonesian case, narrowing at the higher level of expenditure. Thus a lower poverty line shows a larger decline in poverty. In Thailand by contrast, there is very little change in the two curves for the lower levels of expenditure (except at the very lowest levels). Only at the higher levels of expenditure does the 1990 curve lie much below the 1981 curve.

The curves depicted in Figures 24.1 and 24.2 bring out clearly the different distributional consequences of the real growth in per capita consumption expenditures which has occurred in the 1980s in both countries. In Indonesia, the cumulative frequency distribution has shifted downwards by a fairly

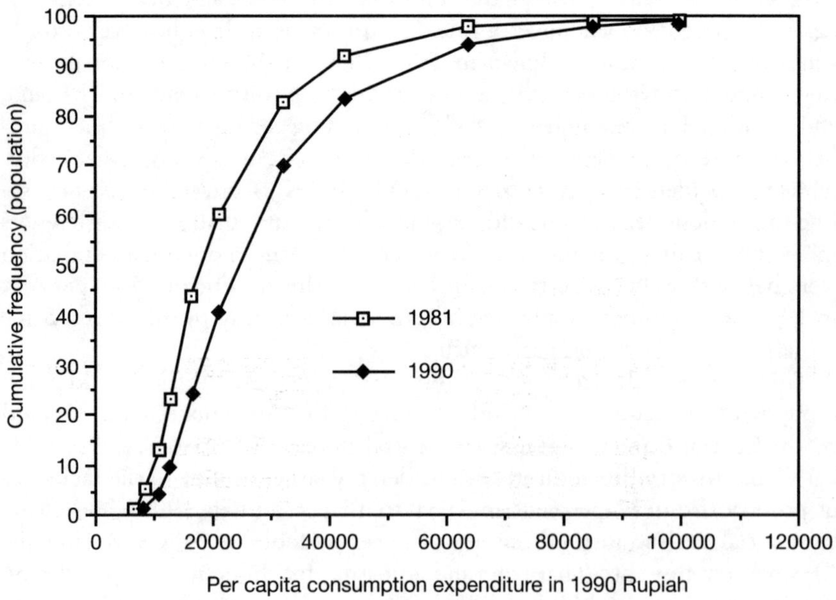

Figure 24.1 Cumulative distribution, Indonesia

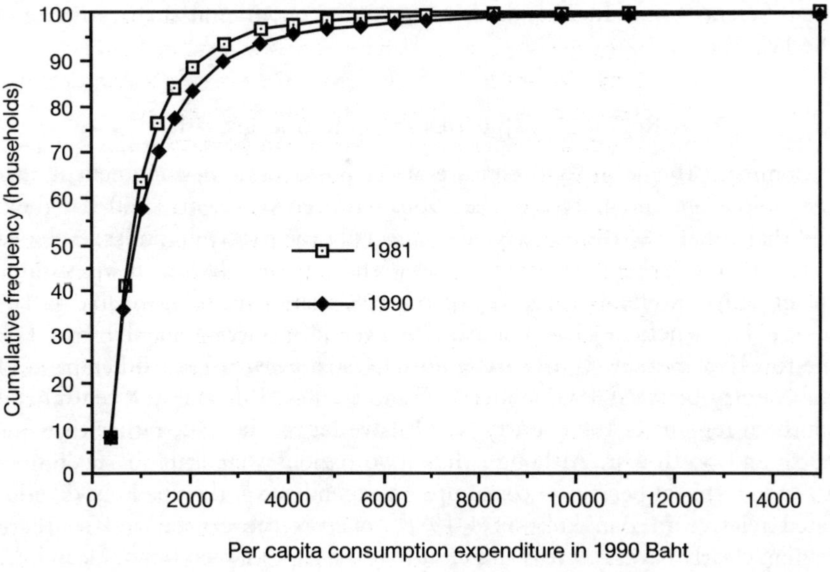

Figure 24.2 Cumulative distribution, Thailand

uniform amount, except for the highest expenditure groups. In other words people in most parts of the expenditure distribution experienced some real increase in consumption expenditures over the decade. In Thailand by contrast, the real improvement was quite minor for households in the bottom part of the distribution, and greater for those in the top three deciles. This evidence of a very skewed distribution of the increased expenditure accruing from economic growth in the 1980s is confirmed by the data on the changing distribution of income by quintile shares. According to Tinakorn, between 1981 and 1988 the share of total income accruing to the lowest 20 per cent of the income distribution declined from 5.4 to 4.5 per cent while the share accruing to the top 20 per cent increased from 51.5 to 54.9 per cent (Tinakorn, 1995, Table 10.4).

EXPLAINING THE DIFFERENCE BETWEEN INDONESIA AND THAILAND

Why did the rapid economic growth experienced by Thailand in the 1980s have so little impact on the real consumption expenditures of those in the lowest deciles of the expenditure distribution? Why did the slower growth in Indonesia which resulted from the post-oil boom period of structural adjustment not have an adverse effect on poverty incidence? In this section, I examine three explanations: differences in the magnitude of regional disparities in the two economies, policies determining access to education, and the differences in living standards in the two economies at the beginning of the 1980s.

Regional disparities in economic growth

A dominant theme in the literature on Thai economic development is that the rapid economic growth of the 1980s has been very centred on Bangkok, and that the rest of the country, and especially the relatively underdeveloped north and north-east of the country has been by-passed. In fact, if we examine the growth of average per capita expenditure, as reported in successive rounds of the Household Socio-economic Surveys, it is clear that the Bangkok metropolitan region (BMR) has enjoyed faster growth than other parts of the country between 1981 and 1990 (Table 24.6). But it is the central and southern regions of the country which have lagged behind, rather than the north and north-east. Although these two regions were still the poorest in 1990 in terms of per capita consumption expenditures, they had not deteriorated relative to Bangkok since 1986, whereas the central and southern regions clearly have. But it is also clear that the gap between Bangkok and the rest of the country is widening. In 1986 per capita consumption expenditures in Bangkok were 82 per cent above the national average; by 1990 they were more than twice as high.[12]

The faster rate of growth of household consumption expenditure in the BMR is a direct consequence of the faster growth of aggregate GDP in the BMR, which is in turn partly the result of the fact that the dynamic manufacturing sector is very largely based there. In 1988, 78 per cent of value added in manufacturing originated from the BMR.[13] In no other country in Asia of comparable size is manufacturing industry so heavily concentrated in the national capital and its immediate vicinity. The poor north-east of the country, by contrast, accounted for only 4.3 per cent of manufacturing value added, but it accounted for 23 per cent of value-added in the slow-growing agricultural sector. In addition the dynamic modern service sector is also

Table 24.6 Annual growth in real per capita consumption expenditures in Thailand, 1981–1990

	1981–86	*1986–90*	*1981–90*
Whole Kingdom	0.4	6.5	3.1
BMR	1.9	7.6	4.4
Northeast	0.4	6.6	3.1
North	1.1	5.6	3.1
Central	–0.1	5.5	0.6
South	1.2	1.0	1.1

Source: *Statistical Yearbook of Thailand, No. 35, 1987–88, Statistical Yearbook of Thailand, No. 39, 1992*, Bangkok: National Statistical Office.

concentrated in the BMR, which in 1988 accounted for 67 per cent of value added in banking, financial services and real estate.

Many recent studies on Thai economic development have tried to find explanations for its extreme Bangkok-centric orientation. Political scientists emphasize the fact that 'adjustments to the institutions of national decision-making have strengthened the central government's control over the provinces and boosted the role of urban industrialists in the policy-making process'. Furthermore, 'the centralised apparatus of government is ill-equipped to resolve many of the collective action problems and information dilemmas associated with enriching a majority of the labour force still employed in agriculture' (Christensen, 1993, p. 2). During the 1980s other problems reinforced the adverse impact of the centralized political system on the rural sector. The land surplus in most parts of the country had largely disappeared, and world prices for most agricultural commodities experienced a decline over the decade. Although the Thai government did reform the system of agricultural taxation, which had had a particularly adverse impact on the rice sector, during the 1980s, the effect of these reforms were not enough to compensate for falling prices.[14] The year 1986 was an especially difficult one for farmers, which explains the very low (in the central region negative) growth in per capita consumption expenditures between 1981 and 1986 outside Bangkok (Table 24.6).

The latter part of the 1980s saw some recovery in the rural economy but it has been argued that the agricultural sector has been largely left to deal with its problems unaided by any government efforts to provide safety nets for those families still largely dependent on agricultural incomes (Christensen *et al.*, 1993, p. 26). In addition, as Krongkaew (1995, p. 43) has pointed out, the long period of agricultural growth based on land extension has meant that successive Thai governments have paid very little attention to the dissemination of yield-increasing technologies, either in the rice sector or in other crops. He argues that use of industrial inputs, such as fertiliser and machinery, will have to accelerate if yields are to increase at the rate which has been achieved in other parts of Asia.

There are a number of contrasts between Indonesian and Thai policies towards rural development in the 1970s and 1980s which help to explain the more rapid decline in poverty incidence in Indonesia. To begin with, although agricultural growth was no faster in Indonesia than in Thailand, prices of key staples such as rice have been protected from world fluctuations to a greater extent than in Thailand through government control of imports and exports. Thus producer incomes did not decline as rapidly, in the early and mid-1980s when world prices of most agricultural commodities fell. This was particularly the case in Java; in other parts of the country producers of export commodities such as rubber and coffee were less protected from world price fluctuations.[15] Industrial growth in Indonesia in the 1980s has been mainly based in Java and in those provinces outside Java where there are substantial endowments of oil, gas, timber and other natural resources.

An abundant supply of cheap labour and relatively well developed infrastructure, has meant that Java and Bali attracted most of the labour-intensive industry oriented to export in sectors such as textiles, garments, footwear and furniture. This in turn has led to a rapid growth in the industrial and service sector labour force in Java over the 1980s, so that by 1990 almost 60 per cent of the total labour force in Java and Bali were employed in those sectors (Table 24.7). In the rest of the country, the proportion of the labour force in agriculture has fallen more slowly, and remained above 60 per cent in 1990. These divergent trends in employment patterns between Java/Bali and the rest of the country imply that, as industrialization proceeds, Java and Bali will account for a steadily declining fraction of the total agricultural labour force. To the extent that this reflects the movement of labour from employment characterized by low productivity and unstable earnings to employment characterized by higher and more regular earnings, it is also probable that over time the population of Java will become more affluent compared with that in other parts of the country, and especially in the eastern part of the country where agricultural productivity growth is constrained by poor soils and lower rainfall. Indeed several recent studies have suggested that the proportion of the poor population located in Java has been falling steadily through the 1980s to a point where the incidence of poverty is now considerably higher in some parts of Kalimantan and Eastern Indonesia.[16] As in other parts of the world, poverty in Indonesia is likely in future to become more a

Table 24.7 Changes in the distribution of the labour force in Indonesia and Thailand, 1980–90

	Indonesia		*Thailand*	
	1980	*1990*	*1980*	*1990*
Percentage in agriculture				
Inner core	49.4	40.8	42.2	32.3
Periphery	65.8	61.3	82.3	75.6
Percentqge in non-agricultural occupations and seeking work				
Inner core	50.6	59.2	57.8	67.7
Periphery	34.2	38.7	17.7	24.4
Percentage distribution of agricultural workers				
Inner core	59.3	53.4	18.2	16.2
Periphery	40.7	46.6	81.8	83.8

Sources: Indonesia: Central Bureau of Statistics (1983, 1991). Thailand: *Report of the Labour Force Survey: Whole Kingdom* July–September 1980 and August 1990 (Bangkok: National Statistical Office.)

function of geographic and economic isolation, and less associated with high population densities.

The same kind of divergent trends which have characterized Java and the Outer Islands in the 1980s can also be found in Thailand. There the contrast is between the BMR and the central provinces on the one hand and the north, north-east and south on the other. By 1990 only about 16 per cent of the agricultural labour force were located in this inner core, and only about one third of the labour force in the inner core gave agriculture as their primary occupation (Table 24.7). But there is a crucial difference between the Thai and Indonesian cases. Because the majority of the poor were concentrated in Java in the 1970s, the faster growth of non-agricultural employment there in the 1980s has had a considerable impact on numbers in poverty. In Thailand, by contrast, the most rapid growth in nonagricultural employment has been in those regions with the lowest incidence of poverty in the early 1980s (Tinakorn, 1995, Table 10.6). Although many young workers in the north and south of the country have migrated to Bangkok and its vicinity to find non-agricultural employment and remitted earnings home, these earnings have not been enough to raise many families above the poverty line.

Access to education

Another important factor which also helps to explain the more unequal nature of the growth process in Thailand compared with Indonesia in the 1980s concerns access to education. Both countries gave high priority to the achievement of universal six-year primary education in the 1970s, and both were able to claim that this target had effectively been reached by the early 1980s. But at the post-primary levels, there has been a marked divergence between Indonesia and Thailand in the 1980s. In Thailand, enrolment growth at the junior secondary level between 1983 and 1990 was very slow, while at the senior secondary level it was negative (Table 24.8). In 1990, there were almost 134,000 fewer young people in upper secondary school than in

Table 24.8 Growth in lower and upper secondary enrolments, 1981–93

	Indonesia		*Thailand*	
	Lower	*Upper*	*Lower*	*Upper*
1981–90[a]	6.5	9.7	2.6	–0.6
1990–93	3.5	–1.3	13.2	8.6

Note:
[a] For Indonesia, the data refer to growth between 1978–79 and 1990.

Source:: Indonesia: *Lampiran Pidato Kenegaraan (Appendix to the State Speech) 1984, 1994* (Jakarta: Department of Information); Thailand: Ministry of Education (1993).

1983. In Indonesia by contrast growth in total enrolments at both levels of secondary school was much faster.

By the early 1990s, the result of these divergent trends was clear in the secondary enrolment ratios in both countries. The gross secondary enrolment ratio (numbers in the secondary system as a proportion of the 13–18 age group) was only 33 per cent in Thailand in 1990 compared with 45 per cent in Indonesia. This was in spite of the fact that in Thailand, the proportion of children completing primary school (as a percentage of first-year entrants) was rather higher (UNDP, 1994, pp. 156–7). In other words, continuation rates from the primary to the secondary system were very low in Thailand. Indeed official data showed that the transition rate from primary to lower secondary school fell in Thailand in the early part of the 1980s and was only 37 per cent in 1985–86, compared with 45 per cent in 1980–81, although it increased to 54.8 per cent by 1990 (Ministry of Education, 1993, Table 24.11).

By 1990, the percentage of the labour force with only primary education in Thailand was higher than in many other parts of Asia a decade earlier, and the gross secondary enrolment ratio lower than virtually anywhere else in East or South-east Asia (Khoman, 1995, Tables 14.9 and 14.10). Thailand's extremely poor performance in secondary education had, by the early 1990s, given rise to a national debate on the future of education policy. Numerous studies pointed out that the main barrier to continuing into post-primary education for most families, especially those in rural areas, was cost (Myers and Sussangkarn, 1992, p. 7). Although rural families are increasingly aware of the importance of post-primary education if children are to compete successfully in an increasingly commercialized environment, they cannot afford the cost of sending children to urban high schools. The policy adopted by the government has been to upgrade rural primary schools into junior high schools by adding on an extra three years to the primary curriculum. Although this approach has met with some disfavour on the part of parents who feel they are being given a second-best alternative, it does appear to have been successful in accelerating the growth of enrolments at the lower secondary level (Table 24.8). Continuation rates have increased from a low of 37 per cent in 1985–86 to 62 per cent by 1991–92. Indeed there is now optimism that the goal set out in the Seventh National Economic and Social Development Plan of 73 per cent continuation into lower secondary school will be surpassed.

These recent improvements will not have much impact on labour force quality in Thailand before the end of the century. At the upper secondary level enrolments have also begun to increase again after a long period of decline. Most of the increase has been in the vocational stream rather than the academic stream, which in part must reflect the judgement of parents and students that vocational training will better equip new entrants to the labour market to find well-paying jobs. In the short run this may be correct, but the evidence from labour market surveys in both Indonesia and Thailand suggests that average earnings for people with academic tertiary qualifications are almost twice as high as earnings for those with upper secondary or vocational qualifications.[17] Clearly those who can afford to continue on to tertiary education are likely to earn far more over their lifetime than those who cannot. Given that in both countries shortages of highly skilled labour, especially in the sciences, will probably further push up graduate remuneration relative to that of other workers, it seems likely that income disparities will remain large in Thailand, and could widen in Indonesia.

Certainly the experience of both countries strongly suggests that rapid industrial growth based on labour-intensive industry raises the opportunity cost of upper secondary education, and encourages young people to leave school at fifteen or sixteen and seek work. This, together with the high cost of upper secondary education, explains the declining enrolments in Thailand since 1983, and the similar trend in Indonesia after 1990. In the short-run this may be desirable, but in the longer run the dangers are obvious. Given the rapid industrial growth in neighbouring countries where wages are much lower than in Thailand, and in some cases lower than in Indonesia, it seems inevitable that both countries will lose their comparative advantage in many labour-intensive manufactures. There will be no alternative to switching the export base to technologically more sophisticated products whose manufacture will require fewer, more skilled workers. Primary school leavers, and secondary drop-outs who have flocked to work as unskilled wage workers in garment, or footwear factories, for example, will find their jobs vanishing to other parts of Asia, and given their poor level of education, they will have little chance of finding work in the faster-growing sectors of industry such as electronics, or in the modern service sector. They will thus be forced to return to unproductive jobs in agriculture or traditional services, further aggravating problems of poverty and income distribution. The evidence indicates that such a process is well underway in Thailand, and may be beginning in Indonesia.[18]

Different starting points

It needs to be emphasized that Indonesia's rapid poverty decline in the 1980s was from a much higher level than Thailand, which in large part reflected the lower per capita GDP in Indonesia. Using the Thai poverty line, 58.7 per cent of the population was under the poverty line in 1981, compared with only 15.2 per cent of Thai households (Table 24.5). Indeed it could be argued that a better comparison would be between Indonesia in the years from 1976 to 1990, and Thailand from the early 1960s to the mid-1970s. Per capita GDP in Thailand in 1962 was $198, compared with $233 in Indonesia in 1976 (both figures in 1975 prices). Meesok (1979, p. 52) has shown that between 1962–63 and 1975–76, the incidence of poverty in Thailand as a whole declined from 57 per cent of the population to 33 per cent.[19] The absolute number of poor people fell also, in spite of the fact that population growth over these years was rather higher than in the 1980s. The decline in the incidence of poverty was especially marked in the north and north-east of the country; in the latter region the incidence of poverty was 74 per cent in 1962–63 and fell to 46 per cent by 1975–76. Meesok (1979, pp. 68–69) attributes this decline to the agricultural growth and diversification which took place in the north-east over these years; she also stresses the importance of growing reliance on non-agricultural sources of income. Similar explanations have been given for the decline in poverty which occurred in Java in the 1980s (Booth, 1992b, pp. 355–6).

It is also striking that, over the period analysed by Meesok, the share of Bangkok in total GDP increased only slightly (Meesok, 1979, Table 2.5). But between 1975 and 1989, the share of Bangkok and the central region of the country in total GDP increased from 53 per cent of total GDP to almost 67 per cent. Thus the composition of total national output has become much more skewed towards the Bangkok area and its surroundings since the mid-1970s. The obvious reason for this is the growing importance of manufacturing and the modern service sector in total GDP, and the declining share of agriculture. In Indonesia, it is probable that continued growth in manufacturing output will skew the distribution of total output more in the direction of Java in future, while much of the rest of the country becomes a relatively neglected agricultural backwater, as has happened in the north and south of Thailand.

CONCLUSIONS

The first general conclusion to be drawn from this paper is that meaningful comparisons of poverty across countries depend crucially on the construction of poverty lines that are comparable, in the sense that they express the cost of the currencies of the countries being compared of a broadly comparable basket of basic goods and services. Given that the definition of 'basic needs' must to some extent vary depending on climate, and cultural and religious factors, as well as on income, the construction of comparable poverty lines is not a straightforward task. In this paper I have argued that the poverty lines adopted for Thailand and Indonesia in the World Bank studies referred to, although ostensibly based on similar calorie intakes, were not truly comparable, and as a result, the poverty incidence estimates were misleading.

A second conclusion concerns the measurement of change in the incidence of poverty over time. It is well established that, because an increase in real per capita income or consumption expenditures over a given period is unlikely to be uniform across the entire income/expenditure range, estimates of changes in the incidence of poverty will depend crucially on the poverty line used. Given this problem it is sensible to use at least two poverty lines, one rather low relative to average income or expenditure, and one closer to the average. An even better practice is to standardize the two distributions on a common set of prices, and prepare two cumulative frequency distributions, such as those given in Figures 24.1 and 24.2. This permits us to see how any average improvement in real household income or expenditure has been spread across the entire distribution of the population.

A third conclusion concerns trends over time in the incidence of poverty and its rate of decline. The Thai experience shows clearly that a continual fall in poverty as economic growth proceeds cannot be taken for granted. If the most dynamic sectors of the economy are concentrated in one part of the country, while a large part of the population still lives in other parts of the country where the agricultural sector dominates both employment and output, then increasing disparities in the regional distribution of income are inevitable. Even with educational and transport policies designed to facilitate the inter-sectoral and inter-regional movement of labour, increasing concentration of GDP in particular regions will probably lead to increasing disparities in household incomes and expenditure. Where such policies are neglected, as they have been in Thailand for much of the past two decades, such disparities are likely to be considerable.

The Indonesian experience of the 1980s suggests that an impressive reduction in the incidence of poverty can be achieved from sustained growth of output and employment in both agriculture, manufacturing and the modern service sector. But as in the case of Thailand, such a rapid decline, relative to output growth, cannot be assumed to continue, especially if the growth of nonagricultural employment opportunities is skewed in the direction of one region. Indonesia in the 1990s may well find itself repeating the Thai experience of the 1980s, with accelerated output growth producing only slight declines in poverty, because the poor are increasingly concentrated in regions which are benefiting only marginally from growth in national output.

NOTES

1 See *The Economist* (London). 15 May 1993, pp. 81–2 and the *Far Eastern Economic Review* (Hong Kong), 18 February 1993.

2 'Official' poverty lines presumably refer to those poverty lines which have been used by planning or statistical agencies in the country concerned. In Indonesia the official poverty line is usually assumed to be that used by the Central Bureau of Statistics in a number of recent publications (e.g. Central Bureau of Statistics, 1992). A critique of the CBS poverty line, together with other poverty line concepts in use in Indonesia is given in Booth (1993). In Thailand there has been little discussion of poverty issues in planning documents until the recently published Seventh Plan (NESDB, 1992), and the most commonly used poverty line was that originally used by Professor Medhi Krongkaew of Thammasat University, and in several unpublished World Bank studies, as well as by Hutaserani and Jitsuchon (1988).

3 See Bidani and Ravallion, 1993, Table 1.

4 See e.g., Feeny, 1990, 82–3.

5 A useful critique of the methodology of setting poverty lines using markups for non-food expenditures is given in Atkinson (1975. 186–90).

6 It is important to emphasize that the comparisons given in this paper use the data on household expenditure (broken down by per capita expenditure classes) for both Indonesia and Thailand. This accords with accepted international practice (van Ginneken, 1994, p. 193). The Indonesian data are taken from the Household Expenditure Surveys carried out by the Central Bureau of Statistics. The Thai data are taken from the Household Socioeconomic Surveys carried out by the National Statistical Office. Both household income and expenditure data are reported in the Thai surveys, but the Indonesian publications only report expenditure data.

7 The new poverty line developed by Krongkaew is considerably higher than that which was used in previous studies, such as Hutaserani and Jitsuchon (1988). In 1988 the new poverty line for the country as a whole was about two thirds of average per capita expenditures as reported in the Household Socioeconomic Survey of that year. The main change in the food component was to take account of increased consumption of rice noodles, meat, eggs, milk and vegetables. The markup for non-food consumption increased because of the higher share of non-food expenditures in total expenditures for all expenditure classes.

8 It appears that Johansen (1993) did not have access to the final tabulations of the 1990 Household Socioeconomic Survey, and used the 1988 distribution to derive the poverty incidence estimates.

9 This procedure has been used in comparative studies of poverty in the developed countries. See Blackburn (1994, pp. 371–2).

10 See Krongkaew (1993). Table 8, for details of how this poverty line is set. For further discussion of trends in the incidence of poverty in Thailand between 1976 and 1988 see Tinakorn (1995, pp. 223–5).

11 Ravallion and Huppi (1991, Figure 1) construct cumulative frequency distributions for per capita consumption in Indonesia in 1984 and 1987. They point out that the poverty lines they use cut the curve at its steepest segment, which means a slight change in the poverty line would have a considerable effect on the head-count estimate of poverty. In addition measured levels of poverty will be very responsive to horizontal shifts in the distribution of consumption.

12 Preliminary data from 1992 Household Socioeconomic Survey indicate that real per capita consumption expenditures in Bangkok in 1992 were 2.42 times the national average.

13 This figure is derived from the regional GDP data prepared by the National Economic and Social Development Board (NESDB).

14 Siamwalla and Suthad (1991) have shown that the net real resource flows from the agricultural sector to the rest of the economy were positive in most years from 1962 to 1982, and only declined from 1983 onwards.

15 Tabor (1992) gives a detailed discussion of the performance of the Indonesian agricultural sector in the 1980s.

16 See CBS (1992), Booth (1993) and Bidani and Ravallion (1993).

17 See Booth (1994, Table 16) for the Indonesian data and Phananiramai and Tonguthai (1994, Table 6) for the Thai data.

18 Thai export data show that, while total exports grew by 13.5 per cent in 1993, labour intensive exports grew by only 6.9 per cent. Exports of medium and high technology products grew by 26.1 per cent in 1993, see *The Nation*, 27 December 1994.

19 Meesok was using income rather than expenditure data to estimate the incidence

of poverty, so the incidences of poverty she reports are not strictly comparable with those in Table 24.8. But broadly her findings would indicate that the headcount measure of poverty in Thailand in the late 1960s was similar to that in Indonesia in 1981, using the Thai poverty line.

REFERENCES

Atkinson, A. B. (1975). *The Economics of Inequality*. Oxford: Clarendon Press.

Bidani, B. and Ravallion, M. (1993). 'A regional poverty profile for Indonesia', *Bulletin of Indonesian Economic Studies*, 29(3) 37–68.

Blackburn, M. L. (1994). 'International comparisons of poverty' *American Economic Review, Papers and Proceedings*, 84(2), 371–4.

Booth, Anne (1992a). *Comparative Assessment of the Incidence of Poverty and Its Change over Time in Southeast Asia*. Canberra: Australian International Development Assistance Bureau (processed).

—— (1992b). 'Income distribution and poverty'. In Booth A, (ed.) *The Oil Boom and After: Indonesian Economic Policy and Performance in the Soeharto Era*. Singapore: Oxford University Press.

—— (1993). 'Counting the poor in Indonesia', *Bulletin of Indonesian Economic Studies*, 29(1), 53–83.

—— (1994). 'Repelita VI and the second long-term development plan', *Bulletin of Indonesian Economic Studies*, 30(3), 1–39.

Central Bureau of Statistics (1983). *Penduduk Indonesia (Population of Indonesia) Hasil Sensus Penduduk 1980, Seri S2*. Jakarta: Central Bureau of Statistics, February.

Central Bureau of Statistics (1991). *Penduduk Indonesia (Population of Indonesia) Tabel Pendahuluan Hasil Sub-Sampel Sensus Penduduk 1990*. Jakarta: Central Bureau of Statistics, October.

Central Bureau of Statistics (1992). *Kemiskinan dan Pemerataan di Indonesia 1976–1990 (Poverty and Inequality in Indonesia, 1976–1990)*. Jakarta: Central Bureau of Statistics.

Christensen, S. R. (1993). 'Democracy without equity? The institutions and political consequences of Bangkok-based development', *Synthesis Reports Volume 3*, 1993 TDRI Year-end Conference on 'Who Gets What and How? Challenges for the Future', Bangkok: Thai Development Research Institute Foundation, December.

Christensen, S. R., Siamwalla, A. and Vichyanond, P. (1993). 'Institutional and political biases of growth-inducing policies in Thailand'. *Fifth International Conference on Thai Studies*. London: School of Oriental and African Studies, July.

Feeny, D. (1990). 'The political economy of regional inequalities in developing economies: the Northeast of Thailand'. *Proceedings of the Fourth International Conference on Thai Studies*. Kunming: Institute of Southeast Asian Studies, 81–114.

Hutaserani, S. and Jitsuchon, S. (1988). 'Thailand's income distribution and poverty profile and their current situations'. Paper prepared for the 1988 TDRI Year-end Conference on Income Distribution and Long-term Development. Bangkok: TDRI, December.

Johansen, F. (1993). 'Poverty reduction in East Asia: the silent revolution', *World Bank Discussion Papers, East Asia and Pacific Region, Number 203*. Washington, DC: World Bank, July.

Khoman, S. (1995). 'Thailand's industrialisation: implications for health, education and science and technology'. In Krongkaew, M. (ed.) *Thailand's Industrialization and Its Consequences*. Basingstoke: Macmillan.

Krongkaew, M. (1993). 'A new poverty profile for Thailand and its welfare implications'. Australian National University, mimeo.

—— (1995). 'Contributions of agriculture to industrialisation'. In Krongkaew, M. (ed.). *Thailand's Industrialization and Its Consequences*. Basingstoke: Macmillan.

Lipton, M. and Ravallion, M. (1995). 'Poverty and policy'. In Behrman, J. and Srinivasan, T. N. (eds) *Handbook of Development Economics, Volume IIIB*. Amsterdam: Elsevier.

Meesok, 0. A. (1979). 'Income, consumption and poverty in Thailand, 1962/63 to 1975/76', *World Bank Staff Working Paper Number 364*. Washington, DC: World Bank, November.

Ministry of Education (1993). *1992 Educational Statistics in Brief*. Bangkok: Educational Planning Division, Ministry of Education.

Myers, C. N. and Sussangkarn, C. (1992). *Educational Options for the Future of Thailand: A Synthesis*. Bangkok: Thai Development Research Institute Foundation, April.

NESDB (1992). *The Seventh National Economic and Social Development Plan 1992–6*. Bangkok: National Economic and Social Development Board.

Phananiramai, M. and Tonguthai, P. (1994). *Labour Welfare in Thailand*. Bangkok: Thai Development Research Institute Foundation, March.

Ravallion, M. (1992). 'Poverty comparisons: a guide to concepts and methods', *Living Standards Measurement Study Working Paper No.88*. Washington, DC: The World Bank.

Ravallion, M. and Huppi, M. (1991). 'Measuring change in poverty: a methodological case study of Indonesia during an adjustment period', *World Bank Economic Review*, 5(1), 57–82.

Siamwalla, A. and Setboonsarng, S. (1991). 'Thailand'. In Krueger, A. O., Schiff, M. and Valdes, A. (eds), *The Political Economy of Agricultural Pricing Policy, Vol 2*. Baltimore: Johns Hopkins University Press.

Summers, R. and Heston, A. (1988). 'A new set of international comparisons of real product and price levels: estimates for 130 countries 1950–85', *Review of Income and Wealth*, 1–25.

—— (1991). 'The Penn world table (Mark 5): an expanded set of international comparisons, 1950–1988', *Quarterly Journal of Economics*, May, 329–68.

Tabor, S. (1992). 'Agriculture in transition'. In Booth A. (ed.) *The Oil Boom and After: Indonesian Economic Policy and Performance in the Soeharto Era*. Singapore: Oxford University Press.

Tinakorn, P. (1995). 'Industrialization and welfare: how poverty and income distribution are affected'. In Krongkaew M. (ed.) *Thailand's Industrialization and Its Consequences*. Basingstoke: Macmillan.

UNPD (1994). *Human Development Report 1994*. New York: Oxford University Press.

van Ginneken, W. (1994). 'Poverty estimates for the ILO's World Labour Report'. In van der Hoeven, R. and Anker, R. (eds.) *Poverty Monitoring: An International Concern*, Basingtoke: Macmillan.

World Bank (1990). *World Development Report*, Washington, D.C.: World Bank.

World Bank (1993). *Sustaining Rapid Development in East Asia and the Pacific* Washington, DC: World Bank.

Part VIII

ASEAN ECONOMIC INTEGRATION

25

THE DEEPENING AND WIDENING OF ASEAN

Chia Siow Yue

Abstract ASEAN's formation in 1967 was motivated by political and strategic considerations and the economic co-operation schemes in the first quarter century produced little impact. Since then there have been efforts to deepen economic integration and widen membership in response to global and regional geopolitical and economic changes. The ASEAN Free Trade Area and Growth Triangles are aimed at improving the region's competitiveness as a production base and investment location. Membership has extended to include Vietnam, and eventually the rest of Southeast Asia. None the less, ASEAN remains small in economic size relative to EU and NAFTA, and this has pushed it to pursue open regionalism and external linkages.

Keywords ASEAN, AFTA, economic integration, trade liberalization, industrial co-operation, growth triangles, open regionalism

INTRODUCTION

ASEAN (Association of Southeast Asian Nations) was formed in 1967 by Indonesia, Malaysia, Philippines, Singapore and Thailand. Brunei joined in 1984 and Vietnam in July 1995. The remaining Southeast Asian countries of Laos, Cambodia and Myanmar are expected to join ASEAN in the next few years.

ASEAN's formation was motivated by the political and strategic environment of the 1960s. The Cold War; regional conflicts and domestic insurgencies propelled the non-communist countries of Southeast Asia to co-operate and provide the underpinnings for economic development. ASEAN has been successful in reducing regional conflicts and promoting regional solidarity, and has played an increasingly influential role in the political and strategic affairs of the Asia-Pacific.[1] A key feature in ASEAN's political success is the 'ASEAN style' of conducting regional relations, emphasizing informality rather than a legalistic framework, adopting the principles of accommodation and consensus in decision making and non-interference in the domestic affairs

Source: *Journal of the Asia-Pacific Economy*, Vol. 1(1), 1996, pp. 59–78.

of its members, and accommodating the needs of members at different levels of economic development. Frequent meetings help reduce sensitivities and develop understanding and bonding. There are some 240 ASEAN meetings of various sorts taking place each year.

Consensus building has also had a convoy effect in slowing the pace of effective economic co-operation. It would be difficult to attribute the economic successes of ASEAN member countries to regional economic co-operation. So far; trade liberalization efforts have had little effect in expanding the share of intra-regional trade, and industrial co-operation schemes have had no noticeable impact on the countries' industrial developments. However, dramatic global and regional geopolitical and economic changes have confronted ASEAN and its members with several challenges. Regional peace and security is being threatened by the rise of regional powers and territorial disputes in the South China Sea. ASEAN has established the ASEAN Regional Forum to help defuse such tensions. On the economic front, ASEAN faces intensified competition for markets and investments and this has spurred the formation of the ASEAN Free Trade Area (AFTA) and growth triangles to improve the grouping's competitiveness as a production base and investment location. ASEAN is also increasingly seeking linkages with other regional groupings to remain relevant and competitive.

The paper first examines the regional economic linkages, focusing on trade and investment, and then discusses the processes and implications of the deepening and widening of ASEAN.

INTRA-REGIONAL TRADE AND INVESTMENT LINKAGES

The ASEAN-6 countries (excluding Vietnam) have highly open economies, as is evident from the high trade and foreign investment penetration ratios shown in Table 25.1. The larger and more inward-looking economies have been embarking on extensive trade and foreign investment liberalization over the past decade.

A notable feature of ASEAN is that extra-regional trade and investment linkages remained quantitatively more important than intra-regional linkages. ASEAN's main trading partners are the OECD countries, particularly the US, EU and Japan. Thus the grouping's economic diplomacy has focused on ensuring the market access threatened by rising regionalism in North America and Europe. For import sourcing of merchandise goods, ASEAN is most dependent on Japan, followed by the US and the EU. For export markets, ASEAN is most dependent on the US, followed by Japan and the EU (Table 25.2). This asymmetrical relationship is particularly evident in the trade in manufactures. In 1992, Japan accounted for 26 per cent and 10 per cent of ASEAN's imports and exports of manufactures

Table 25.1 ASEAN – indicators of economic openness

	Exports/GDP ratio (%) 1992	*Imports/GDP ratio (%) 1992*	*Exports + imports/GDP ratio (%) 1992*	*Inward FDI stock GDP ratio (%) 1992*	*Inward FDI flows/Gross dom. capital formation ratio (%) 1986–91*
Indonesia	27.1	20.5	47.6	55.7	2.4
Malaysia	81.3	53.3	134.6	39.2	9.7
Philippines	18.8	26.9	45.7	7.6	5.7
Singapore	137.1	159.5	296.6	74.8	29.4
Thailand	27.3	37	64.3	11.8	6.3

Source: APEC Economic Committee, Foreign Direct Investment and APEC Economic Integration, June 1995.

respectively, while the US accounted for under 15 per cent and over 20 per cent respectively.

Despite the implementation of the ASEAN Preferential Trading Arrangement (PTA) since 1977, intra-ASEAN trade remains limited. In 1993, such trade accounted for 19.3 per cent of ASEAN's total trade, with a share of 18.1 per cent for imports and 20.7 per cent for exports. The intra-ASEAN share of ASEAN imports has grown significantly since 1970 but not the share for exports. Singapore, the most trade-orientated ASEAN country and the region's entrepot, is the most integrated with the region and accounted for the largest share of intra-ASEAN trade. Excluding Singapore, intra-ASEAN trade falls to less than 5 per cent of ASEAN's total trade. Low trade linkages among the ASEAN-4 (Indonesia, Malaysia, Philippines, Thailand) reflect their low economic complementarity, as they produce largely similar natural resource products and labour-intensive manufactures and compete mainly in the markets of North America, Europe and Japan. With the promotion of export manufacturing and influx of foreign direct investment (FDI) in the past decade, however, regional intra-industry trade is developing rapidly.

The ASEAN region is a major recipient of FDI to the developing world. Table 25.3 shows the stock of inward FDI. In 1992 it amounted to US$136.5 billion, with Indonesia accounting for 46.2 per cent, followed by Singapore (25.2 per cent) and Malaysia (16.6 per cent). The traditional major sources of FDI were Western Europe, the US and Japan. Inflows accelerated in the 1980s, particularly after 1987 (Table 25.4), after the sharp yen appreciation in the mid-1980s. The annual inflow in the 1987–92 period averaged US$9.5 billion, as against an average of US$3.0 billion for 1981–6. In recent years, while Singapore continued to be dependent on FDI from the triad of the US, EC and Japan, the ASEAN-4 experienced a surge in FDI from the Asian newly industrialized economies of Hong Kong, South Korea and Taiwan.

Intra-ASEAN investments remained small relative to inflows from external

Table 25.2 Trade matrix of ASEAN economies 1993

	Brunei	*Indonesia*	*Malaysia*	*Philippines*	*Singapore*	*Thailand*	*ASEAN-6*	*Vietnam*	*Japan*	*EU*	*US*	*World*	*World US$ billion*
						(%) distribution							
Exports													
Brunei	—	0.0	0.1	2.3	8.3	8.6	19.3	0.0	54.2	17.9	1.2	100.0	2.4
Indonesia	0.1	—	1.6	0.8	9.2	1.3	12.9	0.5	30.3	14.4	14.2	100.0	36.8
Malaysia	0.4	1.2	—	1.0	21.7	3.6	27.9	0.3	13.0	14.5	20.3	100.0	47.1
Philippines	0.0	0.4	1.4	—	3.4	1.5	6.7	0.4	16.3	16.9	38.3	100.0	11.3
Singapore	0.8	2.4	13.8	1.8	—	5.6	24.4	1.3	7.3	13.7	19.9	100.0	75.9
Thailand	0.1	0.5	2.8	0.5	12.0	—	16.0	0.3	17.0	17.0	21.6	100.0	37.1
ASEAN-6	0.4	1.2	5.8	1.1	8.9	3.2	20.7	0.7	15.3	14.8	20.1	100.0	210.6
Vietnam	0.0	1.2	2.8	0.4	10.6	2.6	17.6	—	32.3	19.6	0.0	100.0	3.0
Imports													
Brunei	—	1.8	8.0	0.1	26.8	1.5	38.3	0.0	5.4	27.1	20.2	100.0	2.6
Indonesia	0.0	—	1.8	0.2	6.3	0.8	9.2	0.1	22.1	19.9	11.5	100.0	28.3
Malaysia	0.0	1.6	—	0.5	15.3	2.5	19.8	0.2	27.5	11.6	17.0	100.0	45.6
Philippines	0.3	0.6	2.0	—	5.7	1.0	9.6	0.1	22.8	10.3	19.8	100.0	18.0
Singapore	0.2	3.8	15.8	0.6	—	4.0	24.4	0.4	21.0	11.0	15.7	100.0	88.8
Thailand	0.4	1.1	3.6	0.4	6.4	—	12.0	0.2	30.3	14.9	11.7	100.0	46.1
ASEAN-6	0.2	2.1	7.3	0.4	5.9	2.2	18.1	0.3	24.3	13.2	15.0	100.0	229.3
Vietnam	0.0	3.5	2.8	0.8	20.0	2.4	29.5	—	13.1	11.2	0.1	100.0	5.4
Exports + Imports													
Brunei	0.0	1.0	4.2	1.1	18.0	4.9	29.3	0.0	28.7	22.7	11.2	100.0	5.0
Indonesia	0.1	0.0	1.7	0.5	7.9	1.1	11.3	0.3	26.7	16.8	13.0	100.0	65.2
Malaysia	0.2	1.4	0.0	0.8	18.5	3.1	23.9	0.2	20.1	13.1	18.7	100.0	92.6
Philippines	0.2	0.5	1.8	0.0	4.8	1.2	8.5	0.2	20.3	12.8	26.9	100.0	29.2
Singapore	0.5	3.1	14.9	1.1	0.0	4.7	24.4	0.8	14.7	12.3	17.6	100.0	164.6
Thailand	0.3	0.9	3.3	0.5	8.9	0.0	13.8	0.2	24.4	15.9	16.1	100.0	83.2
ASEAN-6	0.3	1.7	6.6	0.8	7.3	2.7	19.3	0.5	20.0	13.9	17.4	100.0	439.8
Vietnam	0.0	2.7	2.8	0.7	16.6	2.4	25.2	0.0	20.0	14.2	0.1	100.0	8.4

Source: IMF, *Direction of Trade Statistics Yearbook*, 1994.

Table 25.3 ASEAN – distribution of inward FDI stock 1980 and 1992

	Indonesia	*Malaysia*	*Philippines*	*Singapore*	*Thailand*	*ASEAN*	*South Korea*	*Hong Kong*	*Taiwan*	*NIEs*	*Japan*	*US*	*EU*	*CER*	*NAFTA*	*APEC*	*World*	*Total*
							(% distribution)											*US$ billion*
1980																		
Indonesia	—	0.3	0.4	1.5	0.1	2.2	0.0	11.5	0.0	11.5	37.5	4.7	9.2	2.9	4.9	59.0	100.0	9.2
Malaysia	0.0	—	0.0	27.7	0.2	28.0	0.1	8.2	0.5	8.7	17.6	6.4	26.6	3.1	6.8	64.1	100.0	6.1
Philippines	0.0	0.0	—	0.4	0.0	0.4	0.5	4.3	0.2	5.0	16.8	54.6	8.9	2.5	58.5	83.2	100.0	1.3
Singapore	0.6	6.1	0.1	—	0.2	7.1	0.0	12.1	0.4	12.6	11.7	22.5	33.1	2.4	22.5	56.2	100.0	5.4
Thailand	0.0	1.1	0.3	4.8	—	6.2	0.3	10.7	0.3	11.3	28.9	35.6	15.9	0.6	35.4	82.2	100.0	1.2
ASERAN-5	0.2	1.6	0.2	8.1	0.1	10.2	0.1	10.3	0.3	10.6	24.7	13.6	19.7	2.7	14.0	62.2	100.0	23.1
1992																		
Indonesia	—	0.2	0.0	3.3	0.2	3.7	4.7	8.3	6.3	19.3	20.7	4.3	10.7	2.1	4.4	50.1	100.0	63.0
Malaysia	3.6	—	0.2	10.4	0.3	14.5	3.3	3.3	17.1	23.7	21.6	9.0	17.9	3.9	9.5	73.7	100.0	22.6
Philippines	—	0.3	—	1.0	—	1.2	1.6	6.6	0.9	9.1	21.0	47.4	10.5	1.8	48.8	81.9	100.0	4.0
Singapore	0.1	3.9	0.3	—	0.9	5.2	0.2	6.1	0.6	6.5	23.3	17.0	23.1	5.5	21.2	61.8	100.0	34.4
Thailand	0.1	0.4	0.1	8.5	—	9.1	0.5	15.4	6.8	22.7	34.0	17.3	10.2	0.9	17.5	84.4	100.0	12.4
ASEAN-5	0.6	1.1	0.1	4.0	0.3	6.3	2.8	7.5	6.5	16.8	22.7	10.7	15.0	3.1	12.0	61.0	100.0	136.5

Source: APEC Economic Committee, Foreign Direct Investment and APEC Economic Integration, June 1995.

Table 25.4 ASEAN – inward FDI flows 1981–92

	1981–6 annual average	*1987–92 annual average*	*1987*	*1988*	*1989*	*1990*	*1991*	*1992*
US$ million								
Brunei	1	(1)	—	1	—	(1)	(1)	(4)
Indonesia	240	999	385	576	682	1,093	1,482	1,774
Malaysia	984	2,268	423	719	1,668	2,332	3,998	4,469
Philippines	74	518	307	936	563	530	544	228
Singapore	1,409	4,093	2,836	3,655	2,773	5,263	4,395	5,635
Thailand	277	1,634	352	1,105	1,775	2,444	2,014	2,116
ASEAN	2,985	9,511	4,303	6,992	7,461	11,661	12,432	14,218
Percentage distribution								
Brunei	0.0	–0.0	0.0	0.0	0.0	–0.0	–0.0	–0.0
Indonesia	8.0	10.5	8.9	8.2	9.1	9.4	11.9	12.5
Malaysia	33.0	23.8	9.8	10.3	22.4	20.0	32.2	31.4
Philippines	2.5	5.4	7.1	13.4	7.5	4.5	4.4	1.6
Singapore	47.2	43.0	65.9	52.3	37.2	45.1	35.4	39.6
Thailand	9.3	17.2	8.2	15.8	23.8	21.0	16.2	14.9
ASEAN	100.0	100.0	100.0	100.0	100.0	100.0	100.0	100.0

Source: APEC Economic Committee, Foreign Direct Investment and APEC Economic Integration, June 1995.

sources, although it is suspected that a sizeable amount of intra-regional investments was not captured by official statistics. These statistics show that ASEAN sources accounted for 16.8 per cent of foreign investments in Malaysia in 1982–7 and 12.6 per cent in 1989–91, as compared to less than 4 per cent for Indonesia and the Philippines (Chia 1993). The low level of intra-regional investments reflects ASEAN's dependence on the advanced countries for capital and technology. In recent years Singapore investments in the rest of ASEAN have seen rapid growth, particularly in Malaysia.

THE FIRST TWENTY-FIVE YEARS OF ASEAN ECONOMIC CO-OPERATION

The regional co-operation agenda of ASEAN's first twenty-five years represented a pragmatic search for acceptable modalities of political, security and economic co-operation. The framework for economic co-operation was established only in 1976 and formal economic integration, whether free trade area or customs union, was considered unacceptable until 1992. The 1976 ASEAN Concord provided for, *inter alia*, economic co-operation in trade and industrial development, banking and finance, food and energy, tourism and transport, and external economic diplomacy including joint approaches on international economic issues. However; substantive progress in regional trade liberalization and industrial co-operation remained limited, reflecting the earlier focus on political-security issues, the wide differences in levels of economic development and industrial competence, and the inward-looking development strategies of most member countries.

Preferential trading arrangement (PTA)

The ASEAN Preferential Trading Arrangement (PTA) was the main instrument to promote intra-regional trade until 1992. Launched in 1977, it contributed little to regional trade expansion and undermined the credibility of ASEAN's intent to liberalize regional trade. The scheme had several weaknesses. First, the import substitution ideology and wide disparities in national tariff levels made high-tariff countries unwilling to cut tariffs for fear of competition and inadequate reciprocity from low-tariff countries. Second, the cumbersome product-by-product approach to tariff reductions produced bizarre results. Tariff lines available for negotiations ballooned with disaggregation of the tariff codes without increases in trade values covered. Tariff reduction offers included irrelevant products such as nuclear reactors and snow ploughs. Subsequent adoption of limited across-the-board tariff reductions led to long exclusion lists which included many products with significant intra-ASEAN trade potential. Third, stringent rules of origin and non-tariff barriers further eroded the effectiveness of tariff preferences. A study by Pangestu *et al* (1992) showed that, out of a total of 12,783 items on the PTA list in 1986, only 337 or 2.6 per cent were granted tariff preferences and only 19 per cent of the total value of these items satisfied the eligibility criteria and actually enjoyed tariff preferences.

In short, the PTA has entailed endless meetings of ASEAN economic officials with limited results. However, to the extent that trade preferences have not promoted the growth of intra-regional trade more than extra-regional trade, discrimination has not been trade diverting or imposed a major welfare loss on ASEAN's traditional trading partners, and ASEAN countries have been able to pursue competitiveness in the global marketplace with minimal distraction.

Industrial co-operation schemes

ASEAN also implemented three industrial co-operation schemes with limited success. The ASEAN Industrial Projects, launched in 1976, was meant to be a showpiece of industrial co-operation but resulted instead in contentious disputes between governments over choice and location of projects. Only two projects were eventually implemented. To avoid an excessive role for government and an emphasis on market sharing which ASEAN countries were not ready to accept, the ASEAN Industrial Co-operation (AIC) and ASEAN Industrial Joint Venture (AIJV) schemes were launched in the 1980s providing for a larger role for the private sector and greater flexibility regarding national and foreign MNC participation.[2] These schemes were not very successful either – problems include continuing government efforts to influence decisions on industrial location, cumbersome and slow bureaucratic approval process and reluctance to engage in regional specialization and production networking.

THE DEEPENING OF ASEAN ECONOMIC CO-OPERATION

ASEAN free trade area (AFTA)

In January 1992, twenty-five years after its formation and in response to external and domestic political and economic changes, ASEAN finally agreed to form a free trade area. First, the end of Cold War and Indochina conflicts has weakened ASEAN's political and strategic underpinnings: previously, regional geopolitical interests kept ASEAN members united and purposeful and the grouping was of strategic interest to the global superpowers. Second, since the early 1980s the ASEAN-4 economies have been undertaking extensive economic reforms, resulting in outward-looking strategies which improved industrial competence and export competitiveness and the convergence of national tariff levels. With the growth of intra-industry trade, ASEAN economies also became more complementary and integrated. Third, the growing emphasis on export manufacturing and foreign investment also caused ASEAN economies to be more concerned about the emergence of trading blocs in Europe and North America and of low-cost production centres in Eastern Europe, China and Indochina.

AFTA will greatly improve the productive efficiency and competitiveness of every ASEAN economy at lower adjustment costs than unilateral liberalization by each country. An ASEAN Free Trade Area (AFTA) will have an integrated regional market of over 400 million people (excluding Vietnam), a combined purchasing power of over US$400 billion growing at 6–8 per cent annually, and a wide range of resource endowment and skills. AFTA will increase ASEAN's attraction as a production base and market for FDI, improve ASEAN's bargaining leverage *vis-à-vis* trading partners, and provide a strategic fallback position should the open multilateral system collapse.

The 1992 AFTA agreement provided for elimination of tariffs and non-tariff barriers within fifteen years from January 1993. Members were given three years to start implementing tariff reductions under the Common Effective Preferential Tariff (CEPT). In response to criticisms that the scheme was inadequate and not bold enough, modifications were made in September 1994: to shorten the time frame for completion of free trade to ten years (2003 instead of 2008); to extend the sectoral coverage to all goods and not just manufactures; and to remove the products in the temporary exclusion list within five years, instead of a review at the end of eight years. In September

1995, Brunei and Singapore proposed that the completion date for AFTA be further accelerated to year 2000, but this has so far met with negative responses from other ASEAN members, reflecting concern over adjustment difficulties facing their domestic industries.

The unweighted average of the CEPT tariff rates was 12.8 per cent in 1993, and ranged from 22.6 per cent for Thailand to 0.4 per cent for Singapore. Tariff reductions cover almost 95 per cent of tariff lines. A general exclusions list covers products exempted on 'public policy' grounds. A temporary exclusion list covers sensitive items, which will be transferred into the inclusion list in five equal instalments starting from January 1996. Tariff reductions follow a dual-track schedule. Under the fast-track schedule, tariffs of 20 per cent and below will be reduced to the target 0–5 per cent within five years (1998) while those above 20 per cent will be reduced to the same level within seven years (2000).[3] Under the normal-track schedule, tariffs of 20 per cent and below will be reduced to the target 0–5 per cent within seven years (2000), while tariffs above 20 per cent will be reduced in two stages, to 20 per cent within five years (1998) and to 0–5 per cent by 2003. For tariff reductions to the 20 per cent level, member countries were free to decide on starting date and frequency and depth of tariff cuts; for tariffs of 20 per cent and below, tariff reductions follow a prescribed schedule. Of the 44,095 CEPT tariff items (Table 25.5), 33.7 per cent are in the fast track, 58.8 per cent in the normal track and 7.5 per cent in the temporary exclusion list.[4] Almost half the fast-track items are textiles and garments. The largest numbers of normal-track items are in base metals and metal manufactures, machinery, electrical appliances and chemicals. The temporary exclusion lists are concentrated in chemicals and plastics and motor vehicles. The average tariff level falls to 4.5 per cent by 1999 and to 2.3 per cent by 2003 (Table 25.6). To enjoy CEPT tariff concessions, a product must do the following: satisfy the reciprocity condition; be on the CEPT inclusion lists of both exporting and importing countries; have an approved tariff reduction schedule; and have at least 40 per cent ASEAN content (single country or cumulative ASEAN basis). Also, quantitative restrictions would be removed upon enjoyment of CEPT concessions,[5] while other non-tariff barriers would be eliminated within five years from enjoyment of concessions.

The AFTA Agreement is short in implementation and technical details and much less ambitious in scope than the NAFTA Agreement; the former covers only fifteen pages while the latter has some 2000 pages. Many inadequacies exist and agreement on implementation procedures needs to be speeded up. First, there is the need to harmonize the tariff nomenclature of member countries and adopt a common definition beyond the internationally agreed HS 6-digit codes. There is also the need to harmonize tariff regimes; as it stands, the reciprocity condition means that tariff preferences will remain largely bilateral and very few CEPT items will reach commonality of preferences for many years. Second, there is the need to clarify the rules of origin.

Table 25.5 Tariff lines in the CEPT by country and sector

Sector	*Brunei*	*Indonesia*	*Malaysia*	*Philippines*	*Singapore*	*Thailand*	*ASEAN*	*% distribution*
Normal track								
Total	3618	4539	5710	3432	3473	5146	25918	58.78
Hs01–24 Live animals, food	826	838	564	294	776	490	3788	8.59
Hs25–27 Mineral products	169	192	163	117	149	204	994	2.25
Hs38–40 Chemicals, plastics	369	347	460	347	295	695	2513	5.70
Hs41–49 Leather, wood, paper	255	284	1754	232	249	350	3124	7.08
Hs50–63 Textiles, apparel	5	0	0	400	0	0	405	0.92
Hs64–67 Footwear	59	110	91	35	59	112	466	1.06
Hs68–71 Stone, ceramics, cement	55	100	68	62	53	85	423	0.96
Hs72–83 Base metals, metal products	586	999	1150	675	623	1217	5250	11.91
Hs84–85 Machinery, electrical products	723	1032	704	784	750	1143	5136	11.65
Hs86–89 Vehicles	1895	121	237	96	124	264	1027	2.33
Hs90–92 Optical, precision instruments	215	298	270	243	227	387	1640	3.72
Hs93–98 Miscellaneous	171	218	249	147	168	199	1152	2.61
Fast track								
Total	2377	2819	2985	960	2183	3531	14855	33.69
Hs01–24 Live animals, food	53	60	157	8	40	74	392	0.89
Hs25–27 Mineral products	5	10	4	7	5	5	36	0.08
Hs38–40 Chemicals, plastics	858	464	1228	607	751	1201	5109	11.59
Hs41–49 Leather, wood, paper	80	51	108	35	82	146	502	1.14
Hs50–63 Textiles, apparel	1009	1803	990	91	975	1758	6626	15.03
Hs64–67 Footwear	0	0	0	0	0	0	0	0.00
Hs68–71 Stone, ceramics, cement	144	248	132	107	142	201	974	2.21
Hs72–83 Base metals, metal products	8	0	1	1	1	2	13	0.03
Hs84–85 Machinery, electrical products	220	156	345	94	165	144	1124	2.55
Hs86–89 Vehicles	0	0	0	0	0	0	0	0.00
Hs90–92 Optical, precision instruments	0	0	0	0	0	0	0	0.00
Hs93–98 Miscellaneous	0	27	20	10	22	0	79	0.18

Temporary exclusion list								
Total	236	1648	621	694	1	122	3322	7.53
Hs01–24 Live animals, food	0	193	18	104	0	28	343	0.78
Hs25–27 Mineral products	9	8	43	43	0	0	103	0.23
Hs38–40 Chemicals, plastics	95	850	123	41	0	0	1109	2.52
Hs41–49 Leather, wood, paper	0	310	108	104	0	0	522	1.18
Hs50–63 Textiles, apparel	0	27	4	268	0	0	299	0.68
Hs64–67 Footwear	0	1	0	23	0	0	24	0.05
Hs68–71 Stone, ceramics, cement	0	12	27	39	0	0	78	0.18
Hs72–83 Base metals, metal products	0	57	112	0	0	3	172	0.39
Hs84–85 Machinery, electrical products	72	48	43	17	0	34	214	0.49
Hs86–89 Vehicles	0	129	143	54	0	57	383	0.87
Hs90–92 Optical, precision instruments	60	8	0	0	1	0	69	0.16
Hs93–98 Miscellaneous	0	5	0	1	0	0	6	0.01
Total	6231	9006	9316	5086	5657	8799	44095	100.00

Source: ASEAN 1995, Vol. 2.

Table 25.6 Average level of CEPT tariff rates by country 1995–2003

Sector	*1995*	*1996*	*1997*	*1998*	*1999*	*2000*	*2001*	*2002*	*2003*
Brunei	2.60	2.60	2.59	2.37	2.05	1.82	0.75	0.46	0.02
Indonesia	12.64	10.45	9.89	7.86	7.28	5.66	4.85	3.85	2.70
Malaysia	7.28	6.64	5.80	5.07	3.28	2.48	0.62	0.47	0.27
Philippines	13.82	10.57	10.07	6.71	5.53	3.91	3.55	3.55	2.80
Singapore	0.00	0.00	0.00	0.00	0.00	0.00	0.00	0.00	0.00
Thailand	16.90	15.12	13.43	10.35	9.41	7.10	5.26	4.12	3.10

Source: ASEAN 1995, Vol. 2.

Administering the rules of origin raises the transaction costs of intra-regional trade as it requires elaborate and cumbersome documentation.[6] The 40 per cent local or ASEAN content rule represents a reasonable compromise between the need for trade liberalization and the need to minimize trade deflection, that is, extra-regional imports entering the ASEAN market via low-tariff member countries and free trade zones. However, it may be argued that trade deflection should not be a major concern when the objective of AFTA is to improve the competitiveness of ASEAN industries rather than to protect ASEAN markets; lower-cost non-ASEAN sourcing of capital goods, intermediate inputs and raw materials would improve ASEAN competitiveness. Third, there is the need to identify and clarify the procedures for removal of non-tariff barriers, which may be a more serious deterrent to intra-regional trade than tariffs.[7] For quantitative restrictions there is possible commitment to tariffication and subsequent tariff reductions. Other non-tariff barriers cover border barriers such as the tedious import documentation and procedures, arbitrary customs valuation and rules of origin, and non-border barriers such as lack of harmonized standards, sanitary regulations, labelling and packaging requirements. So far, ASEAN officials are working on customs valuation systems and procedures, including common customs declaration forms, import and export procedures, the ASEAN Customs Code of Conduct update, elimination of non-tariff barriers relating to technical standards, and harmonization and mutual recognition with respect to sanitary and phytosanitary measures for agriculture products (Chee 1995). Fourth, AFTA requires a dispute settlement mechanism. Disagreements on interpretation of AFTA basic agreements, technical rules and regulations cannot be effectively settled by the ministerial-level commission or ASEAN Secretariat, particularly as the volume of intra-ASEAN trade expands.

The focus of AFTA so far is on liberalizing merchandise trade. AFTA needs also to move into liberalization of trade in services and investment flows as these are of growing interest to every ASEAN member country, and liberalizing intra-regional trade alone may not be the best approach to foster the competitiveness of ASEAN as exporter and as an investment location. ASEAN officials are currently working on a framework agreement on co-operation in services, to include liberalization as well as co-operation in trade in services beyond that agreed upon in the Uruguay Round; an investment co-operation which goes beyond the 1976 ASEAN agreement for promotion and protection of intra-ASEAN investment; co-operation in intellectual property protection and an ASEAN patent and trademark system; and co-operation in finance and banking and transport and communications as trade facilitation measures.

ASEAN growth triangles

ASEAN has created sub-regional growth triangles (GT) as an alternative mode of regional economic co-operation based on the principle of '6 minus x' and focusing on investment co-operation rather than market integration. Three GTs have been established. The southern IMS (Indonesia–Malaysia–Singapore) GT was the first to be developed, covering an area of 23 thousand sq km and a population of over 5 million. The northern IMT (Indonesia–Malaysia–Thailand) GT covers 180 thousand sq km and a population of about 22 million, while the eastern BIMP (Brunei–Indonesia–Malaysia–Philippines) Growth Area covers an area of 700 thousand sq km and a population of over 24 million.

IMS-GT, more commonly known as SIJORI (Singapore-Johor-Riau), comprises the three contiguous areas of Indonesia's Rian islands, Malaysia's southern state of Johor and the city-state of Singapore. During 1990–3 Singapore invested more than US$600 million in Johor and nearly US$350 million in Riau. There was also an influx of other foreign investors. The GT enhances the investment attractions of the sub-region by combining the competitive advantages of their separate parts, integrating the capital, human resources and infrastructure of Singapore with the land, natural resources and labour of Johor and Rian. Geographical proximity and policy co-operation to facilitate investment enable the exploitation of economies of scale and of clustering and specialization according to comparative advantage, and facilitate establishment of production and distribution networks.[8] For business located in Johor and the Riau islands of Batam and Bintan, doing business with and through Singapore is much more cost-efficient and time-saving as Singapore provides world-class transportation, telecommunications, financial and commercial infrastructures and a comfortable and convenient living environment. For Johor and Batam-Bintan, the influx of foreign investments and associated managerial and professional resources raise economic growth, employment opportunities and industrial and tourism prospects. Twinning with Singapore has enabled Johor to become one of the most industrialized and attractive investment locations in Malaysia. The development of Batam and Bintan has facilitated Indonesia's strategy of developing its peripheral islands. For Singapore, the GT has expanded its economic space, facilitated the relocation of industries necessitated by growing land and labour shortages into neighbouring and less unfamiliar business environments and reinforced its role as a regional hub.[9]

There are also problems facing IMS. First, in Johor and Batam-Bintan, the rapid foreign penetration has raised concerns in some quarters over possible centrifugal forces that may undermine national sovereignty and inadequate linkages with the domestic economy. The growing foreign presence and the large influx of workers from other parts of the country also put pressure on housing and infrastructure, raise local costs of living and increase crime and vice. Second, the relocation of industries and consequent large retrenchment of workers in Singapore has created some concern over potential industrial hollowing out, particularly if the retrenched workers cannot readily be redeployed because of economic slowdown and inadequate retraining. Third, there is concern over the sustainability of the IMS-GT. Johor is running out of labour supply while Batam-Bintan has to draw on labour from Java. There is no free trade arrangement between the component areas of IMS, discouraging investors interested in the sub-regional market. The special investment incentives enjoyed by Batam-Bintan were diminished when Indonesia liberalized its investment regime nation-wide in 1994, and the huge Java market and labour supply become stronger magnets to attract foreign investors. Additionally, the opening up of China, India and Vietnam have diverted the interests of Singapore investors.

The IMT-GT covers contiguous areas of west Indonesia, north Malaysia and south Thailand, while BIMP-EAGA encompasses Brunei, east Indonesia, east Malaysia and south Philippines. They are both much larger than IMS-GT in population size and geographically larger and more dispersed. Economic complementarity is less obvious than in IMS-GT as the component areas are more alike in factor endowments and levels of economic and industrial development. There is also a serious lack of integrating transportation infrastructure which could reduce economic distance and transaction costs. Economic co-operation will need to focus less on industrial complementation and more on joint development of infrastructure, natural resources and tourism. For common resources straddling land and sea borders, joint development can minimize ownership disputes and improve environmental management. However, the central challenge in the development of the two sub-regions is mobilizing the financial resources required for infrastructure-related development and demonstrating the commercial viability of various projects.

THE WIDENING OF ASEAN

Expansion of ASEAN membership

Vietnam joined ASEAN in July 1995 and will be acceding to AFTA in January 1996.[10] It has been given an additional three years to complete its

AFTA commitments in view of its level of development and transitional economy status. Laos, Cambodia and Myanmar are expected to join ASEAN over the next few years, so that the regional grouping will cover the whole of Southeast Asia. This extension of membership poses both opportunities and challenges for ASEAN. Politically, a more united Southeast Asia will enhance regional peace and security. A larger membership will also expand the economic size of ASEAN, extending the regional market and its attractions for foreign investment, as well as raising the clout of the regional grouping in external economic relations. The transitional economies of Vietnam, Cambodia, Laos and Myanmar are poor and can benefit from injections of ASEAN capital and expertise. These countries are experiencing an influx of investments and expertise from Singapore, Malaysia and Thailand. But their economies have to prepare for the competition that comes with regional integration. At the same time, an enlarged membership, particularly with new members having distinctly different political traditions and economic systems, will increase the difficulties of reaching consensus on both political and economic issues and ASEAN may need to move towards more formal institutions and frameworks to handle the larger and more diverse membership.

Open regionalism and building external linkages

ASEAN countries are advocates of open regionalism, given their traditional external dependence and the modest size of the grouping. The ASEAN economies are very outward oriented with an average trade/GDP ratio of 96.4 per cent, as compared to 46 per cent for the EU and 19.1 per cent for NAFTA. Intra-regional trade in ASEAN is less than 20 per cent of the grouping's total trade, as compared to almost 60 per cent for the EU and about 40 per cent for NAFTA and this ratio has not changed much in the past two decades. The ASEAN regional market is too small for inward-looking regionalism; in 1993, ASEAN accounted for only 1.9 per cent of world output and 5.7 per cent of world trade, as compared to 30.6 per cent and 19.1 per cent respectively for NAFTA and 26.5 per cent and 34.8 per cent respectively for the EU. Thus the rationale for AFTA goes beyond the enlargement of the internal market. Further, to the extent that ASEAN production is heavily dependent on extra-regional sourcing of capital and intermediate inputs, focusing on intra-ASEAN trade liberalization alone would not significantly reduce production costs. As such, ASEAN countries are simultaneously reducing trade and investment barriers *vis-à-vis* the rest of the world.

Open regionalism is built into the very mechanism of the CEPT scheme. As noted by Chng (1995), a member country which reduces its tariffs to 20 per cent and below, even on an MFN basis, will enjoy CEPT tariff preferences given by its partners. This means that all member countries are encouraged to lower their tariffs on an MFN basis, with intra-ASEAN tariffs being reduced faster and leading to the reduction in MFN tariffs. Since AFTA came into operation in January 1993, several member countries have continued to lower their MFN tariff rates. Singapore in January 1994 removed all its tariffs under AFTA and multilateralized this as part of its Uruguay Round commitments, and Indonesia in May 1995 similarly multilateralized some of its AFTA tariff cuts.

ASEAN countries are among the founder members of the Asia Pacific Economic Co-operation (APEC) forum, whose current membership of eighteen countries spans the Pacific rim and accounts for about half of the world's population and output and 40 per cent of the world's trade. ASEAN countries have much to gain from participation in APEC, as the larger economic grouping includes ASEAN's largest trading partners and investors and membership enables ASEAN to play a central role in forging common positions on regional issues. This role is reflected in the location of the APEC Secretariat in Singapore and alternation of the annual chairmanship of APEC between ASEAN members and other APEC members. However; ASEAN members have been unable to reach a common position with regard to the form and role of APEC. The Malaysian position is that ASEAN and APEC are compatible regional groupings only if the latter remains a loosely structured organization and consultative forum (Ariff 1994).[11] Singapore strongly supports the proposal by APEC's Eminent Persons Group to evolve APEC into an Asia Pacific Economic Community. Indonesia's position was demonstrated during its leadership of the Bogor Summit in November 1994, which resulted in an APEC commitment to achieve free trade by 2010 for developed countries and 2020 for developing countries. The task of the Osaka Summit in November 1995 was to determine the implementation of the free trade objective.

In September 1994 the ASEAN economic ministers agreed to examine possible linkages with the CER, NAFTA and other regional groupings. NAFTA, particularly the US, is economically more important to ASEAN in terms of trade and investment relations than the CER, but, while NAFTA is an ocean away, the CER lies on ASEAN's southeastern boundary. In view of the successful conclusion of the Uruguay Round and establishment of the World Trade Organization (which removed some of the pessimism surrounding multilateralism in recent years), and in view of the APEC proposal for free trade in Asia-Pacific by 2020, one may question the desirability of preferential trading arrangements between APEC sub-groupings. It is a desirable initiative only if such arrangements lead to a faster pace of regional trade and investment liberalization than that agreed upon by APEC. However, such 'accession arrangements' are likely to confront serious obstacles in the near term, due to the problems in harmonizing the scope and pace of liberalization between the groupings and the political sensitivities in some member countries over competition and distribution of benefits and costs.

However, if the focus of the ASEAN-CER and ASEAN-NAFTA linkages is on trade and investment facilitation initiatives, then it should be readily welcomed, as they would be consistent with multilateralism and trade and investment creation. Although some of these initiatives can be dealt with on a bilateral basis, the sub-group-to-sub-group approach economizes on negotiating time. Consultative meetings between ASEAN and CER officials have started to identify practical ways of assisting businesses and expanding trade and investment. They cover areas such as customs procedures, industrial standards, investment promotion, human resource development and visa-free travel.

CONCLUSION

The ASEAN economies have been among the world's most dynamic in the past two decades, with only the Philippines failing to achieve high and sustained economic growth. The economic success of these countries owes much to the ready access to the world's markets, capital and technological resources and to unilateral economic reforms and trade liberalization efforts since the mid-1980s. The main contribution of ASEAN as a regional organization has been in promoting the regional peace and security which have allowed the countries to focus on economic development and the region to become highly attractive to foreign investors.

The dramatic geopolitical and economic changes regionally and globally in the past decade have confronted ASEAN and its economies with several challenges. Regional peace and security is being threatened by the rise of regional powers and territorial disputes in the South China Sea. Hopefully, the ASEAN Regional Forum will be successful in defusing such tensions. On the economic front, ASEAN faces intensified regional and global competition for markets and investments. ASEAN needs to enhance its competitiveness as a production base and investment location. AFTA and the growth triangles are aimed at achieving this objective. And to the extent that the AFTA contributes to the lowering of MFN tariffs and non-tariff barriers, and increased investments improve growth performance, the trade creation effects should outweigh the trade diversion effects and regionalism should contribute to multilateralism. However; AFTA needs to move beyond the CEPT to trade and investment facilitation measures.

ASEAN as a regional grouping is both too big and too small. It is too big in membership in that the large differences in levels of economic development and divergent economic policies among the ASEAN-6 made it difficult to agree on economic integration and the economic co-operation schemes adopted were limited in impact. The subsequent adoption of the so-called '6 minus x' principle allowed some members to opt out of specific co-operation projects not in their national interest. Extending ASEAN membership to include Vietnam and, eventually, Cambodia, Laos and Myanmar, increases the complexities of forging regional consensus, as it further widens the disparities in levels of development and industrial competence and introduces new differences in political regimes and economic systems. To ensure regional peace and cohesion, the richer ASEAN members would need to extend economic and technical assistance to the new and yet-to-be members so that 'levelling up' takes place.

On the other hand, ASEAN is too small to be effective as an economic integration grouping. ASEAN has a population exceeding EU or NAFTA, but its GDP size is less than 10 per cent of that of either grouping. Diversity among members is not enough to provide for regional self-sufficiency in terms of market, capital and technology. Hence ASEAN has to be outward looking and practise open regionalism. ASEAN economic co-operation should move beyond AFTA and take advantage of the *de facto* economic integration process in the Asia-Pacific that results from the growing trade and investment linkages forged by the private sector. ASEAN policy makers need to further reduce barriers to trade and investment flows through liberalization and facilitation measures and encourage their private sectors to be engines of growth. ASEAN needs also to develop strategic trade and investment linkages with other groupings, sub-regions and dynamic economies. To increase its effectiveness in external relations, ASEAN needs to be part of larger groupings in the Asia Pacific region, such as APEC. ASEAN's active participation in the APEC forum and overtures to building linkages with CER, NAFTA and Western Europe are building blocs towards multilateralism.

The ASEAN region is expected to remain buoyant over the next decade. Singapore, a member of the first tier of Asian NIEs, is being graduated by OECD into an advanced developing country in 1996. The other ASEAN economies have entered into the second tier of Asian NIEs. For the Philippines and the transitional economies of Vietnam, Cambodia, Laos and Myanmar, domestic economic reforms coupled with external capital and technical assistance will enable them to become part of the 'East Asian economic miracle'.

NOTES

1 ASEAN has established regular formal dialogues with the US, Canada, EU, Japan, South Korea, Australia and New Zealand. ASEAN's political influence has extended into the wider regional and global forums, an influence out of proportion to its economic strength. This is particularly evident in the Asia Pacific Economic Co-operation (APEC) forum, where ASEAN positions carry considerable weight. ASEAN has also become a focal point for dialogues and arrangements on regional security with the establishment of the ASEAN Regional Forum in 1994.

2 The AIC scheme aims at allocating different production stages of an industry among ASEAN countries. About thirty AIC proposals by the private sector were considered but only one AIC package in the automotive industry was implemented in 1983. According to Hadi (1995), the basic problem was that there was no reason why the markets could not take care of the issue except for trade barriers, and government intervention was used as a substitute for trade liberal-

ization. The second AIC project, based on brand-to-brand complementation was approved in 1988, providing incentives for foreign MNCs, but the major drawback was the non-participation by Indonesia. In 1991 the scheme was extended to include non-automotive products. The AIJV scheme was designed to be more flexible and decentralized and participation requires only two ASEAN countries and non-ASEAN equity of up to 60 per cent is allowed.

3 Initially fifteen product groups were identified for the fast track, namely vegetable oils, chemicals, fertilizers, rubber products, pulp and paper, wooden and rattan furniture, gems and jewellery products, cement, pharmaceuticals, plastics, leather products, textiles, ceramics and glass products, copper cathodes and electronics These have since been extended to include machinery and mineral products.

4 The tariff lines are strictly not comparable across countries and sectors due to differences in level of disaggregation. While Brunei, Indonesia, Malaysia and Singapore have tariff codes disaggregated at the 9-digit level, those of the Philipines are disaggregated at the 8-digit level, and those of Thailand are a mixture of 6-digit and 9-digit codes.

5 A member country is automatically eligible for CEPT concession if the tariff rate on a product it has included in the CEPT is at or below 20 per cent This means its exports of this product to any other member country will be levied the CEPT rate set by those other countries. However, if the tariff rate on a product it has included in the CEPT is above 20 per cent, then it is eligible for concessions only in those member countries that also impose a CEPT rate that is higher than 20 per cent (ASEAN 1995). Since the exchange of CEPT concessions is based on reciprocity, the size of the inclusion list by a member country indicates the coverage of those concessions that it would be eligible to receive

6 The rules of origin rest on the concept of substantial transformation, so that origin is assigned to the country where the last substantial transformation occurred. Substantial transformation may be defined on achieving a threshold proportion of domestic value added, the basis of a change in tariff heading or on the basis of certain manufacturing processes. In a free trade area the rules of origin and local content reduce the probability of trade deflection

7 Sree Kumar (1992) highlighted some of the NTBs in intra-ASEAN trade to include standards testing procedures, customs classifications and valuation procedures subsidy schemes for domestic producers and purchasers, local content rules, and health and safety standards.

8 For a discussion of the factors that led to the emergence of subregional economic zones in East Asia in the 1980s and a comparison of SIJORI with the Hongkong-Taiwan-South China economic zone, see Chia and Lee 1993. The former GT has involved more government intervention than the latter.

9 Singapore's co-operation is also strongly motivated by its heavy dependence on Johor for water supply and its search for new water resources to meet future needs. Riau has agreed to supply Singapore with water from Bintan, which will be jointly developed.

10 Communist Vietnam motivated the formation of ASEAN and was the grouping's arch enemy throughout the 1970s and 1980s. That Vietnam has joined ASEAN in July 1995 is a reflection of the dramatic geopolitical changes in Southeast Asia.

11 Of the ASEAN members, Malaysia has shown the least enthusiastic support for APEC. Prime Minister Mahathir has been advocating the formation of an East Asian Economic Caucus (EAEC), so far without success, mainly because of opposition from the US and Australia, non-response from Japan and lukewarm support from some ASEAN members.

REFERENCES

APEC Economic Committee (June 1995) *Foreign Direct Investment and APEC Economic Integration*, Singapore: APEC Secretariat.

Ariff, M. (1994) 'APEC and ASEAN: complementing or competing?', in Chia Siow Yue (ed.) *APEC Challenges and Opportunities*, Singapore: Institute of Southeast Asian Studies.

ASEAN (1995) *AFTA Reader*, 2 (March) and 3 (September): Questions and Answers on the CEPT for AFTA, Jakarta ASEAN Secretariat

Chee Peng Lim and Teh, R. (1995) *ASEAN and Inter-Regional Linkages* paper presented at the ASEAN Roundtable, August, Singapore: Institute of Southeast Asian Studies.

Chia Siow Yue (1993) 'Foreign direct investment in ASEAN economies', *Asian Development Review*, 11(1).

Chia SiowYue and Lee Tsao Yuan (1993) 'Subregional economic zones: a new motive force in Asia-Pacific development', in C. Fred Bergsten and Marcus Noland (eds) *Pacific Dynamism and the International Economic System*, Washington, DC: Institute of International Economics.

Chng Meng Kng (1995) 'Regional business development in ASEAN: the ASEAN Free Trade Area', *AFTA Reader*, 2.

International Monetary Fund (1994) *Direction of Trade Statistics Yearbook 1994*, Washington, DC: International Monetary Fund

Kumar, Sree (1992) 'Policy issues and the formation of the ASEAN free trade area', in P. Imada and S Naya (eds) *AFTA: The Way Ahead*, Singapore: Institute of South-east Asian Studies

Pangestu, M., Soesastro, H. and Ahmad, M. (1992) 'A new look at intra-ASEAN economic cooperation', *ASEAN Economic Bulletin*, 8 (3).

Soesastro, H. (1995) 'ASEAN economic cooperation in a changed regional and international political economy', in H. Soesastro (ed.) *ASEAN in a Changed Regional and International Political Economy*, Jakarta: Centre for Strategic and International Studies.